THE CAMBRIDGE HIS

COMMUNI

This first volume of *The Cambridge History of Communism* deals with the tumultuous events from 1917 to World War II, such as the Russian Revolution and Civil War, the revolutionary turmoil in post-World War I Europe, and the Spanish Civil War. Leading experts analyze the ideological roots of communism, historical personalities such as Lenin, Stalin and Trotsky and the development of the communist movement on a world scale against this backdrop of conflict that defined the period. The volume addresses the making of Soviet institutions, economy and society while also looking at mass violence and relations between the state, workers and peasants. It introduces crucial communist experiences in Germany, China and Central Asia. At the same time, it also explores international and transnational communist practices concerning key issues such as gender, subjectivity, generations, intellectuals, nationalism and the cult of personality.

SILVIO PONS is Professor of Contemporary History at the University of Rome "Tor Vergata." He is the president of the Gramsci Foundation in Rome and a member of the Editorial Board of the *Journal of Cold War Studies*. His main publications include *Stalin and the Inevitable War* (2002), *Reinterpreting the End of the Cold War* (2005), *A Dictionary of Twentieth-Century Communism* (2010) and *The Global Revolution: A History of International Communism* (2014).

STEPHEN A. SMITH is a historian of modern Russia and China. He is a Senior Research Fellow of All Souls College, Oxford and a Professor of History at Oxford University. His most recent book is *Russia in Revolution: An Empire in Crisis, 1890–1928* (2017). He is currently working on a book on "supernatural politics" that compares the ways in which peasants in Soviet Russia (1917–41) and in China (1949–76) used the resources of popular religion and magic to make sense of the turbulent changes that overwhelmed their lives in the course of the communist revolutions.

THE CAMBRIDGE HISTORY OF COMMUNISM

GENERAL EDITOR

SILVIO PONS, *Università degli Studi di Roma "Tor Vergata"*

The Cambridge History of Communism is an unprecedented global history of communism across the twentieth century. With contributions from a team of leading historians, economists, political scientists and sociologists, the three volumes examine communism in the context of wider political, social, cultural and economic processes, while at the same time revealing how it contributed to shaping them. Volume I deals with the roots, impact and development of communism, analyzing the tumultuous events from the Russian Revolution of 1917 to World War II, and historical personalities such as Lenin, Stalin and Trotsky. Volumes II and III then review the global impact of communism, focusing on the Cold War, the Chinese Revolution, the Vietnam War and the eventual collapse of the Soviet Union. Together the volumes explain why a movement that sought to bring revolution on a world scale, overthrowing capitalism and parliamentary democracy, acquired such force and influence globally.

VOLUME I
World Revolution and Socialism in One Country 1917–1941
EDITED BY SILVIO PONS AND STEPHEN A. SMITH

VOLUME II
The Socialist Camp and World Power 1941–1960s
EDITED BY NORMAN NAIMARK, SILVIO PONS AND SOPHIE QUINN-JUDGE

VOLUME III
Endgames? Late Communism in Global Perspective, 1968 to the Present
EDITED BY JULIANE FÜRST, SILVIO PONS AND MARK SELDEN

THE CAMBRIDGE HISTORY OF COMMUNISM

*

VOLUME I

World Revolution and Socialism in One Country 1917–1941

⋆

Edited by

SILVIO PONS

Università degli Studi di Roma "Tor Vergata"

STEPHEN A. SMITH

University of Oxford

CAMBRIDGE
UNIVERSITY PRESS

CAMBRIDGE
UNIVERSITY PRESS

University Printing House, Cambridge CB2 8BS, United Kingdom

One Liberty Plaza, 20th Floor, New York, NY 10006, USA

477 Williamstown Road, Port Melbourne, VIC 3207, Australia

4843/24, 2nd Floor, Ansari Road, Daryaganj, Delhi – 110002, India

79 Anson Road, #06–04/06, Singapore 079906

Cambridge University Press is part of the University of Cambridge.

It furthers the University's mission by disseminating knowledge in the pursuit of education, learning and research at the highest international levels of excellence.

www.cambridge.org
Information on this title: www.cambridge.org/9781107092846
DOI: 10.1017/9781316137024

First published 2017
Paperback edition first published 2020

Printed in the United Kingdom by TJ International Ltd. Padstow Cornwall

A catalogue record for this publication is available from the British Library.

Three Volume Set ISBN 978-1-316-63458-5 Hardback

Volume I ISBN 978-1-107-09284-6 Hardback
Volume II ISBN 978-1-107-13354-9 Hardback
Volume III ISBN 978-1-107-13564-2 Hardback

Three Volume Set ISBN 978-1-316-63457-8 Paperback

Volume I ISBN 978-1-107-46736-1 Paperback
Volume II ISBN 978-1-107-59001-4 Paperback
Volume III ISBN 978-1-316-50159-7 Paperback

Contents

Plates are to be found between pp. 396 and 397

Plates

Figures

Tables

Contributors to Volume I

Sobhanlal Datta Gupta retired from the University of Calcutta as Surendra Nath Banerjee Professor of Political Science. He is co-Chair of the International Rosa Luxemburg Society, Tokyo–Berlin. Some of his representative works, published recently, include *Comintern and the Destiny of Communism in India 1919–1943: Dialectics of Real and a Possible History* (2006), *Ryutin Platform: Stalin and the Crisis of Proletarian Dictatorship* (2010) and *Marxism in Dark Times: Select Essays for the New Century* (2013).

Michael David-Fox is Professor in the Edmund A. Walsh School of Foreign Service and the Department of History at Georgetown University and Scholarly Supervisor of the Centre for the History and Sociology of the Second World War and Its Consequences at the Higher School of Economics in Moscow. He is the author of *Revolution of the Mind: Higher Learning Among the Bolsheviks, 1918–1929* (1997), *Showcasing the Great Experiment: Cultural Diplomacy and Western Visitors to Soviet Russia, 1921–1941* (2012) and *Crossing Borders: Modernity, Ideology, and Culture in Soviet Russia* (2015).

Geoff Eley is Karl Pohrt Distinguished University Professor of Contemporary History at the University of Michigan. His more recent books include *Forging Democracy: A History of the Left in Europe, 1850–2000* (2002), *A Crooked Line: From Cultural History to the History of Society* (2005), *The Future of Class in History* (2007, with Keith Nield) and *Nazism as Fascism: Violence, Ideology, and the Ground of Consent in Germany, 1930–1945* (2013). He is co-editor of *German Colonialism in a Global Age* (2015).

Donald Filtzer is Emeritus Professor of Russian History at the University of East London. His most recent books are *Hunger and War: Food Provisioning in the Soviet Union During World War II* (2015, edited with Wendy Z. Goldman) and *The Hazards of Urban Life in Late Stalinist Russia: Health, Hygiene and Living Standards, 1943–1953* (2010).

Andrea Graziosi is Professor of History (on leave) at the University "Federico II" of Naples, President of Italy's National Authority for the Evaluation of Universities and Research, Associé of the Centre d'études des mondes russe, caucasien et centre-européen (Paris) and Fellow of Harvard's Ukrainian Research Institute and Davis Center for Russian and Eurasian Studies. He is the author of books on Soviet, East European and Italian history, and the co-chair of the series *Dokumenty sovetskoi istorii.*

JAMES HARRIS is Senior Lecturer in Modern European History at the University of Leeds. He is the author of *The Great Urals: Regionalism and the Evolution of the Soviet System* (1999), *The Great Fear: Stalin's Terror of the 1930* (2016) and *Stalin's World: Dictating the Soviet Order* (2014, with Sarah Davies). He edited *Stalin: A New History* (2005, with Sarah Davies) and *The Anatomy of Terror: Political Violence Under Stalin* (2004).

MARK HARRISON is Professor of Economics at the University of Warwick, Senior Research Fellow at the Centre for Russian, European and Eurasian Studies of the University of Birmingham. His most recent book is *One Day We Will Live Without Fear: Ordinary Lives Under the Soviet Police State* (2015).

ADEEB KHALID is Jane and Raphael Bernstein Professor of Asian Studies and History and Professor of History at Carleton College in Northfield, Minnesota. His most significant publications are *The Politics of Muslim Cultural Reform: Jadidism in Central Asia* (1999), *Islam After Communism: Religion and Politics in Central Asia* (2014) and *Making Uzbekistan: Nation, Empire, and Revolution in the Early USSR* (2015).

ANNA KRYLOVA is Associate Professor of Modern Russian History at Duke University. She is the author of *Soviet Women in Combat: A History of Violence on the Eastern Front* (2010).

HIROAKI KUROMIYA is Professor of History at Indiana University. Kuromiya has authored several books, most recently *The Eurasian Triangle: Russia, the Caucasus and Japan, 1904–1945* (2016, with Georges Mamoulia) and *Conscience on Trial: The Fate of Fourteen Pacifists in Stalin's Ukraine, 1952–1953* (2012).

LARS T. LIH is an Adjunct Professor at the Schulich School of Music, McGill University of Montreal, Canada, but writes on Russian and socialist history in his own time. He is the author of *Bread and Authority in Russia, 1914–1921* (1990), *Lenin Rediscovered* (2006) and co-editor of *Stalin's Letters to Molotov* (1996).

KEVIN MORGAN is Professor of Politics and Contemporary History at the University of Manchester. He is the author of *Bolshevism and the British Left* (2006), *Communists and British Society 1920–1991* (2006, with Gidon Cohen and Andrew Flinn) and co-editor of *Bolshevism, Stalinism and the Comintern: Perspectives on Stalinization, 1917–1953* (2008, with Norman LaPorte and Matthew Worley). His latest book is *International Communism and the Cult of the Individual: Leaders, Tribunes and Martyrs Under Lenin and Stalin* (2017).

MATTHIAS NEUMANN is Senior Lecturer in Modern Russian History at the University of East Anglia. He is the author of *The Communist Youth League and the Transformation of the Soviet Union, 1917–1932* (2012) and co-editor of *Rethinking the Russian Revolution as Historical Divide: Tradition, Rupture and Modernity* (2017, with Andy Willimott).

JOHN PAUL NEWMAN is Senior Lecturer in Twentieth-Century European History and Director of European Studies at Maynooth University, Ireland. He is the author of *Yugoslavia in the Shadow of War: Veterans and the Limits of State-Building, 1903–1945* (2015) and the editor of *Sacrifice and Rebirth: The Legacy of the Last Habsburg War* (2016, with Mark Cornwall) and *The Great War and Veterans' Internationalism* (2013, with Julia Eichenberg).

ALEXANDER V. PANTSOV is Professor of History and holds the Edward and Mary Catherine Gerhold Chair in the Humanities at Capital University in Columbus, Ohio. His publications include *The Bolsheviks and the Chinese Revolution 1919–1927* (2013), *Mao: The Real Story* (2013) and *Deng Xiaoping: A Revolutionary Life* (2015).

BERTRAND M. PATENAUDE is Lecturer in History and International Relations at Stanford University. He is the author of *Stalin's Nemesis: The Exile and Murder of Leon Trotsky* (2010; published in the United States as *Trotsky: Downfall of a Revolutionary*) and *The Big Show in Bololand: The American Relief Expedition to Soviet Russia in the Famine of 1921* (2002).

SILVIO PONS is Professor of Contemporary History at the University of Rome "Tor Vergata." He is the president of the Gramsci Foundation in Rome, and a member of the Editorial Board of the *Journal of Cold War Studies*. His main publications include *Stalin and the Inevitable War* (2002), *Reinterpreting the End of the Cold War* (2005), *A Dictionary of Twentieth-Century Communism* (2010) and *The Global Revolution: A History of International Communism* (2014).

E. A. REES is currently based at the University of Birmingham. He is the author of *Stalinism and Soviet Rail Transport, 1928–1941* (1995), *Political Thought from Machiavelli to Stalin: Revolutionary Machiavellism* (2004) and *Iron Lazar: A Political Biography of Lazar Kaganovich* (2013). He edited *The Nature of Stalin's Dictatorship: The Politburo, 1924–1953* (2003).

TIM REES is Senior Lecturer at the Department of History, University of Exeter. He is the author of *International Communism and the Communist International, 1919–1943* (1998, with Andrew Thorpe) and *Franco's Spain* (1997, with Jean Grugel).

ROBERT SERVICE is Emeritus Professor of Russian History, Emeritus Fellow of St. Antony's College, REES Senior Research Fellow at the University of Oxford, and Senior Fellow of the Hoover Institution, Stanford University. He has published *History of Modern Russia* (2013), *Comrades. Communism: A World History* (2009), *The End of the Cold War* (2015) and *The Last of the Tsars: Nicholas II and the Russian Revolution* (2017).

LEWIS H. SIEGELBAUM is the Jack and Margaret Sweet Professor of History at Michigan State University. He is the author of *Cars for Comrades* (2008) and *Broad Is My Native Land: Repertoires and Regimes of Migration in Russia's Twentieth Century* (2014, with Leslie Page Moch).

STEPHEN A. SMITH is a historian of modern Russia and China. He is a Senior Research Fellow of All Souls College, Oxford and a Professor of History at Oxford University. His most recent book is *Russia in Revolution: An Empire in Crisis, 1890–1928* (2017). He is currently working on a book on "supernatural politics" that compares the ways in which peasants in

Soviet Russia (1917–41) and in China (1949–76) used the resources of popular religion and magic to make sense of the turbulent changes that overwhelmed their lives in the course of the communist revolutions.

Brigitte Studer is Professor of Contemporary History at the University of Bern, Switzerland. Her recent publications are *The Transnational World of the Cominternians* (2015) and "Communisme Transnational," *Monde(s)* 10 (2016) (with Sabine Dullin).

Rex A. Wade is Professor of History at George Mason University, Fairfax, Virginia. He is the author of *The Russian Search for Peace: February–October 1917* (1969), *Red Guards and Workers' Militias in the Russian Revolution* (1984) and *The Russian Revolution, 1917* (2016).

Eric D. Weitz is Distinguished Professor of History at the City College of New York. His major books include *Weimar Germany: Promise and Tragedy* (2013), *A Century of Genocide: Utopias of Race and Nation* (2015) and *Creating German Communism, 1890–1990* (1997).

Nicolas Werth is Senior Researcher (Directeur de recherche) at the Institut d'Histoire du Temps Présent since 1995. He is the author of a number of books on Soviet history, Stalinism and Soviet mass violence. Among his books are *Histoire de l'Union Soviétique: De l'Empire russe à la CEI, 1900–1991* (1990), *L'île aux cannibales. Une déportation-abandon en Sibérie, 1933* (2006), *L'ivrogne et la marchande de fleurs. Autopsie d'un meurtre de masse, URSS, 1937–1938* (2014), *La Terreur et le désarroi: Staline en son système* (2007) and *La route de la Kolyma* (2012). Nicolas Werth participated, with Russian historians, in a number of publications of archival documents, including *Istoriia Stalinskogo Gulaga* (7 vols., 2004) and *Sovetskaia derevnia glazami VChK, OGPU, NKVD* (6 vols., 1998–2012). Forthcoming books in 2017 are *Les révolutions russes* and *Goulag: une anthology* (with L. Jurgenson).

Serge Wolikow is Professor Emeritus at Burgundy University in Dijon, France. He is also the scientific coordinator of the Humanités-Numérique network set up by the French Minister of Higher Education and Research. His latest book is *L'Internationale communiste (1919–1943): Le Komintern ou le rêve dechu du parti mondial de la révolution* (2010).

Preface

If one hundred years after the October Revolution of 1917 communism has become history, it cannot simply be confined to the past. The projects and experiences of world revolution, noncapitalist economies and collectivized societies of the twentieth century are a matter for reflection in terms of historiography, memory and the legacies they left behind. The endurance of communist regimes in some Asian countries and the integration of their economies into globalized capitalism (with the exception of North Korea) have stimulated interest, analysis and questions. This is particularly the case in light of postsocialist China's influence in the world economy and world politics. Indeed, an entirely new phase of scholarship started after the demise of communism in Europe and Russia in 1989–91, with historical research fueled by the opening of the archives. Scholars have investigated, debated and even redefined major topics and periods of communist history on the basis of previously inaccessible evidence. Many collections of documents have been published in several languages. New books and articles have displaced pre-archival literature, thus decisively moving the field of communist studies beyond "Sovietology." A decisive transformation in terms of scholarship is under way. Complaints by historians of communism about the relative backwardness of their own field, when compared with other fields in contemporary history, are in many respects a thing of the past.

Such a transformation has not always been obvious in the last quarter-century. Archival evidence sometimes led historians to embrace a positivist approach that favored accumulation of sources over interpretation, and to use documents in support of already established arguments. The advantage represented by greater distance from the object of study has been counterbalanced by the decreasing interest in it, especially as far as Europe and Russia are concerned. Some might even reject any need to explore the communist experience at all, considering it either irrelevant to our current problems or as an anomaly in the course of European and Russian history.

Others have contended that communism deserves no particular attention because of its manifest failures. Yet assessment of the place of communism remains crucial for framing narratives of the past century, even as scholars assign it different meanings and adopt diverse intellectual perspectives. Historians will continue analyzing how and why communist revolutions, parties, states and societies built mass followings, shaped identities, attracted ordinary people and outstanding intellects, everywhere gave rise to passions of hope and hate, set in motion radical change, spurred modernization, incited violence and genocides, challenged world power and eventually underwent rapid decay, dissolution and profound transformation. Furthermore, to the extent that we recognize the global impact of communism – regardless of our assessment of its outcomes – the issue should have intellectual significance far beyond the bounds of professional historians. The focus on communism helps us understand how our world took shape in the past century, as its history displayed multiple local, national, international and transnational aspects, while connecting Western and non-Western perspectives. Scholars have developed innovative approaches in accordance with the emergence of new historiographical trends, in order to overcome mono-dimensional interpretations inherited from the past, and to place communist history in a multidimensional narrative of twentieth-century history.

The project of *The Cambridge History of Communism* started four years ago, drawing on precisely such insights. This work aims to contribute to the global history of communism. Its purpose is to adopt comprehensive and multiple perspectives, within an inclusive framework of "the global" in history. It aims to understand communism in the context of wider political, social, cultural and economic processes, constraints and vectors, at the same time as acknowledging how communism contributed to shaping them. The chapters combine assessments of classical themes with inquiries into freshly explored issues. They deal with national, regional and international topics, thus unifying scholarly perspectives that were until recently often separated. They focus on Asia and the global South no less than on Europe and Russia. They highlight relationships, interactions and connections while adopting different approaches to social, cultural, economic and political history. While recognizing the Soviet experience as seminal, they devote extensive attention to the other communist experiences, their peculiarities and their increasing diversity.

The Cambridge History of Communism brings together a team of internationally distinguished editors representing different overlapping competences. They helped define the project, organized the volumes and gathered a group of about seventy experts from various countries.

The authors of individual chapters have been selected primarily because of their standing in the various fields of studies on communist history. They include both younger and more established scholars, which is particularly important in order to combine an assessment of scholarly debates with the development of new approaches. Representing various schools of thought, they have been invited to advance their own distinctive approaches and arguments. In the tradition of Cambridge Histories, this work provides synthetic accounts for key periods and topics, while aiming at offering interpretive keys and at being wide-ranging and pluralist. As an authoritative work of reference, it should serve as an ambitious scholarly achievement, written by experts for fellow academics and advanced students, as well as providing an introduction that can be consulted by nonprofessionals.

The Cambridge History of Communism has a basically chronological structure, though several chapters provide long-term overviews and links between the different volumes. Volume I – *World Revolution and Socialism in One Country, 1917–1941* – deals with the period from 1917 to World War II. It includes chapters analyzing momentous events such as the Russian Revolution and Civil War, the revolutionary turmoil in post-World War I Europe, the crisis of the colonial system and the Spanish Civil War. It deals with the ideological roots of communism as well as with historical personalities such as Lenin, Stalin and Trotsky. It addresses the making of Soviet institutions, economy and society while also looking at mass violence and relations between the state, workers and peasants. It introduces crucial communist experiences in Germany, China and Central Asia. At the same time, it also explores international and transnational communist practices concerning key issues such as gender, subjectivity, generations, intellectuals, nationalism and the cult of personality, whose historical significance exceeds its chronological boundaries.

Volume II – *The Socialist Camp and World Power 1941–1960s* – focuses on the period from World War II and the outbreak of the Cold War to the 1960s, but also has many longer-term accounts. It includes chapters dealing with the emergence of Soviet power in the aftermath of the war, anti-fascist resistance, the Sovietization of Eastern Europe, the Chinese Revolution, Chinese modernization, de-Stalinization, Soviet dominance in post-Stalin Eastern Europe, the Prague Spring, the Cuban Revolution, Mao Zedong's personality, the Chinese Cultural Revolution and Cold War anti-communism in the West. It analyzes the political and economic relations between the Soviet Union and the decolonizing world as well as the rise and fall of the Sino-Soviet alliance. It provides an overview of world communism by analyzing national and regional communist experiences in Korea, Vietnam, Latin America, India, Indonesia, Africa, the Arab world and Iran, Yugoslavia, France, Italy and the United States. In addressing all of these single topics efforts are made to supply long-term assessments and also comparative and transnational implications.

Volume III – *Endgames? Late Communism in Global Perspective 1968 to the Present* – covers the period from the 1960s to 1989–91 and to our own day. It includes chapters on the "global 1968," the world impact of the Vietnam War, the role of the Soviet Union in the global Cold War, communist propaganda in the Cold War, Marxist revolutions in Latin America and Africa, communism and genocide in Cambodia, post-Stalin social and cultural developments in the Soviet Union, the decline of Soviet-type economies, reform tendencies in international communism and the Soviet Union, and post-Maoist transformation in China. It deals with Deng Xiaoping's socioeconomic changes and with the failure of Gorbachev's reforms. It looks at the relationship of late socialist experiences and communist cultures to religion, human rights, gender regimes, feminism and environmentalism. It puts a focus on the "global 1989" and on the collapse of the Soviet Union in 1991. It analyzes economic, social and geopolitical developments in postsocialist China. And finally, it offers reflections on the implications of globalization and the legacies of communism.

I am thankful to Juliane Fürst, Norman Naimark, Sophie Quinn-Judge, Mark Selden and Stephen Smith for sharing responsibilities in the project, for their contributions at every stage, and for their invaluable efforts as co-editors of the volumes. I wish to extend my gratitude to all contributors who joined us in making possible the realization of this ambitious work. Michael Watson, our editor at Cambridge University Press, put forward the original idea and then provided advice at crucial moments of the project's development. Elizabeth Hanlon and Cassi Roberts did an essential job in the implementation of the work. Alessandro Larussa helped in keeping order and editing the chapters. The Gramsci Foundation in Rome kindly hosted a workshop in which key topics, concepts and periodizations were debated in depth from different scholarly perspectives. Over several years, I had the chance to discuss this project with many friends, colleagues and experts in Russia, China, the United States, Latin America and Europe. I feel in debt to all of them. This has been a great scholarly and cultural experience, which I hope may bear some lasting fruits.

Silvio Pons

General Introduction

The History of Communism and the Global History of the Twentieth Century

SILVIO PONS

Crucial questions regarding communism aroused intense debates throughout the twentieth century. These concerned the relative importance of ideology, politics and social circumstances in the Russian Revolution and other communist revolutions; the relationship between subjective intentions and longer-term structural processes; the balance between the destruction and achievements brought about by communist experiences; and even the very possibility of defining communism as a unitary phenomenon. The archival opening that took place in the last quarter-century redefined the terms of such debates and provided material for re-posing them – notably from the perspective of the fall of the European communist regimes and the Soviet Union, and from the perspective of China's transformation. However, a deeper revision of our thinking is developing as we make a sustained effort to embed communist history in the wider context of the last century's history, both enriching scholarly understanding and suggesting comparisons, connections and interactions inside and outside the communist world. Such an effort poses old questions in a new light and opens up fresh queries for scholarship.

What follows is a discussion of some relevant issues, which aims to provide a sense of how they are debated by historians. There can be no single prism through which to read this work – still less a summary or consensus of ideas among authors who instead offer a pluralistic landscape of approaches, priorities and interpretations. I will focus on three moments in the interface between communist history and a number of twentieth-century global vectors. First, the context of the "age of wars" as a decisive experience for the establishment of communism as a world network and an alternative project to Western capitalism. Second, the emergence of communism as a global force in the aftermath of World War II and in connections between the socialist camp, the Cold War and decolonization. Third, the multiple trajectories of the decline, fragmentation, collapse, and transformation of communism in the context of growing global interdependence during the late twentieth century and after.

A World Project in the "Age of Wars"

At the end of World War I, the Bolsheviks and their followers thought of themselves as both the heirs of a revolutionary tradition in the lineage of the French Jacobins and Marxism, and as the protagonists of a new cycle of modern revolution set in motion by the cataclysmic consequences of total war. Any assessment of the emergence of twentieth-century communist revolution must properly recognize the importance of wartime experience and its legacy. The uneven and combined development of modern industrial societies, mass politics and imperialism had a history even before World War I, and had already exerted a profound impact on the development of socialist movements. However, the violent collapse of an entire world order invited radical projects for reshaping not only European civilization but also its global domination. The mobilization brought about by the war effort shattered traditional political and cultural patterns and fueled heterogeneous responses. The Bolsheviks provided their own response in terms of world revolution. They claimed Marxist legitimacy while condemning prewar social democracy for its betrayal of internationalism. Lenin's vision of imperialism as an inherently catastrophic global system gave rise to a new kind of internationalism. He envisaged turning the reality of mass violence into the program of a "party of civil war." The Bolsheviks' belief in a regimented intervention to accomplish social revolution had roots in subversive activities under the autocratic regime, but was also a product of the devastating impact of the war on Russian institutions and society. The subjective element and the capacity to mobilize active minorities had a crucial impact as state authority collapsed in the aftermath of the February Revolution. Disputes regarding the Bolshevik Revolution as a *coup d'état* or an outcome of social unrest channeled by revolutionaries will probably continue endlessly. However, historians are inclined to focus more on the political, social and international factors which made possible the consolidation and endurance of revolutionary power.

Militarization became a central feature of revolutionary power as the civil war broke out and mass violence continued beyond the end of the world war.

building organizations in view of longer-term revolutionary scenarios made them particularly dependent on the Soviet Union.

Still, most historians have underestimated the global significance of communists outside power, even if they experienced only defeats – regardless of their compliance or defiance to directives from the "center."[6] The point is not their autonomy from or subordination to Moscow, which has often been the object of inconclusive debates. They did disseminate transnational seeds. The Comintern headquarters in Moscow combined internationalism with cosmopolitan characteristics. Communist parties in different regions and countries were a product of encounters between "professional revolutionaries" who soon started traveling across the world and local groups of militants, activists and intellectuals. Envoys from Moscow interacted and often clashed with established revolutionary groups active in trade unions, factories and urban environments. Moscow was the obvious hub, but the local bureaus provided transnational connections in Berlin and Vienna as well as in Guangzhou, Shanghai and Buenos Aires. Political education passed mainly through Moscow but also occurred elsewhere, for instance through exchanges between the metropolis and colonies of European empires in which there coexisted both integrating functions and conflicting transfers.

At the same time, communists increasingly looked at the Soviet Union and its socialist modernization as a vital horizon for their revolutionary mission elsewhere. The "construction of socialism" was crucial in terms of identity and incentives. It fortified the distance between the social-democratic rescue of the primacy of politics over economics in order to reform capitalism, and the meaning of such a notion in communist culture, which implied anticapitalism, mass mobilization and the use of violence.[7] The Bolsheviks combined state-building as a response to external threats with the perspective of state-led modernization. This itself entailed forced industrialization and further social sacrifices, rationalized on the basis of teleological belief. Stalin's choices closely intertwined "war scares" and extreme pressure for modernization. The original ideal of world revolution came to depend on the success of an inward-looking "revolution from above," and the measure of success was the strength of state security, regardless of its narrow social support.

Class-based categories that had always had both domestic and international implications sparked the peacetime escalation of violence, with

6 Joachim C. Häberlen, "Between Global Aspirations and Local Realities: The Global Dimension of Interwar Communism," *Journal of Global History* 7, 3 (2012), 415–37.

7 Sheri Berman, *The Primacy of Politics: Social Democracy and the Making of Europe's Twentieth Century* (New York: Cambridge University Press, 2006).

deportations, famine and mass death on an unprecedented scale in the aftermath of collectivization, particularly in Ukraine in 1932–33 – which have been the object of an enormous advance in terms of historical knowledge in recent years. Scholarly analyses have also shifted their focus from the top-to-bottom exercise of power to the complexity of interactions between the state and society. The propaganda state employed powerful techniques to mobilize the masses and shape the disciplinary norms of personal conduct. However, discursive strategies and ways of self-identification also implied forms of social negotiation and resistance. The Bolshevik language was only superficially omnipresent and was hardly capable of penetrating society in depth in the Soviet Union. In this light, state-led violence should be seen both as a consequence of class warfare and as a response to failures in attaining effective social mobilization.

The Bolsheviks generally saw the reconstruction of Europe and the European democracies, particularly Weimar Germany, in much the same way as they saw prospects for civil peace in the Soviet Union – namely, as a temporary truce in a volatile state of affairs. Stalin defined his objectives in a way that left no doubt as to the connection between forced modernization and the expectation of a new war, all the more so in the wake of the Great Depression in the West. In 1931 he famously stated, "We are fifty to a hundred years behind the advanced countries. We must make up this gap in ten years. Either we do it, or they will crush us." In 1932, he added that without accelerated industrialization the Soviet Union would be downgraded to a subjugated territory like China.[8] By linking overcoming backwardness with the protection of sovereignty against imperialist threats, Stalin's vision established an archetype for future communist experiences. At the same time, the Bolsheviks' Europe-focused perspective on world power persisted, hindering understanding of the emergence of a new American hegemonic order. This only became an object of reflection among dissidents like Trotsky or, much more sharply, Gramsci in his prison writings in the early 1930s.

Stalin's "revolution from above" raised the enthusiasm and self-confidence of communists. Though dissidents saw "socialism in one country" as a betrayal of world revolution, most communists identified with this notion, in the belief that the creation of a socialist society was an attainable goal. The Great Depression bolstered Stalinist state-building as it confirmed

8 *Stenogrammy zasedanii Politburo TsK RKP(b)-VKP(b) 1923–1938gg.* (3 vols. Moscow: ROSSPEN, 2007), vol. III, 584.

communist messianic prophecies of the breakdown of capitalism. Where Marx depicted capitalist modernity as a simultaneously destructive and dynamic force, communists mainly portrayed a catastrophic and chaotic vision. Even if extreme nationalist forces now became the protagonists of social mobilization in Germany and Central Europe, what counted more for them was that the gigantic Soviet economic and social mobilization had the greatest impact on world dynamics. Not only communists conferred high credibility on a promise of progress focused on the Promethean forces of the Soviet state and industry, unconstrained by private interests. Stalin's modernization appeared to provide the most credible response to the collapse of capitalist laissez-faire, while the crisis of liberal democracy made totalitarian rule more acceptable. Outstanding intellectuals and "fellow travelers" contributed to extending beyond the boundaries of the Soviet Union the idea that Stalinist economic planning and social engineering represented a noncapitalist civilization and an "alternative modernity."

Communists saw the collapsing world order in the 1930s as an inevitable extension of the fall of empires occurring in the wake of World War I. There were several good reasons for establishing such a link in the remaking of the global order.[9] However, Marxist-Leninist ideology created a deterministic mechanism which ironically prioritized the iron laws of history over subjective intervention and the primacy of politics. Communists misunderstood Hitler's rise to power, as they considered radical nationalism as subordinate to the decay of capitalist civilization. At the decisive moment of the Nazi rise to power, they were mainly fighting social democracy. The vision of a permanent state of war decisively affected the establishment of the command economy, the growth of the Gulag system, the displacement and deportation of peoples, the promotion and annihilation of elites, and the emergence of despotic rule over hugely bureaucratized institutions. Historians will continue debating whether Soviet communism is best understood in terms of exceptionalism or shared modernity, but that experience is certainly inseparable from the catastrophic developments of the interwar period.[10]

9 Adam Tooze, *The Deluge: The Great War and the Remaking of Global Order, 1916–1931* (London: Allen Lane, 2014).

10 Stephen Kotkin, "Modern Times: The Soviet Union and the Inter-War Conjuncture," *Kritika. Explorations in Russian and Eurasian History* 2, 1 (Winter 2001), 111–64. See recently Anna Krylova, "Soviet Modernity: Stephen Kotkin and the Bolshevik Predicament," *Contemporary European History* 23, 2 (2014), 167–92; Michael David-Fox, *Crossing Borders: Modernity, Ideology, and Culture in Russia and the Soviet Union* (Pittsburgh: University of Pittsburgh Press, 2015).

These developments shaped the identities of communists well beyond the boundaries of the Soviet Union – even those who forged distinctive revolutionary paths, like the Chinese communists. The 1927 massacre of communists in Shanghai and Guangzhou by the Guomindang was the prelude to a protracted struggle linking guerrilla warfare with the creation of revolutionary base areas for two decades. Within a few years, the Chinese communists fielded organized armies while shifting their social bases toward the peasantry to an extent that Lenin had never imagined. Following the epic experience of the Long March in 1934–35, armed resistance and civil conflicts extended to a new plane. In 1936–37, the coincidence between the Spanish Civil War and the Japanese invasion of China provided a decisive conjuncture for the global extension of the relationship between communists and "international civil war." In both instances, communist parties achieved mass support and decisive influence in the fire of civil war. The paradox was that Spain and China gave fresh impetus to internationalist faith and militant dedication to the fight against fascism and imperialism, while such impetus could become a crime in the Soviet Union.

Stalinism inhibited the internationalist vocation through terror. Yet the planetary extension of the communist movement still persisted in the 1930s. Even the transfer of Soviet patterns and their reception gave rise to multifaceted outcomes. Moscow's disciplinary strategy – establishing a single prototype of the revolutionary party and militancy shaped in conformity with the Soviet model of "democratic centralism" – was subject to strains, adaptation and resistance. As historians increasingly see it, the consequence was much more hybridization than a replication of the original archetypes – as symbols, practices, pedagogies and institutions such as the "cult of personality" had transnational diffusion but also multiple variants when transplanted to other cultures. In Europe, the project of de-social-democratizing workers and intellectuals started out as the imposition of an authoritarian pedagogy from above, but it also eventually gave rise to generational and social variations.[11] We may see here the roots of longer-term ambivalent developments – as communists everywhere antagonized social democrats but their political culture was hardly unified around a single unchanging blueprint. In China, India, Latin America and Africa, the weakness of the tradition of an organized workers' movement and the influence of

11 Brigitte Studer, "Stalinization: Balance Sheet of a Complex Notion," in Norman LaPorte, Kevin Morgan, and Matthew Worley (eds.), *Bolshevism, Stalinism, and the Comintern: Perspectives on Stalinization, 1917–53* (Basingstoke: Palgrave Macmillan, 2008), 45–65.

anti-imperialist nationalism led to the construction of various revolutionary spaces, but neither Marxism nor the Soviet experience offered a clear answer as to what to do with peasants.

Stalin made clear the primacy of the Soviet state interest over the communist movement by concluding the pact with Hitler in August 1939 – a fateful decision which affected his geopolitical thinking and the destiny of the communist revolution well beyond the chronological limits of the alliance. However, after June 1941, as the Soviet Union withstood the Nazi invasion, the prospect materialized of the war dealing a second revolutionary blow to capitalism, a quarter-century after World War I. The ideological and even emotional impact of this prospect should not be missed. Restrained by the Soviet Union's security interests, communists no longer preached civil war as a political program, nor did they openly plan for radical social transformation. They did not prioritize class conflict over national sentiments. But they still experienced war as the main path toward momentous change, and particularly so given that the apocalypse brought about by World War II appeared unrivaled. The barbarian heights of Nazi Germany's genocidal war in the East generated a vital patriotic response among Russians facing a life or death struggle. Stalin's regime adjusted to and exploited these feelings. Instrumental as it was, such appeal to nationalism reflected and encouraged broad support.

In the aftermath of World War II, communism set out a complex, if conflicting, relationship with the nation – thereby engaging the main global political concept of the late nineteenth century, while trying to replace it in the twentieth century. The question of translating internationalism into a national language had been discussed since the creation of the Soviet Union and the birth of communist parties. The prospect of combining class and nation soon emerged, though communists reconciled themselves with national identities only in the mid 1930s, with the popular fronts in Europe and anti-Japanese resistance in China, then opening the way for the effort to become "national" during World War II. The relationship between communism and anti-fascism has been a highly disputed question. Today, narratives of anti-fascism either as a myth and an instrument or as the pole star for all communists hardly fit with a historical understanding of its multiple meanings.[12] Stalin obviously did not see anti-fascism as a priority, but for

12 For such opposite narratives, see François Furet, *The Passing of an Illusion: The Idea of Communism in the Twentieth Century* (Chicago: University of Chicago Press, 1999), and Eric J. Hobsbawm, *Age of Extremes: The Short Twentieth Century, 1914–1991* (London: Michael Joseph, 1994).

many communists it provided an identity superimposed upon the revolutionary calling, in ways that would shape a new generation.

Anti-fascist resistance in Europe and anti-imperialist struggle in Asia emerged as liberation struggles often involving civil wars in which the legacies of nationalist, ethnic and class violence came to a head. When World War II broke out in East Asia in 1937 and in Europe in 1939, Chinese communism was the only crucial mass communist movement surviving outside the Soviet Union, and it was on the defensive. Radical change came in just a few years as the impact of Soviet victory and resistance against fascism gave communism new legitimacy and unprecedented mass dimensions. By the end of the war, its legacy became crucial to Western and even East European communists, though its significance was far from uniform among militants, cadres and leaders. The Soviet presence in Eastern Europe, where anti-communism had strong roots, hardly helped communist parties to gain popular support there, and damaged the credibility of "people's democracies" as distinct from a force under the thumb of Soviet power. Conversely, the impact of Soviet prestige combined powerfully with anti-fascist resistance in Western Europe. We can only understand the enduring mass experiences of French and Italian communism in light of this original twofold impulse. However, anti-fascism was invoked after the war both to build legal mass parties (as in France and Italy) and to legitimate civil war (as in Greece), while its association with "people's democracy" rapidly lost any sense of representing a feasible alternative to the Soviet model in Eastern Europe. Indeed, ideas of anti-fascism as an inspiration for "national paths" never settled the deep ambiguity epitomized by the Soviet model as revolutionaries' ultimate goal.

Communists adopted manifold versions of the nation. In the European continent they followed divergent citizenship-based or ethnic-based concepts, reflecting a cleavage between Western and Eastern Europe. Where European communists constructed their legitimacy as a component of the political nation, as in France, such an idea contrasted with the anti-imperialist concept of the nation, which implied radical social and economic transformation and new forms of postimperial sovereignty. The Chinese communists established anti-imperialist nationalism as the main mobilizing force of their revolution, wedded with pro-peasant social reforms, which promised to exercise a profound influence in Asia and elsewhere in the Third World. Moscow encouraged national self-determination against Western colonial powers, but the same principle hardly applied in the Soviet Union – and soon proved unworkable in its European sphere of influence. Communism interlaced nationalism and the nation-state in multiple ways, with different long-term consequences in the global South, in Eurasia and in Europe.

A Global Force in a Divided World

Communism as state power, forced modernization and a collectivized economy received enormous retrospective legitimacy from the experience of World War II. While celebrating victory, Stalin praised the Red Army, the Soviet system and the Russian people. He made no mention of a connection between war and revolution. He advanced no universalist message – unlike Roosevelt. In private conversations, he talked of spheres of influence and future wars – not revolutions.[13] His priority was building a formidable buffer zone around the Soviet Union as it extended its imperial influence from Korea and north China to Afghanistan and north Iran, while exerting undisputed supremacy in Eastern Europe. Stalin maintained his thinking concerning global antagonism with the West – a view that went back to the interwar conjuncture. Such thinking recognized the possibility only of revolution from above – outcomes charted by an expansive Soviet state. The war moved the practice of Sovietization – a state-led attack on preexisting societies – from the periphery of empire in Central Asia and Mongolia in the interwar period to its western borders, first of all in Poland and the Baltic countries in 1939–40, in the aftermath of the Molotov–Ribbentrop Pact. The collapse of Hitler's empire heralded the re-Sovietization of the Soviet Union's western occupied territories and invited it to fill the geopolitical vacuum left in Europe. The application of the same pattern on a wider scale in Eastern Europe was not planned, but was likely a result of Soviet influence and a consequence of war violence – particularly the destruction of the Jews and the annihilation of former ruling classes.

However, in fact a connection between war and revolution did emerge, indeed one that could not be equated to imperial expansion. Revolution took place in the Balkans – though with opposite outcomes in Yugoslavia, Albania and Greece; in Indochina – as the Viet Minh took power in North Vietnam after fighting the French and the Japanese; and also loomed in China – as the Japanese retreat heralded a clash between the communists and the nationalists. As we now know, Moscow could hardly hold sway over the conduct of local communists in those geostrategic areas. Stalin's break with Tito was

13 Ivo Banac (ed.), *The Diary of Georgi Dimitrov 1933–1949*, trans. Jane T. Hedges, Timothy D. Sergay and Irina Faion (New Haven: Yale University Press, 2003), 357–58.

basically a consequence of Yugoslav autonomy, which threatened to prevent Moscow's control and to affect other East European communists. Stalin also tried to contain revolutionary developments in China in the name of Soviet geopolitical interests, by envisaging a division of the country negotiated with the United States. Nevertheless, World War II continued in bloody civil wars and insurrections for some years not only in China – where it had first started in 1937 – but across the Asian continent including Vietnam and Korea and extending to national liberation movements in the Philippines, Indonesia and Burma. Revolution in China, Vietnam and Korea was the outcome of a cycle of wars which extended beyond World War II in Europe.

By 1949–50, communism played the role of a driving force. Europe and Germany were definitively divided into two blocs by the Cold War, and Sovietization was in its final stage in Eastern Europe. The Soviet bomb quickly put an end to the American monopoly on atomic weapons. The Chinese communists took power and established an alliance between the People's Republic of China and the Soviet Union. The Korean War consolidated the communist alliance by challenging the United States. In terms of economic and technological power, the bipolar order displayed a basic asymmetry, for the United States played the hegemonic role it had discarded a quarter-century earlier and the main poles of industrial and financial power were located in the West and in Japan. The American containment strategy successfully employed the Marshall Plan in the reconstruction of Western Europe and its integration within a US strategic bloc. Nevertheless, in terms of its global drive, communism was on the rise. It had cut off two immense countries from the capitalist world, ruled half of Europe, promoted successful pacifist mobilization, promised to significantly interact with decolonization, maintained its attractiveness to key intellectuals, and benefited from the allegiance of growing numbers of militants on a world scale. In this context, the impact of the Chinese Revolution was central as it demonstrated how communist revolution could be extended to a great semi-colonial country by means of organized popular forces. Even more a revolution "against Marx's *Das Kapital*," the Chinese Revolution provided a global profile to communism no less than had the emergence of Soviet power.

The Soviet Union was no longer an isolated socialist state. Rather, it dominated an international space characterized by coercive transformation – the socialist camp. Soviet power displayed a peculiar framework in Eastern Europe, as countries relatively more advanced in economic development than Russia formed its imperial periphery. Soviet state institutions and developmental patterns also began to be established in China. The latter aspect, as distinct from socialist transformation, had considerable appeal in large areas of the postcolonial world, where nationalist elites were attracted by the promise of overcoming backwardness while maintaining their independence from Western-dominated markets and capital. Historians are abandoning the view that the socialist camp did not interact with the rest of the world because of its isolationism – although this is not to say that the influence of ideology should be discarded. Yet, we now know that Soviet communism went global. The challenge is to better understand *how* it went global.

The death of Stalin in 1953 prompted changes that put the endurance of the communist project to the test. De-Stalinization followed no grand design. Historians see it mainly as an empirical process, which nevertheless opened the way to transnational changes of dramatic magnitude, beyond high politics.[14] The end of Stalinist terror opened up a redeeming thaw in social relations, daily life and culture both within and beyond the Soviet Union, which deeply changed minds and psychologies. The coercion of the postwar economic reconstruction yielded to significant welfare measures. The worst tensions of the Cold War faded away. The encounter between communism and new Third World actors took shape as China was welcomed to the Bandung conference. Soviet assistance in helping to modernize China resembled the Marshall Plan effort in Europe. Prospects for reform and modernization combined with prospects for relaunching the anti-imperialist mission in ways that could balance the crises emerging in the Soviet Union's European "external empire," first of all in East Germany. Khrushchev's demolition of Stalin, mass protest in Poland and Hungary, and the Soviet invasion of Hungary in 1956 were shocking events – momentous changes that imposed a redefinition of narratives, memories and thinking for communists worldwide. Still, communists could believe that history was moving in their direction. Most militants and intellectuals accepted the idea of recovering Leninist principles as opposed to Stalinism. They felt that the opportunities for further development of communism as global force were open, and that Marxism offered the most suitable ideology for unifying mankind.

As a world communist conference was convened in Moscow in 1957 – showing how the communist parties maintained their international tradition

14 Miriam Dobson, "The Post-Stalin Era: Destalinization, Daily Life, and Dissent," *Kritika. Explorations in Russian and Eurasian History* 12, 4 (Fall 2011), 905–24.

and acknowledged Moscow's guidance – Mao Zedong could state that "the wind from the East blows over the wind from the West, for we are strong."[15] The Chinese leader had in mind anti-imperialist movements in the postcolonial world as well as the modernizing impetus symbolized by the Soviet *Sputnik*. Both the Soviets and the Chinese boldly proclaimed that they would overcome the main capitalist economies within a few decades. By the end of the 1950s, the "socialist camp" had evolved into a transnational space interconnected in its political institutions, economic structures, cultural exchanges, material cultures and ways of life – which have to be analyzed both in their powerful drive toward homogeneity and their enormous degree of diversity.

No less importantly, we cannot overlook how the communist confrontation with the West assumed multifaceted dimensions as a result of decolonization. The Cold War contest interacted with new modernization perspectives. The socialist camp's anti-imperialist image capitalized on the Western legacy of colonialism and racism. As development became the prevalent ideology and goal worldwide, Soviet communism had its own cards to play. Historians have focused on the entanglements between the Second and the Third World.[16] A new approach to investing economic resources outside the socialist camp emerged in the Middle East, and it was widely extended elsewhere, from Indonesia to Africa. Socialist progress in the "camp" itself and noncapitalist development in the Third World were intertwined issues, while anti-imperialist nationalism intersected with communist revolutionary aims in multiple ways. Nasser's postcolonial regime in Egypt sided with the Soviet Union while repressing local communists. The war of liberation in Algeria added to the anti-imperialist wave. The Soviet Union established a partnership with Nehru's India. North Vietnam's governing communists sought to extend communist-led movements in a postcolonial order throughout Indochina. A mass communist party played an increasingly influential role in Sukharno's Indonesia. Anti-American revolutionaries took power in Cuba and seemed to open up exciting scenarios in Latin America.

However, in its global drive communism was failing to meet two key challenges of the postwar era. The first challenge was the maintenance of its unity in the face of the Cold War contest and its encounters with

15 *Nasledniki Kominterna. Mezhdunarodnye soveshchaniya predstavitelei kommunisticheskikh i rabochikh partii v Moskve (noyabr' 1957g.)* (Moscow: ROSSPEN, 2013), 570.

16 David C. Engerman, "The Second World's Third World," *Kritika. Explorations in Russian and Eurasian History* 12, 1 (Winter 2011), 183–211.

decolonization. Unity depended first on the Soviet Union's capacity to exercise effective leadership over the "socialist camp" in an inclusive and consensual way. Stalin's legacy of what Charles Maier has called "Leviathan 2.0" – a form of power unconcerned with consensus – still persisted, even if its bases of support within society had been consolidated in wartime.[17] The coercive empire Stalin had created was unmanageable in the absence of fundamental reforms both domestically and internationally, as his successors were well aware. But such changes as were made did not deeply affect its monocratic nature. In spite of attempts to refashion communist legitimacy by means of modernization and growing interdependence, dogmatic inflexibility continued to prevent the Soviet Union from building new forms of hegemony – as distinct from sheer domination – over the movement and the "socialist camp."

Historians have comprehensively analyzed the Sino-Soviet split, showing how post-Stalin changes exacerbated political and cultural divisions well beyond a clash of personalities. Attempts at reform in the Soviet Union and Eastern Europe conflicted in many ways with the Chinese revolutionary path, particularly Khrushchev's effort to emancipate communist ideology from the doctrine of the inevitability of war – which might entail ruinous consequences in the nuclear era – and to provide new peaceful perspectives. Mao was skeptical of de-Stalinization, launched a project of social modernization on the pattern of Stalin's revolution from above, and rejected "peaceful coexistence" as a betrayal of anti-imperialist struggle. Even if the Great Leap Forward failed – replicating in China Stalin's politically induced starvation and mass death – Mao contested Soviet authority from within the communist world. His challenge was a critical one indeed, as he contended for the leadership of world communism. Yet, Khrushchev's reaction also showed the Soviet priority of Cold War bipolarity and intolerance toward autonomous revolutions that threatened Moscow's interests. The state-centric architecture of international communism obstructed any adaptation in terms of "polycentrism" – a formulation suggested by the Italian communist leader Palmiro Togliatti to inspire greater adaptability of the "socialist camp" to global changes, but which was ignored both by the Soviets and by the Chinese. The encounter of communism with decolonization ended up in rivalry between the Soviet Union and China.

17 Charles S. Maier, *Leviathan 2.0: Inventing Modern Statehood* (Cambridge, MA: Harvard University Press, 2014).

The second challenge was the attempt to provide high levels of economic development, productivity and consumption compared with Western capitalism. Even if reforms were circumscribed to economic performance in the aftermath of 1956, there were major efforts to improve living standards and raise life expectancy. Scholars have increasingly devoted attention to the new consumerist impulse that took hold in the Soviet Union, Hungary and East Germany. In global perspective, however, the importance of such developments was lessened as the West experienced the most formidable growth in the history of capitalism. In fact, the postwar global contest between communism and Western capitalism showed mutual ambivalent influences. The welfare-based reform of capitalism in Western Europe's reconstruction was to a significant extent motivated by the influence and fear of communism. It was an anti-communist response totally different from the 1920s, though the red scare hysteria of the earlier era was reproduced in the United States. Yet the reform of capitalism also had the crucial consequences of sweeping away the specter of the Great Depression and reinforcing US hegemony.[18]

The Western combination of prosperity and democracy disproved not only old communist prophecies of capitalist breakdown but also more recent promises of overcoming the capitalist economies. Although the efforts to develop a socialist "soft power" in the aftermath of the post-Stalin insurgencies in Eastern Europe do deserve analysis – as they provide a better understanding of the "socialist sixties" and the advance of transnational connections – their effectiveness should not be overestimated, particularly since the Iron Curtain became more and more porous. At the same time, Soviet and East European projects of forging noncapitalist societies and communities proved frail, and even illusory, in the Third World. Postcolonial elites were much more interested in the Soviet model as a means to promote development than as an end in itself. Sovietization was hardly a usable term or feasible prospect, even outside Europe.

By the end of the 1960s, global communism had impacted on many social, cultural and political developments. Marxism in its multiple varieties was a global language, particularly through its intersection with Third Worldism. The Vietnam War and the Cuban Revolution each catalysed anti-imperialist mobilization elsewhere. However, communism hardly emanated the same sense of a demiurgic force as it had a decade earlier. The prospects of post-

18 Federico Romero, *Storia della guerra fredda. L'ultimo conflitto per l'Europa* (Turin: Einaudi, 2009).

Stalin reforms vanished in 1968 as they found their last and most meaningful manifestation in the Prague Spring and its "socialism with a human face." The attempts to find new forms of socialist legitimacy ended abruptly in a few months. As a consequence of violent repression by the Warsaw Pact in Czechoslovakia, the very notion of reform was banned in the Soviet bloc – to reemerge only in the late 1980s in Moscow. At the same time, Moscow and Beijing represented two different poles and models of communism in competition with each other, particularly in the Third World. Maoism radically reshaped the Soviet concept of modernity and redefined the "two camps" theory underpinning the Soviet Cold War. It did so both by launching an uncompromising anti-imperialist Cultural Revolution and by applying Marxist language to an entirely different vision of relentless North–South conflict. The disputed departure from Stalin's legacy and the impact of decolonization had opened up a cleavage over the very meaning of socialist-led globalization. After half a century, international communism had definitively lost its unity as a political subject and a world movement.

The ending of communist unity revealed more profound changes. As we see now more clearly, the "global 1968" impacted the communist world by heightening its divisions and, no less importantly, by exposing the decline of state-related networks and the emergence of new forms of transnational political activity.[19] Rebellious youth often used the lexicon and even symbols of the communist tradition, but they were not part of the same movement. They echoed the anti-bureaucratic suggestions of the Maoist Cultural Revolution and felt drawn to the anti-imperialist engagement of Che Guevara or Ho Chi Minh. Nevertheless, their relationship to communist establishments was basically a conflictual one. The emergence of a new left never meant creating a base of recruitment for the communist movement – as it had for the World War II resistance generation – nor even inheriting the communist ethos. The relationship between the individual and the collective was dramatically shifting throughout transnational countercultures, even among self-declared revolutionaries. The spirit of unreserved self-sacrifice and the sense of belonging to an embattled army were a thing of the past. Moreover, although reformers in the Soviet bloc did not have much in common with the students' revival of Marxism in the West, they did share with them the insight that the communist project was in crisis. In other

19 Maud A. Bracke and James Mark, "Between Decolonization and the Cold War: Transnational Activism and Its Limits in Europe 1950s–90s," *Journal of Contemporary History* 50, 3 (2015), 403–17.

words, the aftermath of 1968 opened up critical scenarios, even if the capitalist turmoil of the early 1970s would for some time conceal them.

A Failed Alternative in a Globalized World

In post-Stalin times, the history of communism became an increasingly divided and fragmented history in a world of growing interdependence. Diversity eventually prevailed over uniformity in socialist countries despite the apparent homogeneity of one-party states and collectivized economies. The Yugoslav self-management experiment and the Maoist Cultural Revolution pluralized the landscape in diverse ways. Yet pluralism could only mean fracture, as the Sino-Soviet split demonstrated. A variety of divergent experiences affected the trajectories of communist parties, which mainly took shape in terms of narratives of their own identities, the fundamental choices for their strategies and practices, and the relationship with what was left of the Soviet template. Many roots of centrifugal developments could be traced back to World War II, as if the "age of wars" still projected its shadow onto communism, imposing continuity and posing predicaments.

A key to the underlying reasons for fragmentation was the influence of nationalism. Scholars have underlined how the relationship with nationalism that had been forged during World War II increased in importance in Asian communism and affected China's relationship to the Soviet Union and the Cold War.[20] The liberation struggle in Vietnam probably traced the most visible such trajectory, as its internationalist meaning elsewhere in the world was intertwined with its national substance. For some time, the Asian theater appeared the most promising one, to the point of making it possible to believe that the center of gravity of communist revolution was undergoing a critical shift. In Latin America, the Cuban impulse to export guerrillas among the peasantry failed, suffering severe setbacks in the 1960s. In the Middle East and in Africa, communist forces were not the main protagonists of anti-imperialist nationalism even where they had significant influence, particularly in Algeria and South Africa. Asia instead displayed quite dynamic scenarios, in spite of the bloody destruction of Indonesian communism in 1965. Maoism evoked "permanent revolution," while Vietnamese communists successfully carried forward their autonomous armed struggle and civil wars spilled over to the whole of Indochina in the early 1970s. As the

20 Shen Zhihua and Li Danhui, *After Leaning to One Side: China and Its Allies in the Cold War* (Stanford: Stanford University Press, 2011).

Vietnamese, Cambodian and Laotian communists took power in 1975, the global impact of Asian communism contrasted with the apparent decrease in the activism of European and Soviet communism. Only the war between Vietnam and Cambodia in 1979 and the revelation of the genocide carried out by the Khmer Rouge put an end to this trend. However, the cleavage between communist trajectories in Asia, Europe and Russia was destined to remain.

Divisions among communists regarding the inevitability of a Third World War in the nuclear era, and the relative prospects of civil war and legal activity as the path to social and political change, also displayed a global dimension. This itself had roots in World War II. In Western Europe, the French and Italian parties remained influential in spite of capitalist modernization, by means of parliamentary activities, social integration, local government and defense of workers' rights. They cultivated ideas of a "peaceful road" to socialism and distanced themselves from the Soviet model, especially after 1968 and the crushing of the Prague Spring. This was not simply a matter of national strategy. The main implication was that the century's revolutionary legacy had to be reinterpreted by way of structural reforms of capitalist societies, and even by encouraging further changes in Soviet socialism. Peaceful ideas of change were not a European monopoly, as they had developed in India and in Chile by the late 1960s, and were also professed by the Yugoslavs in the nonaligned movement. The violence of the Cold War prevented this from developing further beyond Europe, particularly as the Popular Front government in Chile was destroyed by a military coup with Washington's concurrence in 1973. Anti-imperialist internationalism again took center stage in the global South by the mid 1970s, not only in Asia but also in Africa as a consequence of Cuban intervention in postcolonial Angola and the communists' role in the armed struggle against the racist regime in South Africa. In parallel to this, the Eurocommunist project spoke quite a different language and depicted scenarios of a socialist democracy to be forged in Europe as the forefront of a reformed communism.

In such a multifaceted context, the Soviet Union was obviously a crucial actor. Yet its centrality and orthodoxy came to be widely disputed. In the 1970s, Soviet-type societies showed domestic conservative stability. The adjustment of socialist life both from above and from below was something that had started as soon as the Stalinist terror ended. Scholars have analyzed the gradual emergence of an unwritten social pact exchanging improvements in living standards – particularly the extension of welfare measures and mass consumption – in return for passive acceptance of the regimes' authoritarian framework. Social conformity and consumerist depoliticization combined well with the isolation and repression of dissidents. The Soviet lifestyle and official ideology became increasingly divorced, though this did not necessarily cause upset and could be seen as inherent in the stabilization of a complex noncapitalist urbanized society. "Actually existing socialism" came to signify stagnation and the demise of any communist social project in Eastern Europe and the Soviet Union. The original communist vision of politics as a transformative force came to an earlier ending in Soviet-type societies than it did in the West and the Third World.

The other side of the story was the Soviet contribution to the global Cold War and its expansion in the global South in the 1970s. Brezhnev's project of achieving full superpower status implied detachment from the universalist perspectives still cultivated by Khrushchev, the straightforward use of ideology as *instrumentum regni*, a bipolar status quo in Europe and military confrontation with the West in the Third World – enhanced by the Chinese rapprochement with the United States and Soviet expansionism in Africa. Yet, in light of Arne Westad's study of the global Cold War, scholars have enlarged their perspectives to a plurality of aspects and long-term implications.[21] We should probably see Brezhnev's project as an attempt by the Soviet leadership to build on new sources of credibility – founded on a traditional idea of empire – and on a geopolitical gamble – which assumed that the ideological, cultural and even economic competition in the Third World decisively worked in favor of the socialist camp. This was less inconsistent than it may appear retrospectively. The Vietnam War, the Portuguese Revolution, the end of the Bretton Woods system and the oil shock helped persuade many that the West had worse problems. The failure of Mao's international challenge within the communist movement could only reinforce a sense of supremacy in orthodox communist establishments. However, the Afghan War which started in 1979 and the Polish crisis in the early 1980s showed that such a trajectory was weakly grounded.

Scholars have often emphasized the Soviet imperial overstretch resulting from convergence between the impact of the "Soviet Vietnam" in Afghanistan, the East European countries' huge debts to the West, mass opposition in Poland and Reagan's relaunching of bipolar confrontation. This standpoint is hardly disputable, though it should not lead to deterministic conclusions. However, we are gradually integrating it with an understanding of Soviet

21 Odd Arne Westad, *The Global Cold War: Third World Interventions and the Making of Our Times* (Cambridge: Cambridge University Press, 2005).

communism as a regime in the new century – though devoid of key ingredients such as universalist aims.

Seen in this light, the duality between the Russian and the Chinese revolutions may prove less significant than is often assumed, and different hierarchies of meaning may come into view. The multifaceted trajectories of communism in the late twentieth century led to decline, collapse and transformations. This took place as the Cold War gradually imploded, economic globalization entered an unprecedented historical phase, and a multipolar order began to surface. Communist identities lost their salience as they experienced fundamental changes mainly related to cultural, national and local inheritances – indeed, ones evading classification. They simply dissolved in the new century, as all major political cultures had to redefine their own foundations and deal with sharpened dilemmas of inequality, liberty, sovereignty, development and environmental impacts. We might consider whether it is necessary to develop historical debates on the Russian, Chinese and other communist experiences as reflections on the metamorphoses and vanishing of the past century's revolutionary heritage in our globalized world. Still, we can see now how communist history was intertwined with the global history of the last century. Far from being a deviation from established patterns, communism was a component of global processes and contributed to shaping them in multiple ways. Any historical narrative of globalization will have to take into account this advance in the scholarship, which helps enrich our historical comprehension and render it multidimensional. A hundred years after the Russian Revolution, we cannot comprehend the making of our world without understanding and analyzing communism and its legacies.

Introduction to Volume I

SILVIO PONS AND STEPHEN A. SMITH

The first volume of *The Cambridge History of Communism* concentrates on the history of the Soviet Union and the communist movement from 1917 through to the outbreak of World War II in 1939. Hopes on the part of the Bolsheviks, who seized power in October 1917, that the revolution in Russia would trigger an international socialist revolution ran high in this period. The devastation and suffering caused by World War I radicalized soldiers, workers and peasants across Europe, especially in the defeated countries, and led to the redrawing of the political map, as empires disintegrated and new nation-states emerged. The volume attends to the international implications of the revolution, notably the abortive attempts at communist revolution in Europe between 1918 and 1923, the repercussions in the colonial world, the rise of fascism and the efforts of the Soviet Union to create popular anti-fascist fronts from 1935. A guiding theme is the tension between hopes for international revolution, symbolized in the Comintern (or Third International), which moved from Europe to East Asia in the course of the 1920s to become particularly important in China, and the gradual recognition on the part of the Bolsheviks that they were destined to build socialism in one country, the slogan to which Stalin pinned his colors as he rose to prominence in the Bolshevik party following the death of Lenin in 1924. The volume also situates the revolution in a Eurasian perspective, looking at its impact on Central Asia and the borderlands more generally. Despite the isolation of the Soviet Union, a large swathe of public opinion in the West well understood the potential of international communism to destabilize the capitalist order, especially during the Depression. A number of chapters in the volume treat the multiple interactions between the Soviet domestic context and the international, or even transnational, dimensions, which were set in motion by ideology, policies and organizational practices, the construction of identities, and the idealization of socialist society. That said, the volume is largely concerned with developments within the Soviet Union between the civil war (1918–21) and 1939. The chapters cover the political, economic, social and cultural dimensions that characterized Bolshevik power and the drive to create a socialist society in this period, reflecting the latest research. Since the opening of archives in 1991, following the fall of the Soviet Union, scholars working on Soviet history have had access to a huge amount of new source material, especially for the period after 1921, when censorship and state secrecy meant that sources available to historians became increasingly restricted. Revolutions differ from military coups because the breakdown of state power is total and this opens up a space for mass mobilization. A history of revolution must, then, be a history of an entire society thrown into turmoil, but ultimately a society that is gradually subordinated to a new political power. This is reflected in the volume in essays on the activities and experience of peasants, workers, intellectuals, non-Russian ethnic groups, women and young people – subjects that prior to 1991 were difficult to research. The consequence is to complicate conventional understandings of the relations between state and society, as they evolved through civil war, stabilization in the 1920s, the "revolution from above" that Stalin unleashed in 1928, through to the consolidation of one of the twentieth century's worst tyrannies. And, as will become evident in the subsequent two volumes, this more multifaceted understanding of the evolution of Soviet communism allows us more deeply to appreciate its differences from – as well as similarities with – later communist regimes, highlighting the ways in which later regimes were shaped by inherited patterns of economic development, social structure, cultural and religious traditions and, not least, by the different international conjunctures that emerged after World War II.

*****

The collapse of the tsarist regime in February 1917 was ultimately rooted in a crisis brought about by economic and social modernization of a backward empire, a crisis that was massively exacerbated by World War I. From the 1860s, and especially from the 1890s, the tsarist autocracy strove to keep its place among the major European powers by beginning to industrialize and by modernizing its armed forces. Time, however, was not on its side. From the late nineteenth century the major industrial powers – Germany, the USA, Britain and France – were rapidly expanding their geopolitical and economic might, threatening to reduce Russia to a second-rate power. As Russia's extremely backward society underwent brisk economic, social and cultural change, new social and political forces were unleashed that eroded the social base of the autocracy. Industrialization, urbanization and rural-to-urban migration gave rise to new social classes, notably industrial workers, commercial and industrial capitalists, and the professional middle classes, which did not fit into the traditional system of social estates, dominated as it was by the landed nobility. These emerging social classes demanded that the autocracy treat them as citizens, not as subjects, and grant them civil and political rights. It was these demands, raised in the context of a war with Japan, which led to the outbreak of a massive social and political revolution in 1905. In that year, a liberal movement based in the middle classes, a militant labor movement, mutinies in the armed forces and a colossal peasant movement aimed at dispossessing the landed gentry, built up such momentum that Nicholas II was forced to concede significant political reform in the October Manifesto of 1905. By 1907, order had been restored – the uprising of workers in Moscow in December 1905 and peasant insurgency were ruthlessly crushed, and as the tide of revolution receded, Nicholas began to renege on his promise of a constitutional monarchy.

The years between 1907 and 1914, sometimes called the "Years of Reaction," nevertheless opened up some potential for reform of state and society. After considerable reduction in the representation of peasants and workers in the new parliament, or Duma, the Third Duma proved more willing to work with government, although much of its legislative program was blocked by divisions within the Duma ranks and by stalemate between the Duma and the tsar's ministers. At the same time, tensions between the autocracy and its traditional supporters, the landed gentry and the Orthodox Church, increased. More positively, these years saw the rapid growth of a civil society, evident in the expansion of the press, the proliferation of voluntary societies, the flourishing of the professions and a new consumer culture that cut across class divisions. By the time of the outbreak of World War I, hopes for political reform had faded. Yet despite a resurgence of mass strikes in 1912–14, there were reasons to think that Russia might be moving away from revolution, as the countryside settled down, as industry revived after 1910 and as Russia's armed forces were strengthened. The international environment, however, remained menacing and the problems of managing a multinational empire were becoming increasingly apparent. If World War I had not broken out in July 1914, it is possible that the gulf between the common people and the privileged classes, and that between the privileged classes and government might have been slowly bridged. As it was, the war put paid to any such hope. The demands of "total war" strained the industrial and agrarian economies to the limit, causing price rises, declining real incomes and, crucially, food shortages for people in the cities. The human costs of the war were staggering, with up to 2.25 million soldiers dying in combat, in captivity, or from wounds and disease. Many in the political elite hoped that the outbreak of war might revitalize the constitutional settlement promised in the October Manifesto, but Nicholas's determination to maintain his divinely ordained position as all-powerful autocrat became ever more apparent. On 1 November 1916 Pavel Miliukov, the leader of the liberal Kadet party, delivered a sensational attack on the government in the Duma, listing a series of government failures, and asked: "Is this stupidity or treason?" It was unambiguous evidence that the tsar and court had lost the support of the political and military elites. Meanwhile among ordinary people shortages of subsistence items, rising prices and a general desire to see the end of the war led to political strikes and demonstrations.

The February Revolution of 1917 came about as a result of the machinations of Duma politicians and generals, on the one hand, and mass action on the streets, on the other. In Petrograd, as St. Petersburg was renamed in 1914, women came out on 23 February, International Women's Day, to protest the shortage of bread. Soon workers, students and members of the middle classes were on the streets of the capital, singing the "Marseillaise" and calling for the overthrow of the tsarist government. The die was cast on 27 February when the Volynskii regiment mutinied, inspiring other military units to follow its lead. On that day activists in the Workers' Group of the Central War Industries Committee, in coordination with socialist deputies in the Duma, reconvened the Soviet, which had appeared in October 1905, as a temporary organ to lead the popular movement. Factories and military units began to send delegates to the Tauride Palace, the seat of the Duma, to form the Petrograd Soviet of Workers' and Soldiers' Deputies. On 27 February, too, liberal members of the Duma created a committee, which set about arresting ministers, generals and police chiefs. Mikhail Rodzianko, chair of the Fourth Duma, used his influence to get the generals to persuade the tsar to abdicate. It was out of this Duma committee that the Provisional Government was formed on 2 March.

Rex Wade's chapter offers a detailed account of the events that followed the February Revolution. Suffice to say that out of the confluence of the two forces that made the February Revolution – the political and military elites and the working people and soldiers on the street – there emerged a "dual power." This was the term coined to denote the institutional arrangement under which the Provisional Government had formal authority, but the Soviet Executive Committee real power, since it had the backing of the garrison, control of transport and communications, and general support among the urban populace. For the Provisional Government, the February Revolution represented a political not a social revolution, a revolution that they hoped would expedite the pursuit of war to victory and the ultimate establishment of a democratic state. For the supporters of the Soviet, February was a social as well as a political revolution, a revolution that would redistribute gentry land to the peasantry, improve the conditions of workers and, above all, bring an end to a futile war. It was the question of war that led to the first crisis when the Provisional Government refused to back the plan for a democratic peace formulated by the Menshevik and Socialist Revolutionary (SR) leaders of the Soviet. In a bid to resolve the crisis, the latter joined the government on 22 April. Having joined a coalition in order to strengthen the government's commitment to peace, under the new minister of war, Alexander Kerensky, Soviet leaders found themselves supporting a new military offensive in June. It was the failure of this offensive that rapidly shifted the opinion of workers and soldiers away from the moderate socialists in favor of the Bolshevik party, which had been steadfast in its denunciation of the war as an imperialist war and the Provisional Government as a government of "capitalists and landlords."

The Bolsheviks had entered the public arena during the 1905 Revolution, already fierce critics of the Mensheviks and SRs for their support for the liberal opposition in the "bourgeois phase of revolution." The Bolsheviks, by contrast, were convinced that liberals would betray the revolution and looked to the small proletariat, backed by the peasantry, to push the bourgeois revolution forward in a socialist direction. The unquestioned leader of the Bolsheviks was Vladimir Ilich Lenin, who is discussed in the chapters by Robert Service and Lars Lih. Lenin considered himself a faithful disciple of Marx and the Second International, discussed in the chapter by Geoff Eley, but his belief in the leadership by a disciplined revolutionary party and his defense of dictatorial methods gave his Marxism a rather Russian cast. During the Years of Reaction and World War I, the Bolsheviks were pushed to the sidelines, but Lenin, from his exile in Switzerland, proved indefatigable in his denunciation of the war, which he interpreted as evidence that the global capitalist system was in crisis. Upon his return to Russia in April 1917, after a decade-long absence, he denounced the critical support given to the Provisional Government by the moderate socialists and some in his own party, a government he characterized as one of "capitalists and landowners" and called for transfer of power to the soviets that were growing in the urban centers of the empire. He recognized the deep unpopularity of the war and the likelihood that the masses would turn against the Provisional Government once its inability or unwillingness to tackle their grievances became apparent. However, it was not until the threat of counterrevolution loomed in the shape of General Kornilov, who had formed an alliance of convenience with the Kerensky government in the hope of crushing the soviets, that workers and soldiers rallied around the Bolshevik slogans of "Bread, Peace, and Land," all power to the soviets and an end to the war. In the big cities support for the Bolsheviks – along with their left SR, Menshevik Internationalist and anarchist allies – soared during September. In this period the Bolsheviks proved effective less because of their organizational discipline than because they worked relentlessly in mass organizations such as the soviets, factory committees, trade unions and soldiers' committees.

With the surge in support for his party, Lenin concluded that internationally as well as nationally the time was ripe for the Bolsheviks to seize power. From his hiding place in Finland, where he had fled in the wake of the July Days, he blitzed the Central Committee with demands that it prepare an insurrection, even threatening to resign on 29 September when his demands were ignored. Returning in secret to Petrograd, Lenin on 10 October succeeded in persuading the Central Committee to commit itself to the overthrow of the Provisional Government, but no timetable was set. Preparations for the uprising took on a defensive cast, thanks to Leon Trotsky, brilliant chair of the Petrograd Soviet who had formally joined the Bolshevik party while in jail in August, whose career is analyzed in Bertrand Patenaude's chapter. When on the night of 23–24 October, Kerensky ordered the closure of the Bolshevik printing press, Trotsky declared that action was now imperative to prevent him crushing the revolution. On 24 October reliable military units and Red Guards took control of bridges, railway stations and other key points in Petrograd. By the morning of 25 October all strategic points in the city were under Bolshevik control. At 10.40 p.m., against the background thud of artillery bombardment of the Winter Palace, the Second Congress of Soviets opened. Mensheviks and SRs condemned the overthrow of the government as a declaration of civil war and demonstratively walked out. The seizure of power is sometimes presented as a conspiratorial coup against a democratic government. It certainly had elements of a coup, but it was a coup much advertised, and the government it overthrew had never been democratically elected. Indeed, the Provisional Government was a pathetic shadow of its former self, symbolized in the fact that few of the armed forces were prepared to come to its aid.

The new government made good on its promise of peace and land, but otherwise it quickly found itself moving in an authoritarian direction, partly as a result of mounting political opposition and partly as the economic crisis went from bad to catastrophic. When the SRs won the Constituent Assembly elections, the Bolsheviks did not scruple to shut it down. Soviet power – which they counterposed to the kind of parliamentary regime represented by the Constituent Assembly – was popular, since it was equated with the devolution of power to the lowest levels. But all the pressures on the new government were to centralize power in order to cope with a collapsing economy, and this soon led to clashes with local soviets, many of which were under the control of SRs and left SRs. The Treaty of Brest-Litovsk with the Central Powers, which was imposed by Lenin against the advocates of a "revolutionary war," gave the Bolsheviks only a temporary respite. The formation of a White Volunteer Army, backed by Cossacks, followed by the rebellion of the Czech Legion in May, led to full-scale civil war and saw the Bolsheviks move further in the direction of authoritarian one-party rule. Soviets ceded authority to the party, the Cheka and the Red Army, which was hammered into shape by Trotsky. Some historians interpret Bolshevik authoritarianism as deriving from their ideological commitment to a dictatorship of the proletariat and their determination to hold on to power at all costs, while others see it more as a response to the desperate circumstances of civil war and economic collapse and, especially, to the loss of support in a much depleted working class. So far as the outcome of the civil war was concerned, a victory for the armies of General Anton Denikin and Admiral Aleksandr Kolchak, backed as they were by the Allies, was always a possibility, especially if the advances of the two armies had been successfully coordinated in spring and summer 1919. The Red Army was larger than the White armies, but in qualitative terms it was not superior. It is true that the White leadership was more divided than that of the Red Army and the latter was certainly superior in the sphere of organization. But as much as anything it was the strategic advantage enjoyed by the Reds, who occupied a compact territory, compared with the Whites who were strung out on the peripheries of the empire, that proved advantageous. Crucially, of course, this was a war about the future shape of the international order and, in this respect, the Bolsheviks proved far more effective at projecting their messages of Soviet power and international socialism than did the Whites, who had little to offer the masses on such matters as land, national autonomy, or working conditions. Popular support was not a major factor working to the advantage of the Reds, but neither was it irrelevant: Workers witnessed terrifying examples of White generals hanging strikers, and peasants lived in fear that a White victory would restore the landed gentry. That said, the extent to which the regime faced economically rooted opposition from workers and massive peasant resistance to food requisitioning and conscription should not be underestimated. And once it became clear that the Whites had been defeated, popular discontent would lead to massive peasant insurgency, strikes and, not least, the rebellion by Kronstadt sailors in March 1921. With the Bolshevik power finally established in spring 1921, there would be no going back to the vision of 1917, with the idea of power rooted in soviets, workers' control of production, or a democratically organized army.

A major theme of recent research on the civil war has been that of violence, the theme explored in the chapter by Hiroaki Kuromiya. Between 1917 and 1921, some 10.5 million people lost their lives – mainly from disease and starvation – and a further 2 million went into exile. Civil war killing is often condensed into the image of the Cheka and the red terror, which followed the attempted assassination of Lenin in August 1918. But violence was perpetrated on all sides: by the White armies, their Cossack supporters and ancillary warlords, especially in the Far East; by nationalists seeking autonomy, such as the army of Simon Petliura in Ukraine; in conflicts between ethnic groups in the Caucasus and the western borderlands; by warlords and anarchists, such as Nestor Makhno, in Ukraine; by the "green" bands of irregulars who resisted food requisitioning and conscription, often with an SR coloration; and not least, by peasants defending their local interests often at the expense of their neighbors. After the withdrawal of the Germans from Ukraine, for example, 1919 witnessed an unprecedented pogrom against Jews. Mass violence on all sides was rooted in fear and uncertainty, but it was an expression, too, of the breakdown of state authority, the struggle to survive, a brutalization of daily life and, to some extent, of ideology. Bolshevik violence is seen by Kuromiya as adumbrating the violence of Stalin that was unleashed with forced collectivization of the peasantry (1928–33) and the Great Terror of 1937–38.

Another feature of recent historiography has been to set the Russian Revolution in the context of empire, paying attention to reverberations of the Bolshevik seizure of power on the western borderlands, the Baltic, the Caucasus and Central Asia. The German occupation of Ukraine in early 1918 spurred the Allies to dispatch military contingents to Russia, ostensibly to maintain the war effort on the eastern front, but the signing of the armistice in November 1918 saw Allied intervention actually stepped up, especially in Siberia and the Caucasus. This was a powerful factor that served to internationalize the revolution and to complicate the struggles for national autonomy on the borderlands. It would be hard to argue that the Russian Empire was brought to its knees by national liberation movements – class-based movements were undoubtedly stronger – but in the course of 1917 and the civil war nationalist movements gained in strength, especially in Poland, the Baltic and the Caucasus. Paradoxically, however, the civil war also highlighted internal divisions within nationalist movements, especially regarding land redistribution. And nationalist parties and armies invariably found themselves buffeted by stronger forces, compelling them to turn for support variously to the Central Powers or the Allies, to the Reds or the Whites.

Lenin had insisted that when dealing with the non-Russian peoples of the empire Bolsheviks should avoid Great Russian chauvinism, but this was by no means a counsel observed by all his comrades, not least Stalin himself, commissar of nationalities, and a man socialized in the violent world of the Caucasus. The Bolsheviks lost control of most areas outside the heartland of European Russia between 1918 and 1920, yet by appealing to national self-determination and anti-colonialism, they came to seem to many nationalists to be not ideal allies but the least bad option available. Poland, Finland, the Baltic states, the western parts of Ukraine and Belorussia, and Bessarabia were excised from the former empire, but one of the most surprising outcomes of the civil war – especially in the light of the collapse of the Ottoman, Austro-Hungarian and German empires – was that the Bolsheviks managed to put an empire back together again. At the same time, especially following the creation of a federation of Soviet polities in 1922, this was an empire which institutionalized nationality as a principle of territorial organization and as a defining feature of individual identity. During the 1920s indeed, the Soviet state engaged in vigorous nation-building among the non-Russian peoples, as analyzed in Andrea Graziosi's chapter. In Central Asia, for example, as Adeeb Khalid's chapter shows, national identity gradually came to hold sway over religious, tribal and kin-based identities. An empire of nations thus emerged led by a regime that claimed to be in business to transcend the national principle in favor of proletarian internationalism. After Stalin's rise to power, more conventionally imperial elements came to the fore – such as the overrepresentation of Russians in senior political positions, the presumption of a Russian civilizing mission, and the assumption that sedentary agriculture was superior to pastoralism. Yet this remained an empire of a peculiar type, one that offered universal citizenship to all its inhabitants, regardless of ethnicity.

The Bolsheviks came to power, convinced that capitalism was in terminal crisis, and believing that they were initiating a process of international revolution. They looked in particular to the workers of Germany, Europe's most advanced capitalist power, hopeful that they would rise up and come to rescue of their comrades in backward Soviet Russia. The October Revolution had a massive radicalizing effect on working people in Central and Eastern Europe, devastated by war and inspired by the messages of proletarian emancipation and anti-imperialism. Conversely, it struck fear not only into the old ruling elites but also into those of the new nation-states that were brought into being under the aegis of Woodrow Wilson's Fourteen Points. Czechoslovakia declared independence in October 1918 and the Kingdom of Serbs, Croats, and Slovenes in December of that year. The independent states of Austria and Hungary saw their territories amputated, the implications of which are discussed in John Paul Newman's chapter. But it was in Germany that revolution *à la russe* came closest to being realized. On 29 October 1918, the mutiny of sailors at Kiel set in train the events that led to revolution. As Eric Weitz explains in his chapter, the mutinies and strikes grew to the point where Soviet-style councils emerged. Following the abdication of the Kaiser on 9 November, the Social Democrats proclaimed a republic, but this was soon challenged from the far left by the Spartacist, Karl Liebknecht. By signing agreements with the army, followed by one between the trade unions and the employers, the Social Democrats ensured continuity with the old regime. Irate at the abandonment of the promise to socialize industry, workers took to the streets and, fearing that they would be outflanked from the left, the new communist party launched an ill-advised insurrection, which was ruthlessly crushed by the government. On 5 March, serious fighting again broke out in Berlin and over the next days at least 1,200 people were killed, including seventy-five government troops. Meanwhile in Bavaria, where workers' councils had backed a general strike and an assault on the barracks, the independent socialist Kurt Eisner was assassinated by a right-wing officer. This triggered the proclamation in April of a republic of councils. Supported at first by a socialist coalition, the Soviet republic passed into communist hands for two weeks before the army and the Freikorps purged Munich, killing between 600 and 1,000. Nevertheless, as Weitz shows, the German Communist Party, with some 300,000 members by the mid 1920s, became the largest party outside the Soviet Union. The inner life of communist parties in the interwar period, the normative systems of their socialization, together with the political, ethical and emotional motivations that drove hundreds of thousands to join these parties are the subject of Brigitte Studer's chapter.

In Hungary, a communist regime lasted rather longer at 133 days. Under pressure from a communist party that had grown to 40,000 by March 1919, and faced by foreign occupation, the Hungarian Social Democrats split. A pact of 21 May saw the fusion of the left wing and the communists and the formation of a Soviet government, annulling elections to a Constituent Assembly and creating a proletarian army. Under Béla Kun, the communists became the dominant influence, proceeding on an ultra-left course that entailed a red terror and an attempt to collectivize agriculture. The immediate downfall of the government, however, came as a result of the intervention of the Romanian army. Similar developments – mass mobilization, a split in the socialist party and a right-wing backlash – took place in Italy, where the end of the war saw rapid inflation, shortages of subsistence items and rising unemployment. By spring 1919 there were mass strikes and food riots, providing a context in which the trade unions and the Italian Socialist Party grew rapidly. In Turin and Milan factory councils were formed in the metalworking factories. In Lazio soldiers returning from the front occupied the latifundia, and in the Po Valley landless laborers occupied the lands of large tenant farmers. Landowners and industrialists financed private militias, among them the combat units of Benito Mussolini. The number of strikes continued to rise, peaking in August and September 1920 when widespread occupation of the factories under communist and anarchosyndicalist leadership broke out in response to a lockout by employers. More than in Germany, the backlash had the effect of strengthening the extreme right, when in October 1922 the fascists came to power.

In March 1919, confident that international revolution was just over the horizon, the Bolsheviks called the First Congress of a new (Third) Communist International, known as the Comintern, to promote Bolshevik-style revolution on an international scale. The history of the Comintern is recounted in Serge Wolikow's chapter. Suffice to say that it did not begin serious activity until its Second Congress, which took place from 19 July to 17 August 1920. This Congress, mindful that the revolutionary tide in Europe was ebbing, discussed the possibilities of revolution in the colonial and semi-colonial worlds, the logic being that such revolution might prove a trigger for socialist revolution in the metropolitan centers of the empire. Much debate took place as to whether the communist parties in countries such as India, the Dutch East Indies, or China should subordinate themselves to "bourgeois" nationalist movements, which is a key theme of Sobhanlal Datta Gupta's chapter. In China a powerful nationalist movement arose in May 1919, after the territory that had once belonged to Germany was transferred to Japan. Out of this movement emerged a strengthened Nationalist Party and a tiny Chinese Communist Party, whose members were told – against their better judgement – to join the Nationalist Party on an individual basis. During the 1920s, as prospects for revolution in Europe receded, the Comintern looked increasingly to China to strike a blow against colonialism. In 1926, with Stalin's supporters now in control of the Comintern, the Chinese communists were urged to take power by stealth within the Nationalist Party, while ensuring that unity with the right wing of the party be preserved at all cost. It placed the Chinese communists in a suicidal quandary, and in April 1927 Chiang Kai-shek, leader of the Nationalist Army, crushed his erstwhile allies, spelling the end of the Chinese Communist Party in the cities. In his chapter Alexander Pantsov takes up the story.

Would Marx and Engels have recognized what had taken place in Russia as a Marxist revolution? The Bolsheviks certainly believed they were creating a Marxist revolution, insofar as they sought to overthrow capitalism, private property and the market and claimed that their regime was a dictatorship of the proletariat. Yet the circumstances in which they came to power in no way resembled the conditions for socialist revolution that Marx and Engels had envisaged, as Geoff Eley's chapter explains. They believed that communist revolution would come about largely through structurally determined processes, principally the contradiction between the increasingly socialized character of capitalist relations of production and private ownership of the means of production. They always stressed the importance of revolutionaries in bringing about socialist revolution, but they saw the preconditions for the creation of a socialist society as lying in the development of large-scale production, which could be placed under public control and, above all, in the existence of a sizeable industrial proletariat. The Bolsheviks, of course, recognized that Russia lacked this level of socioeconomic development, but believed that capitalism had achieved a level of development in which socialism would be created internationally and that revolution had broken out first in Russia because it was the "weakest link" in the capitalist chain. Despite Bolshevik victory in the civil war, the failure of the Bolshevik Revolution to spread to Germany led Lenin to rein in his optimism that socialist revolution would break out quickly across the developed world. He remained steadfast in his conviction that the beginnings of communism were to be seen "on all sides," yet he chastised left communists for believing that there was a "direct road" to communism, stressing instead "practical compromises, tacks, conciliatory maneuvers, zigzags, retreats."[1]

*****

At the Tenth Party Congress in March 1921 Lenin remarked that Russia was like a man "beaten to within an inch of his life." Agriculture was devastated and the extremely centralized economy that had met the needs of the Red Army at the expense of the civilian population could no longer be sustained. The Congress ratified a "New Economic Policy" (NEP) which entailed the restoration of the market as a mechanism for adjusting relations between town and countryside, the dismantling of the system of rationing and the encouragement of limited private enterprise. Lenin spoke of the NEP as both a "retreat" and as a policy intended to last "seriously and for a long time." With the NEP, the government priority became one of building a modern, industrial state through short-term sacrifices by the peasantry and the working class. Even before Lenin's death, socialist revolution had been redefined as a project in which the party-state would mobilize the country's human and material resources to pull the country out of economic, social and cultural backwardness as rapidly as possible. However, to many in the party the NEP looked like a return to capitalism. All could agree that the export of grain must be the principal means of financing the importation of the equipment needed for industrialization: The problem was that the peasantry was marketing less grain than it had done before the war. Nevertheless, the NEP enjoyed a heyday between 1924 and 1926, when the peasantry was largely left to its own devices, with even "kulaks" being encouraged to enrich themselves to produce more for the market. In industry production was roughly back to its 1913 level by 1926. The state-owned sector was subject to the principle of "economic accounting," which meant a severe cut in state subsidies, but the industrial commissariats found it hard to resist the temptation to interfere in the operation of industry, to ensure that it was not swamped by the private sector.

The optimal strategy for industrializing the country was the main bone of contention in the struggle between party leaders that took place following Lenin's death in January 1924. The Bolshevik leaders continued to see the international situation as threatening in spite of the treaty with Germany in 1922 and the establishment of diplomatic relations with the Western powers.

1 V. I. Lenin, *Left-Wing Communism: An Infantile Disorder* (1920), www.marxists.org/archive/lenin/works/1920/lwc/.

They thus concluded that Soviet Russia must build up its heavy industrial and defense sectors as fast as possible. Trotsky was the most talented of Lenin's successors but feared being seen as a factionalist, and his inactivity allowed a triumvirate of Stalin, Zinoviev and Kamenev to consolidate their position. He and the left opposition called for priority to be given to the expansion of heavy industry, and to limiting the market through planning. On the right wing of the party, Bukharin looked to a slow expansion of industry (socialism "at the speed of a peasant's nag") by encouraging free trade with the peasants and cooperative forms in agriculture. Increasingly alarmed at Stalin's ambition, Zinoviev and Kamenev joined forces with the left in January 1925, fearful that "kulaks" were benefiting at the expense of the working class. Stalin, who is the subject of James Harris's chapter, endorsed the slogan of "socialism in one country," a slogan that appeared to offer something positive to the growing numbers of young men joining the party who disliked ideological wrangling and who resented the idea that the prospects for socialism might depend on revolution in the more advanced capitalist countries. In October 1926, Stalin made an alliance of convenience with Bukharin, which became less useful once Trotsky and Zinoviev were expelled from the Central Committee in October 1927. Thereafter the Stalin group moved to advocate a far more rapid pace of industrialization, particularly when it became clear in 1928 that grain procurements were falling. With the need to introduce rationing in 1928 the Stalin leadership became convinced that the NEP had failed: Instead of the state sector gradually gaining dominance over the private sector, the reverse was happening. Kulaks were supposedly holding the towns to ransom and in the cities "nepmen," the owners of commercial and small manufacturing enterprises, were prevailing at the expense of the working class.

The forced collectivization of agriculture, which is discussed in Nicolas Werth's chapter, was designed to subordinate the peasantry to the state in order to ensure a steady flow of grain to feed the cities and pay for imports of industrial equipment. The herding of peasants into collective farms and the liquidation of the kulaks as a class provoked resistance on the part of more than 2 million peasants. Several million kulaks were deported. A major result of the disruption was that in 1932–33 a hideous famine broke out in Ukraine, Kazakhstan, the Volga region and the north Caucasus, which led to the loss of some 5.7 million lives. The regime was forced to compromise, by allowing peasants private plots and a limited market for their produce. By 1936 peasants, without the right to a passport, were reduced to something like a premodern "estate" and by the end of the decade they were still eating worse than they had ten years earlier.

Forced collectivization coincided with the first Five-Year Plan. In November 1928 Stalin declared that the Soviet Union must "catch up and surpass" the capitalist countries, otherwise "they will destroy us." The years 1928–32 saw the government seek to transform the entire economy through centralized planning and state mobilization of the human and material resources of the country. An extraordinarily high level of investment was enforced which by the end of the Second Five-Year Plan in 1937 had led to a substantial increase in industrial output. This allowed the Soviet Union to achieve national self-sufficiency and to become a leading military and economic power, ultimately able to defeat Nazi Germany in World War II. However, as Mark Harrison explains in his chapter, the plan was undermined by the constant pressure to increase production targets, and industrial managers were forced to circumvent official supply channels in order to fulfill plan targets. Crash industrialization, moreover, unleashed chaos in society. Millions of people moved from the countryside to the towns, putting intense pressure on housing and supplies, as Lewis Siegelbaum explains. The famine of 1932–33 and the chronic housing shortage led to the introduction of a system of urban residence permits. For the urban population shortages of basic consumer goods were endemic and this was the period that saw the emergence of the queue as a characteristic Soviet institution. Meanwhile the working class grew apace, as Donald Filtzer explains in his chapter, but the modest progress in working conditions that had been achieved during the NEP – notably, the establishment of the eight-hour day – was reversed. Real wages fell, working conditions deteriorated drastically, labor turnover was high, and absenteeism, drunkenness and indiscipline thrived. New managers, many of them former workers, used crude tactics. (Stalin's henchman, Lazar Kaganovich, declared that "the earth should tremble when the director walks around the plant.") For a minority of workers, however, this was the heroic era of building socialism in one country and hundreds of thousands were inspired to take part in socialist competition and to overfulfill production targets.

Stalin's "Great Break" of 1928–32 also witnessed what has been called "Cultural Revolution," discussed in Michael David-Fox's chapter, which shows how the attitudes of intellectuals to communism were similar and interconnected within and outside the Soviet Union. In industry "bourgeois" specialists came under attack and an affirmative action program to promote young workers into management positions was introduced. Male urban youths provided a substantial cohort of supporters of the regime: They were more educated, less care-worn, more enthusiastic and more assimilated into Soviet values than their parents. Matthias Neumann discusses the radicalism of youth in the Soviet Union and across Europe in this period, along with the tensions that this could produce. The Cultural Revolution entailed an onslaught on the "bourgeois" intelligentsia and on pluralism in the arts, which had been maintained in the 1920s. Old hierarchies and old values and habits, especially religious, were excoriated. Many ordinary people struggled to better their educational qualifications, to read improving literature and to acquire the perquisites of "culture," such as a watch, radio, bed, sewing machine, or gramophone. By 1931 the militant phase of the Cultural Revolution was over, and by the mid 1930s there is some evidence of an "embourgeoisement" of party cadres, as they sought to emulate in their dress, home furnishings, language and deportment a style that was considered "cultured."

The 1917 Revolution released many emancipatory impulses that were highly progressive, judged by the standards that prevailed in Europe and the USA in the interwar period. The 1920s gave rise to much experimentation in areas such as education, law, new forms of living, architecture and urban design and health care, and in the arts, literature and music. It was perhaps in the area of gender relations, however, that the revolution had its most visible impact, and this is the theme of Anna Krylova's chapter. The Bolsheviks sought to do away with the patriarchal family: Women's legal status was equalized with that of men; illegitimate children were given equal rights; divorce was made easy. The Women's Department, set up in 1919, sought to liberate working women from the burdens of family responsibilities and involve them in paid work and in the public sphere. Much was said about the "new woman," and women took on roles that challenged the traditional gender order. At the same time, the civil war in some respects reinforced a "macho" culture and in the 1920s male dominance was reinscribed within the party, state and industrial administration. As Krylova shows, however, ideas of women's liberation continued to reverberate through the 1930s, despite the Stalinist regime's restrictions on divorce, a ban on abortion in 1936 and a new emphasis on the family as a bedrock of the new Soviet order. In other areas of social life, too, the 1930s saw a retreat from the utopianism of the early years.

In the course of Stalin's "revolution from above," state-building was completed. E. A. Rees analyzes the complex relations between state administration and the party and the common problems of bureaucracy that beset them. None was more critical of bureaucracy than Stalin himself, yet he oversaw a massive expansion of bureaucracy through central planning and distribution, rationing, the administration of collective farms and the procurement of agricultural produce, and the administration of the internal passport system. At the lower levels of the party-state hierarchy, officials remained poorly educated, unwilling to take the initiative, fearful of those above them and contemptuous of those beneath them. The 1930s, however, stand out, above all, because of the flourishing of Stalin's personal rule, an autocracy of sorts, but one exercised through the party and the secret police. Kevin Morgan analyzes the cult of personality, and explains how it was emulated in communist parties elsewhere. Dissent within the party was almost entirely expunged. The purge (*chistka*) with its probing for the personal and political deviations in the biography of the party member and its encouragement of confession ("recognizing one's errors"), entrenched itself. There was a growing psychology of conspiracy, an obsession with secrecy and the unmasking of hidden enemies.

The Sixth Congress of the Comintern, which met from 17 July to 1 September 1928, claimed that capitalism was now entering a new period of crisis and all cooperation with reformist socialists must end. In Germany the new policy had devastating consequences when the communists refused to cooperate with the Social Democrats to block the rise of Adolf Hitler. The Stalin leadership portrayed the Western powers, particularly France, as warmongers, and as the Depression set in, the Soviet Union became dangerously isolated. The accession of Hitler in 1933 and the suppression of the German Communist Party that followed caused the Comintern slowly to distance itself from sectarian isolation, although it was not until 1935 that the tactic of the "popular anti-fascist front" was finally adopted at the Seventh and last Congress. This was paralleled by new diplomatic efforts on the part of the Soviet government to construct a system of "collective security" to oppose the aggressive plans of Nazi Germany and fascist Italy. In May 1935 a mutual assistance pact was signed between the USSR and France, and in June 1936 a Popular Front government was established, supported by the French Communist Party. In China in December 1936 a second united front was formed between the communists and the Guomindang to combat the threat of Japanese invasion. It was in Spain, however, as Tim Rees explains in his chapter, that the international battle between democracy and fascism was concentrated, after General Franco rose up against the republican government in July 1936. The Comintern actively assisted the republican forces in Spain, and won a degree of admiration for its defense of democracy. Any prestige it gained, however, was undone by its support for the show trials of Zinoviev, Kamenev and others in 1937–38. The extent to which the

Comintern was a tool of Soviet foreign policy was starkly revealed when the Soviet government, convinced that the West would never fight Hitler, signed a nonaggression pact with Nazi Germany on 23 August 1939. War broke out ten days later, but national communist parties were ordered to denounce the war as an imperialist war and to lay equal blame on both sides. In a few months, from March to August 1939, Stalin openly announced his own revision of Marxism – by declaring that the state would not vanish so long as "capitalist encirclement" existed – and definitively established the primacy of great-power interest for the Soviet Union – by concluding an alliance of mutual convenience with Hitler.

This brings us, finally, to the question of the relationship of Leninism to Stalinism. It is beyond question that there was much in Leninist theory and practice that adumbrated Stalinism. Lenin was the architect of the party's monopoly on power; it was he who subordinated the soviets and trade unions to the party; he who would not tolerate those who thought differently; he who dismantled many civil and political freedoms; he who crushed the socialist opposition. At the height of the civil war, Lenin even went so far as to suggest that the will of the proletariat "may sometimes be carried out by a dictator." In other words, Lenin bears considerable responsibility for the institutions and culture that allowed Stalin to come to power. Crucially, he bequeathed a structure of power that favored a single leader, and this made the ideas and capacities of the leader of far more consequence than in a democratic polity. Nevertheless Stalin's "revolution from above" also introduced real *dis*continuity, destroying centuries-old patterns of rural life and wreaking havoc upon urban society. Stalin certainly believed that he was advancing the cause of socialism, yet he presided over the consolidation of a new ruling elite, the restoration of economic and social hierarchies, the reconfiguration of patriarchal authority, the resurgence of a certain Russian chauvinism, the rejection of artistic experimentation in favor of a stifling conformism and the snuffing out of virtually progressive experiments in law and social welfare. Crucially, although the institutions of rule did not change, personal dictatorship, the unrestrained use of violence, the cult of power, paranoia about encirclement and internal wreckers, and the spiraling of terror across every level of society, all served to underline how far the Russian Revolution had traveled since the days of hope in 1917.

PART I

*

ORIGINS

I

Marxism and Socialist Revolution

GEOFF ELEY

Vignette 1: Zhu Zhixin

The first fragments of Karl Marx's writings translated into Chinese (some brief excerpts from the *Communist Manifesto*) were attached to an article of November 1905 by 22-year-old student Zhu Zhixin (1884–1920) in *The People's Journal* (*Min Bao*), which was the organ of the newly formed Revolutionary Alliance (Tongmenghui) of Sun Yat-sen and other exiles in Japan. Zhu followed this introduction to the lives of Marx and Engels (entitled "Short Biographies of German Social Revolutionaries") with a second article on the life of Marx's great rival of the 1860s, Ferdinand Lassalle, together with a series of further commentaries on the progress of socialist parties in Western Europe.[1] Significant interest in European socialist thought, whether among the revolutionary émigrés or radicalized student circles in China itself, seems to have dated from these years. It was a reception almost wholly mediated by translations from Christian socialist and nascently social-democratic publications in Japan, themselves drawing on writings from the United States. Such interest now surged, drawing major impetus from the Russo-Japanese War of 1903–05.[2] The early understandings were loose and eclectic, taking their cues especially from the history and outlook of German social democracy, but with an interest in far wider bodies of social reforming thought too.[3] The impact of the 1905 Russian Revolution then

For general perspective I am greatly indebted to Mrinalini Sinha and Julia Adeney Thomas.

1 See Maurice Meisner, *Li Ta-Chao and the Origins of Chinese Marxism* (New York: Atheneum, 1979), 52; Martin Bernal, *Chinese Socialism to 1907* (Ithaca: Cornell University Press, 1976), 67–68, 107–28.

2 Thus in 1903, the Bookshop published three guides to socialism: *Modern Socialism* by Fukui Junzō (1899); *The Socialist Party* by Nishikawa Kōjiro (1901); and *Socialism* by Murai Chishi (1899). Bernal, *Chinese Socialism to 1907*, 94.

3 See Martin Bernal, "The Triumph of Anarchism over Marxism, 1906–1907," in Mary Clabaugh Wright (ed.), *China in Revolution: The First Phase, 1900–1913* (New Haven: Yale University Press, 1968), 110–12.

decisively shifted the ground of revolutionary thinking in China. Inspiration came again from socialists in Japan, most notably Kōtoko Shōsui (1871–1911) who was then turning to anarchist conceptions of direct action, terrorist thinking and the example of the Russian Socialist Revolutionaries (SRs). Henceforth, under Kōtoko's influence, Chinese revolutionaries also turned toward Russia, replacing versions of Marxist-inclined social democracy with varieties of anarchocommunism inspired both by the terrorist strand of SR militancy and by the thought of Peter Kropotkin, whose works Kōtoko was in process of translating.[4] Between 1906–07 and 1919–20, in other words, *Marxism* per se receded in China as a distinct body of precepts and theory. As a revolutionary exemplar and source of socialist theory, Marx jostled among much wider intellectual company, from Kropotkin and Bakunin to Saint-Simon, the Fabians and Henry George. Budding socialists cleaved increasingly either to revolutionary violence of anarchist coloration or to the social policy socialisms stressing national welfare and development. Before returning to China from Tokyo in spring 1907, for example, Zhu Zhixin had registered exactly this shift in affiliation, moving from embryonic familiarity with the perspectives of West European social democracy toward the direct-action militancy of anarchism instead. It was only later, very dramatically in the turmoil surrounding the reaction to the Paris Peace Conference in 1919, that revolutionaries turned back toward Marx.[5]

Vignette 2: Nguyen Ai Quoc/Ho Chi Minh

Acting for the Association of Vietnamese Patriots in France in January 1919, the future Ho Chi Minh (1890–1969), then known as Nguyen Ai Quoc (Nguyen the Patriot) and working since 1917 in the restaurant kitchens of Paris, petitioned the Paris Peace Conference fruitlessly in support of Vietnamese national self-determination. Already a member of the French Socialist Party (SFIO, Section Française de l'Internationale Ouvrière/French Section of the Workers' International), Nguyen/Ho then gave his support to the Third International's Twenty-One Conditions at the Socialists' Tours Congress in December 1920, joining the new French Communist Party (PCF) as a founding member. He moved in late 1923 to Moscow to work for the Comintern. He served there in the leadership of the short-lived Krestintern

4 Ibid., 123–42.

5 See here ibid., 134–42. For the explosion of Marxism around the founding of the Chinese Communist Party, see esp. Arif Dirlik, *The Origins of Chinese Communism* (New York: Oxford University Press, 1989).

(Peasant International), and kept up a high level of journalistic activity, while delivering a famous critique of the PCF's neglect of colonial matters from the podium of the Third International's Fifth Congress in June–July 1924. Moving next to China in December 1924, he was attached to the Whampoa Military Academy under Mikhail Borodin in Canton, where he formed the Vietnamese Revolutionary Youth League in June 1925. This became the core of the future Indochinese Communist Party, over whose foundation in February 1930 Nguyen/Ho was to preside. Strikingly, as in the Chinese case, these specifically Marxist, or even socialist, affiliations developed at a very late stage. Nguyen/Ho's most illustrious predecessor, the revolutionary Pan-Asian nationalist intellectual Phan Boi Chau (1867–1940), was exploring socialist ideas only by the early 1920s, while the broader nationalist tradition displayed mainly a wide range of nonsocialist constitutionalist, radical-democratic and insurrectionary thinking. Similarly, by having gone west in 1912–18, rather than following an earlier patriotic generation to China and Japan, Nguyen/Ho was exposed on his early travels to an array of influences where socialism was just one among many – rationalist conceptions of freedom and human perfectibility, universalist ideals of civil liberty and democracy, the pursuit of welfare, the advance of science and technology, *progress* in the widest Enlightenment sense.[6] Again, as in China, the turning to Marxism came quite suddenly and late in the day, inspired in 1919–20 by disillusionment with the Paris Peace Conference, the clarifying shock of colonial obduracy and the opening of the communist horizon.

Vignette 3: Manabendra Nath Roy

Finding himself in Mexico City by July 1917, having left India two years before via the Dutch Indies, Japan, China and the United States, the revolutionary nationalist M. N. Roy (1887–1954) completed his passage from Bengal's insurrectionary Swadeshi Movement to an increasingly self-conscious Marxist outlook. Integrating into Mexico City's left-wing anti-colonial and socialist circles during the culminating stage of the Mexican Revolution, Roy headed the infant Mexican Socialist Party in December 1918 while overseeing its conversion into the communist party next year. Recruited for the Third International's Second Congress by Borodin, then chief Soviet envoy to the Americas, he left Mexico in 1919, reaching Berlin in May 1920 en route for

6 Thomas Hodgkin, *Vietnam: The Revolutionary Path* (New York: St. Martin's Press, 1981), 221–22, relying partly on Truong Chinh, *President Ho Chi Minh, Beloved Leader of the Vietnamese People* (Hanoi: Foreign Languages Publishing House, 1966), 10–11.

Moscow. The terms of his disagreement with Lenin at the Comintern Congress in July then set the terms of debate over "the National and Colonial Question" for the coming decade. If revolution in the capitalist West remained primary (Lenin), communists in the colonial world needed to support "bourgeois-democratic nationalism" against Western colonial rule. But Roy, in contrast, placed the Asian revolution first: just as the imperialist economies rested on the system of colonial extraction, so would "the fate of world Communism [depend] on the triumph of Communism in the East."[7] After the Baku Congress of the Peoples of the East in September 1920, Roy was dispatched to Tashkent to organize an Indian Communist Party (CP) and coordinate an anti-British pan-Turkic mobilization, enlisting the nationalist regime in Afghanistan and a revolutionary Muslim "Army of God" aimed toward the Indian Northwest Frontier, where it would connect with the Khilafat movement in India. While the latter fed into the Indian CP's early militancy, the greater ambitions fizzled out, leading to the closure of the Comintern's Central Asian Bureau (the Tashkent School) in May 1921 and its replacement by the Moscow Communist University for the Toilers of the East, with Roy as Director. After some time in Berlin and dispatch to China in 1927, Roy was tarred with the debacle of the CP's suppression by the Kuomintang, falling foul of Stalin's ascendancy and being expelled from the Comintern in 1928–29. Most striking in Roy's ten-year passage through communism was the flux of his affiliations – his restless essaying of revolutionary options and probing of metropolitan and colonial exigencies, in a kind of actualized heterodoxy. His career highlights the open-ended and unfinished quality of the global communist movement in its founding years of 1919–23. The cosmopolitan imaginary of his life between the early 1900s and his final return to India in 1930, reaching across East Asia and the Pacific to the Americas and thence to Berlin, Moscow, Tashkent and Shanghai, was shaped from a "deterritorial" ground of cultural internationalism highly specific to the early twentieth century.[8]

Vignette 4: José Carlos Mariátegui

When the Peruvian journalist-intellectual José Carlos Mariátegui (1894–1930) was blackmailed into European exile by the freshly installed dictatorship

7 Jon Jacobson, *When the Soviet Union Entered World Politics* (Berkeley: University of California Press, 1994), 54.

8 See Kris Manjapra, *M. N. Roy: Marxism and Colonial Cosmopolitanism* (New Delhi: Routledge, 2010), 3–4 and *passim*.

of Augusto Leguía in 1919, he was the feted 25-year-old self-educated editor of the newspaper *La Razón* launched in 1916. By making *La Razón* into the uncompromising voice of labor movement and university reform, he rapidly clashed with Leguía, whose reform-mindedness and tolerance for any forthrightly independent radicalism had soon been exceeded. During his European sojourn (lasting until 1923), Mariátegui passed through France, Germany and Austria, before settling in Italy at the height of the *biennio rosso* (red two years). Already familiar with Marx and enthused for the Bolshevik Revolution and the ideas of Lenin, he luxuriated not only in Europe's revolutionary atmosphere of 1919–23, but in the cultural militancies of modernism too. Henri Barbusse and Georges Sorel were each vital influences. Key interlocutors became Piero Gobetti and Antonio Gramsci, whose weekly newspaper *L'Ordine Nuovo* (*The New Order*, 1919–25) became a model for Mariátegui's own *Amauta*, launched in 1927.[9] Mariátegui was in Italy during the factory occupations of September 1920; attended the Italian Socialist Party's Livorno Congress in January 1921, when the split occurred that produced the Italian Communist Party (PCI); and left Italy as Benito Mussolini came to power, propelled (in Mariátegui's view) by the left's shying away from revolution. During the 1920s his thought showed remarkable scope and originality, ranging across organized and popular religion, education and folk culture, the place and purpose of intellectuals, the importance of the peasantry, the relations among indigeneity, race and national belonging, and the urgency of reconciling the national and the cosmopolitan (including the latter's US and European dimensions), as well as the socialist standbys of economic analysis and political strategy.[10] Yet his impact lacked organized context before the Peruvian Socialist Party was founded in October 1928 (renamed the communist party in 1930), with Mariátegui as general secretary. Comintern contacts dated only from late 1927, and even then Mariátegui guarded the new party's independence. Missing the June 1929 First Meeting of Latin American Communist Parties in Buenos Aires because of illness, he was chided for a range of heterodoxy, whether on the peasantry's progressive

9 *Amauta* was taken from the Quechuan word for "master" or "wise," the title for teachers educated in the "Houses of Knowledge" in Cuzco under the Inca Empire. Quechuan is the main indigenous language of the Andean region of South America.

10 Mariátegui's principal work (1928) has been translated as *Seven Interpretive Essays on Peruvian Reality* (Austin: University of Texas Press, 1971). See also Jesús Chavarría, *José Carlos Mariátegui and the Rise of Modern Peru, 1890–1930* (Albuquerque: University of New Mexico Press, 1979); Nicola Miller, *In the Shadow of the State: Intellectuals and the Quest for National Identity in Twentieth-Century Spanish America* (London: Verso, 1999), 67–70, 117–21, 153–62, 193–95.

potential, the national belonging of indigenous peoples, the capitalist consequences of imperialism, or the revolutionary priorities for Peruvian society (democratic vs. socialist). Thus during the febrile revolutionary conjuncture of 1917–23, Mariátegui's relation to communism, too, was creatively expansive and undecided, with little of the dogmatism that later proved so confining.

Revolution as Parliamentary Preponderance

From the turn of the century, through the cataclysm of World War I and the succeeding revolutionary upheavals, the practical and imaginative contexts for revolution around the globe radically changed. The above four itineraries were emblematic for this larger account. If in each case the intensities of 1917–23 were decisive in convening new possibilities and radicalizing them, then they also reflected longer accumulations of change, with effects mingling and concentrating inside that immediate conjuncture. Some of those longer-range determinations figured the relentlessly expanding penetration of capitalist relations across the globe since the 1850s. Some resulted from the rivalries of world empires since the 1880s and their impact on the given colonial system. Others sprang from the European crisis of liberal constitutionalism before 1914, when the transnational political settlement of the 1860s began to come apart, shaken by novel popular-democratic mobilizations centering on the 1905 Russian Revolution. The first stirrings of anti-colonial nationalism also propelled a global revolutionary surge, hitting Russia in 1905, Persia in 1906–07, Turkey in 1908 and China and Mexico in 1911. Under this press, the larger contexts for thinking about socialist change – the complicated *global* grounds for strategizing revolutionary politics – became ever harder to ignore. After the 1890s, the impact of demands for self-government and social progress in the colonial and neocolonial world remade the ground where socialists needed to act and think. The settled reliabilities of socialist politics, whose terms had solidified institutionally and practically inside the national-state frameworks created since the 1860s, became broken apart and then recast.

Despite all variation in the patterns of popular-democratic politics, including the regionally significant persistence of anarchism and other nonsocialist traditions, a particular model of working-class politics became normalized across Europe in the last quarter of the nineteenth century, one broadly integrating Marx's arguments from the later 1860s and early 1870s. "Marxism" by 1914 stood for many things, but in its prescriptions for the conduct of politics it came from these origins. In the First International's founding debates after 1864, Marx assembled a program which, over time, gave the new socialist parties a template. It included the practical agenda of trade union reforms and labor legislation of his "Instructions" for the delegates to the 1866 Geneva Congress; the resolution on public ownership at the Brussels Congress in 1868; and the resolution of the London Congress in 1871 calling for "the constitution of the working class into a party." Thereto came the negative boundary drawing against older traditions, which Marx devoted so much energy to defeating – liberal-reformist trade union leaders, especially in Britain; French Proudhonists hostile to trade unionism and political action via the state; Mikhail Bakunin and the anarchists, who rejected centralist organizing and the value of party; and the remaining supporters of Auguste Blanqui, with their insurrection hankerings and conspiratorial methods. As the central socialist desideratum, Marx proposed the independent mass party of labor. By the political standards of the time, this was a new departure.

It was vitally keyed to surrounding political transformations of the 1860s. In a new drama of constitution-making, Italy and Germany appeared on the map as unitary states for the first time. After the long hiatus of the reactionary 1850s, labor movements reemerged, including the craft unions of the Trades Union Congress in Britain and workers' associations in the various states of Germany. Labor organizing spread geographically across the continent in the first great European strike wave of 1868–74, aided by liberalizing economic legislation and constitutional reforms, country by country. Popular democracy made a spectacular appearance in the Paris Commune of 1871. What excited Marx in all of this was not just the return of open class conflict, but its palpable connections to politics, offering new openings which the First International then sought to shape. Vital to labor's revival, Marx thought, was the changing constitutional context that enabled it. As a result of the 1860s, liberal constitutionalism gained lasting ascendancy across Europe as a whole, becoming normative for the coming four decades. For the first time, it legalized labor movement activity on a national scale at the level of the state.

This *duality*, between a new understanding of socialist strategy based on the party and the new type of liberal-constitutional polity enabling it to function, decisively framed the socialist mainstream until the new challenges of the pre-1914 decade. In most of Europe the dominant left vehicle became a national social-democratic party in conjunction with nationally federated trade unions, in a new practice that was *centralist*, stressing national rather than local forms of action; *parliamentarist*, privileging the parliamentary arena as the source of sovereignty; and *constitutionalist* in the given meanings of the term, adopting representative over direct means of governing. This preference for centralized forms over the looser federated ones of the 1820s to 1860s made the party into a new theme of left political discourse, with every European country acquiring its national social-democratic party.[11]

By the mid 1890s, the rise of labor movements in Europe had reached a watershed. The main cycle of party foundations was complete, covering Central, Northern and Western Europe; and the next phase was under way, proceeding from Poland and the Balkans in the early 1890s through the Russian Empire to its completion by 1905. The opening of a period of economic expansion after 1895–96 also brought the first period of sustained unionization in Europe. The socialist parties of the first cycle now made steady electoral gains, establishing a parliamentary presence, permeating the public sphere, and deepening their local roots. In the prelude to World War I, those parties experienced a remarkable upswing in electoral success, so that by 1914 seven commanded at least a quarter of their national electorates – those in Finland (43 percent, 1913), Sweden (36.5 percent, 1913), Germany (34.8 percent, 1912), Czech lands (32.2 percent, 1911), Denmark (29.6 percent, 1913), Norway (26.3 percent, 1912) and Austria (25.4 percent, 1911).[12] This north-central European "social-democratic core" revealed a common pattern: single socialist parties organizationally united but ideologically diverse, without serious rivals, and rallying heterogeneous interests around broadly social-democratic values. But elsewhere, matters were more divided. In Britain, locally vigorous socialist initiatives could make small headway against the resilience of a popular liberalism shaped in the 1860s. In Italy and Spain, socialists contended with acute regional disparities, state violence and strong urban anarchist movements. In France, socialists were notoriously fractious, identifying with rival revolutionary traditions, conserving earlier non-Marxist legacies and taking contrasting lessons from the Paris Commune; only in 1905 was that sectarianism overcome, when the Marxist followers of Jules Guesdes joined with the ethical socialism of Jean Jaurès to form the SFIO as a parliamentary party comparable to those elsewhere, recording 16.8 percent of the popular vote in 1914.

11 For a full tabulation, see Geoff Eley, *Forging Democracy: The History of the Left in Europe, 1850–2000* (New York: Oxford University Press, 2002), 63.

12 For complete tabulation, ibid., 66–69. Four other parties surpassed the 20 percent barrier: the Italian (22.8 percent, 1913), Belgian (22.5 percent, 1900), Bulgarian (20.2 percent) and Swiss (20.9 percent, 1913), while the Dutch party reached 18.6 percent (1913).

A crucial source of socialist strength was the party's all-embracing mass base. Between the First International and the self-confident growth accompanying the Second International after 1889, socialists essentially invented the modern political party. The new model of a permanent campaigning organization geared to the fighting of elections now presumed building a continuous presence on the ground, linked to the supporters' everyday social lives. Using the architecture and rhythms of workplace, neighborhood and family, socialists were able to shape collective solidarities with continuity over time, bound together by elaborate machineries of identification. By these means the growing parliamentary strength became connected to a wider coalescence in society. If a special relationship was welded to the consequences of capitalist industrialization, in a compelling narrative of capitalist crisis and the projected socialist future focused on the industrial working class, then socialist support was actually far broader. Sociologically, the appeal was highly ecumenical. Socialists not only spoke across the multiform interests and attitudes separating different categories of *workers* (whether manual laborers in mining, manufacture, transportation and construction, or clerks, shop assistants, uniformed workers, servants and so forth), but appealed to *other popular classes* like the peasantry and petty bourgeoisie as well, and even the lower professions and intelligentsia. Socialism's strength before 1914 was this ability to weave the myriad working-class experiences of societies undergoing rapid transformation into a single story sufficiently inspiring to gather in many other hopes for a better world too.

This imposing machinery of identification and the apparently inexorable progress of socialist parties as popular movements made the "forward march of labor" seem inevitable.[13] If far from homogeneous, working people acquired compelling reasons for seeing themselves as a cohesive class, because their patent powerlessness in society made the ballot box so disproportionately valuable, especially as their other collective resource, workplace combination in unions, remained elusive in most countries until the upheavals of 1910–20. In that sense, the suffrage struggles of 1890–1914 were the engine of political class formation: the Belgian constitution of 1893; universal manhood suffrage in Austria in 1907 and Italy in 1912; Scandinavian liberalizations in Norway (1898), Denmark (1901), Finland

13 Compare the young Eric Hobsbawm's early anthology, *Labour's Turning Point 1880–1900* [1948], 2nd edn. (Hassocks: Harvester Press, 1974), with the later stock-taking in his co-authored *The Forward March of Labour Halted?*, ed. Martin Jacques and Francis Mulhern (London: Verso/Marxism Today, 1981).

(1905) and Sweden (1907); recurring suffrage mobilizations in Germany, especially in 1905–06 and 1909–10. Once workers acquired the vote, it was plain, they also used it, as the remarkable pan-European surge of electoralism in 1907–14 showed. For the pre-1914 socialist parties, using the available parliamentary forms had become axiomatic, whether as a platform for mobilizing the masses or for the winning of short-term reforms. Moreover, this socialist parliamentarianism was shaped around a political imaginary that was *national* in character. The growing masses of workers joining the pre-1914 socialist parties may well have been fervently internationalist. But the "politically defined nation" had become "the effective framework of their class consciousness."[14]

Revolution and Reform Under the Second International

In the debates surrounding the First International the arguments for different types of state organization and different types of labor movement were homologous, contrasting once again with what went before. Until the 1860s, the locally based associational activism of radical democrats and early socialists had coalesced mainly around certain common ideals, focused by newspapers, pamphlets, itinerant lecturers and a few national parliamentarians and other charismatic figures. By the last quarter of the nineteenth century, the very different outlook of the new social democracy now showed analogous convergence around movement and state, with the character of the future socialist constitution being abstracted from socialists' organizational experience under capitalism. Thus, rather than the forms of *direct democracy* that gave greater decision-making to the rank and file at the local level and on the shop floor, both socialist parties and unions decisively chose *representative* forms of national organization; a preference repeated in the parliamentary type of constitution. Likewise, if centralized bureaucracy concentrated the movement's strengths and equalized resources among its stronger and weaker sections, then by the same logic central planning would give the state of the future maximum resources for building socialism.

So far, this was also consistent with what Marx thought in the 1860s and 1870s about revolutionary strategy: Working-class emancipation was above all a *political* question; it required a class-based socialist party; that party was to concentrate the workers' collective strengths in a centrally directed national

14 Eric J. Hobsbawm, *The Age of Empire 1875–1914* (New York: Pantheon Books, 1987), 129.

movement capable of challenging the ruling class. But here discrepancies arose. Marx viewed the existing state as an institutional complex that operated in the interests of capital and for the maintenance of class rule; it could not just be taken over but had to be destroyed. On this score, the later social democrats evinced no such clarity. They either deferred questions associated with the revolutionary assumption of power or backed away from revolution altogether.[15]

This was another vital transition. If a broad agenda of democracy and social reform was the task of the independent parties of labor Marx had advocated, free from bourgeois tutelage or association, then the *revolutionary* entailments were not thought through but consigned to a still to be specified future. Inside that indeterminacy, until the 1890s, socialists still harbored apocalyptic hopes, imagining the inevitability of revolution via earlier nineteenth-century precedents, where social crises led to rapid breakdowns of authority and popular insurrections. Blanqui epitomized such revolutionary psychology, which Marx also shared before the tragedy of the Commune finally fixed his hopes on laws of capitalist development and objective processes of the class struggle. Revolutionary expectations were further fueled by police repression, threats of illegality and concomitant anti-socialist activity, exemplified in the drama of the German Anti-Socialist Law of 1878–90. For August Bebel, a towering personality of the Second International, the *Kladderadatsch* or great collapse of the system was always around the next corner.[16] In place of collapse, however, increasingly came inclusion. By 1900, socialist parties were themselves becoming strong enough to join the "bourgeois" political constellation, winning seats in national elections, participating in parliamentary culture and campaigning for reform. For parties of revolutionaries, accordingly, questions of purity or compromise, maximalism or constructive participation, *revolution* or *reform*, increasingly besieged the agenda.

15 Marx himself never developed his thoughts on the subject systematically. In the event of a revolution, he envisaged a transitional state authority, a "dictatorship of the proletariat," taking decisive and even repressive measures if needed to ensure the revolution's immediate survival. But he used that term as a general synonym for the democratic rule of the working class, as the overwhelming majority of the population, over the rest of society. See Richard N. Hunt, *The Political Ideas of Marx and Engels*, vol. II, *Classical Marxism, 1850–1895* (Pittsburgh: University of Pittsburgh Press, 1984), esp. 363–67; George Lichtheim, *Marxism: An Historical and Critical Study* (London: Routledge & Kegan Paul, 1961), 128; Monty Johnstone, "Marx, Blanqui, and Majority Rule," in Ralph Miliband and John Saville (eds.), *The Socialist Register 1983* (London: Merlin, 1983), 296–318.

16 Vernon Lidtke, *The Outlawed Party: Social Democracy in Germany, 1878–1890* (Princeton: Princeton University Press, 1966), 233.

Controversy erupted over these questions at the close of the Second International's first decade, prompted in 1899–1900 by two instances of "ministerialism."[17] In the so-called Millerand affair at the height of the Dreyfus crisis in 1899, a leading Independent Socialist, Alexandre Millerand (1859–1943), joined a French government of Republican Defense as minister of commerce, thereby polarizing reactions among French socialists and their comrades elsewhere. With the shooting of three strikers in a dispute at Chalon-sur-Saône, their worst predictions seemed confirmed. As Jules Guesde (1845–1922) said, "the war on the working class has never been so implacable as under the Waldeck-Rousseau-Millerand government."[18] Yet for Guesde's main rival in the French movement Jean Jaurès (1859–1914), on the other hand, it was less socialist advocacy per se that demanded priority than the abstract and ethical defense of French liberties at a time when the republic was in danger.

The scandal dominated the International's Fourth Congress in Paris in September 1900, when the SPD wielded its crossnational authority. Wilhelm Liebknecht's first reaction was peremptory: "[A] socialist who enters a bourgeois ministry either deserts to the enemy, or he surrenders to the enemy."[19] But this then gave way to the revolutionary pragmatics of Karl Kautsky (1854–1938), by now the officially credentialed voice of Marxist theory: Providing democratic rights were upheld as a good in themselves, tactical alliances might certainly be approved. To see nonsocialist forces as "one reactionary mass" (in the old Lassallean slogan) was profoundly misconceived, especially as socialists grew stronger, "already powerful enough to influence the course of events, but not strong enough to be the dominant power."[20]

The clearest case for coalition, Kautsky argued, was a national emergency, when a society's "fundamental democratic institutions" were in danger.[21]

17 The Second International convened in Paris in July 1889, at a congress initiated by the SPD with 391 recognized delegates from twenty separate countries, presenting the Marxist face of Europe's emergent socialist parties. Congresses met subsequently in Brussels (1891), Zurich (1893), London (1896), Paris (1900), Amsterdam (1904), Stuttgart (1907), Copenhagen (1910) and Basle (1912). From 1900, a permanent Secretariat sat in Brussels, with an International Socialist Bureau (ISB) to coordinate Congress resolutions.

18 Robert Gildea, *Barricades and Borders: Europe 1800–1914* (Oxford: Oxford University Press, 1987), 400.

19 See Wilhelm Liebknecht to the *Parti ouvrier français*, 10 Aug. 1899, in Institut für Marxismus-Leninismus (ed.), *Dokumente und Materialen zur Geschichte der deutschen Arbeiterbewegung*, vol. IV (East Berlin: Akadamie Verlag, 1967), 31–32.

20 Karl Kautsky to Victor Adler, 5 May 1894, in Friedrich Adler (ed.), *Victor Adler: Briefwechsel mit August Bebel und Karl Kautsky* (Vienna: Wiener Volksbuchhandlung, 1954), 152.

21 Ibid., 116.

In the second instance of ministerialism, an Italian political crisis seemed to meet exactly this criterion. The right-wing government of General Luigi Pelloux, formed after a May 1898 massacre of demonstrators in Milan, unleashed draconian repression against the left, imposed by royal decree. In response, liberals under Giovanni Giolitti and Giuseppe Zanardelli formed a common front with the extreme left. This emerged from elections with big gains, eventually forming a new government in February 1901, endorsed by the Italian Socialist Party (PSI). The Millerand scenario repeated itself. Filippo Turati (1857–1932) pushed social reforms, including a labor office, social insurance, protective laws against female and child labor, and public works. Likewise, however, in defending the constitution Giolitti still used troops against strikers, rapidly exposing the limits of this progressive front. Significantly, in contrast with Millerand, Turati had refused ministerial office as such, and the PSI eventually abandoned the government, thereby preserving the purist protocol.[22]

Thus the scandal over "ministerialism" revealed two models of socialist politics, whose tensions were to recur. The dilemmas were posed inside the SPD by the contemporaneous "revisionist controversy." If by 1900 the SPD was the strongest of Europe's socialist parties and its Erfurt Program the model of its kind, then Kautsky, the latter's architect, was the most prestigious theorist.[23] His commentary on the program, *The Class Struggle*, a "catechism of social democracy," was translated into sixteen languages by 1914, and other Marxists deferred to his views. While building an increasingly elaborate organization and implanting itself in the national polity (becoming by 1898 the largest German party in popular votes), moreover, the SPD remained explicitly revolutionary: Its goal was nothing less than "the *overthrow of capitalist society*."[24] As it advanced in parliamentary strength, though, its revolutionary purity became a problem, for while consistently declaring its apartness from bourgeois society, the party was drawn willy-nilly *into* the "system." Into this developing gap between revolutionary theory and immediate practice came a series of articles by the SPD's veteran intellectual, Eduard Bernstein, published in its premier journal, Kautsky's *Neue Zeit*, and

22 James Joll, *The Second International 1889–1914* (New York: Routledge, 1966), 95.

23 Adopted in 1891, the Erfurt Program became a template for the Norwegian (1891), Swiss (1893), Belgian (1894), Dutch (1894), Swedish (1897) and East European party programs, while the contemporaneous Czech (1888), Austrian (1889) and Hungarian programs (1890) followed similar lines.

24 This was Liebknecht's peroration to the SPD's 1898 Congress. See Raymond H. Dominick III, *Wilhelm Liebknecht and the Founding of the German Social Democratic Party* (Chapel Hill: University of North Carolina Press, 1982), 399.

collected as *The Preconditions of Socialism and the Tasks of Social Democracy*. There Bernstein argued that capitalism had surmounted its tendency toward crisis. The Marxist doctrine of pauperization – ever-widening polarization between rich and poor, inscribed in the labor theory of value – was falsified by modestly improving standards of living. Working-class movements could hope to win reforms under capitalism after all, gradually moving the state toward democracy. Against the catastrophic theory of revolutionary transition, Bernstein proposed a continuous model of improvement, an "evolutionary socialism."[25]

In response, a storm of disagreement came forth, a chorus of orthodox and radical Marxists, Rosa Luxemburg (1871–1919) prominent among them. After some hesitancy, incited by Bebel, Kautsky also joined the fray, and at the SPD's 1899 Hanover Congress Bernstein was officially disavowed. As with the response to Millerand, the real fight was over strategy: Bernstein's critique of Marxist economics mattered less than his political conclusions. If "[the] peasants do not sink; [the] middle class does not disappear; crises do not grow ever larger; [and] misery and serfdom do not increase," then socialists should recruit nonproletarian supporters and make alliances with liberals and other nonsocialist progressives.[26] Indeed, the SPD's future lay precisely in the coalition-building advocated by Turati in Italy, Jaurès in France, or the Fabians in Britain. But Bernstein misread the emotional attachment to revolutionary rhetoric and the party's heritage – both the integrative power of the SPD's revolutionary ethos and the heroic myth of its persecution under the Anti-Socialist Law, not to speak of the actual impediments against reform from the imperial state's continuing anti-democratic intransigence.

Defeating revisionism inspired a powerful rallying of orthodoxy in the SPD, in fact, which hugely constrained coalition-building well into the future. For in Kautsky's treatment this was always a zero-sum game: The primacy of the class struggle precluded alliance with bourgeois parties and vice versa. The alignments around this question in the Second International reflected Europe's map of constitutionalist progress: Those condemning reformism came from countries with weak parliamentary constitutions; their opponents and the abstainers from those where democracy was strong. This already presaged the constellation of 1914–17 too, as the vocal critics of revisionism in

25 Henry Tudor and J. M. Tudor (eds.), *Marxism and Social Democracy: The Revisionist Debate 1896–1898* (Cambridge: Cambridge University Press, 1988), 168–69.

26 Peter Gay, *The Dilemma of Democratic Socialism: Eduard Bernstein's Challenge to Marx* (New York: Columbia University Press, 1952), 250.

the Amsterdam debate of 1904 numbered several who were later to join the wartime revolutionary opposition – Khristian Rakovsky (1873–1941) of Bulgaria, Rosa Luxemburg, and of course Vladimir Ilich Lenin (1870–1924) from Russia.[27] While the Amsterdam debates helped drive the French unification into the SFIO, therefore, its main longer-term effects were divisive, along faultlines becoming ever-clearer during the prewar years. And the impetus in that regard came from the global impingement of imperialism.

Significantly, colonialism first came onto the International's agenda at Paris in 1900 during the Boer War, British imperialism's assault on a *white* settler republic. For neither the exploitation of indigenous peoples in Africa and Asia nor East European nationality questions ever troubled the International's surface until 1907. Nor did the new critiques of imperialism, like Rudolf Hilferding's *Finance Capital* and Rosa Luxemburg's *Accumulation of Capital*, say very much about the colonial world per se, as against the dynamics of metropolitan capitalist crisis. In the light of colonial violence, the Stuttgart Congress in 1907 did condemn "capitalist colonial policies [which] must, by their nature, give rise to servitude, forced labor and the extermination of the native peoples."[28] This debate had a familiar look, with revisionists calling again for flexibility: Bernstein and his fellow SPD reformist Eduard David (1863–1930), the Dutch SDAP's Henri van Kol (1852–1925) and the British Labour Party's Ramsay MacDonald (1866–1937) on one side; Kautsky, SPD leftist Georg Ledebour (1850–1947), the Guesdist Alexandre-Marie Desrousseaux (1861–1955), the Pole Julian Marchlewski (1866–1925) and the British Social Democratic Federation's Harry Quelch (1858–1913) on the other.[29]

Socialists found various ways of accommodating to imperialism. It promoted employment, especially in shipyards, docking, armaments and industries dependent on colonial trade and production, while colonial trade boosted general prosperity. And while positive enthusiasm for "colonialism" among socialists was far rarer, assumptions of racial superiority and acceptance of the "civilizing mission" were not. More seriously, escalating great-

27 See *Internationaler Sozialisten-Kongress zu Amsterdam, 14. bis 20. August 1904* (Berlin: Buchhandlung Vorwärts, 1904), 31–49, in *Kongress-Protokolle der Zweiten Internationale. Band 1: Paris 1889 – Amsterdam 1904* (Glashütten im Taunus: Auvermann, 1975).

28 Julius Braunthal, *History of the International*, vol. 1, *1864–1914* (London: Gollancz, 1966), 318–19.

29 See esp. Preben Karrsholm, "The South African War and the Response of the International Socialist Community to Imperialism Between 1896 and 1908," in Frits van Holthoon and Marcel van der Linden (eds.), *Internationalism in the Labour Movement 1830–1940*, vol. I (Leiden: Brill, 1988), 42–67.

power tensions fed popular patriotism, especially via fears of foreign invasion and national emergencies. Tsarism was a synonym for reactionary backwardness in the European left's collective imagination, and even Kautsky talked of defending German civilization against possible Russian attack. French socialists saw analogous contrasts between French revolutionary traditions and German militarism and authoritarianism, so that when the SPD blocked SFIO anti-militarist initiatives in the International after 1905, relations became seriously frayed. In fact, the issue of preventing war became the vital test of the International's cohesion. If war was to be stopped, armies, munitions and railways had to be immobilized in all combatant countries, and from 1904 calls for a general strike against war never left the agenda.

If socialists proved susceptible to the strength of superordinate national loyalties in the decade before 1914, habituating themselves to the normalizing rhythms and practicalities of living inside the nation, they could also be correspondingly negligent of national minorities. This was not invariably true – Scottish and Welsh radicalisms had a decisive role in shaping the British labor movement, for instance, while social democracies of the subject nationalities of the Russian Empire paralleled the central Russian party amicably before 1914. Yet, the SPD had a poor record of either integrating the German Poles or honoring their separate organizations. And a still more stringent test came from the chaos of allegiances in the Habsburg Empire, where the dominant Germans and Hungarians were only the largest national minorities among many.

Thus when the outbreak of war in August 1914 threw the Second International into disarray, it was not just anti-militarism that was in ruins, but the classical socialist approach to the national question as well. Marxist theoreticians, from Kautsky to Luxemburg, Trotsky to Lenin, had long argued the primacy of internationalism, whether as developmental logic or highest political good: With the maturity of capitalism and the growth of class-consciousness, they believed, workers' national loyalties would surely wither away. Yet, the twenty years before 1914 told to the contrary – in the popular mobilizations around national crises like the Dreyfus affair, or in the tensions and resentments dividing multinational movements like the Austrian and Czech. Socialist leaderships came tacitly to accept the salience of national loyalties too, from Bebel and Jaurès in their different ways to the practicing reformists increasingly running the trade union and party machines. Some right-wing socialists openly and aggressively declared their patriotism. But in most official declarations there was more commonly silence. No congress of the Second International ever placed the "national question" as such onto its agenda. This was what World War I brutally changed, practically overnight.

Revolution as a Non-National and Deterritorial Space

In their programmatic vision of social transformation deriving from the experience of Europe's capitalist industrialization, Marxists of the Second International approached revolution as the necessary consequence of the inevitable capitalist crisis. The *locus classicus* for this operative understanding, the textual authority guiding social democrats in their practical relationship to this fervently desired but structurally determined socialist future, was certainly the SPD's Erfurt Program and its derivatives, along with Kautsky's commentary in *The Class Struggle*. In Kautsky's neo-Darwinian conception of society and its laws of development, the revolutionary opening to the future was inscribed in the necessary movement of history.

As the main motor of change under capitalism, class conflict in these terms was for Kautsky structural and endemic, a permanent and irreducible feature of social life under capitalism. This structural antagonism led to struggles over the social distribution of the value produced in the economy, which assigned people "into two great camps, into two great classes facing each other: bourgeoisie and proletariat."[30] Under deteriorating conditions of capitalist accumulation and profitability, workers' collective mobilizations, organized through their trade unions and the socialist party, relayed pressures to the political system that created openings for change. The most extreme form of such a breakthrough, a crisis of particular and escalating severity, was *revolution*.

Given these assumptions about general proletarianization and the associated immiseration thesis, it was not hard to work this expectation of capitalist crisis into a political narrative of the unstoppable working-class majority. Once thoroughly distributed and embedded in economy and civil society, it was believed, the workers' democratic preponderance would be brought to final fruition by means of universal suffrage, civil freedoms and maximal parliamentary forms. A barricades revolution on the style of 1848 was certainly unworkable, so power could only come via the ballot box, whatever confrontations might be needed along the way to deal with ruling-

30 Karl Marx and Friedrich Engels, *The Communist Manifesto: A Modern Edition*, introd. Eric Hobsbawm (London: Verso, 1998), 35.

class violence, a coup against the constitution, or efforts at suppressing the suffrage.[31] But absent the climacteric of capitalism's general crisis, this image of the revolution was never put to the test before 1914. On the one hand, socialists embraced a practical logic of integration. Yet, on the other hand, with barely a third of their national electorates, even the strongest socialist parties had no prospects of actually forming a government. They dwelled in a kind of limbo: Fixed in opposition, they were permanently on the outside; but access to power could only come from coalition, behind an avowedly limited program, by compromising on the ultimate revolutionary goal.[32]

The resulting dilemma sharpened after 1905, when the settlements of the 1860s finally came apart. In the wake of the revolution in Russia, with strike waves and suffrage mobilizations elsewhere, Europe's socialist parties faced an unruly revival of extra-parliamentary revolutionism. A new industrial militancy stressing direct action and the futility of parliamentary involvement aggressively outstepped the available social-democratic frameworks and disparaged the state per se, disputing its openness for capture. The scale was immense: After the initial takeoff into mass unionism at the turn of the century, a pan-European strike wave began a widening of labor unrest in 1904–07 that in 1910–13 was aggressively continued; if we add the mobilizations accompanying the end of the war, the years 1910–20 become the great age of European unionization, unmatched until after 1945. Under such challenges – along with women's suffrage movements, nationality questions, the international arms race – conventional political alignments came under intense strain. By 1913–14, Europe's parliamentary polities were sliding into chaos – with ten separate ministries in France during 1909–14, for example, and five Italian governments in only four years. In each respect, parliamentary and trade union, popular politics outgrew the patiently cultivated frameworks of action: *Socialist revolution* was exceeding its given containers. Not only the constitutionalist frameworks of the 1860s were breaking down, in other words; socialist parliamentarianism was too.

The revolutionary years after 1917 showed this in many particular ways.[33] Most vital was the break from heavily deterministic conceptions of

31 The classic warranty of this argument during the Second International was Engels's new Introduction to the 1895 edition of Karl Marx's *The Class Struggles in France, 1848–1850* (Moscow: Progress Publishers, 1968), 5–26, which in its published form at the time became tendentiously excerpted by the SPD.

32 For a brilliant explication of this dilemma, see Adam Przeworski, "Social Democracy as a Historical Phenomenon," *New Left Review*, 1, 122 (July–Aug. 1980), 27–58.

33 Space and the terms of this chapter preclude a detailed discussion. But see Eley, *Forging Democracy*, 123–233.

revolutionary crisis and transition. Against that revolutionary fatalism – a waiting on history, an automatic Marxism – the revolutionaries of 1917–23 acted from voluntarist exuberance, a conviction in what Georg Lukács called "the actuality of the revolution," a commitment to *making* the revolution, rather than waiting for it to happen.[34] This was what Antonio Gramsci meant by the "Revolution against Capital," an escape not just from the prison of capitalist society, but from excessively economistic ways of understanding it too.[35] Revolutionary preparedness became less an ability to read the movements of the economy than the attainment of revolutionary *consciousness. Minds* were to be revolutionized. At the outer edge of this new voluntarist revolutionism, the new militants rejected democratic proceduralism, parliaments and parties altogether. "So away with professional leaders, with all organizations that can only work with leaders at the helm," one revolutionist declaimed. "Away with centralism, the organizational principle of the ruling class. Away with all central bodies."[36]

The revolutionary turbulence of those years ripped a huge gap in the long accustomed patterns of political practice, through which popular activism of unprecedented scale and intensity could then rush. This comprehensive political restructuring opened a new space of citizenship and recognition, whether via democratic enfranchisement, the political rights of women, or national self-determination. In the process, many of the Second International's failings and omissions were made far more visible than before. But if we broaden the optic still further, by moving away from the European metropole, the greatest effects will emerge in the revolution's worldwide translation: in the remapping of the revolution's possibilities into a newly *global* political imaginary.

Measured by the Second International's leading activists, within a Eurocentric notation, socialist culture had been nothing if not internationalist. Moreover, the global migrancy of the years before 1914, which brought vast numbers of people across the Atlantic to the Americas and from Britain to its white settler colonies, created particular global circuits for socialist activists, influences and ideas, especially where transnational labor markets were involved. Socialist activists and union militants took their experiences

34 Georg Lukács, *Lenin: A Study in the Unity of His Thought* (London: New Left Books, 1970), 9–13.

35 Antonio Gramsci, "The Revolution Against Capital" (24 Dec. 1917), in Antonio Gramsci, *Selections from Political Writings 1910–1920* (London: Lawrence & Wishart, 1977), 34.

36 Anonymous, "Erlebnisse und Schlußfolgerungen eines Revolutionärs," *Proletarische Zeitgeist* 10 (1931), cited by Manfred Bock, *Geschichte des "linken Radikalismus" in Deutschland. Ein Versuch* (Frankfurt am Main: Suhrkamp, 1976), 97.

and skills from most parts of Europe to the Americas just as they did from Britain to Australia, New Zealand and South Africa.[37] These and other emblematic biographies signified "a genuine international community ... a body of men and women conscious of being engaged on the same historical task, across national and political differences."[38]

Yet, this international community remained Eurocentrically self-limiting, halting at the borders of empire. Europe's socialists acknowledged the relevance of democracy for the colonial world only very exceptionally before 1914: Not only were non-Western voices and peoples of color almost entirely absent from the Second International's counsels, but its parties seldom condemned colonial policy and even positively endorsed it.[39] Socialists commonly affirmed the progressive value of the "civilizing mission" for the underdeveloped world, while embracing the material advantages of jobs, plentiful food, cheaper goods and guaranteed markets brought by colonialism to the metropolitan home.[40] Critical insights into the pervasiveness of imperialist culture were rare indeed, from assumptions about racial hierarchies to genocidal practices and acceptance of colonial violence.[41] Here, the spectacular early twentieth-century stirrings of colonial revolt leveled a powerful rebuke against Europe's left, so that Lenin's readiness in 1916–17

37 See for example the essays of Jonathan Hyslop: "A Ragged Trousered Philanthropist and the Empire: Robert Tressell in South Africa," *History Workshop Journal* 51 (Spring 2001), 65–86; "The World Voyage of James Keir Hardie: Indian Nationalism, Zulu Insurgency, and the British Labour Diaspora 1907–1908," *Journal of Global History* 1, 3 (Nov. 2006), 343–62; "The Imperial Working Class Makes Itself 'White': White Labourism in Britain, Australia and South Africa Before the First World War," *Journal of Historical Sociology* 12, 4 (Dec. 1999), 398–421.

38 Eric Hobsbawm, "Preface," in Georges Haupt, *Aspects of International Socialism 1871–1914* (Cambridge: Cambridge University Press, 1986), xi.

39 The non-European presence in the Second International was confined to the United States, the white settler colonies of Australasia and South Africa, and Japan.

40 This was the argument about "social imperialism" developed by Lenin around the idea of "imperialist super profits" in his writings during the war. See Vladimir I. Lenin, *Imperialism, the Highest Stage of Capitalism* (New York: International Publishers, 1939), originally published in 1916. For pre-1914 socialist thinking, see Hans-Christoph Schröder, *Sozialistische Imperialismusdeutung. Studien zu ihrer Geschichte* (Göttingen: Vandehoeck & Ruprecht, 1973).

41 The detailed picture, country by country, was far more complicated. For Britain, see esp. Stephen Howe, *Anticolonialism in British Politics: The Left and the End of Empire, 1918–1964* (Oxford: Oxford University Press, 1993), and Nicholas Owen, *The British Left and India: Metropolitan Anti-Imperialism, 1885–1947* (Oxford: Oxford University Press, 2007), 1–135; for Germany, John Phillip Short, *Magic Lantern Empire: Colonialism and Society in Germany* (Ithaca: Cornell University Press, 2012), 108–59. For the response of SPD revisionists, see Roger Fletcher, *Revisionism and Empire: Socialist Imperialism in Germany, 1897–1914* (London: George Allen & Unwin, 1984). More generally, Robert J. C. Young, *Postcolonialism: An Historical Introduction* (Oxford: Blackwell, 2001), 71–157, and for a helpful conspectus of the years before 1914, ibid., 115–26.

to extend the principle of national self-determination to the colonial world marked an audaciously novel departure. In that light, the presence of non-Western delegates was an especially vital feature of the Communist International's founding Congress in March 1919, as was its backing for anti-colonial nationalisms. Moreover, this principled and ringing advocacy of the Bolsheviks for the rights of colonial peoples pointedly highlighted the militant disdain of the Peace Conference that was meeting concurrently in Paris, as the Vietnamese, Chinese, Indian and other non-Western petitioners were only too painfully discovering.[42]

The initial call to the founding Congress of the Third International on 24 January 1919 mentioned thirty-nine groups in thirty-one separate countries, all of them European except for the United States, Australia and Japan. Thus far, little had apparently changed. But other groups from the colonial world were then added, so that the fifty-two delegates converging on Moscow on 2–6 March 1919 (from thirty-five organizations in twenty-two countries) gave a far more interesting picture. What this assembly actually represented, of course, was still unclear.

Aside from the existing communist parties in Germany and Hungary, Europe beyond the former Russian Empire was represented by small left-wing sects or nascent groupings with little evident working-class support or standing, sometimes taking the name, but not especially "communist" in the terms soon to be understood. Most delegates came either from former imperial territories already boasting communist parties of their own – these were in Finland, Estonia, Latvia, Lithuania, Belorussia, Poland, Ukraine, Armenia – or from overlapping and contiguous regions of the Middle East, Central Asia and East Asia. Radical nationalists carrying the torch of anti-colonial independence came from Turkestan, Azerbaijan, the Volga Germans, the United Group of the Eastern Peoples of Russia, Turkey, Persia, China and Korea.

Here is where my argument began. With its deliberate appeal to the world's oppressed and exploited peoples, whether under direct colonial

42 See Erez Manela, *The Wilsonian Moment: Self-Determination and the International Origins of Anti-Colonial Nationalism* (New York: Oxford University Press, 2007); and for a corrective, Pankaj Mishra, *From the Ruins of Empire: The Revolt Against the West and the Remaking of Asia* (New York: Picador, 2012); Ali Raza, Franziska Roy and Benjamin Zachariah (eds.), *The Internationalist Moment: South Asia, Worlds, and World Views, 1917–39* (New Delhi: Sage, 2014); Rebecca E. Karl, *Staging the World: Chinese Nationalism at the Turn of the Twentieth Century* (Durham, NC: Duke University Press, 2002). Arno J. Mayer, *Wilson vs. Lenin: Political Origins of the New Diplomacy, 1917–1918* (New York: World, 1964), provides the best introduction; also Jacobson, *When the Soviet Union Entered World Politics*.

rule or subject to variable metropolitan domination, the Bolshevik Revolution entered a world already in motion. Turkey, Persia, China, Mexico – these were the scenes of existing extra-European upheaval, where older state forms, invariably mined by imperialist penetration, were crumbling before nascent nationalist challenge. The Comintern Congress met against a backdrop of anti-colonial insurgency stretching from Egypt all across Asia, usually aimed against Britain: protests in Cairo against martial law and suppression of the newly founded Wafd Party (March); the Amritsar massacre in India's Punjab (April); the Third Anglo-Afghan War securing Afghanistan's independence (May–June); Mustafa Kemal's nationalist uprising in Anatolian Turkey, along with the Kurdish revolt in Mosul (May); the Syrian General Congress in Damascus, in this case aimed against France (May 1919–July 1920); continuing rebellion of Tatars, Bashkirs, Kazakhs, Azerbaijanis and other Muslim peoples in former Russian Central Asia; and last but not least, the May Fourth Movement in China exploding against the refusal of the Paris Peace Conference to consider Chinese claims to Shandong (May–June). On a truly global scale, Britain faced "boiling labor unrest from Winnipeg to Bombay."[43] Amid this global crisis of colonialism, the Bolsheviks were inciting nationalists to democracy, throwing into sharp relief the obduracy of the imperial governments conferring in Paris: Egyptian and Persian delegations, the Bengali polymath Rabindranath Tagore, Indian, Korean and Vietnamese nationalists, Chinese petitioners for Japanese-occupied Shandong – all were spurned or denied access to the table.

For the future understanding of socialist revolution, this brought a profound shift in the operative geopolitical imaginary. If the October Revolution and its aftermath proved the crucible of a new voluntarism, surpassing the old Kautskian determinism in a strategically driven commitment to making the revolution *now*, then the convergent crisis of European colonial order gave this a compellingly *global* dimension. From that same crucible, in other words, came the emergent activism of democratic, communist and radical-nationalist anti-colonial movements in the extra-European world. Across many parts of the globe, but especially in Asia from Persia to Japan, the years 1919–22 saw a fascinating conjunction of socialist, anarchist, indigenous and Enlightenment-influenced thinking about self-determination and self-rule, whose terms shaped the coordinates of Third World revolutionary thinking through the 1930s and 1940s into the era of Bandung.

43 Adam Tooze, *The Deluge: The Great War, America, and the Remaking of the Global Order, 1916–1931* (New York: Viking, 2014), 374.

In these terms M. N. Roy was hardly the sole South Asian revolutionary to be formed by a pilgrimage along the global circuitry of early twentieth-century radical thought. We might add the student-journalist Mandayam Parthasarathi Tirumal Acharya (1887–1951), for example, who from the early 1900s was experimenting with socialist and nationalist ideas from his refuge in the French enclave of Pondicherry, before traveling to London by way of Marseille and Paris in 1907. Intensely active in both public and clandestine revolutionary nationalist circles, first in London and then from 1910 in Paris, with connections to Turkey and Persia, he spent the war years in Berlin, working through the Berlin Committee for Indian Independence, before moving in December 1918 to Petrograd and thence to Moscow. A delegate to the Second Comintern Congress in July 1920, he passed briefly through the Indian Communist Party in 1920–21, but clashed with Roy, and by 1921 was back in Berlin as an anarchosyndicalist. The founding circles of Indian communism disclosed many such stories – the Bengali journalist Muzaffar ("Kakababu") Ahmed (1889–1973), for instance, or the Bombay/Mumbai student Shripad Amrit Dange (1899–1991), or the upper-caste Hindu Abani Mukherji (1891–1937), who was radicalized into socialism by sojourns in Germany and Japan in 1913–15. Each of these trajectories hinged on the European encounter, as inspiration, repulsion, and spur.[44]

When the very firm structures of Second International thought and practice became unlocked during 1905–17 – patterns and routines themselves embedded in the previously stable systems of parliamentary constitutionalism and associated political liberties that coalesced in Europe after the 1860s – there followed a turbulent period of regroupment, whose outcomes long remained unclear. The richness of the indeterminacies came from the gargantuan global consequences of World War I – not just the impact of the war years themselves, but the long-running dynamics of the territorial-political settlement (from Versailles to Sèvres), the geopolitical aftershocks of imperial dissolution all across Eurasia (from East Central Europe through the Middle East and Central Asia to South Asia, China and Japan), and the equally massive fallout from the Bolshevik Revolution. These transformations of 1917–23 accelerated and redirected the flows of influences, people and ideas already in motion from the prewar decade, when revolutions in Russia, Persia, Turkey, Mexico and China enabled a very different worldwide pattern of movement than before.

44 For one brilliant explication, see Benedict Anderson, *The Age of Globalization: Anarchists and the Anticolonial Imagination* (London: Verso, 2013).

For what proved to be a relatively transient historical moment, Bolshevism and the Communist International then offered a framework where remarkably heterogeneous radicalisms could convene, with many different imaginings of what a socialist revolution might be thought to entail. In that sense Moscow was not only "the acropolis of the Communist world," but also a beacon of still-widening nationalist creativity and a Mecca for anti-colonial aspiration.[45] Of course, the moment was fleeting. Notwithstanding Lenin's visionary purpose, which into the 1920s stayed remarkably agile, the strategies and visions of a new revolutionary anti-colonialism drew impetus from the Bolshevik Revolution largely in spite of the Bolsheviks themselves. Once the dust had settled, the latter reverted rapidly enough to earlier Eurocentric assumptions. The meanings of October retracted much of their extra-European, anti-colonial reach. The temporary restabilizing of the mid 1920s, internationally and inside the Soviet Union itself, quickly closed down most of that heady openness of possibility. After the initial experiments and excesses of voluntarism in 1917–23, inside the drama of the immediate revolutionary conjuncture, the freeing of revolutionary strategy from the Second International's pre-1914 economism became captured by Stalinism and fashioned into a reliable program of instrumentally regulated practice: revolution not as the democratic denouement of the final crisis of capitalism, but as the political resource and weapon of the all-knowing Stalinized communist party. The earlier heterogeneity of the anti-colonial radicalisms became a predictable casualty of this Stalinization, sending the cohorts of intellectuals and militants who initially gathered beneath the Bolshevik standard into widely varying future directions. But from the early 1900s to the early 1920s, the meanings of "socialist revolution" had opened briefly and dramatically outwards into an unfinished, cosmopolitan and surprisingly deterritorial space.

Bibliographical Essay

The opening chapters of Archie Brown, *The Rise and Fall of Communism* (London: Bodley Head, 2009), 9–39, and David Priestland, *The Red Flag:*

45 I take the quoted phrase from Kris Manjapra, *Age of Entanglement: German and Indian Intellectuals across Empire* (Cambridge, MA: Harvard University Press, 2014), 180. For another study complicating the dynamics joining the civic, anti-imperial and socialist impulses toward democratic rebellion in the extra-European worlds, see Michelle U. Campos, *Ottoman Brothers: Muslims, Christians, and Jews in Early Twentieth-Century Palestine* (Stanford: Stanford University Press, 2010).

A History of Communism (New York: Grove Press, 2009), 16–102, provide helpful introductions. For the political thinking of Karl Marx and Friedrich Engels in their own time, see George Lichtheim, *Marxism: An Historical and Critical Study* (London: Routledge & Kegan Paul, 1961), along with Richard N. Hunt, *The Political Ideas of Marx and Engels*, vol. II, *Classical Marxism, 1850–1895* (Pittsburgh: University of Pittsburgh Press, 1984), and several of the essays in Eric Hobsbawm, *How to Change the World: Reflections on Marx and Marxism* (New Haven: Yale University Press, 2011), especially the following: "Marx, Engels and Politics" (48–88); "On the *Communist Manifesto*" (101–20); "The Fortunes of Marx's and Engels' Writings" (176–96); and "The Influence of Marxism 1889–1914" (211–60). For the debates among German Social Democrats, see Dick Geary, *Karl Kautsky* (Manchester: Manchester University Press, 1987); Peter Gay, *The Dilemmas of Democratic Socialism: Eduard Bernstein's Challenge to Marx* (New York: Columbia University Press, 1952); and Henry Tudor and J. M. Tudor (eds.), *Marxism and Social Democracy: The Revisionist Debate 1896–1898* (Cambridge: Cambridge University Press, 1988). For French socialism, see Robert Stuart, *Marxism at Work: Ideology, Class and French Socialism During the Third Republic* (Cambridge: Cambridge University Press, 1992). For the general context, see James Joll, *The Second International 1889–1914* (New York: Routledge, 1966). Global dimensions are treated by Kevin B. Anderson, *Marx at the Margins: On Nationalism, Ethnicity, and Non-Western Societies* (Chicago: University of Chicago Press, 2010), while Marcel van der Linden and Jürgen Rojahn (eds.), *The Formation of Labour Movements 1870–1914: An International Perspective*, 2 vols. (Leiden: Brill, 1990), offer comprehensive coverage. Pankaj Mishra, *From the Ruins of Empire: The Revolt Against the West and the Remaking of Asia* (New York: Picador, 2012), surveys the global moment of anti-colonial rebellion in 1919. Together, Helmut Gruber, *International Communism in the Era of Lenin: A Documentary History* (New York: Anchor Books, 1972), and Jon Jacobson, *When the Soviet Union Entered World Politics* (Berkeley: University of California Press, 1994), are an excellent introduction. Perry Anderson, *Considerations on Western Marxism* (London: Verso, 1976), remains a brilliant general conspectus. For the overall context, see Geoff Eley, *Forging Democracy: The History of the Left in Europe, 1850–2000* (New York: Oxford University Press, 2002), especially 3–229.

2

The Russian Revolution and Civil War

REX A. WADE

Communism arose out of the Russian Revolution of 1917. When the revolution began, Vladimir Lenin was in exile in Switzerland, a very minor figure in Russian or world affairs. A year later, in March 1918, he was the head of a new government in Russia and, moreover, renamed his political party "communist." He was also looking at events in Russia as the beginning of a worldwide revolutionary process. Other Bolshevik/communist leaders, such as Leon Trotsky and Joseph Stalin, were making a similar transition from obscurity to world prominence. How did this happen so swiftly in the context of revolution and civil war in Russia?

As 1917 opened, Russia was ripe for revolution. Long-term political, social and economic problems and discontents affected all segments of society and had given rise to revolutionary movements. Then, the disasters of the Great War, with its huge losses of men and dislocation of the economy, magnified all of Russia's problems and discredited the governance of Nicholas II. January 1917 saw all levels of society alienated, a deteriorating economy, a revival of industrial strikes, increasingly resentful soldiers and even talk of a palace revolution. A widespread sense existed that something had to break soon.

That came with the February Revolution. It began out of a wave of industrial strikes in January and February 1917 in Petrograd (the capital, St. Petersburg, had been renamed with the less German-sounding Petrograd at the beginning of the war). These morphed into actual revolution when, on 23 February, "Women's Day," women workers at factories in the Vyborg district of the city marched out from their factories demanding "bread" and called for men at nearby factories to join them. Over the next two days the demonstrations spread until they included most of the industrial workforce, joined by students and broad sections of the urban lower and middle classes. Demonstrators called for an end to the war and political changes as well as solutions to the pressing food supply and other economic problems. Soldiers called out to help break up demonstrations acted with reluctance. Orders to fire into the crowds led to a revolt of the garrison on the morning of 27 February and a turning of the demonstrations into full-fledged revolution.

The Revolution to this point was primarily a popular revolt, with what little leadership it had coming from factory-level activists and isolated individuals who emerged as leaders of demonstrations and attacks on police stations. Neither the revolutionary parties, whose main leaders were in exile, nor the social-political elite provided effective leadership before 27 February. That evening, however, two groups of potential leaders stepped forward. One was a group of mostly liberal and moderate conservative political leaders from the state Duma (a legislative assembly elected on a limited franchise based mainly on wealth). Anxious to contain the street revolution, concerned about its implications for the war effort, but also realizing that this offered a long-awaited opportunity to force Nicholas to reform the political system, on the evening of the 27th they proclaimed the formation of a Temporary Committee of the state Duma that would assume governmental responsibility. At the same time, a multiparty group of socialist intellectuals met in another wing of the Duma building and led workers and soldiers in the formation of the Petrograd Soviet of Workers' and Soldiers' Deputies, a more avowedly revolutionary body committed to turning the street revolt into a sweeping social and economic as well as political revolution.

Over the next three days socialist Soviet leaders worked closely with the liberal and conservative Duma Committee members to consolidate the revolution and form a new government. On 2 March, they agreed on the formation of a Provisional Government to govern Russia until a new governmental system could be created by a Constituent Assembly elected by universal franchise. Nicholas II abdicated the same day.

The new Provisional Government was drawn primarily from the liberal political leadership of the country and dominated by the Constitutional Democratic (Kadet) Party, the main liberal party. Its head, minister-president, was Prince Georgii Yevgenievich L'vov, a well-known liberal public figure. The Petrograd Soviet declined to have its members join, although Alexander Kerensky, a moderate socialist member of the Duma and popular hero of the February Revolution, joined anyway (and later, in July, became its head). The Soviet leaders promised to support the new government insofar as it pursued policies of which they approved. The Duma soon faded as an important political institution, but the Petrograd Soviet continued and commanded the primary loyalty of the industrial workers and garrison soldiers, the main bases of political power. This robbed the Provisional Government of much of its actual authority, creating what quickly was dubbed "dual-authority." In this the government had the generally recognized official authority and responsibility but not the effective power, while the Soviet had the actual power and popular authority but not responsibility for governing. A similar situation developed in cities across the country, with new city governments drawn primarily from liberal-educated society replacing the old tsarist authorities while alongside them local socialist-led soviets of workers' and soldiers' deputies sprang up and wielded real authority.

The new political structure was unstable, but its contours quickly became clearer as a fundamental political realignment took place. Central to this was the emergence of three broad multiparty political blocs: liberals and moderate conservatives, moderate socialists and radical left socialists. The liberal-moderate conservative group dominated the Provisional Government at first, and then from May to October shared it with the moderate socialists. The moderate socialists, predominantly the Menshevik and Socialist Revolutionary (SR) parties – the former Marxists and the latter agrarian-oriented socialists – controlled the Petrograd, Moscow and most other soviets across the country, and also became increasingly influential in the central government and dominant locally. The radical left – Bolsheviks, Menshevik-Internationalists, left SRs, anarchists – initially were a distinctly minority voice, but grew as the liberals and moderate socialists failed to satisfy popular aspirations. Monarchist or truly conservative political parties played little role in 1917.

Within this political realignment, the authority of the Soviet and the overwhelming popular identification with the socialist parties meant that the political future of the revolution hinged on the outcome of struggles for influence among the socialist parties and within the Soviet. Two political leaders returning from exile with fundamentally different programs of revolutionary action, Irakli Tsereteli and Vladimir Lenin, drove the political realignment among the socialists and the development of Soviet policies.

Tsereteli, a Georgian Menshevik, returned from Siberian exile on 20 March and under the banner of "Revolutionary Defensism" led a group that forged the Menshevik-Socialist Revolutionary led bloc of moderate socialists. Key to the Revolutionary Defensist bloc's identity and initial political success was the question of peace. The Revolution released a pent-up demand to end the war and its suffering. The Revolutionary Defensists called for ending the war via a negotiated peace among the warring powers, defense of the country and the revolution until then, and cooperation between the Petrograd Soviet and the government to achieve peace and deal with socioeconomic and other issues. It repudiated the policy of war to victory and spoke to the broad popular desire to end the war, but without Russia's total defeat and possible German domination. From April to September the Revolutionary Defensists dominated the Petrograd Soviet as well as most soviets in other cities. In May they entered the Provisional Government and advocated "coalition government," i.e. one based on an alliance of moderate socialists and liberals. This coalition formed the various cabinets of the Provisional Government from May until the October Revolution.

The radical left was ill-defined and lacked strong leadership until the return of major political leaders from foreign exile. These included Vladimir Lenin of the Bolsheviks as well as some prominent leftist Mensheviks and leftist SRs, who formed radical left wings of those parties in opposition to the dominant moderate wings. Lenin in particular galvanized the radical left. On his return to Russia on 3 April his "April Theses" electrified politics. He criticized the moderate socialist leaders of the Soviet, denounced cooperation with the Provisional Government, and called for rapid movement from the first stage of the revolution toward the second, more radical stage. He also called for abandoning the term "social democrats" in favor of the word "communists" (not actually done until 1918) and for the formation of a new revolutionary socialist International to replace the old International that had effectively collapsed in 1914.[1] The Bolsheviks and other radicals demanded more vigorous efforts to end the war, more rapid and more sweeping social and economic reforms, and called for the Provisional Government's replacement by a socialist government based on the soviets. At first the radical left's extremism was out of keeping with the mood of optimism and cooperation following the overthrow of the autocracy, but its opposition stance positioned it to become the beneficiary of any failures of the Provisional Government and the Revolutionary Defensist Soviet leadership. That came quickly.

The first major crisis of the revolution, the "April Crisis," arose over the war. P. N. Miliukov, the Kadet leader and new foreign minister, argued that Russia's national interests transcended the revolution and required that Russia continue the war to a complete victory. The socialists in the Soviet

1 V. I. Lenin, *Collected Works*, vol. XXIV (Moscow: Progress Publishers, 1964), 21–24.

attacked this policy, while Tsereteli's Revolutionary Defensism provided a seemingly viable, and politically very popular, way to end the war by international negotiation. Miliukov's attempts to defend a policy of war to victory led to massive anti-government street demonstrations from 18–21 April. Soon after, Miliukov and some other liberals were replaced by several leading members of the Soviet, including Tsereteli, forming the first "coalition government" of liberals and moderate socialists on 5 May.

The April Crisis illustrated that the February Revolution had unleased the pent-up frustrations and aspirations of the populace, which found expression in an explosion of popular self-assertion and the formation of thousands of organizations dedicated to articulating the demands of their members. The industrial workers, who had begun the revolution, demanded increased wages, an eight-hour day, better working conditions, an end to the war and other aspirations. Soldiers implemented fundamental changes in the conditions of military service and quickly became ardent opponents of continuing the war. Peasants laid claim to the land and greater control over their villages. The middle classes looked forward to expanded civil rights and a society based on the rule of law. Women demonstrated for the right to vote (which they got in July 2017, making Russia the first of the great powers and one of the first of all nations with universal suffrage). National minorities demanded expanded use of their language and, in some especially important cases, political autonomy within a federal state. A vast array of factory committees, trade unions, soldiers' committees, village assemblies, nationality-based parties, officers' and industrialists' associations, householders' collectives, cultural and educational clubs, economic cooperatives, women's and youth organizations, soldiers' wives, over-age soldiers and others demanded that the government address their needs and hopes. These, and their continuous meetings, represented genuinely popular movements and gave voice to the hopes of the peoples of the empire. They became major forces in the unfolding of the revolution as they asserted themselves and political parties struggled to gain their allegiance. This drove the revolution steadily leftward during 1917.

Popular aspirations and attitudes were reflected in the powerful language and symbolism that developed immediately after the February Revolution. Streets, places and objects were given revolutionary names. Revolutionary songs accompanied most public activity in 1917, while red, the color of revolution since the nineteenth century, was omnipresent in banners, cockades, armbands, ribbons in button holes or pinned to garments and elsewhere. Street demonstrations and marches became part of daily life.

"Festivals of freedom" were popular in the early months (and again after the October Revolution). Words such as "democracy" and "republic" were powerful positive terms, proclaiming a radically new world. Moreover, a universal meaning was assigned to the revolution. Almost the entire political spectrum held the revolution to be not merely a Russian event, but one that would exercise great influence across Europe and the globe, like the French Revolution of 1789 had done earlier. Lenin's belief that the revolution was the beginning of worldwide socialist revolution was only the most extreme form of a commonly held faith that the revolution would change both Russia and the world.

The liberal and moderate socialist political alliance that controlled the Provisional Government after April could not meet the many, often conflicting, aspirations of the population. The general optimism of spring gave way to a summer of discontent. Especially pressing was the war. The Revolutionary Defensists failed in their initial effort to get the warring powers to agree to a negotiated peace. In a desperate effort to show that Russia's views must be seriously considered because it was still a great power of continued importance, they agreed to a military offensive in June. It was unpopular from the beginning and quickly turned into a devastating defeat. This discredited both the government and Revolutionary Defensism among wide swathes of the population. Simultaneously, food shortages, worsening economic conditions, industrial conflict and factory closures, rising crime and public disorders, rural discontent over land distribution and other problems fueled a demand for "All Power to the Soviet." Workers, soldiers and others increasingly turned toward arguments that only a radically different government, based solely on the soviets, could bring peace and meet their various aspirations and needs. This led to the "July Days," massive street demonstrations in Petrograd from 3–5 July demanding a soviet-based, all-socialist government. These began when some units of the garrison, bitterly opposed to the new military offensive, and workers increasingly discontented with the war and the economy, poured into the streets chanting "All Power to the Soviets."

Lower-level Bolshevik activists were prominent among the factory worker and soldier radicals articulating popular discontent and the demand for soviet power, but the Bolshevik party leadership itself had not planned the demonstrations. Faced with the demands from their supporters for action, in the early hours of 4 July the Bolshevik Central Committee (without Lenin, who was resting in Finland), announced its willingness to lead "a peaceful demonstration" in support of an all-socialist government based on the Soviet. Hardly had it done so, however, than the demonstrations floundered on a combination of the unwillingness of the Petrograd Soviet's Revolutionary Defensist leaders to take power, news that troops from the front were arriving to support the Soviet leaders and government, and a sensational release of documents purporting (falsely) to show that the Bolshevik leaders were German agents. Lenin, who had barely returned from Finland, had to rush back there, and stayed in hiding until the October Revolution.

A peculiar and contradictory situation developed after the July Days. Newspaper headlines and political leaders spoke of a conservative reaction, even a possible military dictator. The inside pages, in contrast, revealed a steady radicalization of the population in news articles about the Bolshevik and radical left bloc's capture of one worker or soldier organization after another in reelections. This was seconded by regular reports of rural violence and land seizure, food shortages in cities, renewed industrial conflict, a dramatic increase in crime and public disorders, and growing separatist agitation in some of the minority nationality regions, most importantly Ukraine. Society appeared to be disintegrating and life increasingly insecure.

Governmental political instability magnified these problems. The original cabinet of the Provisional Government had collapsed after the April Crisis and was replaced by the first "coalition" of liberals and moderate socialists on 5 May, still under Prince L'vov. On 2 July (just as the July Days were starting) this cabinet resigned and not until 23 July was a new one formed, led by Alexander Kerensky. Its instability was obvious from the start. Under the slogan of "restoration of order," Kerensky worked with the newly appointed commander of the armies, General Lavr Kornilov. Both wanted to reduce the influence of the Petrograd Soviet, but meant different things by that. Kerensky became convinced that Kornilov was planning a *coup d'état* against him and dismissed Kornilov as army commander on 27 August. An outraged Kornilov sent a small military force against Petrograd, but his attack quickly collapsed. Kerensky's cabinet also collapsed, ushering in nearly a month of renewed governmental crisis.

The Kornilov affair, with its aroma of counterrevolution, sparked an even more insistent demand for soviet power. This catapulted a Bolshevik-led radical left coalition into control of the Petrograd Soviet, the main bastion of revolutionary authority, in September, with Trotsky as chairman. Such radical left coalitions also took over the leadership of the Moscow and many other city soviets and workers' and soldiers' organizations. By mid September, the question was not whether the latest Provisional Government would be replaced, but by whom and in what manner? Ever larger segments of the political elite as well as the general population believed that the time had come for some type of new, all-socialist, soviet-based government. Given that the ascendant Bolsheviks and their allies had repeatedly called for the Soviet to take power, the question now was not so much would they attempt to replace the Provisional Government, but how and when? These questions were debated on street corners, in newspapers and in public meetings.

These very questions tormented Lenin in his Finnish hiding place (an order for his arrest dating from the July Days still existed). He already had turned away from the idea of a broad socialist government in cooperation with the moderate socialists. Believing that the times offered a unique opportunity for a radical restructuring of political power and for a man such as himself, Lenin shifted to a strident demand for an immediate armed seizure of power by the Bolsheviks. This divided the party leadership. A minority supported Lenin. A second position, articulated by Grigorii Zinoviev and Lev Kamenev, two of the most important Bolshevik leaders, favored the more cautious approach of a broad coalition of socialists in a democratic left government, probably created at the Constituent Assembly (elections were scheduled for November). Leon Trotsky, who had joined the party in July and now chaired the Petrograd Soviet, looked to the forthcoming Second All-Russia Congress of Soviets, scheduled for October, as the vehicle for the transfer of power. It was expected that the parties supporting soviet power would have a majority at the Congress, and that the Congress could then declare the transfer of power to itself and create a new, more radical, Bolshevik-led government. Most Bolshevik leaders apparently supported this third option, despite Lenin's demands, and the party's political efforts focused on the forthcoming Congress of Soviets and the selection of deputies to the Congress who would support a transfer of power.

Lenin, frustrated and fearing that an irretrievable opportunity was slipping by, moved from Finland to the outskirts of Petrograd. On 10 October, after hearing Lenin's passionate demands for a seizure of power, the Central Committee of the Bolshevik party passed a resolution stating that an "armed uprising" was "the order of the day." Although this resolution later became central to the myth of a carefully planned seizure of power carried out under Lenin's direction, it was in fact something different. While reasserting the longstanding Bolshevik idea that an armed uprising was a revolutionary necessity, it did not commit the party to any plan for seizing power, nor did it start actual preparations for a seizure of power. Despite Lenin, the party leadership continued to focus on the forthcoming Congress of Soviets as the time, place and vehicle for the transfer of power. This would be the new "revolution" called for not only in the Bolshevik resolution of 10 October, but in hundreds of local workers' and soldiers' resolutions for "All Power to the Soviets." The left SRs and Menshevik-Internationalists, the other important radical left groups, also were looking toward the Congress to make any transfer of power.

The October Revolution began, however, neither in response to any plan of Lenin's nor to any act of the Congress of Soviets, but in response to an action by Kerensky. This was a fortunate break Lenin could not have anticipated. Kerensky's government, apprehensive about the rising demand for soviet power and growing Bolshevik influence, decided on a minor strike against the Bolsheviks on the eve of the Congress. It sent military cadets in the early hours of 24 October to close down two Bolshevik newspapers. Petrograd Soviet leaders declared this a new "Kornilovite" counterrevolutionary plot and called on soldiers and armed workers (Red Guards) to defend the Soviet and the revolution and to ensure the opening of the Congress of Soviets scheduled for 25 October. Throughout the 24th, pro-government and pro-Soviet forces engaged in confused and uncoordinated confrontations over control of key buildings and bridges. The pro-Soviet forces had the greater numbers, morale and determination and with almost no deaths controlled most of the city by midnight.

The character of events changed again on the morning of the 25th. Lenin had been hiding on the edge of the city and unable to participate in events of the 24th. Hearing confused accounts of the events in the city, he made his way to the Soviet headquarters after midnight of the 24th/25th. Lenin pressed the Soviet leaders to offensive rather than defensive action (he may have thought they had initiated events). He then wrote a proclamation declaring the Provisional Government overthrown that was quickly distributed through the city. Lenin had, because of Kerensky's ill-considered action, gotten the armed seizure of power before the Congress that he had wanted but had seemed to have had no chance of achieving.

The Second All-Russia Congress of Soviets opened at 10:40 p.m. on 25 October. As expected, it had a majority in favor of soviet power. The Bolsheviks, however, while the largest party, were not a majority and had to rely on the left SRs and other radical leftists to form a majority. All seemed in place for creating a multiparty, all-socialist government, what "soviet power" had meant throughout 1917. Then, suddenly, Lenin received yet another unpredictable stroke of good luck: The moderate socialist SRs and Mensheviks denounced the Bolsheviks for the events in the streets and walked out. This left the Bolsheviks with an absolute majority and in full control of the Congress, which declared the Provisional Government overthrown and all power to rest in its own hands. Lenin, who had yet to reappear in public, not only had "soviet power" but, unexpectedly, an all-Bolshevik government. This, the Council of People's Commissars, headed by Lenin, was announced at the second session of the Congress on the night of 26–27 October. The innovative name was selected to stress its revolutionary nature, that something new in the world was being born.

Most Russians saw the October Revolution as merely another political crisis, punctuated with the usual street disorders and producing yet another "provisional" government (a term the new government in fact used at first). Nonetheless, the popularity of the idea of soviet power, plus Lenin's and Trotsky's vigorous leadership, let the new Bolshevik government consolidate its position during the following weeks. Soldier and worker support allowed it to turn back attempts to oust it. Locally, radical left-led soviets implemented soviet power in large areas of the country, including Moscow, and gave allegiance to the new Soviet regime. At the same time, the Bolsheviks moved swiftly to meet popular aspirations by a 26 October decree distributing land to the peasants, by allowing workers greater control in the factories, by an informal and then formal armistice with Germany and by other measures. They also introduced repressive measures against real or potential opponents: press censorship, the formation of a political police (the Cheka), repressive measures against the Kadet Party and other actions.

The final act in consolidating power, as well as marking the end of the revolution in the specific sense and the transition to civil war, was the dispersal of the Constituent Assembly. The November elections to the Constituent Assembly and its forthcoming convocation on 5 January 1918 kept alive the idea that Lenin's government was only another temporary – provisional – government. This muted the initial opposition to Lenin's government, but also presented Lenin with a dilemma. The elections gave the SRs a shaky majority in the Constituent Assembly. It was widely believed that any government coming out of it would be the broad socialist coalition that the slogan "All Power to the Soviets" originally meant, and would implement socializing policies. For Lenin and the Bolsheviks, however, accepting the authority of the elections and the Constituent Assembly meant yielding power, which Lenin was unwilling to do. He allowed the Constituent Assembly to open on 5 January, but shut it down by force the next morning. Its dispersal was not necessary for maintenance of a socialist government, or even "soviet power," but it was essential if Lenin and the

Bolsheviks were to retain power and further their own ideal of a world socialist revolution. Simultaneously, Lenin pushed the Bolsheviks to accept the harsh peace terms Germany demanded as the price of ending Russia's involvement in the Great War, pointing out that they had no alternative if their government and its revolutionary agenda were to survive.

During these early months, roughly November 1917 to March/April 1918, the new Bolshevik government implemented a series of socialist-type social-economic policies, such as giving workers more authority in the factories and broadening access to education, as well as others such as changing the calendar to the Gregorian and secularizing marriage and divorce. On 1 December 1917, they created the Supreme Council of the National Economy (Vysshiy sovet narodnogo khozyaystva, VSNKh), charged with planning for and directing the entire national economy and shortly afterward, in June 1918, the Soviet government decreed sweeping nationalization of industry, transportation and mining, and also undertook to establish a system of class-based rationing and consumer cooperatives for food and essential goods. The Bolsheviks saw these measures as not just Russian events, but as of world importance: "We the Russians," Lenin proclaimed in January 1918, "have the honor of being the vanguard of the international socialist revolution" and claimed that the Bolshevik Revolution had "opened a new epoch in world history."[2] To further his vision of this as the beginning of a world radical socialist revolution, Lenin in March 1918 had the Bolshevik party renamed "Communist Party."

Shutting down the Constituent Assembly and these measures ended any possibility of the Russian Revolution playing itself out in the political arena. The Bolsheviks' opponents now had no recourse but to arms, and in early 1918 the revolution of 1917 segued into civil war, or more accurately, civil wars. It was not merely military wars on several fronts involving various opponents, but also an often brutal social and economic class war, a series of ethnic-based conflicts as Ukraine and some other nationality areas declared independence, and had aspects of an international civil war as well as an attempt to create a wholly new type of communist society. We will discuss the several parts of the 1918–21 civil wars period sequentially, starting with the military fighting on which Bolshevik/communist survival depended, and then turn to other aspects.

A preliminary stage of the civil wars came in the "Railway War" of December 1917–March 1918. For this the Soviet government used hastily

2 Lenin, *Collected Works*, vol. XXVI, 72, 479.

organized detachments of Moscow and Petrograd workers' Red Guards, small groups of soldiers and sailors, plus local supporters to attack areas resisting its authority. Moving small detachments along the railway system, in December they assisted Kharkov Bolsheviks in seizing power and declaring a Ukrainian Soviet Republic, then pushed on to defeat the Ukrainian Central Rada's forces and take Kiev in early February 1918, temporarily ending Ukraine's proclaimed independence and bringing it and its food production under Soviet authority. Simultaneously they forced the Volunteer Army, made up mainly of tsarist army officers and Don Cossacks, out of the strategic area south of Moscow. Pro-Soviet forces also took control of areas to the east in the Urals and Siberia. Thus by March 1918, the same month they signed the Brest-Litovsk peace treaty with the Central Powers ending Russia's participation in the Great War, the Bolsheviks and their leftist allies had brought the most important parts of imperial Russia's territory that was not controlled by Germany under "soviet power." They appeared to have triumphed militarily against immediate domestic rivals, protecting what they saw as the base from which communism would spread.

In the late spring and early summer of 1918, however, new and more powerful centers of political and military opposition emerged, Bolshevik-controlled territory shrank drastically, and civil war began in earnest. An early stage involved the Bolsheviks' most politically dangerous opponents, a group of SR leaders who gathered at Samara on the Volga River and in June created Komuch (Committee of the Members of the Constituent Assembly). Based on the SR majority in the Constituent Assembly, they claimed to be the legitimate government of Russia. Komuch, however, had difficulty developing an effective army or government. They got important assistance from the Czechoslovak Legion, which, on its way across Siberia and thence to France to continue fighting Austria–Hungary, revolted against Bolshevik attempts to disarm it. The Western Allied governments, looking for ways to undermine the Bolshevik government and keep Russia in the war, had the Czechs support Komuch. The Czech–Komuch forces won some early battles along the Volga, threatening the new Soviet state, but by early fall the newly organized Bolshevik Red Army defeated them.

At the same time as this early fighting, three important military developments with long-term implications occurred. One was the creation of the Red Army as a formidable fighting force. Under the direction of Leon Trotsky, newly appointed people's commissar of war, the Red Army moved away from the original revolutionary ideals of an all-volunteer army with democratic features, including elected commanders. Trotsky swiftly built a more conventional army with appointed officers, draftees as well as volunteers, and strict discipline. Military officers from the old imperial army, some voluntarily, some coerced, supplemented new revolutionary officers up from the ranks and helped give the Red Army structure as well as leadership. The main innovation was the system of political commissars alongside regular commanding officers (which became a permanent feature of the Soviet army). Under Trotsky's leadership the Red Army quickly became an effective fighting force.

A second development was the appearance in summer 1918 of new and more militarily threatening opponents. These were what came to be known as the White armies, organized and led by conservative officers of the old tsarist army. There were multiple White armies. One of the two main ones, and ultimately the most threatening, the Armed Forces of South Russia (AFSR), formed in south Russia under the leadership of General Anton Denikin during the summer of 1918. The second main White army formed in western Siberia under Admiral Aleksandr Kolchak the following winter. Smaller White armies formed in the Baltic region and in the far north around Arkhangel'sk and Murmansk (supported by small American and British detachments).

The third development involved the Central Powers. German forces occupied Ukraine, Belorussia and part of the Baltic provinces. Turkey moved into parts of the Caucasus region. However, the Central Powers' final defeat by the Western Allies in November 1918 threw the areas occupied by them into new uncertainty, most importantly in Ukraine, where significant nationalist armies reemerged and again threatened the Soviet regime and its communist allies within the old Russian Empire even as Germany's collapse sparked Bolshevik hopes for the spread of communism across war-torn Europe, especially Central Europe.

The decisive military battles of the Russian civil wars came in 1919 between the Red and White armies. In March, Kolchak launched an attack out of western Siberia. Faced with vast distances, poor organization, a relatively small army and peasant and worker revolt behind his lines, Kolchak's offensive quickly floundered. A Red Army counteroffensive in May drove Kolchak's forces back into Siberia and eventual dissolution. Now the poor coordination among the Whites took its toll. Denikin launched his offensive from the south just as Kolchak's offensive from the east faltered, allowing the Bolsheviks to face the two armies sequentially rather than at the same time. Nonetheless, Denikin's AFSR, much better organized, equipped and led than Kolchak's force, drove northward and by November was only about 235 miles from Moscow (to which the capital had been moved in February 1918) and seemed poised to attack it. Now, however, the numerous advantages of the Reds came clearly into play while the handicaps of the Whites became more obvious. Manpower losses by Denikin's best forces, especially the Volunteer Army, could not readily be replaced, while the Red Army, based in the main population centers, grew steadily and by 1919 significantly outnumbered all opponents. Denikin's forces were having trouble with local peasant populations, had seriously overextended their lines, and were engaged in ongoing fighting with Ukrainian nationalist and peasant armies. A Red Army offensive at the end of 1919 thoroughly defeated Denikin's army, bottling up the tattered remnants in the Crimea. A lesser White offensive, by General N. N. Iudenich out of Estonia against Petrograd in October, was repulsed and that army disintegrated.

By early 1920 the Bolsheviks appeared to have won decisively and to be in a position to finish off their opponents quickly, including the nationalist independence movements in Ukraine, the Caucasus and elsewhere (except the Baltic, where German and Allied support for the new states there made that impossible). However, in April 1920 Poland invaded with the aim of annexing parts of Ukraine, Belorussia and Lithuania. After initial defeats, the Bolsheviks rallied and by October drove the Poles back. As the Red Army drove west, for a moment threatening to overrun Poland, it sparked a new, if temporary, hope that this might be the awaited start of the spread of communism into Eastern Europe and beyond. That did not happen, but with Poland repulsed the Red Army quickly drove the last remnants of the AFSR out of Crimea during the spring of 1921, took control of Ukraine and moved to finish off opposition areas in Siberia, the Caucasus and elsewhere where nationalist movements had declared independence. Only in the northwestern region did new independent states survive: Poland, Lithuania, Latvia, Estonia and Finland.

This set the stage for a very different, and chronologically the last, major stage of civil war armed fighting, the 1920–22 war against what has sometimes been termed the "Greens." These were peasant forces that emerged to give military weight to peasant grievances against the Bolsheviks over grain requisitioning and other policies. By summer 1918 the peasants had finished carrying out a thorough agrarian revolution, expropriating and redistributing the land among themselves. The Bolsheviks had encouraged peasant revolution in 1917 and had sanctioned peasant seizure of the land. Once in power, however, the Bolsheviks, like their predecessors, needed the peasants to provide food deliveries for town and army, provide conscripts for the latter and pay taxes. Peasant seizure of land removed the large amounts of grain traditionally put on the market by the former large estates, while the rapid drop in available consumer goods reduced peasant incentive to market grain. Starvation threatened the cities, which suffered large population losses. The Bolsheviks moved to control the acquisition and distribution of foodstuffs for the army and cities, giving the People's Commissariat of Food Procurement dictatorial authority in May 1918. They followed this with a June decree creating Committees of the Poor Peasants. The new committees were intended both to introduce class warfare in the village and to ensure the delivery of grain to the army and cities. All this rested on ideologically based mistaken assumptions about extensive class divisions in the villages, which in fact had been reduced already by the peasants' land redistribution in 1917 and early 1918. As a result, the Bolsheviks had to resort to delivery quotas and outright seizure of foodstuffs, using Red Army detachments, the Cheka and special "Food Detachments" sent out from the cities. The peasants resisted and a spiraling rise of ever bloodier rural violence resulted. During 1920, with the threat of a White victory and return of landlords gone, peasant revolts blossomed across the country, especially in major agricultural districts south and southeast of Moscow. Peasants killed communist officials and peasant armies arose that could emerge quickly and then dissolve back into the villages when government forces appeared. The Bolsheviks responded with brutal suppression, crushing the peasant rebellions by 1922.

Yet another aspect of the civil war and spread of communism involved fighting nationalist movements. The Revolution opened up a new world of opportunities for the ethnically non-Russian peoples of the empire (approximately half of it) to pursue nationalist agendas alongside the broader revolutionary issues. As the authority of the central government disintegrated, especially after the October Revolution, several moved toward some kind of autonomy or even independence. The civil war thus involved nationalist armies fighting against both Reds and Whites, and even each other. Most of these combined Marxism or other socialist ideologies with their ethnic national programs. Socialism and nationalism made potent political partners. Lenin accepted nationality-based movements as a reality of the time and defended the right of national self-determination in the short run, believing that ultimately the advantages of communism would render nationalism meaningless. This set the stage for a complex situation where Bolsheviks sometimes cooperated with local nationalist movements but in other cases opposed them: Ukraine, the Caucasus, Central Asia and the Baltic region saw complex political and ethnic struggles, some independent states and then

Soviet conquest in 1920–22 (except in the Baltic region and Moldova). Intellectually the Bolsheviks "solved" the nationalist problem by putting it within the broader ideology of the spread of communist revolution. Local Bolsheviks emerged as leaders of theoretically independent republics which then, in 1922–24, reformed themselves into the Union of Soviet Socialist Republics (USSR). Lenin saw this as a short-run concession to nationalism that would in time become irrelevant as communism spread and transformed everything. (Instead, ironically, this facilitated the USSR's eventual disintegration and the decline of communism as a world movement.)

The peasants and nationalities reflect the extent to which the traditional military armies and fronts were only a part of the civil war story. The "civil war" was not only a military war, but was also a multisided, often brutal, social-economic class-based war with many "fronts." Part of this grew out of the fact that society had fractured and opposing sides tended to line up along social-economic lines – as workers, property owners, middle class, peasants, landlords, etc. – as well as along ethnic and other divisions. This had begun in 1917 and intensified after the October Revolution and beginning of civil war. On the Bolshevik side this reflected also that they saw themselves as overthrowing the old social-economic order and creating a wholly new type of society, a "socialist" society. As the Bolsheviks developed a theory-based definition of class enemies, the Whites developed a less theoretical but equally deadly class-hatred of Bolsheviks, loosely defined and used indiscriminately for anyone supporting or even suspected of supporting the Soviet regime, especially factory workers. The unfolding of the military civil war intensified these class-war sentiments, which contributed to the great brutality on all sides during the civil war and gave rise to the red terror and the increased role of the Cheka, the secret police and key repressive agency of the Soviet system. All sides in the civil war used terror tactics targeting those seen as supporters or possible supporters of their opponents, often by class definition. The red terror differed from others such as the white terror not only in extent, but also in the Bolsheviks' efforts to develop a theoretical justification based on Marxism and the worldwide class struggle. In 1920 Trotsky published a justification of the use of terror on the basis that it was a continuation of the revolutionary class struggle: "The man who repudiates terrorism in principle . . . must reject all idea of the political supremacy of the working class and its revolutionary dictatorship [and thus] repudiates the Socialist revolution."[3]

3 Leon Trotsky, "Terror and Communism: A Reply to Karl Kautsky," in Rex A. Wade (ed.), *Documents of Soviet History,* vol. II, *Triumph and Retreat, 1920–1922* (Gulf Breeze, FL: Academic International Press, 1991), 90.

The economic collapse, paired with military needs and the leadership's demand for "discipline," also negatively affected the industrial workers, the Bolsheviks' key support base. While exhorting the workers to "iron discipline" and hard work at the workplace, the Bolsheviks introduced measures such as universal compulsory labor and reintroduced hated features of the old regime such as piecework rates, harsh factory discipline and the detested labor books. There were ongoing clashes between workers and Bolshevik authorities. The regime used force to suppress strikes that broke out in 1918 and brought worker trade unions under tight communist party control. These centralizing and authoritarian policies conflicted with workers' activism and aspirations from the revolution of 1917, while the closing of factories in 1918–19 caused massive unemployment and steady worker flight to the countryside (Moscow, Petrograd and industrial cities lost half or more of their populations between late 1917 and early 1921). These clashes caused a dilemma for both workers and the Bolsheviks. The communist party's essential self-identity was as "proletarian" and based on the industrial workers, and party leaders genuinely believed their policies were in the proletariat's long-term interests. Workers, meanwhile, however angry over specific Bolshevik policies, had little alternative to supporting the regime. They hardly wanted a return of the old political-industrial order and feared the "white terror." Worker protests were muted during the critical period of the military civil war, but were still there to break out when the White-capitalist danger was reduced, such as in the wave of strikes that swept Petrograd in early 1921.

Amid discussion of all the violence and brutality of the civil war, and remembrance of what followed under Stalin, it is easy to forget the non-violent and optimistic, even utopian, features of the 1917 Revolution and the early Bolshevik regime and civil war era, to forget that so many believed that they were ushering in a new and better era of human history. Visions of a great cultural transformation on the road to utopia flourished. Bolshevik leaders such as A. V. Lunacharskii, the people's commissar for enlightenment, saw new revolutionary ideals sweeping away "bourgeois" ideas of art, education, family relations and other old cultural and social values, replacing them by new "proletarian" forms as part of a general cultural and social transformation. Indeed, after October the Bolsheviks swiftly abolished all discrimination based on religion or ethnicity, abolished all the titles and ranks that characterized the old system, and announced plans for universal education and health insurance, among other moves toward the glorious new society. Many intellectuals and artists advanced their own ideas about cultural revolution. Debate over exactly what the new world would look like and how to reach it created exciting intellectual and cultural currents alongside the brutality and semi-starvation of the civil war era. Indeed, the conditions of civil and class war, coming on top of the Great War, encouraged a rhetoric of the clash of historical epochs and sweeping utopian visions of a world purged and transformed. Avant-garde art and cultural experimentation flourished alongside visions of a world transformed by new technologies and ideas about the proletariat's transformation and future leadership. The Revolution and civil war swept away old cultural and institutional restraints while encouraging experimentation and utopian dreams of a new world being born.

The civil war also contained elements of an international civil war. The Bolsheviks saw their revolution as the beginning of a worldwide process of revolutions to usher in a new era of human history. Lenin had, before October 1917, responded to internal party criticism of his call for a seizure of power in "backwards" Russia by arguing that the revolution in Russia would ignite a revolution across Europe that would come to the aid of the Russian Revolution. The existing bourgeois-capitalist ruling classes would have to oppose this, and thus the Bolsheviks could place their revolution and the civil war within an international context. The change of the party's official name from Social Democratic (Bolshevik) to Communist in early 1918 underlined this idea. This theory-based vision was reinforced by the reality of Allied military intervention in the Russian Civil War. Small contingents of British, American, Japanese and French troops landed along the far seacoast frontiers to aid the anti-Bolshevik forces. Begun in summer of 1918 as part of the Allied struggle with Germany, the end of that war transformed it into a more ideologically motivated fight against Bolshevism. Although the intervention's goals were confused and its military significance minor, it confirmed Bolshevik notions of an international revolutionary war.

The latter found institutional form in the founding of the Communist International (Comintern) in March 1919. Its founding document declared that the international "imperialist war, which used to oppose a nation to a nation, is being superseded by civil war . . . which opposes one class to another."[4] At the same time the turmoil in Central Europe following the collapse of the German and Austrian-Hungarian empires after November 1918, plus a general European revulsion against the huge costs of the war, led to social conflict, including the emergence

4 *Communist International* 1 (May 1919), 18.

of local communist and other radical movements across Europe. This reinforced Bolshevik visions of a rapid spread of revolution and civil war worldwide, visions which became a central part of early communist thought. It also helped shape much of the history of the twentieth century.

Exactly when to date an end to the Russian Revolution and civil war is difficult, given that elements of civil war continued into at least 1922 and of revolution for even longer. Perhaps March–April 1921 is the best date in practical terms. By then the Whites had been defeated and no alternative regime existed, and most of the breakaway nationalities, including Ukraine, had been brought back under the regime's control. However, at that time the regime was forced to pull back (temporarily) from its more extreme policies and visions of the rapid worldwide spread of communism. The winter of 1920–21 saw widespread worker discontent, strikes and anti-Bolshevik resolutions in factories (on top of the peasant revolts discussed above). Then in March 1921 a revolt broke out among the sailors at Kronshtadt (Kronstadt), the naval base in the harbor of Petrograd. Traditionally among the most reliable supporters of the Bolsheviks from summer 1917 onwards, Kronshtadters now criticized the Bolshevik government as no longer representing the interests of the workers and peasants, and called for new elections to soviets (local and central) that would include other socialist parties, and a reduction of repressive policies generally. The Bolsheviks responded with a military assault on Kronshtadt as well as a crackdown on worker strikes. The Kronshtadt revolt forced the Bolsheviks to face political and economic realities and to shift course radically. On 15 April 1921, at the Tenth Party Congress, Lenin called for a "New Economic Policy" (NEP) by which the Bolsheviks would move to revive the economy and ease general tensions by pulling back from the most extreme revolutionizing policies. Combined with the roughly simultaneous fading of hope for the immediate spread of an international communist revolution, the recent final victory over the Whites, the problems underlying the peasant revolts that were under way and the reintegration of most of the territory of the former Russian Empire into a new Soviet state (with its own complexities), it usefully marks the end of the civil war era. A period of relative stability, the NEP era, followed in the 1920s, during which the Bolsheviks consolidated their rule. Expectations of the spread of communism in Europe and Asia persisted, but now as something not so immediate or so desperately needed for the regime's survival. New upheavals lay in the future, but very different ones from the 1917–21 Russian Revolution, Civil War and founding of communism.

Bibliographical Essay

There is an immense historiography of excellent works on the revolution and civil war. Robert Browder and Alexander Kerensky provide a remarkable document collection in the three large volumes of *The Russian Provisional Government, 1917* (Stanford: Hoover Institution Press, 1961) while the first two volumes of Rex A. Wade, *Documents of Soviet History* (Gulf Breeze, FL: Academic International Press, 1991, 1993), give documents on the civil war era.

Some consider Rex A. Wade, *The Russian Revolution, 1917*, 3rd edn. (Cambridge: Cambridge University Press, 2017), the best one-volume history of the 1917 revolution, while Evan Mawdsley, *The Russian Civil War* (Boston and London: Allen & Unwin, 1987) provides an excellent account of the civil war. Christopher Read, *From Tsar to Soviets: The Russian People and their Revolution, 1917–21* (New York: Oxford University Press, 1991), is an exemplary one-volume history of both the revolution and civil war.

Excellent works on specific topics are many and listing only a small number here involves very difficult decisions. Tsuyoshi Hasegawa, *The February Revolution: Petrograd 1917* (Seattle: University of Washington Press, 1981), provides the best account of that important event. Steve Smith, *Red Petrograd: Revolution in the Factories, 1917–1918* (Cambridge: Cambridge University Press, 1983), stands out among the "social histories" that refocused the historiography of the revolution. Alan Wildman's *The End of the Russian Imperial Army*, two volumes published by Princeton University Press in 1980 and 1987, provides by far the best work on the army in 1917 and early 1918 and its impact on the revolution. The definitive study of the Bolsheviks in the revolution is found in Alexander Rabinowitch's three volumes: *Prelude to Revolution: The Petrograd Bolsheviks and the July 1917 Uprising* (Bloomington: Indiana University Press, 1968), *The Bolsheviks Come to Power: The Revolution of 1917 in Petrograd* (New York: Norton, 1976) and *The Bolsheviks in Power: The First Year of Soviet Rule in Petrograd* (Bloomington: Indiana University Press, 2007), while William Rosenberg's *Liberals in the Russian Revolution: The Constitutional Democratic Party, 1917–1921* (Princeton: Princeton University Press, 1974) is essential reading. *Interpreting the Russian Revolution: The Language and Symbols of 1917* (New Haven: Yale University Press, 1999) by Orlando Figes and Boris Kolonitskii has had a strong impact on the way scholars look at it.

There is a long history of looking at the events in or from the perspective of the provinces. Ronald Suny's *The Baku Commune, 1917–1918: Class and Nationality in the Russian Revolution* (Princeton: Princeton University Press, 1972) is an early and particularly excellent example. Donald Raleigh's two volumes on Saratov, *Revolution on the Volga: 1917 in Saratov* (Ithaca: Cornell University Press, 1986) and *Experiencing Russia's Civil War: Politics, Society, and Revolutionary Culture in Saratov, 1917–1922* (Princeton: Princeton University Press, 2002), have been very influential in shaping the contemporary approach to writing about the revolution and civil war, as has Peter Holquist's excellent, very original *Making War, Forging Revolution: Russia's Continuum of Crisis, 1914–1921* (Cambridge, MA: Harvard University Press, 2002), which uses the Don Cossacks as its focus. Mark Baker looks at peasants and Ukraine in *Peasants, Power, and Place: Revolution in the Villages of Kharkiv Province, 1914–1921* (Cambridge, MA: Harvard University Press, 2016). Adeeb Khalid's excellent *The Politics of Muslim Cultural Reform: Jadidism in Central Asia* (Berkeley and Los Angeles: University of California Press, 1998) reflects the growing interest in non-Slavic peoples during the revolution. Michael Hickey's works on revolution and civil war in Smolensk, of which "The Rise and Fall of Smolensk's Moderate Socialists: The Politics of Class and the Rhetoric of Crisis in 1917," in Rex A. Wade (ed.), *Revolutionary Russia: New Approaches* (New York: Routledge, 2004), is a fine example from among others by him, represent the enormous number of excellent articles that are too often overlooked in reading lists. The ongoing multivolume "Russia's Great War and Revolution" series (Bloomington: Slavica, 2014–) provides essays on a wide range of revolution and civil war topics.

Works focused specifically on the civil war would start with Mawdsley and Kenez, noted above, and continue with Mark von Hagen, *Soldiers in the Proletarian Dictatorship: The Red Army and the Soviet Socialist State, 1917–1930* (Ithaca and London: Cornell University Press, 1990), while Francesco Benvenuti traces the controversies within the communist party about the army in *The Bolsheviks and the Red Army, 1918–1922* (Cambridge: Cambridge University Press, 1988). George Leggett, *The Cheka: Lenin's Political Police – The All-Russian Extraordinary Commission for Combating Counter-Revolution and Sabotage (December 1917 to February 1922)* (Oxford: Oxford University Press, 1981), traces the origins of that important feature of the communist system, while Silvana Malle gives an excellent examination of the Soviet regime under war communism in *The Economic Organization of War Communism, 1918–1921* (Cambridge: Cambridge University Press, 1989).

Foreign affairs were central to the revolution and early Soviet thinking. On the impact of the war and foreign relations on the outcome of 1917, see Rex A. Wade, *The Russian Search for Peace, February–October 1917* (Stanford: Stanford University Press, 1969). For civil war times, see Richard K. Debo,

Revolution and Survival: The Foreign Policy of Soviet Russia, 1917–18 (Toronto: University of Toronto Press, 1979) and *Survival and Consolidation: The Foreign Policy of Soviet Russia, 1918–1921* (Montreal: McGill-Queen's University Press, 1992).

Jonathan D. Smele, *The Russian Revolution and Civil War, 1917–1921: An Annotated Bibliography* (London: Continuum, 2003), provides an excellent extensive annotated bibliography, while the "Further Readings" section of the 2017 edition of *The Russian Revolution, 1917* (Rex A. Wade, Cambridge: Cambridge University Press) gives an extensive list with more recent works included.

For works on Lenin, Trotsky, Stalin and the Comintern, see the essays on those topics.

3

Revolution and Counterrevolution in Europe 1917–1923

JOHN PAUL NEWMAN

Introduction

Depending on one's political agenda, 1917 to 1923 were years of unrealized promise or averted peril. The collapse of the great European and Eurasian empires and the deterioration of established order in many parts of Europe (especially Central Europe) toward the end of the war transformed the into a staging ground for new political and social projects, of the left, the right and – if this term is not anachronistic – the liberal "center." The Bolsheviks' success in Russia and their internationalist pretensions impressed people of all political persuasion; here was an example to emulate, or to avoid, at all costs. But Comintern terminology employed characteristic rhetorical hyperbole when it referred back to the years 1917–23 as the "Red Wave": The revolutionary risings the Bolsheviks inspired in Berlin, Bavaria, Hungary and Slovakia quickly subsided; and Lenin's attempt to breach fortress Europe broke decisively on the banks of the Vistula. In this sense, the political and military response to the communist revolution, the counterrevolution, could – and did – claim success. But here too the record was often disappointing. The counterrevolutionaries, typically spearheaded by a nascent and radical fringe of the right, had their own visions of a utopian future. With the exception of Italy, these right-wing fantasies, violent and supercharged by war, had to give way – if only in the short term – to the liberal democratic capitalist order supported by the war's victorious parties. That liberal democratic order, as Mark Mazower has shown, was ultimately more brittle than had first seemed, except in France and Britain.[1] Nevertheless, in the immediate aftermath of war and revolution, extreme

1 Mark Mazower, *Dark Continent: Europe's Twentieth Century* (New York: Vintage, 2000). On the British and French "exceptions," see Jon Lawrence, "Forging a Peaceable

political currents in Europe were harnessed and channeled by Wilsonian self-determination, arriving at its historical "moment" by the end of World War I.[2] By 1923, the year that last-gasp communist uprisings sputtered out in Germany and Bulgaria, the political center seemed mostly to have held against challenges from both left and right extremes. The communists retrenched; the counterrevolutionaries chalked up an attenuated victory; the defenders of the liberal order heaved a collective sigh of relief.

The significance of these years, then, lies in the creation of a set of political symbols and archetypes, as well as a set of formative experiences, that would continue to define European politics throughout the interwar period. This holds true at all points on the political spectrum. The Red Wave had established communist revolution as an eminently internationalist concern, and as long as the Bolsheviks were in power in Russia, the possibility of another round of revolutionary ferment remained. This was obviously always the goal of the revolutionaries themselves, even if at times that goal was little more than a *fata morgana*.[3] This communist specter haunted the political center, too, whose adherents were insecure about their victory in the period of war and revolution from 1917 to 1923. The ritualized triumphalism of the annual Armistice Day celebrations, which posited a single day in 1918, and a single minute of that day, as the abrupt end of the conflict masked the protracted passage of violence and revolution that took place during 1917–23.[4] In reality, the democratic European *imaginary* was scarred by its traumatic experiences at the end of the Great War and immediately after; and democratic states frequently succumbed to authoritarian impulses when the communist threat was invoked. In this way, the imminent threat of revolution – and the extreme violence – of 1917–23 had circumscribed the borders of liberal politics throughout the continent.

For their part, the counterrevolutionaries, many of whom remained active in the years after 1923, were ready to march across the ground on which the adherents of liberal democracy feared to tread. The years 1917–23 constituted for them a primal scene, one that gave birth to a mythology of violent

Kingdom: War, Violence, and Fear of Brutalisation in Post-First World War Britain," *Journal of Modern History* 75, 3 (Sep. 2003), 557–89; and John Horne, "Defending Victory: Paramilitary Politics in France, 1918–1926. A Counter-Example," in Robert Gerwarth and John Horne (eds.), *War in Peace: Paramilitary Violence in Europe After the Great War* (Oxford: Oxford University Press, 2012), 216–34.

2 Erez Manela, *The Wilsonian Moment: Self-Determination and the International Origins of Anticolonial Nationalism* (Oxford: Oxford University Press, 2007).

3 See Silvio Pons, *The Global Revolution: A History of International Communism 1917–1991* (Oxford: Oxford University Press, 2014).

4 See Gerwarth and Horne, *War in Peace*.

political confrontation – anti-communist, certainly, but also anti-Semitic and typically anti-liberal. Thus the counterrevolution was more than simply the negation of the revolution: Even if it lacked the programmatic rigor of communism, it was nevertheless conceived as a positive political project, one that came to pose as much of a threat to the liberal order as it did to the communists.

The Left Schism

The transnational waves of revolution and counterrevolution that passed over Europe during 1917–23 were, of course, linked inseparably to the years of conflict that preceded them. The war created a new sense of the transformative opportunities brought on by total war, a sense that, *in extremis*, the old political and social norms had failed and would now need to be overturned. The European communist revolutions of 1917–23 thus thrived on the discontent caused by war hardships, and also on the chaotic political circumstances both in their own countries and throughout Europe toward the end of the war and in the years immediately afterwards.

For the left, the Bolshevik Revolution was an ambiguous talisman, one that deepened rather than healed the movement's 1914 schism. After October 1917, social-democratic parties throughout the continent were to "Bolshevize," that is, organize into cadres of professional revolutionaries as prescribed by Lenin, and prepare for an immediate seizure of power in their own countries. Critically, this also meant making a decisive break with left-wing forces that were willing to work within the framework of "bourgeois" political institutions. The break with more moderate left-wing groups in most cases isolated the European communist revolution to the fringes. The postwar democracies could and did incorporate "reformist" left-wing groups such as socialists into parliament and even sometimes into government, but they were considerably less indulgent toward the revolutionary communists. The combined forces of national governments, backed by socialists and the remainder of the nonrevolutionary political left, aligned themselves against the revolution – and this was to say nothing of the considerably more ferocious counterrevolution itself (see below). Such forces make the communist revolution in Europe look less like a Red Wave than an archipelago of distant and isolated islands, within sight of each other but often not materially connected in any meaningful way. And yet it did not seem so at the time: In the chaos of war's end and the dramatic political and social transformations taking place throughout Europe, the threat – or the promise – of communist revolution was real enough. Nevertheless, in the event it was the early and unrepeated seizure of power in Russia that defined the revolutionary agenda throughout Europe.[5]

Lenin and Wilson, Victors and Defeated

The emergence of a rival revolutionary movement in Europe further diminished the prospects of an imminent communist triumph. American president Woodrow Wilson's gospel of a Europe based on principles of the right of peoples (nations) to self-determination found many disciples in the last year of the war. The anti-imperial tenor of Wilson's "Fourteen Points" found an enthusiastic audience in the lands of Central Europe, where war fatigue was at a critical point by the final year of the war.[6] The leaders of the Entente powers, whose victory in the war allowed them to define the peace and the postwar order on their own terms, also eventually adopted Wilson's ideas as a blueprint for the postwar peace.[7] In the European context, the so-called Wilsonian Moment was an alloy of both a popular, mass movement against empire *and* top-down political support for the breakup of empires and the formation or expansion of nation-states (support for which was admittedly late in coming). And in many parts of Europe it was hardly less revolutionary than Lenin's program.

This Wilsonian revolution would come to define the European order after 1918, adopted as it was by the winning parties of the Great War. Like any postwar settlement, the peace made in Paris reflected to a considerable extent the interests of the victorious parties of the Great War, especially Britain, France and the USA, as well as their designated continental allies, the "successor states" of East Central Europe: Czechoslovakia, Yugoslavia, Romania and Poland. It was the prerogative of these "winners" to dictate the terms of peace to the war's defeated states: Germany, Austria, Bulgaria and the Ottoman Empire/Turkey.

For the victor states of the war, communist revolution was perceived as a radical threat to the domestic and international order they were creating in the years immediately after the war. The communist threat was thus

5 Pons, *The Global Revolution*, 16.

6 Aviel Roshwald, *Ethnic Nationalism and the Fall of Empires: Central Europe, Russia, and the Middle East, 1914–1923* (London and New York: Routledge, 2001); Omer Bartov and Eric D. Weitz (eds.), *Shatterzones of Empires: Coexistence and Violence in the German, Habsburg, Russian, and Ottoman Borderlands* (Bloomington: Indiana University Press, 2013).

7 Margaret Macmillan, *Peacemakers – Six Months that Changed the World: The Paris Peace Conference of 1919 and Its Attempt to End War* (London: J. Murray, 2001).

most palpably felt in the successor states of East Central Europe, because those states had gained the most in the peace settlements and therefore had the most to lose in the event of a communist revolution. Anxieties were compounded by the sense of insecurity that quite naturally attended the volatile political climate of postwar Europe. Indeed, in many parts of Europe during 1917–23 the war had not in any meaningful sense ended, as groups of paramilitaries and semi-demobilized soldiers continued to fight beyond the supposed cessation of hostilities in November 1918.[8] Violent ethnic conflicts, often exacerbated by big-power interventions and rivalries, were important features of state-building in this region. In such circumstances it was not difficult to justify harsh and often repressive measures against communists, a political group that could be broadly and nebulously defined to encompass other strata of the political opposition; thus did the anti-communist cause undermine the liberal institutions and political culture of the successor states.

But it was the defeated states of the Great War that were now most prone to the waves of revolution and counterrevolution that passed over Europe during 1917–23. The continuum of war and revolution flowed more rapidly and more violently when buoyed by the shock of defeat in 1918. For the communist revolutionaries, the defeat of 1918 was a bonfire of political vanities in which the rules and pieties of the old order were to be set ablaze, destroyed to make space for the coming communist society. It was, after all, Lenin himself who – alone among wartime political leaders – had hoped for a Russian defeat in the Great War in order to accelerate the inexorable process of revolutionary transformation. For many communist revolutionaries the defeat was a proof of the political and moral bankruptcy of the *ancien régime* and a spur to begin the revolutionary phase. The vanguard of party cadres could spread their message to the people more easily when there was neither victory to stand behind nor gains to consolidate; revolution and defeat made for an explosive compound.

The Counterrevolution

In contrast to their communist enemies, the counterrevolutionaries had no ideological center, no revolutionary program or catechism comparable to that offered by the Comintern. This apparent absence of programmatic purpose, combined with their adherents' ferocious energy, has led some to

8 See Gerwarth and Horne (eds.), *War in Peace*.

argue that the counterrevolution was first and foremost a matter of violent confrontation merely for its own sake, an unfocused – even nihilistic – spasm of rage carried out by men habituated to violence. To be sure, the soldiers of the counterrevolution were in various ways deeply marked by the legacy of the war: whether they were veterans of the conflict who sought to prolong the fighting beyond the armistice or the "postwar generation" of Europeans too young to serve but keen now to emulate and even surpass the older generation in their commitment to violence. Yet the counter-revolutionaries also grasped the sense of Europe passing through a continuum of war and revolution, and like the communists, the counter-revolutionaries had a vision for the new European order, one that coalesced around a looser and more protean kind of politics, united under the broad banners of anti-communism, anti-Semitism and elitism, mediated by local conditions and circumstances, especially an aggrieved or threatened sense of nationalism.

For the counterrevolutionaries this latest phase of the conflict was *sui generis*, however, quite unlike the battles of 1914–17. The new enemy was also a phantasm that was at once ubiquitous and incorporeal. It did not need supply lines or reserve trenches in the manner of conventional armies: The revolution could strike anywhere and at any time. All this gave the revolutionary threat an intangible, uncanny quality. This was, as John Horne and Robert Gerwarth have noted, "Bolshevism as fantasy": a chimera that required constant vigilance and extreme means of combat.[9] There was thus often a lack of symmetry between the actual chance or threat of revolution in any given setting and the extent of counterrevolutionary mobilization and violence. These were not two conventional military forces meeting as equals on the field of battle, this was rather a case of extreme nationalist counter-revolutionaries projecting their own fears and suspicions onto the environment in which they operated. For them, it seemed that communist revolution was animated only by an idea that was impossible to isolate and contain, an idea that the counterrevolutionaries needed to destroy outright. This, then, was a zero-sum battle. As Klaus Theweleit and others have noted, the counterrevolutionaries imagined the communist utopia as an apocalypse that would suck in and destroy all conventions and norms.[10] In this sense,

9 Robert Gerwarth and John Horne, "Bolshevism as Fantasy: Fear of Revolution and Counter-Revolutionary Violence, 1917–1923," in Gerwarth and Horne (eds.), *War in Peace*, 40–52.

10 Klaus Theweleit, *Male Fantasies*, 2 vols. (Minneapolis: University of Minnesota Press, 1987–89).

the October Revolution was crucial: It sent a powerful charge through the political atmosphere of the postwar years.

Because the revolution also threatened their rule, liberal governments in Europe supported counterrevolutionary interventionism within Russia. They could also unleash the counterrevolutionaries against the communist threat in their own countries, but this was often a pact not easily reneged, and the role played by counterrevolutionary violence in stabilizing the postwar order in Europe in many cases damaged the liberal political architecture of European states – sometimes fatally, for once inside the citadel the counterrevolutionaries were not easily expelled. The persistence of such groups beyond the ebbing of the Red Wave of revolution at the end of the war demonstrates that the term "counter-revolution" does not do full justice to the scope and ambitions of the groups in question. To be sure, the primary animus of the counterrevolution was the communist threat, which needed to be eradicated at all costs and without mercy, but the groups and individuals who mobilized against communism did not just seek to turn the political dial back to a prerevolutionary setting which, once reached, would remove their *raison d'être*. In the volatile political environment at the end of the war there simply was no such setting to return to. The call to arms against the Bolshevik threat offered a chance of regeneration, redemption and, at last, victory. This sense of a regenerated, "reborn" conflict was particularly powerful in states that had experienced the shock of defeat in 1918. The counterrevolutionaries saw for themselves a continued purpose in the domestic affairs of their own countries that extended beyond their role as mere military auxiliaries of civilian governments. Like the classical Furies, the counterrevolutionaries stood guard beneath the foundations of the interwar *poleis*, ready to rise again when necessary.

The German Pivot

Once the Bolsheviks had lit the revolutionary fuse in Russia, Germany became the great object of their hopes of an expanded, ongoing revolution. Even if Lenin had revised Marx's predictions for the opening of the socialist revolution away from this modernized, industrialized European powerhouse toward backward Russia, imperialism's "weakest link," he still saw Germany as the pivot of the global revolution. Its large industrial working class and its well-developed, massively supported Social Democratic Party (SPD) were surely ideal kindling for revolution, as was the political and social collapse threatened by the defeat of 1918.[11] Moreover, the Bolsheviks fully understood what havoc a powerful, hostile Germany could wreak upon their own revolution: The punitive terms of the Brest-Litovsk treaty had foretold this in the starkest possible manner.

At the outbreak of the war the SPD had been violently split over the question of whether or not to support war credits.[12] Any notions that the shock of defeat and the example of the Russian Revolution would heal this deep rift and/or move the German left toward a more radical agenda were soon disabused. The defeat and Ebert's republican revolution once again exposed the fractures of the German left. The republican left quickly shed the stigma of their support for war in 1914 and consolidated the democratic, parliamentarian and anti-imperial revolution, becoming an integral part of the new Weimar democracy throughout the 1920s. But the smaller left wing of the German SPD were for the most part unwilling to squander what they saw as an opportunity to repeat the successes of the Bolsheviks in Russia. They formed in December 1918 the German Communist Party (KPD) along Leninist lines, and pushed for revolution "beyond the limited goals of parliamentary democracy."[13]

Like the Bolsheviks, the German communists could draw support – or at least sympathy – from a sizeable segment of German workers and peasants who had been politicized/radicalized by the hardships of the war years and who were receptive to the communists' revolutionary appeals.[14] But the KPD were ultimately unable to alchemize this postwar discontent into a full-blown revolution in the way the Bolsheviks had, and as Eric Weitz notes, each of the communists' three attempts at armed uprising against the republic was a "bigger fiasco than its predecessor."[15] Pro-government troops and Freikorps irregulars ruthlessly suppressed the KPD's abortive "Spartacist Uprising" in Berlin in January 1919. This was less a show of government might than it was of KPD weakness, although the brutality of the government's action and its collaboration with the right-wing counterrevolutionary Freikorps was surely a bad omen. The Bavarian "Soviet Republic" in Munich

11 See Mark Jones, *Founding Weimar: Violence and the German Revolution of 1918–1919* (Cambridge: Cambridge University Press, 2016).

12 See Susanne Miller, *Burgfrieden und Klassenkampf: Die deutsche Sozialdemokratie im Ersten Weltkrieg* (Düsseldorf: Droste, 1974); and, by the same author, *Die Bürde der Macht: Die deutsche Sozialdemokratie 1918–1920* (Düsseldorf: Droste, 1978).

13 Eric D. Weitz, *Creating German Communism, 1890–1990: From Popular Protests to Socialist State* (Princeton: Princeton University Press, 1997).

14 Benjamin Ziemann, *War Experiences in Rural Germany, 1914–1923* (Oxford and New York: Berg Publishers, 2007).

15 Eric D. Weitz, *Weimar Germany: Promise and Tragedy* (Princeton: Princeton University Press, 2007).

lasted barely a month and was smashed in similar fashion, by a joint force of government action and right-wing irregulars. In March 1921, a plan to agitate for a general strike, hatched by the Comintern (which the KPD had joined in December 1920), the so-called March Action, failed to attract national support. The same was true of a series of uprisings in Saxony, Thuringia and Hamburg in autumn 1923; these last significantly whittling away the KPD's membership.[16] When the tide of the Red Wave subsided in 1923, the German Revolution had achieved very little, other than a series of suicidal revolutionary gestures and a pantheon of martyred leaders, foremost of whom were the Spartacist leaders Rosa Luxemburg and Karl Liebknecht. This was an object lesson in the fracturing of the left – a fracturing that the Bolsheviks had exacerbated – and the consequent isolation of the revolution during 1917–23.

What price did the newborn republican democracy pay for its victory over communist revolution? In suppressing the KPD's successive uprisings the Weimar Republic had wielded considerable violence, carried out either by its own troops or, far more ominously, by right-wing paramilitaries deeply exercised by the communist menace in Germany. Many of these groups hated the republicans only slightly less than the communists themselves, a fractional but important distinction that led them to serve alongside – or at least in the same cause as – government troops during 1917–23. The far-right paramilitary counterrevolutionaries had additionally served anti-communist "tours of duty" in the Baltic countries and Poland (see below), finding in the war against Bolshevism the chance to redeem the defeat of 1918 and thereby regenerate the nationalist project. For the veterans of this radical counter-revolutionary movement, the years 1917–23 were recalled (e.g. in memoir literature) as halcyon days of military conquest, brotherly bonding and blood.[17] The counterrevolution had supposedly shown how the communist peril needed to be met on its own terms; that is, with pitiless violence; violence that became ritualized and celebrated for its own sake in the following years. Obviously, the leaders of Weimar democracy, who had shamefully abandoned Germany's war in November 1918, were insufficiently robust to deal with this threat on their own.

This image of a weak Weimar democracy cowed from its birth by powerful anti-liberal, right-wing squads has led some historians to write

16 Matthew Stibbe, *Germany 1914–1933: Politics, Society, and Culture* (Harlow and New York: Longman, 2010), 77.

17 Theweleit, *Male Fantasies*.

off the state as stillborn and, moreover, to draw a single straight line backwards from Nazism to the "vanguard" Freikorps.[18] But to do so is to miss the most salient point about Germany during 1917–23: that its democratic institutions, supposedly so frail, survived both left-wing and right-wing challenges to its order, and that those challenges were themselves the preserve of minority, marginal forces.[19] When Hitler and the National Socialists pointed to the right-wing counterrevolutionaries they created their own false *ex post facto* history of Weimar weakness and popular support for groups after their own heart. In reality, Hitler's "Beer Hall Putsch" of 1923 was hardly less of a fiasco than the failed communist uprisings during 1919–23. As was more often than not the case in Europe in the years of revolution and counterrevolution, a liberal order survived, albeit scathed, in the jaws of extremist challenges.

Italy: The Counterrevolution Triumphant

In contrast to Germany, Italy offers an example of a liberal political culture insufficiently buoyant to stay afloat in the storms of revolution and counterrevolution during 1917–23. At the outbreak of war Italy had been torn domestically between neutralists who wanted to remain clear of the worsening conflict and interventionists who wanted Italy to join the belligerents and thus share with the victors the spoils of war. The advocates of intervention hoped that Italy would achieve in war the final stages of national integration – the great project of the nineteenth-century Risorgimento – by regaining unclaimed *irredenta* in Austria–Hungary. In 1915, and with Italy still wavering between the Entente and the Central Powers, Britain had offered Dalmatian territories to Italy as a return for fighting. This was enough for Italy's political and military leaders to join the war and satisfy the demands of the ever-larger interventionist camp, whose ranks contained quite a few lapsed socialists, including future fascist leader Benito Mussolini. But Italy's entry into the war released a nationalist genie from its bottle. When at the Paris Peace Conference the peacemakers, notably US president Woodrow Wilson, equivocated between Italian territorial demands and those of its neighbors, especially the newly formed South Slav state, the Kingdom of Serbs, Croats

18 See Robert G. L. Waite, *Vanguard of Nazism: The Free Corps Movement in Post-War Germany, 1918–1923* (Cambridge, MA: Harvard University Press, 1952).

19 See, e.g., Benjamin Ziemann, *Contested Commemorations: Republican War Veterans and Weimar Political Culture* (Cambridge: Cambridge University Press, 2013).

and Slovenes,[20] a noisy irredentist clamor could be heard throughout the country. Alone among the victorious states, Italy acted out of insecurity, humiliated nationalist sentiment and thwarted national ambition. It thus sits uneasily among the winners of 1918. As Italian leaders attempted to realize popular demands for the unclaimed lands through the channels of international diplomacy, more direct methods were being employed elsewhere. In 1920, in the port city of Fiume (Rijeka), contested by both Italians and South Slavs, the poet, nationalist and adventurer Gabriele D'Annunzio had launched a military attack on the city, entering Fiume at the head of a small number of elite, battle-hardened veterans of the Italian army and declaring its independence.[21]

Action and attitude over deliberation and substance could serve as an example for the conduct of Italian domestic politics, too. For at home the country seemed to be caught in a maelstrom of civic and workers' unrest. A series of strikes in the industrial north of the country during 1919–20, the *bienno rosso*, had made the country hyperalert to the risk of left-wing revolution. Socialist violence, which included the murder of political rivals, was real, and, as in the German case, demonstrates the significant appeal of communist revolution among many workers and peasants. But the extent of this appeal was greatly exaggerated by the noncommunist democrats and by the counterrevolutionaries. And indeed, the heady brew of domestic and foreign strife gave considerable succor to right-wing counterrevolutionary squads organized in response to the socialist "threat" in Italy. These were the *Fasci italiani di combattimento*, the fascists, uniformed militia groups who apparently possessed no clearly defined political program beyond a set of "negations" (anti-communism, anti-liberalism, anti-Semitism) and an aggrieved sense of nationalism, supercharged by the war.[22] In fact, like the counterrevolution elsewhere, Italian fascism was both a product of war (many of its members were veterans of the fighting, including Mussolini himself) and of the troubling experiences of the postwar period – in this case, the "mutilated victory" abroad and the socialist ferment at home.[23] Like

20 Dragoljub Živojinović, *America, Italy, and the Birth of Yugoslavia (1917–1919)* (Boulder: East European Quarterly, Columbia University Press, 1972).

21 See Michael Arthur Ledeen, *The First Duce: D'Annunzio at Fiume* (Baltimore: Johns Hopkins University Press, 1977).

22 On the "fascist minimum" see Stanley Payne, *A History of Fascism, 1914–1945* (Madison: University of Wisconsin Press, 1995), 7.

23 Alan Kramer, *Dynamic of Destruction: Culture and Mass Killing in the First World War* (Oxford: Oxford University Press), 296–97.

D'Annunzio and his volunteers, the fascists promised to achieve in a more direct manner that which the politicians in Rome could not.

In Italy, as elsewhere, the political center, the revolution and the counterrevolution were three points of a shifting triad. But here, unlike in Germany, the counterrevolutionary threat to the political center was graver and more immediate. There was an inversion between the socialist threat, which had greatly subsided in the months and years after the *bienno rosso*, and the scale and intensity of fascist violence, which continued apace, irrespective of domestic developments, and which would become integral to the movement. All this was missed by the Italian government: The Bolshevik phantasm and the popular nationalist appeal of the fascists themselves unsteadied the liberal center in Italy, which invited Mussolini and his followers into government in 1922, believing that in so doing it could simultaneously galvanize the democratic center against communism *and* tame the fascists. This was a serious miscalculation, essentially the same as the one later made by the right-wing conservative leaders of Weimar with regard to National Socialism in 1933. The fascists would later rewrite this turn and add it to an embellished list of quasi-military conquests, calling it their "March on Rome." In reality, counterrevolution entered the corridors of power in Italy through an open door – and by invitation.

The fragile liberal order in Italy made two fatal mistakes with regard to the fascist threat after the war. First, its leaders misunderstood the fascist movement itself. Benedetto Croce claimed that fascism posed no threat to the established political order, that it was safe, because it had no program.[24] His misreading of the nature of fascism speaks volumes about the more general misunderstanding of the counterrevolution throughout Europe during 1917–23. Such claims presented the counterrevolution as simply a valueless, blunt instrument that could be wielded when necessary. The second mistake stemmed from the first, for as much as the political center saw fascism as a blank slate, it projected its worst fears for revolution and instability onto the socialists, a political group that were in reality deeply divided (not least by the Comintern's stock instruction for a revolutionary fraction to break with the remaining, much larger portion of the socialists)[25] and outmatched by the counterrevolution. This series of miscalculations made a temporary alliance with the fascists seem tolerable, indeed, necessary. In Italy, the

24 Cited in Denis Mack Smith, *Modern Italy: A Political History* (Ann Arbor: University of Michigan Press, 1997), 298.

25 Ibid., 299–300.

counterrevolution triumphed, but only because it had been blessed in its adversaries: a left wing that simply could not compete with fascist violence and a political center with little sense of perspective about the real risk (or lack thereof) of communist revolution.

Austria–Hungary: The Shards of Empire

The various parts of Austria–Hungary would scatter across the categories of victory, defeat, revolution and counterrevolution at the end of the war. In the Habsburg case, the fulcrum of war and revolution arrived in the beginning of 1918, when both Leninist and Wilsonian revolutionary tremors started to reverberate in the Habsburg lands[26] – the former in the guise of "returnee" prisoners of war from Russia who spread rumors of a peasant and workers' revolt against the war (and who were especially effective in Hungary and the Croat lands);[27] the latter in the form of the Wilson's "Fourteen Points," openly discussed by non-German politicians in Vienna and elsewhere.[28] These were seismic signals of a coming catastrophe that fell upon the monarchy at the end of 1918, when war fatigue and nationalist agitation gave radical anti-imperial forces an unstoppable momentum throughout the empire.[29] By this time, all alternative proposals for a restructuring of the monarchy (e.g. those of Emperor Karl) were null and void: The process of Habsburg "decolonization" had reached its most advanced stage.[30] Wilson's vision of national self-determination was hastily (and in many cases violently) applied to the Habsburg lands; its finer details were settled at greater length in the Peace Conference in Paris.

26 For an excellent account of Austria–Hungary's war, see Alexander Watson, *Ring of Steel: Germany and Austria–Hungary at War, 1914–1918* (London: Penguin Books, 2015). On the revolutionary mood in 1918, see Tibor Hajdu, "Socialist Revolution in Central Europe, 1917–1921," in Roy Porter and Mikuláš Teich (eds.), *Revolution in History* (Cambridge: Cambridge University Press, 1986), 101–20.

27 See John Paul Newman, "Post-Imperial and Post-War Violence in the South Slav Lands," *Contemporary European History* 19, 3 (2010), 249–65, and Ivo Banac, "'Emperor Karl Has Become a Comitadji': The Croatian Disturbances of Autumn 1918," *Slavonic and East European Review* 70, 2 (1992), 284–305.

28 Mark Cornwall, "The Great War and the Yugoslav Grassroots: Popular Mobilization in the Habsburg Monarchy 1914–1918," in Dejan Djokić and James Ker-Lindsay (eds.), *New Perspectives on Yugoslavia: Key Issues and Controversies* (New York: Routledge, 2011), 27–45.

29 See Pieter M. Judson, *The Habsburg Empire: A New History* (Cambridge, MA: Harvard University Press, 2016), 385–441.

30 The argument that the Russian war was an early example of decolonization is put forward by Joshua A. Sanborn in *Imperial Apocalypse: The Great War and the Destruction of the Russian Empire* (Oxford: Oxford University Press, 2014).

The drastic political and territorial remapping of Austria–Hungary was of great consequence for the immediate postwar period. New borders crashed around the "shatter-zones" of the Habsburg Empire and generated an impetus for violent ethnic conflict in putative borderlands of the new nation-states.[31] The eventual positioning of borders and the expansions and contractions of various successor-states exposed in the starkest terms who belonged to the victors and and who to the losers of the Great War, which in turn gave momentum to revolutionary and counterrevolutionary remobilization. The political leaders of some national groups were able to realize near-maximalist claims on borders and statehood, notably the Czechoslovaks, Romanians and Poles. Others fared less well, most conspicuously the Austrian Germans and Hungarians, whose "states" had been the ruling moieties of the dual-monarchy but were now vastly truncated dwarf republics facing myriad political and social difficulties at war's end.

Revolution and Counterrevolution in Hungary

The most drastic and violent reversals took place in Hungary. The Hungarians paid one of the heaviest prices for defeat of all the Central Powers, eventually ceding one-third of their prewar territory and one-third of their ethnic population to enlarged and uniformly hostile neighboring states.[32] The fragmentation of the Habsburg monarchy ruptured its existing markets and economic structures, and, it seemed, was set to denude Hungary of many of its "historic" (and Hungarian-populated) lands. And then there were the Carthaginian terms of the peace: Almost every decision at Paris stripped Hungary of yet more of its lands and people, in many cases breaching the supposedly universal law of national self-determination.

Hungary's revolution at the end of World War I initially bequeathed postimperial rule, in a bloodless revolution, to Mihály Károlyi, whose democratic government "firmly embraced Wilsonian idealism,"[33] was well in accord with the Franco-British vision of a "New Europe" of democratic and liberal nation-states, and hoped to head the country into a new era. But the shock of defeat and especially the humiliating and constricted borders of the

31 See Roshwald, *Ethnic Nationalism and the Fall of Empires*, and Bartov and Weitz (eds.), *Shatterzones of Empires*.

32 On Hungary at war, see József Galántai, *Hungary in the First World War* (Budapest: Akadémiai Kiadó, 1989).

33 Peter Pastor, *Hungary Between Wilson and Lenin: The Hungarian Revolution of 1918–1919 and the Big Three* (New York: Columbia University Press, 1976).

new Hungarian state made Károlyi's new era look highly unappealing to many Hungarians. And when Károlyi agreed to yet another partition at Paris, powerful and antagonistic political forces, backed by significant parts of the population, stirred into life. The strange death of liberal Hungary was an object lesson in the perils of reconciling one's country to such seemingly punitive terms (a lesson that Bulgarian agrarian leader Aleksandar Stamboliyski would learn in even harsher terms in 1923; see below).

Hungarian communist leader Béla Kun was the next to take hold of his country's poisoned chalice, coming to power on the back of a Bolshevik-style revolution in spring 1919. Once in charge, Kun installed with ill-considered alacrity a radical program of political and social reforms designed to transform the country, virtually overnight, from a semi-feudal to a workers' and peasants' state. This high-velocity flight toward socialist modernity was a terrible error: Kun was wrong to think that his revolutionary sweep to power gave him license to turn Hungarian society so drastically on its head. Radicalism in Hungary was directed first and foremost outwards, against the Wilsonian order that seemed so excessively hostile to the Hungarians. Bolshevism's chief attractions were its internationalist pretensions, not its domestic political program.

The promise of an international alliance against Entente diktat, then, gave a kind of forlorn hope to many Hungarians that their international standing might improve. For Kun, such a reversal of fortune was a necessity for survival. His existential fears were even more acute than those of Lenin: Thanks to the establishment of the Hungarian "Soviet," the postwar political landscape in Central Europe now featured two antithetical political revolutions, Wilson's and Lenin's, each with their own internationalist ambitions. The situation could not obtain for long; the Hungarian revolutionaries were playing a zero-sum game for the soul of the new order. In his brief time as leader of Soviet Hungary, Kun flailingly attempted to set new revolutionary blazes in neighboring countries, notably in Austria and Czechoslovakia. Kun's only foreign success, a "Slovak Soviet Republic," based in Prešov, lasted for just under three weeks.[34] Kun's own revolution fared little better: It was extinguished after a mere six months.

The counterrevolution came to Hungary in two overlapping waves: The invading army of Romania and, from within Hungary itself, a group of right-

34 Joseph Rothschild, *East Central Europe Between the Wars* (Seattle: University of Washington Press, 1974), 148–49. See also Peter Toma, "The Slovak Soviet Republic of 1919," *American Slavic and East European Review* 17, 2 (Apr. 1958), 203–15.

wing officers and remnants of the *ancien régime* clustered around the city of Szeged, in the south of the country. These latter resembled Kun insofar as they too hoped first and foremost for a dramatic reversal of the postwar catastrophe Hungary was suffering.[35] In all other ways they were utterly different: They did not see salvation in Kun's adaptation of the Soviet model; far from it, they envisaged Bolshevism in Hungary as a nightmare for which violent resistance was a national and moral imperative. Thus Admiral Miklós Horthy, nominal leader of the Hungarian counterrevolution and plaster saint to the Hungarian right more broadly, on retaking the capital for the counterrevolution, promised to punish "sinful Budapest" for its Bolshevik apostasy.

Horthy was true to his word: There was a fearful disparity between the revolutionary "red terror" of Kun's regime – as bad as this was – and the much more ferocious and widespread counterrevolutionary "white terror" that followed. The counterrevolution in Hungary was more than just a military operation whose sole purpose was to decisively remove the Bolshevik threat: It was also about publicly staging and asserting a new kind of politics and a new kind of civilization, one that was staunchly nationalistic, patriarchal and anti-Semitic. There was thus a ritualized and didactic quality to the violence of counterrevolutionary firebrands such as Captain Pál Prónay, who boasted of "roasting Jews on an open spit" all day long. The counterrevolution in Hungary, as elsewhere, quickly conflated Jews and Bolsheviks into a composite national enemy.

All this violence was a means, as Paul Hanebrink has argued, of redeeming "Christian Hungary" through a savage purging of all groups deemed anti- or a-national.[36] It was also a means of redeeming and therefore regenerating national life in the wake of defeat and dismemberment at the end of the war; this, too, was central to the counterrevolutionary project throughout Europe.[37] For Hungary it was a politically formative period indeed, in the worst possible sense. No democratic restoration was possible by 1920; there was no going back to the liberal and reconciliatory Wilsonianism of Károlyi. Moreover, the Hungarian left – and not just its radical wing – was permanently tainted by association with the excesses of Kun's brief Soviet

35 The white terror in Hungary has been extensively analyzed by Béla Bodó; see *Pál Prónay: Paramilitary Violence and Anti-Semitism in Hungary, 1919–1921* (Pittsburgh: University of Pittsburgh Press, 2010) and "The White Terror in Hungary, 1919–1921: The Social World of the Paramilitary Groups," *Austrian History Yearbook* 42 (2011), 133–63.

36 Paul Hanebrink, *In Defence of Christian Hungary: Religion, Nationalism, and Antisemitism, 1890–1944* (Ithaca: Cornell University Press, 2006), 78.

37 On this topic, see Mark Cornwall and John Paul Newman (eds.), *Sacrifice and Rebirth: The Legacy of the Last Habsburg War* (Oxford: Berghahn Books, 2015).

experiment, and was also now construed by the victorious counterrevolutionaries as a foreign, Jewish and anti-national threat to Hungary and its project of regaining lost territories in the interwar period.

Vienna Besieged

In Austria, the end of war reduced the empire to a bloated postimperial capital, Vienna, grafted onto a wizened body politic, exposing the considerable gap between Viennese political modes and those of the rest of the country. Whereas before 1914 the Reichsrat had precariously mediated and balanced competing national and political forces throughout the empire, Vienna now emerged as a small socialist-inclined vessel caught in a tempest of conservative, rural reaction. The potential for military conflict between these two political tendencies was from the start considerable. Both sides wielded sizeable paramilitary forces: on one side the socialist and government-backing Volkswehr, something of a proto-republican army, and on the other, the Heimwehren, rural militia groups from the countryside who formed the Austrian counterrevolution.

As throughout Europe, the international schism between parliamentary social democracy and revolutionary communism cleaved the Austrian left. In Vienna, the dominant political force among the working class was the Social Democratic Party of Karl Renner, the First Republic's premier, who was able to ward of the far-left threat posed to his rule by the Bolshevik inspired workers' and soldiers' soviets throughout the country. Hopes raised by the establishment of the Hungarian Soviet and Kun's interest in an Austrian revolution were soon dashed; the communists were quickly consigned to the fringes of the working-class movement in Austria.[38]

The Austrian counterrevolutionaries were a more formidable and enduring threat.[39] They nursed a hatred of both the republican and radical left, conceiving of the two as lesser and greater evils, while simultaneously exaggerating the threat of full-blown Bolshevik revolution, protection from which was to be provided by the Heimwehren, right-wing militia groups recruited from peasant leagues in Salzburg, Styria and Tyrol. As with its German, Italian and Hungarian counterparts the Austrian counterrevolution seemed to be more adept at organizing and wielding violence than its opponents of the center and

38 Francis L. Carsten, *The First Austrian Republic, 1918–1938: A Study Based on British and Austrian Documents* (Aldershot: Gower, 1986), 26.

39 On this topic, see Janek Wasserman, *Black Vienna: The Radical Right in the Red City, 1918–1938* (Ithaca: Cornell University Press, 2014).

left. The Heimwehren far outnumbered the collective military forces mustered by the Social Democrats and the communists.

The veterans of the revolutionary and counterrevolutionary skirmishing of 1917–23 would also "mature" to become one of the most powerful political blocs in Austria during the 1920s and 1930s.[40] With such forces waiting in the wings, coupled with the humiliation and shock of defeat in 1918, the republic's passage out of empire and into the new epoch of nation-states was a difficult one, and its democratic arc never truly took flight in the coming years. The communist revolution had been decisively warded off, in part with the assistance of the counterrevolutionary Heimwehren – but then these authoritarian groups freighted the democratic institutions of the country with a heavy load in the years that followed. They were ever vigilant, ever bearing a grudge against the republic and ever ready to spring into action once again, if needed.

In the meantime, Austrian national identity, famously otiose while the Austro-Hungarian monarchy was still in existence, never ran deep in the interwar period. Scant water had passed under the bridge between the popular Austro-German hankering for union with Germany in 1918 (denied by the Entente) and the celebrations that greeted the eventual realization of that union in 1938. In the absence of a unifying national identity, social and class divisions continued to cleave Austrian society. The gap between urban and rural strata not only shaped the contours of the Austrian revolution and counterrevolution between 1918 and 1923, it also defined the republic's fraught politics until the authoritarian shift in the 1930s.

Bulgaria: The Squandered Revolution?

Bulgaria had sided with the Central Powers at the end of 1915 and had capitulated to the Entente in September 1918. In contrast to much of the remainder of the Balkans, the Bulgarian Communist Party had emerged at the end of World War I with a sizeable following.[41] This had much to do with

40 Ibid.

41 On the Bulgarian Communist Party, see Joseph Rothschild, *The Communist Party of Bulgaria: Origins and Development, 1883–1936* (New York: Columbia University Press, 1959), and John D. Bell, *The Bulgarian Communist Party from Blagoev to Zhivkov* (Stanford: Hoover Institution Press, 1986). For the remainder of the Balkan communist movements and Greek communism, see D. George Kousoulas, *Revolution and Defeat: The Story of the Greek Communist Party* (London and New York: Oxford University Press, 1965). For the history of the tiny Albanian communist movement (unaffiliated to the Comintern), see Miranda Vickers, *The Albanians: A Modern History* (London and New York: I. B. Tauris, 2011), 141–62. The Yugoslav and Romanian parties are discussed below.

defeat and the unfavorable position of this country in the international order, for having gone to war in 1915 to reclaim lands it had lost in the Second Balkan War of 1913, Bulgaria had in 1918 once again lost territories to its Balkan neighbors. In the national elections of 1919, the Bulgarian Communist Party had won 18 percent of the vote, making it the second largest party behind Aleksandar Stamboliyski's governing Bulgarian Agrarian National Union, and also making it larger than the Bulgarian Socialist Party (with 13 percent of the vote).[42] The Comintern acknowledged this stature by making the Bulgarian communists masters of its affiliate "Balkan Communist Federation,"[43] an office the Bulgarians used to assert national claims on Macedonian lands held by Yugoslavia and Greece (much to the chagrin of those parties). The Bulgarian tail could in this way wag the communist dog.

Conditions for a full-scale revolution in Bulgaria further ripened in the years after the end of the war. Stamboliyski's authoritarian rule increased the number and the vehemence of his enemies throughout the country.[44] But it was his foreign policy that truly outraged nationalist passions in Bulgaria: Stamboliyski's willingness to accept his country's defeat and reduced territory in return for reconciliation to the new national order inflamed large and multifaceted nationalist and revisionist forces in Bulgaria. This camp comprised militarist groups, associations of former army officers and, most formidably of all, the Internal Macedonian Revolutionary Organization (IMRO), the massive autonomist paramilitary group that had established a de facto command in the Petrich district of Macedonia (a territory straddling Bulgaria and Yugoslavia). These combined forces constituted a counterrevolution animated first and foremost by hostility to the Wilsonian order and Bulgaria's place within that order, rather than the threat of communist revolution. They organized a successful coup against the BANU government in June 1923. Stamboliyski himself had the misfortune of falling into the hands of the "Macedonians," who mutilated the leader before killing him and sending his decapitated head to Sofia.[45]

The communists prevaricated throughout this turn of events, and by ultimately opting not to come to the aid of the BANU government, they went a long way to sealing its fate. Belatedly realizing the peril of the

42 Bell, *The Bulgarian Communist Party*, 27.

43 George D. Jackson, Jr., *Comintern and Peasant in East Europe, 1919–1930* (New York and London: Columbia University Press, 1966), 99–100.

44 On this topic, see John D. Bell, *Peasants in Power: Alexander Stamboliski and the Bulgarian Agrarian National Union, 1899–1923* (Princeton: Princeton University Press, 1977).

45 See Joseph Swire, *Bulgarian Conspiracy* (London: R. Hale, 1939).

counterrevolutionary direction upon which the country was now embarked, the communists launched a futile revolution of their own, in September 1923. Its failure was a wake-up call to the Comintern concerning the relative strength of its forces in the region: If the large Bulgarian Communist Party could not effect a successful revolution in the Balkans, it was unlikely that any of its other, far smaller affiliates could. Taking place around the same time as the failed "March Action" in Germany, the Bulgarian revolt caused Moscow to rethink its position vis-à-vis European revolution.

The Habsburg Successor States: Fragile Victors

In the remaining successor states of the Austro-Hungarian Empire, the Kingdom of Serbs, Croats and Slovenes (Yugoslavia), Czechoslovakia, Romania and Poland all became beneficiaries of the Wilsonian peace after the war. This quartet were "victor states" whose leaders would attempt to craft a national politics and international diplomacy that were broadly congenial to the status quo in 1920s Europe.[46] Revolution and counterrevolution threatened to undo the political and territorial gains these states had made at the end of the war. For this reason, the leaders of what we might call "hegemonic" national groups in the successor states (Romanians in Romania, Poles in Poland, Serbs in Yugoslavia, Czechs in Czechoslovakia) acted swiftly and forcefully when confronted with the communist threat: legislating for a quick and extensive land reform which, it was hoped, would satisfy peasant land-hunger and thus limit the appeal of communist revolution. For their part, minorities or national groups that perceived themselves as second-class citizens/subjects in their own countries occasionally turned to communism as a means of protesting their subaltern status (e.g. Macedonians and Montenegrins in Yugoslavia, Ruthenians in Czechoslovakia). And while there were no mass waves of revolution and counterrevolution in this region, yet again an exaggerated sense of communist threat greatly exercised the state-builders of "New Europe," and, of course, the nationalist right.

The sense of peril came first and foremost from abroad, from the vaunted westward expansion of the Soviet Union (a threat most imminently felt by Romania and Poland) and by the establishment of Soviet Hungary. The domestic threat of communism was generally speaking smaller than the international threat, but this did not prevent draconian measures being

46 Although notable territorial disputes still obtained between them, e.g. Teschin, disputed by Poland and Czechoslovakia, and the Banat between Romania and Yugoslavia.

wielded against communists in the successor states.[47] The results were striking: Yugoslav and Romanian communist parties were effectively "broken" by the institutions of their own states in the 1920s. In both cases, violent acts of terrorism created the pretext Belgrade and Bucharest needed to outlaw communism and to wield oppressive measures against its adherents. These measures proved highly effective, bringing down communist numbers from thousands to hundreds, leaving small (but hardened) groups that dissolved even further in the 1920s and 1930s due to interminable fractional and doctrinal squabbling.[48] But "anti-Bolshevik" legislation, often broadly defined, became a stick with which the ruling powers in the successor states could beat not just communists, but also other political opponents. The red menace, in reality a chimera, could be evoked as needed. Thus, as Ivan Berend has noted, the "historical alternative to Bolshevik and populist dictatorships in postwar Central and Eastern Europe was not Western-type democracy but 'white' terror and conservative autocracy."[49] Czechoslovakia alone of the successor states suffered their communists to thrive within the legal framework of the state's politics throughout the interwar period.[50] There was no large-scale repression of communism similar to the kind of outright terror tolerated or wielded in Yugoslavia, Romania, Hungary and Austria.[51]

Front Line: The Baltic Countries and Poland

The battles fought with communism in the Baltic countries, Finland and Poland were of a different order altogether. Here the Bolshevik presence was no mere phantasm evoked to shore up support for right-wing politics or repressive state legislation. These parts were in the crucible of the revolutionary and

47 On the communist parties in Eastern Europe after World War I, see Ivo Banac (ed.), *The Effects of World War One: The Class War After the Great War. The Rise of the Communist Parties in East Central Europe, 1918–1921* (New York: Columbia University Press, 1983).

48 On the Communist Party of Yugoslavia (KPJ) before World War II, see Aleksa Djilas, *The Contested Country: Yugoslav Unity and Communist Revolution, 1919–1953* (Cambridge, MA: Harvard University Press, 1991); on the Romanian party, see Vladimir Tismaneanu, *Stalinism for All Seasons: A Political History of Romanian Communism* (Berkeley: University of California Press, 2003).

49 Ivan Berend, *Decades of Crisis: East-Central Europe Before World War II* (Berkeley: University of California Press, 1998), 139.

50 On the Czechoslovak Communist Party, see Zdeněk Suda, *Zealots and Rebels: A History of the Communist Party of Czechoslovakia* (Stanford: Hoover Institution Press, 1980).

51 See Giovanni Capoccia, "Legislative Responses against Extremism: The Protection of 'Democracy' in the First Czechoslovak Republic (1920–1938)," *East European Politics and Societies* 16, 3 (2002), 691–738.

counterrevolutionary struggle, located as they were on the front line of the ground war with Bolshevism in Europe.

In the immediate postrevolutionary period, the Bolsheviks had enjoyed considerable popular support in parts of the Baltic region.[52] Lenin was rightly hopeful, at least initially, that the Red Wave would continue to surge through the Baltic countries and into Europe itself (or at least to Germany). But, as throughout Europe, nationalism, presented in Wilsonian terms but, at least until 1919, buoyed up by Germany, emerged as the chief rival to the spread of the revolution. And by the autumn of 1918 nationalists, not Bolsheviks, would emerge as the would-be leaders in the Baltic area. The situation was similar in Poland, where a national army led by Józef Piłsudski was emerging as the most powerful political force in the newly formed state. Here, traditional Polish Russophobia would become compounded by the imminent threat of Bolshevik invasion, an admixture whose potency Lenin disastrously underestimated.

The national revolutions in the Baltic countries and in Poland would bear the full brunt of the European war against communist revolution. Both the Bolsheviks and the Entente, who were now essentially in a state of war against one another, correctly saw the Baltic countries and the Polish state as the crucible of the revolutionary conflict. At stake in this conflict were both territory and, potentially, the future of the European order. The success of the newly formed Red Army in the Baltic region and Poland would form the bridgehead into Europe and, importantly, into the German pivot. Bolshevik victory here would mean the incorporation of the Baltic countries and Poland into the Soviet state; defeat could mean the end of the revolutionary project. The war in the East had the character of an existential showdown, one that gave its violence an elemental ferocity. The Baltic countries also became a "tour of duty" for counterrevolutionaries. These were typically demobilized soldiers and officers, mainly from Germany, who saw in the Baltic front a chance of redemption for the defeat suffered in 1918. They too had a keen grasp of the ideological contours of the battle against communism in the East. Their staunch anti-communism found reaffirmation in these violent frontiers, as did certain preconceived notions of a "wild East" at Germany's borders, one that was backward, primitive and dangerous; they were incubators (although by no means the sole factor) of the German approach to occupation here in World War II.[53]

52 Andres Kasekamp, *A History of the Baltic States* (Basingstoke and New York: Palgrave Macmillan, 2010), 96–97.

53 Vejas Gabriel Liulevicius, *War Land on the Eastern Front: Culture, National Identity, and German Occupation in World War I* (Cambridge: Cambridge University Press, 2005).

As Norman Davies has noted, the failures of the Bolsheviks to break the nationalist dam on the River Vistula meant the beginning of a new phase of the communist project, that of retrenchment, consolidation and retreat – although not capitulation. It also forced both communists and nationalists to define, or rather redefine, their programs of state organization and state-forming. As Jerzy Borzęcki has argued, the Treaty of Riga, ending the Russo-Polish War, led the Bolsheviks to reconsider the nature of their state and its relations with the rest of Europe.[54] The Soviet Union became a federalized conglomeration of semi-autonomous national groups, albeit all under the umbrella of a socialist state.[55] For the Poles (and for the Baltic states) the Treaty of Riga demarcated the external borders of their new national state, but it also defined their policies toward national minorities, non-Poles who now comprised almost a third of the population.[56] The Eastern War is remembered as a great defeat for the Bolsheviks and a "miraculous" victory for the Poles. In reality, both sides had suffered sharp blows, both sides had survived: The Poles and the Balts continued to build their nation-states throughout the interwar period, the Bolsheviks survived within the confines of a single country. Both felt the shadow of war and invasion from the other side;[57] neither side was wholly defeated, neither side wholly victorious. This was more broadly true for the whole of Europe: The revolution and the counterrevolution would coexist throughout the interwar period in a state of armed peace. The existential showdown had ceased, at least for the time being, in a stalemate.

Conclusion

What can be concluded from this brief but turbulent period of war, revolution and counterrevolution in Europe from 1917 to 1923? First and foremost, we must be cautious about the apparent stabilization of the European order in the aftermath of these years of violent revolutionary turmoil. As mentioned in the introduction of this chapter, the balance sheet for these years would record an absolute defeat for the communist revolution in Europe, marked by catastrophic failures in Hungary, the Balkans and

54 Jerzy Borzęcki, *The Soviet–Polish Peace of 1921 and the Creation of Interwar Europe* (New Haven: Yale University Press, 2008).

55 See Ronald Grigor Suny, *The Soviet Experiment: Russia, the USSR, and the Successor States* (Oxford: Oxford University Press, 1998).

56 Borzęcki, *The Soviet–Polish Peace of 1921.*

57 Timothy Snyder, *Bloodlands: Europe Between Hitler and Stalin* (New York: Basic Books, 2010).

(above all) Germany. And yet throughout the continent, the differences between the pre-1914 and interwar periods loom large. Lenin famously claimed that the war was a conflict of imperial exploitation in the interests of the tiny financial and political elites, in stark contrast to the emancipatory revolution and war of the Bolsheviks. Perhaps it is more accurate to say that if World War I was a conflict of state ideas, the October Revolution and the conflicts of 1917–23 were battles involving mass, transnational political mobilization. And as we have seen, the war itself opened the floodgates of mass politics and political participation – the local and regional wars that it gave rise to in the years 1917–23 were fought in a highly charged atmosphere of adversarial political confrontation at a mass level; no middle ground existed between the forces of communist revolution and counterrevolution during this period. The center may have held, but it was also vastly diminished. It was in the years of revolution and counterrevolution from 1917 to 1923, rather than the war years themselves, that the "age of extremes" really begins.

Bibliographical Essay

There are several excellent general and comparative accounts of the violence and revolution during the period 1917–23: See especially Alan Kramer, *Dynamic of Destruction: Culture and Mass Killing in the First World War* (Oxford: Oxford University Press, 2008); Robert Gerwarth and John Horne (eds.), *War in Peace: Paramilitary Violence in Europe After the Great War* (Oxford: Oxford University Press, 2012); and Robert Gerwarth, *The Vanquished: Why the First World War Failed to End, 1917–1923* (London: Allen Lane, 2016). Two first-class studies of the ramifications of the collapse of empire in the European borderlands are Aviel Roshwald, *Ethnic Nationalism and the Fall of Empires: Central Europe, Russia, and the Middle East, 1914–1923* (London and New York: Routledge, 2001), and Omer Bartov and Eric D. Weitz (eds.), *Shatterzones of Empires: Coexistence and Violence in the German, Habsburg, Russian, and Ottoman Borderlands* (Bloomington: Indiana University Press, 2013). A good narrative of the experiment in Wilsonian peacemaking at the end of World War I is Margaret Macmillan, *Peacemakers – Six Months that Changed the World: The Paris Peace Conference of 1919 and its Attempt to End War* (London: John Murray, 2001). On Germany during and after World War I, see Benjamin Ziemann, *War Experiences in Rural Germany, 1914–1923* (Oxford and New York: Berg Publishers, 2007); Vejas Gabriel Liulevicius, *War Land on the Eastern Front: Culture, National Identity, and German Occupation in World*

War I (Cambridge: Cambridge University Press, 2005); and Mark Jones, *Founding Weimar: The German Revolution of 1918–1919* (Cambridge: Cambridge University Press, 2016). D'Annunzio's attempt to redefine politics in Fiume under the watchful and concerned eyes of the peacemakers is covered in Michael Arthur Ledeen, *The First Duce: D'Annunzio at Fiume* (Baltimore: Johns Hopkins University Press, 1977). Hungary's red revolution and white counterrevolution are analyzed in Francis L. Carsten, *Revolution in Central Europe, 1918–1919* (Berkeley: University of California Press, 1972), and Béla Bodó, *Pál Prónay: Paramilitary Violence and Anti-Semitism in Hungary, 1919–1922* (Pittsburgh: University of Pittsburgh Press, 2010). For a recent and revisionist study of the longer-term legacies of the counterrevolution in the Austrian capital, see Janek Wasserman, *Black Vienna: The Radical Right in the Red City, 1918–1938* (Ithaca: Cornell University Press, 2014). Communist revolution in East Central Europe and the Balkans is covered in the still generally valid George D. Jackson, Jr., *Comintern and Peasant in East Europe, 1919–1930* (New York and London: Columbia University Press, 1966), and the volume of essays edited by Ivo Banac, *The Effects of World War One: The Class War After the Great War – The Rise of the Communist Parties in East Central Europe, 1918–1921* (New York: Columbia University Press, 1983). The importance of the ending of the Polish–Soviet war in setting the demarcation lines between the communist and noncommunist world is covered by Jerzy Borzęcki in *The Soviet–Polish Peace of 1921 and the Creation of Interwar Europe* (New Haven: Yale University Press, 2008).

4

Lenin as Historical Personality

ROBERT SERVICE

The Struggle for Power

Lenin was baptized Vladimir Ilich Ulyanov in 1870 in Simbirsk, a provincial capital in the mid-Volga region of the Russian Empire. He was of ethnically mixed ancestry; its precise nature is still obscure but it certainly included a Jewish element and possibly also a Kalmyk one. This, though, had practically no effect on his upbringing because his parents identified strongly with Russian cultural and professional trends of the late nineteenth century and strove to integrate themselves and the family that they thought was being constructed through the reforms introduced by Emperor Alexander II since 1861. Vladimir's father Ilya rose from lowly social origins to the post of province schools inspector and was renowned for his energetic promotion of school-building in and around Simbirsk; his mother, whose father was a doctor, was an eager musician and a devoted mother. The children were brought up in an atmosphere dedicated to cultural improvement and educational progress. Each of them excelled at school. The Ulyanovs conformed to the stereotype of a family determined on high attainment for all its members, and the era of reforms made possible their advancement in a fashion that would have been barely imaginable in previous centuries.

Young Vladimir's life was shaken by two events. The first was the death of his father in 1886. This removed some of the household's rigorous constraints on the children's behavior – the boys in particular became distinctly willful. The second, even more traumatic, was the arrest and hanging of the oldest son Alexander for his role in a plot to assassinate Emperor Alexander III in 1887. Alexander II had been killed by agrarian-socialist terrorists six years earlier with the object of destabilizing the whole political order. Alexander belonged to a broadly similar revolutionary conspiracy and although they threw no bomb, the members were punished severely. The Ulyanov family acquired the status of pariahs in Simbirsk. Even so, Vladimir Ulyanov was still allowed to proceed to Kazan University and take up his place in the faculty of jurisprudence. Within weeks he had taken part in a protest demonstration and was expelled from the university. He joined his mother and tried his hand ineffectually at farm management on the estate that his parents had bought. Already, however, he had got involved in revolutionary politics. Like his deceased brother, he was drawn toward the groups that saw the peasantry as standing at the foundations of the possibilities for revolution; he also espoused terrorist activity. At the same time he studied for an external course in law with St. Petersburg University (where he achieved a first-class degree in 1891).

He belonged to a generation when many young revolutionaries were coming to the conclusion that agrarian socialism was an obsolete doctrine for Russia as the country underwent rapid industrialization and acquired factories, mines and railways like other great powers. A revolutionary prospectus resting on the potential of peasants and the village land commune appeared a lot less attractive than in previous decades. The Russian agrarian socialists had anyway always been admirers of Marx – and he himself had offered some encouragement to their leaders.

Under the influence of Georgii Plekhanov, some of them now began to preach that the German variant of Marxism – with its attachment to industry, the working class and the cities – had become appropriate also for the Russian Empire. Bookish intellectuals such as Vladimir Ulyanov joined the little study groups that sprang up in most cities. They pored over tomes by Marx and Engels and became experts in Marxist doctrine and advocates of the need for theoretical purity in applying it. They were equally energetic in investigating Russia's current economic transformation, especially with regard to the social differentiation occurring in the villages as the commercial economy penetrated ever deeper. Ulyanov had never been sentimental about peasants. In the famine of 1891–92 he shocked even his own family with his refusal to participate in relief work: His opinion was that palliative measures simply delayed the development of the toiling masses into revolutionaries.[1] But he never forgot the requirement for Marxists to build a rural dimension into any strategy for basic change in Russia and its empire.

1 V. Vodovozov, "Moë znakomstvo s Leninym," *Na chuzoi storone* 12 (1925), 178.

By 1895 he was operating clandestinely in St. Petersburg inside the Union of Struggle for the Liberation of the Working Class. Although he had contact with several workers who became its members, his priority was to establish his credentials as a Marxist intellectual through writing and discussion. That same December he was arrested and later sent into Siberian exile. By then he had turned into one of the least compromising theoreticians of Marxism in Russia, lambasting those revolutionaries of his generation who persisted in trying to make agrarian socialism into a movement that could challenge the government. As well as Marx and Engels, the Russian Plekhanov and the German Karl Kautsky were contemporary senior writers whose inspiration he acknowledged. He rejected any attempt to moderate revolutionary doctrine. And, with financial help from his mother's landed property as well as her pension, he resolved upon a fulltime career as revolutionary. In Siberia he married fellow Marxist Nadezhda Krupskaia. Continuing his economic studies, he finished *The Development of Capitalism in Russia*, which was legally published in 1899.[2] Ulyanov's sentence came to an end in 1900 and he tried to resume underground revolutionary activity in Russia. When this proved impractical, he moved abroad.

He had the same deep impact on Marxist émigrés as he had achieved before leaving the empire. Undeniably bright and well read in the classics of Marxism, he was also a dynamic organizer with a penchant for leadership. Bald in his twenties, he acquired the nickname of Old Man. His political impatience communicated itself to everyone that he met. He was never going to be content with theorizing about revolution: He aimed to make one in his native country. He lived and breathed the idea that this was a genuine possibility.

His first thought was to align himself with his hero Plekhanov and subordinate himself to his purposes. His second thought was that Plekhanov was incapable of organizing a revolutionary party that would bring about a revolution. His writings called persistently for a tightly centralized, disciplined organization of revolutionaries. Many criticized this as altogether too reminiscent of the terrorist conspiracies of the 1870s and 1880s. Russian Marxists tended to prefer "mass activity"; they believed that the working class as a whole should engage in revolutionary action. Many of them disliked Ulyanov's refusal to announce an unconditional

2 V. I. Lenin, *Polnoe sobranie sochinenii* (Moscow: Gosizdat, 1958–65), vol. III, 1–609.

rejection of terrorist methods. Ulyanov, though, was undeterred. He badgered Plekhanov into agreeing to the setting up of an émigré newspaper which they called *Iskra* (The Spark) with the idea to use the editorials and local Russian news as a means to organize and coordinate a proper party. In essence Ulyanov became its chief editor as he buffeted Plekhanov out of the way. In 1902 he published a booklet, *What Is To Be Done?*, which made his case for his own kind of party. He signed it as Lenin, which was to become the name by which he would be known to history.[3]

There had been a small, clandestine congress of the Russian Social Democratic Workers' Party in Minsk in 1899, but it had left no organizational legacy. Plekhanov and Lenin convoked a second party congress in summer 1903 to rectify the situation. Its proceedings opened in Brussels but were quickly transferred to London when the attentions of the Belgian police became a difficulty. Their evident aim was not only to establish but also to control the new and growing party. Initially the *Iskra* group stuck together and saw off internal party critics such as the Jewish Bund which vainly sought broad organizational autonomy for itself. The Iskraites dominated the central party apparatus elected at the congress. But several among them, notably Lenin's friend Yuli Martov, were disconcerted by Lenin's extreme polemics and conspiratorial maneuvers. The *Iskra* group fell apart. The majority, led by Lenin and supported for a while by Plekhanov, were unperturbed. Calling themselves the Majoritarians (*bol'sheviki* in Russian), they derided the Minoritarians (*men'sheviki*) who advocated a less strenuously ordered party. The strife between the Bolsheviks and the Mensheviks led to a serious factional split inside the party abroad.

Nevertheless Bolsheviks and Mensheviks in the Russian Empire, as distinct from the émigrés, found it possible to collaborate with each other. For them, the matters separating the leaders abroad, though frequently of principle, were an inadequate justification for a lasting schism; and even among his own followers, Lenin was suspected of picking fights unnecessarily. Nonetheless, no one challenged his capacity to write, speak and lead. It was generally recognized that he had a multidimensional talent which was, or could be, of value to the Russian Social Democratic Workers' Party as it increased its recruitment among factory workers and

3 Ibid., vol. VI, 3–190.

miners. Lenin stayed abroad, eagerly noting the intensification of industrial conflict and arguing that events were justifying his earlier strategic proposals. But his verbal intemperance and organizational manipulations caused trouble for him even in the so-called emigration. By 1904, only a year after his victory at the second congress, much of his support had slipped from his grasp. Even many of his Bolshevik adherents were deserting him. Plekhanov too denounced him, and Lenin lost control of the central party apparatus. It began to appear that his potential to lead a party had been exaggerated.

In 1905 the Russian Empire erupted into revolution. Lenin refused to return from Switzerland until after Nicholas II issued his October Manifesto, which appeared to offer a degree of personal security to anti-tsarist militants. Bolsheviks welcomed him eagerly, and Lenin worked out a fresh political strategy of revolution in light of rapidly changing circumstances. Lenin urged the party to aim at setting up a "provisional revolutionary dictatorship of the proletariat and the peasantry." He argued that this was the only way of ensuring that the forthcoming "bourgeois-democratic revolution" against the Romanovs could avoid being compromised by vacillation on the part of the middle classes. The dictatorship, according to Lenin, would establish a regime of full civic rights, land nationalization and progressive capitalism. He envisaged that such a regime would eventually enable the working class to advance to a second revolution of its own, a revolution that would inaugurate socialism. The Mensheviks regarded this as a recipe for civil war and terror. Even so, Lenin proved himself willing to work with them. His own Bolsheviks in his opinion were showing undue inflexibility in their revolutionary tactics. Many refused to enter trade unions or the workers' soviets (or councils). They also declined to participate in the newly announced election to the state Duma. Lenin used the Mensheviks as a counterbalance to the Bolshevik irreconcilables.

With the suppression of the revolutionary tide Lenin returned to the emigration in late 1907. He continued to condone the retention of a united Russian Social Democratic Workers' Party but always ran a separate Bolshevik organization within it; and the Bolsheviks themselves were riven – especially in the emigration – by internal disputes, several of which were initiated by Lenin. His constant object was to control the doctrines and practices of Bolshevism. In 1911, as the Mensheviks became less useful for the purposes of reining in his Bolshevik critics, his patience snapped and he decided to call a party conference in Prague with only a nod in the direction of inviting Menshevik leaders. The resultant Central Committee, ignoring the rights of other factions, proclaimed itself the legitimate supreme agency of the Russian Social Democratic Labour Party. He would have nothing further to do with the Mensheviks. Pushed by Bolsheviks in Russia, he acceded to the setting up of a daily St. Petersburg newspaper to be called *Pravda* (Truth), and he moved to Kraków in Austrian-ruled Poland to kept contact with its editors. He also strengthened links with the Bolshevik deputies in the fourth state Duma. (By then the faction was contesting the elections.) Lenin was itching for a revolution and for it to be led by Bolsheviks, and he refused to hand over Bolshevik funds to the common treasury of the Russian Social Democratic Workers' Party. He wanted politics only on his terms.

His intolerance became notorious even inside his own faction. It was noticed that he characteristically reacted to quite slight disagreements about tactics as if profound philosophical principles were at stake. One reason why the Bolsheviks encountered obstacles to expanding their number of recruits was Lenin's persistent divisiveness. For Lenin, it was as if the greatest priority was to secure total acceptance of his policies. His Bolshevik critics felt that he increasingly overlooked opportunities to cooperate with them in preparing the path toward a revolution against the Romanov monarchy; they came to agree with Mensheviks that his zeal for personal authority vitiated his usefulness as a political leader.

The price he paid was recurrent dissent among the Bolsheviks. In 1909 he had driven his rival Aleksandr Bogdanov from the faction. Bogdanov accused him of being an authoritarian egomaniac.[4] The exodus of militants from the Bolsheviks continued when Europe went to war in summer 1914. To Lenin's consternation the admired German Social Democratic Party voted financial credits to Kaiser Wilhelm's government. Even Kautsky, the party's outstanding theoretician, whom Lenin had always eulogized, refrained from outright condemnation of the German war effort. Lenin broke with the Second International. He castigated those many Bolsheviks who rebutted his call for a "European civil war." His spirit was lifted only by the conviction that the travails of war would lead to revolution in Europe. The diminution of his following therefore failed to demoralize him. As usual he tried to summarize developments in a treatise, *Imperialism as the Highest Stage of Capitalism*,

4 See Robert Service, *Lenin: A Biography* (Basingstoke: Macmillan, 2000), 192–94.

which suggested that the principal capitalist powers had been thrust into military conflict by their competition for world markets. Imperialism, according to Lenin, was the ultimate state of capitalism. In a series of further articles he suggested that economic crises – and indeed world war – would recur until the impoverished working classes of Europe and North America rose against their government and installed revolutionary socialist dictatorships.[5]

At Zimmerwald in September 1915 and Kienthal in April 1916, high in the Swiss Alps, he continued to pursue his case with passion. All participants in these two conferences opposed their national war efforts. Lenin, though, wanted a firm commitment to turning the "imperialist war" into a class-based civil war across the continent. Maneuvering behind the scenes, he opted to organize a cabal of leftists at the conferences, which themselves consisted entirely of the left wing of left-wing socialism, to achieve consensus. Although his style was unchanged, however, his perspective was undergoing alteration. In 1909, in a work of singular philosophical crudity and outdatedness titled *Materialism and Empiriocriticism*, he had argued that the perceptive capacity of the human mind was as accurate as a camera; he had contended that absolute knowledge was attainable and that Marx and Engels had already supplied infallible instruments for this objective. In his wartime notebooks on philosophy he moved over to a more flexible approach to epistemology, basically arguing that ideas – even those of Marxism's founders – could only be found proven when tested out in practice.[6]

This theoretical adoption of experimentalism came from his readings of Hegel and Aristotle. But of course he had always been an experimenter in his active political career. Until World War I, however, he had disguised such a tendency by proclaiming his rigorous attachment to Marxist orthodoxy. In fact his ragbag of doctrines, from the start, had included not only Marxism but also Jacobinism, early nineteenth-century socialist extremism, Russian agrarian socialism and even the centuries-old intellectual (and, if it dare be said, ecclesiastical) tradition that Russia had a unique and universalist destiny in the world. As theory and practice reinforced each other in Lenin's thinking, he was taken aback in his Swiss apartment by the unexpected news that revolution had broken out in the Russian Empire. In previous months he had confessed

5 Ibid., 239–45. 6 His notes are collected in Lenin, *Polnoe sobranie sochinenii*, vol. XXIX.

to wondering whether he would live long enough to hear of this outcome. Suddenly it had happened.[7] Emperor Nicholas II was overthrown, the liberal-led Provisional Government established. Political and civic freedom was announced. What was the best course for Marxists in this extraordinary situation?

Lenin in Power

Lenin had already been considering whether the old Bolshevik notion of a two-stage revolutionary process was valid. The February 1917 Revolution brought him to the point of decision. The Provisional Government, enjoying the conditional support of Mensheviks and Socialist Revolutionaries (and indeed many Bolsheviks), had to be overthrown. He wrote frantically along these lines to the Bolshevik factional leadership in Petrograd (as St. Petersburg had been renamed). At the same time he entered discussions with the German authorities for permission to traverse Germany and make his return to Petrograd via Scandinavia. He and other Bolsheviks found favor in Berlin because they conducted vigorous anti-war propaganda. The deal was done, and Lenin arrived at the Finland station in Petrograd in the early hours of 4 April. In his pocket he had scribbled out what became known as his April Theses.[8]

The fundamental proposal was that the Provisional Government had to give way to a socialist administration. Developing his ideas in articles in *Pravda* and at the Bolshevik April conference, he argued that Menshevik and Socialist Revolutionary supporters of the Provisional Government had betrayed their socialism. He urged that working-class organizations such as the soviets should be turned into the core of the forthcoming socialist regime. In subsequent weeks he stopped talking about the need for a European civil war. He attuned himself to popular opinion, which wanted peace and freedom. Lenin promised to end the war, to give land to the peasantry, to provide the industrial labor force with workers' control and to grant national self-determination to all the peoples of the former Russian Empire. He predicted that socialist revolution in Russia would be quickly followed by revolution across the rest of Europe. A new era in the history of humankind was beginning. Lenin heralded it with fiery aplomb. He rallied the radicals in his own faction to his banner and brought the vacillators into their camp.

7 Ibid., vol. XXVI, 221. 8 Ibid., vol. XXXI, 113–14.

Although he remained a divisive personality in the Russian revolutionary movement, Lenin began to concentrate his energies on turning the Bolsheviks into a party that welcomed everyone who agreed on the need for an immediate second revolution that would inaugurate a socialist order in Russia and bring the Great War to an end. He was sloughing off his old factional obsessions and growing into a brilliant all-round political leader with an instinct for the mood of workers, soldiers and peasants. He spoke at open meetings. He wrote relentlessly for *Pravda*. He raised the spirits of Bolsheviks in the Central Committee and from the provinces – and at the same time he became the bogeyman of those liberals and rival socialists who prayed for the Provisional Government to have success.

Events played into his hands. The Mensheviks would have nothing to do with him and, to his delight, the Bolsheviks were able to form themselves into an entirely separate mass party. The Provisional Government helped him too. First, foreign minister Pavel Milyukov was found to have affirmed his personal commitment to expansionist war aims. This was hugely uncongenial to workers and soldiers. Then the cabinet started a June offensive. This was an unmitigated military disaster. And then the last premier of the Provisional Government, Alexander Kerensky, embroiled himself in a violent dispute with army commander Lavr Kornilov, and only the assistance of socialist agitators – including Bolsheviks – saved him from being overthrown by his own army. Throughout these months, what is more, the economy was collapsing and the administrative and policing agencies fell into shambles. Workers and soldiers started by voting for Mensheviks and Socialist Revolutionaries but by early autumn they were turning to the Bolsheviks, who advocated drastic reforms to stave off famine and bring about peace.

Lenin himself had gone into hiding in early July after the Provisional Government issued a warrant for his arrest as a German spy. He returned clandestinely to the Bolshevik Central Committee on 10 and 16 October to demand that the party exploit its rising popularity in the soviets and immediately seize power.[9] A majority accepted his case. The Provisional Government was overthrown on 25 October 1917 and power was transferred to the Second Congress of workers' and soldiers'

9 *Protokoly Tsentral'nogo Komiteta RSDRP(b): avgust 1917–fevral' 1918* (Moscow: Gosizdat, 1958), 83–105.

deputies. Emerging from hiding in the outskirts of the capital, Lenin became head of the Council of People's Commissars (or Sovnarkom). He issued decrees. He propelled his comrades into revolutionary initiatives. He searched for ways toward peace that would touch off a revolution in Germany. He spoke frequently at open meetings. He published, in early 1918, *The State and Revolution* in his attempt to justify the October Revolution in Marxist terms. The Mensheviks and Socialist Revolutionaries, in the November negotiations with the Bolsheviks, sought to exclude him from any proposed governing coalition; and he was equally eager to exclude the Mensheviks and Socialist Revolutionaries. The only political partnership that Lenin would tolerate was with the left Socialist Revolutionaries who joined Sovnarkom in the middle of the month.

Lenin showed himself to be a bustling governmental leader. He chaired meetings with punctilio and chided Bolsheviks who failed to comply with official policy. But he was also a friendly and encouraging comrade, being devoid of both Trotsky's self-preening arrogance and Stalin's prickly harshness. He was a master of the art of people-management, and he did not fail to understand that if his close associates had a tense relationship with each other, he could more easily manipulate them and dominate discussions.

The problem was that Sovnarkom's writ was confined largely to the cities of Russia. The rest of the country, especially the villages, had yet to declare itself for the Bolsheviks. Shocks continued to be administered to Lenin's pre-October prognosis. When elections were held for the Constituent Assembly in November, the outcome was a disaster for the Bolsheviks, who barely gained a quarter of the votes. Nor was Sovnarkom's foreign and security policy a success. The German High Command issued an ultimatum that Sovnarkom should sign a separate peace on the eastern front and withdraw from the war. Lenin recognized the superiority of Germany's military power and, after months of acerbic dispute in the Bolshevik Central Committee, cajoled his comrades into accepting the German terms in the Treaty of Brest-Litovsk in March 1918.[10] The left Socialist Revolutionaries abandoned the governing coalition in protest, and Lenin also came close to causing an internal split in the Bolshevik party because most leading members had favored "revolution-

10 Ibid., 213 (23 Feb. 1918).

ary war" against imperial Germany. But Lenin held his ground against his left communists, arguing that a "breathing space" had been obtained for the Soviet republic to set about consolidating the October Revolution across Russia.

His policies quickly hardened as the political and military resistance to Sovnarkom sharpened in spring 1918. Lenin, who had been preaching class war with intensifying eagerness, removed the constraints on the new political police known as the Cheka. He urged the creation of "committees of the village poor." Throwing aside his earlier caution, he sanctioned a campaign for the total state ownership of industry. (Banks, large-scale factories and foreign trade were already in the hands of Sovnarkom.) In November the Germans surrendered to the Western Allies and Lenin, disembarrassed of the need to appease the Berlin government, called for the formation of a Communist International. By then Sovnarkom was being attacked by a succession of White armies determined to overthrow the Bolsheviks. Lenin chaired Sovnarkom, which oversaw the implementation of economic and social policy. But it was the party which was truly the supreme arbiter. Power accrued to an inner subcommittee of the Central Committee and Lenin informally headed it. Every grand matter of war, economics, security, culture, administrative appointments and politics came before it. Lenin insisted that the civil war had to be fought politically as well as militarily. By the end of 1919 Russia was conquered by the Reds; by March 1921 nearly all the former Russian Empire was overrun.

Lenin had become the acknowledged authoritative figure in party and government. Although Trotsky was credited as the co-leader of the October Revolution, he was distrusted by many Bolshevik veterans as someone who might seek to use the Red Army against the party itself. Lenin by contrast was revered as the founder of Bolshevism; although he had committed several avoidable mistakes before, during and after 1917, these were overlooked in the euphoria of the victory over the White armies. Although the Bolshevik party remained liable to collapse into debilitating internal disputes, Lenin's opinions acquired a weightiness that no other prominent Bolshevik could match.

The mistaken assumption of the Bolsheviks, shared by Lenin, was that the wartime methods had so demonstrated their worth that they ought to be prolonged into peacetime. Food supplies continued to be expropriated from the peasantry. Peasants revolted, workers went on strike and soldiers and sailors mutinied. Lenin's intuitions about the art of the possible deserted him. In summer 1920 he was primarily responsible for throwing the Red Army at the Poles in a vain attempt to spread the revolution westward in a revolutionary war. The Reds were crushed at the Battle of the Vistula and sued for peace. The rebellious peasants of Russia and Ukraine gave him even greater worry, and in February 1921 he acknowledged the need for a change of strategy and persuaded the Politburo to approve a New Economic Policy (NEP). At its base was the replacement of food requisitioning with a graduated tax in kind set at a level enabling peasants to trade their surplus. Simultaneously Lenin ordered the ferocious suppression of the Tambov rural revolt and the Kronstadt naval mutiny; he also introduced, at the Tenth Party Congress, a ban on factional activity in the party: If the Bolsheviks were going to effect an orderly retreat, his view was that discipline and centralism were unconditional requirements.

Lenin's health was in serious decline by 1921–22 at a time when he had to go on defending the NEP against its Bolshevik critics who wanted either to abandon it or, like Trotsky, introduce more elements of state economic planning. At the same time he sketched a future scenario whereby the NEP would be used to ease the "transition to socialism." Having always based his strategy on some kind of alliance between the urban working class and the peasantry, he urged the need for priority to be given to developing agriculture through the expansion of the rural cooperative network. Somehow or other, he intimated, the way would be prepared for the eventual creation of collective farms without the need for force.[11]

Compulsion, however, remained intrinsic to his basic tenets. He fiercely insisted on retaining the state's capacity to use methods of terror whenever its interests were under threat. Like all other Bolshevik leaders, he continued to take it for granted that the one-party dictatorship was an essential requirement for the defense of the October Revolution. But though he continued to hope for a "European socialist revolution," he planned on the basis that the Politburo needed to attract direct foreign investment in the Soviet economy and avoid a repetition of the 1920 military debacle; he also strove for a political and economic rapprochement with Germany as way of splitting the capitalist powers and speeding the country's postwar reconstruction. While warning his own leftist communist critics about the dangers of

11 Lenin, *Polnoe sobranie sochinenii*, vol. XLIII, 206–24.

"adventurism," he supported efforts to extend the reach of the Communist International through the creation of its parties and network of functionaries around the world. He never wavered in his belief that events since 1917 had confirmed the correctness of the Bolshevik decision to seize power in the October Revolution.

He had not made a clear statement of his evolving strategy before spring 1922 when he suffered a massive heart attack. From his sickbed he was angered by the elaboration of policies by the central party leadership. He detected a lurch into "bureaucratism." He perceived that nations such as the Georgians were being handled in a "Great Russian chauvinist" fashion by the Kremlin. He was exasperated by a proposal to relax the state monopoly on foreign trade. And in each of these matters he blamed Stalin, the party general secretary, as the chief culprit. In the winter of 1922–23, fearing his imminent extinction, Lenin dictated a political testament and appended a codicil calling for Stalin's removal from his post.[12] In March 1923, however, he suffered a further heart attack, which terminated his political career. His physical existence ended on 21 January 1924 after a final convulsion. He was not yet fifty-three years old.

Without Lenin, the Bolshevik party's strategy in 1917 would have been more diffuse and indeterminate. Without Lenin, the revolution against the Provisional Government might have culminated in an all-social coalition government. Without Lenin, the decisions to sign the Treaty of Brest-Litovsk or to initiate the NEP would probably have not have been sanctioned. Without Lenin, there might not have been a Communist International. Without Lenin, the entire philosophical underpinning of dictatorship, terror, ideological certitude and revolutionary optimism and amoralism would have lacked clarity and incisiveness. He was a maker of the twentieth century.

Bibliographical Essay: The Lenin Controversies

Lenin's self-image was of a consistent pupil of Marx and Engels who was doing two main things. One was to defend Marxist ideas from emasculation by those of his followers who failed to understand the essence of his doctrines. The other was to find ways of adapting Marxism to the

12 His last dictated pieces are reproduced ibid., vol. XLV.

contemporary Russian circumstances – at least, this was his purpose until his later years when he assumed that Russia's revolutionary experience had guiding lessons for socialism in every country. His own followers adjusted his image in light of his success in establishing a communist government and built a cult to his greatness which was relayed not only throughout the Soviet Union but to every communist party around the world. Nothing that he did or said in his lifetime was allowed to be rejected or ridiculed. Official Soviet interpretations, through to the end of the USSR in 1991, insisted that he never made a single mistake in his entire political career. Lenin was depicted as the finest intellectual, politician and humanitarian in global history. His doctrines were put on a pedestal as Marxism-Leninism.[13]

Outside the Soviet Union, he was venerated much less widely and his image was often quite the opposite of what was accepted in Moscow. Political refugees from Russia as well as Western political commentators in the main repeated and deepened the charges made against him by his prerevolutionary enemies. The pictures differed from writer to writer but all concurred that he had a lust for power for its own sake and that he was willing to deploy it in the most brutal fashion. Some accepted that he was ideologically motivated but argued that his analysis of Marxism was deeply awry – indeed many claimed that he failed to recognize how the origins of many of his doctrines derived less from Marx and Engels than from the Russian socialist terrorists of the late nineteenth century. Others again suggested that far from having developed Marxist ideas suitable for Russia, Lenin imposed entirely inappropriate ones that help to explain why Russia soon collapsed into an inferno of oppression and exploitation. Anti-communists regarded the October Revolution as a disaster for Russia and the world.

While accepting that Lenin was the originator of the Soviet model of politics, economics and society, they concluded that his USSR constituted a source of one of the most pernicious twentieth-century inventions: the one-party, one-ideology state with a zeal to subjugate its people to its purposes and mobilize them regardless of their own wishes. A term that was used to characterize this from the 1940s was "totalitarianism," and it was applied both to the Soviet Union and to the Third Reich. In other words, the idea was that the structure and practices of a totalitarian state were of greater importance

13 P. N. Pospelov et al., *Vladimir Il'ich Lenin* (Moscow: Gosizdat, 1963).

than whether the rulers belonged to the political far left or the political far right.

What both sides of the debate, pro-Lenin and anti-Lenin, agreed about was that the transformation of Russia through the October Revolution proceeded from actions taken on high and that Lenin was the main actor. Lenin, it was believed, only had to think of a new policy and his communist party offered itself as the automatic realizer of his will. According to this analysis, the party itself had the capacity even before coming to power of manipulating the thoughts of "the masses" and directing them in whatever direction it chose. Official Soviet spokespeople said this in a wholly admiring way since they took it for granted that Lenin was a beneficent genius. Critics of communism saw Lenin in a much darker light and contended that his talent was evil in the extreme. Admirers and detractors alike, however, were at one in proposing that his personal impact was of towering significance. It was a view on politics as a kind of pyramid from the top of which the ruler transmitted his requirements down through all its various levels to its very base.

In the eyes of most communists, Lenin shared this status with no one else. But some of them, especially the Trotskyists (who emerged in the course of the Lenin succession struggle in the 1920s), maintained that Leon Trotsky was either as influential or nearly as influential in making and consolidating the October Revolution; they also contended that Trotsky made extraordinary contributions of his own to Marxism. Trotsky himself made no such claim, except in an indirect fashion, because pragmatic considerations compelled him to present himself to the communist party as merely a follower of Lenin rather than his equal. For Soviet communist interpreters, in any case, Trotsky had never been a true Leninist and quickly turned against the interests of the October Revolution.

The restricted Western focus on one or two communist leaders in the early history of the USSR was paralleled by a distinct lack of primary attention to the general political, economic and social history of 1917. Although it was claimed that the industrial "proletariat" had been crucial to the overturning of Nicholas II and then the Provisional Government, commentators failed to examine workers' conditions of life and work or the nature of their public aspirations. The same was true of the other large social classes in the revolutionary period. Such neglect began to be rectified in the 1970s when research was conducted on the "lower depths" of society. One of the purposes was to knock over the long-worshipped shibboleth that held that everything that happened in the October Revolution was attributable to Lenin (together, perhaps, with Trotsky) and, by extension, to the communist party. A so-called revisionist school of thought came to the fore which challenged the exclusively "top-down" analysis and reasoned that historical causation was multidimensional and multidirectional. Essentially this was an attack on the pyramidal conception of the revolutionary process; its main purpose was to show that what happened in Russia between the February and October Revolutions was not merely the product of the will of a few communist leaders.[14]

It was pointed out that workers between the February and October Revolutions had ideas and made demands of their own. In some cases, the newer writers even implied that Lenin and his party fell in with working-class requirements rather than the other way round. Others highlighted the interaction of party leaders and workers as the tide of revolution washed over them, and it was noted that Lenin drastically altered his policies and discourse in response to the need to attract popular support. Lenin became more elusive of easy categorization but also more like a "normal" politician, albeit a politician of exceptional dynamism and alertness.

Not everyone accepted this normalization of Lenin as a historical figure. A study by Neil Harding asserted that Lenin, a cerebral politician, never did anything without prior elaboration of a fundamental intellectual analysis. Thus it was supposedly his studies of the Russian imperial economy in the 1890s that led him toward the political policies that he recommended to his party. First came the economic exploration, then – by a process of deduction – the ideas about the need for a centralized party and the objective of class dictatorship. When Lenin changed his political policies in 1914–17, it was said, he did so only after a thorough reconsideration of the global economy in the age of imperialism. Such an approach gave primacy to Lenin the thinker, holding that his politics was the inevitable logical product of his basic thought at any given time. One of the motives was to defend Lenin against the conventional charge of having been a power-hungry fanatic without a serious genuine idea in his head. It also presented him as the legitimate successor of Marx and Engels in his

14 Alexander Rabinowitch, *Prelude to Revolution: The Petrograd Bolsheviks and the July 1917 Uprising* (Bloomington: Indiana University Press, 1968); Diane Koenker, *Moscow Workers and the 1917 Revolution* (Princeton: Princeton University Press, 1981); Robert Service, *The Bolshevik Party in Revolution: A Study in Organisational Change, 1917–1923* (London: Macmillan, 1979); Stephen A. Smith, *Red Petrograd: Revolution in the Factories 1917–18* (Cambridge: Cambridge University Press, 1983).

own generation and not as someone who mangled Marxism out of its original shape.[15]

Whereas Harding saw Lenin's writings as an aberration from any original Bolshevik vision, Moshe Lewin maintained that they offered a prospectus for communism with a human face. Lewin saw the shoots of democratic, peaceful, evolutionary growth in his final thoughts. Stephen Cohen's biography of Nikolai Bukharin suggested that this version of Bolshevism could have flourished after Lenin's death if only Bukharin had defeated Stalin in the political struggle between them in 1928–29. Instead, Bukharin was crushed and compelled to recant his opinions, and Stalin had him executed in 1938.[16]

This tender treatment of Lenin by Harding, Lewin and Cohen was until that point at variance with the image of him in the Soviet Union and other communist states, where there had always been a reluctance to give Lenin's economic thought precedence over his political, social, cultural, or foreign-policy thought. The official biography of Lenin as well as the official party history textbook steered clear of identifying or assessing the exact origins of his policies. The emphasis was constantly on Lenin's correctness and no effort was made to examine why he was consistently correct. Indeed, it was treated as political sacrilege to raise any such question. Since the mid 1920s, when his corpse was embalmed and put on display in a mausoleum on Red Square in Moscow, he was treated as if he were the founder of a great new faith. Party scholars were constrained to celebrate and venerate him. Children were indoctrinated with notions about his ineffable goodness. His pictures were in all offices. His statues were installed on main streets and great thoroughfares were renamed after him in every city. Lenin was to be regarded as a model of the perfect communist rather than subject to intrusive scholarly or political inquiry.

This is not to say that his image failed to undergo changes over the decades. Indeed successive party leaders frequently altered it according to their current political interests. In the late 1920s as Stalin mounted to ascendancy in the Politburo, he at first represented himself as a modest, loyal pupil of Lenin as contrasted with Trotsky, Kamenev, Zinoviev and

15 Neil Harding, *Lenin's Political Thought*, 2 vols. (London: Macmillan, 1977–81).
16 Moshe Lewin, *Lenin's Last Struggle* (London: Faber and Faber, 1969); Stephen F. Cohen, *Bukharin and the Russian Revolution: A Political Biography, 1888–1938* (New York: Vintage, 1975 [London: Wildwood House, 1974]).

Bukharin whom he charged with overweening pride and pretension. In the course of the 1930s and 1940s he upgraded his status as Lenin's worthiest successor who made his own original contributions to Marxism. But while encouraging a cult around himself, he maintained the Lenin cult.

The official Soviet interpretation of Lenin and Leninism ossified under Stalin and his collected works appeared in emasculated editions. After Stalin's death in 1953, Nikita Khrushchev called for a revivification of Lenin studies, and a fifth edition of the "full collection of works" as well as a new biography was produced.[17] The saga of the Lenin–Stalin dispute of 1922–23 was revealed and Stalin was denounced as a mass murderer. In truth it was not a full edition because many of Lenin's writings stayed under wraps at the central party archive, especially those which told of his zeal for terror during and after the civil war or of his close relationship with Trotsky, Kamenev, Zinoviev and Bukharin. A monocult of Lenin replaced the binary cult of Lenin and Stalin, and scholarly and media commentary remained within reverential limits. This situation prevailed in every respect after Khrushchev's fall from power in 1964 except that books tended to downplay the disagreements between Lenin and Stalin – the new party leader Leonid Brezhnev even toyed for a while with the idea of rehabilitating Stalin's reputation.

In 1985, when reforms began under Mikhail Gorbachev, Stalin was again denounced and Gorbachev called for a renovation of Soviet communism in line with Lenin's precepts. Gorbachev was a sincere admirer of Lenin, and increasingly he and his favored historians also concentrated on the ideas that Lenin was developing in 1922–23. A stream of hidden documents and memoirs flowed into public debate. Lenin was still eulogized as the greatest individual in the history of humankind, but he at least began to appear in a more believable psychological light than ever before in Soviet history. In Gorbachev's opinion, Lenin's deathbed writings adopted a democratic, gradualist approach to revolutionary change and spurned the terror-based and dictatorial features of his earlier doctrines and practices.[18] While genuinely believing in this version of the past, Gorbachev failed to confront the evidence that Lenin never really abandoned his commitment to dictatorship, terror and one-party rule.

17 Lenin, *Polnoe sobranie sochinenii.*
18 Mikhail Gorbachëv, *Perestroika i novoe myshlenie dlia nashei strany i dlia vsego mira* (Moscow: Politzdat, 1987).

When the USSR collapsed at the end of 1991, the gates were opened in Russia and the other successor states to analyses that identified Lenin and the October Revolution as an undiluted catastrophe for the country. President Boris Yeltsin castigated the years since 1917 as a "totalitarian nightmare," and his defense advisor and historian Dmitrii Volkogonov led the way in depicting Lenin as a misanthropic near-maniac. Yeltsin frequently contemplated Lenin's removal from his dedicated museum. Even the communist party started to consign Lenin to oblivion, although it was gentler in its treatment of Stalin.

Volkogonov's books were close in their analytical framework to that put forward earlier by Richard Pipes, and Volkogonov attained widespread popularity in Western countries.[19] Pipes's portrait of Lenin and the October Revolution was challenged by Robert Service who urged that it overlooked the complex intersection of ideological objectives, party-political constraints and licenses, and personality traits and circumstantial luck. Lenin in Service's depiction was error-prone as well as doctrinally driven and compelled to maneuver cleverly in pulling his party along with him – the difficulties in imposing the NEP on the Bolsheviks being a remarkable example. He never fully triumphed over those difficulties before he died. On the other hand, there were times, as in the October 1917 Revolution and the Brest-Litovsk controversy, when his handling of the party brought about outcomes which were less amenable to any kind of reversal. And about the deep long-term impact of such policies, in Russia and around the world, there can be little doubt.[20]

Whereas Volkogonov provided an account that postulated the misanthropic and fanatical essence of Lenin, there have been attempts in the UK and the USA to resume the theory-first approach initiated by Harding. Moira Donald argued that the primary intellectual influence on Lenin, after Marx and Engels, was their German follower and chief theoretician of the German Social Democratic Party, Karl Kautsky. Whereas Harding traced

19 Richard Pipes, "The Origins of Bolshevism: The Intellectual Evolution of Young Lenin," in Richard Pipes (ed.), *Revolutionary Russia* (Cambridge, MA: Harvard University Press, 1968), 28–62; Richard Pipes (ed.), *The Unknown Lenin: From the Secret Archive* (New Haven: Yale University Press, 1996); Dmitrii Volkogonov, *Lenin: politicheskii portret* (Moscow: Novosti, 1994) and *Lenin: Life and Legacy* (London: HarperCollins, 1994).

20 Robert Service, *Lenin: A Political Life*, 3 vols. (Basingstoke: Macmillan, 1985–95); Service, *Lenin: A Biography*.

a doctrinal lineage from Marx and Engels through Plekhanov to Lenin, Donald insisted that Kautsky rather than Plekhanov was the great lasting influence. What is more, she rejected the notion that Lenin emasculated Kautsky's thought in the process of incorporating it in his writings and speeches; and like Harding, she denied that the Russian agrarian-socialist terrorists of the late nineteenth century had a primary impact upon Lenin and his Bolshevism.[21]

Lars Lih took a somewhat different line of analysis while concurring that Lenin was uninfluenced by revolutionary thinkers other than Marxists. His main object was to highlight Lenin's attempt to provide a realistic strategy for the rising labor movement. Lih challenged any notion that Lenin displayed elitism in his attitude to the role of workers in the party.[22]

Lenin's frequent somersaults in policy have led to various interpretations of his career. Whereas Soviet spokespeople argued that Lenin changed in no fundamental respect except marginally insofar as he adapted to changing circumstances in Russia and the world, Pipes suggested that the stages of his career were so diverse that there was not one but several successive and different "Lenins," especially in the years around the turn of the century.[23] Harding countered this by arguing that Lenin's Marxism remained notably consistent in the early years and that the first big rupture in Lenin's thinking about revolutionary strategy occurred as late as 1914 – accordingly there were essentially two Lenins, or possibly three if his dictated deathbed notes are included.[24] As numerology entered the analysis, Service contended that there was only one Lenin and that the changes in his doctrines, policies and practice were secondary to a constancy in most of his basic attitudes and assumptions; and he challenged the idea, common enough from the 1970s onward in the West and from the late 1980s in the USSR, that Lenin's last articles changed anything very fundamental in his worldview.[25]

Lenin was controversial in his time and continues to provoke controversy today. Boris Yeltsin, Russia's first postcommunist president, mooted the

21 Moira Donald, *Marxism and Revolution: Karl Kautsky and the Russian Marxists, 1900–1924* (New Haven: Yale University Press, 1993).

22 Lars T. Lih, *Lenin Rediscovered: What Is To Be Done? In Context* (Boston: Brill, 2005).

23 Pipes, "The Origins of Bolshevism."

24 Harding, *Lenin's Political Thought*, vol. II, "Introduction."

25 Service, *Lenin: A Political Life*; Service, *Lenin: A Biography*.

possibility of moving his physical remains from the mausoleum on Red Square and burying him in the earth. This proposal was never fulfilled after Yeltsin's political popularity dipped and he decided to avoid courting unnecessary trouble for himself; and Vladimir Putin allowed the whole matter to fade from public discussion.

5

Bolshevik Roots of International Communism

LARS T. LIH

During the first decade of its existence, Bolshevism defined itself as the Russian branch of "revolutionary social democracy." The first step away from a mythologized to a historical understanding of the roots of world communism is to understand this self-definition. Prior to World War I, social democracy was an international workers' movement dedicated to achieving socialism and represented by political parties in most of the major "civilized" countries (primarily Western Europe, Russia, the USA and Japan). The present-day connotations of "social democracy" are misleading when talking about the outlook and reputation of social democracy before 1914. Prewar social democracy saw itself and was seen by others as a radical threat to the existing order.

The flagship party of social democracy was the *Sozialdemokratische Partei Deutschlands* (SPD). The SPD grew up in the 1870s and 1880s, and by the 1890s it had survived a period of intense government persecution to become the largest political party in Germany. By this time, a loose organization of national social-democratic parties called the Second International had risen up (the First International had been founded in the 1860s by Karl Marx and others). In the 1890s, a broad reformist current began to call for a revision of the traditional revolutionary rhetoric of social democracy (hence "revisionism"). Since there was now an explicitly nonrevolutionary wing of social democracy, the more orthodox and Marx-based wing began to call itself "revolutionary social democracy." The Russian Bolsheviks saw themselves as disciples of the West European revolutionary social democrats, whose works were eagerly translated into Russian. Karl Kautsky, the acknowledged spokesman for revolutionary social democracy, had so much prestige among the Bolsheviks that he can almost be called an honorary Bolshevik (until the outbreak of the world war in 1914, after which he was hated as a "renegade" as much as he was earlier admired).

Nevertheless, there were some fundamental contrasts between the situation in Western Europe and the situation faced by the Russian Bolsheviks. The West European social-democratic parties operated legally and enjoyed sufficient political freedom (freedom of speech, press, assembly) to carry out impressive agitational campaigns and to sustain a flourishing socialist press. The Russian Bolsheviks were forced to be creative as they adapted an inspiring foreign model to a very different political and social environment.

The Bolshevik party took power in Russia in October 1917, and this date constitutes a fundamental before-and-after watershed in the history of Bolshevism. The present chapter, an examination of Bolshevik outlook and practice, is therefore divided into two main sections: "Old Bolshevism" (before October 1917) and "State Bolshevism" (from October 1917 to Lenin's death in early 1924). Each section is further divided into four subsections corresponding to distinct aspects of Bolshevism: its class scenario, its transformational aims, its concept of the party's mission, and its view of the global context of revolution in the early twentieth century.

The most fundamental of the four aspects of Bolshevism is the *class scenario*, that is, its assessment of the social forces in Russia acting for and against revolution. The class scenario of Old Bolshevism was tested by the struggle for power in 1917 and afterwards, and – at least in the view of the Bolsheviks themselves – passed with flying colors. In contrast, the *transformational aims* of the revolution were very malleable: sometimes more ambitious, sometimes less so. In the years after October, Bolshevik spokesmen were ready to admit that the experience of power led to surprises and disappointments, so that many dreams of social transformation had to be deferred. Of all the four aspects, the *party mission* was the most strongly affected by the conquest of power, leading to the creation of a new political phenomenon, the party-state. Old Bolshevism had looked up to international social democracy and the German SPD in particular as models to emulate, while State Bolshevism presented itself as a model party to the entire world. The Bolshevik view of the *global context for revolution* also underwent a major change of perspective when the party found itself the head of a worldwide communist movement. Despite these major shifts in perspectives, there is an underlying continuity on all four levels, as the following pages will show.

Old Bolshevism (1904–1917)

Class Scenario

Before the Revolution of 1905, Russian social democrats asked themselves this question: What social forces in Russia are working *for* an anti-tsarist revolution, and which forces are working *against* it? The Revolution of 1905 itself was a vast popular upheaval that led to the introduction of a quasi-legislature (the state Duma), but it did not topple the tsar or lead to far-reaching social change. In the postrevolutionary period, the social democrats reframed their question: What does the experience of 1905 tell us about the social forces needed for a decisive repetition of 1905, one that would carry the revolution "to the end" (*do kontsa*), that is, accomplish all the transformational aims realistically possible?

Since they were committed Marxists, the Bolsheviks naturally framed their answers in the form of a class scenario: They identified the major classes in Russian society, assigned them class interests or motives for action, assessed the degree of their organization and awareness, and weighed the outcome of their future interactions. Some classes were completely predictable: The landowning gentry (*dvorianstvo*) would oppose a far-reaching revolution that included radical land reform, while the industrial workers would support it. All the more crucial was the role of what might be called the swing classes: the peasants and the liberal bourgeoisie.

According to the analysis worked out in greatest detail by Lenin in works such as *Two Tactics of Social Democracy in the Democratic Revolution* (1905), the peasants were potential supporters of a thoroughgoing revolution, since their land-hunger could only be satisfied by the removal of tsarism's chief social support, the landowning gentry. The liberal bourgeoisie were also supporters of an anti-tsarist revolution, since tsarist political backwardness hampered the emergence of a dynamic modern, "bourgeois" society. Due to their education, organization and position in society, the liberals saw themselves as the natural leaders of the anti-tsarist "liberation movement." According to the Bolshevik analysis, however, liberal leadership would make it impossible for the revolution to be carried out "to the end," because a thoroughgoing revolution of this type would damage bourgeois interests in all sorts of ways.

The implication of this reading of class motives was clear: The task of the socialist proletariat, organized and led by Russian social democracy, was itself to assume the role of revolutionary leadership. Leading the revolution meant enlisting the peasantry as supporters and thereby denying any peasant support to the liberals. It also meant establishing a temporary revolutionary government based on the workers and peasants that would beat back the inevitable tsarist counterrevolution and carry out basic transformational measures.

The Bolshevik revoutionary strategy can be contrasted with the class scenario of the other main wing of Russian social democracy, the Mensheviks. The Mensheviks argued that the revolution could only be carried out to its maximum possible extent if the proletariat were not isolated from the other progressive forces in society. For the Mensheviks, the peasantry could barely be counted as one of these progressive forces, since it was culturally backward, very unorganized and interested only in land. On the other hand, there was no inherent barrier to a de facto alliance with progressive "bourgeois" forces such as the liberals, because purely socialist and therefore divisive aims were not on the agenda. The Mensheviks warned the Bolsheviks not to scare off the liberal revolutionaries with over-radical rhetoric. The Bolsheviks retorted "don't try to frighten us by pointing to the frightened liberal." The Bolsheviks thought it was useless to try to keep the liberals onside, because they would be driven by class interest to cut short the revolution long before it had been carried out "to the end." The liberals would surely make some sort of deal or agreement (*soglashenie*) with the forces of the tsarist order, and any socialists who made an alliance or "agreement" with the liberals would end up indirectly supporting the counter-revolution. The accusation of *soglashatel'stvo* ("agreementism") became central to Bolshevik polemics in 1917.

The class scenario is the heart of Bolshevism. In the words of the Bolshevik Lev Kamenev, one crucial aspect of the class scenario of Old Bolshevism was the insistence that the proletariat should and would "raise all issues and all struggles to the level of *a struggle for the vlast*'" [Kamenev's emphasis].[1] *Vlast'* is often translated "power," but *vlast'* means something more than just the simple ability to get people to do what you want. A *vlast'* is rather the sovereign authority in a country, the final decision-making center with a monopoly of the legitimate use of coercion. Old Bolshevism envisioned only a temporary revolutionary government, not a permanent one, but it was already thinking in terms of state power.

1 Lev Kamenev, "Piat' let," in Lev Kamenev, *Mezhdu dvumia revoliutsiiami* [1910] (Moscow: Tsentrpoligraf, 2003), 587–96.

The Bolshevik class scenario was not only a pragmatic political strategy – just as important, it was a highly emotional, even romantic vision of class leadership of the Russian *narod* (the people, including both peasants and urban workers) by the socialist proletariat and its party. This quality is revealed by a succinct summary of the Bolshevik class scenario given in 1912 by Joseph Stalin (at the time a mid-level Bolshevik activist): The only way to obtain political freedom is through a "broad movement of the *narod*, led by the *vozhd* [leader] appointed by history for it, the socialist proletariat."[2]

Transformational Aims

The point of a revolution is to make possible some necessary or desirable transformation of social, political and economic institutions. Like all revolutionary social democrats of this era, prewar Bolsheviks were inspired by an image of a fully socialist society. According to the Marxist logic of history, a socialist society could only be achieved by a *particular class agent*, namely, the proletariat, who therefore had a world-historical mission to take state power and introduce socialism. The final goal – fully socialist society – lies at the end of a long and difficult journey. At each step of the way, some transitional goals will be urgent and others can be deferred. What is fundamental is not any particular goal, but rather *the very possibility of traveling down this path* – a possibility ultimately guaranteed by proletarian state power.

According to Marx, *only* the proletariat could carry out a socialist revolution. Nevertheless, many tasks vitally important for the ultimate success of the proletariat's mission could be carried out with other classes as allies. A basic assumption of revolutionary social democracy might be called "the axiom of the class ally." This axiom is stated concisely by Karl Kautsky in a highly influential 1906 article on Russian revolutionary dynamics: If circumstances are such that the proletariat can achieve revolutionary victory only with the help of another class, then, "as a victorious party, [the proletariat] will not be able to implement any more of its program than the interests of the class that supports the proletariat allow."[3]

2 I. V. Stalin, *Sochineniia*, vol. II (Moscow: Gosudarstvennoe Izdatel'stvo Politicheskoi Literatury, 1946), 213–18.

3 Karl Kautsky, "The Driving Forces of the Russian Revolution and Its Prospects," in Richard B. Day and Daniel Gaido (eds.), *Witnesses to Permanent Revolution: The Documentary Record* (Leiden: Brill, 2009), 567–608.

For both Kautsky and the Bolsheviks, the peasantry was an indispensable ally for the so-called democratic revolution in Russia, a revolution whose goals included overthrowing the tsar, uprooting all remnants of feudalism and serfdom in Russian society and setting up a democratic republic. These were necessary, exciting and ambitious goals – but they represented only the opening stage of the path to socialism. Thus the alliance with the peasantry simultaneously *enabled* the accomplishment of democratic goals and *prevented* the accomplishment of socialist goals. Nevertheless, the limits imposed by the peasant ally were *open-ended*, that is, no limits were set in advance that defined how far the peasants would follow the lead of the proletariat. The Bolshevik class scenario relied on a relatively optimistic reading of the peasantry as a class ally, in comparison to the situation in Western countries or to the assessment of the Russian Mensheviks.

From the point of view of revolutionary social democracy, *political freedom* – basic rights of speech, press, assembly and so forth – was an essential transitional goal. A party such as the German SPD was unthinkable without political freedom; according to Karl Kautsky, anyone who underestimated political freedom or who did not strive to attain it was an enemy of the proletariat. Strange as it may seem, given later developments, Lenin and the Bolsheviks completely agreed with Kautsky on this issue. Bolshevik agitational literature insisted on the benefits of political freedom and in fact paid considerably more attention to this issue than to evocations of the socialist utopia. An eloquent example is *To the Rural Poor*, a pamphlet Lenin wrote in 1903 to present the social-democratic message to the peasantry.

Mission of the Party

In the early 1930s, Joseph Stalin directly intervened in the writing of party history to insist that the Bolsheviks had always been a new type of party, with an organization and outlook in complete contrast to the other socialist parties in Russia and Western Europe. Cold War academic scholarship took up the theme of "a party of a new type," although of course with the value signs reversed. According to this academic consensus, Lenin rejected Western social democracy because he did not believe the workers were receptive to the revolutionary message. He therefore singlehandedly invented a new type of party – the vanguard party – in which membership was restricted to "professional revolutionaries" recruited from the intelligentsia.

Newer research takes more seriously the Bolshevik's self-description as the Russian branch of international revolutionary social democracy. Lenin and the Bolsheviks strongly believed in the party ideal that was embodied in the German SPD. They were prevented from imitating these ideals by repressive conditions in Russia, but so were all the other Russian socialist parties. As a result, the Bolsheviks were not very distinctive in organizational terms.

All European social-democratic parties were vanguard parties in the sense that they did not see their mission as simply reflecting the opinions of the working class as a whole, but rather as spreading the socialist message. Thus they recruited into the party only those whom they considered to be the elite of the working class, that is, workers who consciously accepted the socialist message and were willing to propagate it to their less enlightened comrades. These parties developed a range of innovative techniques for spreading the socialist "good news," such as an impressive socialist press, expertly staged mass rallies and a host of cultural societies, including socialist singing groups and sports teams. Taken together, these techniques can be called a permanent campaign in support of the socialist "good news."

Due to Russia's repressive conditions, the Russian socialist underground could only offer paltry imitations of the permanent campaign, relying on smuggled-in newspapers and clandestinely organized rallies. Only a very robust faith in the workers' receptivity to the social-democratic message could justify Lenin's hopes for the pivotal revolutionary role of the weak and vulnerable Russian underground. Also crucial to the successful functioning of the socialist underground was the *professional revolutionary*. Lenin put this term into circulation in his *What Is to Be Done?* (1902), but the movement as a whole immediately made it a central term in their vocabulary, because it corresponded to a reality that everyone recognized but that hitherto lacked a name. The role of the professional revolutionary was essentially to connect up local organizations both with each other and with overarching leadership bodies. Their job was to provide literature, give instruction and directives, and perhaps most important, give isolated local organizations a sense that they truly belonged to a greater whole, to a movement with a national and international dimension. This functional role was certainly not the brainchild of Lenin. On the contrary, it was the product of anonymous trial and error by a generation of Russian activists striving to apply the German model of a right and proper workers' party to the harsh conditions of tsarist Russia.

Global Context

The Bolsheviks did not pay special attention to the global context until the years preceding the outbreak of war in 1914. When they did adopt what could be called a global class scenario, they once again affirmed their identity as revolutionary social democrats by taking over a scenario that found its most eloquent expression in the writings of Karl Kautsky. According to Kautsky's account, the whole world was moving into a new era of wars and revolutions. All sorts of revolutions were simmering: socialist revolution in Western Europe, revolutions for national independence in Europe, anti-colonial revolutions in the rest of the world. These various revolutions were tightly interlocked, with war serving as a powerful catalyst. Russia had a special role to play in this complicated system of interaction, since its "democratic" anti-tsarist revolution would send shock waves in all directions: toward the "East" and its anti-colonial struggle as well as toward the "West" and its imminent socialist revolution. In turn, the proletarian revolution in Western Europe would (it was hoped) vastly accelerate Russia's own journey along the path to socialism.

In 1914, the West European social-democratic parties chose to support their own "bourgeois" governments rather than fight for revolution. The Bolshevik reaction to what they considered to be the betrayal of the Western Europe socialist parties was to declare the death of the Second International and to insist on the need for a new and purified International. They certainly did not repudiate their loyalty to revolutionary social democracy – rather, they reaffirmed it and condemned the other parties for their failure to live up to it. According to the Bolshevik diagnosis, the mistake of revolutionary social democracy was to believe it could coexist in one organization with the socialist "opportunists," that is, the reformist wing of the Second International.

In 1916, Lenin published a short book entitled *Imperialism: The Highest Stage of Capitalism*. Lenin made little claim to originality, since from his point of view his opponents were the ones who had shamefully betrayed the prewar consensus of revolutionary social democracy ("the views now held by Kautsky and his like are a complete renunciation of the same revolutionary principles of Marxism that he championed for decades").[4] Lenin's economic analysis served as underpinning for the following political conclusions: War is inevitable as long as capitalism exists; the present

4 V. I. Lenin, *Imperialism: The Highest Stage of Capitalism*, Preface to the French and German editions, www.marxists.org/archive/lenin/works/1916/imp-hsc/pref02.htm.

war was "imperialist" in its motivations and therefore revolutionary socialists should not choose sides; the economies of the imperialist countries had become highly centralized, thus demonstrating that conditions were ripe for a socialist revolution in Western Europe. All these political conclusions strengthened Lenin's case for a new and genuinely revolutionary Communist International.

State Bolshevism, 1917–1924

In October 1917, the Bolsheviks took over state power and did not relinquish it until 1991. Lenin became incapacitated in early 1923 and died in January 1924. By that time, the Bolsheviks had emerged bloody but unbowed from a civil war, made many shifts and compromises in economic policy, founded a new Socialist International and forged a new relationship between party and state.

Acquisition of state power increased the options open to the Bolsheviks in many ways, since they now had control over powerful means of coercion and the state bureaucracy. Possession of power also imposed heavy constraints. As a radical underground party or as a campaigning opposition party, the Bolsheviks were free to be ideologically rigid and to make all sorts of unfulfillable promises. As a governing party, they had to compromise, adapt to unpleasant realities and assume responsibility for unpopular policies. We will look at these contradictory effects in each of the four aspects of the Bolshevik outlook: the class forces they saw as friends and foes, the relation between transformational aims and actual state policies, the mission of a party now saddled with the burdens and opportunities of power and the translation of a global vision into practical foreign policy.

Class Scenario

The heart of the original Bolshevik class scenario was the assertion that only a worker/peasant *vlast'* (the energizing center of state power) could carry out the necessary tasks of the revolution to the end. The Bolsheviks now had their *vlast'*, and their first and overwhelming priority was to protect it – to ensure that it was not overthrown by counterrevolutionaries or that its essential class content was diluted. The question of the *vlast'* was thus an either/or affair: You either had it or you didn't. There was a striking contrast between this issue and the issue of how to carry out the aims of the revolution. As suggested by the metaphor of the path to socialism, policies of social transformation were a more-or-less affair. The Bolsheviks claimed to be on the only path that led to socialism, but they made no promises about the speed of the journey or about lack of detours.

The Bolsheviks were ready to justify violence that ensured the survival of the worker/peasant *vlast'*. In their readiness to use violence to defend a valued set of political institutions, the Bolsheviks can be compared to other "patriotic" defenders of national states. As Bolshevik spokesman Nikolai Bukharin announced, "we are for revolutionary violence ... The October revolution was violence of the workers, peasants and soldiers, against the bourgeoisie. And such violence against those who have oppressed millions of the toiling masses is not wrong – it is sacred."[5] In contrast, when it came to social transformation, there was much less motivation to resort to violence. There was little incentive to court unpopularity over policies that were not related directly to survival.

According to the Old Bolshevik class scenario, a thoroughgoing revolution required (a) political leadership by the socialist proletariat represented by the party, (b) mass support from the peasantry who saw the revolutionary *vlast'* as a defender of its basic gains and (c) denial of any possibility of political leadership to Russian elites. The Red Army is the most striking embodiment of this strategy. Who could have predicted that a gaggle of urban plebian extremists would put together and lead to victory an army manned by peasant recruits and officered by tsarist military professionals? The Red Army was the Bolshevik class scenario in action.

The vehicle for the class power of the workers and peasants was the soviets, a new made-in-Russia political institution. Soviets first sprang up during the 1905 Revolution as elective "councils" representing exclusively the working classes yet laying claim to various governmental tasks. After the fall of the tsar in early 1917, the soviets instantaneously reemerged in Petrograd (St. Petersburg, renamed during World War I), although the Petrograd Soviet also represented the overwhelming peasant rank and file of the tsarist army. During 1917, the Bolsheviks campaigned on a platform of "All Power to the Soviets!" (*vsia vlast' sovetam!*). After the October Revolution, the peasant countryside was also brought into a nationwide network of soviets.

5 Nikolai Bukharin, *Program of the Communists (Bolsheviks)* (1918); available online under the title *Programme of the World Revolution*, www.marxists.org/archive/bukharin/works/1918/worldrev/index.html.

Lenin himself had even greater ambitions for the soviets than just as a vehicle for class power in revolutionary Russia. During 1917, he wrote a book entitled *State and Revolution* that made the case for the soviets as the highest type of democracy with worldwide relevance, due to institutional features such as frequent reelections, massive participation of workers and peasants in governmental affairs, salary caps for officials and so forth. Soon after the Bolshevik conquest of power, the soviets lost most of their democratic vitality, due primarily to domination by a single party with a monopoly of political power. "Soviets" just became another word for "governmental institutions." Lenin and other Bolshevik leaders acknowledged this state of affairs in 1920, blamed the civil war and looked forward to "revitalizing" the soviets in peacetime.

Nevertheless, Soviet Russia could accurately be described as a "worker/peasant *vlast*'" in several crucial aspects. The whole stratum of landowners had been liquidated as a class, the former educated elite was completely barred from power, the new government institutions were increasingly staffed by workers and peasants, many of the policies of the new government aimed at gaining support from these classes (for example, mass literacy campaigns), and the workers and peasants were celebrated continually in song and story.

Policies toward the peasantry were the most crucial aspect of the Bolshevik class scenario, but they were also intimately tied up with the aims of the revolution, so discussion of these policies will be deferred for the moment. Next in importance was the Bolshevik attitude toward the *spetsy*, the newly coined term for "specialists," both military and civilian. In 1917, the Bolsheviks had railed against "agreementism" or cooperative coalition with Russian elites. But how could you hope to run a modern society without giving elites an independent voice? The Bolsheviks found a way to do this, at enormous cost: turn military, technical and organizational elites into *spetsy*, that is, individual specialists deprived of any political influence but willing to work under Bolshevik political direction.

On the side of the *spetsy*, we can trace an evolution on the part of the majority from the civil-service strikes and outright sabotage of the early days of the revolution to sullen cooperation, along with much more enthusiastic participation by a minority (although many of the former educated elites were permanently lost to Russia through death or emigration). The evolution on the Bolshevik side was also rocky, and most oppositional groupings within the party were worried that *spetsy* would gain too much influence and dilute the class content of the revolutionary *vlast'*: the left communists in early 1918, the military opposition in 1919, the democratic centralists in 1920 and the worker opposition in 1920–21.

The extent and direction of revolutionary violence was also determined by the class scenario. Bolshevik violence was institutionalized most visibly in the Cheka, the political police whose name was shorthand for Extraordinary Commission for the Struggle Against Counterrevolution, Sabotage and Speculation. The Cheka was only one source of the extraordinary violence from all quarters that inundated "Russia drenched with blood" (to use the title of a Soviet novel published in the 1920s).[6] Bolshevik violence was determined by the class scenario in three principal ways. First, the scenario mandated the defense by any means necessary of the survival of the worker/peasant *vlast'*. Second, the scenario identified friends and foes by class indicators, and those who were designated foes often became hapless targets of official and unofficial violence. Third, defense of the worker/peasant *vlast'* meant placing very heavy burdens on the workers and peasants themselves: army conscription, grain levies, long working hours under bad conditions, all amidst demoralizing economic breakdown. These burdens, even for a common cause, could not be enforced without heavy reliance on force.

The Bolsheviks had their hands full applying violence to ensure the survival of the worker/peasant *vlast'*. There were few resources left over to enforce grandiose aims of transformation, even without the official taboos against violence used in this way. From the point of view of the Bolsheviks, violence and terror were protective policies forced on them by enemies determined to destroy the worker/peasant *vlast'*. Nevertheless, these policies were responsible for one of the new and unexpected features of Soviet power: the complete lack of any independent political and social life. No rival political party, no social organization genuinely free of state direction, was allowed to survive, since they were seen as potential threats to the beleaguered worker/peasant *vlast'*.

Transformational Aims

In late 1920, Bolshevik leader Leon Trotsky gave a speech on the occasion of the third anniversary of the October Revolution. His remarks eloquently reveal the distinction made by Bolsheviks between the class scenario and

6 Artem Veselyi, *Rossiia, krov'iu umytaia: roman; fragment* (Moscow: Khudozhestvennaia literatura, 1990; original complete publication 1932).

transformational aims. From the point of view of class power, the three years since the revolution was a story of heroic if hard-fought victory. From the point of view of transformational aims, the same period represented a tragic deferral of revolutionary dreams:

> We went into this struggle with magnificent ideals, with magnificent enthusiasm, and it seemed to many people that the promised land of communist fraternity, the flowering not only of material but spiritual life, was much closer than it has actually turned out to be ... Three years have gone by – three years, during which the whole world of our enemies tried to hurl us back across that fateful historical threshold we had crossed ... We stood firm, we defended the first worker and peasant state *vlast'* in the world ... If back then, three years ago, we were given the opportunity of looking ahead, we would not have believed our eyes. We would not have believed that three years after the proletarian revolution it would be so hard for us, so harsh to be living on this earth.[7]

Trotsky's attitude reflected a Bolshevik consensus. This fact needs to be stressed, because the older scholarship paints a very different picture. According to these scholars, the Bolsheviks started off with moderate policies in early 1918 and then became more and more radical in their transformational aims. By 1920, the Bolsheviks were in a veritable state of "euphoria" (a term often found in scholarly accounts) about "war communism," that is, the system of harsh economic measures put in place to support the war effort and combat the economic crisis; they identified such measures as "shortcuts to communism" or even communism itself. Only after the legalization of free trade in grain in spring 1921 did the Bolsheviks realize that ruined, devastated Russia was not the socialist paradise. "Silently, with a heavy heart, Bolshevism parted with its dream of war communism."[8]

The reality is quite different. The Bolsheviks in power started off with the hope of "gradual but unremitting" steps toward socialism, but very rapidly became aware that the deepening crisis was forcing retreats, compromises and detours. This necessity did not please the Bolsheviks, but it also did not threaten their inner self-identification. The survival

7 L. Trotsky, "Tri goda bor'by i ucheby," in L. Trotsky, *Sochineniia*, vol. XVII, part 2 (orig. Moscow 1926), www.magister.msk.ru/library/trotsky/trotl820.htm.

8 Isaac Deutscher, *The Prophet Armed: Trotsky, 1879–1921* (Oxford: Oxford University Press, 1954), 514. According to Robert Conquest, "grain procurement by force ... was regarded by the Party, from Lenin down, as not merely socialism, but even communism": Robert Conquest, *The Harvest of Sorrow: Soviet Collectivization and the Terror-Famine* (New York: Oxford University Press, 1986), 48.

of the worker/peasant *vlast'* was the essential task, while the path to socialist transformation was always seen as a more-or-less affair. Neither in 1920 nor earlier did the Bolsheviks experience any particular euphoria about achieved social transformation nor did they have hallucinatory illusions about a leap into communism. The introduction of the New Economic Policy (NEP) in 1921 was not a sharp turnaround but another detour of the same type as previously. The real turning-point was in 1923–24 when the worst of the crisis was over and real decisions had to be made about the further course of socialist transformation. The evolution of Bolshevik policy can be illustrated by looking at the crucial issue of the peasantry.

The Bolsheviks and the Peasants

The peasants were the central issue for the Bolsheviks after 1917, not only because they were the large majority of the nation, but because they constituted the link between the Bolshevik class scenario and their transformational aims. Any claim to be traveling toward socialism, at whatever speed or degree of directness, required some sort of rationale that explained the role of the peasant. According to the axiom of the class ally, the proletariat could only go so far along the path to socialism as permitted by the perceived class interests of any necessary class ally. The Old Bolshevik class scenario assumed that the peasantry as a whole supported "democratic" aims but not "socialist" ones. The Bolsheviks never rejected the axiom of the class ally or the necessity of majority support. Within these constraints, there were two possible ways the class scenario could envision peasant support for socialist as well as democratic aims:

(a) *Class differentiation.* The peasantry breaks up into proto-bourgeois exploiters and proto-proletarian wage workers. Stimulated by the economic crisis, the landless peasants (*batraki*) forge ahead with advanced forms of collective agricultural production such as communes or *sovkhozy* ("state farms" based on landowner estates and run by local poor peasants).

(b) *Class leadership.* Just as the proletariat had earlier convinced the peasants that democratic revolution would benefit them, it could now convince them that they would be benefited by various steps toward socialism carried out by the worker/peasant *vlast'*. Tractors, electrification and efficient state regulation could bring a majority of the peasants on board, even without significant class differentiation.

Both these possible solutions were well within the logic and spirit of the Bolshevik class scenario, if only certain adjustments were made in the empirical reading of the situation. Both potential strategies were adumbrated by Lenin after his return to Russia in spring 1917, and both were tried out. The first one failed, was seen to fail and was decisively rejected for the short and medium term. The other became the beacon of Bolshevik peasant policy and was enshrined in Lenin's final articles of early 1923.

In Lenin's April Theses of 1917, he revealed his hopes for progress toward socialism based on class differentiation when he called for special soviets for *batraki* (landless agricultural workers) and for model farms run by such soviets. In spring 1918, the Bolsheviks fanned the flames of class war in the villages by creating Committees of the Poor (*kombedy*) restricted to poor peasants. The *kombedy* were given the very practical tasks of creating a foothold for Soviet power in the villages and ensuring that rich peasants were forced to provide grain quotas, but Lenin himself viewed them from the perspective of his hopes for peasant class differentiation. In the summer and fall of 1918, he stated that the Russian Revolution was entering a new phase: For the first time it could be called truly socialist, since the peasantry was dividing along class lines. Lenin's hopes were ironic, because the party as a whole was already moving away from any practical reliance on class war in the villages.

At the beginning of 1919, Lenin was still very hopeful that peasant communes and the state farms (*sovkhozy*) set up on former landowner estates would reveal the advantages of collective production. By the end of the year, however, he was completely disillusioned by these experiments and asserted that peasants were completely justified in scorning them. At the same time, he insisted in the strongest terms that any coercion used to create communes and the like was an absurd outrage. Thus by the beginning of 1920 – a year before the introduction of the NEP – the class differentiation strategy for putting Russia on the path to socialism had been decisively abandoned in the short and medium term.

In contrast to these abortive policies was the class leadership strategy, one that was based even more squarely on the Old Bolshevik class scenario: leading the peasant majority down the path to socialism by demonstrating the advantages of socialism for the peasantry and the economy as a whole. The germ of this strategy can also be found in some of Lenin's pronouncements of spring 1917; he argued that measures such as nationalization of the banks were not only steps toward socialism but also would receive immediate peasant support. In order for this strategy to become mainstream policy, however, a shift in Bolshevik perception of the peasantry had to take place.

This shift, which can be called "the rise of the middle peasant," is one of the unreported stories of the civil war. It took place primarily in the second half of 1918 and the first half of 1919, and it was originally motivated by practical searches for solutions to difficult policy problems such as ensuring grain supply. Instead of focusing on what they thought the peasants would *become* (rural capitalists and proletarians), the Bolsheviks sought a *modus vivendi* with the "middle peasant," that is, the peasant-as-such, the small landowning communal peasant who was going to be around for a long time. Prior to spring 1918, even the term "middle peasant" was barely present in Bolshevik discourse. In spring 1919, a much ballyhooed "turn to the middle peasant" was trumpeted at the Eighth Party Congress.

This discursive shift was reflected in policy changes. In late 1918, the *kombedy* were disbanded. Demands for grain from the villages remained very high and burdensome, but for that very reason the Bolsheviks tried to find methods of working *with* village institutions instead of splitting them (the so-called *raverstka* method). At the end of 1920, debates around the creation of village "sowing committees" to help combat the famine showed a striking contrast with the outlook of 1918. The Bolsheviks now openly made a wager on "the industrious owner" (*staratelnyi khoziain*) and rejected the "loafer" (*lodyr'*). They explicitly based agricultural policy on the long-term predominance of peasant farms as opposed to communes and state farms.

The original class scenario predicted that the peasantry as a whole would support the revolution and allow it to successfully defend itself against its enemies. According to the class scenario as amended by the civil war experience, it was the middle peasant who provided this crucial support. Looking back in 1920, Bolshevik spokesman Yevgenii Preobrazhenskii wrote that in summer 1918, when the rich peasants who originally supported the revolution became disenchanted, the whole fate of the revolution depended on the choice of the middle peasant.

> Over the whole course of the civil war, the middle peasantry did not go along with the proletariat with a firm tread. It wavered more than once, especially when faced with new conditions and new burdens; more than once it moved in the direction of its class enemies. [But] the worker/peasant state, built on the foundation of an alliance of the proletariat with 80% of the peasantry, already cannot have any competitors for the *vlast'* inside the boundaries of Russia.[9]

9 Yevgenii Preobrazhenskii, "Social Base of the October Revolution," *Pravda* (7 Nov. 1920).

After Preobrazhenskii wrote his article in late 1920, the Bolsheviks undertook one more major attempt at accommodation with the peasant majority: the introduction in spring 1921 of the NEP. The effective end of the civil war in late 1920 meant that the burdens and restrictions of the civil war were no longer justifiable in the eyes of both peasants and workers – and, from the point of view of the party, the same circumstance allowed the state to take the risk of losing control of the grain supply. Widespread peasant rebellions and worker discontent in early 1921 brought the point home to the Bolsheviks. In response, they introduced the first of many policy changes associated with the NEP: the temporary dismantling of state-organized exchange (the grain monopoly), with a concomitant decriminalization of a free market trade in grain.

Looking back over events since October 1917, we see that whenever forced to choose between socialist ideals and peasant support, the Bolshevik chose peasant support. Immediately after the October Revolution, they gained peasant support by letting the peasants break up large estates (much to the scorn of Western socialists, who saw the breakup of large production units as economic regression). In 1919, they moved away from "class war in the villages" to an accommodation with "middle peasants." In 1920, they based long-term agricultural policy on small-scale peasant agriculture rather than socialist experiments. In 1921, they retreated further by allowing free trade in grain.

The Bolsheviks certainly did not give up on their socialist goals, but they now hoped to attain them via class leadership of the peasant majority. The peasants would now be lured down the path to socialism by advantages coming from socialist industry such as tractors and electrification. In late 1920 (that is, prior to the NEP), Lenin came up with a famous slogan that encapsulated this strategy: "Communism is Soviet power plus electrification of the whole country."[10] This theme of partnership with the peasants in socialist construction is still prominent in Lenin's final writings of 1923, particularly "On Cooperation."[11]

The class leadership strategy animated the idea of "socialism in one country" that became party dogma shortly after Lenin's death. In one respect, "socialism in one country" contradicted the prewar class scenario

10 Speech of 21 Nov. 1920: V. I. Lenin, "Our Foreign and Domestic Position and Party Tasks," www.marxists.org/archive/lenin/works/1920/nov/21.htm. This speech illustrates many of the themes of the present chapter.

11 V. I. Lenin, "On Cooperation," www.marxists.org/archive/lenin/works/1923/jan/06.htm.

that saw the peasantry as a roadblock on the road to socialism. But the distinctive aspect of the prewar Bolshevik scenario was not this assumption, but rather the idea of *open-ended* class leadership of the peasantry by the socialist proletariat. Because of this, the Bolsheviks were able to gradually convince themselves that there were no limits to how far the peasants could travel down the road to socialism, given proper leadership.

Mission of the Party

The conquest of power led to fundamental changes in the party's sense of itself as well as its internal organization. Control of the state was an unprecedented experience not only for the Bolsheviks but for any socialist party. One result was the unexpected and innovative institution of the party-state, in which one party monopolized political life by outlawing any potential rivals and also amalgamated with state institutions at all levels.

A central cause of this outcome was the sudden disappearance of "the historic *vlast'*," that is, the Romanov dynasty that had ruled Russia for more than three hundred years. The collapse of this dynasty during the February Revolution meant the absence of any legitimate authority at all. All candidates for a new *vlast'* – Provisional Government, Constituent Assembly, the various White governments, peasant rebels and the Bolsheviks – had to answer the insistent question: Why should anyone obey your orders? The Russian Revolution and its aftermath should therefore be seen under the aegis not of Marx (class mission) or of Locke (consent of the governed), but of Hobbes (urgent need for a single, uncontested sovereign authority).

A successful candidate for creating a new *vlast'* had to pass a number of tests. Did it possess a confident sense of mission, have a secure social base in the population, control sufficient coercive power to enforce its will and to ward off rivals, have the ability to maintain organizational integrity on a national scale and – not least! – demonstrate a minimum of governmental competence? One by one, the other contenders failed to meet one or all of these tests. The Bolshevik party had a sense of mission and a strong base in the proletariat; the class scenario pointed the way to parley these into control over the ultimate means of coercion in the form of the Red Army, and they had little compunction about applying coercion.

The Bolshevik experience in the socialist underground gave them the capacity for maintaining organizational integrity under very trying circumstances. When we read about the party congresses after the revolution, we should remember to be amazed that the Bolsheviks knew how to use congresses to keep a nationwide organization together. The greatest challenge facing this disparate group of ex-professional revolutionaries was governmental competence. We have already seen the basic solution to this challenge: enlisting military and civilian *spetsy* and using their technical skills without allowing even the slightest political autonomy. This strategy led to an inherent tension between party and state, since the party felt it must act as watchdog at all levels over a bureaucracy that they fundamentally did not trust.

The party's new status as arbiter of the state meant a drastic change in the party's internal life. The freewheeling debates and groupings of prewar Bolshevism shifted fairly rapidly to a new emphasis on monolithic unity and strict disciplined centralism. The new party norms were encapsulated in the "anti-faction resolution" passed by the Tenth Party Congress in early 1921 that also introduced the NEP. Although occasioned by specific party disputes, the anti-faction resolution sprang more fundamentally from the realization that a party so deeply involved in the everyday life of the state and so worried about presenting a united front in the face of hostile forces could not afford the luxury of "factionalism," that is, genuine internal debate. Along with factionalism many other features of healthy party life were lost.

These profound changes led to a decided shift in the meaning of the party organizational norm "democratic centralism." Before the revolution, the emphasis of the term was "*democratic* centralism": It expressed an aspiration toward democratic control from below that was admittedly not possible in an underground organization. Accordingly, in the eyes of party activists, "democratic centralism" was only really applied in the times when the party had legal status but was not yet in power: 1905–07 and 1917. Only after the conquest of power did tightly disciplined centralism of the type we associate with communist parties become both possible and necessary. Under these circumstances, the emphasis in party usage now became "democratic *centralism.*"

One core feature of the mission of revolutionary social democracy had always been spreading the message through the various techniques we earlier described as "the permanent campaign." The Bolsheviks remained true to this sense of mission after the conquest of power, but it now had radically different policy consequences. Before the revolution, the Bolsheviks were determined fighters for the political freedom that would allow them to mount the campaigns, rallies, agitational pamphlets, press and cultural societies that parties like the SPD employed to spread the message in a hostile environment. After the conquest of power, the Bolsheviks relied on the same techniques as before, but now backed up with state resources. One of these state resources was coercive prohibition of any messages coming from hostile sources. Thus, the same old goal of spreading the good word made the Bolsheviks champions of what might be called "state monopoly campaignism," and therefore enemies of political freedom. Much of what we associate with a totalitarian "propaganda state" – the incessant campaigns, the ubiquitous "agitprop" – had its roots in the innovative practice of prewar social democracy, but now applied without any limit or rival.[12]

Global Context

In 1917, Bolshevik spokesmen said quite explicitly that the Russian Revolution was doomed to defeat unless there was a corresponding socialist revolution in Europe. The years immediately following the October conquest of power brought a big disappointment and a big surprise: No successful revolution occurred in Western Europe nor was likely to occur in the foreseeable future, yet Soviet power survived nevertheless.

One of the Bolsheviks' primary goals after October 1917 was to create the new, opportunist-free International of their dreams. The meaning of the new International in Bolshevik eyes was profoundly modified as the revolutionary fever chart rose and fell. There was no immediate revolutionary response to the October Revolution in Europe, forcing the Bolsheviks to sign the oppressive Brest-Litovsk treaty with Germany in early 1918. Nevertheless, the Bolsheviks had not yet lost their optimistic hopes for European revolution and they were overjoyed with the November Revolution in Germany in late 1918. Their high expectations were not seriously compromised by the crushing of the Spartacist revolt in Germany in January 1919, and they hastily proceeded to organize the founding congress of the new Third or Communist International (Comintern). The title "communist" both here and in the new official title of the Bolshevik party was a deliberate rejection of the term "social democracy," yet for all that, the renaming was an *affirmation*, not a rejection, of what prewar revolutionary social democracy had once stood for in Bolshevik eyes.

12 See Peter Kenez, *The Birth of the Propaganda State: Soviet Methods of Mass Mobilization, 1917–1929* (Cambridge: Cambridge University Press, 1985).

The Comintern had been founded in the expectation of an imminent revolutionary outbreak. The hastily improvised First Congress in 1919 represented only small isolated parties who nevertheless felt that a massive tide of world revolution was carrying them forward. The confident predictions of world revolution made by Bolshevik leaders in spring 1919 were quickly and profoundly disappointed. The crucial turning-point in the Bolshevik outlook came in August 1919 with the collapse of the Hungarian Revolution. After that failure, Bolshevik leaders no longer promised their constituency in Russia that an international revolution would soon solve their problems.

The Second Congress of the Comintern in summer 1920 was a more substantial and representative affair, yet already the Bolshevik leaders realized that there no longer existed a direct revolutionary situation comparable to Russia in 1917. The new International was forced to come to grips with the same challenge that had faced the old one: how to be a revolutionary party in a nonrevolutionary situation. Just for this reason, the Second Congress spent much time in drafting rules for maintaining revolutionary purity. These were the famous "Twenty-One Conditions" that had to be accepted by any party wishing to join the new International. The Comintern congresses that followed (the Third in 1921 and the Fourth in 1922) further registered the cooling of expectations for revolution any time soon.

As the expectations for immediate revolution died down, the foreign policy of Soviet power was governed less by the global class scenario and more by the standard concerns of state security and prosperity. The Bolsheviks certainly did not lose their hopes for world revolution, but we can perceive a steady shift of world communism's center of gravity from Western Europe to the global "East," that is, to colonies and ex-colonies from Egypt to China. A concrete sign of this shift was the Congress of the Peoples of the East that took place in Baku in late 1920. In the last article published by Lenin before his incapacitating stroke in March 1923, he comforted himself that "The outcome of the struggle will be determined by the fact that Russia, India, China, etc., account for the overwhelming population of the globe . . . In this sense, the complete victory of socialism is fully and absolutely assured."[13]

13 V. I. Lenin, "Better Fewer, but Better," www.marxists.org/archive/lenin/works/1923/mar/02.htm.

Looking back at the trajectory of the four levels of the Bolshevik outlook, we can see an underlying unity despite dramatic shifts along the way. The heart of the Bolshevik class scenario was the image of the socialist proletariat and its party as leaders of the peasantry down the path that would eventually lead to full socialism. The Bolsheviks saw both the civil war and the peacetime economy as examples of this leadership. Dreams of socialist transformation were never abandoned, but they were consciously deferred both during the civil war and during the NEP.

The remaining two levels had more of a direct impact on the world communist movement, since this movement was defined by its acceptance of the Russian Bolshevik party as a model. Communist parties in power reproduced the party-state and the "state monopoly campaignism" pioneered by the Bolsheviks. The ideal of a centralized, opportunist-free International in an era of war and revolutions remained potent even after postwar stabilization in Europe. The shift of world communism away from Western Europe toward the global "East" was already noticeable in the first years of the new International.

Bibliographical Essay

A firm grasp of revolutionary social democracy and the SPD model is necessary for any student of Bolshevism. Standard works in English are Vernon Lidtke, *The Alternative Culture: Socialist Labor in Imperial Germany* (New York: Oxford University Press, 1985); Gary Steenson, *"Not One Man! Not One Penny!" German Social Democracy, 1863–1914* (Pittsburgh: University of Pittsburgh Press, 1981); Carl Schorske, *German Social Democracy, 1905–1917: The Development of the Great Schism* (Cambridge, MA: Harvard University Press, 1970); and Kevin J. Callahan, *Demonstration Culture: European Socialism and the Second International, 1889–1914* (Leicester: Troubador Publishing, 2010). More and more of the works of Karl Kautsky are becoming available in English. Fundamental to understanding the Bolshevik class scenario is Kautsky's 1906 article "The Driving Forces of the Russian Revolution and Its Prospects"; this seminal text can be read in Richard B. Day and Daniel Gaido (eds.), *Witnesses to Permanent Revolution* (Leiden: Brill, 2009), 567–608, along with commentaries by Lenin and Trotsky (the young Stalin also wrote one). Lenin greatly admired Kautsky's 1909 book *The Road to Power* (Chicago: Bloch, 1909) even after he considered Kautsky as a political enemy. Kautsky's views on the global context of revolution and their impact on the Bolsheviks is set forth in Lars

T. Lih, "'A New Era of War and Revolution': Lenin, Kautsky, Hegel and the Outbreak of World War I," in Alexander Anievas (ed.), *Cataclysm 1914: The First World War and the Making of Modern World Politics* (Leiden: Brill, 2014), 366–412.

The best way to get a feel for the Bolshevik outlook is to read their writings and speeches. Lenin is of course fundamental, but other Bolshevik writers are often more representative of the Bolshevik movement as a whole. Lenin's most famous works are discussed briefly in this chapter (*To the Rural Poor, What Is To Be Done?, Two Tactics, Imperialism, State and Revolution,* "On Cooperation"), but often he is more revealing in his speeches, especially during the years in power. His addresses to party audiences each year on the anniversary of the revolution are particularly instructive. Anthologies of his writings include Robert C. Tucker, *The Lenin Anthology* (New York: Norton, 1975), and Paul Le Blanc (ed.), *Revolution, Democracy, Socialism: Selected Writings of V. I. Lenin* (London: Pluto, 2008) (each contains an important introduction).

The website Marxists Internet Archive has extensive English-language texts for a wide range of Bolshevik writers. An underused source for Old Bolshevism is the first three volumes of Stalin's *Collected Works*: try to think of him as just a typical Bolshevik propagandist rather than a future dictator. Trotsky's writings from 1917 to 1921 often give a different impression than the retrospective picture found in his later writings. Zinoviev's *History of the Bolshevik Party* (1924) tells the story of Old Bolshevism from the point of view of Lenin's closest lieutenant. A four-hour speech Zinoviev gave in late 1920 in Halle has recently been translated in Ben Lewis and Lars T. Lih (eds.), *Zinoviev and Martov: Head to Head in Halle* (London: November Publications, 2011); Zinoviev's remarks on this occasion throw much light on the rapidly evolving Bolshevik view of the global context as well as on domestic policy (Zinoviev is far from "euphoric"). Nikolai Bukharin's *Program of the Communist Party* (1918) and *The ABC of Communism* (1920) that he co-authored with Yevgenii Preobrazhenskii were semi-official statements of the ambitious Bolshevik aims and the results achieved to date. The essential reading for the early years of the Communist International are the series of Congress proceedings edited by John Riddell.

The views set forth here about the Bolshevik outlook are thoroughly documented in Lars T. Lih, *Lenin Rediscovered: What Is to Be Done? In Context* (Leiden: Brill, 2006) and *Deferred Dreams* (forthcoming); both books have a full review of the relevant literature. A thankfully shorter overview is Lars T. Lih, *Lenin* (London: Reaktion Books, 2011). Representative Cold War interpretations of Bolshevism are Alfred Meyer, *Leninism* (New York: Praeger, 1962), and Martin Malia, *The Soviet Tragedy: A History of Socialism in Russia, 1917–1991* (New York: Free Press, 1994); a more idiosyncratic reading can be found in Neil Harding, *Leninism* (Basingstoke: Macmillan, 1996). Besides the ongoing series from Alexander Rabinowitch about the Bolsheviks in Petrograd, recent scholarship has little to say about Bolshevism per se. The exceptions to this observation are excellent biographies of lesser-known Bolsheviks. A recent example is Barbara Allen, *Alexander Shlyapnikov, 1885–1937: Life of an Old Bolshevik* (Leiden: Brill, 2015); a biography of Mikhail Tomskii by Charters Wynn is in preparation.

6

Stalin as Historical Personality

JAMES HARRIS

Controversy will always surround the figure of Joseph Stalin. In his tenure as general secretary of the Soviet Communist Party, he directed an extraordinary transformation of the USSR. He took charge of a largely illiterate, peasant society barely out of feudalism and devastated by foreign invasion and civil war. In the nearly thirty years of his tenure, the Soviet Union became a military and economic superpower. It almost single-handedly defeated Europe's greatest army in World War II. It came to lead the world in major categories of heavy industrial production. Soviet science, culture and sport won international recognition. The Soviet developmental model was adopted in Asia, Africa and the Americas. But this transformation was obtained by callously violent means. Millions of peasants died in the process of the collectivization of agriculture and famine induced by excessive state grain collections. The rapid pace of industrialization was achieved by means of suppressing living standards. The revolutionary state that had promised the liberation of working people from exploitation became a hypercentralized dictatorship prone to react with extreme violence to the slightest whiff of dissent. A network of concentration camps known as the Gulag expanded rapidly through the 1930s. Between 1936 and 1938, in a period commonly known as the Great Terror, the regime summarily executed three-quarters of a million people, and incarcerated over a million more in the Gulag. It is impossible to establish a precise figure, but Stalin's regime was directly and indirectly responsible for tens of millions of deaths.

What was Stalin's role in all this? To what extent can the achievements and the suffering of the Soviet interwar period be attributed to him alone? Did Stalin single-handedly strangle the democratic, liberationist strains of Bolshevism to create a personal dictatorship? Did the violent change of the period derive from defects in Stalin's personality? The answers are far from straightforward. For many historians, and much of the general public, Stalin is understood simply as a monster, driven by a lust for power and a paranoid fear of opposition to his emerging personal dictatorship. We can surely agree that Stalin was not a good man, but the focus on one individual, however successfully he concentrated political power, oversimplifies complex historical and moral issues. He certainly accumulated extraordinary personal power. He came to exercise it with a high degree of autonomy, but in the twenty-five years we have had access to party and state archives, we have surely now established that he did not act alone. Stalin was not particularly unique among his Bolshevik peers. They were not pacifists. For the most part, they were prepared to resort to extreme violence in defense of the revolution. And very few Bolsheviks were committed democrats. As a leader, Stalin was not a seeker of consensus, but the party membership did not expect to be consulted in affairs of state. If we seek to understand the violent transformation of the USSR in the 1920s and 1930s, focusing on the psychopathology of the leader will necessarily provide incomplete answers. Stalin was not a devil among angels. He was not a radical among moderates. The emergence of his personal dictatorship, and the extremely violent exercise of power, needs to be understood in its social, cultural and political context. The object of this chapter is to draw a sketch of that context.

For many years, psychohistory was the pith of the Stalin biography and the core of the "monster" narrative: The beatings young Stalin received at the hands of his drunkard father made him heartless and cruel; the results of childhood illness and accidents – his pockmarked face, withered hand and limp – made him the object of mockery among his early peers and instilled in him a deep memory for slights and a deep impulse to exact revenge; his modest origins contrasted with those of much of the early Bolshevik intellectual elite and this drove him to try and better them by devious means.[1] Most recent work has abandoned this approach. In many respects, Stalin's childhood was a happy one. There is no particular reason to conclude that his relationship with his parents was troubled. Indeed, they and the extended family went to great lengths to further his education and open opportunities for advancement. Stalin was an excellent student, and never lost his love of learning. There was no particular reason for him to feel insecure in the company of Bolshevik intellectuals. He was ambitious and capable, and as

1 The most influential of the early biographies was that of Stalin's arch-enemy Leon Trotsky, *Stalin: An Appraisal of the Man and His Influence* (New York: Harper and Brothers, 1941).

he was drawn into the social-democratic movement, it should come as little surprise that he would rise rapidly in the ranks of the Bolsheviks.[2] In short, historians are no longer inclined to look for explanations of the peculiar outcomes of interwar Soviet history – the origins and nature of Stalinism – in the youth of the future dictator.

There are other common images of Stalin that have fallen into disuse. In his account of the Russian Revolution, the Menshevik Nikolai Sukhanov referred to Stalin as a "grey blur, looking up now and then dimly and not leaving any trace."[3] The tendency, reinforced by Trotsky's writings, was to portray Stalin as a mediocrity, a creature of the bureaucracy, who pulled levers behind the scenes while much greater men acted out the revolution. He was publishing articles and pamphlets in aid of the social-democratic movement from the age of twenty-three in 1901.[4] He played a role in the revolutionary movement in the Caucasus, and participated in party congresses in Finland (1905), Stockholm (1906) and London (1907). At that stage he was by no means in the front rank of the movement. He never lived or worked among the social-democratic grandees in foreign exile, but it was enough that in 1912, Lenin drew him into the Bolshevik Central Committee. After the February Revolution, Stalin was at the center of events in the capital. His rise to the front rank of the movement can in part be attributed to his loyalty to Lenin at a time when planning for the October coup was fraught with controversy. But Stalin was also valued for his skills as a writer, and perhaps more significantly for his organizational skills, which were particularly valuable given the extraordinary scope of Bolshevik ambitions in a period of political and social chaos.

In revolution and civil war, Stalin did not have a dramatic and romantic role like Trotsky, forming and leading the Red Army. His military record on the southern front and the Soviet–Polish war was mixed at best.[5] Rather, he continued to distinguish himself for his efforts to forge a functioning network of new state institutions to govern the expanding territory under Bolshevik control. The experience made him a strict centralist. At the time of the October Revolution, the Bolsheviks did not have

2 See for example Robert Service, *Stalin: A Biography* (Basingstoke: Macmillan, 2004).

3 Nikolai N. Sukhanov, *The Russian Revolution, 1917: An Eyewitness Account*, vol. I (New York: Harper Torchbooks, 1962), 230.

4 See I. V. Stalin, *Sochineniia*, vol. I (Moscow: Gosizdat, 1951).

5 When Kliment Voroshilov asked Stalin's permission to publish the leader's "military writings," Stalin flatly refused. At least in the mid 1930s, he preferred not to draw attention to that part of his career.

a coherent vision of how to organize a functioning government. How should the central state apparatus be organized? How should it represent local soviets? How should the economy be managed? There was a desperate shortage of needed skills at all levels, and the lack of clarity in administrative functions often led to total breakdown of local government. In the sessions of a constitutional commission established by Sovnarkom in late March 1918, the left Socialist Revolutionary (SR) participants were keen to establish that the new constitution should enshrine the principle of proletarian participation from below through the soviets. The Bolsheviks on the commission shared Stalin's concerns that the SR plan proposed by M. A. Reisner would "make permanent the confusion and disorder that currently predominates in cities and provinces, and lead to the absolute collapse of any power. Right now we need a strong, muscular power."[6] In the end, the first Soviet constitution said more about the responsibilities of the people to the state, than the state to the people, and was devoted largely to defining the roles of institutions from the bottom to the top of the administrative pyramid.[7]

The 1918 constitution may have helped, but it did bring order to Soviet governance. Much of the small pool of Bolshevik administrative talent was drawn into the Red Army to fight the civil war. Then, as the war drew to a close, Bolshevik forces were transferred to civilian duties, but because their numbers had been seriously affected by wartime losses, and because the boundaries of the new state were expanding tremendously, they were spread very thinly. Not only was there a shortage of capable administrators, but those in place continued to be prone to in-fighting. Officials wanted to give orders, not to take them. Struggles for power erupted at all levels in the drive to capture the "responsible positions" within and among organizations. Local officials fought cadres sent in from Moscow. New recruits to the party refused to accept the seniority of members with underground experience. Soviet Executive Committee chairmen refused to follow the directives of the party committee secretaries; local economic councils (*sovnarkhozy*) fought with local trade unions. Defeating the Whites was one thing, but if the Bolsheviks were to achieve any of their revolutionary aims, the chaos had to be sorted as a first priority. In April 1922, on Lenin's initiative, Stalin was

6 Gosudarstvennyi arkhiv Rossiiskoi federatsii (GARF), f. 6980, op. 1, d. 5, l. 9.

7 A. Ia. Vyshinskii (ed.), *Konstitutsii i konstitutsionnye akty RSFSR, 1918–1937* (Moscow: Izdatel'stvo vedomostei Verkhovnogo Soveta RSFSR, 1940).

appointed general secretary of the party and charged with sorting out the mess.[8]

There remains a deeply entrenched popular image of the consequences of appointing Stalin as general secretary. Back in the 1940s, Isaac Deutscher argued that Stalin was able to use the secretary's "power over appointments" to pack party offices with his "friends, henchmen and followers."[9] Since that time, the dominant view has been that Stalin's rise to power was a victory of machine politics over the ideas of his more capable Bolshevik peers.[10] And yet, the archives show no direct evidence that the Secretariat ever made appointments on the basis of factional loyalties. Rather, the record-assignment department was assigning well over 1,000 officials a month, such that no personal connection with the general secretary could be formed.[11] The conflict department, meanwhile, was receiving 150 reports per month of regional organization paralyzed by in-fighting (*skloki*).[12] The Secretariat was not coping with the tasks before it, such that the organization was seen as a bureaucratic millstone, rather than the pathway to influence and power.

Stalin did not turn the organization around in an instant. The demand for skilled and authoritative cadres remained high, and largely unmet. Secretariat officials admitted that in the vast majority of cases, they were assigning party members blindly (*sovershenno sluchaino*).[13] However, the Secretariat made considerable advances in dealing with *skloki*. It continued to intervene in a minority of cases where the work of local organizations had completely broken down, but it reduced the number of cases of catastrophic in-fighting by empowering the party first secretaries to resolve disputes as they saw fit. While there is no evidence to suggest that the Secretariat was enforcing conformity to any set of policies or "political line," the decision to reinforce the power of party secretaries was hardly conducive to political diversity or open discussion. This played a critical – and underappreciated – role in the

8 Rossiiskii gosudarstvennyi arkhiv sotsial'no-politicheskoi istorii (RGASPI), f. 17, op. 2, d. 78, l. 2.

9 Isaac Deutscher, *Stalin: A Political Biography* (London: Oxford University Press, 1949), ch. 7.

10 See for example Adam B. Ulam, *Stalin: The Man and His Era* (New York: Viking, 1973), or more recently Christopher Read, *The Making and Breaking of the Soviet System* (Basingstoke: Macmillan, 2001).

11 *Trinadtsatyi s''ezd RKP(b), mai 1924 goda. Stenograficheskii otchet* (Moscow: Gosizdat, 1963), 120.

12 Conflicts were usually rooted in personal antagonisms rather than matters of political principle. "Otchet org-instruktorskogo otdela TsK za period vremeni s maia 1920 goda po 15 fevralia 1921 goda," *Izvestiia TsK* (5 Mar. 1921), 7–9.

13 RGASPI, f. 17, op. 69, d. 140, l. 30.

Lenin succession and Stalin's rise to uncontested power. In the early 1920s, the situation in the Politburo was similar to that of party committees in the provinces. The Lenin succession was yet another power struggle among ambitious party leaders. But the situation in the provinces was different insofar as relative educational levels were considerably lower there. The finer points of the policy debates within the party elite did not particularly engage middling and lower party officials. In the mid 1920s, they were busy rebuilding the war-torn economy and establishing a functioning administrative apparatus. For many, policy debates were a distraction, or at worst, they threatened to give rise to local *skloki*. Statutes governing the rules of "intra-party democracy" dictated that local control commissions were responsible for printing and distributing proposals and platforms in advance of party meetings. But governed as they were by the party majority in any given locality, they often sat on them, and only promoted the views of the majority.[14] They also did their best to restrict the range of policy debate in the local press and to present alternative policy platforms in an unfavorable light.

It has to be stressed here that no evidence either in central or in local archives has come to light to suggest that this was orchestrated by the center, or by Stalin personally.[15] Indeed for a time in the mid 1920s, oppositionists excluded from the party by regional control commissions for factional activity were being restored by the Central Control Commission.[16] But it does seem clear that Stalin understood well what was happening, and took advantage of it, in particular publicly making it obvious that he accepted the logic of local actions:

> Democracy is not something appropriate to all times and places ... Democracy demands a certain minimum of culture [*kultur'nost'*] from the members of [Party] cells and organizations as a whole ... Of course we need to retreat from it ... If we were to permit the existence of group struggle, we would destroy the Party, turn it from a monolithic, united organization into an alliance of groups and factions. It would not be a Party, but rather the destruction of the Party ... Not for one minute did Bolsheviks ever imagine the Party as anything but a monolithic organization, cut from one piece, of one will ... In the current conditions of capitalist encirclement, we need not

14 See for example Tsentrdokumentatsii obshchestvennykh organizatsii Sverdlovskoi oblasti (TsDOO SO), f. 6, op. 1, d. 176, ll. 8, 10, 88; d. 6, l. 23; d. 848, l. 31, 89, 96.

15 The correspondence between the center and provinces, between Stalin and regional leaders, is substantial and well explored.

16 TsDOO SO, f. 424, op. 1, d. 204, l. 20; d. 205, l. 375ob.; d. 229a, l. 59; d. 304a, ll. 4–13.

> only a united Party, but a Party of steel, capable of withstanding the onslaught of the enemies of the proletariat, capable of leading the workers into a decisive struggle.[17]

Party secretaries were pleased to repeat Stalin's phrases about the importance of party unity and use them to legitimize the repression of any challenge to their power. Stalin had reinforced their power, but the Secretariat, and Stalin personally, was the figure secretaries turned to with their concerns, about grain collections, investment in the industrial economy and other issues. Through the 1920s, Stalin was cordial and solicitous, offering whatever help he could.[18] Stalin was building a relationship that would serve him well in the Lenin succession. The logic was clear. Regional party secretaries made up almost half of the Central Committee, and party statutes dictated that the Central Committee "elected" the Politburo.[19]

How then did this play out in Stalin's victory in the succession struggle? Historians have tended to take their cues once again from Trotsky. They have echoed Trotsky's view that Stalin was a political opportunist devoid of his own ideas, interested only in power for its own sake. He took the ideas of the right to defeat the left, and then he took the ideas of the left to defeat the right. We have already seen above that Stalin is now taken more seriously as a political thinker and Marxist-Leninist, but what is not as well reflected in the contemporary historiography is the story of the gradual leftward drift of party opinion in the 1920s. The NEP was a retreat, but it worked. The partial retreat to capitalism and the growing power of capitalist "elements" (especially the so-called nepman and the better-off peasant, or kulak) grated with the Bolsheviks and much of the working class, but the NEP brought a rapid economic recovery. When Trotsky and then the United Opposition attacked the NEP and proposed to accelerate industrialization by squeezing the capitalist elements, memories of the 1923 Scissors Crisis were still strong, and the party elite sensibly hesitated to put the recovery at risk.[20] Besides, the

17 *Trinadtsataia konferentsiia rossiiskoi kommunisticheskoi partii (bolshevikov)* (Moscow: Krasnaia nov', 1924), 93, 100–1.

18 For example, RGASPI, f. 558, op. 11, d. 36, ll. 95, 103; d. 153, ll. 21–22, 28–29, 34–35, 55, 57–58.

19 Technically, the Politburo itself presented slates of candidates to the Central Committee, but when the Politburo was divided, as it was through much of the 1920s, the Central Committee could have a decisive role in determining who was excluded and who remained in the party's highest decision-making body.

20 The Scissors Crisis refers to a period of rising prices for industrial goods and falling prices for agricultural production. Prices unfavorable to peasants discouraged them from marketing grain and raised the specter of famine. Many Bolsheviks worried that Trotsky's plans would reopen the "scissors."

Politburo majority, with Stalin at the helm, claimed that targets for efficiency savings within industry would generate as much new investment as the left projected. Why take the risk? The policy argument mattered, but what was happening behind the scenes mattered more. Finding that their literature was not being distributed and their ideas printed in the press rather selectively, the left resorted to printing their own and organizing clandestine meetings in the center and regions. Not only were they violating party statutes, but they had engaged in the patterns of in-fighting (*sklochnichestvo*) that local party secretaries were now well practiced in combating.

In its finer detail, the policy debate in the 1920s was a quite sophisticated exchange of ideas on the future of the revolution, but in the newspaper headlines and slogans for the consumption of the rank and file and broader public, it descended into the universal campaigning habit of mutual character assassination. The left presented Stalin as a bureaucrat, threatening to sell out the revolution to the capitalist elements. Stalin in turn presented them as "splitters" and pessimists, threatening to undermine ongoing progress by undermining party unity and discipline. Stalin and the Politburo majority were able – just – to orchestrate the expulsion of the left in 1927 because the general secretary was perceived by many to be a helpful and solicitous "boss"; because changing course was a risk without an obvious payoff and because they did not want to encourage local opponents of their power. Then, once the leaders of the left had been convicted of violating party rules – of "conspiring against the party" – the full force of the political police, the OGPU (Ob"edinennoe gosudarstvennoe politicheskoe upravlenie), was brought to bear. Lists of left oppositionists were compiled and they were put under surveillance.[21]

Between 1925 and 1927, as the left was being squeezed out of political life, the limits of the NEP were becoming more obvious. Factories and infrastructure damaged in the war had largely been restored and the economy was approaching capacity. Much greater investment would soon be needed to build new capacity and infrastructure. At least initially, Stalin asserted that funds could be found in efficiency savings within industry itself. National economic plans had been on the cards since the civil war. They were being put into effect by 1927, and under the pressure of higher party authorities, they were gradually made ever more ambitious. Particularly on the issue of just how ambitious the plans could be, divisions again emerged within the

21 Roman Podkur, "Povstanskyi rukh ta opozytsiini politychni uhrupovannia v informatsiinykh dokumentakh ChK-GPU (pochatok 20-kh rr.)," *Z arkhiviv VUChK-GPU-NKVD-KGB* 2–4 (2000), 390–97.

party elite. Bukharin and the "right" were worried lest pushing too far too fast would threaten the fundamental basis of the NEP economy and would lead to bottlenecks and shortages. Stalin and others farther to the "left" were absorbed by the potential of the planned economy to be more efficient and effective than capitalism. After all, producers would be working together in unison rather than competing one with another for markets.[22]

In this new phase of political struggle, Stalin had several obvious advantages. He had said that growth rates could be sustained, and by most appearances it looked like he was right. The logic of the struggle against the left applied again. If it works, why change? But there were other more significant reasons why Stalin carried the support of both the party elite and the rank and file. Regional leaders – making up about half the party Central Committee – were attracted to the projected central investment in local economies. Indeed, they competed for it, and each promising to make more for less, created a pressure to make the plans yet more ambitious.[23] The acceleration of the plans was by no means a smooth process. In 1927–28, a sharp fall in grain collections threatened to derail the plan in its first year. Stalin declared that the better-off peasants (kulaks) were trying to undermine the plan for *political* motives, and he proposed to seize grain from them by force. As some engineers, planners and other specialists were expressing doubts about the realism of economic plans, Stalin again proposed harsh measures against them. Stalin was increasingly promoting a politics of class warfare, fully aware of its resonance among the working class and the rank and file of the party. They had never entirely made their peace with the NEP and the compromises with capitalist "elements."[24] It was not difficult for Stalin to whip up excitement about a "socialist offensive" that would accelerate the construction of socialism and drive out the capitalist elements. Supporters of the "right" were horrified, but kept in check, demonized as splitters and doubters standing in the way of real progress.

Stalin's relationship with the party rank and file was particularly secure. Many were barely literate, such that the finer points of what was at times

22 The best recent work on this period includes David Priestland, *Stalinism and the Politics of Mobilization: Ideas, Power and Terror in Inter-War Russia* (Oxford: Oxford University Press, 2007); Erik van Ree, *The Political Thought of Joseph Stalin: A Study in Twentieth-Century Revolutionary Patriotism* (London: Routledge, 2002).

23 James Harris, *The Great Urals: Regionalism and the Evolution of the Soviet System* (Ithaca: Cornell University Press, 1999).

24 See for example Anne Gorsuch, "NEP Be Damned! Young Militants in the 1920s and the Culture of Civil War," *Russian Review* 56, 4 (1997), 564–80.

a sophisticated and esoteric policy debate were lost on them. From an early stage of the leadership struggle, Stalin carefully presented himself as Lenin's best and most faithful disciple. Stalin's efforts to "codify" Leninism in self-serving and accessible ways must not be underestimated. As he gradually cemented his popular reputation in this way – the representation of his opponents as mere "oppositionists" and "anti-Leninist" – the more Stalin was able to rally the greater mass of this group. His contributions to a cult of Lenin shifted smoothly by the end of the 1920s to his own leader cult. Stalin's victory over the right, and the left for that matter, was not in any sense the realization of "inner party democracy" in the sense of an open discussion of competing political ideas, but the point here is that Stalin was able to take advantage of a broader sense that debate – understood as *sklochnichestvo* – was pointless and even counterproductive when policy seemed to be working. One may attribute this lack of enthusiasm for democracy to deeper authoritarian strands in Bolshevism, or some "backwardness" in Russian political culture, but one should not lose sight of parallel events in Europe. In this same period, democratic institutions collapsed in Italy, Spain and Poland and shortly thereafter in Germany, not least because democracy was perceived to cause more problems than it solved.[25]

Stalin's ambition to succeed Lenin as leader cannot be doubted, but the traditional story of his rise needs revising. There were no obvious, opportunistic U-turns in his views. There was naturally some shift in the views of all policymakers as the NEP brought economic recovery, and the challenge of building new factories and infrastructure was discussed. Stalin remained in the majority and his policies seemed to work in practice. He could reasonably portray his challengers as squabblers, *sklochniki* wantonly sowing disunity, where party unity and discipline were key to continued success. Stalin was not able to use the Secretariat to pack party bodies with his supporters, though the Secretariat did bring him into constant contact with senior party figures in the provinces, where the discourse of *sklochichestvo* resonated profoundly. They were occupied from day to day with the business of economic management in their regions. Some did have sympathy with the left or the right, but while policy was bringing good results, and new investment and growth were on the horizon, few were interested in rocking the boat. In short, through the 1920s, Stalin's policies and his leadership had

25 See for example Zeev Sternhell (ed.), *The Intellectual Revolt against Liberal Democracy, 1870–1945* (Jerusalem: Israel Academy of Sciences and Humanities, 1996).

significant support within the party and the working class – support that was rooted in a sense of forward movement and real achievements.

By the end of the 1920s, Stalin's victory in the Lenin succession seemed complete, though it is important not to exaggerate his power at that stage. Nearly a decade later, at the 1937 celebrations on the twentieth anniversary of the October Revolution, Stalin made a speech to his inner circle and a few guests in which he reminisced about his path to power. He claimed that Trotsky's mistake had been to address his arguments to the Central Committee, logical as that may have been. Stalin then noted the overwhelming support he had among the rank and file. In 1927, 720,000 party members voted in favor of the "Central Committee line" which he had authored; 4,000–6,000 voted for Trotsky. He then raised a toast to the rank and file (*seredniak*).[26] And yet what is most interesting in Stalin's words is in the subtext. Within the party masses, thousands had voted against him. Tens of thousands had harbored doubts. More significant still though was what the toast implied about the party elite. Without their approval he could not have orchestrated the removal of Trotsky, Zinoviev, Kamenev, Bukharin and others, but Stalin didn't think their support was so solid, or so certain. As we shall see, the historiography has tended to simplify what remained a dynamic situation and to assume that Stalin's victory in the Lenin succession was complete at the end of the 1920s.

After his defeat in 1927, Trotsky was forced into exile – a move that Stalin would come bitterly to regret. Stalin thought exile would sever ties between Trotsky and his followers, but they appeared somehow to be sustained, and Trotsky gained almost total freedom to observe events in the USSR and criticize Stalin's handling of them.[27] Former oppositionists in the USSR could be silenced much more easily. They were subject to GPU surveillance, making any kind of organized action against the leadership almost impossible. And yet, Stalin's concern about grumblings of dissent heightened in the early 1930s. Because his support within the upper echelons of the party derived in part from the perceived success of his policies, he had reason to be unsettled when things started to go wrong. Forced pace collectivization descended into a civil war with the peasantry.[28] In the summer of 1930, industrial production not only slowed, it began to

26 RGASPI, f. 558, op. 11, d. 1122, ll. 158–74.

27 Copies of the bulletins reporting on Trotsky's actions abroad can be found in Anastas Mikoian's personal archive, RGASPI, f. 84, op. 1, d. 135, ll. 3–51.

28 See for example Lynne Viola, *Peasant Rebels Under Stalin: Collectivization and the Culture of Peasant Resistance* (Oxford: Oxford University Press, 1990), ch. 4.

contract. Sergei I. Syrtsov, a candidate member of the Politburo, publicly raised serious concerns about flaws in planning that subtly cut against the grain of Stalin's insistence that the plan was entirely realistic. Syrtsov faced no immediate public rebuke, but as the economic crisis deepened, he was conscious of being isolated from policy discussions. In October he made the mistake of expressing his anger to a group of colleagues, one of whom, B. Reznikov, denounced him. The letter of denunciation accused Syrtsov of asserting that a growing group in the party elite might attempt to remove Stalin. "It's unimaginably vile," Stalin wrote to Molotov. "All the evidence suggests that Reznikov's version of events is true. They played at organizing a coup."[29]

The episode did not shake Stalin's conviction that his economic policy was correct, and that any expression of doubt was a manifestation of what was then labeled the right "deviation." At the same time, Stalin coldly assessed the relative strength of his position. Now that the right had been defeated and the Politburo unified, he had less reason to worry about the correlation of forces in the Central Committee or the broader party elite. Rather than step back from the extraordinary ambitions of the first Five-Year Plan, forced collectivization was resumed, and Stalin insisted that nothing less than 100 percent plan fulfillment would be accepted. On his direction, the party press insisted that current policy was "uniquely correct" and encouraged organizations to "watch [their] ranks" and "expose" (i.e. denounce) those who would criticize the plan or who doubted it could be fulfilled.[30] And yet, given that the plan was palpably unrealistic, the intransigence of the center put local organizations and enterprises in an impossible position. Not only were they afraid to pass on the sort of information necessary for effective decision-making at the top, but also because they had to meet impossible targets to keep their jobs, they had little choice but to lie to the center, hide capacity, exaggerate the need for supplies, and engage in other behaviors that looked to the center like a form of wrecking.

Stalin's strategy did not address concerns about central policy. It only made it politically impossible for officials to express them publicly or in internal correspondence. And it did little to improve plan fulfillment.

29 L. Kosheleva, V. Lel'chuk, V. Naumov, O. Naumov, L. Rogovaia and O. Khlevniuk (eds.), *Pis'ma I. V. Stalina V. M. Molotovu, 1925–1936 gg.* (Moscow: Rossiia molodaia, 1995), 231.

30 I. V. Stalin, "Politicheskii otchet," in I. V. Stalin, *Sochineniia*, vol. XII (Moscow: Gosizdat, 1952), 357–61; "S''ezd razvernutogo sotsialisticheskogo nastupleniia," *Bol'shevik* 13 (1930), 4–5.

Relentless pressure to meet grain collection targets contributed directly to the famine of 1932–33 in which millions of peasants died. The few local officials brave enough to insist that targets were too high were accused of being "infected with kulak sentiments."[31] In July 1932, former left oppositionists with connections in Gosplan smuggled an extended criticism of state economic policy abroad, where it was published in Trotsky's journal *Bulletin of the Opposition*. What made the episode particularly troubling for Stalin was that the document contained a wealth of statistical material that had been circulated among a relatively small number of leading economic officials. It served notice to Stalin that former oppositionists were not just grumbling quietly behind the scenes. They appeared to be making contact with disaffected leading officials. Worse was to follow. In mid September, the OGPU obtained a copy of an even more vitriolic oppositionist document calling for the violent overthrow of the regime. The author, Martem'ian Riutin, had been removed from the Central Committee in 1930 for oppositionist activity, though he had apparently renounced his views. However, Stalin was given reason to believe that Riutin had not only held to his views, he had also continued to discuss them with leading officials in the party and state apparatus. Riutin's closest colleagues were arrested and interrogated, and the case put before the Central Control Commission, which concluded that his anti-Stalin diatribe had been passed "from comrade to comrade, group to group, from city to city, calling for . . . the preparation of an attempt to oust Stalin and other leaders of the party and Soviet government."[32]

There were other, perhaps more serious, worries for Stalin relating to the international situation. Here again, he was not alone in his interpretations and responses. The concept of "capitalist encirclement" was not his invention. Following the end of the civil war and the retreat of invading foreign forces, Soviet leaders took it for granted that the capitalist states on their western and southern frontiers would only be preparing for the next opportunity to invade. Soviet intelligence agencies had some notable

31 V. Danilov, V. Vinogradov, L. Viola, L. Dvoinikh, N. Ivnitskii, S. Krasil'nikov, R. Manning, O. Naumov, E. Tiurina and Khan Chzong Suk (Han Jeong-Sook) (eds.), *Tragediia sovetskoi derevni: Dokumenty i materialy v 5 tomakh, 1927–1939*, vol. III (Moscow: Rossiiskaia politicheskaia entsiklopediia, 2002), 199–200. For examples of Stalin's correspondence with regional officials at this time, see Rossiiskii gosudarstvennyi arkhiv ekonomiki (RGAE), f. 7486, op. 37, l. 147; RGASPI, f. 558, op. 11, ll. 40–41.

32 A. Artizov (ed.), *Reabilitatsiia: Kak eto bylo, ii. Fevral' 1956-nachalo 80-kh godov. Dokumenty* (Moscow: Mezhdunarodnyi fond "Demokratiia," 2003), 394–98.

successes. They had moles in the General Staffs of the French, Polish and Japanese armies, and an assortment of agents, mostly communist sympathizers, well placed in many European governments. They regularly intercepted communications of the Japanese military attachés in the Soviet Union with their commanders in Tokyo and those of US diplomats in Russia, Japan and France with the State Department. But the agencies tended see aggressive intentions from the capitalist states where none existed. In early July 1926, the head of the OGPU Feliks Dzerzhinskii wrote to Stalin asserting that "there is an accumulation of evidence which indicates with doubtless (for me) clarity that Poland is preparing a military assault on us with the goal of seizing Belorussia and Ukraine."[33] The war scare of 1927 is often treated as Stalin's invention, cynically employed to disarm the right and drive through the "Great Break," but the evidence suggests that Bukharin and others on the right were similarly convinced by the "evidence" that war was imminent.[34]

Reports from Soviet intelligence agencies in the early 1930s sustained the sense of threat. When Japan invaded Manchuria in the autumn of 1931, it looked as though there was a new, eastern front in the threat from the capitalist powers. The evidence seemed pretty compelling. The OGPU had intercepted a letter from Yukio Kasahara, the Japanese military attaché in Moscow to the General Staff in Tokyo advocating a war against the USSR and the annexation of the Soviet Far East and western Siberia. To make matters worse, Kasahara observed that "the countries on Soviet western borders (i.e. at a minimum Poland and Romania) are in a position to act with us."[35] A month later, Voroshilov wrote to his deputy Ian Gamarnik informing him of further (unconfirmed) reports to the effect that the Japanese "were in the midst of intensive preparations for war this spring. We also have evidence of the preparations of the White Guards, who boast that they can contribute 130,000 troops to an invasion force. They are proposing the creation of a 'Russian' government in the Far East."[36] Meanwhile, the

33 RGASPI, f. 76, op. 3, d. 364, l. 57.

34 Michal Reiman, *The Birth of Stalinism: The USSR on the Eve of the "Second Revolution"* (Bloomington: Indiana University Press, 1987), appendices; Sarah Davies and James Harris, *Stalin's World: Dictating the Soviet Order* (New Haven: Yale University Press, 2014), 100–06.

35 RGASPI, f. 558, op. 11, d. 185, ll. 1–9.

36 A. V. Kvashonkin, L. P. Kosheleva, L. A. Rogovaia and O. V. Khlevniuk (eds.), *Sovetskoe rukovodstvo: Perepiska, 1928–1941* (Moscow: ROSSPEN, 1999), 167–68 (13 Jan. 1932). Defense spending had been steadily increasing in the course of the Five-Year Plan, but leapt forward in 1932, nearly tripling from 845 million rubles to over 2.2 billion rubles.

Western press was publishing reports of a Franco-Japanese pact, and the Soviet embassy (*polpredstvo*) in Paris received information to the effect that France was supplying Japan with arms on a grand scale.[37] Elections in Germany brought further setbacks for the communists and signs of deepening nationalism and anti-communism. While the possibility of German participation in the anti-Soviet coalition hung in the air, Poland gave every indication that preparations were under way for an autumn invasion. Resistance to the grain collection targets in Ukraine was encouraging the Poles to send many small groups across the border with the aim of organizing resistance and ultimately a broad peasant rebellion.[38] In mid August 1932, Stalin told Lazar Kaganovich that the Ukrainian Party and the OGPU had to break resistance to the grain collections immediately: "If we don't take measures to correct the situation, we could lose Ukraine."[39] Stalin was not being "paranoid." He was responding to a consistent and compelling stream of foreign intelligence indicating that war was imminent.[40]

In this context, the murder of Politburo member Sergei Kirov on 1 December 1934 was doomed to send shock waves through the party elite. We now know that Leonid Nikolaev was unhinged, and acting alone, but Stalin was not inclined to see it that way. Five months earlier, Kaganovich reported to Stalin, who was on vacation at the time, that a certain A. S. Nakhaev, the commander of a division of Osoaviakhim in Moscow, attempted to get his men to take arms against Soviet power. They didn't follow him and Nakhaev was arrested immediately. Kaganovich assumed he was suffering some kind of breakdown, but Stalin insisted that the NKVD (Narodnyi Komissariat Vnutrennikh Del, People's Commissariat for Internal Affairs) had to dig deeper:

> Of course (of course!) he's not working alone. We have to hold him to the wall and force him to tell the whole truth – and then punish him severely . . . The Chekisty make a mockery of themselves when they discuss his "political views" with him. (This is called an interrogation!)[41]

37 S. V. Morozov, *Pol'sko-Chekhoslovatskie otnosheniia, 1933–1939* (Moscow: Izdatel'stvo MGU, 2004), 165.

38 James Morris, "The Polish Terror: Spy Mania and Ethnic Cleansing in the Great Terror," *Europe-Asia Studies* 56, 5 (2004), 751–66.

39 RGASPI, f. 558, op. 11, d. 188, ll. 31–51.

40 V. V. Dam'e, N. P. Komolova and N. L. Petrova, *Komintern protiv fashizma. Dokumenty* (Moscow: Nauka, 1999), 291–97.

41 O. V. Khlevniuk, R. U. Devis (R. W. Davies), L. P. Kosheleva, E. A. Ris (E. A. Rees) and L. A. Rogovaia (eds.), *Stalin i Kaganovich: Perepiska. 1931–1936 gg.* (Moscow: ROSSPEN, 2001), 429.

As in the Riutin case, Stalin was particularly concerned to know who associated with him, whom he shared his political thoughts with, and who influenced him. With Nikolaev, as with Nakhaev, Stalin excluded the possibility that he acted alone. Stalin's influence over the investigation was obvious, not because he explicitly dictated its outcome, but because the NKVD relied on torture and confession the outcomes were almost certain to confirm the leader's suspicions. In the Nakhaev case, Stalin had told Kaganovich that "[h]e must be a Polish-German agent (or Japanese)." Why then did Stalin dismiss the possibility of a foreign connection to the Kirov assassination? He did not do so immediately. Over the phone from Moscow, before he had even traveled to Leningrad, he had asked if Nikolaev was carrying any foreign items. He would have quickly learned that Nikolaev's wife Milda Draule was Latvian. But Stalin remained unconvinced that Nikolaev was acting on behalf of hostile capitalist powers. While the international situation was not good, it was not at a critical phase where the assassination of Soviet leaders would help pave the way for a successful invasion. Besides which, employing an ex-party member such as Nikolaev would have been unprecedented. Foreign governments had long tended to use Whites to conduct acts of terrorism in the USSR. Rather, in Stalin's view, the recruitment of disaffected party members – Nikolaev had been purged in April 1934 – was the *modus operandi* of the former oppositions.

Nikolaev duly "confessed" that his decision to assassinate Kirov had been influenced by Trotskyists in the Leningrad party organization. Arrests spread to the Leningrad Komsomol, which had had strong ties to Zinoviev's Leningrad opposition. The NKVD developed a picture of a widespread "Trotskyist–Zinovievite" organization with "centers" in Moscow and Leningrad. The testimony of those under interrogation suggested that the Trotskyist–Zinovievite group calculated that the Stalin leadership would not be able to cope in the event of war against the USSR, and that in such an event Kamenev and Zinoviev would inevitably come to power. After the trial of those supposedly directly involved in the murder, a further trial of those who had "inspired" the murderers took place. It concluded that the "Leningrad counterrevolutionary Zinovievite group was systematically cultivating a hatred of the party leadership and particularly Stalin" and bore a "moral and political responsibility for the Kirov murder."[42]

42 "O dele Leningradskoi kontrrevolutsionnoi zinov'evskoi gruppy Safarova, Zalutskogo i drugikh," *Izvestiia TsK KPSS* 1 (1990), 42–43.

The information Stalin was receiving about the international situation and the activities of former oppositions was worrying, but the news from other quarters was rather more heartening. The famine had ended and the persistent crises in the industrial economy characteristic of the first Five-Year Plan were replaced with relatively stable growth. The colossal investment of the early 1930s was bearing fruit not just in terms of the output of heavy industry, but also in terms of military production and the ability of the Soviet state to defend itself in the event of invasion.[43] Stalin was guardedly optimistic about the future, and encouraged a confident, defiant tone in public statements on the international situation.[44] As the investigation into the Kirov murder progressed and further evidence of the "counterrevolutionary" conduct of the former left opposition was presented to him, Stalin was not initially inclined to worry. Through 1935, Nikolai Yezhov, then head of the Central Committee Cadres Department, was trying to convince him and other senior officials that Zinoviev and Kamenev were not merely morally complicit in the murder of Kirov, but had taken part in the planning; that Trotskyists were directing counterrevolutionary actions from abroad, and that Genrikh Iagoda, head of the NKVD, was underestimating the present danger to the lives of Soviet leaders. Stalin was satisfied by the reassurances he was receiving from Iagoda.[45]

But things appeared to take a serious turn for the worse in late 1935 into 1936. The intercepted correspondence of Japanese military attachés indicated clearly to Stalin that the militarists, an ascendant force in Japanese politics, were stepping up plans for a war against the USSR. Their increasing military expenditure, their efforts to negotiate a peace deal with China and a nonaggression pact with the United States all reinforced the impression that they were serious about an invasion.[46] Meanwhile, German rearmament was proceeding at a breakneck pace, the Rhineland was remilitarized, universal military conscription was announced, and there was no let-up in Hitler's anti-communist rhetoric.[47] The start of the Spanish Civil War in July 1936 was interpreted as the unfolding of a world war "meticulously"

43 R. W. Davies, *The Industrialisation of Soviet Russia,* vol. VI, *The Years of Progress: The Soviet Economy, 1934–1936* (Basingstoke: Palgrave Macmillan, 2014).

44 See for example *Izvestiia*, 25 Jan. 1933; *Pravda*, 27 Jan. 1933. See also Kosheleva et al. (eds.), *Pis'ma Stalina Molotovu*, 245, for Stalin's approval of the confident tone.

45 J. Arch Getty and Oleg V. Naumov, *Yezhov: The Rise of Stalin's "Iron Fist"* (New Haven: Yale University Press, 2008), ch. 9.

46 RGASPI, f. 558, op. 11, d. 185, ll. 126–32.

47 RGASPI, f. 558, op. 11, d. 188, ll. 55–56; d. 446, ll. 130–44.

planned by the fascists.[48] As the threat of war grew, Stalin was given more to worry about at home. Yezhov had not been put off his determination to "prove" the existence of a grand conspiracy to overthrow the regime. Indeed, he developed a new angle indicating that the large community of political émigrés was littered with German and Polish spies.[49] The arrest of V. P. Ol'berg, a German political émigré with links to Trotsky, gave Yezhov the chance to link the foreign threat with the former left opposition. Ol'berg confessed to counterrevolutionary activity and began to name scores of co-conspirators. As the investigation progressed, "evidence" emerged of Trotsky's links with fascist governments and cooperation with the Gestapo in the organization of acts of terrorism against Soviet leaders.[50]

In the standard narrative, it is assumed that Stalin directed these investigations and dictated the "confessions" that the NKVD interrogators were to obtain, but the archival record tells another story. Stalin, who had initially rejected Yezhov's theories of conspiracy, was gradually won over as he received transcripts of interrogations. Stalin was surprised and appalled by what he read:

> Did you read the testimony of Dreitser and Pikel'? What do you think of the bourgeois dogs [*burzhuaznye shchenki*] in the camp of Trotsky-Mrachkovskii-Zinoviev-Kamenev? They want to "remove" all Politburo members, these, to put it mildly, shitheads [*zasrantsy*]! It's ridiculous, isn't it? The depths to which people can sink . . .[51]

Because Stalin and others in the leadership believed that they were dealing with experienced conspirators who would leave little or no material evidence of their counterrevolutionary crimes, they continued to rely on confessions obtained under torture. And because some former oppositionists genuinely despised Stalin and discussed among themselves the prospects of returning to power, the realities of the "conspiracy" were easily exaggerated and twisted out of all proportion, but in a way that the leadership found wholly credible. Why, after all, had Trotsky founded the Fourth International? Why was he splitting the international communist movement just as the USSR was under threat of invasion? Why was he

48 Karl Radek in *Izvestiia*, 1 Aug. 1936. The text was approved by Stalin. For more detail, see Davies and Harris, *Stalin's World*, 123–30.

49 Naumov and Plotnikova, *Lubianka: Stalin*, 468–69, 489, 495, 506–08, 565–66, 738–42, 751.

50 Ibid., 744–47; *The Case of the Trotskyite–Zinovievite Terrorist Centre* (Moscow: People's Commissariat of Justice, 1936), 88–92 (V. P. Ol'berg), 75, 103 (N. Lur'e).

51 Kvashonkin et al. (eds.), *Sovetskoe rukovodstvo*, 333–34. The similar reactions of Voroshilov and Kaganovich can be found here.

dividing republican forces with his engagement in the Spanish Civil War? Was that not a gift to the fascists? Stalin and his inner circle were ready to believe that the former oppositions wanted a war between the fascists and communists because it presented their best hope of unseating Stalin and fashioning their return to power.

In the autumn of 1936, Yezhov finally succeeded in unseating Iagoda and taking control of the NKVD. An arch conspiracy theorist was now at the helm of the political police. Logically, he sought to remove Iagoda loyalists from the organization, including all the regional NKVD chiefs. That opened another can of worms. Since the early crises of the first Five-Year Plan, when regional organizations had been under unrelenting pressure to meet unrealistic plan targets, they had engaged in a series of adaptive practices: degrading the quality of production, delivering incomplete production, lying about any spare capacity, exaggerating needs for inputs and investment, subverting central campaigns like Stakhanovism that complicated plan fulfillment and so on. At the apex of the regional organizations, the first secretaries organized around themselves closed, and fundamentally corrupt, cliques in order to hide these adaptive practices and manage information flows to the center. The regional NKVD chief was the linchpin of the clique, with the power to take repressive action against anyone who might leak unfortunate information to the center. When Yezhov removed them and put in his own men, it was inevitable that the darker secrets of the regional organizations would leak out. In the next nine months or so, through the summer of 1937, a faint whiff of scandal became an unholy stench. In that time, much of the Bolshevik elite was arrested and subject to NKVD interrogation, generating the usual warped and exaggerated "confessions." Stalin and his inner circle failed to see that the adaptive practices of the party and state elite were the product of the unrealistic plans which they had so ruthlessly enforced. Instead, they concluded that much of senior officialdom was part of the "conspiracy" against the revolution.[52]

Neither Stalin nor anyone in his inner circle were "paranoid" in the sense of having some chemical imbalance in the brain, but they had inherited and reinforced an information-gathering system that fed them a detailed, consistent and grossly exaggerated picture of the threats facing them and the revolution they were leading. Things were looking bleak indeed in 1937 – much bleaker than they were in reality. War was on the horizon, and

52 Harris, *Great Urals*, ch. 7; Davies and Harris, *Stalin's World*, ch. 1.

there seemed to be vast and interconnected conspiracies ready to aid the enemy in the event of an invasion. Stalin's response was viciously brutal, but ultimately characteristic of the movement he led. The "red terror" of the civil war period had been justified in broadly similar terms. If the revolution were to be overturned, the forces of international capital would set back the liberation of working people – not just of the USSR, but of the whole world – by generations. Of course the red terror was conducted in the context of civil war whereas Stalin's terror was prophylactic, but the lessons of the last world war were clear. The old regime lost power because it had not adequately secured the home front before hostilities began. Stalin and his inner circle were determined not to make that mistake.[53] Following this profoundly misguided logic and misinformed by an intelligence system led by an arch conspiracy theorist, hundreds of thousands of innocent Soviet citizens lost their lives in the so-called mass operations of 1938.[54] The incidence of arrest and execution fell sharply in 1939 and never returned to the levels of 1936–38, but Stalin and the Soviet leadership continued to believe that the regime faced an array of foreign and domestic enemies bent on removing him and putting an end to Soviet power and the world revolution. Indeed, the Nazi invasion and ultimate Soviet victory served to convince them that they had been right about the conspiracy and that their actions had been necessary and effective.[55]

In all, millions had been killed, not just in the terror, but in collectivization and the famine, in the labor camps of the Gulag and in the repression of dissent. Policy discussion had been closed down and a personal dictatorship emerged to replace the consultative party bodies – the congresses and conferences, Central Committee and even the Politburo fell into disuse. There can be no doubt that Stalin bears primary responsibility for all this and for that reason, Stalin's personality matters. It is far from clear or simple, though, how to address the subject. The dominant public perception of Stalin as an evil monster may be true, but it is not helpful if we seek to explain Soviet political violence and the evolution of the dictatorship in the interwar

53 Oleg Khlevniuk, "The Objectives of the Great Terror," in Julian Cooper, Maureen Perrie and E. A. Rees (eds.), *Soviet History, 1917–1953: Essays in Honour of R. W. Davies* (Basingstoke: Palgrave Macmillan, 1993), 158–76.

54 For more on the mass operations, see Paul Hagenloh, *Stalin's Police: Public Order and Mass Repression in the USSR, 1926–1941* (Baltimore: Johns Hopkins University Press, 2009); David Shearer, *Policing Stalin's Socialism: Repression and Social Order in the Soviet Union, 1924–1953* (New Haven: Yale University Press, 2009).

55 See for example *Molotov Remembers: Inside Kremlin Politics. Conversations with Felix Chuev*, edited and with an introduction and notes by Albert Resis (Chicago: I. R. Dee, 1993), 260, 278–79.

period. It is frankly counterproductive if we ignore the context and conclude that these things were merely products of the defects in one man's character: a lust for power, paranoia, or some other psychopathology.

Stalin did not lack political ambition. He put himself forward as Lenin's successor and did not hesitate to smear his opponents and inhibit their ability to promote their views, but he could not have done that if party members, and particularly party first secretaries, had not shared his view that party unity should take precedence over party democracy. In the 1920s, Stalin's policies seemed to be working. The party rank and file was broadly receptive of his efforts to present himself as the one true Leninist, and of his commitment to "build socialism."

But things turned badly against the Politburo majority in the early 1930s. Collectivization met ferocious resistance and famine followed. The industrial economy was in crisis and the threat of war appeared to be growing. Support for Stalin waned. He took some conciliatory measures, reducing the targets in the second Five-Year Plan, introducing the private plot and so on, but his instinct was to put discipline over democracy, and enforcement over conciliation. The information-gathering system Stalin had inherited when he came to power was set up to identify the threat of counterrevolution, and it tended systematically to exaggerate that threat. Stalin tended to reinforce those flaws, but he was not the most fearful of Soviet leaders and certainly not paranoid. From well before 1917, Bolshevik leaders shared the conviction that revolution would bring reaction, and that they could not shrink from violence in defense of what they had achieved. As his intelligence apparatus delivered an ever more detailed and compelling picture of fascist forces gathering for invasion, and as the Kirov murder seemed to signal the spread of a domestic "fifth column," Stalin concentrated political power and lashed out in defense of the revolution. The consequences were appalling, and utterly counterproductive both for Soviet power and for its defensive capabilities. Lenin, Trotsky, Bukharin or others may well have acted differently, but Stalin's authoritarianism and propensity to violence had deep roots in Bolshevism.

Bibliographical Essay

The Soviet state always carefully controlled information about its leaders and the functioning of the political system. Writing the history of Stalin's rule was a daunting task further complicated by the political sympathies of readerships split between a left broadly sympathizing with the aims of the revolution and a right convinced of its evils. Early biographers of Stalin include Trotsky's excoriating *Stalin: An Appraisal of the Man and his Influence* (London: Harper & Brothers, 1941) and Henri Barbusse's hagiographic *Stalin: A New World Seen through One Man* (London: John Lane, 1935). In the context of the early Cold War, Trotsky's influence on the historiography was palpable, most notably in Isaac Deutscher, *Stalin: A Political Biography* (London: Oxford University Press, 1949).

After Stalin's death, Khrushchev presided over a release of information intended to reinforce his program of "de-Stalinization," in which the violence of the Stalin era was blamed on the excessive concentration of power in the hands of the dictator. It was a political sleight of hand. Khrushchev was reinforcing his own power by reassuring the Soviet political elite that their roles in the horrors of the Stalin era would remain secret. Robert Conquest's *The Great Terror: Stalin's Purge of the Thirties* (London: Macmillan, 1968) fell for the trick. Personalizing the story of Soviet political violence made compelling popular history, and more than any other work it cemented the simplistic "Stalin as monster" narrative in the public imagination.

In the 1970s and 1980s, "revisionist" historians chipped away at this dominant view. In *Education and Social Mobility in the Soviet Union, 1921–1934* (Cambridge: Cambridge University Press, 1979) Sheila Fitzpatrick established that the Stalin regime had significant social support. Moshe Lewin, *The Making of the Soviet System: Essays in the Social History of Interwar Russia* (London: Methuen, 1985), examined the social and cultural roots of Stalinism. In *The Origins of the Great Purges: The Soviet Communist Party Reconsidered, 1933–1938* (Cambridge: Cambridge University Press, 1985), J. Arch Getty explained the violence of the 1930s in terms of a response to bureaucratic recalcitrance and political chaos.

The opening of the archives in 1991 transformed the study of the Stalin era. In place of a relatively narrow body of primary sources, historians suddenly had access to tens of millions of files in central and regional archives. Such was the volume of material, it was inevitable that it would take generations to digest. In those first years, the most significant works on the subject were collections of documents. Some of the best in English were published by Yale University Press in the "Annals of Communism" series, for example, J. Arch Getty and Oleg Naumov (eds.), *Road to Terror: Stalin and the Self-Destruction of the Bolsheviks, 1932–1939* (New Haven: Yale University Press, 1999); Lynne Viola, V. P. Danilov, N. A. Ivnitskii and Denis Kozlov (eds.), *The War Against the Peasantry, 1927–1930: The Tragedy of the Soviet Countryside*

(New Haven: Yale University Press, 2005); and Matthew E. Lenoe, *The Kirov Murder and Soviet History* (New Haven: Yale University Press, 2010).

More recent studies of Stalin, such as Erik van Ree, *The Political Thought of Joseph Stalin: A Study in Twentieth-Century Revolutionary Patriotism* (London: Routledge, 2002), and Sarah Davies and James Harris (eds.), *Stalin: A New History* (Cambridge: Cambridge University Press, 2005), have departed from the Trotskyist mold, to take the leader more seriously as a Marxist thinker. Some studies, such as Stephen Kotkin, *Stalin: Paradoxes of Power, 1878–1928* (New York: Allen Lane, 2015), and Oleg Khlevniuk, *Master of the House: Stalin and His Inner Circle* (New Haven: Yale University Press, 2009), continue to emphasize Stalin's impulse to build a personal dictatorship in the shaping of the Soviet political system, while others assert that Stalin was focused on realizing his vision of the revolution rather than seeking power for its own sake: Sheila Fitzpatrick, *On Stalin's Team: The Years of Living Dangerously in Soviet Politics* (Princeton: Princeton University Press, 2015); Sarah Davies and James Harris, *Stalin's World: Dictating the Soviet Order* (New Haven: Yale University Press, 2015).

We are still a long way from digesting the contents of archives, though recent work has advanced our knowledge of Stalinism in important respects. Jan Plamper's *The Stalin Cult: A Study in the Alchemy of Power* (New Haven: Yale University Press, 2012) is a masterful exploration of one critical instrument of Stalinist rule. Gábor Rittersporn's *Anger, Anguish and Folkways in Soviet Russia* (Pittsburgh: University of Pittsburgh Press, 2014) and Wendy Goldman's *Terror and Democracy in the Age of Stalin: The Social Dynamics of Repression* (Cambridge: Cambridge University Press, 2007) and her *Inventing the Enemy: Denunciation and Terror in Stalin's Russia* (Cambridge: Cambridge University Press, 2011) examine the social and political tensions that intensified the political violence of the Stalin era. In *Practicing Stalinism: Bolsheviks, Boyars and the Persistence of Tradition* (New Haven: Yale University Press, 2013), J. Arch Getty has argued that the roots of Stalin should be sought in prerevolutionary traditions and patterns of leadership.

7

Trotsky and Trotskyism

BERTRAND M. PATENAUDE

Leon Trotsky was a Russian revolutionary, a Soviet communist leader and a Marxist theorist. A prolific writer and a spellbinding orator, he was a central figure in the Russian Revolution of 1905 and the October Revolution of 1917, the organizer and leader of the Red Army in the Russian Civil War, the heir apparent to Soviet leader Vladimir Lenin and the arch enemy and then vanquished foe of Joseph Stalin in the succession struggle after Lenin's death. Exiled from the USSR in 1929, he sought to rally his followers behind the banner of a new International that would challenge the Kremlin's leadership of world communism. He was murdered by a Stalinist agent in Mexico in 1940.

The Young Trotsky

Trotsky was born Lev Davidovich Bronstein on 26 October (7 November) 1879, in the village of Yanovka, in Kherson province, southern Ukraine, near the Black Sea. The fifth of eight children (of whom only four survived into adulthood), Bronstein was the son of a successful Jewish landowner and farmer, a profile untypical of the vast majority of Russia's Jews living in urban centers in the Pale of Settlement, in the western borderlands of the Russian Empire. His father was all but illiterate; his mother, from Odessa, was modestly educated. Lev Bronstein was raised in relative comfort on the family's large and prosperous farm. Unlike most Russian Jews, he grew up speaking a blend of Ukrainian and Russian but no Yiddish. These circumstances help explain his lifelong self-identification as an internationalist, rather than as a Jew.

In 1888, Bronstein was sent to study at a *realschule* sponsored by German Lutherans in Odessa, where he lived with the family of his mother's nephew, a liberal intellectual who, together with his wife, introduced the boy to the world of books and literature and taught him to speak proper Russian. The school's teachers and student body were a diverse national and ethnic community, an environment that enhanced the boy's cosmopolitan sensibility. A precocious youth, he was a rebellious student who at times found himself in trouble with school authorities, though he graduated with good grades. He completed the final year of his secondary education in nearby Nikolaev, a smaller and more provincial city, in 1895–96. It was there that he was drawn to political radicalism, joining a circle of students and workers who gathered in an orchard on the outskirts of town to discuss and debate radical politics.

By 1897, Bronstein had shed his initial resistance to Marxism and helped organize a social-democratic group called the South Russian Workers' Union, which agitated among workers for higher wages and shorter hours. A police raid of the circle in January 1898 rounded up Trotsky and some 200 of his confederates. He spent the next two years in prisons in Nikolaev, Kherson and then Odessa, with extended periods in solitary confinement. In December 1899 he was sentenced to four years in exile in Siberia. He spent the next six months in a Moscow transit prison, where he first heard of Lenin and read the latter's newly published *The Development of Capitalism in Russia*.

Bronstein settled in the town of Verkholensk, above Lake Baikal in eastern Siberia. He lived with Aleksandra Sokolovskaia, a fellow member of the Nikolaev circle, whom he married in the Moscow prison. In exile, Bronstein, a voracious reader and keen student of languages, completed his conversion to Marxism. Establishing contact with like-minded exiles, he wrote leaflets for a group called the Social Democratic Siberian Union. He became a regular contributor to *Vostochnoe obozrenie* (Eastern Review), a local newspaper in Irkutsk, the largest town in the region, publishing pseudonymously signed essays on Siberian social life and also literary criticism.

In 1902, Bronstein received his first issues of *Iskra* (The Spark), a Marxist newspaper published by Russian social democrats in London, and also a copy of Lenin's newly appeared *What Is To Be Done?* Their arrival coincided with his decision that summer to flee Siberia, leaving behind his wife and their two daughters. He traveled using a false passport that identified him as Trotsky, a name he later claimed he wrote in at random, taking it from one of his jailers in Odessa. In Samara on the Volga Trotsky made contact with social democrats, and before long Lenin heard their reports about the talented young man they had nicknamed The Pen and summoned him to London.

Trotsky arrived there in October 1902, and for a brief period became Lenin's protégé and began contributing articles to *Iskra*. He was dispatched to the continent to lecture and meet fellow social democrats. In Paris his guide around the city was Natalia Sedova, a Russian art student who became his companion and comrade for the rest of his life.

In the summer of 1903, Trotsky was a delegate to the Second Congress of the Russian Social Democratic Labour Party, the occasion of the fateful split of the party into Bolshevik and Menshevik factions. On the crucial votes, Trotsky sided with Julius Martov, Pavel Axelrod and other delegates soon to become known as Mensheviks, who supported a definition of party membership more broadly inclusive than Lenin's and who opposed his moves to assert control over *Iskra*. In the wake of the congress, Trotsky launched extremely bitter polemical attacks against Lenin, whom he accused of behaving imperiously and of advocating a dangerous form of centralism bound to lead to dictatorship. In a lengthy pamphlet titled *Our Political Tasks*, published in Geneva in 1904, Trotsky called Lenin "malicious," "hideous," "dissolute," "demagogical" and "morally repulsive," and compared him to Robespierre. In a memorably prophetic formulation, he warned where Lenin's conspiratorial methods would lead: "[T]he party organization substitutes itself for the party, the Central Committee substitutes itself for the organization and, finally, a 'dictator' substitutes himself for the Central Committee."[1]

Trotsky had sided with the Mensheviks, yet he soon cut his formal ties to the group and assumed the status of an independent Marxist. As such, he became a persistent advocate of party unity, even though his violent condemnation of Lenin would seem to have closed off the possibility that he could effectively play the role of conciliator. Although he was a free agent, in the coming years he would maintain closer personal relations with individual Mensheviks and would publish in Menshevik newspapers.

Trotsky in 1905

Trotsky first came to prominence in the Russian Revolution of 1905. He arrived in St. Petersburg, the Russian capital, in October, after a general strike had been declared. The St. Petersburg Soviet of Workers'

1 Isaac Deutscher, *The Prophet Armed: Trotsky, 1879–1921* (London and New York: Verso, 2003), 77; Baruch Knei-Paz, *The Political and Social Thought of Leon Trotsky* (Oxford: Oxford University Press, 1978), 186, 199.

Deputies, established that same month, became his base of operations. Formally Trotsky was the Soviet's deputy chairman, but in fact he was its true leader. He was especially conspicuous as an orator with a theatrical flare. On the day Tsar Nicholas II issued the October Manifesto, promising an elected national assembly, Trotsky, addressing a large outdoor audience, dismissed the tsar's concession as "merely a scrap of paper" as he crumpled a copy in his fist.[2] As biographer Dmitri Volkogonov observes of Trotsky in 1905, "He gave the impression that this was not his first revolution."[3]

Trotsky and the members of the St. Petersburg Soviet were arrested on 3 December. He spent nearly ten months in prison awaiting trial, first in Kresty and then in the Peter and Paul Fortress. He used this time to read deeply in the European classics – his taste for French novels springs from this period – and also to produce his most original theoretical contribution to Marxism, the theory of "permanent revolution." The revolutionary events of 1905 confirmed Trotsky in the notion he had begun to develop the previous year – under the influence of Alexander Helphand, a Munich-based Russian-Jewish Marxist whose pen name was Parvus – that Russia was on the brink of a seizure of power, not by its feeble bourgeoisie, but by its workers, who had demonstrated that they were not only capable but ready to lead the way. Trotsky shared Lenin's belief that Russia's proletariat, not its bourgeoisie, would have to make the bourgeois revolution; but he now went further, asserting that a proletarian dictatorship would push forward and make both the bourgeois and socialist revolutions in rapid succession.

Trotsky's thinking seemed to contradict orthodox Marxism's assumption that a socialist revolution could take place only in an advanced capitalist country. In fact, Trotsky's analysis was more radical still. Although it was common wisdom among Marxists that Russia had entered the capitalist stage of development, Trotsky argued that because of the preponderant role of the state and of foreign capital in Russia's modernizing economy, capitalism had in fact failed to take root there. As a result, Russia's bourgeoisie, rather than being anchored to an urban middle class, remained tethered to the countryside, which explained its deficiencies as a political force. At the same time, Russia, as a latecomer to modernization, had been able to adopt advanced forms of industry, its modern factories incubating a highly concentrated

2 Deutscher, *The Prophet Armed*, 107.

3 Dmitri Volkogonov, *Trotsky: The Eternal Revolutionary* (New York: Free Press, 1996), 39–40.

proletariat capable of mass action.[4] Trotsky's theory incorporated an international dimension. Russia's telescoped bourgeois and socialist revolutions, he surmised, would serve as a detonator of revolution in Europe's advanced capitalist countries. In fact, said Trotsky, the Russian Revolution's ultimate success would depend on its westward spread; left isolated in Russia, the proletarian dictatorship would be swallowed up by the peasant mass.

Trotsky's theory of permanent revolution first appeared in print in a little-noticed collection of essays, *Results and Prospects: The Moving Forces of the Revolution*, published in Russia in 1906. At the moment it appeared, the spotlight was on the trial of the St. Petersburg Soviet members, which began on 19 September, and was climaxed by Trotsky's testimony, which took the form of an impassioned speech defending the insurrection and attacking the tsarist government for its tolerance of assassinations and incitement of pogroms. The guilty verdict was delivered on 2 November, and the defendants were sentenced to Siberian exile for life. En route to Siberia, Trotsky managed to escape and make his way to St. Petersburg and then abroad.

By the fall of 1907 Trotsky, along with his wife and their two sons, had settled in Vienna. Trotsky supported himself and his family through his journalism, mostly by contributing pseudonymously to *Kievskaia mysl'* (Kievan Thought), a liberal newspaper popular in Russia. All the while, he remained an independent Marxist seeking to reunite the Bolshevik and Menshevik factions. His most famous attempt at conciliation was his role in sponsoring a conference of social democrats held in Vienna in August 1912 known as the August Bloc. Lenin's Bolsheviks, who in January had expelled the Mensheviks and declared themselves to be the Social Democratic Labour Party, refused to attend the Vienna gathering, and in any case, the Mensheviks were also prepared to go their separate way.

Trotsky's finest journalistic reporting from this period was his war correspondence, for *Kievskaia mysl'*, from the front lines of the First and Second Balkan Wars, in 1912–13. At the outbreak of World War I in August 1914, Trotsky avoided detention in Austria as an "enemy alien" by moving to Switzerland, and soon he resettled in France. Trotsky analyzed the war and its revolutionary prospects in an influential

4 In his *History of the Russian Revolution*, published in the early 1930s, Trotsky coined the term "the law of combined development" as a label for this phenomenon of backwardness. See Knei-Paz, *The Social and Political Thought of Leon Trotsky*, 89, n. 81.

pamphlet titled *The War and the International*, in which he predicted that the conflict would lead to the collapse of the capitalist system and a European-wide revolution. He advocated the principle of national self-determination and predicted the rise of a postwar "United States of Europe." Lenin and the Bolsheviks, meanwhile, were calling for turning the "imperialist" war into a civil war and for the formation of a new International to replace the discredited Second Socialist International, a position considered far too radical by the Mensheviks, supporters of a democratic peace. The social democrats gathered in September 1915 at a conference in Zimmerwald, Switzerland, a village outside Bern, where Lenin's radical position was in the minority, but where it also became apparent that Trotsky and Lenin shared a sense of the international revolutionary possibilities created by the war.

Red October

In September 1916 Trotsky was expelled from France to Spain, and from there he sailed in January 1917 to New York City, which is where he learned of the collapse of the Russian autocracy. Returning to Russia in May, Trotsky became an associate member of the executive of the revived Petrograd Soviet, now hovering in uneasy counterpoint to the Provisional Government. Lenin, who had returned to Russia in April, was calling for "All Power to the Soviets." He and Trotsky were now brought together by circumstances: For Lenin the attraction was Trotsky's radical view of the revolutionary situation, his experience in revolution, and his skill as an orator and revolutionary organizer; for Trotsky, lacking an organizational base, the chief draw was Lenin's Bolshevik party. For the moment, Trotsky was the leader of a group of disaffected social democrats he had formed in 1913 called the Inter-Borough Organization.

In the wake of the July Days unrest, Trotsky was arrested on 23 July for alleged associations with the Bolsheviks. He was released from prison on 4 September, after the failed military putsch in late August known as the "Kornilov affair." While he was in prison, the Inter-Borough Organization had merged with the Bolshevik party, so Trotsky had become a Bolshevik and been elected to the party's Central Committee. On 9 September the Bolsheviks won a majority in the Petrograd Soviet, and on 23 September Trotsky was elected the Soviet's chairman. Lenin, in hiding in Finland since the post-July Days crackdown, was now lobbying strenuously for an armed insurrection, but Trotsky advised waiting in order to time the seizure of power to coincide with the convening of the Second All-Russian Congress of Soviets, scheduled for late October. Trotsky's idea was to cloak the insurrection in democratic legitimacy and bring along the largest possible number of supporters. In the meantime, Trotsky was a whirlwind of activity, especially as an orator, addressing audiences all over the city and securing support for the Soviet, notably from the Petrograd garrison. A Menshevik eyewitness testified that he "seemed to be speaking simultaneously in all places. Every Petrograd worker and soldier knew him and heard him personally. His influence, both on the masses and at headquarters, was overwhelming."[5]

In early October the Petrograd Soviet established the Military Revolutionary Committee to coordinate the defense of the capital. Under Trotsky's leadership the committee became the chief instrument for organizing the insurrection. After Lenin emerged from hiding and arrived in Petrograd on 10 October, the Bolshevik Central Committee passed a resolution, by a vote of 10 to 2, in favor of an armed seizure of power. The Congress of Soviets opened on 25 October. That night, Lenin and Trotsky informed the delegates of the seizure of the Winter Palace by the Red Guards. As some of the delegates walked out of the hall, Martov and his fellow Mensheviks accused the Bolsheviks of carrying out a putsch and protested that some kind of political compromise ought to be agreed. Trotsky disdainfully dismissed his former comrades. The Bolshevik triumph, he declared, was a mass insurrection, not a coup. No compromise was necessary. "To those who have left and to those who tell us to do this we must say: You are bankrupt. You have played out your role. Go where you belong from now on: into the dustbin of history!"[6]

Trotsky in Power

In the new Soviet government, Trotsky became people's commissar of foreign affairs, reportedly boasting, "I shall publish a few revolutionary proclamations and then close shop."[7] The most pressing matter was the

5 Nikolai Sukhanov, quoted in Volkogonov, *Trotsky*, 84.

6 In the original Russian source Trotsky uses the term *"sornaia korzina istorii,"* literally rubbish can, or waste basket, of history. Nikolai N. Sukhanov, *Zapiski o revoliutsii*, 3 vols. (Moscow: Respublika, 1991–92), vol. III, 337. "Dustbin" is the most commonly used rendering in English, along with "ash heap." Deutscher (*The Prophet Armed*, 259) prefers "dustheap."

7 Deutscher, *The Prophet Armed*, 271.

war with Germany. A ceasefire was agreed and negotiations with representatives of the Central Powers got under way at Brest-Litovsk. The Germans offered the Soviet government punishing peace terms, setting off an acrimonious debate among the Bolshevik leadership. Lenin wanted to sue for peace in order to give the revolution a chance to survive; other Bolsheviks preferred to prosecute a "revolutionary war" in the hope of igniting revolution in Europe. Trotsky carved out a middle position, summed up in the slogan "neither war nor peace," and this compromise broke the deadlock. At the end of January 1918, Trotsky's explanation of his government's position stunned his interlocutors at Brest-Litovsk. But the filibustering came to an end on 18 February, when the Germans renewed their military offensive, forcing the Soviet government to sign the extraordinarily harsh Treaty of Brest-Litovsk and surrender a huge swathe of vital territory in European Russia, including Ukraine.

Trotsky resigned as foreign affairs commissar and became people's commissar of war, as the revolution's enemies gathered on the periphery. He set about forging a genuine army out of the remnants of the peasant tsarist army and the proletarian Red Guard units from Moscow and Petrograd. He arranged for former officers of the Russian Imperial Army to be enlisted into the ranks of a Red Army desperately in need of their expertise and experience. In order to ensure their loyalty, Trotsky attached to the ranking officers trustworthy Bolsheviks designated as political commissars. Leaving strategy and operations mostly to the experts, he reserved for himself the role of supreme agitator, rushing from front to front in his armored train to shore up morale and inspire the fight. Along the way, he acquired a reputation for brutality, especially for his merciless treatment of deserters. Units retreating without orders might face summary justice and a firing squad, not excepting commanding officers and commissars.

The image of Trotsky as the bloody Red warlord was a favorite of anti-Bolshevik propagandists. Especially notorious was his decision to use the wives and children of former tsarist officers as hostages in order to command their allegiance. White Guard propaganda made the most of the fact that the Red warlord was a Jew, thereby tapping into popular perceptions about "Jewish Bolshevism." Trotsky's actions as war commissar also embroiled him in controversy with fellow communists and led to his first clashes with Stalin, who was chief political commissar on the southern front. Trotsky's lowest point came in the summer of 1919, when he suffered a series of political setbacks just as the White armies were closing in and an impatient Lenin was reproaching him for the Red Army's reversals on the battlefield.

He offered his resignation as war commissar, which the Central Committee rejected. Trotsky's fortunes revived in October, when he successfully lobbied for and then organized and led a defense of Petrograd at a time when Lenin and others had been prepared to sacrifice the former capital. For his role in leading the Red Army to victory he was awarded the Order of the Red Banner.

Trotsky's reputation for ruthlessness extended to his treatment of class enemies. He was a staunch defender of the communist government's use of coercion and terror. His most elaborate defense took the form of a 1919 pamphlet called *Terrorism and Communism*, written in response to German social democrat Karl Kautsky's anti-communist pamphlet of the same name which accused the Bolsheviks of setting up a dictatorship of a party, not of a class, and using it to terrorize the population. Trotsky, despite his prescient warnings before 1917 about the dangers of Lenin's centralism leading to "substitutionism," now appeared to have no doubt that the interests of the communist party were identical with those of Russia's proletariat. He defended the party's methods as legitimate means to worthy ends. Excesses were an inescapable feature of every revolution, he maintained.

As the civil war wound down, Trotsky proposed to apply to Soviet Russia's acute economic crisis the kind of draconian measures employed by the Red Army. He called his program the "militarization of labor," envisioning the compulsory deployment of demobilized soldiers to industrial "fronts" that most needed them. Compulsion and coercion were not only justified, he argued, but inevitable, indeed desirable, during the transition from capitalism to socialism. Trotsky's proposals met strong resistance in the Central Committee, but Lenin backed him up. Appointed interim people's commissar of transport in March 1920, Trotsky prescribed similar shock methods for the revival of Soviet Russia's ravaged railway system. He also took a hard line in the bitterly fought internal party debate in 1920 concerning the question of whether to grant Soviet trade unions a measure of autonomy. Trotsky took the view that such autonomy was unnecessary under a proletarian dictatorship, while Lenin took the opposing view, leading to clashes between the two leaders.

The economic crisis of the winter of 1920–21, which sparked worker protests and peasant rebellion, persuaded the Soviet leadership to introduce limited trade, the first step in the introduction of a mixed market economy known as the New Economic Policy (NEP). But before the reforms were introduced, the sailors of the fortress island of Kronstadt, the main base of the Baltic Fleet in the Gulf of Finland, rose in revolt. The sailors there had played a vital role in the revolutionary events of 1917. Trotsky, who was their favorite, honored them at the time as "the pride and glory of the revolution." Now they were demanding genuine elections to the soviets, the cessation of political terror and the kind of limited free trade the Bolsheviks were about to introduce. A special target of their wrath was "bloody Field Marshal Trotsky."[8] The Bolsheviks portrayed the uprising as an act of counterrevolution, and Red Army troops crossed over the ice to crush it. Afterwards, hundreds of rebels were executed without trial.

Succession Struggles

The communist party introduced the NEP at its Tenth Congress in March 1921, where the delegates also voted to impose a ban on internal factions. In the economic debates of the 1920s, Trotsky consistently took a position on the left of the spectrum, advocating a faster pace of industrialization, more economic planning and a tighter rein on capitalism in the countryside. At this time Trotsky was a member of the Politburo and the Central Committee of the Communist Party, remained people's commissar of war, and was a member of the Executive Committee of the Communist International. Lenin and Trotsky were widely perceived as the country's top two leaders. Lenin suffered a stroke in spring 1922, and his deteriorating health set off a power struggle. By the time of his death, a triumvirate of Stalin, Lev Kamenev and Grigorii Zinoviev had combined to check the heir apparent. Within a few years Trotsky would suffer a total political defeat and be expelled from the USSR.

Several related factors explain Trotsky's precipitous downfall, beginning with his ineptness as a politician. He was much more effective operating among the masses in a time of revolutionary upheaval than he was maneuvering in the corridors of power of an established government. His status as a lone wolf in the years before the October Revolution ensured he had almost no practice at intra-party politics. And his personality was a handicap. He had very few personal friends, tended to be awkward and stiff in personal relations, and his irrepressible haughtiness alienated people. After his defeat, Trotsky preferred to believe he had lost power to a political machine rather than a person, but Stalin, while he

8 Paul Avrich, *Kronstadt 1921* (Princeton: Princeton University Press, 1970), 60, 176.

lacked Trotsky's intellectual gifts, was a master of political intrigue. Their political struggle was a one-sided contest.

As a latecomer to the Bolshevik party, moreover, Trotsky had no organizational base within the party, whose membership was expanding with new party cadres much more likely to be loyal to Stalin, who was appointed the party's general secretary in 1922. Trotsky felt inhibited from asserting himself by the ban on party factions, which he nonetheless continued to support. The autumn of 1923 seemed to offer him his most opportune moment to act, in the wake of the failed communist insurrection in Germany, a fiasco Trotsky attributed not to inapposite historical analogies between revolutionary Russia and Weimar Germany, but chiefly to inept Kremlin leadership. When, that same autumn, Trotsky and his followers, calling themselves the left opposition, blamed Soviet economic mismanagement on the hierarchy of party secretaries obstructing inner-party democracy and warned that a bureaucratic "degeneration" was strangling the revolution, they were denounced for engaging in factionalism.

The above factors help explain Trotsky's baffling passivity in the face of mounting political danger, as he squandered opportunities to defend himself.[9] In April 1922 when Lenin nominated Trotsky to be deputy chairman of the Council of People's Commissars, he declined the invitation. Several months later, Lenin, in ill health and ill at ease with Stalin's centralist designs for administering the Soviet state, encouraged Trotsky to challenge Stalin at the upcoming party congress over the high-handed methods he had used to subdue the Georgian comrades. Trotsky failed to take action. He later insisted that to have asserted himself politically would have been interpreted as a power grab, but his reticence may also be explained by his confident assumption that in the end he would be recognized as Lenin's successor. Lenin may have inadvertently encouraged this thinking with his so-called political testament of December 1922, in which he singled out Trotsky as "probably the most able man in the present Central Committee," although in the same document Lenin also noted Trotsky's "excessive self-confidence" and his tendency to be "too much drawn to the purely administrative aspect of affairs" and to set himself in opposition to the Central Committee. Lenin's letter expressed concern that Trotsky and Stalin, the party's "two most

9 Knei-Paz (*The Social and Political Thought of Leon Trotsky*, 379) aptly remarks: "Why Trotsky did not strike out with more than words against the new, post-Lenin leadership of the 'triumvirate', why he did not attempt to make a real thrust for power, remains the great enigma both of his personality and of his political judgment."

eminent leaders," would eventually clash and cause a schism in the party. In early January, concerned about the "unbounded power" Stalin had accumulated, Lenin added a famous postscript calling for Stalin's removal as general secretary.[10] This seemed to place the ultimate weapon in Trotsky's hands, yet he failed to take advantage of it.

At critical moments in the succession struggle Trotsky suffered bouts of fever and lethargy that put him *hors de combat*. Trotsky's contemporaries and his biographers have suspected a psychological dimension to this mysterious illness: perhaps an indication that Trotsky had no stomach for political in-fighting. This mysterious illness was never more consequential than in January 1924, when Lenin died, and Trotsky, convalescing in the Black Sea resort of Sukhumi, Georgia, failed to return for the funeral. Lenin's burial in the makeshift wooden mausoleum on an arctic Red Square was a defining event in Soviet political history, yet Trotsky was nowhere to be seen.

In May 1924, in an attempt to disarm his critics within the party leadership, Trotsky stood before the Thirteenth Party Congress and declared that, "In the last instance, the party is always right, because it is the only historic instrument which the working class possesses for the solution of its fundamental tasks . . . One can be right only with the party and through the party because history has not created any other way for the realization of one's rightness. The English have the saying, 'My country, right or wrong.' With much greater justification we can say: My party, right or wrong."[11] But was it really Trotsky's party? The image of Trotsky quietly encouraged by his opponents was that he was something of a closet Menshevik. Trotsky tried to make the case for his impeccable Bolshevik credentials in an essay he published in the autumn of 1924 called *The Lessons of October*, which highlighted his vital role in the events of the crucial year 1917 and at the same time pointed to the failings of Zinoviev and Kamenev, the two Central Committee members who had voted against the October uprising. The triumvirs responded with an orchestrated campaign against Trotsky that spotlighted his disagreements with Lenin going back to 1903. The insults that Trotsky once hurled at Lenin were now hauled out for inspection, cringe-worthy quotes that must have raised eyebrows among the newer recruits to the party at a time when Lenin was being transformed into a near-sacred figure.

10 Isaac Deutscher, *The Prophet Unarmed: Trotsky, 1921–1929* (London: Verso, 2003), 57–58; Volkogonov, *Trotsky*, 242–43.

11 Deutscher, *The Prophet Unarmed*, 115.

Toward the end of 1924, Stalin began to promote the slogan "socialism in one country" as an alternative to Trotsky's "permanent revolution." Stalin, while not making a case for Russian economic self-sufficiency or abandoning the idea that the final victory of Soviet socialism would require international revolution, promoted "socialism in one country" as an argument for Soviet Russia's capacity for self-reliance in the short term, in conditions of peace and stability, against the backdrop of what was perceived to be the relative stabilization of international capitalism. Trotsky's theory was now turned against him, as Stalin used it to portray him as a pessimist, someone who believed that Russia could not even proceed to build socialism without the assistance of the Western proletariat. In fact, Trotsky, while remaining more sanguine about the immediate prospects of international revolution, was a consistent advocate of a faster-paced industrialization, more economic planning and tighter curbs on capitalism in the countryside, which gave his rivals a pretext to depict him as a reckless super-industrializer who "underestimated" the importance of the peasantry. Yet, somewhat contradictorily, Trotsky's theory of permanent revolution was now used to paint him as a defeatist at home and at the same time a reckless adventurer in championing socialist revolution abroad.

In January 1925 Trotsky, expecting to be sacked, resigned as war commissar. His hopes revived in 1926 when the triumvirate collapsed and Zinoviev and Kamenev combined forces with him in a so-called Joint Opposition against Stalin and Nikolai Bukharin. But these joint forces were largely spent forces, and the opposition failed to gain traction, despite openings offered by Soviet foreign policy failures, especially in Britain and China. In Britain, when a general strike broke out in May 1926, the Stalin–Bukharin leadership, persuaded that capitalism had entered a period of relative stabilization and perceiving the strike as a capitalist provocation, decided against using Anglo-Soviet trade union connections to exploit the situation. Trotsky, who believed Britain was ripe for revolution, sharply criticized the Politburo for its timidity. China's communists, meanwhile, had been instructed by the Comintern to enter into an alliance with Chiang Kai-shek's nationalist movement, the Kuomintang. Stalin and Bukharin counseled moderation, believing that China must first work to achieve a bourgeois-democratic revolution. Trotsky, ever impatient, derided such thinking as a form of Menshevism, and when, in April 1927, Kuomintang forces massacred tens of thousands of communists and workers in Shanghai, the Kremlin had to scramble to justify itself and adjust its policy. Yet Trotsky was unable to capitalize on the China debacle.

At a stormy Politburo meeting in October 1926, at which Stalin labeled the Joint Opposition a "social-democratic deviation" and demanded that they admit their errors and recant, Trotsky, who had not lost his touch when it came to striking dramatic poses, delivered a fiery rebuttal that culminated with him pointing a finger at Stalin and declaring "The First Secretary poses his candidature to the post of gravedigger of the revolution!"[12] prompting Stalin to rush out of the hall and slam the door behind him. The next morning, 26 October, the Central Committee voted to remove Trotsky from the Politburo. A year later he was dropped from the Central Committee, and in November 1927 he and Zinoviev were ousted from the communist party, with Kamenev and hundreds of other oppositionists soon to follow.

In January 1928 Trotsky was exiled to Alma Ata, in Kazakhstan. He was joined there by his wife and their older son, Lev. Hundreds of Trotsky's supporters were similarly exiled as the rout of the Joint Opposition was completed. As Trotsky kept up contact with his fellow exiles, trying to maintain the morale and the unity of the opposition, Stalin adopted a "left course" in economic policy whose centerpiece was the coercive requisition of grain from the countryside. Soon Trotsky learned that onetime allies were abandoning him, justifying their defections by the idea that Stalin was carrying out the left opposition's program. As the capitulations mounted, Stalin decided to exile his nemesis from the USSR. In February 1929, Trotsky and his wife and son Lev sailed to Turkey. He would never see Russia again.

The Lion and the Labyrinth

Trotsky spent the next four years in Turkey, living in a house on Prinkipo Island (today Büyükada), on the Sea of Marmara. He devoted much time to writing analyses of Soviet and international developments, mostly for the *Bulletin of the Opposition*, the political organ of the Trotskyist movement headquartered in Berlin. Trotsky was assisted in this work by his son and loyal lieutenant Lev Sedov, whose name now became closely linked to his father's. To earn money to support himself and the *Bulletin*, Trotsky agreed to publish an autobiography, and then followed it with a panoramic history of the Russian Revolution. These books, translated into several languages, brought in much-needed income and served as a platform for Trotsky to

12 Deutscher, *The Prophet Unarmed*, 248.

defend his place in history, now under assault by Stalin's falsifiers, as the emblematic duo "Lenin and Trotsky" was being replaced by "Lenin and Stalin."

In 1929, meanwhile, Stalin's economic program took a radical turn in the form of a crash industrialization drive under the Five-Year Plan and the coerced collectivization of the peasantry. Trotsky, reading the triumphant newspaper headlines out of the USSR, did nothing to inhibit the perception that Stalin was continuing to engage in theft from the left opposition's playbook, although in fact Trotsky's economic proposals in the 1920s never strayed beyond the NEP framework, whereas Stalin's revolution from above put an end to NEP. Stalin's "Great Break" was accompanied by a radical shift in Comintern policy that directed communists to treat social democrats as "social fascists," a policy that would facilitate the rise of Hitler's National Socialists. Trotsky was a vociferous critic of the new policy and, after the Nazis came to power in 1933, warned presciently about National Socialism's dangerous appeal in Germany and beyond. In July 1933, Trotsky was able to secure permission to move to France, but by the summer of 1935, as Paris and Moscow sought a rapprochement, he was forced to move again, this time to Norway.

It was in Norway that Trotsky wrote his highly influential analysis of Stalin's USSR, *The Revolution Betrayed*. The book applauded the "unprecedented tempo of Russia's industrial development" and the emergence of a nationalized planned economy and collectivized agriculture, while criticizing the needlessly violent methods used to accomplish those ends and denying that these achievements added up to the attainment of "socialism," as Stalin had proclaimed. In Trotsky's view, despite rising bureaucratic privilege and economic inequality, the USSR remained a workers' state, albeit a "degenerated workers' state." Only the Stalinist regime, the product of Soviet Russia's prolonged isolation, was objectionable. Trotsky condemned Soviet police repressions and state terror, and even classified the USSR and Nazi Germany as "totalitarian" twins that bore a "deadly similarity." He advocated a revolution to overthrow Stalin's ruling bureaucracy and restore "Soviet democracy," but he had in mind a narrowly political, as opposed to a social revolution. The USSR, in other words, far from being a lost cause, was still retrievable for the revolution. Red October remained untarnished.[13]

13 Leon Trotsky, *The Revolution Betrayed*, trans. Max Eastman (Mineola, NY: Dover, 2004), 1, 208, 210, 218.

The Revolution Betrayed was completed just before the start of the first Moscow show trial, in August 1936, when sixteen leaders, including Zinoviev and Kamenev, were accused of the most fantastic of crimes, such as treason, conspiracy, assassination, wrecking and sabotage. The indictment claimed that Trotsky and Lev Sedov were at the center of the conspiracy. The accused were charged with establishing a "Trotskyite–Zinovievite Terrorist Center." "Trotskyism" now became the ultimate heresy, as phrases like "Trotskyist wreckers and spies" haunted Soviet newspaper headlines. All sixteen defendants confessed to their crimes and were convicted and executed, while Trotsky and son Lev were convicted *in absentia*. Trotsky himself was as yet out of Stalin's reach, but Trotsky's family members and former associates in the USSR were swept up in the terror.

After the Moscow trial, the Norwegian government, keen to avoid antagonizing the Kremlin, placed Trotsky under house arrest and moved to expel him. He sailed to Mexico, the only country that would offer him asylum, arriving there in January 1937, just as the second Moscow trial was about to begin. Artists Diego Rivera and Frida Kahlo, his patrons, put up Trotsky and Natalia at a home they owned in Coyoacán, a suburb of Mexico City. Although the Mexican government was welcoming, the Mexican communists, whose ranks in these years would swell with refugee fighters from the International Brigades in Spain, were hostile and sought to undermine his exile status.

Trotsky's plight struck a chord with *Trotskysant* intellectuals in the United States repulsed by the ghoulish theater produced by Stalin's Kremlin. These so-called New York intellectuals saw Trotsky as the humane face of Soviet communism who represented the original ideals of the October Revolution betrayed by Stalin's dictatorship. The fact that Trotsky happened to be a Jewish intellectual strengthened the connection. The appeal owed much to Trotsky's literary works, not least *Literature and Revolution*, his 1923 survey of the Soviet literary scene which advocated relative tolerance, limited censorship and respect for literary tradition. It was here that Trotsky introduced the label "fellow travelers" to designate writers who, while sympathetic to revolution's ideals, would be able to progress only so far along the road to socialism.

The receptive atmosphere in New York literary circles helped make possible the formation of the "Commission of Inquiry into the Charges Made against Leon Trotsky in the Moscow Trials," a New York-based panel of liberal-to-left individuals known as the Dewey Commission, after its chairman, John Dewey, the American philosopher and public intellectual.

Dewey and other commission members took testimony from Trotsky at his Coyoacán residence for one week in April 1937. In December, the Commission announced its verdict: The trials were a frame-up; Trotsky and his son were not guilty as charged. Trotsky celebrated his victory, yet at the same time he was forced to defend himself when his critics revived the memory of Kronstadt, and his role in the suppression of the rebellion, and by extension in the rise of Stalinism. Trotsky was busy parrying this criticism when, in February 1938, he received the devastating news that his son Lev had died under mysterious circumstances in a Paris hospital while recovering from surgery. Trotsky blamed his death on foul play by Stalin's NKVD (Narodnyi Komissariat Vnutrennikh Del, People's Commissariat for Internal Affairs).

After the Nazis stormed to power in 1933, Trotsky changed his mind about remaining inside the Comintern as the left opposition. The only way forward, he decided, was to build a Fourth International, to replace the communist Third International, uniting the Trotskyists – the self-styled "Bolshevik-Leninists" – into an organization that would become the true standard-bearer of proletarian internationalism. Formally the organization came into existence only in the summer of 1938. At the time, there were no significant Trotskyist parties anywhere, and worldwide there were at most a few thousand full-fledged Trotskyists spread out among numerous marginal organizations in many countries and often riven by factionalism, making them vulnerable to NKVD penetration.

The French Trotskyists, the most important "section" of the embryonic Fourth International in the early 1930s, had been crippled by a factional split. Trotsky had advised its members to join the French Socialist Party as a temporary haven from the blows of the French communists and there to build a base of supporters. The maneuver, which came to be known as the "French turn" and which took place in August 1934 and was replicated in other countries, was controversial throughout the Trotskyist movement. In France, as elsewhere, it led to a minority split. After the formation of the Popular Front, Trotsky encouraged his French followers to break away and establish a separate party, which happened in early 1936, although this new entity soon underwent a split. By 1938, the United States was home to what was easily the largest Trotskyist group in the world, although its total membership probably never exceeded two thousand, by generous estimates. The Socialist Workers' Party was headquartered in New York, with a branch in Minneapolis, Minnesota, where the US Trotskyists had put down roots in the labor movement during that city's great truckers' strike of 1934.

The formal establishment of the Fourth International took place on 3 September 1938, in a village outside Paris. The meeting, attended by twenty-one delegates representing Trotskyist "sections" in eleven countries, lasted a single day. This was a modest beginning, by any measure, and the Trotskyists themselves regarded the new venture with skepticism, but Trotsky preferred the optimistic view. Just as World War I had carried the Bolshevik party to power in 1917 on a wave of revolution, the next world war would precipitate a revolutionary tidal wave that would sweep the Bolshevik-Leninists to victory. Trotsky's view of the matter was summed up by the title he gave to his new organization's programmatic statement: "The Death Agony of Capitalism and the Tasks of the Fourth International." The Munich agreement at the end of September 1938 prompted Trotsky to predict the likelihood of a Nazi–Soviet pact. When the pact came, in August 1939, followed by the German invasion of Poland on 1 September, which started World War II, Trotsky failed to appreciate the enormous shock it produced among his own followers. Their disillusionment deepened with the Soviet invasion of Poland, which began on 17 September, only two and a half weeks after the German assault from the west, and demonstrated that the pact was no mere nonaggression treaty, but an aggressive military alliance.

Trotsky's analysis of these events took the form of a long article, "The USSR in War," completed on 25 September. In it he declared that if World War II did not spark a proletarian revolution in the West, or if the proletariat were to take power but then surrender it to a privileged bureaucracy as in the USSR, this would confirm the emergence of a new form of totalitarianism. In that case, Trotsky acknowledged, "nothing else would remain except only to recognize that the socialist program based on the internal contradictions of capitalist society ended as a Utopia."[14] This uncharacteristically pessimistic note took his followers by surprise, as did his analysis of the latest events in Europe. In Trotsky's view, the Red Army, far from behaving like a mirror image of the Wehrmacht in Poland, was serving as a vehicle for progress there by expropriating the large landowners and nationalizing the means of production, and thus objectively spreading the features of socialism abroad.

Most of Trotsky's American comrades found this judgement difficult to square with what common sense told them about the Soviet subjugation of

14 Leon Trotsky, *In Defense of Marxism: Against the Petty-Bourgeois Opposition* (New York: Pathfinder Press, 1970), 14–15.

Poland – and, before long, of the three Baltic states. Trotsky further exacerbated the discord among his followers when he justified the Soviet invasion of Finland, on 30 November 1939, as the Red Army taking the side of the workers and peasants in a Finnish civil war and introducing workers' control in industry. Given this state of affairs, Trotsky said, the Bolshevik-Leninists must continue to lend the USSR their "full moral and material support."[15] This struck most of his American followers as fantastic. Trotsky had intended his article to heal a factional split in the Socialist Workers' Party, but instead this and his other efforts at conciliation helped ensure that the party's dissenting minority faction broke away to form a separate political party.

These events distracted Trotsky from completing a biography of Stalin he had reluctantly agreed to undertake for an American publisher in order to pay for the new home he moved into in 1939 after his political split with his volatile benefactor, Diego Rivera. Meanwhile, against the backdrop of a national election campaign in Mexico, in the winter and spring of 1940 the tone of the anti-Trotsky campaign turned violent. Meetings of the communist party and its front organizations were punctuated by shouts of "Death to Trotsky!" Heightened vigilance and increased security at Trotsky's new home failed to prevent a nighttime armed assault by Mexican communists in May 1940 that nearly killed Trotsky. In preparing to defend against another such assault, Trotsky and his staff failed to detect an NKVD assassin in their midst: a Spaniard named Ramón Mercader posing as a Canadian businessman romantically involved with a New York Trotskyist known to Trotsky, a relationship the operative used to maneuver himself into Trotsky's entourage. On 20 August, he arranged to be alone with Trotsky in his study, where he struck him on the head with an ice axe. Trotsky died of his wounds the next day.

Long Live Trotsky!

Trotsky's Fourth International lived on, although its influence, never more than marginal to begin with, continued to dissipate further, especially as Trotskyist groups around the world exhibited a propensity to split into ever smaller splinter groups, factions and tendencies on the political fringe. Trotsky's widow, Natalia, broke with the Fourth International after its leadership hailed the Korean War as a fight against American imperialism

15 Ibid., 62.

and classified Eastern bloc countries as "workers' states." "I do not see his ideas in your politics," Natalia wrote to the Executive Committee in submitting her resignation in 1951.[16] The Fourth International itself split in 1953 into the International Secretariat and the International Committee, the latter including the Socialist Workers' Party in the United States and the largest Trotskyist groups in the United Kingdom and France. Ten years later a "unity congress" succeeded in bringing the two groups together under the United Secretariat of the Fourth International, although the schism was never fully healed and the splintering continued. In the post-Stalin years, self-described "Trotskyist" groups proliferated in dozens of countries worldwide, but these were insignificant in size and had a marked tendency to spawn groupuscules. The collapse of the USSR did nothing to turn their fortunes around.

After Stalin's death in 1953, Khrushchev's de-Stalinization led to the political rehabilitation of selected victims of Stalin's repressions – though not the defendants in the major purge trials, and certainly not Trotsky, whose name and image had since Stalin's time been thoroughly erased from history books, museums and films. Yet Trotsky remained useful as a Soviet bogeyman, and "Trotskyism" as the ultimate heresy. When Mao Zedong accused Khrushchev of "revisionism" and challenged his leadership of the world communist movement, the Kremlin condemned the Chinese communists for their "neo-Trotskyist deviation."[17] Trotsky's status behind the Iron Curtain as the supreme heretic was dramatized by Milan Kundera in his 1967 novel *The Joke*, in which a male student sends a postcard to a female classmate that includes the prankish exclamation "Long Live Trotsky!" – a bit of mischief that lands him in a military work brigade.

Trotsky and Trotskyism came back into vogue in leftist circles in the West during the revolutionary year 1968, when Trotsky's intense countenance appeared ubiquitously on political posters, especially on the streets of Paris. Trotsky's enduring appeal to a later generation of left-leaning intellectuals in the West (most of the American *Trotskysants* of the 1930s had become Cold War liberals) was in part due to the influence of Isaac Deutscher's absorbingly written, sympathetic biographical trilogy of Trotsky published in the 1950s and 1960s. The Trotsky revival was brief, but it bore fruit during the following decade in the form of several new biographies of and other books about Trotsky in English.

16 *New York Times*, 9 May 1951. 17 *Time*, 10 Apr. 1964.

Yet in the USSR Trotsky remained a devil figure. In the late 1980s when General Secretary Mikhail Gorbachev's policy of *glasnost'* encouraged historians to fill in the "blank spots" of Soviet history, Old Bolsheviks who had gone down in the purge trials were rehabilitated, but Trotsky remained anathema. In a speech he delivered in November 1987 to mark the 70th anniversary of the Bolshevik Revolution, Gorbachev stated that Trotsky "had, after Lenin's death, displayed excessive pretensions to top leadership in the party, thus fully confirming Lenin's opinion of him as an excessively self-assured politician who always vacillated and cheated." Trotsky's ideas, said Gorbachev, were "essentially an attack on Leninism all down the line."[18] In the new atmosphere of openness Gorbachev had fostered, however, Trotsky was no longer taboo, and Soviet journalists and historians began to publish articles about his role as Lenin's essential comrade in 1917 and as the organizer of the Red Army, as well as the fact that the Kremlin had orchestrated his murder. Trotsky's own articles began to appear in print, and in post-Soviet Russia his books became available and biographies of him were published, by which point in time, with the entire Soviet experiment in disfavor, they were completely harmless.

The fascination with Trotsky as a historical figure persists, as evidenced by his not insignificant footprint in Western popular culture. His last years in Mexico have proven to be especially fertile ground, with their tragic story line of the wandering exile destroyed by the monstrous regime he helped create. The Mexico sojourn continues to inspire Trotsky's appearance in works of Western fiction, including Saul Bellow's breakthrough novel *The Adventures of Augie March* (1953), Barbara Kingsolver's *The Lacuna* (2009) and Cuban novelist Leonardo Padura's *The Man Who Loved Dogs* (Spanish 2009/English 2014). One early such novel was behind the 1972 feature film *The Assassination of Trotsky* (1972), in which Richard Burton played the lonely exile as a brooding bore. Trotsky's affair with Frida Kahlo, which was featured in the 2002 movie *Frida*, has brought Trotsky to the attention of a wider audience, although not in a way he could have imagined or desired.

The circumstances of Trotsky's violent death continue to transfix. "Whatever happened to Leon Trotsky?" asked the lyric in the new wave 1977 song "No More Heroes" by The Stranglers, and answered: "He got an ice pick that made his ears burn." The fact that the actual murder weapon was a "mountain-climber's axe" is the running joke of David Ives's short one-act

18 *New York Times*, 8 Nov. 1967.

comedy-drama *Variations on the Death of Trotsky* (1991). Ives's play is one of those Trotsky moments that inspired Christopher Hitchens to observe that "Even for educated readers, Leon Trotsky survives as part kitsch and part caricature."[19] A more recent instance of the man of October serving as a comedy hook was the Canadian film *The Trotsky* (2009), in which a high school student believes himself to be reincarnation of Trotsky. Long live Trotsky, indeed.

Bibliographical Essay

Trotsky is the subject of a celebrated biography by Isaac Deutscher: *The Prophet Armed: Trotsky, 1879–1921* (1954), *The Prophet Unarmed: Trotsky, 1921–1929* (1959), *and The Prophet Outcast: Trotsky, 1929–1940* (1964). All three volumes were republished by Verso in 2003. Deutscher's trilogy is magnificent, but also deeply flawed due to its hagiographic treatment of Trotsky's ideas, actions and personality. Time and again, the author is too willing to give Trotsky, his tragic hero, the benefit of the doubt. Nonetheless, Deutscher's influential biography is one of a kind and not to be missed. Biographies of Trotsky in English or English translation abound. The best starting place is Joshua Rubenstein's intelligent brief overview, *Leon Trotsky: A Revolutionary's Life* (New Haven: Yale University Press, 2011). Dmitri Volkogonov, *Trotsky: The Eternal Revolutionary*, trans. and ed. Harold Shukman (New York: Free Press, 1996), draws on Russian archival sources available only to the author to create a portrait quite unlike any other.

Baruch Knei-Paz, *The Social and Political Thought of Leon Trotsky* (Oxford: Oxford University Press, 1978), offers an exhaustive, acutely observant and indispensable analysis of Trotsky's theoretical writing. Trotsky's works available in English translation and worth reading include *My Life: An Attempt at an Autobiography* (Mineola, NY: Dover, 2007); *Literature and Revolution* (Chicago: Haymarket Books, 2005); *The Revolution Betrayed*, trans. Max Eastman (Mineola, NY: Dover, 1937); and *In Defense of Marxism: Against the Petty-Bourgeois Opposition* (New York: Pathfinder Press, 1970). Trotsky's *History of the Russian Revolution*, trans. Max Eastman (Chicago: Haymarket Books, 2008), is a hugely detailed account of 1917 that is unmistakably Marxist in its interpretation of events and best appreciated as a work of literature. Trotsky's Balkan war reporting has been compiled in *The War*

19 Christopher Hitchens, "The Old Man," *The Atlantic* (July/Aug. 2004).

Correspondence of Leon Trotsky: The Balkan Wars 1912–13 (New York: Pathfinder Press, 1981).

Among the best memoirs by people who knew Trotsky well is that of Jean van Heijenoort, *With Trotsky in Exile: From Prinkipo to Coyoacán* (Cambridge, MA: Harvard University Press, 1978), written by his closest secretary/comrade during his years in exile. Max Eastman, an American socialist who knew Trotsky in the early Soviet years and wrote a portrait of his youth, offers fascinating character sketches of him in "Great in a Time of Storm: The Character and Fate of Leon Trotsky," in *Heroes I Have Known: Twelve Who Lived Great Lives* (New York: Simon & Schuster, 1942), 239–59; and "Problems of Friendship with Trotsky," in *Great Companions: Critical Memoirs of Some Famous Friends* (New York: Farrar, Straus and Cudahy, 1959). For a critical assessment of Trotsky by an American Trotskyist who served as his secretary in Turkey, see Albert Glotzer, *Trotsky: Memoir and Critique* (New York: Prometheus Books, 1989). Soviet people's commissar of education Anatoly Lunacharsky profiled Trotsky in a 1923 volume translated into English as *Revolutionary Silhouettes*, trans. Michael Glenny (New York: Penguin, 1967).

Exhaustive coverage of the myriad groupings that populated the international Trotskyist movement, tracing their evolution from Trotsky's exile years through to the final phase of the USSR, is provided in Robert J. Alexander, *International Trotskyism, 1929–1985: A Documented Analysis of the Movement* (Durham, NC: Duke University Press, 1991).

8

Communism and the Crisis of the Colonial System

SOBHANLAL DATTA GUPTA

Birth of the Comintern

The fall of the worldwide colonial system is generally associated with the end of World War II in 1945. The collapse was the result of a crisis of colonialism, which was largely precipitated by the anti-colonial struggle of the people in the colonies, spreading primarily across Asia and Africa. Initially, in most of these countries the thrust of the struggle had a nationalist orientation. The seizure of power by the Bolsheviks in Russia in October 1917 had an electrifying impact on the struggle of the colonial peoples. This was manifest in more than one way. First, the Soviet government proclaimed that the USSR stood by colonial peoples and would extend all possible support to their cause. Second, the formation of the Communist International (Comintern) in 1919, with its headquarters in Moscow, led to the formation of communist parties in the colonies, and this opened up an alternative perspective for the people in the colonies vis-à-vis nationalism. Third, the struggle of the colonial people for the first time in history was viewed in the spirit of internationalism, when, besides the Russian Communist Party and the Comintern (1919–43), communist parties of the metropolitan countries came forward to extend their support to the cause of the colonial people.

Two issues became deeply relevant in this context. First, as the Comintern and the communist parties in the colonies under its guidance and control acted as major catalysts of anti-colonial struggle, how were they to work out an understanding of the colonial question that was distinct from that of nationalists? Second, the communist parties of the metropolitan countries were required in principle to support the cause of the anti-colonial struggle, but in practice this led to tensions that to a large extent vitiated the relations between the communist parties in the colonies and those in the metropole.

The birth of the Comintern in 1919 envisaged the project of a world revolution but how did the colonies figure in this dream? Was the problem of colonialism recognized on its own terms, demanding a strategy of revolution that would conform to the peculiarities of the different colonies, or was it considered simply as an appendage to the grand project of world revolution, which, it was believed, was destined to begin somewhere in Europe, notably in Germany? To be more exact, how did the Comintern work out its understanding of the colonial question – in the mirror of Eurocentrism or in terms of the uniqueness of the colonies? Now that the archival holdings of the Comintern are to a large extent accessible to scholars, it is possible to refresh our understanding of the colonial question and throw new light on it.

The manifesto of the First Congress of the Comintern highlighted the importance of the colonial question but also pointed out that "the hour of proletarian dictatorship in Europe" would also constitute the hour of liberation of the colonial people, the colonial question being considered as an appendage to the European revolution. But opinions expressing a different understanding of the colonial question also figured, however marginally, at the inaugural Congress. Thus Mustafa Subhi (Turkey) pointed out that the destiny of the European revolution was also dependent on the fate of the revolutionary movements in the East. The vision of an outbreak of revolution in the East, with direct military help from Soviet Russia, also figured in Lenin's initial perception of the colonial question, following the victory of the October Revolution. He highlighted the importance of secretly sending money and weapons to the countries of the East by way of aiding the liberation struggle in the colonies and it was on his initiative that Lev Karakhan drew up a proposal whereby the Central Committee of the Russian Communist Party was to allocate large sums for Bolshevik agitators to be sent to the Eastern countries. Thus, a trip to China or Korea was estimated to cost ten thousand gold rubles, while Persia, India and other Asian countries had their own costings.[1]

The defeat of the German Revolution and the retreat of the revolutionary forces across Europe put an end to the projected dream of imminent world revolution, and this made it imperative for the Russian Communist Party and the Comintern to pay special attention to the national liberation movement in the backward, colonial countries. The social basis for the creation of a mass

1 Sobhanlal Datta Gupta, *Comintern and the Destiny of Communism in India, 1919–1943: Dialectics of Real and a Possible History*, 2nd revised and enlarged edn. (Kolkata: Serribaan, 2011), 70–75.

workers' party was absent in these countries, yet the experience of the Russian Revolution, coupled with Lenin's assurance that Soviet Russia was the only principled ally of the oppressed nations, sparked an enthusiastic response. Thus, according to one estimate, already by the end of 1921, communist parties had been formed in China, Korea, Dutch East Indies (Asia), Egypt and South Africa (Africa), Argentina, the Caribbean and Mexico (Central and Latin America) and Turkey.[2]

Forging an Anti-Colonial Strategy

It was the Second Congress of the Comintern (1920) which may be considered to have inaugurated the entry of the East into the European circuit in an altogether new perspective, the principal text articulating this being the "Colonial Theses," originally drafted by Lenin and subsequently adopted at the Congress with some amendments. Through this document it was possible for the first time, as Sanjay Seth has said, for the East to project itself no longer as the West's essentialized Other but in terms of its own subjectivity, so that the destiny of the proletarian revolution in the West now got linked directly to the anti-imperialist struggle in the colonies.[3] Also adopted were the "Supplementary Theses" drafted by M. N. Roy, but in a drastically modified form. The two sets of theses represented opposing viewpoints, leading to what is known as the Lenin–Roy debate, the significance of which was substantial. First, Lenin's formulation that the Comintern was required to extend support to nationalist movements in the colonial countries was rejected by Roy, a position shared by Ahmed Sultanzade (Iran) and Giacinto Serrati (Italy). Roy's understanding was that bourgeois nationalism in the colonies was an accomplice of imperialism and wholly reactionary, so that extension of support to the nationalist forces on the part of communists amounted to betrayal. Second, while Lenin made a distinction between bourgeois-nationalist, that is, reformist movements, and national-revolutionary, that is, radical movements against imperialism, for Roy in the colonies what mattered was the distinction between nationalist and proletarian currents, since in countries like India industrialization had sufficiently developed to create embryonic classes. Third, for Lenin, the

2 See "Introduction," in Tim Rees and Andrew Thorpe (eds.), *International Communism and the Communist International 1919–1943* (Manchester: Manchester University Press, 1998), 2.

3 Sanjay Seth, *Marxist Theory and Nationalist Politics: The Case of Colonial India* (New Delhi: Sage, 1995), 58–59.

agenda in the colonial countries was to militarize the peasantry through the organization of peasants' soviets rather than to harbor the dream of a proletarian revolution, since industrialization was yet to take off. By contrast, for Roy the agenda in the colonies was proletarian revolution under the leadership of the communist party.

There was a strong feeling shared by many delegates, notably Roy and Pak Chin-sun (Korea), that victory of the revolution in the colonies was a necessary condition for the triumph of the revolution in the West, and that it was, therefore, imperative for the European proletariat to extend all possible aid to the struggles of the colonial people. The "Directives on the Nationality Question and the Colonial Question," passed by the Congress and signed by Lenin in 1920, emphasized that all communist parties should come to the help of the bourgeois-democratic liberation movements in the colonies, but also wage a battle against the influence of all reactionary and mediaeval elements in these countries. This was assumed to extend to struggles against Pan-Islamism and similar trends. Further, while support should be extended to the peasant movement in the backward countries, the aim should be to give them a revolutionary character. In addition, links should be forged between these movements and the European proletariat. Finally, while the local communist parties should build up temporary alliances with national liberation movements, they must not merge with them, and must unconditionally maintain the independent character of the proletarian movement.[4]

One month after the conclusion of the Second Congress in August 1920, the colonial question again came up for a detailed examination at the First Congress of the Peoples of the East, held at Baku in the Caucasus. Although neither Lenin nor Roy attended the Congress it bore the imprint of the ideas projected at the Second Congress, touching upon the sensitive question of extension of support to nationalist movements and the goal of revolutionary struggle in the colonies. Especially significant was the stress laid by a number of delegates on the importance of building up peasant soviets in the East in the light of Lenin's "Colonial Theses." One consequence of the Congress was the establishment of the Council of Propaganda and Activities of the Peoples of the East (its predecessor was the Council of International Propaganda which worked from Tashkent

4 "Leitsätze über die Nationalitätenfrage und die Kolonialfrage" [Directives on the Nationality Question and the Colonial Question], in *Leitsätze zum II. Kongress der Kommunistischen Internationale* (Petrograd, Smolny: Verlag der Kommunistischen Internationale, 1920), 50–59.

during 1919–20), whose objectives were: the publication of a journal called *Narody Vostoka* (Peoples of the East), establishment in Baku of a university of social sciences for activists in the Eastern countries, publication of pamphlets and extension of support to the national liberation movements in the East. Further, it acted as the auxiliary apparatus of the Executive Committee of the Communist International (ECCI), maintaining links with communist and revolutionary parties and groups of the Near and Middle East.

The ebbing of the revolutionary tide in the West and the turn of the Comintern toward the East led to the creation of a number of special institutions. This had begun with the setting up of the Eastern Department of the Comintern, which was created by a decision of the ECCI on 11 December 1919. On 5 June 1920, by a decision of the Small Bureau, the Turkestan or Tashkent Bureau of the Comintern was established, in the activities of which M. N. Roy, G. Safarov and Ya. Sokolnikov played a major role. Thereafter, between the Third Congress in 1921 and the Fourth Congress in 1922, the importance of the Eastern Department grew steadily. On 15 January 1921 the "small bureau" of the Comintern – the five-person executive – decided to create a Department of the Near East, and on that same day the Turkestan Bureau was also brought under this department. After the Third Congress in August 1921, it was suggested to establish Departments of the Near and Middle East as well as North Africa to develop a more detailed strategy. On 2 June 1922 the Eastern Department was put under the leadership of Safarov and by the beginning of 1922 there existed two departments responsible for the conduct of the Comintern's Eastern policy, namely, the Department of the Near and the Middle East and the Department of the Far East, the latter being known in some Comintern documents as the Far Eastern Secretariat. However, in mid 1922 it was felt that the growing importance of the colonial question required the setting up of a unified Eastern Department of the ECCI in which there would be three relatively independent sectors, namely, Near East, Middle East and Far East, and this arrangement continued until the Fourth Congress, held in 1922. The Eastern Department existed until 1926, when, consequent on a decision of the Presidium of the ECCI on 24 March 1926, it was replaced by the Eastern Secretariat, which functioned until 1935.

A crucial role in lending material support to the Comintern's Eastern policy was played by the Communist University of the Toilers of the East (KUTV) in Moscow, formed on 21 April 1921, under the Commissariat of Nationalities headed by Stalin, following a resolution of the All-Union Central

Executive Committee of the Russian Communist Party. This had two distinct aims: (a) preparation of the national cadres for the Asian republics and regions of the Soviet Union; and (b) preparation of cadres for the communist parties of Eastern countries outside the Soviet Union. With departments located at Tashkent, Baku and Irkutsk, it was engaged in training and orienting the cadres of the communist parties of the Eastern countries in the spirit and outlook of the Comintern. The KUTV provided major support in working out a colonial policy for the various regions of Asia. Furthermore, in the declaration of a "Scientific-Historical Group" in 1925, the task of the KUTV to develop a revolutionary scientific – as opposed to a bourgeois scientific – analysis of the East was spelled out, bourgeois science supposedly reflecting the exploiters' view of the East. The KUTV became the embryo of future Soviet Oriental studies, and in 1936 gave birth to the Scientific Research Association on the Study of National-Colonial Problems (NIANKP), established on the basis of a resolution of the ECCI Secretariat. In addition, a Scientific Research Association (NIA) was formed in KUTV in early 1927, which came to be known as the "scientific laboratory" of the Eastern communists. Its main task was the preparation of teachers and scientific workers for the East, with two sections respectively for the Soviet East and for Eastern countries beyond the Soviet Union.

In contrast to the Second Congress, the Comintern's Third Congress of 1921 adopted no document on the colonial question, as the Eastern question figured only briefly, causing resentment among many delegates. Although three theses were submitted for discussion in the Congress by Roy (India), Ahmed Sultanzade (Iran) and Zhang Tailei (China) they did not figure in the official proceedings. Only one discussion on the Eastern question was allowed on 12 July. The texts of the theses[5] indicate that, while Roy broadly stuck to his earlier position, expressing deep skepticism about the nationalist forces in the industrially advanced colonies, which could at any moment compromise with imperialism, and championing the cause of a proletarian revolution in association with the landless peasantry, the position of the Chinese Communist Party was rather different. Zhang Tailei underscored the importance of a "united national front" and argued that in the Near and Middle East and also in advanced Eastern countries, which included India and China, Roy's strategy of fighting on two fronts, namely, against imperialism and the indigenous bourgeoisie, was wrong,

5 The texts of the theses are available in *To the Masses: Proceedings of the Third Congress of the Communist International, 1921* (Leiden: Brill Nijhoff and Hotel Publishing, 2014), 1181–93.

although the communists should aim to win over the masses from the hegemony of the nationalist bourgeoisie. The Fourth Congress of the Comintern (1922) did allow Roy to present a "Report on the Eastern Question" and the differences between his and the Comintern's position were quite evident. Roy's report highlighted the following: First, the "Colonial Theses" of the Second Congress had erroneously placed all colonial countries in one bloc and prescribed a single universal strategy of revolution. For him, the colonies were divided into three groups, namely, those which were "nearing to highly developed capitalism," marked by a rising bourgeoisie and a class-conscious proletariat; colonies where capitalism's development was rather low, feudalism being still the backbone of society; and a third group characterized by the predominance of "primitive conditions." Moreover, echoing the position of the original version of his "Draft Supplementary Theses" presented at the Second Congress, Roy came close to viewing the bourgeoisie in countries like India, Egypt and Turkey as counterrevolutionary, and strongly pleaded for communist parties to assume leadership of the anti-imperialist struggle in countries like India, where, he believed, capitalism was sufficiently developed. Finally, while not opposing the Comintern's general strategy of building up an anti-imperialist united front, Roy underscored the necessity of liberating this front from the leadership of the "timid and hesitating bourgeoisie" and of bringing the masses more actively to the forefront.

The focus of the "Theses on the Eastern Question" adopted by the Fourth Congress of the Comintern was different, characterized by caution in relation to Roy's rather ultra-left position. The central strategy outlined was that of building up an anti-imperialist united front against colonial rule, with a special section devoted to the importance of the agrarian question, which was considered to be the key to the revolutionary movement in the backward countries of the East, highlighting the necessity of an agrarian revolution to mobilize the vast masses of the peasantry. Notwithstanding these differences within the Comintern, the East came to assume a prominent position in the aftermath of the Fourth Congress. This was evident in the strengthening of the Eastern Department. A resolution of the Fourth Congress stated that henceforth "special attention will have to be given to the activities of the Eastern Department and the head of this Department will belong to the Presidium." Thereafter Safarov, to whom the Presidium of ECCI had in 1921 given the task of organizing the Middle Eastern and Far Eastern sections of the Comintern, became a member of the Colonial Commission of the Fourth Congress and was elected to the ECCI, and, according to a decision of the Presidium on 2 June 1922, was put in charge of the Eastern Department. Thus, in a report dated 12 December 1922, prepared by M. Grol'man and K. Troianovskii, it was stated that earlier in the work of this department there was hardly any definite plan or distribution of work and, consequently, now for the first time, a unified, all-embracing structure was to be created with corresponding delimitation of functions. On 4 May 1923, Karl Radek was given the charge of this department and Grigorii Voitinskii was made his deputy. The Eastern Department now covered the following regions in three sections: The Near Eastern section dealt with Turkey, Egypt, Syria, Palestine, Morocco, Tunis, Algeria and Persia; the Middle East section covered British India, Indochina and Indonesia; the Far Eastern section handled Japan, Korea, China and Mongolia. While each section had its own commission on the basis of either country or region, the ECCI and the Eastern Department relied in their work on a number of regional bureaus and secretariats. Again, for a systematic study of the situation in different countries and the activities of the communist parties, it became the practice to establish temporary and permanent commissions within the framework of the Eastern Department and its sections.

The Comintern's understanding of the colonial question took a new turn at the Fifth Congress (1924), following Lenin's death. The "Report on the National-Colonial Question," presented by Dmitry Manuilsky, the official spokesman of the Comintern, was questioned by Roy. First, while for Manuilsky colonialism, and the anti-colonial struggle, was viewed as a homogeneous concept, Roy reiterated his earlier position, namely, the threefold division of the colonies. Second, while Manuilsky affirmed the position of the Second Congress that direct links between the nationalist struggle in the colonies and the Comintern had to be forged, Roy stuck to the position that the Comintern should lend its support to organizing parties of workers and peasants.

The irreconcilable differences between Roy and Manuilsky eventually prevented the Fifth Congress from taking any position on the colonial question. Meanwhile Stalin's entry into the Comintern, his report at the Fourteenth Conference of the VKP(b) on 9 May, and his speech to the students at the KUTV on 18 May in 1925 introduced a new angle to the Comintern's understanding of the colonial question. First, differing with Manuilsky he pointed out that the bourgeoisie in the colonies had split into a revolutionary and a reactionary wing, that a differentiated notion of the bourgeoisie needed to be accepted, and that in the leadership of the anti-colonial struggle proletarian hegemony had to be established. Closely similar to Roy's position, this was in tune with the spirit of "Bolshevization" of the Comintern, which was the guiding spirit of the Fifth Congress.

The impact of "Bolshevization" on the shaping of the colonial question was manifest in the further reorganization of the Eastern Department, as the East was fast emerging as a major factor in the Comintern's strategy. On 8 March 1924 the ECCI Presidium chose F. Petrov (F. F. Raskol'nikov) as the chief of the Eastern Department and Voitinskii as his deputy, the other members being Roy, Sen Katayama, M. G. Rafes and B. A. Vasil'ev. Then, in a report (marked "strictly secret") sent by Petrov and Voitinskii on behalf of the Eastern Department to the Presidium of the ECCI on 16 May 1925, the necessity of the following measures was highlighted: to strengthen the work of the Eastern Department and to primarily entrust Roy with the necessary responsibility in this regard; to establish a better linkage between the Eastern Department and the Presidium, the Secretariat, and the Orgburo of the ECCI; to effect organizational links between the Eastern Department and the Colonial Commissions of the West European communist parties in order to guide their political activities; to increase the number of qualified functionaries in the Eastern Department for agitational-propagandistic and organizational work; and to organize in the KUTV the publication of Marxist-Leninist literature for the countries of the East. Following a resolution of the ECCI Presidium on 24 March 1926, the work of the Eastern Department was diversified and its work was divided, in pursuance of a decision taken on 8 July 1927, into the following regional secretariats, namely, Anglo-American and Eastern. While India, west Africa, Indonesia and Korea came under the Anglo-American division, the Eastern Division included China, Mongolia, Palestine, Syria, Persia, Egypt and the remaining African countries. The Anglo-American Division was headed by G. I. Petrovskii, while the Eastern Division was led by Petrov, Roy being a member of both the divisions.

Between the Comintern's Fifth and Sixth Congresses (1928) another development took place which was quite significant for the colonies. This was the establishment of the League against Imperialism (LAI) in 1927 in Brussels, which was virtually a front organization of the Comintern. Willi Münzenberg was the key figure in organizing its activities which were primarily aimed at lending support to the cause of the colonial peoples. The LAI espoused the idea of an anti-imperialist popular front, cutting across party affiliation, and this gained the support of such luminaries as Albert Einstein and Jawaharlal Nehru.

The Comintern's Sixth Congress (1928) took place under the shadow of "Bolshevization," taking an "ultra-left" turn, in accordance with Moscow's view that capitalist development had now entered a new "third period" of crisis. This had implications for policy on the colonial question. In the "Theses on the Revolutionary Movement in the Colonies and Semi-Colonies" the ultra-left position of the Comintern on the colonial question was starkly evident, although there continued to be sharp differences within the Comintern on the colonial question. It can be surmised that at least two factors contributed to this ultra-left turn. The immediate cause was the setback of the Comintern in China, when the united front between the Chinese Communist Party and the nationalist Guomindang collapsed in 1927, resulting in the brutal massacre of the communists. The other factor was the struggle being waged by Stalin within the Soviet Communist Party against the "right," represented by Bukharin and his followers. The ultra-left turn was strikingly evident in the complete dismissal of nationalism in the colonies, as "class versus class" now became the new slogan. This affected the policy of the LAI too, as was evident at its Second Congress, held in 1929, which dismissed nationalists as lackeys of imperialism. Münzenberg was marginalized in the Comintern and the LAI was put in jeopardy, as its nationalist supporters were isolated, preparing the ground for its eventual collapse and disintegration.

By the time of the Seventh Congress held in 1935 it was realized, following the coming to power of the Nazis in Germany, that the need of the hour was for a united front/popular front. The attitude of the communists toward anti-colonial nationalism now shifted in a more positive direction, but the entry of the Soviet Union into the war from 22 June 1941 and the Comintern's description of the new situation as a "People's War" led to a tricky situation in many colonies where nationalism was an important force. As the communist parties were now under an obligation to defend the cause of the Soviet Union and support the Allied Powers, in countries like India this was perceived by many as tantamount to the communists collaborating with British imperialism, which led to nationalists accusing communists of being "traitors," and to the isolation of the communists from the mainstream anti-colonial struggle.

Metropolitan and Colonial Communist Parties

As the communist parties in the colonies gradually took shape under the aegis of the Comintern, the relation between these parties and the communist parties of the metropolitan countries emerged as a rather ticklish issue. The Comintern leadership repeatedly criticized the metropolitan communist parties for inadequate anti-colonial work, for giving insufficient support to the anti-colonial struggle, and for failing to educate the European proletariat about the importance of anti-colonialism for its own emancipation. As early as the First Congress Nikolai Bukharin published an article entitled "The Communist International and the Colonies" in *Pravda* on 6 March 1919, which highlighted the importance of revolutionary movements in the colonies for the metropolitan countries and warned against the false consciousness of the metropolitan proletariat vis-à-vis the colonies.[6] At the Second Congress serious concern was expressed about the rather indifferent, if not negative, attitude of representatives of some European parties toward the importance of the colonial question.

At the Fourth Congress a number of delegates representing the communist parties of Turkey, Iran, Britain and Indonesia alleged that many European communist parties did not pay sufficient attention to anti-colonial work. Delegations from thirteen countries, including three in Europe, launched a collective protest, endorsed by Safarov and Trotsky, which highlighted the urgency of breaking European communist parties from a pro-colonial stance. The discussion on the colonial question at the Fifth Congress also featured criticism of the attitude of the West European communist parties toward the struggles of the colonial people by Roy (India) and Ho Chi Minh (French Indochina). While Roy mainly criticized the British Communist Party's stand on the colonial question, Ho Chi Minh castigated the French, British, Dutch and Belgian communist parties for their failure to be guided by the spirit of internationalism. The critique of the indifference of the metropolitan communist parties was married to a sharp critique of the role of the nationalist bourgeoisie in the struggle against imperialism. At the Sixth Congress Sen Katayama (Japan) pointed out that, while Lenin had forcefully emphasized that the metropolitan country must in every manner promote the revolutionary movement in the colonies, the Communist Party of Great Britain (CPGB) had so far "sinfully neglected" Ireland and India, as had the Dutch

6 John Riddell (ed.), *Founding the Communist International: Proceedings and Documents of the First Congress, March 1919* (New York: Pathfinder-Anchor Foundation, 1987), 307–08.

Communist Party in regard to Indonesia. The members of the Indian delegation were somewhat less condemnatory, saying that it was high time that the CPGB paid full attention to the movement in India, and helped in the organization of a strong communist party there and strengthened closer contacts.

As regards the French Communist Party (PCF) there was a major gap between official pronouncements and its mobilizational activities. The French empire embraced Vietnam in Southeast Asia and a large part of the Arab world, including Syria, Algeria and Morocco. Among the first Vietnamese communists Ho Chi Minh, Bui Lam, Nguyen van Tao and many others were members of the PCF and Nguyen van Tao was even elected a member of its Central Committee. Indeed it was only in April 1931 that the Communist Party of Indochina (ICP) ceased to be a section of the PCF and became officially recognized as an independent section of the Comintern. Ho Chi Minh had been sent to Moscow by the PCF and became an important figure in the Comintern. Together with Mikhail Borodin, Moscow's Comintern emissary, he was instrumental in organizing the anti-colonial struggle in Vietnam under the auspices of the ICP. For Ho Chi Minh it proved an uphill task to work out his own strategy within Comintern guidelines, in accord with the traditions and culture of his homeland. This was manifest on two levels. In 1925 he established the Thanh Nien (Vietnamese Revolutionary Youth League), which focused on the idea of a new Vietnamese society, with an emphasis on anti-imperialism (national independence from French occupation) and anti-feudalism (land to the tiller). However, this strategy came in for severe criticism especially after the Comintern's Sixth Congress in 1928. The commencement of the "third period" led to a break with the Thanh Nien strategy, as left-wing sectarianism raised its head, subordinating the cause of national unity against French colonialism to domestic class struggle. In 1930 the Nghe Tinh Soviet movement, an abortive communist uprising against French colonialism, ended in disaster. The period after the Sixth Congress witnessed a clear division within the ICP between a group that became the majority, which questioned the idea of giving priority to forging national unity and the Comintern position in the name of internationalism and class struggle, and a minority, represented by Ho Chi Minh and his associates, which became suspect in the eyes of the Comintern. Ho was dubbed a "nationalist," and his position that violence against the landowners and the bourgeoisie be kept to a minimum and that they be neutralized was labeled "opportunist." It was only after the

Seventh Congress of the Comintern (1935) that it became possible for Ho Chi Minh to revive his earlier strategy. In July 1939 he submitted a report to the Comintern on the ICP's strategic line during the Popular Front period which stressed that the main agenda was national liberation and that the main contradiction was one between imperialism and the Indochinese masses. The eventual result was the establishment of the Viet Minh front in 1941, which aimed to fight the Japanese and the French occupation forces.

The situation in the French-controlled Arab world was very different. There communist groups and parties were small, scattered and fragmented, while local nationalist forces were quite strong among the masses. Consequently, the Comintern urged the embryonic communist parties to work closely with these local forces. Two episodes deserve attention. One was the uprising of the Druze in Syria in 1925–27 under the leadership of Sultan Amir Hasan Atrash. It was a bloody confrontation with the French authorities that was wholly supported by the Syrian Communist Party. The other episode was the uprising of the Moroccan Rif people in 1921–26 under the leadership of Emir Abd-el-Krim against repressive Spanish and French rule, which was supported by the Algerian and Tunisian communists on the advice of the Comintern. In Algeria the PCF was largely instrumental in the formation of the Algerian Communist Party in 1936, but it always treated the Algerian party as an appendage of the PCF, its argument being that the emancipation of the Algerian people largely depended on the liberation of the French working class. Officially the PCF in its resolutions and pronouncements endorsed the positions of the ICP, the Syrian Communist Party and the uprising in Morocco. But, as Martin Thomas has shown, the party was torn between the Comintern's directive that French colonial policy be attacked and the fear of police persecution at home. Thus although in the pages of *L'Humanité*, the PCF's endorsement of the anti-colonial struggle in the French colonies was evident, what actually happened was that the PCF entrusted Jacques Doriot, a firebrand, militant campaigner against French colonial policy, with the responsibility of organizing the anti-colonial work of the PCF virtually on a personal basis, thus absolving the party leadership of any further responsibility. In fact, the PCF's anti-colonial work became almost synonymous with the activities of Doriot until 1934, when he was expelled from the party for his alleged defense of the Popular Front line, which prior to 1935 ran counter to Comintern policy. Again, during the Popular Front period, in the case of

Algeria, as anti-fascism became the priority, the anti-colonialism of the PCF was once more downplayed.[7]

On this issue one comes across a striking parallel with the position of the Portuguese Communist Party (PCP). With regard to the Portuguese colonies of Africa the PCP campaigned vigorously against the fascist regime of António de Oliveira Salazar, calling for its overthrow, but was not in favor of the independence of the colonies. The argument underlying this position was twofold.[8] First, Portugal, despite having built up an empire in the past, now was itself an oppressed country, since it was financially dominated by other advanced European powers. In PCP documents Portugal was, at times, described as a semi-colony marked by a dual status, oppressor and oppressed. Second, the need of the hour was to break with fascism and in this anti-fascist struggle the entire Portuguese nation, which included the colonies, had to stand united. In the interwar period the issue of liberation of the colonies thus was not recognized as an autonomous issue.

In the Dutch East Indies the relation between the Indonesian Communist Party (PKI), Asia's oldest communist party, and the Communist Party of the Netherlands (CPH) was rather different. From the very beginning Dutch communists like W. van Ravesteyn, Henk Sneevliet, Adolf Baars and Pieter Bergsma were in close contact with the Comintern and played a decisive role in the formation of the PKI in 1920. One key issue underlying the PKI–CPH relationship was the attitude toward Sarekat Islam, a Pan-Islamic organization opposed to Dutch colonial rule. While Sneevliet and Bergsma favored a positive attitude, there were others in the CPH who looked upon such religious-nationalist organizations with deep suspicion. Within the PKI, one section represented by Tan Malaka and Darsono believed that in the fight against colonial repression Sarekat Islam, although a religious movement, was a potential ally, since it had a strong popular base and it also contained radical elements, as evidenced in its understanding that colonialism was sinful capitalism. Indeed, the strategy of this wing of the PKI was to convert sections of Sarekat Islam into red bastions, which came to be known as Sarekat Rakjat, through which the Communist Party would make inroads among the toiling masses, the majority of whom were Muslim. But a more militant wing, represented by Muso Manowar and

7 Martin C. Thomas, *The French Empire between the Wars: Imperialism, Politics and Society* (Manchester: Manchester University Press, 2005), 9.

8 José Neves, "The Role of Portugal on the Stage of Imperialism: Communism, Nationalism and Colonialism (1930–1960)," *Nationalities Papers* 37, 4 (2009), 485–99.

Alimin bin Prawirodirdjo, rejected the idea of any such negotiation with nationalism and Islam. Interestingly, the Comintern, while officially not endorsing the idea of any alliance between the PKI and Sarekat Islam, did not, in practice, oppose it. In 1926, because of the adventurism of the militant wing of the PKI, which was not supported by the Comintern, an abortive communist uprising was staged, which ended in disaster. But eventually the PKI recovered ground by forging an alliance with nationalism in Indonesia represented by Sukharno and Mohammad Hatta in the 1940s during the period of Japanese occupation.

The domineering role of the communist parties of the metropolitan countries was most clearly evident in the relation between the CPGB and the Communist Party of India (CPI). While the destiny of Indian communism became inseparably linked with the twists and turns in the Comintern, it was the mediating role of the CPGB which was crucial in communicating the Comintern's line to the CPI at decisive moments. The CPGB's relations with the Indian communists were not always smooth, especially while M. N. Roy acted as the spokesman of the CPI in the Comintern (until his expulsion in 1929). This is explained by the fact that from the mid 1920s the CPGB was being projected by the Comintern as a counterweight to Roy, eventually paving the way for the CPGB to emerge virtually as the CPI's guardian. This was facilitated by the fact that after Roy's exit from the Comintern, it was Rajani Palme Dutt and Ben Bradley of the CPGB who emerged as the spokesmen of India in the Comintern. However, following the Soviet Union's entry into the war after 22 June 1941, when the "imperialist war" was renamed a "people's war," for the CPI it was difficult to accept the CPGB's position that the CPI should lend support to British war efforts and suspend the anti-colonial struggle. Eventually the CPI did accept this position, despite intense debates and confusion within its ranks. But like the PCF, the CPGB too was accused of Eurocentrism by the Comintern leadership, its main allegation being that the average CPGB member was guided by the spirit of "Empire-consciousness." Now that the archives of the CPGB are open to scholars two things are evident. First, the top CPGB leadership was strongly inclined toward extending full support to the anti-colonial struggle of the Indian masses, Dutt, Bradley and Philip Spratt being some of the key figures in this regard. A good number of CPGB activists like Bradley and Spratt went to India and played an active role in the organizational work of the CPI. But they admitted and lamented the fact that despite the adoption of resolutions and the issuance of statements, adequate mobilization for anti-colonial work on the part of the CPGB was lacking, as the average British worker could not connect to the cause of anti-colonialism in India.[9] Second, it was the CPGB's, more precisely Dutt's, understanding of Gandhi that decisively shaped the CPI's strongly negative perception of Gandhi too. Dutt in his *India Today* (1940) portrayed Gandhi as a reactionary figure, a skilled manipulator who cleverly used his mass appeal to serve the interests of the Indian bourgeoisie, who opposed modernity, and who was virtually a lackey of British imperialism. *India Today* became almost a Bible for the Indian communists for many generations and it was this position represented by the CPI in its programmatic documents that to a large extent led to its isolation from the mainstream nationalist movement.

In the case of the Communist Party of Philippines, the situation was different again. Besides the Comintern, the Communist Party of the United States (CPUSA) also played an active role in promoting the cause of anti-colonialism against the United States. At the end of 1924, when the Labor Party was formed in the Philippines, William Elliot (Alfred Wagenknecht), representative of the CPUSA, arrived in Manila on the Comintern's instructions to organize trade unions and he, along with Alimin and Tan Malaka of the PKI, was largely instrumental in drawing up the manifesto of the Labor Party. This was followed by the arrival of Harrison George, a Profintern representative and an American communist, who helped build up a communist group under the leadership of Antonio D. Ora and Crisanto Evangelista. In 1930 the communist party was formed. Up to 1937 the Communist Party of the Philippines emphasized a militant policy of confrontation with the US authorities, inviting severe repression. In 1937, an American communist, James Allen, in a letter to the communist party proposed an alliance with the newly formed Socialist Party. In 1935 an autonomous transitional government had been granted by the United States and, following the socialist–communist merger, the Communist Party of the Philippines was reorganized, as Evangelista became its chairman and Abad Santos of the Socialist Party became its vice-chairman. Eventually the party played a crucial role in organizing the Huk resistance against the Japanese occupation during World War II and it faced severe repression during and after the war. The deep involvement of the CPUSA in the organization of the Communist Party of the Philippines is explained by the fact that as early as 1925 the ECCI at its Fifth Plenum had resolved

9 Datta Gupta, *Comintern and the Destiny of Communism*, 187–92.

that the CPUSA must support the liberation movement in countries opposed to American imperialism.

Despite many setbacks, twists and turns, and eventually the collapse of the Soviet Union in 1991, it is an incontrovertible fact that the Bolshevik Revolution, primarily through the formation of communist parties in the interwar period, decisively contributed to the crisis and fall of the colonial system. If one takes stock of this phenomenal event, then a number of conclusions follow. First, in their early years in the negotiations with nationalism, the communist parties in the colonies were largely guided by a deep sense of distrust and an adventurist dream of socialist revolution on the model of the October Revolution. In the process, despite the Comintern's advice to the contrary on a number of occasions, they invited persecution and became isolated from the mainstream of anti-colonial struggle. The Egyptian Communist Party, for example, in its assessment of the Wafd, branded it as an agent of imperialism and was ruthlessly suppressed. The idea of a united front against colonialism was anathema for most of the communist parties. The same thing happened in the case of the PKI.

Second, to a large extent the Comintern's shift from the strategy of a united front (1920–22) to that of "class against class" via "Bolshevization" (1924–34) contributed to this animus against anti-colonial nationalists. At the same time, it is also undeniable that the anti-colonialism of the communist parties flourished following the Comintern's adoption of a popular/united front line in 1935. The underlying explanation was simple. In most of the colonial countries the influence of the communist parties was small compared to that of the nationalist and noncommunist parties and groups. The understanding of the Seventh Congress opened up a new opportunity for the communist parties to forge alliances with these forces and to build up their own mass base among the workers and peasants, and sometimes this eventually paid dividends. The communist parties of India, Indonesia, Indochina, the Philippines, Syria, Egypt and Algeria, to cite a few examples, gained enormously as they joined hands with the nationalist forces in their respective countries in their struggle against imperialism and succeeded in coming out of their isolation of the "third period." Thus, in India the communists allied themselves with the Congress, in the Philippines the communists and the socialists built up an alliance, in Algeria the communist party joined the North African Star, a radical nationalist organization, in Indonesia the PKI joined forces with the nationalists and in Tunisia the communists agreed to work within the Neo-Destour, a nationalist revolutionary party.

Third, as affiliates of the Comintern, communist parties were bound to toe the line of the International, even if it did not square with the realities of the given situation. But there were exceptions. In Vietnam and Indonesia, for example, the Comintern's presence was not as strong as it was in the case of India, thanks to the domineering role of the CPGB. Those parties that could build up a relatively autonomous space and connect with the masses emerged as a major force in the future. Those that did not (i.e. India) eventually declined. The communist movement in the colonies was mostly weakened by the internecine conflict of two lines, i.e. class (anti-capitalism) versus nation (anti-imperialism), commonly viewed as "left" versus "right," and international versus local. In the Arab world "Arabization" – as well as the indigenization of the communist parties more generally, especially in Africa – became an important issue. The Comintern promoted an indigenous Arab leadership but was not in favor of a single Arab communist party, such as was called for in 1931 by a conference of the communist parties of Syria and Palestine. The call was motivated by the fact that a single party was seen as being necessary to confront the unity of the "reactionary" national bourgeoisie of the Arab world. The Comintern Secretariat in a resolution entitled "Tasks of Communist Parties of Arab Countries in the Fight for a Popular Anti-Imperialist Front," adopted in 1936, advised the PCF to follow the line of Arabization of the communist movement in Algeria and Tunisia and reminded the French comrades that they were "helpmates, not leaders or nannies."[10] Within the Syrian Communist Party there was a powerful trend, especially among the rank and file, which subscribed to the idea of single Arab communist party, but leadership came round to the view that this was a wrong understanding, since, despite similarities in respect of culture and language, there were major differences between Arab societies and so formation of a single Arab communist party would amount to a denial of this pluralism.

In the case of South Africa, unlike Algeria, since there was no big brotherly presence of the CPGB, indigenization of the communist party through black Africans was gradually achieved.

Finally, in the formation of communist parties in the colonies it was by no means always the case that the Comintern played the major role. In the

10 A. Reznikov, *The Comintern and the East: Strategy and Tactics in the National Liberation Movement* (Moscow: Progress Publishers, 1984), 232.

establishment of the communist parties of Thailand and Cambodia, for example, it was Chinese and Vietnamese communists who played the crucial role, just as in the case of Burma, it was the Communist Party of India that was largely instrumental in its formation.

To conclude, for all the communist parties of the colonies the introduction of Marxist ideas was a major challenge, considering the overall backwardness of the countries of Asia and Africa. Despite failures and setbacks in many places, however, they succeeded in leaving their mark on history.

Bibliographical Essay

For a documentary understanding of the Comintern and the colonial question between 1919 and 1922 the most authentic works are John Riddell (ed.), *Founding the Communist International: Proceedings and Documents of the First Congress, March 1919* (New York: Anchor Foundation, 1987); *The Communist International in Lenin's Time: Proceedings and Documents of the Second Congress, 1920*, 2 vols. (New York: Pathfinder Press, 1991); *To the Masses: Proceedings of the Third Congress of the Communist International, 1921* (Leiden: Brill Nijhoff and Hotel Publishing, 2014); *Toward the United Front: Proceedings of the Fourth Congress of the Communist International, 1922* (Chicago: Haymarket Books, 2011). William Duiker's *The Communist Road to Power in Vietnam* (Boulder: Westview Press, 1981) and Ruth M. McVey's *The Rise of Indonesian Communism* (Ithaca: Cornell University Press, 1965) still are the two best volumes on communism in Vietnam and Indonesia respectively. On the French Communist Party's understanding of the colonial question *The French Empire Between the Wars: Imperialism, Politics and Society* (Manchester: Manchester University Press, 2005) by Martin Thomas is full of deep insights. On the Portuguese Communist Party's understanding of the colonial question literature is lacking. However, one very good reading is José Neves, "The Role of Portugal on the Stage of Imperialism: Communism, Nationalism and Colonialism (1930–1960)," *Nationalities Papers* 37, 4 (1991), 485–99. On communism in India, the Comintern, and the role of the CPGB, two important contributions are Neil Redfern, *Class or Nation: Communists, Imperialism and Two World Wars* (London and New York: Tauris Academic Studies, 2005), and Sobhanlal Datta Gupta, *Comintern and the Destiny of Communism in India 1919–1943: Dialectics of Real and a Possible History*, 2nd revised and enlarged edn. (Kolkata: Seribaan, 2011). On the League against Imperialism and Willi Münzenberg the best work is the monumental two-volume study

"We Are Neither Visionaries Nor Utopian Dreamers": Willi Münzenberg, the League Against Imperialism, and the Comintern, 1925–1933 (Lampeter: Edwin Mellen Press, 2013) by Fredrik Petersson. On communism and anti-colonial struggle in Africa and the Arab world in the interwar period literature is rather scanty. Still G. G. Kosach's "The Comintern and the Communist Parties of Arab Countries in the 1920s and 1930s," in R. A. Ulyanovsky (ed.), *The Comintern and the East: A Critique of the Critique* (Moscow: Progress Publishers, 1981), and A. Reznikov's *The Comintern and the East: Strategy and Tactics in the National Liberation Movement* (Moscow: Progress Publishers, 1984) would enlighten the reader.

9

The Comintern as a World Network

SERGE WOLIKOW

Unlike other international labor organizations, the founding members of the Comintern proclaimed from the outset that it was to be the global party of the revolution. As this objective proved impossible to attain, the organization gradually became an appendix of Soviet politics before disappearing totally in 1943. Nonetheless, for several decades of the twentieth century, it left a significant if not lasting trace upon the international communist movement. Regarding political forms, the initial, very centralized structure served as a model for dissemination, then as a means that differentiated political organizations across the world that claimed to be communist.

The Comintern did not emerge as a ready-made global revolutionary party. Three factors urged Bolshevik leaders to hasten the decision to found a new International: first, the initiative of several socialist parties to relaunch the Second International at Bern in February 1919; second, the fragile position of Soviet power which found itself surrounded; and third, their conviction of an imminent world revolution. The Moscow Conference, held from 2–6 March 1919, was thus transformed by the Bolsheviks into a founding event.

Imminent the world revolution may have been, yet at first, the structure of the new International was weak and limited. Its organization was fragile, even more so as it was not based on organized parties. The only communist force in Europe outside the Soviet Union was that of the German communists, but they were hostile to what they regarded as a premature political move. In fact, the main support, both in human and material terms, came from the Russians themselves. An Executive Committee and a Bureau were set up in order to ensure the management of the organization and to develop its activity under the presidency of Grigorii Zinoviev, the Bolshevik leader who fought with Lenin on the international front during the war. Every year a Congress, made up of delegates of the various sections, met to decide on strategic action for the organization. Subsequently a secretariat and bureau were set up in Kharkov and in Berlin.

During its first year, the Comintern was merely a symbol and a flag rather than an active organization. It gave European leaders reason to worry and the labor movement reason for hope. However, the revolutionary wave that the Bolsheviks were counting on did not wash across Europe: In 1919 the ephemeral Soviet Republics of Hungary and Bavaria failed and were crushed. There was nonetheless active social mobilization and large fractions of the socialist parties opted in favor of this Third International. After a terrible year, the Red Army (created in early 1919 and led by Trotsky) contained and defeated the White Armies and managed successfully to counter an offensive by the Polish army. Thus in 1920 the Red Cavalry headed for Warsaw while in Moscow, communist party delegates and other movements gathered for the Second Congress of the International Communist Movement.

Centralized Governing Bodies

The structures of the Comintern were instituted during the Second Congress in July 1920: both the central organization and the national sections, i.e. the country-specific communist parties. In the subsequent congresses of 1921 and 1922, further modifications were made to the leadership organs. These were defined in detail in a resolution during the Fourth Congress in November 1922. The central organization of the Comintern was subsequently subject to many regular and significant modifications, which have long been underestimated given the secrecy surrounding its management.[1]

The highest authority of the International – the World Congress – was initially planned to take place annually. Its rather general duties were set out thus in 1920: "[I]t discusses and decides the more important questions of program and tactics connected with the activity of the Communist International." In the early years, this frequency was respected. During each congress, the strategic orientations, tactics and moves of the International were discussed and defined. Gradually, however, the real guidance and leadership of the Communist International (CI) shifted to more restricted organizations run by permanent staff based in Moscow. The composition and the duties of the Executive Committee of the Communist International (ECCI) were defined during the Second Congress in 1920: Elected by the Congress, its role was to

1 G. M. Adibekov, E. N. Charnazarova and C. C. Chirinia, *Organizatsionnaia struktura Kominterna, 1919–1943* (Moscow: ROSSPEN, 1997).

direct the International. At the outset, it had a limited number of members: five members from the Bolshevik party, the communist party of the country where the ECCI resided, plus a dozen other members, one from each of the main parties.[2]

The ECCI was in charge of directing the organization's affairs between congresses. It published a periodical, *Communist International*, as well as a weekly, *International Correspondence*. It also had the power to control the activity of the national sections and to exclude all parties or party members who violated the decisions of Congress. Individuals or groups thus sanctioned could nonetheless appeal to Congress. However, in effect this system soon proved to be insufficient. As the number of national sections grew, so too did the ranks of their representatives in the ECCI. Its tasks now required specialization while still maintaining smooth continuity. The composition of the ECCI was thus modified in 1921. It now comprised twenty-four members and ten deputy members of which a minimum of fifteen were required to reside permanently in Moscow. Further modifications in 1922 meant that the ECCI was now to meet periodically in enlarged sessions. As these were open to representatives of all parties, special delegations were formed and sent out especially for the occasion. These enlarged sessions, known as ECCI plenaries, were initially designed to cover specific questions that the Congress had not found the time to deal with. However, from 1925, they became a substitute for the Congress, which was far less frequently convened: Eighteen months went by between the Fifth Congress and the Sixth, in 1928, and seven years passed before the Seventh and last Congress was held in 1935.

Work Departments and Bolshevization

At around the same time there was a change in the mode of leadership, especially following the Fifth Congress in 1924 during which the new statutes of the Comintern were adopted. The preeminence of the Executive Committee over the various national organizations increased and centralization, begun in 1922, was reinforced. There were now seventy-two members instead of thirty-seven in the ECCI; it was given additional powers and met four to six times a year. This was to the detriment of the national sections, whose activity was now subject to the decisions of the

2 "Statuts de l'Internationale communiste, adoptés au 2e Congrès de l'IC," in *Manifestes, Thèses et Résolutions des Quatre premiers congrès mondiaux de l'Internationale Communiste 1919–1923* (Paris: Librairie du Travail, 1934).

ECCI and whose congress meetings diminished in frequency. In fact, from as early as 1920, the real political direction came from a "Steering Committee" renamed the Presidium in 1921 and endowed with a secretary and a president. Grigorii Zinoviev was president from 1920 to 1926, followed by Nikolai Bukharin until early 1929, then V. M. Molotov, Dmitry Manuilsky, and finally Georgi Dimitrov. Several departments were created, notably for organization, agitprop, information and the press. These provided an efficient means for the Comintern to lead and monitor the communist parties whose job it was to put into application the decisions of the International. Delegates were sent out to support local leaders, and the choice and prestige of these emissaries depended on the seriousness of the issues and the urgency of the measures required. Thus, Jules Humbert-Droz was sent to Paris and then to Rome in 1922, A. I. Gural'skii in 1924 and Stepanov (S. M. Minev) in 1929. And when it came to solving problems within the ranks of the French leaders, Manuilsky himself traveled to Paris in 1922, 1925 and 1931.

This management system was differentiated and yet highly centralized. During the Second International the Executive Committee had acted as a coordinator for the often conflicting aims and activities of local parties. This was no longer the case. The First International with its national sections still served as an explicit reference for the CI, but these sections were no longer as versatile as they had been in the 1860s. They were now specific political organizations, well-structured parties that became national sections of a centralized world party. During the Third Congress it was stated that central committees of local parties were subordinate to the ECCI, as much in terms of political orientation as in the appointment of their leaders.

In the mid 1920s, during the brief period when Bukharin took over as secretary after Zinoviev had been removed, the globalization of communism was inseparable from the actions of the Comintern. A peak was reached during the Sixth Congress with discussions about a program for the international communist movement.

In early 1926 the Executive Committee's duties were thoroughly reorganized. Changes included the setting up of regional secretariats in charge of a number of parties. The eleven secretariats, reduced to eight in 1928, included the Latin Secretariat – headed by Humbert Droz – whose role it was to guide and monitor the communist parties of France and Belgium. Other secretariats included one for the English-speaking European countries, one for Germany, one for North America, one for Spain and Latin America and one for the East, thus ensuring that each geographical zone had its own specific secretariat and was properly monitored. In 1928 the West European Bureau (WEB) was developed in Berlin and directed by Dimitrov.

At the same time a "Political Secretariat" was formed, which provided a basis for the real leadership of the Comintern, along with a "political commission" and a small committee in charge of preparing or finishing the work of the Secretariat, notably in terms of recruiting agents or making concrete adjustments to the decisions taken. The Comintern leadership had access to a web of hundreds of technical and political collaborators. Recent research in the archives has revealed the diversity and extent of this network. The figures should no doubt be treated with caution, but in the second half of the 1920s 346 people worked for the Secretariat, whereas fifteen years later the figure had risen to 429. The growth in numbers arose more from a proliferation of administrative tasks than from a development in real activity.[3] The practical management of business within the Comintern headquarters in Moscow, which was essential to the smooth running of the organization, became progressively more complicated as a result of increased centralization and the differentiation of parties and their activities. The international liaison department was in charge of organizing the travel arrangements of the Comintern envoys as well as distributing information and financial support. The technical infrastructure involved forging documents, sending and receiving radio-telegrams, guarding secret crossing points and so forth. This department was directed by O. A. Piatnitskii, who was also head of the organization section until he was pushed aside in 1935.

During the early years the national delegations taking part in the meetings expressed each party's point of view and the CI monitored their political activities from time to time, nonetheless sending an emissary to attend their congresses and whenever serious leadership problems arose. This procedure, offering a voice to the various parties via their representatives, was backed up by a system of special commissions charged with consulting the delegates and approving decisions taken about their activities by the Comintern executive board. The commissions, first constituted during the statutory meetings on the fringe of the plenary sessions, mainly dealt with questions regarding the management and orientation of the communist parties involved. In July 1924 during the Fifth Congress, the "Souvarine Commission" was set up.[4] During the 6th and 9th

3 Peter Huber, "Les organes dirigeants du Komintern: un chantier permanent," in Serge Wolikow (ed.), *Une histoire en révolution? Du bon usage des archives, de Moscou et d'ailleurs* (Dijon: EUD, 1996), 225.

4 Boris Souvarine, member of the Political Bureau and head of the French Communist Party, sided with Trotsky against the position of the French Communist Party leaders. The commission judged him in lieu of the French Communist Party and excluded him from the Comintern for a year.

Plenums and the Sixth Congress of the Comintern, "French commissions" were created whose members included major international leaders. Similarly, during the 7th Plenum a "German commission" was formed in order to modify the leadership of the German Communist Party (KPD).

Already by this time, decisions were prepared beforehand at the Presidium or the Secretariat as well as within the framework of the Russian Communist Party delegation. From 1926, this delegation defined the position of the Russian representatives in the ECCI. They were particularly vigilant against the "opposition" – that is, the groups supporting Trotsky or Zinoviev. In 1926 these two factions converged to form the Unified Opposition. In March 1926 at the 6th Plenum of the Comintern, it was in the name of the Russian delegation that Stalin criticized the choice of leaders of the French Communist Party. During the 7th Plenum in autumn 1926, the Russian delegation examined the case of the KPD leadership and certain leaders were accused and expelled, notably Ruth Fischer, who was a close ally of Zinoviev.[5] Later on Manuilsky and Molotov represented the Russian delegation at the CI meetings and gave regular reports on the situation in the USSR, the policies of the Russian Communist Party and its point of view on the situation of various other parties. After 1929, the whole organization became even more cumbersome with the multiplication of commissions set up to interview the delegations that were specially formed to report on the situation of their respective political parties. Generally speaking, the national leaders were interviewed beforehand by the Presidium and their regional secretariats, not to mention the interviews held in small groups at the level of the Political Secretariat. All in all, it was an extremely bureaucratic procedure.

Permanent representatives of the national parties took their seats alongside the national delegations and the leaders of the CI. Between 1921 and 1939, the permanent national representatives had a prominent position, called upon to follow the political affairs of their party and to report regularly to the various offices they were assigned to. Some parties, although they were not important in terms of numbers, still had permanent representatives because of the strategic importance of their countries. This was the case with Britain.[6] The inclusion of these representatives within the CI organization and their

5 A. Vatlin, *Komintern: idei, resheniia, sud'by* (Moscow: ROSSPEN, 2009), 149–63.

6 John McIlroy and Alan Campbell, "The British and French Representatives to the Communist International, 1920–1939: A Comparative Survey," *International Review of Social History* 50, 2 (2005), 203–40.

sporadic communication with their own parties led them to adopt the theses of the CI leaders rather than represent their parties' interests. Their role diminished during the 1930s and as a result their status was modified: The permanent delegates took on the role of intermediaries or advisors rather than representatives. To obtain more precise information about the parties and ensure that all decisions taken by the CI were applied locally, permanent envoys were hurried off to check up on the communist parties: Eugen Fried was sent to Switzerland in spring 1929, then to France in autumn 1930. Andor Berei was sent to Belgium.[7] Most Comintern envoys were moved from one party to another. Their role was to ensure that all national parties faithfully toed the CI line. They were also instructed to bring stability to the organization by ensuring its smooth running and the the selection of reliable executives, who were now systematically selected on the strength of their bibliographical questionnaires. The most promising candidates were chosen to attend the International Lenin School in Moscow and lived there for a period of eighteen months to two years.[8]

Restructuring and Decline in Activity

Following the Seventh Congress in July and August 1935, the central structures of the CI underwent a final major change. According to the official discourse, the decrease in centralization was in order to encourage more autonomy for the local sections. This seems contradictory in view of Stalinization and the purges affecting the CI. Recent progress in research and easier access to the archives has helped shed light on this paradox, which strives to cover up the fervent Stalinization of the Comintern and the weakening of its basic structures.

By the end of 1935, the structures put in place after 1926 were transformed.[9] The regional secretariats were replaced by personal secretariats. The Executive Committee played a smaller role and the enlarged plenary meetings ceased. The Presidium, on the other hand, met far more frequently. Other modifications followed from 1933 onwards.

7 Annie Kriegel and Stéphane Courtois, *Eugen Fried. Le grand secret du PCF* (Paris: Seuil, 1997).

8 Serge Wolikow and Jean Vigreux, "L'Ecole Léniniste Internationale: une pépinière de cadres communistes," *Cahiers d'histoire, revue d'histoire critique* 79 (2000), 45–56.

9 CE Presidium Session, 13 Oct. 1935, speech of P. Togliatti, in Rossiiskii gosudarstvennyi arkhiv sotsial'no-politicheskoi istorii (RGASPI), 495/2/201, quoted in Aldo Agosti, *Togliatti negli anni del Comintern (1926–1943). Documenti inediti dagli archivi russi* (Rome: Carocci, 2000).

The agitprop department was scrapped and the organization department radically changed. In October 1935 most of the specialized departments (agriculture, women, cooperatives, etc.) disappeared – only the cadres and the propaganda departments surviving. The duties of the various commissions were transferred to the personal secretariats. Dimitrov, in addition to his functions as secretary general, was in charge of liaising with the Chinese Communist Party. Manuilsky's secretariat now covered Western and Southern Europe and had charge of the communist parties in France, Belgium and Luxemburg. André Marty headed the secretariat for the Anglo-American states. These secretariats covered every region in the world, ensuring both the continuation of the Comintern's global ambitions and the reinforced bureaucracy of the management system. Finally, an agent of the NKVD, M. A. Trilisser, alias Moskvin,[10] was brought in to the Secretariat; Nikolai Yezhov was installed in the ECCI and its Presidium, where he became the official representative of the Soviet party. He presided over the control commission of the party before taking over as commissioner for internal affairs. He was responsible for organizing and coordinating the Great Terror which affected both Soviet society and the apparatus of the Comintern on which he had a firm grip. At the Seventh Congress there was mention of "the necessity of transferring the center of gravity of its work [referring to the CI] to the elaboration of political orientation and fundamental tactics" and conversely, "of avoiding, as a general rule, direct involvement in the internal affairs of the organisation of communist parties."[11]

This affirmation should be interpreted with caution, given that none of the official documents from the Seventh Congress mitigates the principles of centralization or the preeminence of the leadership of the CI with regard to the various communist parties. Furthermore, reference to the archives reveals that these parties were still carefully controlled even if the methods had evolved. Communist party representatives were now in direct contact with the secretaries of the Executive Committee and attended the Presidium sessions. In 1935 Palmiro Togliatti, alias Ercoli, even suggested that their attendance be made permanent, but in fact they continued to

10 Trilisser came from the NKVD (the People's Commissariat for Internal Affairs). He was with the ECCI for a long time, in charge of underground work. He became one of the Comintern secretaries and was responsible for administrative workings and the international liaison service. From 1936, he headed the commission in charge of Comintern staff control, in other words, repression. He was finally arrested in November 1938 and sentenced to death in 1940.

11 Agosti, *Togliatti negli anni del Comintern*.

attend only the sessions concerning their respective parties. The much-proclaimed suppression of the CI delegates at communist party meetings is a good example of the ambiguity of the decisions taken at that time. The case of Eugen Fried is revealing. In his diary, Dimitrov recounts his encounter with Fried. We learn that he remained in Paris, now occupying a leading position in the French Communist Party while still maintaining direct links with the Comintern to which he provided reports about the French situation. Officially the role of the permanent delegates was maintained and the major communist parties were still represented in Moscow, but when it came to dealing with specific questions, it was the party leaders who were summoned to the Presidium in Moscow. In this way, the central organization kept abreast of developments on the international scene – whether it was the Spanish, British or Chinese Communist Party – and continued to have the upper hand. In the case of Spain, the Comintern sent out an increasing number of special envoys from the early 1930s onwards: André Marty, Victorio Codovilla and later, during the civil war, Togliatti.[12] The same vigilance was maintained toward the French Communist Party. His cadres section, now tightly controlled by the Comintern cadres department, itself under the strict authority of Moskvin (Trisiller), made sure that militants to be promoted to positions of national responsibility were subject to close scrutiny. The leaders in the organization section of the French Communist Party were frequently in Moscow meeting Dimitov in person.[13] Part of their activity involved studying personal files transmitted by the national sections, especially prior to a congress. The cadres department played a key role in gathering the mountain of files on suspected Trotsky supporters.

From Decline to Dissolution

Just as the organization of the Comintern evolved to become more Soviet-controlled, so the second decade was marked by a gradual dwindling of its autonomous activity and its increasing subordination to the preoccupations of the Soviet state, especially its international policies. At first the existing structures served this manipulative purpose but by 1935 they were adapted

12 Antonio Elorza and Marta Bizcarrondo, *Queridos camaradas. La Internacional Comunista y España, 1919–1939* (Barcelona: Planeta, 1999), 337 ff.

13 "Discussion with French comrade Armand," 1 Sept. 1938, in Ivo Banac (ed.), *The Diary of Georgi Dimitrov 1933–1949*, trans. Jane T. Hedges, Timothy D. Sergay and Irina Faion (New Haven: Yale University Press, 2012), 74.

and reduced, as the image of international communism appeared increasingly controversial. The influence of the USSR pervaded the Comintern. Its specific function remained, however, despite the automatic alignment of its policies to those of the Soviet Communist Party. Meanwhile, the latter began to merge into the Soviet state.

Stalin never openly intervened in the running of the International. Unlike other Soviet leaders, he remained in the back seat of the CI assemblies, speaking only to deliver reports on the situation of the USSR. His real political influence was only felt when voiced by Molotov, Manuilsky or Piatnitskii, usually over supposedly national questions such as German Communist Party policies.

Nevertheless, the entire political life of the organization declined within a few years and then ceased altogether. The hitherto usual debates and extensive reports of executive activity during the enlarged sessions of the Executive Committee also came to a halt. It would be another four years before a report was published on the work of the Seventh Congress of the CI in 1935 – and even then, much was omitted or summarized and several speakers and attendees were simply not mentioned. For these "ghosts," this was the second "disappearance" as many of them had already been taken away during the ever-growing repression and dark events that the International experienced during and after 1936.

For indeed, the Comintern did not escape the climate of terror and physical intimidation that affected the Soviet population as a whole, and communist party executives in particular. Soviets suffered the most, whatever their position in the party, from middle ranks to the top leaders. But other CI members were also targeted. Some were removed from the political arena prior to being arrested. This was true for Russians such as Piatnitskii and V. G. Knorin as well as the Hungarian Béla Kun – all three had been critical of the new orientation of the CI. Having been removed from their senior posts after the Seventh Congress in 1935, they were arrested and shot two years later. The Polish communists were also eliminated in 1937, the dissolution of their party having been approved by the leaders of the CI.[14] This liquidation was organized as part of the plan to combat Trotskyism, a decision taken by Stalin that Dimitrov and the Comintern leaders ratified. This act tragically symbolized the abdication and submission of the CI to the

14 William J. Chase, *Enemies within the Gates? The Comintern and the Stalinist Repression, 1934–1939* (New Haven: Yale University Press, 2001).

policies of the Soviet regime. With Moskvin (Trilisser), from the NKVD, the Soviet police state was truly consolidated. Although some dividing lines persisted to separate the sections of the secret services and the diplomatic services, the machinery of the Comintern was effectively under the control of the former. In late 1938 Moskvin was killed in his turn, as was Yezhov, who had simultaneously been a member of the Presidium and commissar of internal affairs. This was the punishment meted out to the leaders responsible for and involved in the purges. Following this, top leaders, notably Dimitrov and Manuilsky would never take the slightest political initiative without the prior approval of Stalin, who thus led the Comintern policies from 1937.

Within a few years, the whole process of subordination was accomplished without resolving the underlying problems – the conflicts of interests or the logic of the action undertaken. The difficulties and failures arising from these hidden and uncontrolled factors were attributed to enemies and dissident leaders who had voiced doubts or had not anticipated quickly enough the change in orientation.

The contradictions between Soviet politics and the situation of communist parties remained after 1934, although, following the Seventh Congress of the Comintern, an effort to counter fascism led to both a merging of orientation and a certain impetus for joint action. On the other hand, there were ever-growing drifts in the internal politics of the various communist parties. The gap was also widening between the politics of the Popular Front, advocated by the International, and the interior politics of the Soviet Communist Party. The question of whether or not the French Communist Party should take part in the government was often brought up between 1935 and 1938, with the Comintern arguing against it while the French Communist Party was in favor. However, although the Soviet Communist Party was no longer as inspirational as it had been for communist parties in other countries, the French party nonetheless remained true to the USSR.

The perspective of a new world war pushed the Comintern to direct its activity toward international relations and to adhere closely to USSR foreign policy. Soviet diplomacy – whose policies since 1935 had leaned toward collective security and maintaining the status quo – partially changed direction after 1938. The Soviet government, prioritizing interests of state, signed a nonaggression pact with Germany on 23 August 1939. This agreement with the National Socialist Reich took the Comintern by surprise. Rather belatedly and with great difficulty, its leaders managed to broadcast the new official line denouncing the existence of two opposing "imperialist" camps, though somewhat sparing Germany. It was Stalin who imposed this sudden turn on

Dimitrov in early September 1939,[15] breaking with the anti-fascist stance maintained until this time. Recent research based on telegrams exchanged between the Comintern leaders and Stalin shows how his sudden, brutal U-turn put the communist parties, at least the European ones, in considerable disarray. Dimitrov's diary details the atmosphere of the time as well as Stalin's obsessions and the acute subordination and marginalization of the Comintern.

Ever since 1937, Stalin had shown great suspicion with regard to the Comintern's activity. He claimed that they were working with the enemies of the USSR. "All of you there in the Comintern are playing right into the enemy's hands."[16] He used this view to justify the repression of the Comintern leaders and also to express his doubts about the organization per se. In early September 1939, when the war had begun to affect Europe, Dimitrov, Manuilsky and Otto Kuusinen worked on a document about anti-fascist action, intended for the communist parties. But Stalin, flanked by Molotov and Andrei Zhdanov, summoned Dimitrov on 7 September and informed him of the new situation and the new line that the Comintern was to take. Bluntly, he explained his view of the tactics and conditions that the Soviet Union and – in solidarity with them – the communist parties must adopt, by seeking to exploit the rivalry between capitalist countries. The politics that Dimitrov had advocated since 1934 were swept aside as antequated. Stalin undermined the popular-frontist position of the Comintern, by aligning the interests of the USSR with the revolutionary perspectives of communist parties in capitalist countries. However, he made a clear distinction between the situation in the USSR and that of the communist parties elsewhere in the world. These other communist parties must defend the USSR above all, even against their own states. The war was seen as eradicating the distinction between fascist and democratic countries, so Stalin was no longer concerned about the communist battle against fascism. From this time on, not a single Comintern document was signed by Dimitrov without first being reviewed and modified by Stalin in person. Indeed, Stalin gave Dimitrov direct orders about the concrete tasks he had to perform. Nevertheless, the Comintern's activities evolved unexpectedly and in conditions of ever-greater complexity.

There was increased centralization of decision-making within the Comintern, controlled by Stalin and his close entourage, Molotov and

15 N. Lebedeva and M. Narinskii, *Komintern i Vtoraia mirovaia voina* (Moscow: Pamiatniki Istoricheskoi mysli, 1994).
16 Banac (ed.), *Diary of Georgi Dimitrov*, 11 Feb. 1937, 52.

Zhdanov. However, the situations that called for decisions were becoming increasingly diverse. The new official line defined the war as a conflict between two imperialist camps, from both of which the communists were told to distance themselves. This meant that the Comintern had to mold its politics exactly to the Soviet Union model. Yet communists in different countries were facing constantly evolving situations. War had pushed most parties underground, complicating communications. The Comintern transmission service now relied on the NKVD and on Soviet diplomats working in foreign embassies, and the organization's actions were coordinated by the use of a radio-telegram system which was often disturbed by military action. Of strategic importance at the outset of the war was the slow restoration of the network in Brussels under Fried, which continued in occupied France in the winter of 1940–41 under Jacques Duclos. During autumn 1939 and the early months of 1940, there were still fairly regular meetings of the Presidium, where problems faced by communist parties in putting the new line into effect were discussed. These meetings soon became more restricted and concentrated on specific problems faced by individual parties. Interviews and documents, which until this point had been general, began to deal with a multitude of country-specific cases, in which the Comintern and Soviet diplomacy began to take an interest from autumn 1940. Indeed, they realized that the international situation was not evolving as expected and in view of the complexity of things, they almost exclusively turned to bilateral contacts and meetings. This meant that directives sent to the various communist parties could no longer be the same – there was no longer real international unity. For the first time since 1919, the Comintern hesitated and finally renounced the idea of adopting a single call for 1 May 1941. Dimitrov notes: "I spoke to Zhdanov about the CI call for May 1st. We both feel that in the present context it is no use issuing a Comintern statement." A few days later, Stalin used Zhdanov as an intermediary to demand that a separate text be addressed to each party, the contents of which he prescribed. It was necessary to differentiate according to the country (at war, out of the war zone, occupied, etc.). There was no hesitation regarding the basic directives: "[T]he imperialist war is the business of the imperialists; the people's peace is the business of the working class and the people – the war of the people of Greek and Yugoslavian people against imperialist aggression is a just war, etc."[17] On 19 April the directives for 1 May proceedings were written and sent by encrypted telegram to New York, Brussels, London and Amsterdam. The telegram gave an explicit account of the Comintern's position and

17 Ibid., 18 Apr. 1941, 155.

explained the decision to not take a common stance. The various parties were told to come up with the appropriate slogans for their situation.

This change in strategy coincided with the decision that Stalin announced to the All-Union Communist Party Politburo about transforming the international organization. Reminding them that they had allowed the United States Communist Party to separate from the Comintern in November 1940 so as not to be considered an organization under foreign control, he suggested that this move be generalized by creating independent parties that were even free to change their names. And all this was said in the box of the Bolshoi Theater! "The parties take their leave of Dimitrov. That won't be too bad. On the contrary. It would be convenient to make the communist parties totally independent rather than sections of the CI. They should become national communist parties with different names – the Workers' Party, the Marxist Party etc. The name does not matter. What's more important is that they integrate with their people and concentrate on their own specific tasks."[18] From that moment on, Stalin envisaged the disappearance of the organization: "From the point of view of the interests of the Comintern institutions, this may not be pleasant, but it isn't their interests that decide."[19] Dimitrov's diary provides precious information about the way in which Stalin tested the real impact of the initiative he unfolded in theory.

> Raised for discussion with Ercoli [Togliatti] and Maurice [Thorez] the issue of discontinuing the activities of the ECCI as a *leadership body* for Communist parties for the immediate future, granting *full independence* to the individual Communist parties of individual countries, converting them into authentic *national* parties of Communists in their respective countries, guided by a Communist program, but resolving their own concrete problems in their own manner, in accordance with the conditions in their countries, and themselves bearing responsibility for their decisions and actions. Instead of the ECCI, having an organ of *information and ideological and political backing for the Communist parties*.[20]

The French and Italian leaders agreed with his analysis and Dimitrov welcomed their positive reactions. In fact, there was nothing surprising in it, since they had each implicitly supported this course of action in their own way in the 1930s, especially regarding the conduct of their respective parties toward the fight against fascism and their political alliances. "Both feel that this way of posing the problem is basically valid and are perfectly aware of the present position of the international labour movement."[21] In the following

18 Ibid., 20 Apr. 1941, 155. 19 Ibid., 156. 20 Ibid., 21 Apr. 1941, 156. 21 Ibid.

weeks Dimitrov talked to Manuilsky and then to Zhdanov, now deputy general secretary of the Communist Party of the Soviet Union (CPSU). The question was to find a way of justifying and publicly explaining the termination of the Comintern's activities. In the USSR, as abroad, the impact of such a decision was anticipated with concern.

> The resolution must be grounded in principle, for we will have some serious explaining to do abroad as well as among our own Soviet Communists as regards why such a step is being taken. There used to be a Comintern with its own considerable history; then suddenly it ceases to exist and function as a united international center.[22]

Arguments were required to stave off criticism and "all possible blows by the enemy ought to be anticipated, for instance, that this is supposedly a mere maneuver, or that the Communists are rejecting internationalism and the international proletarian revolution."[23] The change also needed to appear genuine and initiated by several parties rather than top-down. "It matters a great deal on whose initiative this is to be done: on the leadership's own initiative or on the proposal of a number of Com[munist] parties. It seems the latter would be better. The matter is not so urgent: there is no need to rush; instead, discuss the matter seriously and prepare."[24]

Finally, the onset of the German invasion meant that the question was temporarily postponed – until 1943, at which point, given the change of context with the USSR now at war, it was easy to implement an expeditious procedure sealed in secrecy.

When the USSR entered the war, it gave Stalin the opportunity to accentuate the turn toward patriotism in Soviet politics. The communist parties that had not taken full measure of the new shift and had cleaved to the last to the theory of an imperialist war were now summoned to reconsider their analysis and to support their own governments so long as they were allies of the USSR. The British and Swedish Communist Parties were therefore severely criticized for opposing the Churchill government or for having displayed an attitude of neutrality. Communist parties worldwide were called to defend anti-fascist politics and to side with the USSR for national defense. The Comintern mobilized all its means and systems to apply the policies adopted including transmissions and the dispatching of militants and executives to infiltrate occupied countries and operate behind military lines. The Comintern ran a radio service for various countries involved in the

22 Ibid., 12 May 1941, 162. 23 Ibid. 24 Ibid., 163.

war. Its leaders closely followed the policies of the main parties for which they adopted precise directives. Thus the French Communist Party was closely monitored by the secretary general of the Comintern, with the participation of Thorez himself, even though he never appeared officially since his presence in the USSR could not be publicly acknowledged. This secret came out later though, when, in the summer of 1941, Churchill and de Gaulle refused the Comintern's request to send him to Great Britain. Although the work of the Comintern was far from negligible, its political effectiveness was weakened by its desire not to be seen as such. The day after the military parade of 7 November 1941 as the German troops were advancing toward Moscow, Dimitrov noted in his diary: "No need to emphasize the Comintern."[25]

By the time the staff and equipment of the Comintern were transferred to Ufa in October 1941, its problems of management and budget restrictions were beginning to show. The decision to dissolve the organization and the implementation of this measure took place in the spring of 1943, in just a few weeks during the months of May and June. The decision was first reached at a meeting between Dimitrov, Molotov and Manuilsky on 8 May. "We discussed the future of the Comintern. Reached the conclusion that the Comintern as a direct[ing] center for Com[munist] parties in the current conditions is an impediment to the Com[munist] parties' independent development and the accomplishment of their particular tasks. Work up a document dissolving that center."[26]

During the next few days the documents prepared by Dimitrov and Manuilsky were submitted to Stalin and then to the Presidium. It was decided that the various parties be consulted either through their representatives in Moscow or by telegram. The agreement was unanimous and the decision of the Presidium was soon made public in *Pravda* on 10 June. A commission charged with winding up Comintern affairs transferred most of the organization's activities to an international information section of the Soviet Communist Party Central Committee. Aleksandr Shcherbakov was to be the official director and Dimitrov and Manuilsky his deputies. Speaking to Reuters, Stalin stated that this dissolution "unmasked the slanderous remarks of the enemies of communism about the labour movement according to which communist parties did not work in the interests of their people but on orders from abroad."[27]

25 Ibid., 7 Nov. 1941, 204. 26 Ibid., 8 May 1943, 270.

27 Ibid., 12 June 1943, 280; 29 May 1943, www.revolutionarydemocracy.org/rdv8n2/dimitrov.htm.

The disappearance of the Comintern marked the end of the existence of a supranational, independent communist organization. This event, precipitated by the world war, was the culminating point of a strategic evolution that allowed the failure of a project built upon a centralized network of national sections, in favor of an international movement coordinated solely by the Soviet Communist Party.

Despite its demise, the Comintern left a lasting imprint on the international communist movement in the essential domains of party organization and militant culture – to such an extent in fact, that decades later, the influence remained for the most part.

It helped to spread two main forms of communist organizations throughout the world: communist parties and mass organizations. The former depended directly on the Comintern, the latter on independent organizations themselves controlled by the Comintern. From its outset this organization founded communist parties according to the same model, a prototype that was formalized with the implementing of Bolshevization from 1924. Mass organization were designed to place different economic, social and cultural activities under communist influence, and gradually developed as the Commintern sought to emerge from isolation. Thus in 1921, for instance, it organized help for the starving populations, and in 1927 it created the Anti-Imperialist League, designed to widen its influence on colonized nations.

The Creation and Development of Parties: From Europe to the Outer Regions, 1920–1924

During the Second Congress of the CI in Moscow in 1920, the central subject of discussion was the constitution of communist parties. These discussions, and the decisions reached, gave shape to how the parties were to function as national sections of the Comintern. In order to comply, they were to call themselves communist parties and to greatly modify their activities which to date had been similar to those of the socialist parties. The Congress thus adopted the "Twenty-One Conditions" of entry into the Third International. These gave strict instructions for the actions to be taken within each party. The aim was to constitute parties that had a truly revolutionary aim and a desire to take political power.

The communist parties were to be disciplined and determined, to combine legal and illegal activities, and to break with the parliamentary system while remaining vigilant about elections. They were to subordinate political and media activity to that of the party line and to get away from reformist politics while trying to win over the former members of socialist parties to the communist cause. The need for a proletarian party was reiterated after much debate. Indeed, given the role of the socialist parties during the war, the development of a plethora of committees, councils and soviets in various countries could lead to the belief that the partisan organization was outdated. But the extent and complexity of the revolutionary clashes as well as the Bolshevik experience in Russia justified the necessity for an organization charged with stimulating, organizing and leading the struggle for political power.

Adopting the Twenty-One Conditions for entrance to the CI was the subject of great debate within the socialist parties of every country during communist party constitutive congresses. The latter, usually propelled by a revolutionary minority wanting to join the Third International, were sometimes excluded only to form a new party calling itself communist.

The second phase of the construction of communist parties took place during the Fifth Congress in 1924 when "Bolshevization" became the general credo. The idea was to restructure the communist parties so that they were capable of satisfying the revolutionary objectives set out in 1920. As these objectives had not been met, the methods used by communist parties were criticized following Lenin's death, especially since the perspective of a revolution seemed remote after the fiasco of "German October," i.e. the failed revolution in Germany in 1923.

By infiltrating workplaces and creating units within factories, as well as a reinforced ideological discipline, it was hoped that the parties would be able to seize any future opportunities for a revolution. The organization bureau of the International led by the hardened Bolshevik Piatnitskii played a decisive role in pushing through these transformations. The hasty implementation of these changes shook most of the parties in 1924–25. The new, much-lauded and highly recommended Bolshevik party model was a far cry from the way the party had been run in 1917. First, it was far more centralized and of an overtly monolithic nature. Given that the priority at the time was to combat Trotsky, the reorganization of the communist parties was carried out hastily and in a bureaucratic way. It was met with skepticism, even hostility, by large fractions of the labor movement and notably by those unions that were not organized in the tradition of Russian socialism. Many of the leaders who voiced their disagreement about the new communist party objectives were excluded.[28] The new organization of the CI, designed to lead all action,

28 See, for instance, the letter from 250 unionists and party executives protesting to the Comintern leaders.

dominated union activity, subordinate now to the objectives of the party. Despite everything, this period was essential and seminal: The structures, organization modes and activities set up at this time lasted, almost unchanged, until the dissolution of the CI – and even beyond, as communist parties often used them right up until the 1960s. The reason for this longevity cannot simply be put down to the force of inertia or the respect for tradition. It indicates the historic impact of this reorganization, promoted in the 1920s by the CI. In Europe, Asia and Latin America[29] it created revolutionary organizations, able to act in politically dramatic situations, organizations more used to civil war, foreign occupation and repression than the regular practice of political democracy. In fact, Western Europe was precisely where the reorganization was most difficult to enforce and party activity hardest to change, most likely due to the existence of a degree of political democracy that made such changes seem neither necessary nor pertinent.

The expansion of communist parties outside Europe amounted to a number of precocious attempts, often unknown or at any rate underestimated, since the initial results were limited. Hence the geographical rooting of the communist parties in the world, subject to diverse local conditions as well as the strategic fluctuations of the Comintern, was unevenly distributed. Nonetheless, the first attempts at communist construction are always interesting, whether they be in Iran, India, China, Palestine, North and South America, or North and South Africa – if considered within their wider, twentieth-century historical framework.

First we need to put into context the Congress of the Peoples of the East, held in Baku in September 1920, under the auspices of the Comintern just after its Second Congress. The event in Baku, just south of Soviet Russia, close to Turkish and Arab worlds and not far from the Indian subcontinent,[30] brought together more than 2,000 delegates, present in spite of the tough obstacles put in their path by the British authorities, as well as the Turkish and Iranian states. So much so that several delegates died and never reached the Congress, and others were killed when they returned to their countries. The communists constituted over half of the total number of delegates. Others represented national movements. Most came from the Caucasus and Central Asia but there were also delegations from China, India and the Arab world. The communists belonged to newly formed parties from zones

29 Daniela Spenser, "Las vicisitudes de La Internacional Comunista," *Desacatos* 7 (2001), 133–48.

30 Edith Chabrier, "Les délégués au premier congrès des peuples d'orient," *Cahiers du monde russe et soviétique* 26, 1 (Jan.–Mar. 1985), 21–42.

controlled by the Red Army and the Bolsheviks, but also from neighboring countries such as Turkey or Iran. There were also many immigrants from Western Europe, the USA and, most of all, from Russia. They were divided and their movements embryonic.

Throughout the Congress, there was strident opposition to the major Western powers, particularly against Britain. There were also tensions between the Bolshevik conception of a world revolution centered on the idea of proletarian revolts in industrialized countries and the revolutionary fight of local parties for their own national independence. This was notably true for Muslim movements of Russia and contiguous Central Asia. The Congress produced two manifestos, the establishment of a Propaganda Council and longlasting action resulting in the creation of an Institute of Propaganda in Tashkent. The University of the Toilers of the East was also set up with branches in Baku and in Irkutsk and soon attracted hundreds of students. In December 1922, following the Fourth Congress of the Comintern, the Eastern Bureau was created to coordinate and lead communist action in the zones dominated by the great Western powers, using the strategy of a common anti-imperialist front. It had three divisions: North Africa, Middle East, and South and Southeast Asia. It was headed successively by Radek, Voitinskii and Raskol'nikov.

During the decade of the 1920s, several communist parties were set up in zones outside Europe. These included areas close to the USSR where it was often Russian immigrants who set up parties that often met with brutal repression, particularly since they were often oppressed by both the local authorities and the French or British powers. This was notably the case in the Middle East. In India, despite British influence, Marxist ideology was spread by the communists in large industrial centers such as Bombay (Mumbai). After a difficult start, the development of communism in China was far stronger, but it had to face hard trials and very violent repression. This considerably reduced its influence at the end of the 1920s. Yet again, the Comintern was there to support this chaotic evolution where the stakes were high and the scope well beyond China alone.

"Auxiliary" Organizations

The difficulties of the Russian Revolution and the disappointment of the world revolution led the CI executive to quickly set up mass organizations affiliated to the International. Thus the Red International of Labor Unions

(Profintern) (1921) and the Workers' International Relief Organization (1922) were, followed in 1923 by the Communist Women's International, an international women farmers' organization, and in a different register, the Young Communist International, which had been set up in Berlin in 1919, but was moved to Moscow after the failed German Revolution. It was regarded as a school for the future executives of the CI. In fact, in 1921, during the Third Congress of the Comintern, the creation of the so-called auxiliary organizations was the consequence of the awareness of political changes, notably in Europe. The idea of conquering the masses took the concrete form of a series of initiatives by the Comintern leaders to set up organizations capable of challenging the influence of the reformist movements. These new organizations were nonetheless strictly controlled, directly or indirectly, by the Comintern. For instance, the management of the Profintern, created in summer 1921, was entrusted to Solomon Lozovskii, a hardened union leader who was familiar with the West European labor movement. This international union initially made concessions to the French revolutionary unionists to entice them into joining, but it very soon changed its tune to shadow the politics of the Comintern and to adopt a union model based on that of the party. The fact that the Second Congress in summer 1921 was held in Moscow and not in Berlin was also an indication of the desire to regain control of an organization that was deemed to be a den of dissent.

The development of auxiliary organizations continued with the Workers' International Relief (MOPR), as well as an international sports organization, Sportintern, founded in 1924, and the League against Imperialism in 1927. Other organizations were also founded in the 1920s and 1930s, such as, for instance, the International Association of Friends of the Soviet Union, the International Association of Revolutionary Writers and Artists, and the World Committee against War and Fascism. In this way the CI was able to exercise indirect influence to counter the increasing popularity of European social democracy which steadily gained followers from 1922 to 1923 until the Great Depression in 1929. At the end of the first postwar decade, the activity and the size of these auxiliary organizations had considerably diminished. The failure was striking because for almost all the national sections of these organizations, the numbers were far below those of their socialist counterparts, whether it be the unions, the youth movements, or the sports associations. In fact, when they were first established at the time of the CI's anti-imperialist United Front, the communist organizations had been designed as open structures, capable of including noncommunist members in their folds. With the world economic crisis and class war, these organizations, their influence fading, were sacrificed for the sake of unity at the time of the Popular Front. This organizational model nonetheless served as a reference for the creation of large, international, communist-influenced front organizations after World War II.

The disappearance of the Communist International did not mark an end to international communism – rather, the organization gave way to national parties and was finally forgotten. It is essential to consider the footprint and legacy of the International on the communist movement if we are to understand the history of communism in the twentieth century. If 1943 marked the end of an era and a turning-point in an evolution that had begun well before this date, the influence of the CI continued to leave its mark on communist movements in the following decades. It bequeathed exceptional power to the Soviet Communist Party. This internal position of the communist movement was reflected in the global situation, where the USSR became the second global superpower as a result of its involvement in the world war, the sacrifice of its people as well as the fact that it was a symbol of hope for those struggling against national annihilation and massacres not only in Europe but also in the Far East. This new prestigious position was such that, for a long while, it validated the Soviet model set up during the time of the CI and silenced any criticism. The communist partisan system was now subordinated to the international politics of both the USSR and the new communist states. In Latin America and Western Europe, the political strategies that came into play during the Cold War had an immense bearing on the actions of communist parties. Even though these parties were not in power, they were greatly influenced by the diplomatic imperatives of Stalinist politics, as may be seen by the episode of the division of Yugoslavia – one of many examples of the lasting influence of the Communist International.

Bibliographical Essay

For a long time, the history of the Comintern focused on directions and discussions in governing bodies which were published and aired in weekly or monthly magazines that translated official documents into several languages. The general history of the Comintern described central strategy considered in this documentation and party tactics analyzed through the positions and interventions at events including the Chinese Revolution, the English general strike, the war in Spain and the election of European communist parties. For studies of the early 1900s, general works include: Aldo Agosti, *La Terza*

Internazionale: Storia Documentaria (Rome: Editori Riuniti, 1974); Aleksandr Iurevich Vatlin, *Die Komintern 1919–1929: Historische Studien* (Mainz: Decaton Verlag, 1993); Kevin McDermott and Jeremy Agnew, *The Comintern: A History of International Communism from Lenin to Stalin* (Basingstoke: Macmillan, 1996); P. Broué, *Histoire de l'Internationale communiste* (Paris: Fayard, 1997); and Natal'ia Lebedeva and Mikhail Narinskii, *Il Komintern e la seconda guerra mondiale* (Perugia: Guerra, 1996).

With the opening of the archives, valuable histories of the Comintern include: Serge Wolikow (ed.), *Une histoire en révolution? Du bon usage des archives de Moscou et d'ailleurs* (Dijon: Éditions Universitaires de Dijon, 1996); G. Adibekov, E. Charnazarova and K. Chirinia, *Organizatsionnaia struktura Kominterna, 1919–1943* (Moscow: ROSSPEN, 1997); Serge Wolikow, Bernhard H. Bayerlein, Georges Mouradian and Brigitte Studer, "Les archives du Komintern à Moscou," *Vingtième Siècle. Revue d'histoire* 61 (1999), 126–32; Serge Wolikow, with Bernhard Bayerlein, Mikhail Narinskii, and Brigitte Studer, *Moscou, Paris, Berlin, 1939–1941: Télégrammes chiffrés du Komintern* (Paris: Tallandier, 2003); Serge Wolikow, "Historia del comunismo. Nuevos archivos y nuevas miradas," in Elvira Concheiro, Massimo Modonesi and Horacio Gutiérrez Crespo (eds.), *El Comunismo: otras miradas desde América Latina* (Mexico: UNAM, 2007); and Serge Wolikow, Alexandre Courban and David François, *Guide des archives de l'Internationale communiste, 1919–1943* (Dijon: Archives Nationales-MSH Dijon, 2009).

Over the 1990s and 2000s, many publications have highlighted the functioning of the governing bodies of the Comintern and analyzed more accurately the internal activity of the central organization and its relationship with national sections, and the policy of the USSR. See Serge Wolikow, "Le regard de l'autre, le Komintern et le PCF," in Mikhail Narinsky and Jürgen Rojahn (eds.), *Centre and Periphery: The History of the Comintern in the Light of New Documents* (Amsterdam: International Institute of Social History, 1996), 189–202; and Antonio Elorza and Marta Bizcarrondo, *Queridos camaradas: La Internacional Comunista y España, 1919–1939* (Barcelona: Planeta-De Agostini, 2006).

Much light has been shed on the interactions between center and periphery as well as the terms of the Comintern's global approach. The opening of the Stalin archives has led to renewed analysis of the links between the policy of the Soviet Union and the Comintern, incorporating the history of international relations and that of communism. For the history of Stalinist repression and how the Comintern was affected and deeply weakened by it, see William J. Chase, *Enemies Within the Gates? The Comintern and the*

Stalinist Repression, 1934–1939 (New Haven: Yale University Press, 2001); Fridrikh I. Firsov, "Dimitrov, the Comintern and Stalinist Repression," in Barry McLoughlin and Kevin McDermott (eds.), *Stalin's Terror: High Politics and Mass Repression in the Soviet Union* (New York: Palgrave Macmillan, 2003), 56–81; and Norman Laporte, Kevin Morgan and Matthew Worley (eds.), *Bolshevism, Stalinism and the Comintern: Perspectives on Stalinization, 1917–53* (Basingstoke: Palgrave Macmillan, 2006).

The global history of communism in the twentieth century is examined in Serge Wolikow, *L'Internationale Communiste (1919–1943): Le Komintern ou le rêve déchu du parti mondial de la révolution* (Paris: Éditions Ouvrières, 2011), and Silvio Pons, *The Global Revolution: A History of International Communism, 1917–1991* (Oxford: Oxford University Press, 2014).

With the development of digital humanities, parts of the archives of the Comintern are available online on the RGASPI site: sovdoc.rusarchives.ru/; and for French records, on the site of MSH Dijon Pandor, pandor.u-bourgogne.fr/.

10

The Popular Fronts and the Civil War in Spain

TIM REES

> Our desire is that all the organizations of the Popular Front be strengthened. Our desire is that all anti-fascist forces be consolidated, wherever they are to be found. Although I know that this can lead to criticism of our position, of our actions, never, never, can it be said that a single member, not a one, has been attracted to the party by the promise of advancement or the lure of personal gain.[1]

These words were spoken as part of a rousing closing speech made by Jesús Hernández, a leading figure in the Spanish Communist Party (PCE), at a party plenum held in March 1937. At the time Spain was nine months into its brutal civil war which raged on until the final defeat of the republican side at the hands of General Franco's Nationalists in April 1939. The plenum was held partly to publicize the growing strength of the communist party but its central theme, echoed by all the speakers present, was to extol support for the Popular Front as an alliance of all the political parties and trade unions that supported the republic. In evoking the idea of the Popular Front, and the language of anti-fascism which accompanied it, the PCE was following policies common to the international communist movement. In the context of the war in Spain, Hernández hammered home the message that cooperation was the key to ultimate victory and that the PCE was providing a selfless example in working toward that common goal, all of which was reflected in the title of his speech: "Everything Within the Popular Front."

This plenum, and another held in November 1937, presented the PCE as not just at the heart of the conflict in Spain but as part of a worldwide struggle being led by the international communist movement against the threat of

1 Partido Comunista de España, *Todo dentro del Frente Popular* (Valencia: Ediciones del Partido Comunista de España, 1937).

fascism. The fact that Franco was actively aided by Germany and Italy added to the sense that the civil war encapsulated all the great ideological and international conflicts that had built up by the late 1930s. As a result, the defense of the democratic republic appeared to offer the chance to strike a blow against the seemingly inexorable advance of far-right and fascist movements. While this feeling was strongly shared among liberals and leftists of all political persuasions, making the commitment to support the republic one of the great international causes of the time, it struck a particular chord with communists. This was symbolized by the dispatch of the famous International Brigades of volunteers from around the world – predominantly but not exclusively communists – organized by the Communist International (Comintern). Their decision to fight in Spain resulted in great part from the prominence given by the Soviet Union and the international communist movement since the mid 1930s to the need to counter the spread of fascism. The establishment of virulently anti-democratic and anti-communist regimes in Germany by the Nazis in 1933 and in Austria in 1934 by Engelbert Dollfuss were the shocks that had finally prompted Soviet and communist leaders into action. In particular, a remilitarized and aggressive Germany under Adolf Hitler presented a direct threat to the USSR and his rise to power had involved the destruction of the largest non-Soviet communist party. The lesson that Soviet and communist leaders took was that the USSR and communist parties were too weak by themselves successfully to resist the rise of fascism. Under Stalin the USSR had become internationally isolated, convulsed by the internal changes unleashed by his rule. Meanwhile, the official policy of the Comintern and its member communist parties since 1928 had been to promote "Bolshevik-style" revolution around the globe and to reject all ideological and political alternatives, including participation in "bourgeois democracies" such as the Spanish republic created in 1931. Now communist leaders increasingly accepted the need to seek alliances with other powers, particularly the Western democracies, and with other political movements on the liberal-left. Their dilemma, however, was how best to do this in ways that were compatible with the ideological integrity and wider aims of the communist cause. In May 1935 this led to the signing of a mutual assistance pact between the USSR and France in a vain attempt to contain German expansionism. Later in July–August of the same year, the Comintern held its seventh and last world Congress in Moscow to discuss, among other matters, the stance of the international communist movement toward fascism. Decisions taken at that Congress paved the way for communist participation in anti-fascist political alliances with other groups, subsequently known as popular fronts, and raised the possibility that they might also become part of democratic governments.

The war in Spain marked the highpoint of this popular front approach and is often cited as a prime example of the shift in this direction that the Comintern had taken at its seventh world Congress. During the conflict, communist propaganda lavishly celebrated the role of the PCE as heroic and lauded it as an example of what could be achieved through anti-fascist unity and adherence to the Popular Front. The achievements of other popular fronts at the time were similarly highlighted. Here the principal achievements came through successful participation in electoral politics. Most notable was the victory in the French National Assembly elections of May 1936 of a Front Populaire alliance of center-left parties. This included the formation of a separate Popular Front committee in colonial Senegal that included local communists and which supported the unsuccessful candidacy of the Senegalese socialist Lamine Guèye in the same elections. Less well known, but as significant in its own right, was the electoral and political left-wing coalition initially formed in Chile in 1937. In the congressional elections of that year the Popular Front was narrowly defeated, as was its candidate in the presidential contest that followed shortly afterwards. However, in 1938 the candidate of the Popular Front, Pedro Aguirre Cerda of the Radical Party, finally captured the presidency with a small majority.

The association of the popular front concept with these dramatic developments has made it the most famous of the "lines" adopted by the Comintern throughout its existence. Even decades later, official histories, commemorations and memoirs viewed communist involvement in the "good fight" against fascism as a moral example still to be emulated and admired. This favorable propaganda justified the activities of the Comintern and its member parties and provided evidence subsequently of communism's anti-fascist credentials. However, closer examination of popular fronts in Spain and elsewhere suggests that their creation and nature were far from straightforward, and their activities and achievements mixed. In fact, even to talk of a coherent popular front strategy that was orchestrated and consistently applied by the Comintern is misleading. The Seventh Congress of the Comintern produced no such clear and transparent guide to action for its member parties. Instead the popular front idea evolved and changed by choice and circumstance. Nor did communist parties necessarily play a leading role in the formation and direction of the political alliances which took the name of popular front. Likewise, the relatively few popular fronts that were created were often quite different in practice despite their shared commitment to the cause of anti-fascism. Wartime Spain, in particular, represented a special situation that produced a unique form of the popular front and of communist involvement in it.

What all the popular fronts did share in common was their ultimate failure, alongside the Soviet policy of alliances with the Western democracies. They were not cohesive alliances and all proved unsustainable in the face of internal political differences and deep dilemmas over policy. The Spanish example, in particular, followed a very distinctive course and demonstrated the limited ability of the communists decisively to influence developments. Despite the optimistic hopes of Hernández and other Spanish party leaders in 1937, the civil war ended ignominiously in internal fighting within the republican side that finally destroyed the Popular Front; the result was a crushing defeat that helped hasten the final end of the Comintern itself. The experiment of "popular frontism" in France had already fallen apart under the weight of internal divisions during 1938, followed by the final dissolution of the Chilean example in early 1941. Their immediate successes tended to be correspondingly short-lived and, at best, they delayed rather than prevented the spread of "fascism."

The Seventh Congress of the Comintern was called at a time of grave uncertainty for the international communist movement and the Soviet Union. The new head of the Comintern, Georgi Dimitrov, had witnessed at first hand the rise of the Nazis and the suppression of the German Communist Party (KPD). In Czechoslovakia and France there were growing calls from factions within their communist parties to abandon the attacks on other organizations as "social fascists" and traitors to the working class previously promoted by the Comintern in favor of greater meaningful cooperation. Within the trade unions, in particular, there were also examples of grassroots joint actions involving communist and socialist activists in order to defend workers' rights and to defend wages and working conditions as the effects of economic depression deepened. Meanwhile, the USSR also faced a corresponding threat from a resurgent Germany to the west and an increasingly threatening Japanese presence to the east. For Stalin and his coterie, concern with the security of the Soviet Union was matched by a preoccupation with the tremendous domestic pressures unleashed by the campaigns for collectivization and forced industrialization. While these fears and uncertainty about the immediate future motivated the decision to call a congress, Dimitrov and other leading figures in the Comintern were also aware that the revolutionary idealism of Bolshevism was at the heart of its appeal. The need to "recognize reality," had therefore to be balanced by the continuing affirmation of the fundamental tenets of communist political doctrine and identity.

No dramatic "about turn" in Comintern policy was actually announced at the carefully managed Congress, attended by 513 representatives from sixty-five communist parties. Rather the Comintern leadership signaled new priorities in response to the threat of fascism while theoretically retaining full support for the central aim of spreading Bolshevik-style revolution around the globe. Most of the themes discussed were indistinguishable from previous congresses: attacks on the leaders of other working-class organizations, particularly socialists, as traitors to the cause of real revolution; vehement rejections of "Trotskyism" and other deviations from Leninist orthodoxy; and belief in the USSR as the homeland of socialism and in the inspirational leadership of Stalin. The most controversial item was André Marty's defense of the recently signed agreement between the USSR and France, which was criticized by some delegates as a capitulation to the capitalist and imperialist powers. Otherwise nothing in the language or terminology used departed from the established political lexicon of communist orthodoxy; instead change was introduced by subtle redefinitions and changes of emphasis. In his report Dimitrov used a definition of fascism previously agreed upon by the Comintern's executive, famously describing it "as the open terrorist dictatorship of the most reactionary, most chauvinistic and most imperialist elements of finance capital." While this made clear that fascism was rooted in capitalist society, it also suggested that it could not be seen as simply a form of bourgeois rule like any other. Instead it posed a violent and immediate threat which required a shift in communist tactics which Dimitrov argued should be based upon the creation of a "united front of the working class" which could lead to the formation of "anti-fascist people's fronts."[2] The concept of the "united front" was already familiar, and had been used in various forms since the founding of the Comintern in 1919. It was significant that veteran delegates at the Congress, such as Jules Humbert-Droz, were not permitted to speak for fear that they would point out what was now proposed actually marked a step back to a position that the Comintern had held in the early 1920s. The final resolutions of the Congress expressed the new formula as "the creation of a broad anti-fascist popular front on the basis of the proletarian united front." Also included in passing were the possibilities of electoral cooperation with non-working-class political parties and communist

2 Georgi Dimitrov, "The Fascist Offensive and the Tasks of the Communist International in the Struggle of the Working Class Against Fascism," in Georgi Dimitrov, *Selected Works*, vol. II (Sofia: Sofia Press, 1972).

involvement in "bourgeois governments," but these steps were only to be agreed on a case-by-case basis. Also discussed were the legitimate use of armed force in the face of fascist violence and the formation of workers' militias for the purposes of defense.

Stalin's lukewarm approval, echoed by loyal communist party leaderships, was a sign of his personal disinterest but also of the general uncertainly about what actually was changing. Though no grandiosely titled "popular front" strategy was, in fact, adopted at the Congress, this did not mean that its practical consequences were actually negligible. Most significant was the endorsement of a less dogmatic and prescriptive approach to political tactics on the part of the Comintern. Giving greater priority to the struggle against fascism helped communist parties to take a more flexible attitude toward their activities. This was further reinforced, at least rhetorically, by a call from Dimitrov for party leaderships to take more responsibility for their own actions and to make decisions based upon a self-assessment of local political conditions. This did not mean that parties had *carte blanche* to do as they liked, far from it. But it did mean they could explore a greater range of political opportunities and tactics in the name of anti-fascism. What these subsequently entailed in practice were matters of interpretation and compromise, as the prescriptions that the Congress had offered were far too vague to serve as any kind of clear blueprint for action. Nevertheless, it was this more permissive atmosphere that subsequently enabled at least some communists to respond more flexibly to local political opportunities.

It quickly became evident that creating "united fronts" of the working class as a prerequisite for "people's fronts" was unrealistic and even offers of limited joint action were mostly rejected. Nor were all communists enthusiasts for collaboration; compromise and negotiation did not sit easily with Bolshevik diehards and many activists were uneasy. In the case of the Chinese Communist Party (CCP) there was outright rejection when Comintern leaders encouraged the party to seek accommodation with Chiang Kai-shek's Nationalists, with whom they were engaged in a civil war. Only an attack on China by Japan in 1937 would bring them together in a fragile alliance of convenience. Years of attacks on other working-class parties by communists could also not simply be overcome overnight. Overtures to the Labour and Socialist International for cooperation were rejected, as were offers of joint action by the overwhelming majority of socialist parties. Although there were sympathetic voices within socialist ranks, there was also a deep well of distrust of communist motives based on past experience, which reflected a bitter rivalry between sibling movements that also claimed to speak for the working classes.

For many socialists, communist anti-fascism appeared as just a tactical facade behind which lay the same old hegemonic intentions. In addition, the small size and marginal importance of the great majority of communist parties reduced even further the appeal of any kind of partnership with them. The spread of right-wing dictatorial regimes in Europe and the Americas, alongside the large areas of the globe under authoritarian colonial rule, severely limited the number of countries in which it was even possible to organize and act openly. In liberal-democratic Scandinavia, the Low Countries, Britain and Ireland, where the threat from the far right was relatively weak, there was little incentive for noncommunists to cooperate. Even in Czechoslovakia, which was the only part of Central Europe not under authoritarian rule and with a strong communist party, offers of unity and cooperation were rejected by the socialists. Consequently, unity on communist terms was therefore overwhelmingly rejected and it was only in very specific circumstances that it proved possible to create alliances.

The Popular Fronts that were formed in France, Spain and Chile during 1936 and 1937 were actually loose electoral alliances, in which communists mostly played minor and variable roles, rather than ones based upon united fronts of the organized working class. Their creation was driven only partly by a desire to forestall the spread of fascism, though anti-fascist rhetoric was certainly part of the ideological glue that bound them together. More important was blocking the political right, in whatever guise, from government at times of acute economic crisis and social polarization. Only in France was the role of the Communist Party (PCF) truly crucial. A large and well-organized party, with an independent trade union federation (CGTU), the PCF was an established force on the political left. When its leader, Maurice Thorez, began to call for a Front Populaire (in one of the first uses of the term) from 1934 the groundwork for cooperation with the socialist movement was already being laid through local cooperation between trade unions and later by joint candidacies in municipal elections. While the Comintern could now endorse these actions, it was also clear that a communist–socialist election pact was incapable of defeating the coalition of the conservative–right that seemed poised to take power as the existing government faltered. It was only when the middle-class Radical Party and a number of smaller leftist parties added their weight that a Popular Front was finally agreed to fight the April 1936 elections.

In contrast, the much smaller Chilean Communist Party (PCCh) and the Spanish PCE were in no position to play such pivotal roles to bring about popular fronts. Calls from the party leaders, Carlos Contreras Labarca and

José Díaz, for united fronts and people's fronts were initially rejected or ignored, particularly by the Chilean and Spanish socialist parties. In Chile, it was the defeat of the disunited center-left parties in the March 1937 congressional elections, plus the prospects that the right would also win forthcoming presidential elections, that provided the impetus for a Popular Front. Its key creators were the radical and socialist parties, with radical-socialists, democrats and communists playing only lesser roles. The PCE was even more fortunate in finding itself as part of the Spanish Popular Front, given that it played no active part in its creation. Instead in Spain it was the socialist and left republican parties which were at the heart of negotiations in late 1935 to form an electoral alliance – or rather to re-form on new terms the electoral and government coalition that had brought the republic into being in 1931, but which had collapsed in 1933. A disastrous attempt in October 1934 to oust the resulting center-right government had ended in failure, provoking a brief workers' rising in the mining region of Asturias which had been crushed by the army and police forces. Subsequently, the PCE had erroneously tried to claim credit for this "October Revolution," gaining some credibility with the Comintern as a result. It certainly shared the same fate as all the other parties of the left in finding its leaders imprisoned or in exile and its press silenced. The calling of new elections for February 1936 then provided the impetus to form an electoral coalition to keep the right from power. Initially, the PCE was excluded from negotiations by the republicans and moderate wing of the Socialist Party (PSOE). However, for his own purposes the leader of the socialist left, Largo Caballero, insisted that the PCE be brought into the Popular Front, alongside a host of other smaller movements of the far left. Otherwise, the party would have remained isolated. This was a decision that Caballero was later to regret bitterly as it unwittingly gave the PCE a credibility that it otherwise lacked. The degree to which the PCE had no say in this process was made evident when its vehement objections to the admittance of the "Trotskyists" of the POUM (Workers' Party of Marxist Unification) were simply ignored. Consequently, the PCE appeared as a very incidental force in an unwieldy electoral bloc that ranged from moderate republicans to both orthodox and dissident communists.

This rather fragile unity was reflected by electoral platforms that were compromises designed to avoid disputes between the coalition partners and to maximize popular appeal. Keeping the right from power and containing the lurking threat of fascism reflected the only really common aims. The electoral program of the Spanish Popular Front also included promises of an amnesty for those imprisoned after the October rising. Though broadly "progressive" in outlook, there was little otherwise in the agreed programs of the Popular Fronts that could be identified as specifically reflecting the aims and aspirations of their communist participants. Equally, however, there was nothing in them that was particularly objectionable. More positively, there was a commitment to economic and social reform though often with little in the way of specific policies. Cultural differences also played a significant part in drawing together the participants in these Popular Fronts, and in differentiating them from their opponents. The most obvious example was in terms of the deep clerical–anticlerical divisions within Chile, France and Spain, with the Popular Fronts presenting themselves as champions of "modern" values against religious reaction. This encompassed matters far beyond just the position of the Catholic Church and included attitudes toward gender roles, education, the family and sexual relations. The acquiescence of the communists gave a strong impression that they had tacitly accepted "bourgeois" norms, prompting some criticism from within party ranks. This was reinforced by the increasing use of "national" and "patriotic" symbols by communist parties, though in ways that tried to reinterpret them in anti-fascist and revolutionary forms. This addressed deeper questions about how communists could reconcile a commitment to the creation of a universal proletarian civilization with the existence of liberal nation-states, particularly when one of the most effective charges against them had been that they were "unpatriotic." The French Popular Front, in particular, promoted the idea that it was saving the nation from forces linked to threatening outside powers – a description that could equally apply to the PCF and its links to the USSR. Not surprisingly, the French party, but also others, struggled to find a middle ground over how they related to "their" nations.

Willingness to accept these broad "anti-fascist" electoral positions might have given the impression that communists had quietly surrendered any real commitment to a separate revolutionary mission and identity. But any appearances that communist ideology had been decisively "diluted" or "toned down," as has sometimes been argued, masked a more complex reality. While the communists accepted these agreements in order to be included in Popular Fronts this did not therefore mean they had forsworn their ultimate ambitions, as was demonstrated during the electoral campaigns themselves. While they fulfilled their obligation to support all the parliamentary or presidential candidates from their respective Popular Front coalitions under the common programs, they continued to campaign separately on their own issues, including the abolition of private property and the creation of future Soviet-style regimes. In communist eyes tactical support for the Popular Front did not alter their long-term strategic aims nor did they cease to see themselves as essentially revolutionaries. In fact, the inclusion of communist candidates in all the electoral slates presented to voters in Spain and France in February and April–May 1936 actually enhanced their political profiles and gave them new platforms from which to espouse their ideological views. Similar opportunities were given to the Chilean communists during the presidential campaigns of 1937 and 1938. Communist activism was also crucial in strengthening the leftist character of the Popular Front and in identifying this with communism. For the PCE, in particular, this was to prove a crucial boost to the party's credibility, helping it to emerge from political marginality toward becoming an established force alongside its anarchist and socialist rivals. However, party leaders and the Comintern were acutely aware of the "danger" posed by an increasing accommodation with the bourgeois regimes they existed to overthrow and with other political movements that they were still striving to supplant. And this fear helped guide their actions during the euphoria of the so-called Popular Front springs that followed.

These electoral victories did not lead directly to governments that were representative of the Popular Front alliances that had produced them. In every case the goal of keeping the right from power was achieved, and also brought the PCE seventeen parliamentary deputies, having previously had only one, while the PCF gained seventy-two seats. The election of Aguirre Cerda to the presidency in Chile in 1938 served the same essential purpose, though rather bizarrely his victory was achieved with the last-minute endorsement of his candidacy by the Chilean Nazi Party. The question then was how far cooperation would continue subsequently in terms of forming and supporting new governments. In Spain the issue did not arise as there was never any intention to form a coalition government of the Popular Front, which to all intents and purposes ceased to exist having served its electoral purpose. Instead, the left republican parties formed a minority government, with no representation from the working-class movements including, crucially, the socialists. Similar circumstances applied in Chile in 1938 when the PCCh was denied cabinet positions in the government headed by Aguirre Cerda in which the radicals were utterly dominant, save for a few minor positions given to the socialists. In contrast, in June 1936 the PCF was directly offered ministerial posts in a coalition government by the socialist leader Léon Blum. Considerable discussion with the Comintern followed before the leaders of the PCF finally declined the offer on the grounds that acceptance would compromise their ideological integrity and be met with hostility by party members. Instead the new administration was formed by the socialists and radicals alone. It was clear in every case that mutual wariness between communists and noncommunists continued to run deep.

The position adopted by the Comintern was, in effect, that the popular front was fine as a defensive shield in the anti-fascist struggle but it should not to be allowed otherwise to inhibit communists' freedom of action. The ambiguous position initially proved advantageous in the face of rising social and political tensions. Freed from the constraints of government, the communists were able to become fully involved in waves of worker protests and demands for increased social welfare. The communist trade union federation in France and the communist factions within the socialist unions in Spain often played leading roles, responding in many cases to pressures from their grassroots memberships. In France, cooperation with the socialist union federation led to a general strike and factory occupations in May–June 1936 that ended in agreements with employers conceding a range of improvements in wages and conditions of work. Spain also saw a steep rise in strike activity and land invasions during the spring, with communists acting alongside their more numerous anarchist and socialist counterparts. The large May Day parades mounted in the major cities of both countries publicly celebrated these achievements, demanded solidarity with the Soviet Union and exhorted further advances in the struggle against fascism. In Chile the PCCh also played a key role in urban and rural labor disputes, pressing in particular for agrarian reform. By placing pressure on the new governments, communist parties became part of a de facto left opposition in both the street and from within parliament. In Spain the PCE shared an almost identical position to Caballero's wing of the socialists, closely linked to the unions, which called for a socialist transformation of society.

A surge in communist popularity and strengthened organizations were the immediate rewards, further reinforcing the sense that the parties involved had chosen their positions wisely. All the parties gained members, most notably and dramatically in the case of the PCE whose ranks nearly quadrupled between March and July 1936. This upward trajectory, which continued into 1937, finally turned the PCE into a "party of the masses" on a scale which began to match the socialists. The profiles of those joining were also broadly similar: predominantly young, mostly male trade unionists with no previous political affiliations; this was exactly the constituency previously dominated by the left wing of the socialist movements. In Spain this marked the beginning of a complex process of cooperation and rivalry by which the communists were to displace Largo Caballero's section of the socialists. Communist unions or union factions, as in Spain, also flourished. This included the spread of communist unionism into the countryside for the first time, mostly among rural laborers but also with the formation of peasant leagues in Chile. Inevitably these developments impacted upon relations with other working-class movements, particularly the socialists. In Spain this was accompanied by a realignment of political organizations with novel consequences. The growing youth section of the PCE formally joined its socialist counterpart in a new body, the United Socialist Youth (JSU), whose formation in April 1936 was facilitated and approved by the Comintern. There were also unapproved negotiations between four small "Marxist" groups in Catalonia, including the Catalan section of the PCE, which finally resulted in their merger into a new party, the Unified Socialist Party of Catalonia (PSUC) in July 1936. The leaders of the PSUC sought recognition from the Comintern as a party separate from the PCE; when this was finally granted in 1939 Spain became the only country with two communist parties. In Spain, at least, it seemed that the long-sought project of a single party of the working class under communist tutelage was finally making progress.

These communist successes came at a price in terms of tensions with their anti-fascist partners and in exacerbating social and political divisions. To their electoral allies the French and Spanish communists appeared opportunistic and unreliable. This mistrust was at its deepest with their respective socialist parties, which feared that under the banner of cooperation the communists' intentions were as predatory as ever. Their growing prominence, both within and without the institutions of government and the state, also helped fuel anti-communism and the rise of the radical right. The Comintern's policy that communist parties should form armed "self-defense" organizations both reflected and contributed to a corresponding spread of violence. But this did not mean that communist leaders were blind to the risks that were being run. Parties were also warned of the dangers of provocations by the right amidst instances of sporadic violence. In France and Chile these never reached the point of a complete breakdown in order, but the fears were real. In May 1936 the Comintern, concerned at the signs of growing polarization and political violence in Spain, specifically informed the PCE leaders that they needed to avoid weakening the authority of the government, presided over by the left republican parties, to the point that it might collapse and open the door to fascism: It was to prove a prescient warning.

The sudden outbreak of civil war in Spain produced conditions that not only led to a revival of the Popular Front but were to transform its nature and the role of the communists within it. Following the attempted military coup of 17–18 July 1936 that sparked off the war, there was a near-collapse of state authority. In those areas that had not fallen to the insurgents and their right-wing allies, the ensuing power vacuum was filled by a patchwork of organizations that assumed local authority. At the forefront were the trade unions and the political parties of the left, particularly where they exercised armed force through militias or retained the support of local police and military forces. Within the emerging loyalist zone this decisively reinforced the importance of the working-class movements, and marked the relative eclipse of the middle-class republican parties in terms of their real influence. An immediate casualty of the war was the all-republican government placed into office after the February elections. The nature of local control varied hugely, depending upon the mix of organizations and political groups in any given village, town, or city neighborhood. Representatives formed ad hoc committees to deal with the practical problems of running their localities, replacing or displacing the previous system of government and authority in the process. The demands upon them were huge: ensuring security and defense, organizing production and work, and meeting the practical needs of the local population. While sheer necessity was a primary driver, this also represented a radical and unplanned alteration to existing social and political structures. In areas such as the city of Barcelona and the region of Aragón where they predominated, many anarchists and the dissident communists of the POUM consequently viewed this as an opportunity finally to achieve their different revolutionary goals.

Anti-fascist cooperation accordingly gained a new urgency in what quickly became a life-and-death struggle for survival and to shape the future of Spanish society. Members of the PCE and the Catalan communists in the newly formed PSUC were active participants in these developments, sometimes taking prominent roles in places like Madrid and Valencia where they had a strong presence. Likewise, members of the party militia, the Workers' and Peasants' Anti-Fascist Militia (MAOC), swelled by a rush of new volunteers, were quickly caught up in the initial confused fighting. Communists also joined local committees and were enthusiastic participants in activities such as the seizure of property from suspected nationalist supporters and other "security" measures. But how the conflict was to be conducted, particularly in terms of any reconstituted system of government, was a question that those on the republican side were immediately forced to confront in the face of the advancing insurgents. The problem was that, while they were united in their desire to defeat their "fascist" opponents, they were not all in agreement as to how best that was to be achieved, nor to what final end.

A return to a revised form of popular front was an obvious answer. While there was a broad consensus that cooperation was a necessity, the ensuing process of reconstituting political alliances proved problematic. As the largest political movement, allied to a strong trade union federation, it was clear that the Socialist Party would have to be at the heart of any effective coalition. However, when Largo Caballero agreed to form a new national government it took protracted negotiations before a new cabinet was announced in early September 1936. One stumbling block was whether the PCE could be persuaded to participate. Initially, the collapse of the rising in large parts of Spain, including most of the major cities, mistakenly convinced PCE leaders that the insurgency would soon implode – a message that the Comintern's advisor, Vittorio Codovilla, also passed on to Moscow. Even after it became clear that this was not the case, the Spanish communists saw no need to alter their existing political stance. Accordingly, when offered government posts the PCE rejected the offer on the understanding that this was Comintern policy. It was only after consultation with Moscow that this decision was reversed in line with the assessment by the Comintern and Soviet leadership that the grave threat posed by fascism in Spain now justified such involvement. It was similar thinking, matched by growing evidence of the extent of Axis aid for the nationalists, which also prompted the exceptional offer of Soviet military aid to the republicans – a policy that ran counter to the nonintervention promoted by the Western Allies and which was to fatally undermine Stalin's attempts to reach an accord with them.

Two communist minsters, Jesús Hernández and Vicente Uribe, subsequently joined the first truly representative Popular Front government in Spain. This new precedent was later to be followed in Chile when communists joined a similar coalition government with none of the prohibitions that had previously been placed on the French party. Along with socialists, Caballero's government also contained left republicans, Catalan nationalists and three members of the anarchist Confederación Nacional del Trabajo (CNT). Enticing anarchist ministers into the government had proved an even greater task, requiring them to compromise their deepest principles at the cost of dividing the anarchist movement in the process. To make matters even more complicated, separate coalition governments were also created in the autonomous regions of Catalonia and the Basque Country. Regional nationalists headed both of these administrations, in alliance with republicans, socialists and communists. In the Basque Country, the regional section of the PCE played only a minor role holding no significant ministerial positions. In contrast, in Catalonia the Catalan communists within the newly formed PSUC were a more important component of the coalition, particularly as the regional CNT refused to participate. Even so, PSUC leaders were unable to prevent, despite their vociferous objections, the inclusion of a representative, Andreu Nin, from the Trotskyist POUM. In practice, therefore, what emerged was not a single cohesive popular front but a plurality of individually negotiated popular fronts that varied in composition and with overlapping, and potentially competing, areas of authority.

Like all the other loyalist groups, the Spanish communists were forced to radically rethink their political position in the light of these new circumstances. The choices they faced were not easy, particularly in terms of their self-identification as revolutionaries and their previous reluctance to compromise too deeply with the "bourgeois" republic to whose defense they were now committed. The most obvious was the absolute commitment to the Popular Front, now radically reimagined as not just an electoral alliance but the basis for a reconstructed state. Achieving and preserving unity was of paramount importance in winning the war, and the Comintern constantly reminded the PCE and PSUC leaderships of this. But this was now taken to mean the translation of the Popular Front into every institution of authority, including the military forces. This redefined the republic itself as no longer just a "bourgeois" democracy but as an anti-fascist regime with "progressive" features which included state direction of the economy, the redistribution of landed estates, and forms of workers' control under government supervision. This led to the idea that the Spanish and Catalan communists were promoting a "democratic republic of a new type," sensitive to the concerns of more enlightened members of the middle class, but essentially dedicated to the interests of the working class and poor peasantry. This redefinition also allowed the Spanish communists to vigorously defend a switch from previously attacking the parliamentary regime to now defending it. Moreover, they also presented the war not as a civil war at all but as a war of "national liberation" against the Axis powers and their fascist allies within Spain. Although falling short of the full Bolshevik ideal, this allowed the communists to argue that they were still acting as revolutionaries – while simultaneously rejecting as "absurd" the revolutionary claims of the anarchists and POUM. This reformulation was undertaken in consultation with the Comintern and particularly with Palmiro Togliatti, its deputy leader and representative in Spain during the second half of the war, giving it wide importance as a further refinement of communist thinking about the Popular Front and its potential as a route toward a socialist society.

It was really only at this point that the Comintern embraced the Popular Front fully, though this did nothing to dispel the suspicion in the eyes of noncommunists that this was a subterfuge. The PCE and PSUC continually defended themselves against charges of opportunism and sectarianism made in response to their rapid rise to prominence during the early phase of the war. Indeed, by the spring of 1937 communists were found holding positions of responsibility in all the organizations and institutions created by the republic, including the army, police and security services. The numbers of party members had also grown rapidly to make the PCE a truly mass party after years of marginality and its members also played key roles within other organizations. In addition, the PCE sponsored a swathe of so-called mass organizations open to all comers and which provided a variety of health and welfare services, produced propaganda and purported to represent groups such as "anti-fascist" women and peasants. The PCE also continued to argue for the creation of a united party of the working class, meaning the fusion of the communists with the socialists – a proposal that was entirely dismissed by the socialists. It was not so surprising, therefore, that other members of the Popular Front coalition – particularly the anarchists and left socialists – found the PCE threatening and possibly duplicitous in its intentions.

The PCE presented itself as making great sacrifices in order to preserve the Popular Front, but this was balanced by an increasingly aggressive stance toward anyone perceived to threaten its unity. It was a natural corollary to the changes in communist thinking that anyone who did not fully support the Popular Front that represented "the people," and the creation of a state based upon it, was either a "fascist" or was acting in ways that consciously or unconsciously aided fascism. Communist rhetoric and actions were accordingly uncompromising toward anyone labeled a fascist, promising their destruction as enemies of "the anti-fascist people." By definition this included anyone in the nationalist camp, but it also included elements within the republican side such as "uncontrollable" anarchists who rejected a centralized war effort and, above all, the Trotskyists of the POUM. Coinciding with the turn toward the terror in the USSR, which also engulfed the Comintern, the PCE and PSUC conducted a vigorous campaign against their rivals in the POUM, arguing that they should be excluded from the Popular Front and suppressed as disguised fascists. Doing anything about this was, however, another matter. There was to be a persistent tension between what the party leadership, and the Comintern, desired and the ability to realize those desires within the confines of coalition politics. Despite the growing prominence of the Spanish and Catalan communists, they were never in a position to dictate government policy at any level – at least not without running the risk of fatally undermining the Popular Front by alienating other parties in it. In particular, the need to keep the bulk of the anarchists on board and to keep good relations with the socialists was always of fundamental importance. This was to lead to continued frustrations and it rather confirmed the communist fear that alliances posed a potential trap in terms of pursuing their own aims and political identity.

The wartime Popular Front in Spain never proved the stable and cohesive coalition, united in its purpose, that the communists had hoped for. Lots of different factors contributed to this, not least the tensions and rivalries between the socialists and anarchists. The underlying pressures came, however, from the failure to turn the tide of the war in favor of the republicans. By the spring of 1937 this focused in particular on Largo Caballero's leadership of the government, and specifically on his insistence on retaining the additional role of minister of war. Critics from the right of his own party, allied to the republicans and communists, gradually withdrew their support for him, demanding a greater drive toward centralizing the war effort. In May this growing political crisis was compounded by the outbreak of street fighting in Barcelona (the so-called May Days) where local tensions exploded into confrontation between forces of the regional government and local anarchists and supporters of the POUM. Although suppressed by force, this precipitated the temporary withdrawal of anarchist ministers and a cabinet coup that removed Caballero from power. The new socialist prime minister, Juan Negrín, from the right of the party, pursued a policy of centralization which included taking greater control over Catalonia and reducing the power of the trade unions. The government, strongly urged on by the communists, also banned the POUM (and ignored the murder of Andreu Nin by Soviet agents) and marginalized the anarchists. Although the same organizations remained represented in the Popular Front, and in the coalition government, this effectively signaled a realignment in which the right of the Socialist Party took power from the left and the communists and republicans shifted their allegiances accordingly. Nevertheless, despite some significant attempts to seize the military advantage, the war continued to go against the republicans. In March 1939 the government was overthrown in an internal military coup, backed by a range of supporters who had become disillusioned with the failure to end the war and who desired a negotiated peace with Franco. Strongly proclaiming their anti-communist credentials, they were rebuffed and the remnants of the republic collapsed. This internal rupture and decisive military defeat brought a bitter final end to the Popular Front in Spain. Summoned to Moscow and fearful of retribution, the leaders of the PCE and Comintern advisors naturally blamed everyone but themselves for its failure.

As it was, the anti-fascist alliances elsewhere already seemed to be in a state of decay. In France the Popular Front had finally dissolved in August 1938 following mounting and irreconcilable policy and political differences among its participants. The PCF had increasingly opposed the government, dominated by the more conservative Radical Party after Blum lost power in June 1937. Disagreements covered domestic labor and economic policies, the failure of France to aid the Spanish republic in the civil war, and the signing of the Munich agreement – the last of which led to a disastrous general strike called by the communist unions. Similar tensions also pulled apart the Popular Front in Chile during 1940. As a consequence, the PCCh fought the 1941 congressional elections alone but, nevertheless, gained seats for the first time. However, the Soviet and Comintern leadership were not concerned for long with these failures as the signing of the Nazi–Soviet pact in August 1939 immediately made anti-fascism an embarrassment rather than a priority. Instead the Comintern urged its member parties to denounce the subsequent outbreak of war in Europe as a capitalist conflict and to oppose the war efforts of the Western democracies, sowing consternation and confusion among the ranks of communists around the world. While dramatic and shocking, this reversal marked the final abandonment of a policy of political alliances and cooperation that already seemed exhausted. The achievements of the various Popular Fronts now appeared fleeting as the international communist movement found itself once again thrown into crisis and uncertainty. With its functionaries decimated by the Soviet terror and lacking any clear role after the civil war in Spain, the Comintern itself was moribund and completely sidelined by Stalin.

From a communist perspective, the Spanish Civil War saw the popular front idea taken to its most developed form as the potential basis for a new type of the "anti-fascist" state. However, this was not really the result of any conscious strategy but largely occurred as a reaction to circumstances not previously envisioned. Indeed, it would be wrong to describe the Comintern as having adopted a popular front "strategy" as such, let alone one that led inexorably to this political outcome – this only appeared to be the case with the benefit of hindsight. Nevertheless, the more pragmatic approach adopted by the Comintern to political alliances and joint actions in the name of anti-fascism was important. To a great extent this reflected the communist experience of popular fronts as a whole, where a more accurate description of the changes after 1935 was later summed up by a prominent Spanish communist, Santiago Carrillo, as having introduced "firmness and strategic intelligence into the project of change of that period."[3] Nor was this simply a passing phase. Instead, this more flexible attitude and the notion of the Popular Front (or something very like it) were to become enduring features of international communism and part of the established political lexicon of the left more generally – although it required the Axis attack on the USSR in June 1941 to see a decisive revival. Suddenly, the demands of war and resistance to occupation placed opposition to fascism even more strongly at the forefront of Soviet and communist priorities. At this point the communist role in the war in Spain, and the idea of the Popular Front more generally, once again became a model to be applauded and applied. The forms that these were to take – from the "anti-fascist people's democracies" of postwar Eastern Europe to the ill-fated Popular Unity government of Salvador Allende in Chile during the 1970s – were never exact repetitions of the experiences of the 1930s. Likewise, the central unsolvable dilemma of "popular frontism" endured: how to achieve genuine cooperation for an apparently greater good while preserving the assumed purity of communist ideals.

Bibliographical Essay

The popular front period of the 1930s is of such significance that all the histories of the Comintern and the international communist movement deal with it. For good recent examples see Serge Wolikow, *L'Internationale Communiste (1919–1943): Le Komintern ou le rêve déchu du parti mondial de la révolution* (Paris: Éditions Ouvrières, 2011); Silvio Pons, *The Global Revolution. A History of International Communism, 1917–1991* (Oxford: Oxford University Press, 2014); and Kevin McDermott and Jeremy Agnew, *The Comintern: A History of International Communism from Lenin to Stalin* (Basingstoke: Macmillan, 1996). In many ways the best starting point for more specific research are the essays in Serge Wolikow and Annie Bleton-Ruget (eds.), *Antifascisme et nation. Les gauches européennes au temps du front populaire* (Dijon: Éditions universitaires de Dijon, 1998); Martin Alexander and Helen Graham (eds.), *The French and Spanish Popular Fronts:*

3 Santiago Carrillo, *Memorias* (Barcelona: Planeta, 1993), 14.

Comparative Perspectives (Cambridge: Cambridge University Press, 1989); and Helen Graham and Paul Preston (eds.), *The Popular Front in Europe* (Basingstoke: Macmillan, 1987). On the change in Comintern policy, E. H. Carr, *The Twilight of the Comintern, 1930–1935* (Basingstoke: Macmillan, 1982) remains a useful starting point. Much light is also shed by the documents in A. Dallin and F. I. Firsov (eds.), *Dimitrov and Stalin, 1934–43: Letters from the Soviet Archives* (New Haven: Yale University Press, 2000), and in Ivo Banac (ed.), *The Diary of Georgi Dimitrov 1933–1949*, trans. Jane T. Hedges, Timothy D. Sergay and Irina Faion (New Haven: Yale University Press, 2003). On the connections between Soviet foreign policy and Comintern policy see Jonathan Haslam, "The Comintern and the Origins of the Popular Front, 1934–35," *Historical Journal* 22 (1979), 673–91, and Silvio Pons, *Stalin and the Inevitable War, 1936–1941* (London: Frank Cass, 2002). For an overview of Chile see Paul Drake, "Chile 1930–1958," in Leslie Bethell (ed.), *The Cambridge History of Latin America*, vol. VIII, *Latin America since 1930: Spanish South America* (Cambridge: Cambridge University Press, 1991), 267–310, and Manuel Loyola and Jorge Rojas (eds.), *Por un rojo amanecer. Hacia una historia de los comunistas chilenos* (Santiago: Impresora Vals, 2000). Overviews of the Popular Front in France, with considerable discussion of the communist role, include: Julian Jackson, *The Popular Front in France: Defending Democracy, 1934–1938* (Cambridge: Cambridge University Press, 1988); Jean-Paul Brunet, *Histoire du Front populaire, 1934–1938*, 2nd edn. (Paris: Presses Universitaires de France, 1998); Serge Wolikow, *Le Front Populaire en France* (Paris: Éditions Complexe, 1999); and Danielle Tartakowsky and Michel Margairaz (eds.), *L'avenir nous appartient. Histoire du Front populaire* (Paris: Larousse, 2006). On the PCF, see Stéphane Sirot, *Maurice Thorez* (Paris: Presses de Sciences Po, 2000), and Jacques Girault, *Des communistes en France (années 1920 – années 1960)* (Paris: Publications de la Sorbonne, 2002). Good overviews of the Spanish Popular Front are provided by José Luis Martín Ramos, *El Frente Popular. Victoria y derrota de la democracia en España* (Madrid: Pasado y Presente, 2012), and in Eduardo González Calleja and Rocío Navarro Comas (eds.), *Política, sociedad, conflicto y cultura en la España de 1936* (Granada: Editorial Comares, 2011). Communist involvement in the civil war and Popular Front is covered by Tim Rees, "The Highpoint of Comintern Influence? The Communist Party and the Civil War in Spain," in T. Rees and A. Thorpe (eds.), *International Communism and the Communist International, 1919–43* (Manchester: Manchester University Press, 1998), 143–67; Fernando Hernández Sánchez, *Guerra o revolución. El Partido Comunista de España en la guerra civil* (Barcelona: Crítica, 2010);

Stanley Payne, *The Spanish Civil War, the Soviet Union, and Communism* (New Haven: Yale University Press, 2004); Lisa A. Kirschenbaum, *International Communism and the Spanish Civil War* (Cambridge: Cambridge University Press, 2015); and Frank Schauff, *Der verspielte Sieg: Sowjetunion, Kommunistische Internationale und Spanischer Bürgerkrieg 1936–1939* (Frankfurt: Campus Verlag, 2005).

PART II

*

PATTERNS AND EXTENSIONS

11

Communism, Violence and Terror

HIROAKI KUROMIYA

Terror and violence are endemic to dictatorships. In the history of political violence, the Soviet practice marked a new stage: Political violence was ideologically justified and exercised by the first communist state in world history.[1] Backed by Moscow, communists elsewhere also resorted to violence as a political weapon. At the root of communist violence was ideology predicated on the theory of class struggle as the driving force of history. No Soviet leaders refrained from advocating the use of terror against class enemies. However, ideology did not always dictate the scale of terror. Violence ebbed and flowed dependent on many factors, and often Bolshevik terror had little to do with the ideology of communism per se. The Great Terror (1937–38), for example, struck far more workers, peasants and national minorities than "class enemies." Far from following the Marxist prediction of the withering away of the state, the Soviet state hypertrophied, supported by the seemingly almighty secret police (whose name changed from the Cheka [Emergency Commission for Combating Counterrevolution and Sabotage] to the GPU/OGPU [State Political Administration] and, from 1934, to the NKVD [People's Commissariat of Internal Affairs]).

Although Marxism may not have predetermined the scale of terror in the Soviet Union, the terror is not explicable without considering the role ideology played in the process. To be more exact, communist dictators, like all other dictators, adjusted or revised their ideology to suit their political needs. That was the case from the very beginning. The civil war that

1 One of the most incisive studies of the entire phenomenon of Soviet political terror is Nicolas Werth, "A State Against Its People: Violence, Repression, and Terror in the Soviet Union," in Stéphane Courtois, Nicolas Werth, Jean-Louis Panné, Andrzej Paczkowski, Karel Bartošek and Jean-Lois Margolin, *The Black Book of Communism: Crimes, Terror, Repression*, trans. Jonathan Murphy and Mark Kramer (Cambridge, MA: Harvard University Press, 1999), 33–268.

followed the October Revolution became the first stage of the Bolshevik application of prescriptive terror: Anyone opposed or suspected of being opposed to the revolution was branded as a class enemy and counterrevolutionary, and terrorized. It was also at this time that the Bolsheviks employed deportation as a means of dealing with political "enemies" en masse and confined them to concentration camps, or labor camps, which subsequently became known as the Gulag.[2]

Even though its full scale has not become known until recently, Soviet terror was such that the first communist state in world history came to signify in Western consciousness a place of unbridled political terror. Soviet political violence also presaged the immense terror committed by the followers of Soviet communism in the latter half of the twentieth century.

The Scale of Terror

From the beginning of its existence, the Soviet government exercised political terror extensively. Although the Bolshevik seizure of power in October 1917 in Petrograd itself may have been relatively bloodless, the struggle for power that followed in the country as a whole culminated in the bloody civil war, accentuated by red and white terror, and wars of conquest (in Poland, Georgia and elsewhere). Perhaps the most prominent casualties of the Bolshevik terror were the Romanov family: The former tsar Nicholas II and his family were murdered by the Bolsheviks in 1918. In areas where the old regime was restored (in Ukraine under Hetman Pavlo Skoropadskyi, for example), White terror was equally fierce, targeted at workers, peasants, Jews and others who benefited from the Bolshevik Revolution. To determine precisely the scale of terror during this period is nearly impossible. Everywhere the absence of stable authority aggravated the terror. Available statistical data are limited and it is often impossible to tell direct battle casualties from targeted killings. It is equally complicated, for example, to distinguish the casualties of Red Army terror from those of the White Army and other anti-Bolshevik groups. Many fighters shifted their allegiance from

2 Based on his study of the de-Cossackization of the Don Cossacks, Peter Holquist emphasizes that Bolshevik terror should be placed within the larger, pan-European trend of political states "to practice prophylactic political hygiene upon their respective populations." See Peter Holquist, "'Conduct Merciless Mass Terror': Decossackization on the Don, 1919," *Cahiers du monde russe: Russie, Empire russe, Union soviétique, États indépendants* 38, 1–2 (1997), 127–62.

one camp to another. After their defeat, the Whites conducted detailed research and estimated that red terror killed 1.7 million.[3] The victims included "class enemies" such as former land and factory owners, clergy, officers, soldiers, political opponents and teachers as well a large number of workers and peasants who stood up to Bolshevik rule. Recent estimates by Russian historians list a far lower figure of no more than 50,000.[4] The true figure is likely somewhere between these two extremes.

The scale of Bolshevik political terror from 1921 onward is somewhat easier to estimate because there exist official data compiled by the Soviet secret police, though they are far from complete or definitive. The so-called Pavlov–Mozokhin data count 757,432 executions (out of 3,155,985 convictions) for political crimes from 1921 through 1941.[5] An additional 1,817,496 people were sent to prison and the Gulag in the same period (see Table 11.1).

Clearly, Stalin's "revolution from above" with its rapid industrialization and wholesale collectivization of agriculture led to the dramatic escalation of terror from 1930 onward: It was a frontal assault against the old social structure, inevitably inviting resistance, which, in turn, invited further state violence.[6] The figures listed in Table 11.1 undercount the actual numbers, however. For example, many executed kulaks at the time of collectivization and de-kulakization in the late 1920s and early 1930s are not included, nor are the more than 20,000 Polish prisoners of war killed in 1940 (victims of the Katyn massacres). Many of those who were tortured to death in prison and elsewhere are also unlikely to be counted among these figures. Furthermore, in 1933, at the time of the Great Famine (*Holodomor* in Ukrainian), the Pavlov–Mozokhin data list "only" 2,154 executions. Yet the actual figures are likely to be ten times higher.[7] Michael Ellman estimates that the total figure for

3 S. P. Mel'gunov, *Krasnyi terror v Rossii, 1918–1923*, 2nd edn. (Berlin, 1924), 138–39.

4 See, for example, O. B. Mozokhin, *Pravo na repressii. Vnesudebnye polnomochiia organov gosudarstvennoi bezopasnosti. Statisticheskie svedeniia o deiatel'nosti VChK-OGPU-NKVD-MGB SSSR (1918–1953)* (Moscow: Kuchkovo pole, 2011), 40.

5 Here I rely on the Pavlov data, although for most years there are no or few differences between the Pavlov and Mozokhin data. For details, see Stephen G. Wheatcroft, "Great Terror in Historical Perspective: The Records of the Statistical Department of the Investigative Organs of OGPU/NKVD," in James Harris (ed.), *The Anatomy of Terror: Political Violence Under Stalin* (Oxford: Oxford University Press, 2013), 287–305.

6 This point is emphasized by Nicolas Werth, *La terreur et le désarroi. Staline et son système* (Paris: Perrin, 2007).

7 See Aleksei Tepliakov, "Dinamika gosudarstvennogo terrora v SSSR v 1933," *Vestnik novosibirskogo gosudarstvennogo universiteta. Seriia istoriia, filologiia* 12, 1 (2013), 50–54.

Table 11.1 *Number of People Convicted and Executed in Cases Investigated by the OGPU/NKVD*

Year	Convicted	Sentenced to be executed
1921	35,829	9,701
1922	6,003	1,962
1923	4,794	414
1924	12,425	2,550
1925	15,995	2,433
1926	17,804	990
1927	26,036	2,363
1928	33,757	869
1929	56,220	2,109
1930	208,069	20,201
1931	180,696	10,651
1932	141,919	2,728
1933	239,664	2,154
1934	78,999	2,056
1935	267,076	1,229
1936	274,670	1,118
1937	790,665	353,074
1938	554,258	328,618
1939	24,720	2,552
1940	18,371	1,649
1941	35,116	8,001

Source: GULag (Glavnoe upravlenie lagerei) 1917–1960 (Moscow: MFD, 2000), 432–34 (typographical errors corrected).

executions for 1937–38 alone is approximately 1 million.[8] Therefore the Pavlov–Mozokhin data have to be treated as merely approximate.

The most intense years of terror were the years of the Great Terror in 1937–38. According to the Pavlov–Mozokhin data, during these two years 681,692 people were sentenced to be executed, or 90 percent of the executions from 1921 through 1941. These two years alone accounted for 42.6 percent of all the convictions during the two decades. In addition, 31,456 people, many of whom belonged to the Soviet elite, were executed from 1 October 1936 to 30 November 1938 by the Military Collegium of the Supreme Court. [9] They

8 See Michael Ellman, "Soviet Repression Statistics: Some Comments," *Europe-Asia Studies* 54, 7 (Nov. 2002), 1151–72 (1162).

9 *GULag (Glavnoe upravlenie lagerei)*, 435. Some or even many of these may also be counted in the Pavlov–Mozokhin data, however.

include those tried as foreign spies at numerous, often sensational show trials. The most famous of the show trials were the three held in 1936–38 against many Old Bolsheviks and old comrades of V. I. Lenin's such as G. E. Zinoviev, L. B. Kamenev, G. L. Piatakov and N. I. Bukharin. These two years were extraordinary years even by Soviet standards, and will be discussed in detail later in this chapter.

The terror against the so-called politicals was in fact a relatively small portion of the terror inflicted on the population in the first decades of Soviet communism. Many nonpolitical behaviors were criminalized, with the result that there was virtually no difference between politicals and common criminals. In August 1932, for example, when famine gripped the country, the government issued a law for the "protection of socialist property," which stipulated execution (or ten years' incarceration under extenuating circumstances) for the theft of, say, a few sheaves of wheat from the collective farm fields. Although the law was not implemented as rigorously as it was envisioned, this led to hundreds of thousands of convictions. Another example was the 1940 draconian labor law that criminalized unauthorized absenteeism and tardiness.

These criminalized masses of people filled the infamous Gulag. Thanks to Aleksandr Solzhenitsyn's famous trilogy, *The Gulag Archipelago*, published in the 1970s, the Gulag (rather than mass killings) became the symbol of communist terror in the consciousness of the West. Forced labor camps were already functioning during the civil war, the most famous being the Solovki orthodox monastery complex, turned into prison and labor camps in the White Sea. Initially the number of inmates was relatively small. On 1 January 1920, for example, there were 8,660 inmates in the Russian Soviet Federative Socialist Republic (RSFSR), rising to approximately 60,000 in October 1922.[10] From 1921 to 1929, secret police action alone accounted for 175,584 people sent to prisons and labor camps or into exile.[11] Furthermore, there were numerous instances of "forced labor without deprivation of freedom." In 1928, for instance, there were 208,899 such cases.[12]

With the beginning of wholesale collectivization and de-kulakization in the late 1920s and early 1930s (see Table 11.2), the Gulag population increased sharply (see Table 11.3), and was supplemented by numerous special

10 George Leggett, *The Cheka: Lenin's Political Police* (Oxford: Clarendon Press, 1981), 178.
11 *GULag (Glavnoe upravlenie lagerei)*, 432.
12 Michael Jakobson, *Origins of the Gulag: The Soviet Prison Camp System 1917–1934* (Lexington: University Press of Kentucky, 1993), 84.

Table 11.2 *Number of Prisoners in NKVD Camps*

Year	As of 1 January	Average per year
1930	179,000	190,000
1931	212,000	245,000
1932	268,700	271,000
1933	334,300	456,000
1934	510,307	620,000
1935	725,483	794,000
1936	839,406	836,000
1937	820,881	994,000
1938	996,367	1,313,000
1939	1,317,195	1,340,000
1940	1,344,408	1,400,000
1941	1,500,524	1,560,000

Source: Istoriia stalinskogo Gulaga, konets 1920-kh – pervaia polovina 1950-kh godov, vol. IV (Moscow: ROSSPEN, 2004), 110.

Table 11.3 *Number of People Confined in Colonies and Prisons of the NKVD as of 1 January*

Year	In colonies	In prisons
1935	no data	240,259
1936*		457,088
1937*		375,488
1938*		885,203
1939	355,243	352,508
1940	315,584	186,278
1941	429,205	470,693

Source: Istoriia stalinskogo Gulaga, vol. IV, 109 and V. N. Zemskov, "Demografiia zakliuchennykh, spetsposelentsev i ssyl'nykh (30–50-e gody)," *Mir Rossii* 4 (1999), 113.

* Denotes combined figures for colonies and prisons.

settlements (colonies) for exiles (see Table 11.4), variants of the Gulag.[13] The spread of the Gulag across the entire country, especially to northern Russia, Siberia, Central Asia and the Far East, formed an archipelago of camps, dotting the Eurasian continent. The Gulag was a correctional facility,

13 See Lynne Viola, *The Unknown Gulag: The Lost World of Stalin's Special Settlements* (Oxford: Oxford University Press, 2007).

Table 11.4 *Number of People Convicted in Cases Investigated by the OGPU by Occupation (1925)*

Workers	12,919
Peasants	26,106
Capitalists	948
Professionals	3,948
Government employees	8,638
Clergy	895
Pupils	243
Other citizens	18,194
Red Army officers	242
Red Army soldiers	520

Source: Mozokhin, *Pravo na repressii*, 373.

based on the belief that forced labor would transform "enemies" (deemed correctable) into Soviet citizens. Labor was to ensure redemption. Yet by any measure the Gulag was more a hell than a purgatory. The prospect of death from cold and hunger was ever present. The Gulag also served to deploy free (or at least cheap) labor forces to remote areas of the country where it was difficult to attract free labor. Whether it was economically rational or not is a question difficult to answer, just as it is difficult to determine conclusively whether modern slavery (in the United States in the early nineteenth century, for instance) was economically profitable. In any case, the Gulag was used to isolate and confine the politically suspect and the socially marginal from Soviet society.

This is far from the full extent of terror. Several million people died during the famine of 1932–33, called *Holodomor* (killing by famine) in Ukraine which was especially hard hit by the famine. Certainly, the famine, engineered by Moscow or not, constituted naked state terror: At the time Moscow even refused so much as to acknowledge the famine and accepted no outside assistance. Those individuals who received private help from abroad were arrested then or later.

More generally, one can estimate that between 1930 and 1936 as many as 12 million people were convicted by Soviet courts, tribunals and nonjudicial organs.[14] There are numerous other cases of forced evictions of undocumented individuals and politically suspect people from cities and

14 Oleg V. Khlevniuk, *The History of the Gulag: From Collectivization to the Great Terror*, trans. Vadim Staklo (New Haven: Yale University Press, 2004), 305–06.

deportations (of ethnic minorities such as Poles, Germans and Koreans, for example) from border regions to Siberia, Central Asia and other remote parts of the Soviet Union). In addition, 2.5 million or so "kulaks" and "socially harmful elements" were exiled. Most of these people were not among the 12 million convicted between 1930 and 1936 mentioned earlier. Before the Great Terror, one in every six Soviet adults was likely to have been subject to various forms of repression. What followed was the Great Terror and the repressive period of the immediate prewar years. In one year from June 1940 to June 1941, more than 3 million people were convicted under the draconian labor law. Altogether from 1930 to 1940 as many as 20 million people, including repeat offenders, were sentenced to "forced labor without deprivation of freedom," and suspended sentences.[15] In the same period, about 1 million people died in camps and exile. On the eve of the German invasion of 1941, 4 million people were confined in labor camps, special settlements and exile. An additional 2 million people were engaged in some form of correctional labor without being confined.[16]

In the history of political terror in the world, Soviet communist terror stands out in that it represents the first mass murders in world history committed by a secular ideological state that professed Marxism. The terror was committed not in wartime (except for 1918–20 and 1939–45), but in peacetime and much of it against the citizens of the Soviet Union. Whether the colossal scale of Soviet terror is extraordinary by world standards is difficult to determine. Even before the modern era mass murders were commonplace.[17] In the twentieth century alone, we have the genocide of Armenians, the Nazi Holocaust and mass murders in Mao Zedong's China, in Pol Pot's Cambodia and elsewhere that implicitly or explicitly followed the Soviet precedent. There were other politically motivated mass murders in Indonesia, Uganda and many other parts of the globe, some of which were directed against communists.

Because Stalin deliberately isolated the Soviet Union from the outside world, the world community failed to grasp the full scale of his political terror, even while aware of the famine of 1932–33, the Great Terror and many other acts of brutality such as collectivization and de-kulakization as well as the existence of the Gulag. Even though in 1956 Stalin's successor Nikita

15 Ibid., 305. 16 Ibid., 328.

17 Whether it was modern technology that enabled mass murders has been a controversial subject. See Jörg Baberowski (ed.), *Moderne Zeiten? Krieg, Revolution und Gewalt im 20. Jahrhundert* (Göttingen: Vandenhoeck & Ruprecht, 2006).

Khrushchev denounced Stalin's terror in his secret report to the communist party, it was not until the collapse of the communist regime in 1991 that Moscow acknowledged the full scale and scope of Soviet terror.

Moscow's careful manipulation of world opinion had much to do with its success in concealing the truth. It employed overwhelming propaganda against imperial powers which were seen as scheming against the first socialist state in world history. It disarmed ideologically many believers in socialism and communism outside the Soviet Union, who subsequently ignored the terror or downplayed it. Against the background of the Great Depression that struck the capitalist world in 1929 and continued to paralyze it for much of the succeeding decade, the seemingly dynamic economic development of the Soviet Union contributed to a political and ideological paralysis in the West. Deep secrecy surrounded the terror which was carefully hidden by elaborate methods of obfuscation.

Ironically, in the years leading up to World War II, it was the United States that aided in the Soviet cover-up of terror. The United States had long been wary of Japan's expansion in Asia since its victory over Russia in 1905. Unlike most Western powers, however, Washington did not recognize the Soviet government even after it consolidated its power. Japan's aggression into China in 1931 changed Washington's stance toward Moscow. Washington claimed its own stake in Asia and especially in China and saw Moscow as a counterweight against Japan. This meant that Washington came to terms with Moscow and resumed diplomatic relations in 1933. All the while, Washington, under the presidency of Franklin D. Roosevelt, strategically kept silent about the millions of deaths in the Soviet Union in 1932–33 and deliberately minimized Stalin's terror throughout the 1930s and during World War II, an important historical episode now almost completely forgotten.[18]

The Victims

Soviet communism's terror under Stalin was so extensive that almost every family was touched in one way or another. Was the terror indiscriminate or arbitrary? In other words was it "stochastic"? Some scholars claim so. Unlike

18 This episode is discussed extensively in Tim Tzouliadis, *The Forsaken: An American Tragedy in Stalin's Russia* (New York: Penguin, 2008).

the Nazi terror, which targeted certain groups of the population (such as Jews, communists and homosexuals), the Soviet terror appears to have affected almost every category of people. Nevertheless, the Soviet terror was almost certainly not stochastic. While it is true that terror spread and affected people seemingly randomly, this was in large measure due to the sloppiness and ineffectiveness that were exacerbated by the pressure for fulfilling quotas. The "kulak operation" of 1937–38 specified target numbers of people to be arrested or executed (affecting formerly de-kulakized peasants and other people Moscow deemed politically dangerous). Moscow's intention at least was to direct its terror against clearly defined groups of people.

When the communist party successfully seized power in October 1917, it knew that it would face armed resistance. That is why some key figures such as Zinoviev and Kamenev argued against Lenin's plan for the seizure of power. As predicted, after the seizure of power, the Bolshevik coup met with stiff resistance from the anti-communists. Unlike the relatively bloodless revolution in the capital, the process of establishing communist power elsewhere proved difficult and bloody. The anti-Bolshevik forces were aided by foreign (capitalist) countries that intervened in the Russian Civil War. The Bolsheviks accepted this development as an inevitable part of the class struggle against class enemies, both internal and external. Even were they to fail to maintain power, they felt justified in fighting. Otherwise, they asked, what kind of revolutionaries were they? If they outlived the Paris Commune of 1871 (which lasted some seventy days), they could console themselves with the knowledge of having fought harder and better than the Communards of the nineteenth century.

In their fight for survival, the Bolsheviks sought to eliminate alleged class enemies by terror: factory owners, landowners (including numerous Cossacks) and other property owners as well as many professionals (such as bankers, professors, engineers and military officers, who were regarded as privileged classes) and the clergy whose loyalty the Bolsheviks believed rested with the old regime. All opposition political parties were suspect starting with the Cadets (constitutional liberals) and conservative Octoberists and ending with socialists such as the Socialist Revolutionaries (SRs), the left Socialist Revolutionaries (with whom the Bolsheviks formed a brief coalition government after the seizure of power), and the anti-Bolshevik Mensheviks. Terror against such people is hardly surprising though not justifiable by the circumstances of war. After all, the Bolsheviks, strongly influenced by Jacobinism, believed genuinely in "the dictatorship of the proletariat" and practiced it.

Yet the proletariat itself was not immune to Bolshevik terror. The collapse of the economy and the brutal rule by the Bolsheviks led to numerous industrial actions by angry and hungry workers all over the country, including those in the cradle of the revolution, Petrograd. They were mercilessly repressed. Moreover, having gained land and freedom from exploitation thanks to the Bolshevik Revolution, the peasants were extremely unwilling to part with their produce. To feed the famished cities and workers, the Bolsheviks resorted to requisition by armed detachments. This led to bitter armed conflict between the peasants and the communist government. Most tellingly, in early 1921, the Kronstadt sailors, the staunchest supporters of the Bolsheviks in the capital in 1917, rebelled against the Bolshevik government. They, too, were violently crushed. Already by this time, most of the inmates in the burgeoning Gulag were workers and peasants: On 1 November 1920, of the 17,000 inmates for whom statistical data are available, 39 percent and 34 percent were workers and peasants respectively.[19] This picture does not change during the decade of relative peace in the 1920s (see Table 11.4).

Thus 54 percent of the convicted were workers and peasants. Moreover, in the same year 92 percent of the convicted were noncommunists, and 80 percent were illiterate or had only elementary education.[20] In the pre-World War II decade, from de-kulakization to the Great Terror and the enforcement of draconian labor laws, the majority of victims were ordinary people – workers and peasants as well as "marginal people" such as the unemployed, vagabonds and prostitutes.[21]

Thus, from the very beginning of the Soviet communist regime, the majority of the victims of its terror belonged to the common people (excepting the 1–2 million people who fled or were forced to flee abroad in the wake of the revolution and the civil war). True, they accounted for the vast majority of the population. Yet it is also symptomatic of the way in which the communist government quickly turned into a dictatorship against its own people. This in turn necessitated the establishment of a vast surveillance network of secret police, which compiled detailed data on countless

19 Leggett, *The Cheka*, 178.

20 Mozokhin, *Pravo na repressii*, 373–74. Ninety percent of the convicted were men.

21 See esp. Rolf Binner, Bernd Bonwetsch and Marc Junge, *Massenmord und Lagerhaft. Die andere Geschichte des Großen Terrors* (Berlin: Akademie Verlag, 2009).

numbers of politically suspect individuals.[22] The communist dictatorship against its own people did not mean that it enjoyed little popular support: It was still able to mobilize fighting forces (the Red Army) from among the workers and peasants to beat the Whites on the battlefield. More generally, faced with the choice between the Bolsheviks and the old regime, the population ultimately chose the former as the lesser evil. The outcome reflects the centuries-old culture of Russia in which power is "conceived not in terms of law but in terms of coercion and hegemony," or in terms of "masters and men." So it is not that Bolshevik power betrayed the people but that the revolution turned out to be a "people's tragedy," which they themselves "helped to make."[23]

The Bolshevik restoration of prerevolutionary power relations between masters and men did not mean that the Bolsheviks became de-ideologized. They in fact remained committed to, and reasoned according to, their ideology. Even the 1920s, when the government sought to establish civil peace instead of civil war and implemented pacifying measures, turned out to be far from peaceful. Political show trials had begun as early as 1921 with the trial of leaders of the Ukrainian SRs who had resisted Moscow's aggression into Ukraine in 1918. It was followed by the more famous show trial of the SRs in Moscow.[24] Moscow had not refined its techniques yet: Some of the accused stood up to defend themselves and others. Still, many of hallmarks of future show trials, which highlighted communist justice in the Soviet Union and later in Eastern Europe under communist rule, were evident: fabrication of evidence, use of agents provocateurs willing to testify in public against the defendants, conduct of trial dictated by a script from above, predetermined sentencing and the like. Although legal experts were concerned about the danger of "substantive justice" as opposed to bourgeois "formal justice," the logic of revolutionary, substantive justice always overrode everything else. This logic generated views on "objective enemies": Anyone, whether worker or peasant, disloyal to the Soviet government was "objectively" a friend of its enemy, the capitalists, and therefore a class enemy.

22 See V. S. Izmozik, *Glaza i ushi rezhima: gosudarstvennyi politicheskii kontrol' za naseleniem Sovetskoi Rossii v 1918–1928 godakh* (St. Petersburg: Izd-vo SPbUEF, 1995).

23 These quotes are from Orlando Figes, *A People's Tragedy: A History of the Russian Revolution* (New York: Viking, 1996), 808–09.

24 See Marc Jansen, *A Show Trial Under Lenin: The Trial of the Socialist Revolutionaries, Moscow 1922* (The Hague: Nijhoff, 1982).

In the early 1930s, especially during the grave famine crisis of 1932–33, the logic of objective enemy underwent a subtle yet important change to include many communists themselves. It was then that the target of terror was no longer just the "class enemy" but also the "enemy of the people," a class-neutral category. Although the term "enemies of the people" had long been used by the Bolsheviks (and others), Stalin gave it new currency and applied it to numerous communist party members, calling them enemies "with a [communist] party membership card in their pockets." It was also then that Stalin began to apply similar supraclass, class-neutral concepts of enemy such as "fascist spies" and "hirelings of the capitalists." This made it possible to terrorize communists en masse, including many of the Old Bolsheviks as well as those formerly in Lenin's closest political circles, allowing Stalin to take out the high command of the Red Army in 1937–38. Party members in responsible positions were far more likely to be subjected to terror than were low-ranking nonparty members. As is often mentioned, of the 1,966 delegates to the Seventeenth Congress of the Communist Party, 1,108, or 56.6 percent, were arrested as "counterrevolutionaries." The ratio of repression was even higher for the 139 members and candidate members of the Central Committee elected by the Congress: 70 percent (or ninety-seven persons).[25]

Many instances of Bolshevik mass terror may be characterized as "genocidal."[26] De-Cossackization and de-kulakization are just two examples. At the time of the Great Terror, many of the de-kulakized who had survived in camps and exile were executed. So were the clergy: In 1937–38 as much as 80 percent of the arrested Orthodox clergy appear to have been executed.[27] Likewise, certain national minorities were targeted for destruction: ethnic Poles, Germans, Latvians, Greeks, Finns, Estonians and other mainly diaspora nationalities. In the two years of terror, according to official statistics (which are almost certainly not exhaustive), 335,513 individuals were convicted. Of them, 247,157 or 73.66 percent were executed. Of these "national operations," by far the largest was the Polish operation in which 139,835 people were indicted, and 111,091 or 79.44 percent were sentenced to be shot. The Polish operation accounted for 41.7 percent (of

25 See "O kul'te lichnosti i ego posledstviiakh. Doklad Pervogo sekretaria TsK KPSS N. S. Khrushcheva XX s'ezdu KPSS 25 fevralia 1956 g.," *Izvestiia TsK KPSS* 3 (1989), 137.

26 See Norman M. Naimark, *Stalin's Genocide* (Princeton: Princeton University Press, 2010).

27 See Rolf Binner and Marc Jung, "Vernichtung der orthodoxen Geistlichen in der Sowjetunion in den Massenoperationen des Großen Terrors 1937–1938," *Jahrbücher für Geschichte Osteuropas* 52, 4 (2004), 524.

the indicted) and 44.9 percent (of the executed) for all the national operations.[28]

Given that in 1937 there were 636,220 ethnic Poles in the Soviet Union, it may appear that more than 17 percent of ethnic Poles were executed in 1937–38. This is somewhat misleading. Not all of the victims of the Polish operation were ethnic Poles. Numerous Russians, Ukrainians, Belarusians and others who had any association or contact with ethnic Poles or Poland were executed according to the Polish operation. (The same was true of other national operations.) Likewise, numerous ethnic Poles were repressed according to the German and other operations, including the "kulak operation." There is no doubt that diaspora nations were targeted by the Great Terror. Having received a memorandum from the secret police chief Nikolai I. Yezhov in September 1937 that 23,316 people ("Polish refugees, Polish political émigrés, prisoners of war [from World War I and the Polish–Soviet War of 1919–21], contacts with Polish consuls, and others suspected of spying for Poland") had been arrested, Stalin cheerfully noted: "To Yezhov. Very good! Dig up and clean out, henceforth too, this Polish espionage filth. Eliminate it *in the interests of the Soviet Union*."[29]

In all cases of mass operations, no evidence was required to arrest, indict and execute individuals. Numerous individuals, for example, were executed for telling innocent political jokes. After the Soviet Union collapsed almost all victims of terror (except for the police officials who actively engaged in the terror and subsequently were killed by Stalin on charges of, for example, foreign espionage) were exonerated as a group.

In executing terror, the Soviet secret police deployed numerous secret agents and informers. Writers and other cultural figures were surrounded by dozens of informers. This is relatively well known. Much less known is the provocation the secret police employed and the provocateurs deployed to create enemies from innocent people. Even after the demise of the Soviet Union, very little information on these matters has been released. This seems to be the final taboo of the history of Soviet terror. Undoubtedly, many people voluntarily denounced other people to the police for various reasons.

28 See N. V. Petrov and A. B. Roginskii, "'Pol'skaia operatsiia' NKVD 1937–1938 gg.," in A. E. Gur'ianov (ed.), *Repressii protiv poliakov i pol'skikh grazhdan* (Moscow: Zven'ia, 1997), 33 and 40.

29 *Lubianka. Stalin i Glavnoe upravlenie gosbezopasnosti NKVD, 1937–1938* (Moscow: Mezhdunarodnyi fond Demokratiia, 2004), 352, 359 [emphasis in the original].

Yet many others were clandestine informers and provocateurs employed, or coerced into service, by the police.

The following example is suggestive. At the time of the Great Famine, ethnic Poles fled Belarus to western Siberia. Suspicious of them, the local police engaged in provocation. They detailed a secret informer (named "Pushnin") to marry a local Polish girl and insinuate himself into the Polish community. Then, masquerading as a representative of Polish Military Intelligence, he filled in questionnaires on all adults of the Polish community and had them sign the papers, which he hid in a prearranged place agreed upon with the police. Pushnin the provocateur then staged a flight from the village, as the police uncovered "clandestine activities" of Polish intelligence in the community. The police duly "discovered" the questionnaires in the "hiding place" and arrested all the Poles, including Pushnin's wife, listed on the questionnaires. The police accused them of being members of the fictitious "Polish Party of People's Heroes." In connection with this affair, more than 3,000 people were repressed in western Siberia.[30] Similar operations are legion.[31] The full scope and scale of these ultra-secret operations in the Soviet Union remain unknown, however.

Why the Terror?

The Bolsheviks never flinched from terror. The following statement by the secret police in 1919 is indicative: "We reject the old system of morality and 'humanity' invented by the bourgeoisie to oppress and exploit the 'lower classes.' . . . To us, everything is permitted, for we are the first to raise the sword not to oppress races and reduce them to slavery, but to liberate humanity from its shackles. . . . Blood! Let blood flow like water!"[32] Of course, the secret police ultimately raised its sword against humanity. Stalin's right-hand man in the 1930s, Viacheslav M. Molotov, left revealing remarks regarding his role in the mass killing of the 1930s. Interviewed in 1971, Molotov surprised his sympathetic listener by readily acknowledging that he had signed death warrants against untold numbers of Soviet

30 See L. I. Gvozdkova, *Istoriia repressii i stalinskikh lagerei v Kuzbasse* (Kemerovo: Kuzbassvuzizdat, 1997), 182–83.

31 Another, earlier example is V. I. Isaev, *"Oni khoteli ubit' Stalina." OGPU protiv nemetskikh studentov v pokazatel'nom sudebnom protsesse 1925 g.* (Novosibirsk: Izd-vo SO RAN, 2005).

32 Quoted in Werth, "A State against its People," 102.

citizens,[33] meanwhile denying, until his death in 1986, the very existence of the secret protocol to the 1939 nonaggression (Molotov–Ribbentrop) pact with Nazi Germany, to which he was signatory. As a Marxist, Molotov was too ashamed to admit the imperialist protocol that divided up Eastern Europe with Nazi Germany. However, he did not hesitate at all to admit that he, along with Stalin and others, was responsible for the mass murders of the 1930s.

The terror committed by both Red and White during the civil war is perhaps understandable, if not justified, in light of the circumstances of war. The *modus operandi* of the Soviet government after it won the civil war was that there remained unknown numbers of enemies in the country who were assisted by foreign capitalist powers and that these enemies had to be eliminated. This assumption was a convenient one for Stalin and his coterie as they tried to protect their own power by removing as an enemy anyone opposed to them. The turmoil caused by collectivization and de-kulakization was compounded by the presence of millions of dispossessed and displaced individuals scattered all over the country. It was indicative of this atmosphere that in April 1930 Karl B. Radek, a prankster and loose tongue, addressed Stalin in his letter from Voronezh: "Dear Stalin! Don't be scared by the red ink [of this letter]. This is not a threat from a de-kulakized person, just a request to remind you of [your?] promise that in two–three months I can return to Moscow."[34] It was in January 1933, in the midst of the famine crisis, that Stalin articulated the need to intensify enemy-hunting:

> [T]he last remnants of moribund classes – private manufacturers and their servitors, private traders and their henchmen, former nobles and priests, kulaks and kulak agents, former White Guard officers and police officials, policemen and gendarmes, all sorts of bourgeois intellectuals of a chauvinist type, and all other anti-Soviet elements – have been tossed out.
>
> But tossed out and scattered over the whole face of the USSR, these "have-beens" have wormed their way into our plants and factories, into our government offices and trading organizations, into our railway and water transport enterprises, and, principally, into the collective farms and state farms. They have crept into these places and taken cover there, donning the mask of "workers" and "peasants," and some have even managed to worm their way into the party.

33 See *Sto sorok besed s Molotovym. Iz dnevnika F. Chueva* (Moscow: Terra, 1991), 439–40.

34 Rossiiskii gosudarstvennyi arkhiv sotsial'no-politicheskoi istorii (RGASPI), f. 558, op. 11, d. 789, l. 20.

> What did they carry with them into these places? They carried with them hatred for the Soviet regime, of course, burning enmity toward new forms of economy, life, and culture.[35]

Therefore, according to Stalin, it was necessary to find and destroy these cleverly hidden enemies. In his view, if there were a grain of suspicion about someone's political loyalty, it was a big deal. According to Khrushchev, when he rejected as unreliable the "mad rambling" of a party member ("sick person") about "enemies of the people," Stalin "flared up, got very angry, and came down hard on me, [saying] 'Not to have confidence in such a person is wrong.' . . . 'Ten percent of the truth is still the truth. It requires decisive action on our part, and we will pay for it if we don't act accordingly.'"[36]

The secret police used provocation as a clever way to uncover the true color of cleverly hidden enemies. (Once the suspect was in custody, the remaining 90 percent of the "truth" could be beaten out of him or her.) Unfortunately, information on police operations is scarce. It is easy to understand why the discussion of provocation is the last taboo of the history of the Stalinist terror. For one, while there is consensus about the need to exonerate innocent victims and commemorate them, it is awkward and shameful to reveal that untold numbers of individuals denounced, willingly or not, fellow citizens, or were forced to engage in framing and incriminating them through provocation and ruse. For another, such operations involved reprehensible police tactics: The police often coerced helpless and desperate individuals (such as wives of arrested men) and criminals into service. As a result, implicit consensus still obtains in the former Soviet republics that these awkward issues are best left untouched. There is no doubt, however, that provocation was part and parcel of terror operations under Stalin.[37] Stalin carefully hid this and other mechanisms of terror and mobilized (by force and persuasion) the masses of people against the alleged "enemies of the people." It is due to the failure to see through Stalin's disinformation, misinformation and camouflage that some Western historians claim, preposterously, "democratic" elements in the Great Terror and that others see it as having been "easy" and "simple" for

35 I. V. Stalin, *Sochineniia*, vol. XIII (Moscow: Gosizdat, 1951), 207.

36 Sergei Khrushchev (ed.), *Memoirs of Nikita Khrushchev*, vol. I, *Commissar, 1918–1945* (University Park: Pennsylvania State University Press, 2004), 117.

37 See discussion by Hiroaki Kuromiya, *The Voices of the Dead: Stalin's Great Terror in the 1930s* (New Haven: Yale University Press, 2007).

foreign countries to recruit spies and organize subversion in the Soviet Union in the 1930s![38]

Dangerous though they were, in Stalin's view, the "cleverly hidden enemies" could be severely constrained by the Soviet secret police. Stalin understood, however, that he had little control over external enemies (foreign capitalist countries). He also understood that the most dangerous moment for his power would be when internal and external enemies joined hands against him. He sought to make sure that this would never happen. If confrontation with world capitalism was to come (and, as a Marxist, he was convinced that it was inevitable), he had to be certain that the rearguard was secure. This was the context for the Great Terror of 1937–38.

The Great Terror is an extraordinary event even in the annals of terror in the Soviet Union. It did not flow from normal or even heightened police operations. Rather, it was mass killings as a precautionary measure to ensure the security of the rear to prepare the country for war and place it on a war footing. Enemies had to be eliminated or neutralized, according to Stalin, *before* war began. Otherwise it might turn out to be too late.

It is likely that Stalin learned a lesson from the experience of the Chinese communists or quite possibly experimented in China several years before he launched the Great Terror. The "Futian events" in China in 1930–31 refers to Mao Zedong's massacre of tens of thousands of communists and soldiers as "ABs" (anti-Bolsheviks). The massacres took place during a beleaguered war against the Chinese Nationalists. Such massacres would appear to be nothing but the actions of a mad man. Yet Mao justified them by using the old Chinese saying *ningke cuo sha yi qian bu ke shi yi ren louwang* ("it is better to kill 100 people wrongly accused than to allow one guilty person to escape the net"). As Philip Short reminds us, Stalin's Great Terror, coming several years after Mao's terror, eerily resembles the Chinese incident.[39] Oddly, Mao's terror appears to have worked to break the Nationalist encirclement. Stalin's advisors and observers were placed in Mao's camp. The Chinese communists under Mao and their Soviet advisors sent a note to Moscow that the terror had strengthened the revolutionary forces.[40]

38 See, for example, Wendy Z. Goldman, *Terror and Democracy in the Age of Stalin: The Social Dynamics of Repression* (New York: Cambridge University Press, 2007) and Sarah Davies and James Harris, *Stalin's World: Dictating the Soviet Order* (New Haven: Yale University Press, 2014), 64.

39 Philip Short, *Mao: A Life* (New York: Henry Holt & Company, 1999), 281 and 283.

40 RGASPI, f. 514, op. 1, d. 689, ll. 25–29 (report in Chinese from the Central Bureau of the Soviet District of the Chinese Communist Party dated 12 December 1931).

The Great Terror in the Soviet Union followed Mao's logic that internal cleansing was a requisite for victory over enemies. Stalin also appears to have learned a lesson from the experience of the Spanish Civil War in which he covertly took part. The war, as seen from Moscow, was characterized by "anarchy, partisan and subversive and divisionist movements, relative erosion of the frontiers between front and rear, betrayals." The Spanish case demonstrated to Stalin "direct proof that there existed, and was very obvious, just such a threat from within."[41] Expanding on the Chinese and Spanish experience, Stalin insisted repeatedly that internal "enemies" had to be dealt with *before* war broke out: Otherwise it might be too late. Bukharin, who would become the chief defendant at the third Moscow show trial, clearly understood Stalin's logic and had declared at the time of the first Moscow show trial (Kamenev–Zinoviev trial) in 1936:

> I am happy that this entire business [of destroying "our enemies"] has been brought to light before war breaks out and that our [NKVD] organs have been in a position to expose all of this rot before the war so that we can come out of war victorious. Because if all of this had not been revealed before the war but during it, it would have brought about absolutely extraordinary and grievous defeats for the cause of socialism.[42]

Stalin branded Kamenev, Zinoviev, Bukharin and countless others as foreign spies and had them executed. Stalin, however, did not believe in his own rhetoric. In October 1938, after killing many of his rivals as well as hundreds of thousands of others, Stalin appeared triumphant and spoke unusually frankly of the "ten, fifteen, twenty thousand" supporters of Bukharin as well as of "as many, possibly more, Trotskyites," who were sentenced to death: "Well, were they all spies? Of course not. Whatever happened to them? They were cadres who could not stomach the sharp turn toward collective farms and could not make sense of this turn, because they were not trained politically, did not know the laws of social development, the laws of economic development, the laws of political development."[43] Stalin made it clear that the

41 On Stalin's lesson from the Spanish Civil War, see Oleg Khlevniuk, "The Objectives of the Great Terror, 1937–1938," in Julian Cooper, Maureen Perrie and E. A. Rees (eds.), *Soviet History, 1917–53: Essays in Honour of R. W. Davies* (New York: St. Martin's Press, 1995), 163 and 165.

42 Quoted in J. Arch Getty and Oleg V. Naumov, *The Road to Terror: Stalin and the Self-Destruction of the Bolsheviks, 1932–1939* (New Haven: Yale University Press, 1999), 309.

43 RGASPI, f. 17, op. 163, d. 1217, ll. 51–52. This speech was published in *Voprosy istorii* 4 (2003), 21.

crime of the executed was that they had lost faith in the rightness of the party and therefore were potential traitors. They had to be killed, according to Stalin's logic.

Bukharin and other prominent Bolsheviks executed by Stalin knew his logic perfectly well. Radek once frankly told an American diplomat why political killing in general was necessary for Stalin. According to Loy W. Henderson:

> Radek said that in his opinion the old tsarist police were unbelievably stupid. They arrested Bolshevik leaders again and again only eventually to release them or allow them to escape. Bukharin agreed. He said, "Yes, our Stalin was arrested several times yet he lived to destroy the police who had failed to destroy him." Radek continued, "But we Bolsheviks are not so stupid. When we arrest enemies of the state we either execute them or we put them away so that no one ever hears of them again." Bukharin again agreed. Neither one of them apparently had any idea that within the next three years Bukharin would be executed and Radek would be sentenced to ten years in prison.[44]

In 1938 Bukharin incriminated himself and was executed. Radek was "put away" and no one ever heard from him again: In 1939 Radek was killed in prison by Stalin's order. Although Bukharin, unlike most other Old Bolsheviks, denied the grotesque accusation that he was a foreign spy, he accepted Stalin's logic: His sacrifice was necessary for the sake of the survival of the Soviet Union against fascism, a logic Arthur Koestler developed in his famous fictionalized account *Darkness at Noon* in 1940, two years after Bukharin's death.

Stalin left no stone unturned. Anyone with the remotest possibility of showing disloyalty to his regime became suspect, a candidate for recruitment by foreign countries. Even hooligans were politically dangerous, according to this reasoning. As the NKVD chief Genrikh G. Yagoda said in 1935, there was "merely one step" in the transition "from a hooligan to a terrorist," and "hooliganism" was "an element leading to the emergence of diversionary groups."[45] Incarceration was not enough. In 1937–38 the secret police went after those already confined in the Gulag and killed tens of thousands just in

44 George W. Baer (ed.), *A Question of Trust: The Origins of US–Soviet Diplomatic Relations. The Memoirs of Loy W. Henderson* (Stanford: Hoover Institution Press, 1986), 426.

45 Quoted in V. N. Khaustov, "Deiatel'nost' organov gosudarstvennoi bezopasnosti NKVD SSSR (1934–1942 gg.)," Akademiia federal'noi sluzhby bezopasnosti doctoral dissertation (1997), 334.

case.[46] The goal of the mass operations of the Great Terror was to secure the rear by eliminating any political danger in preparation for war. Anyone potentially susceptible to foreign influence was considered a security risk. The Great Terror became in a sense an operation of "total counter-espionage."[47] Even before the Great Terror, Soviet counterintelligence was so pervasive and thorough that there was virtually no possibility of foreign spies infiltrating the country. Stalin insisted otherwise, however.

Stalin's terror was not merely a domestic affair. He sent special assassins abroad to kill important émigré leaders and others opposed to his power. During the civil war in Spain from 1936 to 1939 numerous people were thus murdered.[48] Stalin also exported terror abroad, especially to Xinjiang (Chinese Turkestan) and the first Soviet satellite state, the Mongolian People's Republic. The Mongolian Great Terror, carried out under the direct control of Moscow, was proportionately far harsher than that in the Soviet Union. Official data show that 20,474, or almost 3 percent of the population (approximately 700,000), were killed.[49] Applied to the Soviet Union, that would mean 4.5 million executions. Stalin imagined that many Mongolians including the large population of lamas in the country were potential allies of Japan and destroyed them. His insistence that Mongolia would be used by the Japanese as a staging ground for invasion into the heart of the Soviet industrial–military complex, western Siberia, meant that Stalin terrorized this tiny country with impunity.

Although Stalin pursued absolute security, he was a realist and understood that absolute security was impossible: It would have meant no one but himself left alive. Such was impossible. The Great Terror had to end at some point, and Stalin indeed ended it in the autumn of 1938. Stalin's goal was the total subjugation of the population to his power through terror. In 1929 Stalin went out of his way to defend the famous play by Mikhail Bulgakov, *Days of the Turbins* (or *The White Guard*), one of his favorites, which sympathetically portrayed the anti-Red Turbin family in Kyiv during the civil war: the play was good and important, according to Stalin, because it demonstrated to the audience the "all-conquering power of Bolshevism"

46 See Binner, Bonwetsch and Junge, *Massenmord und Lagerhaft*, 658.

47 See Hiroaki Kuromiya and Andrzej Pepłoński, "Stalin und die Spionage," *Transit: Europäische Revue* 38 (2009), 20–33.

48 See Ronald Radosh, Mary R. Habeck and Grigory Sevostianov (eds.), *Spain Betrayed: The Soviet Union in the Spanish Civil War* (New Haven: Yale University Press, 2001).

49 See *Ulsyg aiuulaas khamgaalakh baĭguullagyn azhild garch baĭsan aldaa zavkhralyg shalgasan düngiĭn mukhaĭ nuutslagdsan iltgêl* (Ulaanbaatar: Urlakh êrdêm, 2002). This was a secret report written in 1961 which was not published until 2002.

(*vsesokrushaiushchaia sila bolshevizma*).[50] Stalin's terror had its limits but was a priceless political tool, because it demonstrated to the Soviet people that it was useless to resist his power.

Conclusion

The end of the Great Terror did not mean the end of terror in general. The Soviet government continued killing thousands of people. In 1940, after it destroyed Poland in collusion with Nazi Germany, it summarily executed the cream of the Polish POWs. Simultaneously it criminalized millions of workers for their alleged tardiness and truancy.

Soviet violence contained elements of routine (and even intensified) policing, economic instrumentality and social engineering. It derived in large part from the urgent need to modernize the country's economy (so as to be able to catch up and overtake the most advanced enemy countries of the capitalist camp) and to cleanse the country of undesirable and "parasitic" elements (such as criminals and the unemployed – the government guaranteed employment, hence the principle "He who does not work, neither shall he eat"). Throughout the period, the violence tended to assume excessive dimensions. Because the government did not trust its own bureaucracy to implement radical policies such as collectivization and de-kulakization, it was guided by the conviction that excesses are better than moderation: While moderation might fail policy implementation, excesses would not, and once the task was accomplished, certain individuals were to be held accountable for the excesses. Such was the case in 1930 (collectivization and de-kulakization) and 1937–38 (the Great Terror). The de-kulakization campaign was so traumatic for the entire population that even Stalin later hesitated to recommend it to East European communists.[51] While the use of excesses led to inordinate human sacrifice, none of the elements of excess (policing, economic instrumentality and social engineering) is particularly unusual for any modern dictatorship. The Soviet government used the modernizing, transformative and prophetic ideology of communism to justify its terror. Terror became routine.

The mass killings of 1937–38, however, were anything but routine. Stalin was forced to adjust and revise the Marxist ideology to suit his political needs in order to justify an even greater degree of terror. He prepared carefully for it. In 1934, fearful of the contemporary implications of "revolutionary

50 See Iu. I. Shapoval, *Ukraina XX stolittia. Osoby ta podii v konteksti vazhkoi istorii* (Kyiv: Heneza, 2001), 107, 108, 122. See also Stalin, *Sochineniia*, vol. XI, 328.

51 See Hiroaki Kuromiya, *Stalin: Profiles in Power* (Harlow: Longman, 2005), 189.

defeatism" Lenin had used to fight tsarism, Stalin attacked the allegedly pro-German, anti-Russian treatise of Friedrich Engels.[52] Simultaneously, the image of "enemy" shifted decisively from class enemy to class-neutral "enemy of the people" and foreign spy. This allowed Stalin to eliminate anyone suspected of disloyalty, from Lenin's former comrades to workers, peasants and vagabonds. It was a clear manifestation of Stalin's use of *raison d'état* to safeguard, through terror, his power, and its embodiment the Soviet Union, in anticipation of external threat.

Stalin and his clique remained proud of the mass killings they had sanctioned to the very end of their lives. They insisted that the Great Terror saved the Soviet Union from defeat in the war. Molotov was most vocal. Interviewed in the 1970s, he still defended the terror by insisting that Stalin let "an extra head fall" so that there would "be no vacillation at the time of war"; "Stalin played it safe" (*Stalin perestrakhoval delo*).[53] Untold innocent heads fell as a result of Stalin's "over-insurance," which, Molotov insisted, was "permissible for the sake of the fundamental matter, if only to retain power!" (*vse eto dopustimo radi osnovnogo: tol'ko by uderzhat' vlast'!*).[54] Ultimately, however, Stalin understood the negative consequences of the Great Terror and did not order another. A routine of terror resumed, with some exceptions (such as the Katyn massacres).

Meanwhile, the communist terror had a devastating impact on individuals, their families and friends, and the psyche of the population as a whole. Virtually no family escaped the terror. The terror, reinforced by the isolation of the Soviet Union from the outside world, left the population no alternative but to live with the regime on its terms.

Bibliographical Essay

There is a large amount of literature on the subject in many languages. Numerous people, Soviet citizens and foreigners alike, inside and outside the Soviet Union, suffered terror. Millions of people perished, but millions did survive and some of them have left their accounts. The best-known work is written by one of them, Alexander Solzhenitsyn. His famous trilogy *The Gulag Archipelago 1918–1956: An Experiment in Literary Investigation* (New York: Harper & Row, 1974–78) draws on his own and countless others' reminiscences and accounts. Hiroaki Kuromiya's *The Voices of the Dead: Stalin's Great Terror in the 1930s* (New Haven: Yale University

52 Ibid., 114. 53 *Sto sorok besed s Molotovym*, 416. 54 Ibid., 402.

Press, 2007) seeks to retrieve the lost voices of the executed. The most comprehensive and judicious scholarly treatment of terror under Soviet communism is Nicolas Werth, "A State Against its People: Violence, Repression, and Terror in the Soviet Union," in Stéphane Courtois, Nicolas Werth, Jean-Louis Panné, Andrzej Paczkowski, Karel Bartošek and Jean-Lois Margolin, *The Black Book of Communism: Crimes, Terror, Repression*, trans. Jonathan Murphy and Mark Kramer (Cambridge, MA: Harvard University Press, 1999). Some important documents related to the Great Terror are translated in J. A. Getty and O. V. Naumov, *The Road to Terror: Stalin and the Self-Destruction of the Bolsheviks, 1932–1939* (New Haven: Yale University Press, 1999). A concise account of Stalin's terror as genocide is Norman M. Naimark, *Stalin's Genocide* (Princeton: Princeton University Press, 2010). The most extensive oral testimonies of the *Holodomor* of 1932–33 are assembled in James E. Mace and Leonid Heretz (eds.), *Oral History Project of the Commission on the Ukraine Famine*, 3 vols. (Washington, DC: US Government Printing Office, 1990).

Statistical data are always incomplete and can be misleading. The most useful analysis of statistical data on Soviet terror are Stephen G. Wheatcroft, "Great Terror in Historical Perspective: The Records of the Statistical Department of the Investigative Organs of OGPU/NKVD," in James Harris (ed.), *The Anatomy of Terror: Political Violence Under Stalin* (Oxford: Oxford University Press, 2013), 287–305, and Michael Ellman, "Soviet Repression Statistics: Some Comments," *Europe-Asia Studies* 54, 7 (2002), 1151–72.

The most detailed, albeit not comprehensive, account of the Great Terror is Rolf Binner, Bernd Bonwetsch and Marc Junge, *Massenmord und Lagerhaft. Die andere Geschichte des Großen Terrors* (Berlin: Akademie Verlag, 2009), which attributes the Great Terror to internal and social factors. By contrast, Oleg Khlevniuk, "The Objectives of the Great Terror, 1937–1938," in Julian Cooper, Maureen Perrie and E. A. Rees (eds.), *Soviet History, 1917–53: Essays in Honour of R. W. Davies* (New York: St. Martin's Press, 1995), 158–76, sees the Great Terror as a response to the threat of war. For the export of the Great Terror to Asia (Mongolia and Xinjiang), see Hiroaki Kuromiya, "Stalin's Great Terror and the Asian Nexus," *Europe-Asia Studies*, 66, 5 (2014), 775–93.

There is also a voluminous literature on the Gulag. Apart from Solzhenitsyn, Oleg V. Khlevniuk, *The History of the Gulag: From Collectivization to the Great Terror*, trans. Vadim Staklo (New Haven: Yale University Press, 2004), and Lynne Viola, *The Unknown Gulag: The Lost World of Stalin's Special Settlements* (Oxford: Oxford University Press, 2007), are the most updated accounts based on declassified archival documents.

One of the most revealing accounts left by Soviet leaders directly involved in the terror under Stalin is *Molotov Remembers: Inside Kremlin Politics – Conversations with Felix Chuev*, edited with an introduction and notes by Albert Resis (Chicago: Dee, 1993).

12
The Soviet Government 1917–1941

E. A. REES

The Council of People's Commissars (known as Sovnarkom) was the nominal government of Soviet Russia from the October Revolution onwards. Its role changed over time within the confines of the communist one-party state. Sovnarkom's powers and its relationship with the Politburo, the supreme body of the party, was not set from the outset, but evolved in response to changing circumstances. This chapter examines three phases in Sovnarkom's development. These coincided with particular subperiods in the development of the Soviet economic system. This was related also to shifts in the balance of power between the two organizations that also in part reflected the authority of the organization and its leader. The first phase, under V. I. Lenin, from 1917 to 1924, saw the establishment of war communism and the shift to the New Economic Policy (NEP); the second phase, under A. I. Rykov, from 1924 to 1930, saw the consolidation of the NEP and the shift to the command economy; the third phase under V. M. Molotov, from 1930 to 1941, saw the consolidation of the command economy and the major upheaval of the Great Terror, rearmament and preparations for war.

Sovnarkom Under Lenin

Sovnarkom, chaired by Lenin, was from the outset recognized as the principal body of government, effectively the cabinet which ruled through an extensive structure of commissariats, which represented in a modified form the ministries inherited from the Provisional Government.[1] In March 1920 the Council of Labor and Defense (STO) was set up with Lenin as its chair. The STO became the effective economic cabinet, and had oversight over the chief economic commissariats, responsible for finance, planning, food supply

1 T. H. Rigby, *Lenin's Government: Sovnarkom 1917–1922* (Cambridge: Cambridge University Press, 1979).

and trade as well as the Supreme Council of the National Economy (Vesenkha) which oversaw nationalized industries.

In July 1923 Sovnarkom had Lenin as chairman with five deputy chairmen: V. Ya. Chubar', L. B. Kamenev, M. D. Orakelashvili, A. I. Rykov and A. D. Tsurupa. There were ten members of Sovnarkon, each a head of a commissariat: NKProd – food supply; NKIndel – foreign affairs; NKPS – transport; NKVneshTorg – external trade; NKRKI – the workers' and peasants' inspectorate; Vesenkha – industry; NKTrud – labor; NKPT – posts and telegraphs; NKFin – finance; and NKVMDel – military and naval affairs. At this time Lenin chaired the STO and was assisted as vice-chairman by L. B. Kamenev. The STO had a further eight members – the heads of the commissariats of finance, military and naval affairs, two representatives of Vesenkha, transport, Gosplan (the State Planning Commission) and the TsSU (the Central Statistical Administration).

The overlapping composition of Sovnarkom and the STO, and the fact that Lenin chaired both meant that substantive economic matters could be resolved by the STO and then be ratified by Sovnarkom as a matter of course. The fact that four leading figures of the Politburo (Lenin, Trotsky, Kamenev and Rykov) were also members of Sovnarkom and the STO meant that these individuals could decide key economic issues in Sovnarkom–STO which would then be approved by the Politburo. Of seven full Politburo members, three were neither Sovnarkom nor STO members – Joseph V. Stalin as party general secretary, G. E. Zinoviev, head of the Leningrad party organization and head of the Communist International, and M. P. Tomskii, head of the trade union movement.

Sovnarkom was in theory appointed by the legislative body the Central Executive Committee (TsIK) which was elected by the Congress of Soviets, a kind of parliament, which was elected by the people. In reality the parliament had little power. The consolidation of the one-party state and the outlawing of opposition parties after 1921, confirmed the dominance of Sovnarkom. TsIK provided a facade of democratic accountability and ratified the legislation approved by the executive. The most important committee of TsIK was the budget committee which was established in 1925. While Sovnarkom and TsIK represented the public face of power, the real power was exercised behind the scenes by the party, most notably by the Politburo which dealt with the most sensitive political issues: foreign policy, defense policy and internal security matters. While Lenin was the leading figure in the Politburo and Sovnarkom–STO the division of power between party and governmental bodies was not clearly demarcated.

In 1917 the Bolsheviks came to power professing a belief in the future abolition of the state, the creation of a system of direct participatory democracy of the commune state, with citizens involved not only in decision-making but also in the administration of public affairs. Lenin in *State and Revolution* offered a naive conception of state administration and economic management (based on the German war economy) whereby administrative functions could be progressively simplified and made amenable to democratic control and performance by ordinary citizens. In the first year of Soviet power the Bolsheviks were to be rudely disabused of these illusions. But the Bolshevik regime from its inception was not a law-governed state; the state itself was conceived as the embodiment of the proletarian dictatorship.

During the era of war communism, the Soviet regime came to rest on four principal administrative pillars – the party, the Red Army, the Cheka, and the state bureaucracy. During the civil war the regime took open resort to terror, and willingly justified this in ideological terms.[2] A surrogate role was assigned to the soviets and trade unions. During these years the state bureaucracy was greatly expanded, reflecting the nationalization of all industry in June 1918, brought under the control of the Supreme Council of the National Economy and its administrative agencies that managed entire branches of industry (*glavki*) and state-appointed managers. NKProd (the People's Commissariat of Food Supply) developed a vast apparatus that oversaw food requisitioning and food rationing. This era saw the heady debates on the abolition of money, the market and private ownership and their replacement by state administration and distribution.

This transformation in the character of the regime prompted heated debate from diverse groups within the party: the military opposition, the workers' opposition and the democratic centralists. All of these groups stressed the importance of party and soviet democracy, and reliance on proletarian cadres in running the state institutions. The collapse of the economy provoked a major crisis in the winter of 1920–21, with mass popular discontent in the towns, large-scale peasant revolt in the countryside, which triggered a major change in policy, the abandonment of war communism and the retreat to the NEP.

The Bolsheviks, having seized power, outlawed all right-of-center parties, including the Octobrists and Kadets in 1917. In 1921, the one-party state was consolidated with the left-of-center parties, the Mensheviks and Socialist

2 Richard Pipes (ed.), *The Unknown Lenin: From the Secret Archives*, with the assistance of David Brandenberger; documents translated by Catherine A. Fitzpatrick (New Haven: Yale University Press, 1996).

Revolutionaries being banned. Within the ruling communist party, a new tough regime was instituted, with the banning of political factions, and the establishment of mechanisms to police the party's own membership to discipline and purge its ranks: the Central Control Commission.

The Soviet state inherited large elements from the authoritarian practices of the Russian state.[3] The public sphere was severely circumscribed, with only limited scope for social organizations, such as trade unions or soviets, or the media to act as counterweights to the state administration. The Soviet state was from its inception beset by a problem of legitimacy. With this went a greater reliance on coercive means, the resort by the state to terror and the growing concentration of power within the party-state apparatus.

The NEP saw the retreat to a mixed market economy which lasted until 1928. The inflated state bureaucracy was drastically pruned, as the system of state rationing and requisitioning was ended. Small and medium-scale industry was transferred back into private hands through leasing. State enterprises were required to operate on the market, subject to tight credit controls, and required to conform to the discipline of profitability. As a check on a headlong retreat into a capitalist economy the State Planning Commission (Gosplan) was established. From 1921 the Commissariat of Finance exercised tight discipline aimed at balancing the budget, securing revenues, curbing excessive expenditure and stabilizing the currency. Within the framework of the NEP a certain degree of autonomy was allowed for individual groups within the economy, for the peasants with surpluses to trade and private businessmen (nepmen). The People's Commissariat of Foreign Trade enforced the state's monopoly of foreign trade when trade relations with the West were revived.

In two key articles in 1923, "How We Should Reorganize the Workers' and Peasants' Inspection" and "Better Fewer But Better," Lenin outlined his concerns: the incompetence of communist administrators placed in charge of state and economic institutions; the regime's reliance on former specialists inherited from the old regime; and the inability of the party to control the state administration. The state, he argued, needed urgently to improve the quality of its cadres; communist officials should become qualified and proficient in administration. The task of training cadres was assigned to the People's Commissariat of Workers' and Peasants' Inspection (NKRKI), which was to be linked to the party disciplinary body, the Central Control

3 Oleg Kharkhordin, "What Is the State? The Russian Concept of Gosudarstvo in the European Context," *History and Theory* 40, 2 (2001), 206–40.

Commission (TsKK), and which in turn was to be linked to the party Central Committee and Politburo. This hybrid body (TsKK–NKRKI) was also expected to involve ordinary rank-and-file workers in investigating the work of state and economic institutions and advancing proposals for their improvement. The body was intended as a link between the government – Sovnarkom – and the party Politburo.

L. B. Krasin, the commissar of foreign trade, roundly criticized Lenin's scheme for its "primitive" understanding of administration, which drew on the military model of administration, and its obsessive concern with ensuring party control over the state and over the bourgeois engineers, technicians and administrators within its employment. Krasin was accused of seeking to weaken the party's power and of eroding communist ideology in favor of a technocratic approach. He frankly declared that it was better for the communist party to achieve reconciliation with these specialists than to rely on arrogant and incompetent party officials.[4]

Lenin's scheme of 1923 for managing the state administration was predicated on the assumption that it was possible to create a self-regulating one-party dictatorship. In the event, the agency that he had proposed to set up as part of the self-regulating mechanism, TsKK–NKRKI, was placed under the control of V. V. Kuibyshev, one of Stalin's allies. In the succession struggle after Lenin's death Stalin used the party Secretariat and Orgburo and TsKK to wrest control of the party and state apparatus. This produced a concentration of decision-making powers within the party-state machine, with no countervailing institutions able to check its operation.

Sovnarkom Under Rykov

On Lenin's death the chairmanship of Sovnarkom was assumed by Rykov, and the chairmanship of the STO by Kamenev. Joint sessions of Sovnarkom–STO became a way of facilitating coordination between the two bodies, The mid 1920s saw the economy return to prewar levels of production. This provided the basis for an increasingly intense debate on the future of the NEP which became embroiled in the struggle for the succession.

From 1924 onwards Sovnarkom, under Rykov, was increasingly challenged in key policy areas and lost ground to the Politburo. The first significant indication of this shift came in November–December 1925. A report

4 E. A. Rees, *State Control in Soviet Russia: The Rise and the Fall of the Workers' and Peasants' Inspectorate, 1920–34* (Basingstoke: Palgrave Macmillan, 1987), 52–54.

compiled by the Central Statistical Administration (TsSU) revealed that counter to the official party position, the kulaks dominated the supply of marketable grain. This confuted the official party view that the NEP had benefited mainly the middle peasants. A counterreport was compiled by NKRKI which confirmed the party's assessment of the situation. As a result, the TsSU position was discredited, paving the way for political influence over the details of policymaking and on the statistical compilation of information.[5]

The Fourteenth Party Congress was styled the congress of industrialization. From 1926 onwards the chairmanship of Sovnarkom and the STO were combined by Rykov. Thereafter the Politburo increasingly intervened in the sphere of economic policy. The allocation of large investments to prestige projects such as the Dnepr hydro project (Dneprostroi) required Politburo authorization. It provided the basis for strengthening the planning agency Gosplan. As industry returned to prewar levels of output by 1927 the demands for enlarged investment to ensure the restoration of old plant and to build new ones became a major preoccupation of Vesenkha, headed from 1926 by Kuibyshev.

Politburo intervention in economic policy was instrumental in producing the "left turn" of 1928. Sovnarkom and the STO themselves remained under Rykov, staunch defenders of the NEP. The all-union commissariats of finance and trade remained strong supporters of the NEP. This was true also of the People's Commissariat of Agriculture of the Russian Soviet Federative Socialist Republic (RSFSR), under A. P. Smirnov from 1923 to 1928.[6] The trade union movement under Tomskii was a supporter of the NEP. Within the party N. I. Bukharin became its ideological defender.

The fate of the NEP revolved around the future direction of the Soviet regime. In this struggle power shifted dramatically from Sovnarkom–STO to the Politburo. This was achieved through a politicization of issues and an attack on what was defined as "rightist" tendencies in government: The grain crisis of 1927–28 was turned into a campaign against the "kulaks"; the war scare of 1927–28 heightened emphasis on strengthening the country's defenses; the Shakhty trial developed into an attack on "bourgeois specialists"; the Smolensk affair was turned into an attack on political degeneration in provincial party bodies. As late as 1928 a high proportion of the administrative personnel in government and economic management were

5 Ibid., 123–27.

6 James W. Heinzen, *Inventing a Soviet Countryside: State Power and the Transformation of Rural Russia, 1917–1929* (Pittsburgh: University of Pittsburgh Press, 2004).

those inherited from the old regime. The Shakhty trial initiated a purge of nonparty specialists and the advancement of a younger generation of administrators, many of whom were workers from the bench.[7] A new generation of administrators were advanced in the state apparatus, the economic agencies, the trade unions and the new collective farms.

The NEP was terminated in 1928–29 with the adoption of the first Five-Year Plan and the launch of agricultural collectivization and "dekulakization" of November–December 1929. Within Sovnarkom and the STO the initiative in promoting industrialization was taken up by Gosplan and Vesenkha. In this the commissariats committed to the NEP, notably the Commissariat of Finance, were increasingly overruled. The formation of the first Five-Year Plan involved dramatic clashes among the all-union commissariats and titanic struggles between different regional lobbies to secure investment for the modernization of their regions. The most dramatic struggle was that between the Urals regional party and industrial lobby in conflict with the Ukrainian interests to secure maximum investment for the modernization of the metallurgical industry.[8]

The left-turn of 1928–29 generated intense interdepartmental conflicts over questions of policy and resource allocation. In these years Stalin relied to a large extent on the TsKK–NKRKI, headed by his fellow Georgian G. K. Ordzhonikidze, to act as a policymaking center in opposition to the main economic commissariats. In a series of dramatic developments, the senior officials of TsKK–NKRKI, armed with radical proposals to transform the economy, took over the key economic commissariats. In 1929 Ya. A. Yakovlev took over the running of the new all-union Commissariat of Agriculture (NKZem USSR). In 1930 Ordzhonikidze and a team of senior officials from TsKK–NKKI took over the running of Vesenkha. In 1931 A. A. Andreev, head of TsKK–NKRKI, took over the running of the troubled transport commissariat (NKPS).[9]

Industrialization and agricultural collectivization from 1929 onwards saw a relentless centralization of administration with Sovnarkom–STO and Gosplan as the main coordinating centers. Vesenkha established its dominance over industry. The direction of agricultural policy was taken over by the new NKZem USSR, while the task of building the new collective farms

7 Sheila Fitzpatrick, "Stalin and the Making of a New Elite, 1928–1939," *Slavic Review* 38, 3 (1979), 377–402.

8 James R. Harris, *The Great Urals: Regionalism and the Evolution of the Soviet System* (Ithaca and London: Cornell University Press, 1999).

9 Rees, *State Control in Soviet Russia*, ch. 7.

was entrusted to the all-union Kolkhoztsentr, and the creation of machine tractor stations was overseen by Traktortsentr. These institutional pressures led to the unrealistic targets set during the first Five-Year Plan and the over-optimistic projections that led to the collectivization of agriculture.

Sovnarkom Under Molotov

In December 1930 Molotov replaced Rykov as chairman of Sovnarkom. The idea that Stalin should combine the post of party general secretary and chairman of Sovnarkom was mooted but was rejected by Stalin himself. Combining the two posts would have placed an almost intolerable administrative load on his shoulders. With Molotov as head of Sovnarkom and the STO he had a reliable deputy who could attend to the detailed work of economic management. The command economy hugely increased the administrative load of the economic commissariats, the planning agency, the supply organizations, and the workload of Sovnarkom and the STO. With the defeat of the right opposition the governmental apparatus, which had been a rightist stronghold, was purged.

The issuing of joint Sovnarkom–Central Committee decrees on major issues became a common feature of government. Sovnarkom occupied a clearly subordinate role to the Politburo. It lost any vestige of influence over internal security, defense and foreign policy. Even in the realm of economic policy the Politburo arrogated to itself the right to decide issues of importance, and intervened directly to ensure the correct interpretation and implementation of policies. It involved a shift to direct control over production targets, control over supply and allocation, and control over prices and investment. Sovnarkom's powers were increased as the command economy saw a great transfer of power over local enterprises from republican and regional authorities to the all-union commissariats.[10]

The second Five-Year Plan reflected a more realistic approach to planning, with a conscious attempt to avoid the wildly exaggerated targets which had been set for the first Five-Year Plan. Sovnarkom and Gosplan were entrusted with enforcing planning discipline. Gosplan drew up the plans and, with Sovnarkom and the STO, made sure that enterprises met their targets and ensured supply of materials, machinery and finished products to their intended destinations. The Commissariat of Finance tightly controlled state

10 E. A. Rees (ed.), *Centre–Local Relations in the Stalinist State, 1928–1941* (Basingstoke: Palgrave Macmillan, 2002), ch. 1.

revenue collection and ruble issue, and Gosbank imposed strict limits on the supply of credit to state enterprises.

After 1917 Sovnarkom's meetings were held in the Kremlin. By the 1930s Sovnarkom and Gosplan occupied a large American-style skyscraper office block on Prospekt Marksa in central Moscow. All the major commissariats occupied buildings in the city center, and had their own newspapers and journals. Individual commissariats had very clearly developed identities, shaped by their function and status, which were reinforced by intense interdepartmental rivalries. Powerful political figures who headed such agencies over a prolonged period of time placed their own imprint on their development. The Soviet state was highly bureaucratized with strong corporatist elements.

The repression of bourgeois specialists continued with a series of trials in 1930–31. Stalin's speech "New Conditions – New Tasks in Economic Construction," delivered to a conference of business executives in June 1931, signaled an end to the judicial harassment of bourgeois specialists.[11] The development of the Soviet industrial economy saw the growth of the managerial and technical stratum. After the famine crisis the years 1934, 1935 and 1936 saw a gradual improvement in the economic situation, and with that an easing of political repression. In May 1935 Stalin emphasized administrative order and stability of cadres. The key to economic success, he argued, was the caliber of officials; the slogan that "cadres decide everything" was counterposed to the slogan that "technology decides everything."[12]

The concept of "revolution from above" was derived from Engels's comments on Bismarck's use of the Prussian state to accomplish the unification of Germany which the "revolution from below" had failed to secure. In Soviet Russia this strategy was intended to consolidate socialism while providing a rationalization for the expansion of the power of the party-state.[13] The elimination of the private sector in industry and agriculture, and the suppression of private trade involved an unprecedented extension of state power. The command economy established a degree of control more extensive and more permanent than anything attempted under war communism.

11 I. V. Stalin, *Sochineniia*, vol. XIII (Moscow: Foreign Languages Publishing House, 1955), 53–82.

12 J. V. Stalin, "Address to Red Army Academy Graduates," in J. V. Stalin, *Problems of Leninism* (Peking: Foreign Languages Press, 1976), 772.

13 E. A. Rees, *Political Thought from Machiavelli to Stalin: Revolutionary Machiavellism* (Basingstoke: Palgrave Macmillan, 2004), 223–24.

Economic controls were buttressed by social controls with the introduction of internal passports and residence permits from 1932 onwards. The administration of the economy was based on state ownership and planning, but money was not abolished, and the market retained a residual role; in particular, the collective farm market which was legalized in 1933 and the labor market remained relatively unregulated until 1939.

By 1935 Sovnarkom had sixteen members. The increase reflected the changes brought in by industrialization and the collectivization of agriculture. Two commissariats were responsible for the collective farms and another for the state farms. Vesenkha was divided into three commissariats – heavy industry, light industry and the timber industry. Two commissariats were created, responsible for internal and external trade. Water transport was given its own commissariat. By 1939 Sovnarkom had twenty-four members reflecting the inclusion of new economic commissariats and new regulating agencies.

The absorption of Sovnarkom into the minutiae of economic management made the role of formal meetings of the council more cumbersome. Under Lenin and Rykov, Sovnarkom generally met formally on a weekly basis. In 1930 there were just 38 meetings of Sovnarkom. From 1932 onwards the sessions were held fortnightly. By 1939 the meetings were held monthly. The establishment of the command economy greatly increased the administrative load on Sovnarkom and the STO. In 1931 Sovnarkom issued 1,187 decrees (*postanovlenii*), and in 1940 it issued 2,717 decrees.[14] As formal sessions of Sovnarkom declined in importance heads of commissariats commonly absented themselves from meetings and sent deputies in their stead.

Sovnarkom's business was increasingly handled by committees and commissions. Sovnarkom had a number of standing commissions covering a panoply of different fields: defense, administration, labor and health, education and culture, agriculture and forestry, industry, construction, transport and trade. The STO had a less elaborate committee system, but included important bodies such as the State Committee for Agricultural Procurements and the Committee for Prices. The Committee for Agricultural Procurement, set up in 1932, was chaired by Kuibyshev (head of Gosplan), and in 1933 was transferred from the STO to Sovnarkom. The setting of grain procurement targets for different provinces often provoked intense lobbying, with Stalin himself playing a key role in fixing

14 Derek Watson, *Molotov and Soviet Government: Sovnarkom, 1930–1941* (Basingstoke: Palgrave Macmillan, 1996), 56.

the targets. In 1938 the Committee of State Procurement was taken over by the People's Commissariat of Procurement. The STO also had committees on fuel, construction, freight, regulation of trade, standardization, state reserves and inventions. Its railway projects included the Moscow to Donbass trunk line.

While Sovnarkom had nominal control over economic policy, the Politburo itself encroached on its sphere of decision-making. Powerful commissariats such as Vesenkha and NKTyazhprom (the People's Commissariat of Heavy Industry) under Ordzhonikidze often sought to circumvent decisions of Sovnarkom by appealing its decisions directly to the Politburo. In 1934–36 the two powerful economic commissariats – heavy industry (under Ordzhonikidze) and rail transport (under L. M. Kaganovich) – frequently worked in tandem making it difficult for the government to impose its will on them. Sovnarkom and Gosplan strove to bring these high-spending commissariats under control. Thus disputes between Politburo members in the 1930s generally reflected sharp interdepartmental rivalries.

The focus of Sovnarkom through the period of Molotov's tenure was industry. Agriculture, transport and communications, supplies and finance occupied subordinate positions. Even here crucial issues – the setting of targets for the Five-Year Plan and for the annual plans, the setting of grain procurement targets – were deemed to be of such importance that they were approved by the Politburo, and often by Stalin personally. Sovnarkom also had responsibility for routine administrative appointments and dismissals. It acted as a problem-solving center, resolving interdepartmental disputes, and responding to petitions from individual enterprises and from the regions.

The spheres of responsibility of Sovnarkom and the Politburo were only vaguely demarcated. Economic issues deemed of political significance were decided by the Politburo while routine matters of economic management could be delegated to Sovnarkom and the STO. Under Molotov there was no real instance where the governmental body dissented from the policies espoused by the Politburo. The draconian legislation directed at the theft of collective farm property in 1933 came from Stalin and the Politburo. The Politburo had precedence over Sovnarkom on vital issues of internal security, defense policy and foreign policy.

In technical matters, however, Sovnarkom's areas of competence were extended. In the 1930s its role in the cultural and educational sphere significantly expanded. This reflected both an extension of state activities, but also in part the transfer of functions previously performed by other agencies, especially the commissariats for enlightenment at the republican level.

Sovnarkom oversaw this area through permanent commissions – cinema (1929), radio (1933), arts (1936), physical culture (1936), agricultural exhibitions and higher education. Overlapping and reinforcing control was provided by party bodies and through the unions organized to oversee culture.

Sovnarkom had oversight of specialist regional administrative bodies, such as the Central Asian Council, and the administration of the northern (Arctic) sea route. It oversaw major construction projects. It had control over roads, auto transport and civil aviation. It oversaw technical issues such as weights and measures, standardization, the hydrometrological committee and geological research and cartography. It had responsibilities for issues of health and medicine. It also had charge of population resettlement, evaluating state reserves and estimating labor reserves.

The problem of enforcing official policies saw the development of a whole series of control mechanisms to supervise the line administrators. In 1934 dissatisfaction with the work of the party and state control agencies – TsKK–NKRKI and Sovnarkom's Commission of Implementation – led to their abolition. In their place was created a separate Commission of Party Control and the Commission of State Control. These two bodies were narrowly confined to the tasks of monitoring the implementation and performance of state and economic agencies. Control exercised by the NKVD (the People's Commissariat of Internal Affairs), the Procuracy and the Commissariat of Justice were intensified. In 1935 the NKVD was also given a seat on Sovnarkom.

Collectivization and de-kulakization were also instrumental in the extension of the forced labor system which used criminals and political prisoners.[15] The Gulag (the chief administration of camps) was in effect a state within a state. It became an intrinsic part of the Stalinist economic system with major sectors – such as timber felling, goldmining, construction (railways, canals, hydro complexes) and whole industrial complexes (Norilsk, Vorkuta) – under its control. Many of the major construction projects – e.g. the Belomor canal and the Moscow Volga canal – were carried out by Gulag labor. Although under the control of the OGPU/NKVD, and thus nominally under the supervision of Sovnarkom, the key decisions regarding the management of the system were referred to Stalin and Molotov jointly. High-level decisions were approved by the Politburo rather than Sovnarkom.

15 Oleg V. Khlevniuk, *The History of the Gulag: From Collectivization to the Great Terror*, trans. Vadim A. Staklo (New Haven: Yale University Press, 2004), ch. 1.

Political–Administrative Relations in the Stalinist State

The Communist Party of the Soviet Union (CPSU), as the only legal party, was transformed from being a forum of political debate into an agency responsible primarily for regulating the state apparatus. Party control took various forms: (1) The Secretariat and Orgburo exercised oversight of administrative appointment (*nomenklatura*), and controlled the implementation of policy through its staff of instructors and inspectors who were charged with checking policy implementation and reporting to higher authorities through the Central Committee's departments of agriculture, industry, trade and transport, that were set up in 1934; (2) the Secretariat's departments, linked to the political administrations established in 1933, exercised direct control over the political departments (*politotdely*) in agriculture, rail and water transport, analogous to the system of party control over the armed forces; (3) high-powered Politburo and Central Committee investigative commissions were sent to investigate particular policy trouble spots during collectivization and the famine years; (4) party bodies at republican, city, province, district and local level down to the party cells in the institutions and workplaces also had a role in managing the administrative system and exposing shortcomings.

Politburo commissions and joint Politburo–Sovnarkom commissions assumed a key role in decision-making and in drafting legislation. Some were virtually permanent bodies, such as the Commission for Defense. The hard currency commission had a key role in shaping the country's foreign trade policy. A high-level joint Politburo–Sovnarkom commission was charged with resolving the rail transport crisis and met on a regular basis from 1934 to 1935. There were also ad hoc Politburo commissions, set up as the occasion required, which from the early 1930s onwards played a major role in drafting legislation.

People's commissars (*narkoms* or ministers), in the 1920s and 1930s, were men who had made their careers in the revolutionary underground or as political commissars during the civil war. Although formally appointed by TsIK on the recommendation of Sovnarkom, they were in fact appointed by the Politburo, with Stalin having a decisive say. Typically, they occupied their posts for many years: Gleb Krzhizhanovskii headed Gosplan from 1923 until 1930; G. F. Grin'ko was commissar for finance from 1930 to 1937; K. E. Voroshilov was commissar of defense from 1926 until 1940; Ordzhonikidze headed the industrial commissariat from 1930 to 1937; M. M. Litvinov was commissar of foreign affairs from 1930 to 1939.

Powerful commissars jealously guarded their institutions as their personal fiefs. In 1934–36 Ordzhonikidze, head of NKTyazhprom, and Kaganovich, head of NKPS, succeeded in keeping the control agencies – the Procuracy, the Commission of Party Control, the Commission of Soviet Control and the NKVD – from interfering in their institutions. This reflected an alliance of institutions underpinned by the close friendship of Ordzhonikidze and Kaganovich. In 1936 the balance was decisively tilted against them. NKTyazhprom and NKPS were the first commissariats to be heavily purged. Ordzhonikidze's inability to protect his cadres was undoubtedly a factor in his suicide in 1937.[16]

The USSR in the 1920s did not have a particularly large state administrative apparatus in comparison to other advanced countries. In many ways the USSR, like other peasant countries, was undergoverned, especially in the provinces and rural areas, and it was thus more reliant on periodic campaigns and the threat of coercion to impose its will. The party secretaries in the republics and regions were appointed by the center but possessed some measure of discretion, operating in some ways like tsarist provincial governors but acquiring a whole new set of responsibilities related to the management of the planned economy. After 1930 no figures were published of the number of those employed in the state administrative apparatus. Political struggles within the state institutions themselves were common, reflecting ideological divisions and cliental allegiances. Many commissariats became battlegrounds between contending administrators and specialists from different generations.

With the fusion of politics and administration and the concentration of power at the center, all frustrations with the way the regime operated tended to be focused on the political leadership. The leadership responded by blaming policy failures on lower-level officials. The regime deployed a strong anti-bureaucratic rhetoric and had frequent resort to the disciplining and punishing of subordinate officials. In March 1930 Stalin blamed the excesses of collectivization on errors perpetrated by local party officials. In 1932–33 he blamed the famine crisis on local officials, and in 1939 he blamed the excesses of the purges on N. I. Yezhov, head of the NKVD.

The dominance of the party-state apparatus, while placing enormous power in the hands of the political leadership, also posed the danger of inertia, which might impede the leadership's ability to impose its policy

16 E. A. Rees, *Iron Lazar: A Political Biography of Lazar Kaganovich* (London: Anthem Press, 2012), chs. 9 and 10.

priorities. In 1921 the switch from war communism to the NEP involved dismantling the powerful People's Commissariat of Food Supply (NKProd) and building up the Commissariats of Finance (NKFin) and Trade (NKTorg). Similarly, Stalin in launching the "left turn" in 1929 undercut those institutions most supportive of the NEP (the Commissariats of Finance and Trade) and built up other institutions that were committed to the new line (Vesenkha, Gosplan, TsKK–NKRKI). While policy under the NEP was to some extent shaped by the influence of powerful lobbies, after 1929 shifts in policy were attained by building up powerful institutions that could carry those policies through. Political priorities remained supreme.

In the 1930s Sovnarkom and Gosplan performed the main coordinating role in the economy. Vesenkha/NKTyazhprom – the Commissariat of Heavy Industry – was far and away the most powerful of the economic commissariats. In 1929, it swallowed up all profitable republican and local enterprises. There was also a very clear hierarchy among the republican and regional administrative agencies. In the 1930s Moscow city and province enjoyed great favor in terms of resource allocation. These years also saw a significant shift of economic power from Ukraine to the Russian Federation, especially with the creation of the second industrial base around the Urals–Kuznets combine. One key aspect of administrative relations in this period was the intense rivalry between the territorial administration (republics, provinces and cities) and the dominant all-union economic commissariats.

The famine of 1932/33 coincided with a dramatic decline in the regularity of formal meetings of the Politburo, Orgburo and Secretariat.[17] This betokened a shift to a system of personal dictatorship as the main locus of decision-making became the meetings in Stalin's private office in the Kremlin, with Stalin able to summon officials at will.[18] Stalin's correspondence with his leading deputies Molotov and Kaganovich for the 1920s and 1930s provides detailed insight into the way the leading group worked.[19] This is supported

17 Oleg V. Khlevniuk, *Master of the House: Stalin and His Inner Circle*, trans. N. Seligman Favorov (New Haven: Yale University Press, 2009).

18 Stephen G. Wheatcroft, "From Team Stalin to Degenerate Tyranny," in E. A. Rees (ed.), *The Nature of Stalin's Dictatorship: The Politburo 1924–1953* (Basingstoke: Palgrave Macmillan, 2004), ch. 3.

19 Lars T. Lih, Oleg V. Naumov and Oleg V. Khlevniuk (eds.), *Stalin's Letters to Molotov 1925–1936* (New Haven: Yale University Press, 1995); R. W. Davies, O. V. Khlevniuk, E. A. Rees, L. P. Kosheleva and L. A. Rogovaya (eds.), *The Stalin–Kaganovich Correspondence* (New Haven: Yale University Press, 2003).

by the accounts provided by Molotov, Kaganovich, A. I. Mikoian and lower-level administrators.[20] Stalin emerges from these accounts as a dominating personality who was closely involved in all major facets of decision-making.

Stalin of course could not decide everything and had to delegate power. Like any dictator, he needed a dependable administrative apparatus through which to govern. The central party machinery, the administration of Sovnarkom, the central commissariats and the territorial administrative tiers continued to function. From the early 1930s onwards Stalin's influence in the fields of defense, foreign policy, internal security and appointments was immense. His role in the decision to abolish rationing in 1935 was central, but his role in initiating the Stakhanovite drive of 1935 was marginal.[21] In agriculture, which was treated as a resource base, his control was exercised through his discretion in approving procurement targets, determined by the state's Committee for Agricultural Procurement, which in effect set the level of repression to be applied to the collective farm workers. In industry, where adjustments in the targets for one sector held repercussions for the whole plan, his role was more limited, and here a rather different pattern emerges: Already from 1933 onward the task of managing industrial policy was largely delegated to Sovnarkom (Molotov), Gosplan and NKTyazhprom.

The Great Terror 1936–1938

During the Great Terror of 1936–38, according to official figures, at least 680,000 people were executed. Most of these victims came from lower social groups. However, high-level officials suffered disproportionately. The administrative elite were decimated. Virtually no institution, in the center, republics, or localities, escaped unscathed. A new generation of officials was promoted to replenish the staffs of the administrative and economic structures. Stalin at the Eighteenth Party Congress in March 1939 asserted that since the previous congress in 1934 the party had succeeded "in promoting to leading state and Party posts over 500,000 young Bolsheviks,

20 F. Chuev, *Sto sorok besed s Molotovym. Iz dnevnika F. Chueva* (Moscow: Terra, 1991); F. Chuev, *Tak govoril Kaganovich. Ispoved' stalinskogo apostola* (Moscow: Otechestvo, 1992).

21 R. W. Davies and O. Khlevnyuk, "The End of Rationing in the Soviet Union, 1934–1935," *Europe-Asia Studies* 51 (1999), 557–609; R. W. Davies and O. Khlevnyuk, "Stakhanovism and the Soviet Economy," *Europe-Asia Studies* 54 (2002), 867–903.

members of the Party and people standing close to the Party, over 20 per cent of whom were women."[22]

Stalin after 1937 was no longer simply a dictator. He now held the lives of his colleagues in his hands. On 14 April 1937 the Politburo on Stalin's initiative approved the creation of two commissions aimed at speeding up decision-making. Foreign policy matters were to be resolved by a commission comprising Stalin, Molotov, Voroshilov, Kaganovich and Yezhov. Economic policy matters were to be decided by a commission comprising Molotov, Stalin, Chubar', Mikoian and Kaganovich. This removed the formal obligation of gaining the assent of the Politburo.[23]

From 1937 the state administration underwent important changes. First, NKVD control and surveillance was entrenched as a permanent and extensive feature of the system of rule. In 1938 officials of NKVD took over the running of the Commissariat of Water Transport, and established a strong presence in the Commissariat of Rail Transport (NKPS), in the Commissariat of Timber and in the Commissariat of Posts and Telegraphs.[24] Second, the Gulag was extended as an omnipresent component of the state and economic system. Third, a "state of siege," with draconian legislation, including severe new labor laws, was instituted. Fourth, the priority placed on rearmament profoundly shaped economic and social policy with the return to taut planning. From 1937 repression was routinized into the "normal" day-to-day management of state–society relations, where the state's actions were bound by no law and were often capricious and unpredictable. It was a society in which the cult of the leader loomed large, and in which the fear of internal enemies and of external enemies shaped popular consciousness.

Moreover, from December 1936 the industrial commissariats were drastically subdivided. Whereas in 1930 there was just once commissariat responsible for all-union industry (Vesenkha), by 1941 there were twenty-two branch industrial commissariats, including four devoted specifically to the defense industries.[25] Similarly many of the republics and larger territorial

22 J. V. Stalin, "Report to the XVIIIth Party Congress," in *Problems of Leninism*, 922.

23 E. A. Rees, "Stalin as Leader, 1937–1953: From Dictator to Despot," in Rees (ed.), *The Nature of Stalin's Dictatorship*, 203.

24 Mark B. Tauger, "The People's Commissariat of Agriculture," in E. A. Rees (ed.), *Decision-Making in the Stalinist Command Economy, 1932–37* (Basingstoke: Macmillan, 1997), 148–49, 258–59; E. A. Rees, *Stalinism and Soviet Rail Transport, 1928–41* (Basingstoke: Macmillan, 1995), 193–94.

25 E. A. Rees and D. H. Watson, "Politburo and Sovnarkom," in Rees (ed.), *Decision-Making in the Stalinist Command Economy*, 24.

administrative units (*krais*) were subdivided into smaller province (*oblast*) units.[26] These steps were intended to strengthen the center's control, and to make local agencies more responsive to local needs. But this entailed a huge increase in Sovnarkom's responsibilities in coordinating the economic commissariats and the republican and regional territorial administrations.

The task of coordinating the economic commissariats prompted dramatic changes in the structure of government. In November 1937 the STO was abolished and was replaced by Sovnarkom's Economic Council, whose membership was the same as that of Sovnarkom. In April 1940 five new specialist branch economic councils were established: engineering (chair V. A. Malyshev); defense industries (chair N. A. Voznesenskii); consumer goods (chair A. N. Kosygin); metallurgy and chemicals (chair N. A. Bulganin); and fuel and electricity (chair M. G. Pervukhin).[27] These five chairmen were to go on to play a prominent role in the future management of the Soviet government. Stalin personally took a close interest in rearmament and the development of the defense industries.

The purge, the strengthening of the role of the NKVD and the subdivision of the commissariats all served to break up institutions that were seen as having developed a corporate entity, fostering institutional interests and departmentalistic outlooks. This attitude was reflected more widely. In May 1939 Litvinov was dismissed as people's commissar of foreign affairs and replaced by Molotov. On taking up his appointment Molotov announced his intention to purge the commissariat of Jews, an indication that the staff of the commissariat by their cosmopolitan, pro-Western outlook, were no longer considered fit to carry out the new policy which was to seek a rapprochement with Nazi Germany.[28]

The administration of the armed forces underwent dramatic changes. In 1934 the People's Commissariat of Military and Naval Affairs was renamed the People's Commissariat of Defense. During the terror the armed forces were subject to a drastic purge, and NKVD and party control over the army was strengthened.[29] In December 1937 a People's Commissariat of the Navy, headed by P. A. Smirnov, was established. In May 1940 the longstanding commissar of defense Voroshilov was ousted and replaced by S. K. Timoshenko.

The Great Terror placed Stalin in a dominant position. He closely oversaw the conduct of the purges. From 1936 onwards he oversaw the Soviet

26 Stalin, "Report to the XVIIIth Party Congress," 918. 27 *Izvestiya*, 18 Apr. 1940.

28 Derek Watson, *Molotov: A Biography* (Basingstoke: Palgrave Macmillan, 2005), 153–57.

29 Roger Reese, *The Soviet Military Experience: A History of the Soviet Army 1917–1991* (London and New York: Routledge, 2000).

rearmament drive, and he was instrumental in concluding the Soviet–Nazi pact. The concentration of power in his hands went alongside the decline of the Politburo as a decision-making forum. In May 1941 Stalin replaced Molotov as chairman of Sovnarkom, thus combining the leadership of party and state bodies, which made his position unassailable.[30] But he could not function without subordinates to run the great institutions of the party, state, and military and secret police.

Soviet "Bureaupathology"

The Soviet state administration after 1928 became a control-dominated system, the worst confirmation of Krasin's warnings of 1923. This reflected in part the tsarist state tradition and the difficulty of central control over an immense territory. In the Soviet era the sphere of state activity greatly increased. Taut planning created additional strains with consequent distortions in policymaking, with operative officials evading controls and subverting the controllers. The tightening up of control was directed against what was perceived as waste, inefficiency, mismanagement, and corruption. But tight control produced its own consequences: demoralization, lack of initiative, the development of more elaborate evasion strategies by operative officials, and the concealment of errors.

Official policy moved in cycles between tightening control (1917–21, 1928–33, 1936–41) and relaxation (1922–28, 1934–36). The Soviet regime's obsessive concern with control nurtured the worst feature of what V. A. Thompson characterized as "bureaupathology," with consequent distortions in information flows vertically and horizontally, irrationalities in decision-making and the resort to ever more desperate methods of control to enforce compliance with central directives.[31] Soviet economic commissariats, trusts and enterprises displayed all the features common to monopolistic organizations, where producer sovereignty, not consumer sovereignty, prevailed. Attempts to overcome these problems included the development of "control from below," through incentive systems to stimulate shock work and Stakhanovism among workers as a way of forcing up production targets

30 O. V. Khlevniuk, *Politbiuro. Mekhanizmy politicheskoi vlasti v 1930-e gody* (Moscow: ROSSPEN, 1996).

31 The ideas of V. A. Thompson are discussed in Rees, *State Control in Soviet Russia*, 4–5. See also E. A. Rees, "Politics, Administration and Decision-Making in the Soviet Union, 1917–1953," in E. Volkmar Heyen (ed.), *The Yearbook of European Administrative History, 2004*, vol. XVI (Baden-Baden: Nomos, 2004), 259–90.

and raising efficiency. These campaigns caused considerable disruption to production and probably did more harm than good.

At the time, policy failures, waste and inefficiency were seen as the product of organizational failings, individual incompetence, or in extreme cases sabotage and wrecking. The response was invariably to further strengthen controls. But tighter controls only reinforced existing response strategies: the evasion of responsibility; the referral of decisions to higher authority; concealment; rule breaking; covert activities – managers resorting to the black market for supplies of goods in short supply; and efforts to subvert the control agencies. Strategies of mutual protection (so-called family circles) proliferated. There was a constant danger of the party becoming drawn into "petty tutelage," with the party substituting itself (*podmena*) for the operational agencies; with the result that the party was often overwhelmed by administrative detail and lost its political focus.

Under Stalin's dictatorship the structures of collective leadership were progressively dismantled. It required the creation of more fluid relations, which freed Stalin to intervene in policy matters as and when he desired. But the party-state apparatus could not function as a whole on this basis. The apparatus needed structure, order and stability. As a result the Stalinist administrative system combined at different levels apparently contradictory principles of organization: fluidity versus hierarchical order. The process of policy formation, the conflict between operative and control agencies, adversely influenced the rationality of decision-making. Official ideology, with its self-confirming logic, distorted reality, creating a one-sided consideration of policy options, and inclined the regime to adopt policies with high collateral costs.

Conclusion

Under Lenin from 1917 to 1924 Sovnarkom occupied a central position, alongside the Politburo, as the key center of decision-making. It oversaw the management of the state and economy, and exercised control over internal security policy and foreign policy. Lenin's personal authority gave Sovnarkom a role equal to the Politburo in importance. The transition from war communism to the NEP in 1921 drastically changed the role of Sovnarkom in economic management, but its authority and prestige remained undiminished. Rykov became chairman of Sovnarkom on Lenin's death but lacked his authority. In the mid 1920s Sovnarkom managed in effect a mixed economy, which it regulated primarily through its control over taxation and prices and wages. The "revolution from above" saw an unprecedented extension of the power of Sovnarkom over all aspects of the state-owned, planned economy. Under Molotov, Sovnarkom was aligned ever closer to the Politburo. At the same time Sovnarkom was turned into an administrative agency with key political issues – internal security, foreign policy, defense – being reserved for the Politburo.

With the growth of Stalin's personal power from 1932 onwards there was no area of policymaking in which he could not intervene with decisive effect if he so willed. As the Politburo itself declined, so Sovnarkom remained as the indispensable administrative and coordinating center of the state as regards economic and general administration. The NKVD emerged as a separate body responsible for internal security. The People's Commissariat of Defense had oversight of the armed forces. The party Secretariat and Orgburo continued as coordinating centers and agencies of party oversight with control over appointments.

Stalin presided over a system of government with pronounced polycratic features. In this the party, the government, the military and internal security forces had their own spheres of authority. But often agencies had overlapping responsibilities and were frequently in competition with one another. But attempts to depict Stalin as a "weak dictator," buffeted by factions and institutional pressures, are wide of the mark.[32] Some scholars argue the state's reliance on coercion and terror was evidence of its weakness. This is to confuse issues. A regime that was able to win a protracted civil war, to collectivize its peasantry and to withstand a major military invasion was not a weak state. The strength and weakness of states cannot be assessed in isolation from a consideration of the prudence and wisdom of the policies they pursue. The imposition of collectivization, de-kulakization, inevitably provoked strong resistance in the countryside, and food shortages in 1932–33 ignited localized urban protest. Official policies required coercive force. In these circumstances the reliability of state agencies, such as the military and the secret police, could not be taken for granted.

The decision-making process that evolved had certain strengths, which accounts for its longevity and its survival in difficult circumstances. It was a permanent system of crisis management. It gave Stalin enormous control

32 The Nazi dictatorship has also been depicted as a polycratic system stimulating a debate as to whether Hitler was a strong or weak dictator. See Ian Kershaw, *The Nazi Dictatorship: Problems and Perspectives of Interpretation*, 2nd edn. (London: Edward Arnold, 1989), 60, 65; Jonathan Harris, "Was Stalin a Weak Dictator?," *Journal of Modern History* 75, 2 (2003), 375–86.

over the policy process. It allowed for a quick response. Once a policy line was chosen there was no prevarication. It placed the onus on the lower tiers of the administrative hierarchy to respond as diligent and enthusiastic executors of the center's will. The obverse side of this was the weaknesses of a system that was over-centralized and over-dependent on one figure. Processes of consultation and the taking of advice depended on Stalin's willingness to heed the opinions of others. The costs of policies (economic and human) were not a primary concern. Policy failures were often perpetuated and not corrected. Stalin's personal rule coexisted with, and indeed depended on, what remained a highly formalized and bureaucratized system at the level of the operative institutions, the party and government apparatus, the ministries and the republican and regional administrations.[33]

The Soviet administrative system was a species of developmental administration, albeit within the framework of an ideocratic communist one-party state. What emerged was a "control centered" administrative system, which manifested in its most acute forms all the features of "bureaupathology" which carried serious implications for rationality in decision-making. The exaggerated targets set for the economy, and the inherent inefficiencies of the state-owned, centrally planned economy generated demands for improved performance and greater adherence to official policy. Tension and conflict between the control agencies and the police agencies on the one hand and the operative, economic commissariats on the other became an established feature of the system, and contributed to the cycles of repression which were a hallmark of the era.

Bibliographical Essay

The main study of the Soviet government under Lenin is T. H. Rigby's *Lenin's Government: Sovnarkom 1917–1922* (Cambridge: Cambridge University Press, 1979). The main study of these institutions under Molotov is Derek Watson's *Molotov and Soviet Government: Sovnarkom, 1930–1941* (Basingstoke: Palgrave Macmillan, 1996). There is no comparable study of Soviet government under Rykov. On the STO see Derek Watson, "STO (The Council of Labour and Defence) in the 1930s," *Europe-Asia Studies* 50, 7 (1998), 1203–27. On the management and regulation of the government apparatus see E. A. Rees, *State Control in Soviet Russia: The Rise and the Fall of the Workers' and Peasants' Inspectorate, 1920–34* (Basingstoke: Palgrave Macmillan, 1987), and D. R.

33 Rees (ed.), *The Nature of Stalin's Dictatorship*, chs. 2 and 7.

Shearer *Industry, State and Society in Stalin's Russia, 1926–1934* (Ithaca and London: Cornell University Press, 1996). On interdepartmental conflicts within the Soviet government, see P. R. Gregory (ed.), *Behind the Façade of Stalin's Command Economy: Evidence from the Soviet State and Party Archives* (Stanford: Hoover Institution Press, 2001); Sheila Fitzpatrick, "Ordzhonikidze's Takeover of Vesenkha: A Case Study in Soviet Bureaucratic Politics," *Soviet Studies* 37, 2 (1985), 153–72; and E. A. Rees (ed.), *Decision-Making in the Stalinist Command Economy, 1932–1937* (Basingstoke: Macmillan, 1997).

13

Migration and Social Transformations in Soviet Society 1917–1941

LEWIS H. SIEGELBAUM

In the narrative of the October Revolution and socialist construction that became standard, indeed obligatory in the Soviet Union, the Bolshevik party, the vanguard of the Russian proletariat, mobilized the workers of Petrograd and key units of the armed forces to seize the Winter Palace, overthrow the Provisional Government and proclaim soviet power. After a brief "breathing spell," the fledgling Soviet government set about defending the revolution from its many enemies both domestic and foreign. It dispatched Red Guard and Red Army units to the various fronts of the civil war. It then guided peasants and workers through the reconstruction of the economy based on Lenin's New Economic Policy (NEP). Beginning in the late 1920s, it directed its cadres to assist poor peasants in collectivizing agriculture, resettle "kulaks" in remote areas, and recruit workers to new and expanded industrial facilities, a process that continued throughout the 1930s.

This narrative, long criticized by historians outside the Soviet Union and now in post-Soviet Russia too, nevertheless has proven hard to dismiss entirely. Its periodization persists in a wide range of accounts. Those that reverse its signs, condemning the Bolsheviks and the Soviet government for what Soviet historians once praised, impute to them the same degree of agency: *They* mobilized, dispatched, directed, resettled and recruited. Whether for good or ill, the social transformations that occurred in the aftermath of 1917 thus had to be state-initiated and led. The workers and peasants – to say nothing of other social aggregations – could only follow or resist, but otherwise not participate in their own transformations.

Was this actually so? This chapter uses migration and more broadly geographic displacement as a lens through which to examine the nature and extent of social transformations from World War I until the Great Patriotic War. Migration, whether undertaken on an individual or familial basis, usually has had broad effects on both sending and receiving communities, altering *inter alia* the gender balance, available labor supply, age at marriage, family structure and economic wherewithal. Collectively and cumulatively, such effects could be either transformational or, on the contrary, stabilizing. It might seem strange, however, to use migration as an index of social transformation in the Soviet context, especially if we seek to depart from the emphasis on state-led initiatives. The Soviet state, after all, took great pains to rationally distribute the population to maximize resource development. It also exerted considerable effort to move entire diaspora nationalities away from international borders and remove dangerous "social elements" from its "regime cities." At least for the Stalin era, migration became virtually synonymous in public discourse with deportation and the Gulag.

It would be foolish indeed to deny the importance of state control of migration and its use of coercion to enforce that control. Coercion was crucial to what Leslie Page Moch and I have called the state's migration *regimes* – its policies, practices and infrastructure designed to both foster and limit human movement.[1] In seeking to organize and structure migration, the state categorized people according to its own lights, inscribing them as itinerants and nomads, resettlers, special settlers, bearers of residence permits, and later in the Soviet era, recipients of special pay increments, young specialists assigned for a given number of years to a particular job and place, and temporary urban residents (*limitchiki*). But migration also resulted from migrants' *repertoires*. By repertoires I mean migrants' practices, their relationships and networks of contact that permitted them to adapt to particular migration regimes and even bend those regimes to their own purposes. Marked by geographic origin, confession, gender, kinship, friendship and professional identity, repertoires are visible in peasants sending men to the city, in scouts inspecting territory designated for family settlement, in the rhythms of seasonal mining and harvest migration, and in other practices that transcended the revolutionary divide.[2]

Regimes and repertoires related to each other in different ways. Sometimes, as most clearly demonstrated in the case of civilians fleeing war, repertoires instigated regimes. Indeed, as Peter Gatrell recently reminded us, the refugee crisis of the Great War posed "challenging

1 Lewis H. Siegelbaum and Leslie Page Moch, *Broad is My Native Land: Repertoires and Regimes of Migration in Russia's Twentieth Century* (Ithaca: Cornell University Press, 2014).

2 See V. P. Danilov, "Krest'ianskii otkhod na promysly v 1920-kh godakh," *Istoricheskie zapiski* 94 (1974), 55–122; on the scouts see Lewis H. Siegelbaum, "Those Elusive Scouts: Pioneering Peasants and the Russian State, 1870s–1953," *Kritika* 14, 1 (2013), 31–60.

questions" about who counted as a refugee, how relations would be managed between refugees and host communities, and to what extent distant kin would become involved that "have continued to dominate discussions of refugee crises ever since."[3] Unprecedented rural-to-urban migration in the early 1930s similarly brought forth a regime to cope with the numbers and needs. But regimes could induce repertoires too, such as when soldiers and deportees responded to their parlous situations by escaping in one or another manner. Some repertoires worked in tandem with regimes, such as those of resettlement and seasonal migration; others undermined – or in the language of the day, "sabotaged" – the intent of the regimes. This dialectical dance produced much social and political change.

The remainder of this chapter tracks different groups of Soviet citizens on the move, some uprooted and others uprooting themselves, some following paths marked by previous generations and others blazing new paths. All were subjected to one or another migration regime and responded to their circumstances by applying their own repertoires. They thereby made their own history, albeit not in conditions of their own choosing. They may have done more than that: The most comprehensive effort to date to compare "crosscultural migration" in Russia to the rest of Europe, China and Japan between 1900 and 1950 finds that Russia's rate was significantly higher.[4] It is intriguing to think about the ways that so much movement could have been both cause and consequence of the making and transformation of a new society.

1914–1924

Nearly seventy years ago, Eugene Kulischer described the summer 1914 Russian offensive into Eastern Prussia and Galicia as "a gigantic wave [that] came from inner Russia and flowed beyond the 'watershed'" that marked the usual geographic division between peoples who moved west to the German lands and North America and those who moved east to the industrial centers of Russia and new farmland beyond the Urals. Kulischer was the first

3 Peter Gatrell, *The Making of the Modern Refugee* (Oxford: Oxford University Press, 2013), 26.

4 Jan Lucassen and Leo Lucassen, "Measuring and Quantifying Cross-Cultural Migrations: An Introduction," in Jan Lucassen and Leo Lucassen (eds.), *Globalising Migration History: The Eurasian Experience (16th–21st Centuries)* (Leiden: Brill, 2014), 33. "Cross-cultural migration" is defined on 14–20.

to consider soldiers as migrants. As Joshua Sanborn reminds us, none other than Leo Tolstoy regarded "murders" and "movements" as "the core social processes of warfare." But excepting Kulischer who was not a credentialed historian, Sanborn probably was right when he wrote in 2005 that "historians of migration have been even less receptive to the notion that soldiers can be analyzed as migrants than historians of armies have been to the idea that soldiers can be analyzed as murderers."[5]

Sanborn's own work has helped to bring historians to their senses. They increasingly are recognizing that soldiers experience not only geographical displacement, but also social dislocation and relocation. Their training replaces previous norms of behavior with a new set of militarized values – unquestioning obedience to authority, capacity to murder on command and fortitude under fire – and in this sense, like other migrants, they cross cultures. Reinforced by the replacement of their civilian garb by uniforms, new forms of address and rituals, and a predominantly homosocial environment, this shift has psychological dimensions pointing in the direction of brutalization. Yet, as with other forms of migration, military migrants have employed a variety of repertoires to mitigate the negative effects of the regimes to which they were subjected, and these often had life-saving consequences.

From a little over a million, the number of men in the Russian imperial armed forces grew to over 3.9 million in the summer of 1914. By the time of Russia's withdrawal from World War I in 1918, nearly 15 million men had served in the active army, of whom some 2 million were stranded abroad either as prisoners of war or as internees.[6] Letters from home gave soldiers a connection with their peacetime lives and personae, and like other emigrants, soldiers wrote home – more so than ever before, for World War I came on the heels of a great move forward in literacy, most pointedly among recruits, over two-thirds of whom were literate in the case of Russia.[7] Soldiers needed to hear from home, to learn about their farms and families; they were anxious particularly because in addition to men, requisitions of livestock had taken their toll on the production of

5 Eugene M. Kulischer, *Europe on the Move: War and Population Changes, 1917–47* (New York: Columbia University Press, 1948), 30; Joshua A. Sanborn, "Unsettling the Empire: Violent Migrations and Social Disaster in Russia During World War I," *Journal of Modern History* 77 (June 2005), 290–324.

6 Eric Lohr, *Russian Citizenship: From Empire to Soviet Union* (Cambridge, MA: Harvard University Press, 2012), 136, 148.

7 Joshua A. Sanborn, *Drafting the Russian Nation: Military Conscription, Total War, and Mass Politics, 1905–1925* (DeKalb: Northern Illinois University Press, 2003), 144.

food and fodder. Otherwise, they felt as if they were, in the words of one soldier, "cut off from the whole world."[8]

As the army dug deeper and deeper into the pool of young men, draftees used every sort of strategy to stay home or get home. They inflicted wounds on themselves, gave themselves hernias, paid bribes, jumped off troop trains and melted into civilian crowds during transfers. In the spring of 1916, the government decided to recruit Muslim subjects in Turkestan for support and labor services, thereby provoking a ruinous rebellion. The Kazakhs and Kirgiz certainly had no stake in the tsar's battle or otherwise serving a state that had taken so much of their land for use by settlers. This conscription thus proved a distraction from the war effort rather than contributing to it: Tens of thousands of Central Asians and over 3,500 Russian settlers lost their lives in the uprising, and an estimated 300,000 refugees fled across the border into China.[9]

The war situation shifted drastically in 1917 as the revolution intensified in Petrograd. The offensive that Russia's allies insisted upon and Minister of War Alexander Kerensky vociferously defended proved a bust when inestimable but significant numbers of soldiers sabotaged, deserted and mutinied. The Bolsheviks' seizure of power is unimaginable apart from the old army's effective demobilization. The ensuing civil war is equally inconceivable without new mobilizations and "violent migrations" by both the Red and White armies. Of course, desertion took its toll on the fighting capacities of both sides. By the end of 1919, deserters from the Red Army alone numbered 1.7 million. Most, about three-quarters, simply had failed to appear for induction. Another 18–20 percent fled from conscription points and rear units, which meant that only 5–7 percent deserted from frontline combat units. Some deserters returned home to rejoin their families and assist with farm tasks, but men conscripted by one side sometimes defected to the other.[10]

8 Sanborn, "Unsettling the Empire," 299.

9 Martha Brill Olcott, *The Kazakhs* (Stanford: Hoover Institution Press, 1987), 101–26; Daniel Brower, "Kyrgyz Nomads and Russian Pioneers: Colonization and Ethnic Conflict in the Turkestan Revolt of 1916," *Jahrbücher für Geschichte Osteuropas* 44, 1 (1996), 41–53.

10 Mark von Hagen, *Soldiers of the Proletarian Dictatorship: The Red Army and the Soviet Socialist State, 1917–1930* (Ithaca: Cornell University Press, 1990); Orlando Figes, "The Red Army and Mass Mobilization During the Russian Civil War," *Past and Present* 129 (Nov. 1990), 168–211; Nicolas Werth, "Les déserteurs en Russie: violence de guerre, violence révolutionnaire et violence paysanne – 1916–1921," in S. Audoin-Rouzeau, A. Becker, C. Ingrao and H. Rousso (eds.), *La violence de guerre, 1914–1945: Approches comparées des deux conflits mondiaux* (Brussels: Éditions Complexe, 2002), 99–116.

On top of this, soldiers engaged in violent migrations of their own making by forming or joining freelance groups, sometimes identifying themselves as "anarchist," and sometimes as "Green." The extent and importance of such groups tended to be overshadowed in Soviet times by the ideologically more palatable conflict between Reds and Whites. When Soviet historians did refer to them, the two most common terms they employed were "partisans" and "bandits." Partisans were, by definition, groups allied with the Red Army; bandits lent themselves to "use by enemies of Soviet power to undermine civil and military measures of the Soviet government [and] disorganize the Red Army's rear as expressed in . . . mass disorders, arson, killing of party and soviet employees, sabotaging of railroad lines, etc."[11] Such was the protean nature of loyalties, though, that bandits could become partisans, or, as was more common after the defeat of a White army, partisans could become bandits. Hardly any area did not see partisan–bandit activity, but south-central Ukraine, Tambov province in the central agricultural region and western Siberia (including parts of the Urals and current Kazakhstan) saw the most probably because food procurement efforts were at their most intense in those regions.

Violent migrations of soldiers extended outward – to the western border and beyond in the summer of 1920 when the Red Army chased the invading forces of independent Poland all the way to Warsaw; south to Dagestan and other Transcaucasian territories some of which had brief spells of independent statehood; and east into Turkestan to quell various "Basmachi" rebellions. Conventionally, the Russian Civil War is supposed to have ended in 1921, but it would be more appropriate to extend Peter Holquist's notion of a "continuum of mobilization and violence" that began with World War I at least to 1924, especially in reference to these outlying regions of the former empire.[12]

The same periodization applies to civilians whom the violent migrations of soldiers transformed into refugees and deportees. The number of people counted within Russian political space as refugees burgeoned during the war, reaching 6.3 million by July 1917. This figure did not include the approximately 1 million individuals – mostly ethnic Germans and Jews – forcibly cleared from the Polish and Baltic provinces, and in the case of Germans even from the major cities of European Russia. Although massed

11 S. S. Khromov (ed.), *Grazhdanskaia voina i voennaia interventsiia v SSSR* (Moscow: Nauka, 1983), 53, 424–25; quotation from 53.

12 Peter Holquist, *Making War, Forging Revolution: Russia's Continuum of Crisis, 1914–1921* (Cambridge, MA: Harvard University Press, 2002).

and seemingly faceless to many observers, refugees saw themselves as, and were, distinct from one another in origin, outlook and identity. We know that women and children made up the vast majority, but the archives provide only an approximation of their volume, direction and emotional bearing. Traveling in wagons, on horseback, in boxcars and on foot, the refugees aroused contradictory emotions among the host population – pity at their homelessness and hunger, fear of contamination, resentment at their intrusion and claim to resources. Such attitudes intensified ethnic and national consciousness among refugee communities, all the more so in that associational activity on their behalf emphasized the national basis of their victimization and salvation.[13]

Soviet Russia's withdrawal from the war made "reevacuation" home a more realistic prospect for many refugees from Poland and the Baltic provinces, while the collapse of the German Empire less than a year later had the same effect on their self-appointed leaders' aspirations for national independence. Still, a complex of new regimes of migration slowed homeward journeys. People without documents suffered infinite delays. Historians speak of three waves of refugees – those from World War I, from the civil war and from the famine of 1921–22 – but it is important to realize that the waves were not just successive; they were cumulative and from 1921 began to merge. The regional offices of Moscow's *Tsentrevak* attended to not only world war and civil war refugees but also local industrial workers, agricultural settlers, former prisoners of war, and deserting and demobilized soldiers. The numbers and proportions were bound to vary from one region to another depending on the intensity of fighting, the availability of foodstuffs and whether rail lines functioned.[14]

Out-migration depleted the country's major cities of millions who fled starvation, returning to the villages they had left earlier in search of work and a better life. By 1920 Petrograd's population stood at just 722,000 or 38 percent of its total for 1910, and Moscow's dipped from 1.5 million to just over a million. Were these urban-to-rural migrants refugees too? Or what about citizens Logina, Tserkina and Mikulin who sent an appeal to the commissar of agriculture in August 1922? The "old tsarist government," they wrote, had

13 Peter Gatrell, *A Whole Empire Walking: Refugees in Russia During World War I* (Bloomington: Indiana University Press, 1999); Nick Baron and Peter Gatrell (eds.), *Homelands: War, Population and Statehood in Eastern Europe and Russia, 1918–1924* (London: Anthem, 2004).

14 Gennadii Kornilov, "Refugees in the Urals Region," in Baron and Gatrell, *Homelands*, 156–78.

forced them to live in poverty (*bedstvovat'*) and in the midst of World War I to abandon their native village in Vilna province for Siberia. They settled in Tomsk province where they spent the next six years. In 1921, an (unspecified) "White attack" caused them to flee back home. However, home now was under Polish rule, and sure enough, they found Polish families living in the houses they used to inhabit. They took up temporary residence in tents, but wrote to request assistance to return to Siberia.[15] How do we categorize this trio of unfortunate families? As resettler-returnees? As refugees who after reevacuating themselves turned out to be refugees again? Best not to get too fussy about categorization.

What is clear is that in the years 1914–24 military and revolutionary mobilizations induced a tremendous amount of mobility, which affected not only the migrants themselves but also the host societies that absorbed them. These processes do not fit easily into the standard narrative of war, revolution, civil war, state- and party-building, war communism and its replacement in 1921 by the NEP. But their salience to social transformation is indisputable. For this is how millions of peasant draftees became violent migrants; how village and town dwellers became refugees separated from their "national" homelands; how workers abandoned the cities in search of food; and how family structures cracked, extruding an entire class of orphans (*besprizorniki*) who wandered from one city to another engaging in various repertoires of survival. This also was how, detached from parental supervision, young males assumed positions of authority and thereupon embarked on career migration, sent by party and state bureaucracies that needed their expertise particularly in outlying parts of the country.[16]

1924–1928

Not until the mid 1920s did peasants seeking better agricultural conditions elsewhere receive state support, as had been the case before 1914. Indeed, despite much fanfare about planned resettlement replete with fantastical target figures, the resettlement regime run by the Commissariat of Agriculture closely resembled its tsarist predecessor. Once again, the state relied on peasants' scouts to represent the interests of their clients by making application for scouting certificates that gave them the right to reduced fares

15 Rossiiskii gosudarstvennyi arkhiv ekonomiki (RGAE), f. 478, op. 7, d. 700, l. 118.

16 See for example Eduard M. Dune, *Notes of a Red Guard*, trans. and ed. Diane P. Koenker and Stephen A. Smith (Urbana: University of Illinois Press, 1993).

on the railroad and to choose parcels of land. As under the tsars, so in the 1920s, higher authorities "categorically" enjoined those on the ground to "struggle against irregular [*samovol'nye*] resettlers" whose actions disrupted the rational distribution of land among those from overcrowded areas. But as before, a substantial number of peasants employed a repertoire that took advantage of the state's scheme without conforming to its rules; they traveled at their own initiative and bore the expenses associated with irregular resettlement.[17]

In *re*settling, peasants both before and after the revolutionary upheavals were seeking not social transformation but rather the reproduction elsewhere of a familiar way of life associated with extensive grain cultivation on household plots held either in communal or familial tenure. They thereby were pursuing a profoundly conservative agenda, one that had no chance of fulfillment during the continuum of crisis from 1914 to 1924 but that seemed possible again in the relatively pacific circumstances of the mid 1920s. Between the spring of 1924 and the fall of 1929, Soviet authorities tallied some 900,000 resettlers. Cheliabinsk, with its extensive facilities to register, feed, bathe, disinfect, educate and in other ways minister to settlers, remained the main entry point for travel to Siberia and the Far East, which together accounted for the lion's share of resettlers. The chief sending regions included the central black earth provinces, the middle Volga and the West (Belarus, Briansk oblast).[18] As impressive as the volume of people voluntarily relocating might seem, from the perspective of Soviet planners eager to develop the natural resources of certain remote regions (the far north, parts of the Urals and western Siberia for example), it was inadequate.

In the meantime, peasants revived other patterns of migration – maintaining a foothold in the village while working seasonally somewhere else, and abandoning the village altogether for urban employment. Within a year or two of the introduction of the NEP, opportunities for seasonal employment began to pick up. In 1923–24 Soviet authorities recorded only 215,000 seasonal migrants (*otkhodniki*) in agriculture – a far cry from the nearly 4 million before the war who tramped to the wheat and sugar beet fields of the south – but nearly 1.4 million in nonagricultural pursuits such as construction, mining

17 RGAE, f. 478, op. 7, d. 2958, ll. 1–4; E. H. Carr, *Socialism in One Country, 1924–1926*, 2 vols. (Harmondsworth: Penguin, 1958), vol. 1, 556, 558.

18 N. I. Platunov, *Pereselencheskaia politika sovetskogo gosudarstva i ee osushestvlenie v SSSR, 1917–iiun' 1941 gg.* (Tomsk: Tomskii gosudarstvennyi universitet, 1976), 80–85; Carr, *Socialism in One Country*, 561–62.

and logging. Data compiled for the years of "high NEP" (1925–27) show a return to the status quo ante for nonagricultural employment, but the persistence of far lower rates in agriculture – one in ten of all seasonal migrants, compared with nearly half before the war.[19] No obvious transformations here either, but rather the persistence in the eyes of communist activists of economic backwardness. Efforts by the party to introduce new hiring methods and provide seasonal workers a more cultured environment more than met their match in the *artels* and their elders.

Urban population growth due to in-migration started before 1924, though at what point new migrants began to outnumber returnees remains unclear. By 1926, more than 2 million people were living in Moscow of whom 1.8 million were registered as permanent residents. Moreover, whereas before the revolution the sex ratio had been skewed toward males reflecting their predominance among seasonal migrants, the first Soviet census showed a slight majority of women and a higher proportion of married couples living together. This and other phenomena associated with the NEP – higher levels of employment and unemployment, a burgeoning underworld of gangsters and prostitutes, the proliferation of barely legal "nepmen" – did indicate social transformation, but not of the sort communist authorities could approve of.

Finally, these years also saw forced migration in the form of expulsions of former noble landowners. However, the mildness of the operation is telling. Minutes from the 1925 session of the Central Executive Committee's Presidium reveal considerable disagreement over how to carry it out and against whom. Some landlords moved out as the legislation stipulated; some appealed, postponing their departures; and some apparently transformed themselves into game and forest wardens, horse breeders, or whatever was required to stay on. In comparison to what kulaks would face a few years hence, the whole process seems gentle and humane. Among the 220 families liable for expulsion in Moscow province before 1927, only forty-five in fact were expelled; in Smolensk only 215 of 665. When the campaign concluded at the end of 1928, it had removed only about a third of the more than 10,000 families liable to expulsion.[20] This was social transformation that communists could approve of, but lacking an effective enforcement mechanism, they backed off.

19 Danilov, "Krest'ianskii otkhod," 79–80.

20 I. N. Lozbenev, "Vyselenie byvshikh pomeshchikov iz mest ikh prozhivaniia v regionakh tsentral'noi Rossii v 1925–1927 godakh," *Rossiiskaia istoriia* 1 (2009), 81–86.

1928–1941

Backing off did not sit well with the ascendant Stalin faction, and in 1928 they made their move. No more compromises or coalition-building within the party; no more coddling of the kulaks or diaspora nationalities. If people were needed to develop resources, why let their unwillingness to do so get in the way? "There are no fortresses the Bolsheviks cannot storm." Historians have identified this mentality as the driving force of Stalin's "revolution from above" by which the party prosecuted the collectivization of agriculture and forced-pace industrialization. What has been underappreciated about this revolution is the extent to which it depended on unhinging people and moving them around. Indeed, deracination – tearing up people's ties to particular places – played a particularly important role in shaping Soviet society in the Stalin era.

A state intent on uprooting peasants and redistributing them according to its lights required reliable personnel in the villages. This was why the first people roused into motion were the "cadres."[21] They consisted of over 200,000 "new people" – the Twenty-Five-Thousanders recruited from the factories by party and trade union committees, plus larger numbers of political activists and demobilized Red Army soldiers – who, after receiving crash-course training, fanned out across the countryside. Most Twenty-Five-Thousanders became collective farm chairmen or deputy chairmen, but because of what Lynne Viola calls a "famine" in rural leadership, they took on additional responsibilities such as accounting, bookkeeping, agronomy and political education. They rarely met with a warm reception. Long workdays, near constant dousing of bureaucratic fires, lack of supplies, lateness in receiving their salaries and stupendous exhaustion were the rule. Like other sorts of migrants, not all stuck it out. But of the original contingent of over 27,000 who committed themselves in 1930 to staying for two years, 11,000 remained in the countryside beyond 1932.[22]

Collectivization set millions of peasants in motion. Either out of fear of starvation or actual hunger, whether recruited by some industrial organization or simply turning up at a construction site's hiring office, peasants left their native villages as soon as they could obtain permission or without any

21 Kate Brown, *A Biography of No Place: From Ethnic Borderland to Soviet Heartland* (Cambridge, MA: Harvard University Press, 2003), 115–16.

22 Lynne Viola, *The Best Sons of the Fatherland: Workers in the Vanguard of Soviet Collectivization* (New York: Oxford University Press, 1987).

permission at all. Many went after outside earnings to supplement income from the garden plot that collectives conceded to peasant families. They thereby become embroiled in a tug of war between collective farm administrators, desperate to control "their" peasants, and recruiters. Initially, *kolkhoz* management had the upper hand, but in June 1931 the Soviet government tilted the balance in favor of recruiters when it decreed that kolkhozes had to include provisions for *otkhodniki* in their annual plans and publicize opportunities; administrators could not deduct off-farm earnings from seasonal migrants or saddle them with additional responsibilities; and family members had equal rights to goods and services distributed by the kolkhoz. But whoever dictated the regime of temporary labor, seasonal migrants continued to employ repertoires to maximize opportunities and minimize disasters: They changed jobs with amazing frequency, sometimes because the work was too arduous or the living conditions unbearable, at others to search for "the long ruble."[23] Stephen Kotkin, in reference to such labor fluidity, observed that "the train, that ally of the Bolshevik leadership and its bureaucrats and planners, was being used against them: Construction workers were using the trains to tour the country."[24]

They also frequently overstayed their visas, as it were, joining the long parade of peasants along the route toward Soviet working-class formation. They built the new blast furnaces and rolling mills while living in tents and barracks. After the completion of such giant *stroiki*, those who stayed on stood a decent chance of moving into an apartment erected alongside the factory, eventually. In such manner did towns like Magnitogorsk rise from nothing within a few years, although none exactly duplicated the steel city behind the Urals. Established cities were another story. They burst their seams with newcomers during the first Five-Year Plan and on throughout the 1930s. Moscow's numbers jumped from 2.2 to 3.7 million people during the first Five-Year Plan. These figures do not include its suburbs – counting them, Moscow grew to 4.5 million by 1939 and added 2 million peasants to its

23 Sheila Fitzpatrick, "The Great Departure: Rural–Urban Migration in the Soviet Union," in William Rosenberg and Lewis H. Siegelbaum (eds.), *Social Dimensions of Soviet Industrialization* (Bloomington: Indiana University Press, 1993), 15–40; Sheila Fitzpatrick, *Stalin's Peasants: Resistance and Survival in the Russian Village after Collectivization* (New York: Oxford University Press, 1994); Gijs Kessler, "The Peasant and the Town: Rural–Urban Migration in the Soviet Union, 1929–40," 2 vols. (Ph.D. dissertation, European University Institute, 2001).

24 Stephen Kotkin, "Peopling Magnitostroi: The Politics of Demography," in Rosenberg and Siegelbaum (eds.), *Social Dimensions of Soviet Industrialization*, 85.

population in the process.[25] If in the new towns men outnumbered women, then in Moscow with its more varied economy and heterogeneous labor force, the reverse was true.

Absorbing the millions of newcomers without much in the way of housing construction put living space at a premium. This was not so much urbanization as the "ruralization of the cities," less a process of proletarianization than of transforming Moscow, say, into a "peasant metropolis."[26] At least during the first Five-Year Plan. The Soviet state reacted to the sheer, unprecedented – and uncontrollable – volume of human movement with an aggressively restrictive regime of migration control. In the summer of 1931, it introduced organized recruitment (*orgnabor*) to recruit peasant manpower for specific industrial and construction projects in specific numbers. More sweepingly, the internal passport became the legal requirement for residence in an expanding list of important cities, labeled "regime cities," at the end of December 1932. A residence permit (*propiska*) issued by local authorities confirmed the right of passport holders to urban residence; those found without the appropriate documents faced expulsion.[27]

Some 12 million residents of twenty-eight regime cities received passports by August 1934. The document showed the name of the bearer, along with age, nationality, social position, permanent residence and place of employment. When first introduced, passport registration caused thousands of people to leave the regime cities because their social position rendered them ineligible or they anticipated deportation. Nonetheless, the passport was not entirely effective as a mechanism of control; country people continued to find their way to regime cities. Many traveled as noncollectivized peasants (*edinolichniki*), not bound by kolkhoz rules, others obtained passports and urban registration "by informal means" after being hired at the gate by a new employer, or stayed on in town after military service or education. Where there was a will, there were

25 Stephen Kotkin, *Magnetic Mountain: Stalinism as a Civilization* (Berkeley: University of California Press, 1995); David Hoffmann, *Peasant Metropolis: Social Identities in Moscow, 1929–1941* (Ithaca: Cornell University Press, 1994), 7.

26 Moshe Lewin, *The Making of the Soviet System: Essays in the Social History of Interwar Russia* (New York: New Press, 1994), 218–21.

27 Nathalie Moine, "Passportisation, statistique des migrations et contrôle de l'identité sociale," *Cahiers du monde russe* 38, 4 (1997), 587–600; Paul M. Hagenloh, "'Socially Harmful Elements' and the Great Terror," in Sheila Fitzpatrick (ed.), *Stalinism: New Directions* (London: Routledge, 2001), 286–308; and David R. Shearer, *Policing Stalin's Socialism: Repression and Social Order in the Soviet Union, 1924–1953* (New Haven: Yale University Press, 2009).

many ways, and, after a brief hiatus in 1933, peasants found their way to regime cities again, thwarting authorities' attempts to shift migration to open cities.

This brings us to the least fortunate group of peasants – the well-to-do, identified by the collectivizers and their agents in the village as kulaks. If not executed *in situ* or shuffled off to the expanding network of facilities run by the Gulag administration, kulaks were liable to expropriation and deportation with their families in convoys of converted boxcars to remote parts of the country (the north, the Urals, Kazakhstan, western Siberia). There, as "special settlers" (*spetsposelentsy*) and later as "labor settlers," they mined coal and various metals, cut timber and built canals. Or, they didn't. They died from malnutrition, cold and despair. And they escaped.

People escaped from the special settlements early and often – over half a million people during the years 1932–34, or about one in six of all special settlers. Such prodigious leakage hints at the intolerable conditions in the settlements; it also implies that escape was not that difficult. Obtaining false documents from relatives and the local population or fashioning them themselves, escapees forged signatures of the commandants in charge of "security." Among escapees, able-bodied young people predominated. Some who were caught and sent into exile a second time found a way to escape again. The OGPU offered bounties to informers and punished escapees with penalties up to confinement in labor camps, but the hemorrhaging remained heavy until conditions in the settlements improved toward the middle of the decade.[28]

This particular migrant group actually experienced two transformations – from well-to-do peasants to special settlers; and from special settlers to fugitives. How did they travel and where did they go? In most cases it is not possible to know because, like the surprisingly large number of escapees from the Gulag (129,000 in 1933–34 alone), these runaways tried their best to avoid detection. The few accounts we have indicate that they headed home and relied on the train to cover the major portion of their journeys. From towns in the far north and Urals like Arkhangel'sk, Kotlas, Syktyvkar and Molotov, escapees seeking to return to their homes in the Belorussian SSR

28 T. I. Slavko, *Kulatskaia ssylka na Urale, 1930–1936* (Moscow: Mosgorarkhiv, 1995); Sergei Krasil'nikov, *Serp i molokh: Krest'ianskaia ssylka v zapadnoi sibiri v 1930-e gody* (Moscow: ROSSPEN, 2003); N. A. Ivnitskii, *Sud'ba raskulachennykh v SSSR* (Moscow: Sobranie, 2004); I. I. Klimin, *Rossiiskoe krest'ianstvo v zavershaiushchii period sploshnoi kollektivizatsii sel'skogo khoziaistva (1933–1937 gg.)* (St. Petersburg: VVM, 2012).

passed through Vologda, Kirov, Gor'kii and even Leningrad and Moscow, before leaving the trains in Vitebsk, Minsk and Orsha. Strangers drove them in carts, ferried them across rivers, fed them and hid them when local activists, the police, or the OGPU came round. When they did reach their own district or village, they more often than not did not return to their own home – which they found either occupied by another family or too dangerous to reoccupy – and so they moved in with relatives and merciful neighbors, or they moved on.[29]

The mass deportation of kulaks ended in July 1931 after which other categories of people populated the special settlements. Chief among them were "déclassé elements" extruded from urban areas, and people from western border regions considered unreliable either on the basis of class or national affiliations. Déclassé elements emerged from the passportization of residence in "regime cities." Passportization had the twin objectives of halting in-migration to these cities and cleansing them of socially marginal or harmful "elements." Individuals "not carrying out socially useful labor," kulaks who had fled from the countryside, and a variety of disenfranchised groups known as *lishentsy* (former tsarist police and White Army officers, private traders, clerics) were barred. They had to leave for a nonregime city or the countryside within ten days or face a fine and possible deportation.[30] The proliferation of regulations, in other words, engendered a proliferation of outlaws. Large-scale ethnic cleansing began in the western border regions in 1935 and continued on and off for nearly three years. It resulted in the removal of a third to a half of all those defined as ethnic Finns, Poles, Germans and other nationalities from the special zone originally defined as 22 km but eventually encompassing territory up to 100 km from the border. It culminated in the wholesale deportation of Koreans from Far Eastern borders in late 1937. In their internal correspondence, Soviet authorities repeatedly used the metaphor of cleansing to refer to the forcible removal from a given territory of groups they identified as kulak, anti-Soviet, counterrevolutionary and anti-kolkhoz but also "unreliable" which almost always bore an ethnic specificity.[31]

29 A. L. Zaerko, *Pobegi iz ada* (St. Petersburg: Nevskii prostor, 2003).

30 Golfo Alexopoulos, *Stalin's Outcasts: Aliens, Citizens, and the Soviet State, 1926–1936* (Ithaca: Cornell University Press, 2003). Tat'iana Smirnova, *"Byvshie liudi" Sovetskoi Rossii: Strategii vyzhivaniia i puti integratsii 1917–1936 gody* (Moscow: Mir istorii, 2003).

31 Terry Martin, *Affirmative Action Empire: Nations and Nationalism in the Soviet Union, 1923–1939* (Ithaca: Cornell University Press, 2001); Pavel Polian, *Against Their Will: The History and Geography of Forced Migrations in the USSR* (Budapest: Central European University, 2004). For the relevant NKVD memoranda see *Politbiuro i krest'ianstvo,*

After spending weeks traveling in those inevitable boxcars, many newcomers found their housing inadequate, if built at all, and the steppe "bare" and "naked," which added to their sense of disorientation and vulnerability. They named their settlements after their home villages, but this hardly helped accustom them to such a radically different environment. Ultimately, their attitudes about where they lived had less to do with the lack of living space or the scarcity of consumer goods than with the coerced nature of their departure and the unfamiliarity of the landscape. Little wonder then why some chose to flee. Still, for every special or labor settler who escaped, others stuck it out by adapting. A far less spectacular response, adaptation is nevertheless what decades later enabled former deportees to speak with pride about their accomplishments, even those who spoke with bitterness about what the state had done to them. In Kazakhstan, Polish and German deportees adapted their skills in animal husbandry and in grain cultivation to a different climate and topography; in Uzbekistan, Korean deportees built an irrigation system that enabled them to adapt their skills in rice and vegetable cultivation.

Finally, what was a catastrophe for some turned out to be a lifesaver, or at least an opportunity, for others. Abandoned by deportees, vast stretches of land and the equipment used to cultivate crops needed fresh hands. The involuntary resettlement of some made possible – indeed imperative – the voluntary resettlement of others. This symbiotic relationship of some people being moved out and others being moved in, of deportation and resettlement, of depopulation and repopulation, would become endemic to resettlement policy in the 1930s and 1940s. Red Army soldiers about to complete their terms of service became some of the chief recruits for collective farms located both in strategically sensitive border regions such as the Far Eastern krai, Karelian Autonomous SSR and Leningrad oblast and in the fertile Kuban.[32] Already accustomed to taking orders and not yet having returned to their homes, they represented to Soviet authorities an attractive alternative to the Cossacks who had performed similar functions in earlier centuries.

As with so many other tasks assumed by the Soviet bureaucracy, including population removal, this exercise in population insertion proceeded on the

vol. II, 432–43; N. L. Pobol' and P. M. Polian (eds.), *Stalinskie deportatsii, 1928–1953* (Moscow: Materik, 2005).

32 V. Danilov, R. Manning and L. Viola (eds.), *Tragediia sovetskoi derevni, kollektivizatsiia i raskulachivanie: Dokumenty i materialy v 5 tomakh, 1927–1939* (Moscow: ROSSPEN, 2002), vol. III.

basis of quotas. Simultaneously, recruiters wooed collective farm families to western Ukraine and the Donbass by offering them a waiver on all tax arrears, cancellation of obligatory milk and meat deliveries for a year, use of horses from the common stables, free transportation to destination, a loan of up to 100 kg of grain to each family and provision of credits to purchase domestic animals.[33] Generally, they overfulfilled their quotas, and not because they had to twist arms. On the contrary, they had difficulty keeping up with peasant requests for information, accommodating scouts sent out by families to inspect the recently vacated lands, and preventing families from joining the convoys outside official strictures (*samovol'no*).

Why? Why did peasants from the western oblast want to leave their homes for Dnepropetrovsk? Soviet authorities worried that independent householders, kulaks and other anti-Soviet elements were trying to sneak away without fulfilling their tax and other obligations to the state. They were not entirely wrong. Everyone, not only anti-Soviet elements, and not only in the western oblast, but also peasants throughout the newly collectivized countryside desperately sought relief from the obligations imposed on them. Many must have seen resettlement to Ukraine, the Kuban and other parts of the country that were sparsely populated thanks to recent famine and deportations as their only chance for survival. The persistence of these practices despite the state's radically revised resettlement regime illustrates one of the fundamental truths about this form of migration, namely its dependence on cultural repertoires that could translate the state's grandiose schemes into terms both comprehensible by potential migrants and to their advantage.

Up to this point, the people undergoing social transformation did so via either voluntary or coerced migration. Also encountered have been migrants who by moving from one place to another successfully avoided transformation. What though of itinerants, people whose way of life was bound up with moving either now and then or at regular intervals? What of the Roma, known better in those times as gypsies, and of mobile pastoralists, otherwise known as nomads? For these people, becoming sedentary – either voluntarily or more commonly by coercion – represented social transformation. The regime of migration to which they responded, in other words, was a regime of anti-migration.

33 Ibid., vol. IV.

To begin with the Roma, the All-Union Central Executive Committee and Council of People's Commissars repeatedly issued decrees in 1926, 1928, 1932 and 1936 encouraging them to make the transition to "a working, settled way of life" (to cite the title of the first decree). Each would proclaim the advantages of doing so and list various material incentives. The very repetition of the decrees, however, suggests that the gap between intentions and fulfillment remained yawning. Neither the Commissariat of Agriculture, nor the Kolkhoz Center, nor the Resettlement Administration, nor any other state bureaucratic agency seemed willing to tackle the issue with sufficient dedication and funding. How to explain such rare diffidence? The widely dispersed nature of Roma communities and their essentialization as inveterate nomads and con artists goes some way. In any case, despite the heroic efforts of a few Romani activists, only a small number of the kolkhozes set up for Roma survived for more than a couple of years. It is not hard to understand why: When faced with the grim prospect of life on some underfunded collective farm, many would choose tried-and-true methods of survival.[34]

Not much more successful were efforts in the 1930s to sedentarize the reindeer-herding small peoples of the north. To Soviet officials, the annual migratory cycle of the *tundroviki* seemed grossly inefficient and uncivilized. In a burst of revolutionary optimism, party missionaries decided to collectivize and sedentarize the savages simultaneously. But the remoteness of the region and severity of its climate worked against their ambitions, as did the indigenes' mobility and their unwillingness to comprehend the advantages of consolidated farms. The reckoning for the Evenki and other northern peoples would come in later decades when the industrialization and despoliation of the region enforced changes in migration and work patterns that profoundly disrupted their lives.[35]

Nomads elsewhere in the USSR did not have to wait that long. Already hemmed in by Slavic peasant settlers in the late imperial period, the Kazakhs of the steppe region adapted to their strained circumstances by reducing or eliminating entirely their reliance on summer pasturage and increasing their

34 Brigid O'Keeffe, *New Soviet Gypsies: Nationality, Performance and Selfhood in the Early Soviet Union* (Toronto: University of Toronto Press, 2013); Nikolai Bessonov, "Tsygane v Rossii: prinuditel'noe osedanie," in O. Glezer and P. Polian (eds.), *Rossiia i ee regiony v XX veke: territoriia – rasselenie – migratsii* (Moscow: OGI, 2005), 631–40.

35 Yuri Slezkine, *Arctic Mirrors: Russia and the Small Peoples of the North* (Ithaca: Cornell University Press, 1994); David G. Anderson, *Identity and Ecology in Arctic Siberia: The Number One Reindeer Brigade* (Oxford: Oxford University Press, 2000).

cultivation of grain. But by the mid 1920s, after the dust from the October Revolution had settled, Kazakh society had "re-traditionalized." Clan and subclan ties took on a new vitality, and clan heads (*bais*) correspondingly reasserted their authority. According to the 1926 census, over 97 percent of Kazakhs lived in rural areas, and two-thirds of households were classified as semi-nomadic because they moved with their herds to summer pastures in a classical pattern of transhumance.

In 1928, the communist party's Kazakh section decided to launch an offensive against the "feudal" power of the *bai*, followed in December 1929 by its resolution to sedentarize Kazakh nomads on collective farms. The equivalent of de-kulakization in the rest of the Russian Soviet Federative Socialist Republic (RSFSR) and among Russians within Kazakhstan, "debaiization" struck at the heart of kinship solidarities that governed Kazakh nomadic society. The collectivization of livestock herds nearly wiped them out owing to lack of fodder, shelter, organization and, in many cases, will. Deprived of their traditional livelihoods, many herdsmen and women became refugees – *otkochevniki* in state parlance. True wanderers, they rustled cattle and otherwise preyed upon the kolkhoz population; they gravitated toward the cities, the industrial sites and construction projects; and they traveled by the hundreds of thousands north to Siberia and the Urals, south to Uzbekistan and east to China. And they died. According to the successive censuses of 1926 and 1937–39, the ethnic Kazakh population within Kazakhstan dropped from 3.7 million to 2.1 million.[36]

Conclusion

It is impossible to tell the story of social transformations during the Soviet Union's formative decades without acknowledging the enormous role of the party-state, its ideologically inspired agendas, and its power to realize them. What this chapter has argued is that the state's major undertakings of those decades – civil war, collectivization, industrialization and mass terror – depended for their success on people moving or being moved. It also has stressed that having assumed so much responsibility for displacing and relocating its citizens, having separated so many of them from their

36 Olcott, *The Kazakhs*; Niccolò Pianciola, "Famine in the Steppe: The Collectivization of Agriculture and the Kazakh Herdsman, 1928–1934," *Cahiers du monde russe* 45, 1–2 (2004), 137–92; Isabelle Ohayon, *La sédentarisation des Kazakhs dans l'URSS de Staline: Collectivisation et changement social (1928–1945)* (Paris: Maisonneuve & Larose, 2006).

homes, the Soviet state did a poor job in those decades of delivering on its promises to provide the necessary resources to make lives better or even to sustain life.

Yet, people were not putty in the hands of the state. While not denying the forcefulness of state coercion in the name of security and expanded production, this chapter has highlighted ordinary people's resourcefulness – in disembarking at the "wrong" station, bonding with distant kin, evading surveillance, adjusting to new environments and otherwise taking advantage of opportunities presented by crises. Nearly forty years ago, Charles Tilly wrote rather grandly "the history of European migration is the history of European social life."[37] Analogously, it could be said that the lens of mobility yields fundamental insights into the social transformations experienced by the Soviet Union's citizens in the formative period of that country.

Bibliographical Essay

Soviet studies and migration did not dwell in the same scholarly space until quite recently. Both scholarly communities are probably to blame. With the exception of the Great Migration of African-Americans from the southern states to northern cities in the 1910s through the 1960s, internal migration long tended to play second fiddle to immigration in migration studies. Among Russianists, seasonal migrants and migrants to the cities figured in labor and urban histories, and the more recent literature on the Gulag and other carceral regimes has included useful information on the logistics of deportation. But attempts to encompass various forms of migration and their interdependence have been few and far between. For a European-wide perspective, see Eugene Kulischer, *Europe on the Move: War and Population Changes, 1917–47* (New York: Columbia University Press, 1948); for a recent analysis of internal migration in "Russian political space" throughout the twentieth century, see Lewis H. Siegelbaum and Leslie Page Moch, *Broad Is My Native Land: Repertoires and Regimes of Migration in Russia's Twentieth Century* (Ithaca: Cornell University Press, 2014).

The contribution of World War I to the downfall of tsarism is an old topic, but it has been infused with new life in recent years by attention to soldiers as

37 Charles Tilly, "Migration in Modern European History," in William McNeill and Ruth Adams (eds.), *Human Migration: Patterns and Policies* (Bloomington: Indiana University Press, 1978), 68.

"violent migrants" and to refugees as both socially destabilizing and significant to claims for national independence. See especially Joshua A. Sanborn, "Unsettling the Empire: Violent Migrations and Social Disaster in Russia During World War I," *Journal of Modern History* 77 (2005), 290–324; Peter Gatrell, *A Whole Empire Walking: Refugees in Russia During World War I* (Bloomington: Indiana University Press, 1999); Nick Baron and Peter Gatrell (eds.), *Homelands: War, Population and Statehood in Eastern Europe and Russia, 1918–1924* (London: Anthem, 2004); and Peter Gatrell, *The Making of the Modern Refugee* (Oxford: Oxford University Press, 2013). For the chronological extension of the war-induced "continuum of crisis," see Peter Holquist, *Making War, Forging Revolution: Russia's Continuum of Crisis, 1914–1921* (Cambridge, MA: Harvard University Press, 2002).

Deracinating people became an important part of the Stalin revolution, with enormous implications for social transformation. The dimensions of this policy and its execution have been analyzed most thoroughly in Pavel Polian, *Against Their Will: The History and Geography of Forced Migrations in the USSR* (Budapest: Central European University Press, 2004), and most brilliantly in the following works: Kate Brown, *A Biography of No Place: From Ethnic Borderland to Soviet Heartland* (Cambridge, MA: Harvard University Press, 2003); Lynne Viola, *The Unknown Gulag: The Lost World of Stalin's Special Settlements* (New York: Oxford University Press, 2007); and David R. Shearer, *Policing Stalin's Socialism: Repression and Social Order in the Soviet Union, 1924–1953* (New Haven: Yale University Press, 2009). An older historiography analyzed the unprecedented migration of peasants to the cities. It includes David Hoffmann, *Peasant Metropolis: Social Identities in Moscow, 1929–1941* (Ithaca: Cornell University Press, 1994), and Stephen Kotkin, "Peopling Magnitostroi: The Politics of Demography," in William Rosenberg and Lewis H. Siegelbaum (eds.), *Social Dimensions of Soviet Industrialization* (Bloomington: Indiana University Press, 1993), 63–104.

Finally, publication of valuable collections of documents, some with extensive commentary, on the deportations of kulaks and borderland peoples include V. Danilov, R. Manning and L. Viola (eds.), *Tragediia sovetskoi derevni, kollektivizatsiia i raskulachivanie: Dokumenty i materialy v 5 tomakh, 1927–1939* (Moscow: ROSSPEN, 1999–2006), and N. L. Pobol' and P. M. Polian (eds.), *Stalinskie deportatsii, 1928–1953* (Moscow: Materik, 2005).

14
Foundations of the Soviet Command Economy 1917–1941

MARK HARRISON

The early years of the Soviet command economy provide a textbook case in the interplay of beliefs, interests, policies, institutions and outcomes. Based on their beliefs, political actors decided what was in their interests and made policies that changed institutions (understood as Douglass North's "rules of the game").[1] Institutions and policies together changed outcomes. Completing the loop, the actors interpreted the outcomes, drew lessons and adjusted policies. We will start from what is most easily observed, the outcomes.

Outcomes

In 1913 the Russian Empire was the world's largest country in territory and the third largest in population (after China and India). Using dollars and international prices of the year 1990 as a standard of value, Figure 14.1 shows average incomes in 1913 just below $1,500. It is often said that Russia was the poorest of the European powers, and this is true, but it also overstates Russia's backwardness. On a global yardstick, Russia was just an average country in everything but size. Russian incomes were close to the global average, similar to those of most Latin Americans and Japanese, and far above those of most Africans, Indians and Chinese. Notably, the Russian average was well above the $400 that the late Angus Maddison set as characteristic of a society at "bare-bones" subsistence.[2]

1 Douglass C. North, *Institutions, Institutional Change and Economic Performance* (Cambridge: Cambridge University Press, 1990), 3.

2 Angus Maddison, *Growth and Interaction in the World Economy: The Roots of Modernity* (Washington, DC: AEI Press, 2005), 5–7. According to Maddison, average world incomes were $1,524 in 1913 and $1,958 in 1940, both years measured in the same international dollars and 1990 prices. Data from www.ggdc.net/maddison/maddison-project/orihome.htm.

In an unequal society many fell below the average, but Russia then was more equal than Russia today. In 1904, the incomes of Russia's bottom 40 percent were half the average; on the basis of that proportion, most of Russia's poor could still exist above the $400 floor in a typical year.[3] The poorest of the poor could sink below the floor. Not all years were typical and from time immemorial Russia suffered from severe episodes of regional famine, the most recent in 1891. Thus, destitution tended to be periodic and local. On average, life expectancy was short – around thirty years for a Russian born in 1897.[4] High levels of infant and child mortality were an important factor in poor average prospects.

At the end of our period, on the eve of World War II, not everything had changed. Soviet borders were quite similar to those of the Russian Empire. Between 1917 and 1940 there were great exchanges of territory, most of which were subsequently reversed. In the outcome, the Soviet population was still the world's third largest.

In the economy, there was growth. In 1940, output per head was 50 percent above the 1913 level. This improved on the performance of the global mean, which went up by just one-third.

There was growth, but growth was volatile. Figure 14.1 shows, for example, that four-fifths of the increase in national income from the beginning to the end of our period was achieved in a single explosive spurt that lasted just four years (1934 to 1937).

In 1940 the Soviet Union's national product was not just larger than before. There was a great movement from farms to factories and offices. In 1913, agriculture and trade, shown in Figure 14.2, accounted for three-fifths of the Russian economy. By 1940 their share had shrunk to one-quarter. Industry, transport and services went up from one-quarter to three-fifths. Most of this shift was compressed into the period of the first Five-Year Plan, from 1928 to 1932.

Output expanded, but consumption barely increased. Household consumption made up four-fifths of national expenditure in 1913; by 1940 it had fallen to barely more than one-half. Figure 14.3 shows the change in uses of resources. Consumption gave up resources to government outlays, civilian and military, and to investment in the capital stock, most of it now state-owned or controlled. Again, most of the change in uses of national income

3 Peter H. Lindert and Steven Nafziger, "Russian Inequality on the Eve of Revolution," *Journal of Economic History* 74, 3 (Sep. 2014), 797.

4 *Naselenie Rossii za 100 let (1897–1997). Statisticheskii sbornik* (Moscow: Goskomstat Rossii, 1998), 164.

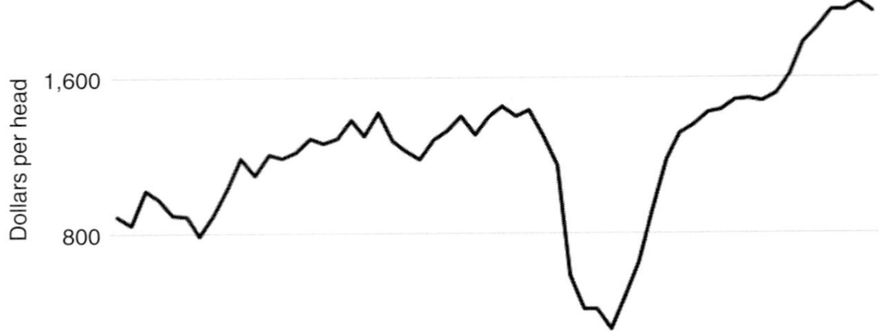

Figure 14.1 Russia and the Soviet Union: Real National Income per Head in International Dollars and 1990 Prices
Source: A. Markevich and M. Harrison, "Great War, Civil War, and Recovery: Russia's National Income, 1913 to 1928," *Journal of Economic History* 71, 3 (2011), 693, and Appendix, Table A39. Figures are for Russian Empire territory (excluding Finland and Poland) to 1917, and for Soviet interwar territory otherwise.

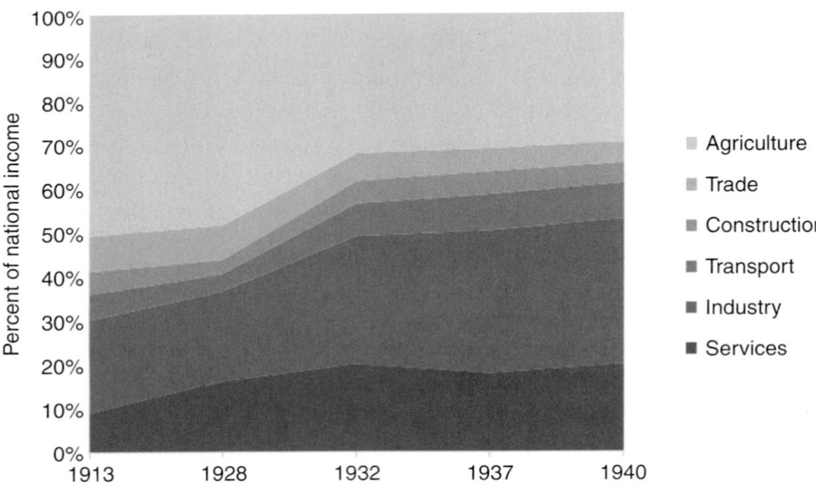

Figure 14.2 Russian and Soviet National Income by Origin, 1913 to 1940, Percentage of Total
Source: A. Markevich and M. Harrison, "Great War, Civil War, and Recovery: Russia's National Income, 1913 to 1928," *Journal of Economic History* 71, 3 (2011), 680, and Richard Moorsteen and Raymond P. Powell, *The Soviet Capital Stock, 1928–1962* (Homewood, IL: Irwin, 1966), 622–23. Percentage shares are calculated at 1913 prices for 1913 and 1928, and at 1937 factor costs for 1937 and 1940.

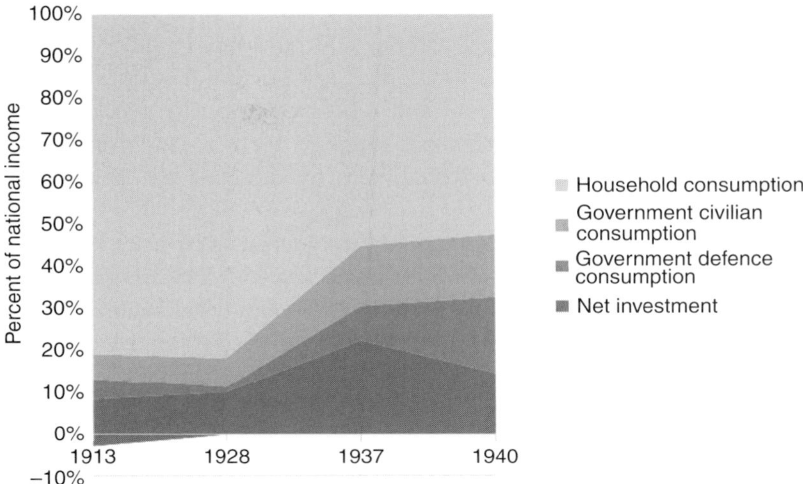

Figure 14.3 Russian and Soviet National Income by End Use, 1913 to 1940, Percentage of Total
Source: R. W. Davies, Mark Harrison and Stephen G. Wheatcroft (eds.), *The Economic Transformation of the Soviet Union, 1913–1945* (Cambridge: Cambridge University Press, 1994), 272. Percentage shares are calculated at current prices for 1913, and at 1937 factor costs for 1928 to 1940. The shaded area that appears below the horizontal axis in 1913 represents that part of net investment financed by foreign saving, matching the deficit in the current account of the balance of payments.

was squeezed into a relatively short timespan, which the figure shows as 1928 to 1937. Observations of higher frequency might show that the main changes were even more compressed.

The changes in the structure of the Soviet economy were far-reaching and abrupt. Their size and speed have no parallels in the economic history of market economies in peacetime, where structural change has generally proceeded at a much more leisurely pace. A comparison among Figures 14.1–14.3 suggests, however, that when structural change was most rapid, in the early 1930s, there was little economic growth.

It is not easy to compare the inequalities of welfare across the Soviet population of 1940 with those in the Russian Empire of 1913. In Russia's market economy, access to goods and services depended largely on purchasing power, which can be measured. In the Soviet economy entitlement was based much more on political, social and employment status. At the same time distribution by status became secret. Most entitled were the party elites in Moscow and the provinces who could draw freely on public resources for their household needs. Stalin lived modestly, but he never had to stand in line. Public employees in large factories and government offices received many benefits, including access to goods at low government prices and free housing, child care, medical care and other services. The security police regularly sampled their attitudes and reported them to Stalin personally, who responded to evidence of discontent by directing the shipment of additional supplies.[5]

The entitlements of collective farmers, in contrast, were few. They were required to work much of the year for the collective for little or nothing, and were expected to feed themselves from restricted family land allotments. No one responded to their discontents. In times of hunger they died when others went without. The Soviet Union suffered two more famines within our period, one in 1921 and another in 1932–34. By the numbers of premature deaths, both were worse than the famine of 1891.[6]

Least entitled were the millions swept up into labor camps and penal colonies because they violated Soviet laws on state property or work discipline, or because they fell into the social and ethnic categories that Stalin designated from time to time as more likely to contain enemies. These were executed or imprisoned for varying terms; if imprisoned, they were worked as slaves, sometimes to death.

For those that survived, conditions of life generally improved. The 1930s saw determined efforts to educate the public in health and disease prevention and to provide a basic infrastructure for public health. By 1940, adult heights were increasing and life expectancy at birth was more than forty years.[7]

Behind the outcomes of 1940 were the policies and institutions of the Soviet command economy. State property and centralized distribution squeezed private ownership and trade into the background and the underground. The new institutions arose from discretionary political actions on a vast scale. Discretionary interventions are often short-lived; to persist, they must be institutionalized in new rules of the game. The Soviet command economy that existed on the eve of World War II institutionalized the political interventions of the preceding years.

5 Paul R. Gregory, *The Political Economy of Stalinism: Evidence from the Soviet Secret Archives* (Cambridge: Cambridge University Press, 2004), 92–97.

6 R. W. Davies and Stephen G. Wheatcroft, *The Years of Hunger: Soviet Agriculture, 1931–1933* (Basingstoke: Palgrave Macmillan, 2004), 402–15.

7 Robert C. Allen, *Farm to Factory: A Reinterpretation of the Soviet Industrial Revolution* (Princeton: Princeton University Press, 2003), 132–52; Elizabeth Brainerd, "Reassessing the Standard of Living in the Soviet Union: An Analysis Using Archival and Anthropometric Data," *Journal of Economic History* 70, 1 (Mar. 2010), 83–117.

Table 14.1 *Top Ten Powers in the International System, 1913 and 1940, by the Compound Index of National Capability*

	CINC in 1913 (%)	Rank	CINC in 1940 (%)	Rank	Change in CINC (%)	Rank
USA	22.0	1	20.2	1	−1.8	8
Germany	14.3	2	17.1	2	2.8	1
Russia/USSR	**11.6**	**3**	**13.7**	**3**	**2.1**	**2**
UK	11.3	4	9.5	4	−1.8	7
China	9.6	5	9.3	5	−0.4	5
France	6.8	6	7.6	6	0.8	4
Austria–Hungary	4.5	7	–	–	–	–
Japan	3.4	8	5.1	7	1.7	3
Italy	3.4	9	3.0	8	−0.4	6
Turkey	1.8	10	–	–	–	–
Spain	–	–	1.2	9	–	–
Canada	–	–	1.2	10	–	–
Top ten, total	88.6	–	87.9	–	–	–

Source: The National Material Capabilities (ver. 4.0) dataset, described by J. David Singer, Stuart Bremer and John Stuckey, "Capability Distribution, Uncertainty, and Major Power War, 1820–1965," in Bruce Russett (ed.), *Peace, War, and Numbers* (Beverly Hills, CA: Sage, 1972), 19–48; www.correlatesofwar.org/.

As discussed in the bibliographic essay that ends this chapter, economists and economic historians have often evaluated the Soviet economy from the perspective of civilian economic growth and consumer welfare. But this is not how Lenin and Stalin typically expressed their ambitions for the economy. They saw Russia surrounded and penetrated by internal and external enemies working together against the revolution. The goal they set was to rebuff these enemies by "overtaking and outstripping the advanced countries" in aggregate production and military power, which counted for much more than individual wellbeing.[8]

Table 14.1 illustrates the progress made from the perspective of national power. The table uses the composite index of national capability (CINC), developed by the Correlates of War project to capture "the ability of a nation to exercise and resist influence." At each point in time, the CINC score combines six indicators of a country's relative weight in the international

8 V. I. Lenin (in 1917), *Polnoe sobranie sochinenii* (hereafter *PSS*), vol. XXXIV (Moscow: Gosizdat 1969), 198, echoed by I. V. Stalin (in 1927), *Sochineniia*, vol. X (Moscow: OGIZ, 1949), 302.

system: total population, urban population, iron and steel production, energy consumption, military personnel and military expenditure. On this measure the table reports the "top ten" powers in 1913 and 1940.

In both years global power was highly skewed, so that the top ten countries gathered nearly 90 percent of global power. From start to finish, there was little change in the top ten. The Austro-Hungarian and Ottoman (Turkish) Empires dropped out after World War I, and their places were taken by two lightweights, Spain and Canada. Stalin's policies did not improve the global rank of Russia (the Soviet Union), placed third after the United States and Germany and before the United Kingdom in both 1913 and 1940. What did change was relative distance. The Soviet Union and Germany both gained on the United States, the world leader, and both opened their lead over the UK. In fact, the Soviet Union registered the second largest gain (after Germany) in relative strength.

In light of the war that followed, this achievement would later be widely hailed as a justification of Stalin's efforts to build industrial and military power in relative isolation from the world economy.

Antecedents and Definitions

At the turn of the twentieth century, the concept of a command economy was unknown in the English language. Of the semantic equivalents in use today, "central planning" was the first to appear, coming into usage in 1916.[9] This was the year of Germany's experiment in economic planning for the Hindenburg program of war-industry construction.

World War I was the first conflict in which industrialized powers fought each other to a standstill, and it was the first in which government-controlled economic mobilization was decisive. The overriding need to assure the supply of war gave rise to common features of a command economy in several countries, more notably in Britain and Germany, less so in Russia, before the Bolshevik Revolution took place. The economic demands of the

9 Based on their frequency in the Google Books English-language corpus, inspected through the Google Books N-gram Viewer, books.google.com/ngrams/, and described by Jean-Baptiste Michel, Yuan Kui Shen, Aviva Presser Aiden, Adrian Veres, Matthew K. Gray, the Google Books Team, Joseph P. Pickett, Dale Hoiberg, Dan Clancy, Peter Norvig, Jon Orwant, Steven Pinker, Martin A. Nowak and Erez Lieberman Aiden, "Quantitative Analysis of Culture Using Millions of Digitized Books," *Science* 331, 6014 (Jan. 2011), 176–82. "Command economy" first appeared in Franz Neumann, *Behemoth: The Structure and Practice of National Socialism* (London: Victor Gollancz, 1942). Thanks to Peter Wardley for this reference.

war were unprecedented: By 1917, government purchases stood at nearly 40 percent of GDP in Britain, 50 percent in France and 60 percent in Germany.[10] But these governments did more than just purchase a large share of the economy's output. In addition, they intervened on the supply side so as to turn their offers to buy into offers that could not be refused, the definition of a command.

The complex nature of a modern economy implied that such efforts could not be limited to the market for final goods and services, and controls were gradually extended back along the supply chain to the markets where intermediate products and raw materials, food, labor, capital issues and bank credit, transport and shipping space, and foreign exchange were traded. In all those markets a common-sense or "business-like" approach implied the fixing of quantities while holding prices below the level that would clear the market, replacing the tendency to equilibrium with administrative rationing based on political priorities.

The main driver of a command economy was the government's aim to monopolize the economy's resources and punish their diversion to private goals. Government demands were unprecedented, but they did not make a command economy if private suppliers could turn the government down or negotiate a higher price. Government offers to buy from private firms became more forceful when the government built and subsidized its own shipyards and arsenals, or denied materials and labor to uncooperative firms. The pressure on those firms to comply was reinforced when government-sponsored cartels established priorities that favored the firms supplying the government by channeling scarce intermediate goods in their direction. As for farmers, government officials intervened in the private selling of food by fixing maximum prices and minimum entitlements for the urban population. In the labor market, the government drafted able-bodied men for military service and also, increasingly, for war work in factories and mines. In monetary policy and in markets for domestic credit and foreign exchange, there was financial repression: favorable terms for approved borrowers regardless of ability to repay, with others denied credit.

Taken together, these elements, which all seemed to arise naturally in a context of patriotic fervor, promised to give government officials colossal authority to steer resources away from private uses. To realize the authority

10 Stephen Broadberry and Mark Harrison, "The Economics of World War I: An Overview," in Stephen Broadberry and Mark Harrison (eds.), *The Economics of World War I* (Cambridge: Cambridge University Press, 2005), 15.

was not straightforward, however. It placed great demands on the state's capacity to implement new policies and enforce new rules without succumbing to corruption or resorting to violence.

Imperial Russia in the War

How much of this command system already existed in Russia before 1917, when the Bolsheviks took power? The answer is: only a little.

The Bolsheviks inherited an economy in decline. By 1917, Russia's real national income was down by around one-fifth from its peacetime level.[11] This sounds bad, and in fact it was bad: The Russian economy was being slowly pulled apart by the demands of total war.

On the demand side, Russia's 9 million soldiers required to be fed, armed and deployed. But Russia's economy was far flung and its productivity lagged behind that of its rivals. In wartime most of the working population was employed in farming or fighting. Fighting took resources directly from farming; food supplies were undermined by the large-scale conscription of young men and horses into military service. Domestic taxes could not meet the war's demands, so the imperial government covered the deficit by borrowing extensively. Britain and France supplied funds; so did Russia's central bank, which printed money to match. This boosted the war effort for a time, but inflation then took off, reaching 6 percent monthly in 1916 and early 1917.[12]

As for Russia's industries, in wartime they struggled to satisfy war contracts. They did not have the capacity to continue to supply the farming population with manufactured consumer goods and agricultural implements as well, and this damaged the farmers' incentives to supply food to the war effort. The damage was accentuated by the defeats of 1915, which led to the loss of much farmland, while millions were displaced and fled to the east, creating an additional burden of refugees. Food became scarce, particularly in the towns. At this point the economy began to disintegrate.[13]

11 Markevich and Harrison, "Great War, Civil War," 680.

12 Mark Harrison and Andrei Markevich, "Russia's Home Front, 1914–1922: The Economy," in Adele Lindenmeyr, Christopher Read and Peter Waldron (eds.), *Russia's Home Front in War and Revolution, 1914–1922*, vol. III, *National Disintegration and Reintegration* (Bloomington: Slavica, 2016).

13 Peter Gatrell, *Russia's First World War: A Social and Economic History* (Harlow: Pearson Longman, 2005).

The decline in the Russian economy during the war years up to 1917 sounds bad, but it is possible to make too much of it. The problems that Russia encountered in mobilizing for total war were not unique and were apparent in all the European powers that retained a significant sector of peasant farmers. In fact, the margin of economic decline was smaller in Russia than in Austria, Finland, France, Germany, Hungary and Turkey.[14] In other words, while the military situation that the Bolsheviks inherited was absolutely dire, and was made worse by their own agitation among the soldiers, the economic situation was no worse than that found elsewhere on the continent.

At the end of the monarchy, Russia still had a market economy. The main factor directing the war mobilization of resources was the money that the imperial government threw at the war. As noted, this alone did not make a command economy. It is true that the war also gave rise to a few innovative policies and institutions that can be read with hindsight as the antecedents of a command economy in Russia before the Bolsheviks took power. At the time, however, these steps were tentative, with little political will or administrative capacity behind them, so that outcomes were hardly affected.

Most significant were the imperial government's efforts to prioritize food for the soldiers and workers. Bread was rationed in Petrograd and Moscow from 1916, but rations were not honored unless bread was available, which made the exercise meaningless. The availability of bread was compromised by the low fixed prices that the government wished to prevail. The government set quotas of grain to be supplied from every region at the low fixed prices, but at those prices the peasants in those regions would not sell to anyone. The quotas were voluntary at first, but became statutory in November 1916. In March 1917 the Provisional Government declared a state monopoly of grain. When the farmers resisted, so that supplies fell short or were diverted into illegal channels where prices rose freely, the government did not enforce the quotas, the fixed prices, or the monopoly. "Until the October Revolution," according to Silvana Malle, "market rules virtually prevailed."[15]

14 Markevich and Harrison, "Great War, Civil War," 690; for country studies, see Broadberry and Harrison (eds.), *Economics of World War I.*

15 Silvana Malle, *The Economic Organization of War Communism, 1918–1921* (Cambridge: Cambridge University Press, 1985), 324.

First Steps

Following the October 1917 Revolution, the Bolsheviks quickly established three elements of a command system: the principle of unconditional confiscation of private property, the control of industrial supply and the control of food produce that was judged to be surplus to the farmers' own basic consumption. In sharp contrast to the imperial and Provisional Government, the Bolsheviks were willing to use considerable violence to impose their principles.

Confiscation served several purposes, including the expropriation of enemies, the gain to the public purse and the reward of supporters. Early Soviet decrees transferred the estates of the aristocracy and church to the state, but most of this property was immediately privatized when the peasants took what they wanted. The Bolsheviks raided the banking system in search of real and paper valuables. Some of this accrued to the state, but again much was taken by the raiders for themselves.[16] The value of such items under new ownership was greatly diminished, as is generally the case for stolen goods.

In industry there was a wave of nationalizations. Within a month of the revolution, a government decree established a ministry of industry, the Supreme Council of the National Economy (Vesenkha). The ministry quickly bred a number of specialized "chief committees" responsible for the supply of materials such as coal and iron, and a territorial apparatus charged with implementation of orders.[17] At first the Bolshevik administration aimed only to regulate private industry, as in the German war economy of the time. Nationalization of industry proceeded faster than intended. In some cases, the private owners or managers fled; in other cases, gangs of workers chased the owners away. The workers declared the facilities to be public property, and introduced management by elected committees.[18] Determining that elective management was ineffective, Vesenkha declared itself the legal owner and took responsibility.

The establishment of Vesenkha was followed by measures to nationalize the banks (January 1918), to affirm state monopolies over domestic trade in

16 Sean McMeekin, *History's Greatest Heist: The Looting of Russia by the Bolsheviks* (New Haven: Yale University Press, 2009); Elena Osokina, *Zoloto dlia industrializatsiia: Torgsin* (Moscow: ROSSPEN, 2009).

17 Eugène Zaleski, *Planning for Economic Growth in the Soviet Union, 1918–1932* (Chapel Hill: University of North Carolina Press, 1971), 24–36.

18 E. H. Carr, *The Bolshevik Revolution, 1917–1923*, vol. II (London: Macmillan, 1952), 62–79.

foodstuffs and all foreign trade (April), and to seize the "commanding heights" of large-scale industry and transport (June).

The extension of state ownership and regulation had implications for food policy. Within weeks, the new state became responsible for feeding millions of soldiers and urban residents, many of them its employees. The Bolsheviks took over the already existing grain quotas and price controls that, until now, had had little or no effects on the actual distribution of food. Failure to feed the workers and soldiers had already brought down the Russian monarchy and the Provisional Government. Not wishing such events to be repeated, between January and June 1918 the Bolsheviks instituted a "food dictatorship" based on requisitioning food stocks and their centralization under government control.[19]

These elements of a command economy were in place by the early summer of 1918. The attempts to coordinate industry and to ration food resembled measures already adopted in Germany, where Lenin and other Bolsheviks now saw a template of economic as well as military modernization.[20] They went much further, however, in their radical disregard for property rights and civil rights. Resisters faced unrestrained violence, an element new to Russia and the other European economies at war. In matters of food supply Lenin motivated extreme penalties by reference to "enemies of the people" in agriculture and trade, working hand in glove with the foreign enemy to strangle the revolution.[21]

Context and Results

In the confused circumstances of the time, because the result looked like a war economy, it was always tempting to suppose that it was driven by the immediate demands of war, like the war economies of the industrialized powers. This interpretation was offered by Lenin himself when, after the event, he denounced "that peculiar war communism, forced on us by extreme want, ruin and war."[22] He meant to suggest that the command economy was not a free choice but a necessary wartime evil.

19 Lars T. Lih, *Bread and Authority in Russia, 1914–1921* (Berkeley: University of California Press, 1990), 126–37.

20 Lenin, *PSS*, vol. XXXVI (Moscow: Gosizdat, 1974), 132; see also Malle, *Economic Organization*, 298–300.

21 Summary execution: Lenin, *PSS*, vol. XXXV (Moscow: Gosizdat, 1974), 311–12, 314, and 358; "enemies of the people": vol. XXXVI, 506.

22 Lenin, *PSS*, vol. XLIII (Moscow: Gosizdat, 1970), 220.

This story is refuted by timing, however. At the end of 1917, Russia's economy was in no worse shape than that of any other continental power, where no such measures were taken or contemplated. By March 1918, Soviet Russia had made peace with Germany and the Bolsheviks did not anticipate rebellion in Russia. A revolt of Czechoslovak troops in Siberia at the end of May turned out to be the signal, but even so the civil war was slow to unfold, and there was little serious fighting through the rest of the year.[23] As late as October, Lenin was planning a Red Army of 3 million men for the next spring to support the German Revolution – not to suppress counterrevolution in Russia.[24] Thus the context of the first attempt to establish a Soviet command economy was not a domestic emergency but rather the mistaken belief that foreign and domestic threats had receded, leaving the emergency in the past.[25]

It is true that, once the civil war was in full swing, the scope of the command economy was further enlarged. By 1920, public ownership of industry extended to small artisan establishments with one or two workers.[26] The government had first call on the labor services of the citizens through military levies, requirements to perform public works and the control of public employment, where workers were under a military style of discipline.[27] Tougher regulation was in preparation.[28] Agriculture remained in private hands, but farmers were obligated to deliver up their food produce above a subsistence norm for government distribution to others. The government was preparing to impose sowing plans on individual farms. Trade was now a government monopoly: The government had the right to buy all important commodities at fixed prices. These were orders that could not be refused, either because the seller was also a government employee, or because the buyer could shoot the seller. In industry, government priorities over intermediate goods were enforced by a centralized authority, Vesenkha, which managed the government-

23 While the civil war is conventionally dated from the end of May or June 1918, its low intensity in the remainder of the year can be judged from the fact that the Red Army incurred only 8,000 permanent losses in 1918 compared with 368,000 in 1919 and 1920, based on an incomplete count reported by G. F. Krivosheev et al., *Grif sekretnosti sniat': Poteri Vooruzhennykh Sil SSSR v voinakh, boevykh deistviiakh i voennkykh konfliktakh: Statisticheskoe issledovanie* (Moscow: Voenizdat, 1993), 30–31.

24 Lenin, *PSS*, vol. L (Moscow: Gosizdat, 1970), 186.

25 Christopher Read, "Leninism, Stalinism and the Problem of Transition: Spring 1918 and 'The Immediate Tasks of the Soviet Government,'" working paper (University of Warwick, 2012).

26 Malle, *Economic Organization*, 65. 27 Zaleski, *Planning for Economic Growth*, 19.

28 Malle, *Economic Organization*, 485–88.

owned production facilities and drove out private enterprises. Soldiers and urban residents depended on a government ration for their food requirements.

Some elements of the command economy were still missing, however. Rations fell short, so that the black market flourished. Inflation accelerated. The Bolshevik government was even less able to raise taxes to cover its spending than the governments that came before it, and there was no attempt at financial repression.

Also missing was competent, clean administration. If the Bolsheviks had the will to make the command economy work, they lacked the state capacity. Direct evidence of this is the violence and corruption that surrounded their relationship with peasant farmers. The new regime had so little competence and legitimacy that it could impose its requirements only by subjecting resisters to exemplary punishment. In order to motivate the violence, it gave a substantial share of the food obtained to the perpetrators as incentive.

Under these conditions the command economy did not work. The state struggled to monopolize resources. As fast as it gathered them into its hands, the same resources flowed back into private uses like sand through a sieve. Officials, managers, workers and farmers diverted them to eat or barter or resell. You could call it corruption or a loot chain, but often it was just people who were cold and hungry, fighting over scraps to help their families survive.

When the loot chain was able to function, at least someone got a benefit. Even worse was the alternative, when the resources that the government aimed to capture vanished into thin air, so that no one gained. This happened when the supplier lost any interest in producing goods that would otherwise be seized or stolen. It happened, clearly, in agriculture, where peasant farmers, forced to sell below cost, unable to buy anything in exchange through legal channels, responded by further cutting back the area under crops, so that even less food was produced than before.

Confirmation of this mechanism is found in the trend of the aggregate economy under the new command system. After the October 1917 Revolution, but before the civil war battles that began with 1919, the Russian economy fell over a cliff. Russia's national output, which declined by one-fifth in three years of the world war, dropped by two-fifths in 1918 alone, and continued to drop further. Large-scale industry, transport and construction, the sectors of the economy that were most engaged with the supply of war, disappeared, returning the economy to a premodern structure.

Incomes fell to a premodern level too, less than $600, equivalent to that found in the poorest economies in the world today, leaving many at or below Maddison's "bare bones" subsistence.[29]

The command economy, and not the wars to which it supposedly responded, caused Russia's "worst economic disaster of the twentieth century."[30] Just as output collapsed before the serious fighting began, it also failed to recover when the fighting went away. By the end of 1920 the anti-Bolshevik forces were essentially defeated but the economy stagnated at a dangerously low level.[31] Pockets of hunger and disease appeared and then spread uncontrollably. In 1921 harvests failed across the southern and eastern regions. More than 5 million people died.[32]

A Breathing Space

At the Tenth Party Congress of March 1921, Lenin announced a "breathing space."[33] The requisitioning of food surpluses from farmers would cease. Instead, a graduated tax would be levied in proportion to the harvest. The food obtained through taxation would fall short of what was needed to feed the towns and the army, so the remainder would be acquired through market exchange. By means of this New Economic Policy (NEP), the Bolsheviks aimed to restore incentives to agriculture and to replace the conflict-laden struggle with the peasant farmers over food supplies with trade based on mutual benefit.

The elimination of one element of the command system had implications for other elements. These implications emerged only gradually. Meanwhile, two factors slowed down the process of policy reform. The harvest failed, precipitating widespread famine. Agricultural recovery began in 1922. And policy reform was not immediately extended to public finance. Government spending was maintained, revenues fell even shorter than before, and the expectation of ever-widening budget deficits precipitated hyperinflation. Stabilization was achieved only in 1923.

29 Markevich and Harrison, "Great War, Civil War," 680. 30 Ibid., 698.

31 Fighting continued after 1920, but only on the periphery and at much lower casualty rates for the Red Army: 238,000 permanent losses in 1921 and 1922, compared with 702,000 from 1918 to 1920 (almost all in 1919–20), based on relatively complete data reported by Krivosheev et al., *Grif sekretnosti*, 54.

32 S. G. Wheatcroft and R. W. Davies, "Population," in Davies et al. (eds.), *Economic Transformation*, 63.

33 Lenin, *PSS*, vol. XLIII, 69.

By the mid 1920s, however, the Soviet economy had achieved a substantial recovery. It now looked quite different from the years of "war communism." Food distribution was no longer a public monopoly, and small private traders were thriving. Industry produced consumer goods for sale to urban working households and to farmers in the countryside. Public sector workers were demobilized, and private enterprise was allowed back into small-scale production. For most people, in other words, economic life became almost normal, even if the politics of the new regime remained somewhat strange.

Off the streets and behind closed doors, important elements of the command economy remained in place. Large-scale industry, transport and banking were still in state ownership. The business of industry was delegated to managers, but the business of management remained highly political. It is not that profit-seeking was unimportant; in every branch of industry, managers were now pressed to cover costs and raise productivity faster than wages. The Soviet government's peacetime priority was to secure its regime by building military and industrial power. This required funding for industrial projects and re-equipment, and food for growing numbers of industrial and construction workers and soldiers. The government aimed to fund investment by increasing industrial profits, and to feed the workers and the army by getting more food from the countryside. Lower prices of manufactured goods would encourage farmers to sell more food voluntarily, but the same lower prices implied lower profits from industry unless industrial costs could be pushed down by even more. The most important influences on industrial costs were wages and work effort, so managers faced relentless pressure to force employees' efforts up while restraining wages.

But the pressure that managers faced did not come from the market; it came from the ruling party and its "regime of economy."[34] Managers did not face pressure from buyers, because high and rising public investment created excess demand and a sellers' market. They were not under pressure from competitors, because entry into the domestic market was regulated to protect them. They were not pressed by creditors, because government subsidies would cover any losses. The pressure came from policy. If the basic rule of a command economy is that policy takes precedence over market equilibrium, then that rule never went away.

34 E. H. Carr and R. W. Davies, *Foundations of a Planned Economy, 1926–1929*, vol. I (London: Macmillan, 1969), 357–75.

Under the NEP the pressure on the markets for food and labor was considerably relaxed. At the same time the Bolsheviks made major investments in three aspects of state capacity. First was a special agency to coordinate targets for the economy's final products with supplies of intermediate goods: the State Planning Commission (Gosplan), which Lenin authorized just two months before announcing the NEP. Gosplan found precedents in Lenin's utopian electrification plan of 1918, and in the experience of coordinating industry during the civil war years. Although Gosplan would be famous for its long-term projections, most of its early activity consisted of trying to solve detailed matching problems of inter-industry supply.[35] A result was the famous "material balances" methodology for balancing supply and demand for goods on paper.[36]

The regime made a second investment in the supply of competent, noncorrupt officials. The key figure here was Stalin, party general secretary from 1922. The system that he created reserved all important positions in the government and the economy for party members and made their careers. Centralized personnel files identified the competences, records of achievement and failings of the thousands available. Government appointments promoted and rewarded the competent and loyal party members and planted them everywhere. To Stalin, his biographer Stephen Kotkin notes, competence and loyalty were the same thing, because the measure of competence was clear understanding, unswerving acceptance and detailed implementation of party policies.[37]

In a third investment, Stalin's Secretariat also codified the Soviet regime of secrecy.[38] A command economy is protected by secrecy. If the public has the facts and knows who makes the decisions, every command can be appealed and bargained. It is true that any government likes to keep secrets, not only in military and intelligence affairs. Every politician and business executive values confidentiality. But Soviet secrecy was unusually pervasive and outstandingly effective. The extension of state ownership turned a vast swathe of normally confidential business facts into government secrets. The "conspirative norms" that Bolshevik decision-making took from the underground and applied directly to

35 Zaleski, *Planning for Economic Growth*, 40–41.

36 R. W. Davies and Stephen G. Wheatcroft (eds.), *Materials for a Balance of the Soviet National Economy, 1928–1930* (Cambridge: Cambridge University Press, 1985).

37 Stephen Kotkin, *Stalin*, vol. I (London: Penguin, 2014), ch. 10.

38 G. A. Kurenkov, *Ot konspiratsiia k sekretnosti: Zashchita partiino-gosudarstvennoi tainy v RKP(b)-VKP(b) 1918–1941 gg.* (Moscow: AIRO-XXI, 2015).

government completely excluded modern concepts of "freedom of information" and "right to know." And government secrecy, being identified with state security, was managed by the security police.

The system of secrecy put economic decisions beyond public challenge. It complemented Stalin's personnel system because the way a person handled secret communications became a measure of competence and loyalty. Finally, the need to screen managers for access to secret communications embedded the security police in the market for qualified personnel.

The personnel and secrecy regimes that Stalin established in the 1920s had implications far beyond the economy. They became the bedrock of the Soviet political monopoly and, while he lived, of Stalin's personal authority. But they do also have an economic aspect that has been little noted. The lack of a personnel system in the first years of the Bolshevik dictatorship was surely a factor in the disastrous end of Lenin's attempt at a command economy. Stalin's creation of a personnel system in the 1920s helps to explain how the latter succeeded when he tried a command economy again. Throughout its existence the Soviet command economy was plagued by its low information capacity, and this can be traced to the secrecy regime that underpinned it from the 1920s.

Four Crises

During 1928 Stalin, now the central figure in the Bolshevik regime, abandoned the NEP and launched a second attempt at a command economy. Like the first attempt, the second one was violent and destructive, but with a different outcome: once it began there was no breathing space, and after several years a new economic system was in place.

The return to a command economy marked the resolution of four crises: the leadership struggle, a crisis over grain supplies, a war scare, and a crisis over the loyalty of key industrial personnel. The leadership struggle that followed Lenin's last illness was resolved in Stalin's favor. In December 1927 Stalin sealed the victory over his opponents on the left of the party, and turned to settle his account with former allies, now critics, on the right. Around him emerged a close-knit clique that it is convenient to call "Team Stalin."[39] The team included Viacheslav Molotov (prime minister), Klim

39 Stephen G. Wheatcroft, "From Team Stalin to Degenerate Tyranny," in E. A. Rees (ed.), *The Nature of Stalin's Dictatorship: The Politburo, 1924–1953* (Basingstoke: Palgrave Macmillan, 2004), 79–107.

Voroshilov (defense), Sergo Ordzhonikidze (industry), Lazar Kaganovich (railways), Anastas Mikoian (trade) and Valerian Kuibyshev (planning).

The grain crisis followed from the economic tensions already described. Administrative pressure failed to lower costs and raise productivity in industry by enough to pay for increasingly ambitious industrialization plans. As much as the regime tried to hold down the prices of industrial goods, there was little incentive for the peasants to sell food to the state's purchasing agents. The reason was the industrialization plans already mentioned: After industry had supplied the goods required for investment, there was not enough capacity to produce the goods that would satisfy peasant demands. During 1927 the regime began to take back control of the food market, arresting traders and putting them on trial. With 1928, Stalin and other leaders fanned out to the Urals and Siberia to boost food supplies by requisitioning. The return to compulsion brought trials of resisters, linked to accusations of sabotage and betrayal to the foreign enemy. In June 1929 the state reasserted its legal monopoly over the grain trade.

The industrialization plans, and a solution to the grain crisis, were rendered more urgent by external tensions, but the mechanism at work was not the obvious one. The 1920s saw periodic war scares, most notably in 1927. These were mostly just scares, not real threats. For the Bolsheviks the foreign enemy was an article of faith, not a testable hypothesis, so they did not need real threats in order to believe in the likelihood of war.

The war scares mattered otherwise. They served to flash urgent warnings to Stalin and those around him about the mood in the country. The channel for the warnings was security police reports that signaled sharp upticks in mass discontent whenever rumors of war circulated.[40] The Bolshevik leaders did not forget the last war, when hunger at home and military setbacks abroad had sparked a revolution. They determined to insure themselves against any repetition. Here the war scares were useful. Political leaders used them to stigmatize critics as traitors. And military leaders used them to develop war plans with more ambitious requirements for industrial mobilization.

The heightened awareness of risks to the security of the regime thus had implications for both foreign and domestic policy. International capital, Stalin

40 N. S. Simonov, "'Strengthen the Defence of the Land of Soviets': The 1927 'War Alarm' and Its Consequences," *Europe-Asia Studies* 48, 8 (Dec. 1996), 1355–64.

maintained, having failed to overthrow the regime by invasion, was now trying to overthrow it by stealth, by sabotaging its economic plans. "We have internal enemies. We have external enemies," he declared in the spring of 1929. "This must not be forgotten, comrades, for a single moment."[41] The answer to foreign enemies was to rearm, but this would take years. An *interim* solution was to identify the enemies within and eliminate them.[42]

April 1928 saw the first show trial of alleged saboteurs, who were managers and engineers, many of them foreign, from the mining town of Shakhty in the Donbass. Several were executed.[43] There was collateral damage. The Soviet Union's foreign relations were damaged. At home industrial relations were poisoned because managers and engineers in every workplace fell under suspicion and lost authority. Stalin paid the price to deliver an unmistakable message: Any resistance to regime plans aligned resisters with the foreign enemy, placing them outside the community.

The Plan Is the Law

Stalin's command economy emerged in the 1930s through several key processes: the centralized planning of industry and services, the collectivization of agriculture, the detachment of the economy from foreign trade, the spread of forced labor, the embedding of the security police in the economy and rearmament.

Most famous of Stalin's plans was the "first five-year plan for national economic development," compiled by Gosplan and approved at a party conference in April 1929.[44] The Five-Year Plans can be seen from many angles. From the side of final outputs, there was a set of ambitious targets: The first Five-Year Plan envisaged doubling national income and trebling the output of investment goods, while lifting consumption per head by two-thirds. From the side of capacity, there was a utopian vision of the future, captured by hundreds of large-scale industrial and infrastructural projects. From the side of intermediate requirements, the plan was built on a framework of optimistic assumptions for productivity, harvests, foreign trade and international relations. On all matters, successive Five-Year Plans gave less and less detail as the economy was ruled more and more by secrecy. But the point was not in the detail because from yet another side the Five-Year Plan

41 Stalin, *Sochineniia*, vol. XI (Moscow: OGIZ, 1949), 62.

42 Mark Harrison, "The Dictator and Defense," in Mark Harrison (ed.), *Guns and Rubles: The Defense Industry in the Stalinist State* (New Haven: Yale University Press, 2008), 1–30.

43 Kotkin, *Stalin*, vol. I, ch. 14.

44 Zaleski, *Planning for Economic Growth*, 58–147.

was not a technical blueprint; it was an instrument to mobilize the masses against enemies.

From this time Stalin used periods of heightened political and economic mobilization to identify and isolate the persons he could not trust. It was not a metaphor when, in 1931, he called on the party to "thrash" the "so-called wise men, who talk to you about realistic plans and so on."[45] Political leaders, economic officials and ordinary citizens were exposed to arrest and punishment when they cast doubt on ambitious targets or failed to struggle toward them.

While Five-Year Plans were never unimportant, they were invariably pushed off course by unforeseen circumstances and unintended consequences. The economy was managed from day to day by officials in the industrial ministries and the bargains they made. As industry grew and became more complex, Vesenkha was divided into many specialized ministries. Serious disruption was managed above the ministers by Team Stalin, which sometimes pushed back with still more radical measures, and sometimes adapted to what could not be changed.

Radical pushback was expressed in decisions of 1928 to take grain by force when it did not come from the market, of 1930 to mobilize for "the five-year plan in four years," and of 1932 to press for the grain quotas when the harvest failed. At other times there was adaptation. Associated with the Five-Year Plan was a utopian vision of a moneyless economy with physical products rationed to industry and consumers alike, based on collective management, rigid obedience and heroic self-sacrifice. After 1931 this vision retreated in stages. By the mid 1930s Soviet industry had individually responsible managers and profit-and-loss accounts. Employees were paid in money based on results. Money could be spent in government stores where prices were low and shelves were often bare, or at higher scarcity prices in a restricted sphere of private trade.[46]

But adaptation was limited. The limits are shown by the first attempt to reform the command economy, which transpired as early as 1931.[47] On becoming minister for industry, Ordzhonikidze quickly became convinced that industry was too centralized. Instead of relying on supplies planned from

45 R. W. Davies, *The Soviet Economy in Turmoil, 1929–1930* (Basingstoke: Macmillan, 2004), 75.

46 R. W. Davies, "Changing Economic Systems: An Overview," in Davies et al. (eds.), *Economic Transformation*, 18–20.

47 R. W. Davies, *Crisis and Progress in the Soviet Economy, 1931–1933* (Basingstoke: Macmillan, 1996), 11–18, 201–28, 265–70, 345–46.

above, he proposed, industrial managers should go to a wholesale market to buy intermediate goods on their own authority. To give them the right incentives, their costs would be funded by payments from satisfied buyers, not from the state budget.

These proposals resemble the unsuccessful attempt to introduce wholesale trade in industry sponsored by a later prime minister, Aleksei Kosygin, in 1965.[48] In his time Ordzhonikidze was defeated by many adversaries. Below, the prospect of freedom from controls paralyzed industrial suppliers while encouraging buyers to make outrageous demands that could not be met. Above, Stalin and Molotov did not want to give up discretionary control over detailed allocation. This was decisive. In early 1933 the Politburo dismissed Ordzhonikidze's radical advisors, leaving him isolated.

This account has dwelt on times when things went badly, but there were also times when things went well. In the mid 1930s the harvest recovered and food became less scarce. Many of the great projects of the first Five-Year Plan were completed. Production and living standards rose together. "Life has become better, comrades," Stalin declared in 1935. "Life has become more joyful."[49]

The Peasantry

The ability of subsistence farmers to withhold food surpluses from sale was a major obstacle to mobilization of the war economies from 1914 to 1918.[50] In the collectivization of Soviet agriculture, the Bolsheviks removed this obstacle, bringing 120 million subsistence farmers under the command system.

"Collectivization" comprised three distinct innovations.[51] First was a return to forced procurement. This was done outside the law in the Urals and Siberia in 1928, and then legislated for the whole country in 1929. The immediate returns were considerable. In 1928, 1929 and 1930 government agents stripped the countryside of food. As food became scarce, its price rose, a warning signal from the market. The Bolsheviks interpreted rising prices as sabotage, not scarcity. They intensified the food seizures. Hungry peasants

48 Vladimir Kontorovich, "Lessons of the 1965 Soviet Economic Reform," *Soviet Studies* 40, 2 (Apr. 1988), 308–16.

49 Stalin, *Sochineniia*, vol. XIV (Moscow: Pisatel', 1997), 84.

50 Broadberry and Harrison, "Economics of World War I," 18–22.

51 R. W. Davies, *The Socialist Offensive: The Collectivisation of Soviet Agriculture, 1929–1930* (Basingstoke: Macmillan, 1980), and R. W. Davies, *The Soviet Collective Farm, 1929–1930* (Basingstoke: Macmillan, 1980); Davies and Wheatcroft, *Years of Hunger*.

ate animal feedstuffs, and then the animals that could not be fed. The horse population collapsed, disrupting plowing and harvesting. In 1932, poor weather triggered a famine, killing around 6 million. In contrast to the famine of 1921, there was little international awareness and no official acknowledgement.

Another innovation was a campaign to "liquidate the kulaks as a class." The kulaks (more prosperous peasants) were expropriated and excluded from rural society. Under a decree of February 1930, 2 million people were eventually resettled or imprisoned. The survivors suffered persecution and discrimination for a generation. The signal to the people was that the traditional market route of individual self-improvement was closed forever. Only those willing to align their efforts with the command system would survive. Even this was a false promise, as the famine proved.

The third innovation was collectivization itself. The first Five-Year Plan aimed to bring up to one in five peasant households into the collective farm sector. This target, which seemed ambitious beforehand, had two drivers. One was modernization: If the state was to invest in agriculture, it intended to retain control over the uses of new machinery. Another was control over food: The evidence suggested that larger farms based on collective cultivation would yield bigger surpluses for industrialization. As tensions rose during 1928 and 1929, the second motivation overrode the first. The Five-Year Plan target was overtaken as Stalin signaled a more radical target, "wholesale collectivization." Collectivization covered half of all family farms in early 1930 (before a temporary retreat), and 90 percent by 1936.

Collectivization greatly enhanced the state's control of grain and cattle farming and of the uses of the harvest. But it did little or nothing to cover the immediate costs of industrialization, partly because it was destructive, so that privately owned horses had to be replaced by state-funded tractors, and partly because the private food market was not completely eliminated, leaving open a channel for resources to flow back to the farming population.[52]

Most significant for the future was reversal of the traditional ranking of claims on grain and meat. This reversal became Stalin's guarantee against the peasants' withdrawal from the market if war broke out. Before collectivization, the farmer decided what to eat and what could be sold as surplus. Under

52 Michael Ellman, "Did the Agricultural Surplus Provide the Resources for the Increase in Investment in the USSR During the First Five Year Plan?," *Economic Journal* 85 (Dec. 1975), 844–63.

collectivization, the farm first delivered the food that the state required; then the farmers shared whatever was left.

Collectivization also involved experimentation and adjustment. Grain and cattle farming was collectivized, but from 1931 peasants were granted small allotments and the right to sell their own produce on the free market. This gave urban consumers a vital channel to unrationed supplies of eggs, fruit and vegetables.

Enemies

During this time two more elements of the command economy were set in place: the security police and forced labor. The Gulag, the chief administration of labor camps, was established in 1930 to handle the hundreds of thousands of kulaks deported and imprisoned with their families. The numbers in labor camps, mainly occupied in mining and construction, rose from less than 200,000 in 1930 to 1.9 million in 1941.[53] The expansion was not, as some thought, led by demands for more forced labor.[54] The state did not have economic plans that could only be implemented by forced labor, and security chiefs did not lobby for more detainees. Rather, new imprisonments were dictated by waves of political mobilization, and an economic purpose was then found for the prisoners.[55]

Forced industrialization and collectivization also fixed the roles of the security police in the economy. Stalin understood that many employees represented security risks, because they had been disenfranchised, expropriated, had lost family members, or had suffered themselves. The security police had to manage these risks in the workforce. Every state-owned factory and office acquired a "first department," responsible for secrecy and security. The security police vetted personnel and looked into all cases of plan disruption or failure, including accidents and delays, for signs that enemies or disloyal elements were at work and, if so, to remove them.[56] But they did not become co-responsible for management or economic performance; this was the managers' job.

53 V. P. Kozlov et al. (eds.), *Istoriia Stalinskogo Gulaga*, vol. IV (Moscow: ROSSPEN, 2004), 130.

54 S. Swianiewicz, *Forced Labour and Economic Development: An Enquiry into the Experience of Soviet Industrialization* (London: RIIA and Oxford University Press, 1965), 161–62.

55 Paul R. Gregory and Mark Harrison, "Allocation under Dictatorship: Research in Stalin's Archives," *Journal of Economic Literature* 43, 3 (Sep. 2005), 737–38.

56 Hiroaki Kuromiya, *Stalin's Industrial Revolution: Politics and Workers, 1928–1932* (Cambridge: Cambridge University Press, 1988).

A similar mechanism for oversight was implanted in rural society. Ownership of tractors and combines that the state allocated to farming was vested in local equipment depots (MTS). The MTS supplied neighboring farms with machinery services in return for a share of the crop. Every MTS acquired a "political department" of security officials responsible for surveillance and security in the locality.[57]

Driving the Soviet command economy was always the Bolshevik conception of the foreign enemy. The ruling ideology preached that capitalism meant war. The war atmosphere was reinforced by frequent war scares. These served to confirm the existence of enemies against whom loyal subjects were expected to unite, and to expose and isolate slackers and resisters, branding them as fifth columnists.

Some enemies were real. In the 1920s there was active hostility to the Soviet Union in Russia's former western colonies from Poland to Finland. By annexing Manchuria in 1931, Japan emerged as an enemy on the eastern border. In Germany Hitler made no secret of his plan to expand eastward. With each reassessment the Red Army increased its mobilization requirements, which were then translated into ever more ambitious plans for rearmament.

These were not just war preparations. Between 1938 and 1940 the Red Army fought several actual wars. It defended the eastern border against Japan. In the west, it seized territory from Poland, Romania and Finland, and occupied the entire Baltic region. The annexations brought more millions of people under the command system.

In the last years before 1941 large swathes of the civilian economy were converted to war production and the assembly of thousands of airplanes, tanks and guns, and millions of shells. What would later be called the Soviet military–industrial complex, 500 factories and institutes in 1928, grew to 1,000 facilities in 1936 and 2,000 in 1941.[58] In the late 1930s national output was stagnating (Figure 14.1) and the supply-side composition of the economy did not change (Figure 14.2), so war preparations drew resources away from both investment and consumption (Figure 14.3).

57 I. E. zelenin, "Politotdely MTS – prodolzhenie politiki 'chrezvyshaishchiny (1933–1934 gg.)," *Otechestvennaia istoriia* 6 (1992).

58 Keith Dexter and Ivan Rodionov, *The Factories, Research and Design Establishments of the Soviet Defence Industry: A Guide, Version 17* (University of Warwick, Department of Economics, 2016), warwick.ac.uk/vpk/. On other aspects, see Harrison (ed.), *Guns and Rubles*.

Conclusions

The Soviet command economy attempted to realize an idea that first arose in World War I: that the state could monopolize all of an economy's resources for a great public purpose. There were two main phases of institution-building, separated by a "breathing space." The first phase began in 1918 and lasted through 1920; the second began in 1928 and lasted through the 1930s. The second attempt was more persistent than the first, and the results were more durable, apparently because the breathing space that preceded it allowed several years of investment in new organizations and systems.

The Soviet command economy was rooted in the Bolsheviks' beliefs, examples and experiences. Of their beliefs, most powerful was the Bolshevik conception of the enemy. A war economy was required because they expected to be permanently at war. The economy would be subject to continuous attempts at penetration and infiltration and had to be organized for defense against internal and external enemies acting together. This was a general belief, not requiring any particular evidence. It was strengthened when signals of enemy activity could be found. But it was not weakened when evidence was lacking, because lack of evidence promoted the suspicion that the enemy was at work in unseen ways.

What would a war economy mean in practice? In the Bolshevik concept of economic policy, political priorities would suppress the market equilibrium in the interests of the state. This concept had already found practical expression in the war economies that emerged across Europe in 1916 and 1917, in Russia as in Germany and elsewhere. From these examples the Bolsheviks worked out what they wanted: a war economy, more like Germany's than Russia's, but more centralized and more ruthlessly enforced than either. The result was a war economy but, unlike its antecedents, it was built on the expectation of future war rather than on war in the present. Designed to overcome Russia's weaknesses in World War I, it would prove itself in World War II.

Finally, the Bolsheviks brought their own experience from the underground, where they had learned conspiratorial decision-making in secret, unaccountable cabals. Achieving power, expecting their internal and external enemies to conspire against them, they raised secretiveness and conspiracy to the level of government.

Such beliefs, examples, and experiences largely explain the permanent elements of the Soviet command economy. These included the priority of state ownership over private property rights and of state plans over private goals; waves of political mobilization of resources into high-priority activities; centralized rationing of capital goods and intermediate supplies (including imports) based on state priorities; rewards based on the fulfillment of quotas and on political status; personnel selection based on competent loyalty; and decisions made and communicated in secret.

Not all of Stalin's innovations were permanent. Forced labor is one element that was prominent in our period but was de-emphasized later. Likewise, food was typically rationed to urban consumers in emergencies (which, because of Stalin's other policies, were frequent), but not at other times.

The Soviet command economy shows experimentation and learning from mistakes. Lessons were learned from the failures of the Russian economy in 1914–17 and of the Soviet economy in 1918–20. Bribing people or killing them on the spot did not make an effective command system. A command economy needed clear, secure lines of command and control, and competent, loyal administrators to assure those lines. There followed a search for perfection, but the command economy was never perfected. The fate of the reforms that Ordzhonikidze proposed as early as 1931 illuminates the dead end into which most reformist ideas would vanish.

Why, despite its deficiencies, did Stalin want a command economy? It gave him what he wanted. Through industrialization, he acquired a powerful defense industry, a multimillion army, thousands of aircraft and tanks, and nuclear weapons. The collective farms ensured that the defense industry and the army would be fed first when the country was under attack. The economy's centralized institutions for oversight and enforcement guaranteed his authority. Here was the command economy's comparative advantage: the production of economic and military power.

Bibliographical Essay

One of the most remarkable projects in the history of any country is the *History of Soviet Russia* from 1917 to 1929 in nine volumes (London: Macmillan, 1950–69) begun by E. H. Carr in the 1940s and continued by R. W. Davies in his *Industrialization of Soviet Russia* from 1929 to 1936 in fourteen volumes (Basingstoke: Macmillan, 1980–2014); a fifteenth volume up to 1940 is in preparation. Even without access to Soviet archives, Carr's work was so diligent and precise that it remains an essential work of reference. Carr took on Davies as a collaborator for the last volumes completed before his death. In his own work Davies benefited eventually from access to Soviet archives and also from collaboration with Stephen Wheatcroft and Oleg Khlevniuk.

The collapse of the Soviet state in 1991 opened up many former Soviet archives for independent historical investigation. Surveys of the resulting progress in our understanding of the Soviet economic system include Paul R. Gregory and Mark Harrison, "Allocation under Dictatorship: Research in Stalin's Archives," *Journal of Economic Literature* 43, 3 (2005), 721–61; Michael Ellman, "The Political Economy of Stalinism in the Light of the Archival Revolution," *Journal of Institutional Economics* 4, 1 (2008), 99–125; and Andrei Markevich, "Economics and the Establishment of Stalinism," *Kritika* 15, 1 (2014), 125–32.

Economists have tended to describe the Soviet economy as a developmental state that provided civilian public goods and pursued civilian economic growth, although inefficiently. This tradition is exemplified by M. H. Dobb, *Soviet Economic Development since 1917* (London: Routledge & Kegan Paul, 1948); Alexander Gerschenkron, *Economic Backwardness in Historical Perspective: A Book of Essays* (Cambridge, MA: Belknap Press, 1962); and, more recently, Robert C. Allen, *Farm to Factory: A Reinterpretation of the Soviet Industrial Revolution* (Princeton: Princeton University Press, 2003).

In contrast to this approach, research in former Soviet archives has given greater salience to power and security as factors in Soviet economic institutions and policies. Paul R. Gregory, *The Political Economy of Stalinism: Evidence from the Soviet Secret Archives* (Cambridge: Cambridge University Press, 2004), has analyzed Stalin's economic decisions in light of his quest for internal security. The needs of external security are emphasized by Lennart Samuelson, *Plans for Stalin's War Machine: Tukhachevskii and Military-Economic Planning, 1925–1941* (Basingstoke: Macmillan, 2000); David R. Stone, *Hammer and Rifle: The Militarization of the Soviet Union, 1926–1933* (Lawrence: University Press of Kansas, 2000); John Barber and Mark Harrison (eds.), *The Soviet Defence-Industry Complex from Stalin to Khrushchev* (Basingstoke: Macmillan, 2000); and Mark Harrison (ed.), *Guns and Rubles: The Defense Industry in the Stalinist State* (New Haven: Yale University Press, 2008).

The archival revolution is still recent, but Vladimir Kontorovich and Alexander Wein, "What Did the Soviet Rulers Maximise?," *Europe-Asia Studies* 61, 9 (2009), 1579–601, maintain that Western economists should have reached the same conclusions long before, based on the published goals of Soviet leaders and the outcomes of their policies.

Three works commend themselves to entry-level readers. The final edition of Alec Nove's *Economic History of the USSR, 1917–1991* (Harmondsworth: Penguin, 1992) remains a vivid and compelling narrative of the Soviet economy from beginning to end. A thematic textbook on the Soviet economy up to 1945 is R. W. Davies, Mark Harrison and Stephen G. Wheatcroft (eds.), *The Economic Transformation of the Soviet Union, 1913–1945* (Cambridge: Cambridge University Press, 1994). Although not limited to the Soviet economy or to our period, the third edition of Michael Ellman's textbook on *Socialist Planning* (Cambridge: Cambridge University Press, 2014) is fully revised in the light of the Soviet archives and pays more attention to military affairs.

15

The Soviet State and Workers

DONALD FILTZER

The hierarchical class structure of the modern Soviet Union emerged out of the twin processes of forced collectivization and industrialization during the first three Stalinist Five-Year Plans (1928–41). Industrialization was a time of rapid social mobility. Millions of peasants moved into the working class, and hundreds of thousands of both workers and peasants left the ranks of the toilers to take up posts as low-level managers or party officials, from which many advanced still further up the social ladder of power and privilege. Hundreds of thousands more enrolled in the new technical institutes that trained the new generation of engineers, scientists, economists, technicians and industrial managers demanded by industrialization. Irrespective of the route they followed, what we see is that people of proletarian or peasant origin left their class and joined the ranks of the intelligentsia and party elite. Once there, they adopted a different social role. They managed the society and extracted their privileges from the social product created by that overwhelming mass of the population at the base of the social pyramid who remained peasants and workers. Although the decades after the 1930s still allowed for relatively high levels of social mobility within the pyramid, the shape of the pyramid did not change. By the late 1960s and 1970s the Soviet Union had a clearly discernible inherited class structure: The social group into which you were born was the social group in which you very likely would remain.[1]

Industrialization and collectivization had evolved as quite separate policies. In fact, the original variants of the first Five-Year Plan did not foresee, much less incorporate, collectivization as part of their assumptions or calculations. As the policies unfolded, however, they became inextricably linked. In

1 Donald Filtzer, "Privilege and Inequality in Communist Society," in Stephen A. Smith (ed.), *The Oxford Handbook of the History of Communism* (Oxford: Oxford University Press, 2014), 505–21, here 507–14.

the minds of Stalin and those in the leadership in favor of forcing the pace of industrialization, collectivization would satisfy a number of aims. It would rationalize agricultural production, and thus provide a surplus of food for export and to feed the growing number of workers in the towns, whose standard of living would therefore rise. It would also release labor power from the countryside to work in construction and industry. When peasant resistance led to widespread destruction of crops, seed corn and livestock these plans collapsed. The agricultural surplus available to finance industrialization disappeared (although this did not prevent the government from continuing to sell grain abroad in order to buy foreign machinery), and collectivization became a net drain on industrial investment. This left a drastic cut in consumption and an equally sharp increase in the intensity of labor as the main internal resources of accumulation. Living standards fell and conditions inside the factories and on building sites dramatically worsened.

Collectivization did, however, disgorge from the countryside millions of peasants who supplied new labor power for construction, industry, mining and transport. This new workforce had to be taught skills, but it also had to be tamed, disciplined and socialized into the rhythms and routines of industrial production within the specific contours of the Stalinist authoritarian system. This proved to be a tumultuous process. Resentment against collectivization and the appalling working and living conditions that workers old and new encountered forced workers to develop a wide range of mechanisms through which they could attenuate these hardships: moving frequently from job to job in search of better conditions; going absent from work; refusing to obey instructions; and most critical of all, asserting partial control over the pace and organization of work itself, thereby partly nullifying the regime's ongoing drive to increase the intensity of labor. The early years of industrialization also saw a large number of strikes and mass protests. The regime used force to quell the strikes and protests, but the other symptoms of recalcitrance it tried to bring under control largely through economic sanctions: up until the end of rationing in January 1935, by tying good behavior and work performance to the receipt of rations and housing, and after that point by offering monetary rewards and privileges to those who could break production records. At the end of the 1930s, as accelerated military spending placed renewed downward pressure on the standard of living, labor turnover and absenteeism again began to rise. After a vain attempt to curb absenteeism by reasserting the economic sanctions of the early 1930s, in

June 1940 the regime made job-changing and absenteeism criminal offenses. These measures granted the regime a partial victory during the war and early postwar years, but once Stalin died workers again began to usurp considerable control over the labor process. This was to be a major source of instability in the Soviet economy right up until its disintegration during *perestroika*.

Forging a New Workforce

The breakneck speed and voluntaristic targets of the industrialization drive led to the mass influx of a totally new wave of workers drawn overwhelmingly from sections of the population, primarily the peasantry, that had little or no prior experience of industrial life. The sheer scale of this transformation can be seen in Table 15.1.

During the eight years 1928–36, the number of industrial workers more than doubled. It increased by over one-third during the calendar year of 1930 alone. The increase in the number of construction workers was proportionally even larger: from around 630,000 in 1928 to just under 2.5 million in 1932, after which the number contracted to 1,740,000 in mid 1935, as many of the new factories begun during the first Five-Year Plan came to completion and the Gulag system of labor camps began to take over some of the functions of

Table 15.1 *Workers in Large-Scale Industry, 1928–1936*

Year	Number of workers	Workers as % of 1928	Women workers	Women as % of 1928	Women as % of all workers
1928	2,531,900	100.0	725,900	100.0	28.7
1929	2,788,700	110.1	804,000	110.8	28.8
1930	3,116,200	123.1	885,000	121.9	28.4
1931	4,256,400	168.1	1,271,500	175.2	29.9
1932	5,271,300	208.2	1,735,400	239.1	32.9
1933	5,319,700	210.1	1,826,200	251.6	34.3
1934	5,215,000	206.0	1,918,400	264.3	36.8
1935	5,658,300	223.5	2,321,900	319.9	41.0
1936	6,173,000	243.8			

Figures are for 1 January of each year, except 1935, which are for 1 July.
Source: *Trud v SSSR. Statischeskii sbornik* [Labor in the USSR: Statistical Handbook] (Moscow, 1936), 91.

the civilian construction industry.[2] This lower figure still represented a near tripling of the construction workforce in just seven years.

Until 1929 and 1930, many of these new workers had come from the urban unemployed; others were nonworking dependants of urban families enticed into employment by the collapse of the standard of living and the need for a second or even third wage in order to survive. By 1930, however, these sources were exhausted. From then on the bulk of the new workers came from the countryside: peasants who either fled, or were recruited from, the newly organized collective farms. The new workers were generally young: By 1933 over 41 percent of all industrial workers were under the age of 22.[3] They were also increasingly female. Between 1932 and 1935 women accounted for virtually the entire increase in the industrial workforce; by 1939 women constituted 43.9 percent of industrial workers.[4]

The mass entry of women into industry, and to a lesser extent into mining and construction, had profound immediate and long-term consequences. In the short term, they facilitated the process of accumulation through the hyperexploitation of industrial labor power. The voracious demand for new workers alongside the collapse in real wages (see below) created both opportunities and compulsion for families to supplement the main (usually male) wage with the labor of wives and teenage dependants. While these extra incomes partially offset the fall in real wages, this also allowed the regime, in the words of one historian, to "realize the output of two workers for the price of one," thus substantially augmenting the size of the surplus available for investment.[5]

In the longer term, women entered industries where women previously had had only a minor presence, most notably coalmining, machine-building and metalworking, and iron and steel. Here they made up between 25 and 30 percent of all workers. Yet within these industries they occupied the least skilled and lowest-paid jobs.[6] At the same time, textiles, garments and other

2 *Trud v SSSR. Statischeskii sbornik* (Moscow, 1936), 245. The figure for 1928 is interpolated from the total of workers and clerical employees given in the handbook's figure 13.

3 A. G. Rashin, "Dinamika promyshlennykh kadrov SSSR za 1917–1958 gg.," in *Izmeneniya v chislennosti i sostave sovetskogo rabochego klassa* (Moscow: Izdatel'stvo Akademii Nauk SSSR, 1961), 7–73, here 18. The figure includes apprentices.

4 Ibid., 59.

5 Wendy Z. Goldman, *Women at the Gates: Gender and Industry in Stalin's Russia* (Cambridge: Cambridge University Press, 2002), 105.

6 Percentages are from Donald Filtzer, *Soviet Workers and De-Stalinization: The Consolidation of the Modern System of Soviet Production Relations, 1953–1964* (Cambridge: Cambridge University Press, 1992), 64. For marginalization into low-skilled work, see Goldman, *Women at the Gates*, 194–202.

branches of light industry where women had always been the majority of workers, became even more "feminized," as skilled men left to take higher-paying jobs, often unskilled, in heavy industry. There was thus established a pattern that was to characterize Soviet industry for the remainder of the USSR's existence. Women were segregated horizontally into specific, low-paid industries; within industry as a whole they were segregated vertically into low-skilled, low-paid and usually heavy manual work with limited prospects for promotion.[7]

Working and Living Conditions and Workers' Responses

The rapid increase in the number of workers was largely unplanned. The original Five-Year Plan had anticipated that the increased number of employees (workers as well as clerical staff) in industry and construction would have barely soaked up the pool of urban unemployed by 1933. By 1930, however, the annual plans had been pushed up so high that industry was already suffering from severe labor shortages.[8] What type of environment did these workers encounter once they entered the towns? We focus here on three aspects: working conditions, food supply and housing.

Let us look first at working conditions. Lacking adequate resources to fulfill the Five-Year Plan's impossibly ambitious targets, the regime tried to compensate through a policy of unrelenting speed-up. At the heart of this policy was the hyperindividualization of labor incentives through the mass application of piece rates, even in lines of work – for example, equipment repair – where piece rates were not just ineffective but counterproductive. Workers were typically assigned what the Soviets called "norms," that is, hourly or daily targets for the number of items to be produced. Each item had a job price, so that a day's earnings would be determined by the number of pieces multiplied by the job price. By setting the targets high and the job prices low, workers were placed under enormous strain just to eke out a subsistence wage. The policy was enforced through the system of shock work (*udarnichestvo*). Shock workers (*udarniki*) were workers – almost all of them young –who were encouraged to exert themselves to the maximum in order

7 Filtzer, *Soviet Workers and De-Stalinization*, ch. 7.

8 Eugène Zaleski, *Planning for Economic Growth in the Soviet Union, 1918–1932* (Chapel Hill: University of North Carolina Press, 1972), 317, 342–43. R. W. Davies, "The End of Mass Unemployment in the USSR," in David Lane (ed.), *Labour and Employment in the USSR* (Brighton: Wheatsheaf, 1985), 19–35, here 29–31.

to exceed their norms by very large amounts. For this they received not just extra pay, but more important in a situation of universal shortages, privileged allocations of food, housing, footwear, clothing, theater tickets, rest home passes and places for their children in local kindergartens.[9] On their own these incentives were not sufficient to encourage ordinary workers to emulate shock workers' records, not the least because outside Moscow and Leningrad the "privileges" shock workers received were often meager or nonexistent.[10] What gave the policy its bite was the widespread practice by managers of taking shock workers' production records and then making them the new targets for everyone. Norms were raised and piece rates cut, so that workers now had to work considerably harder simply to maintain their previous earnings.

The effects of this policy were extraordinarily damaging. First, the system provoked considerable opposition among rank-and-file workers, opposition that occasionally spilled over into physical assaults, some fatal, on shock workers and line managers. In most instances these protests were merely verbal, voiced at factory meetings, and usually couched in terms of contrasting the state's industrialization policies with the official propaganda that in a proletarian state, workers should be masters of production, not treated as slaves. Second, speed-up and the drive to set records caused inordinate damage to machinery, waste of materials and energy, and a sharp deterioration in product quality, as workers cut corners and pushed their equipment to the maximum in order to meet their targets. The deterioration of quality proved a major drain on economic output. Defective items had to be remedied or totally remade; generally, however, shortages of parts and components compelled managers to use defective products anyway, so that, in the words of one observer, "whole factories are being erected out of defective construction materials and equipped with machines made from defective metal."[11] Third, of equal or even greater importance in the long term was the systemic disruption that shock work, and the push for plan overfulfillment in general, caused. Whether in a coalmine, a building site, or a factory, production required coordination

9 *Trud* (7 Apr. 1931); *Voprosy truda* 2 (1931), 77 (I. Troitskii); *Sotsialisticheskii vestnik* (25 Feb. 1934). *Sotsialisticheskii vestnik* was a Menshevik émigré newspaper originally published in Berlin, and after Hitler came to power, in Paris.

10 Elena Osokina, *Our Daily Bread: Socialist Distribution and the Art of Survival in Stalin's Russia, 1927–1941* (Armonk, NY: M. E. Sharpe, 2001), 88; *Trud*, 10 Aug. 1931, 7 Sep. 1931, 5 Jan. 1932, 5 July 1932; *Rabochii Rostov* (9 May 1932); A. Kromskii, *Na bor'bu s tekuchest'iu i progulami* (Samara, Russia, 1933), 38.

11 Khristian Rakovsky, "The Five-Year Plan in Crisis," *Critique* 13 (1981), 13–53, here 24.

between different interdependent links in the production process. If shock workers fulfilled their targets by 150 percent and the other interlinked stages in production were fulfilled by only 100 percent, then the excess production of the shock workers was of little practical use. The same was true on a more macro scale. If one section of a factory overfulfilled its plan by vast amounts and other sections linked with it did not, here, too, the excess output of the record-breaking section merely used up raw materials, energy, machinery and tools to little purpose. Coordination and calculation broke down. This became a systemic feature of the Soviet system until the country's collapse in 1991.

In addition to the physical strain, workers were also hungry. In theory, collectivization should have led to an improvement in living standards by increasing the supply of food and rationalizing distribution through the state and cooperative trade networks. The opposite took place, as food production plummeted, while the exodus to the towns meant that by the time of the 1932–33 famine the number of urban residents needing to purchase food had grown by roughly 50 percent.[12] In fact, serious food shortages had started to appear even before collectivization, following the poor harvests of 1927 and 1928, to which those peasants with a marketable surplus had responded by hoarding grain. In the spring of 1928 the regime introduced bread rationing in certain towns in Ukraine and southern Russia, and more extensive rationing in Leningrad and Moscow in 1929. By early 1930 rationing had been extended to the whole of the country, giving workers basic entitlements to bread (the main staple of the diet), sugar, kerosene (needed for cooking and in some homes also for heating), soap, herrings, pasta products, butter, tea, meat, eggs, textiles and other essential consumer items.[13] But entitlement to rations did not mean that workers could actually obtain them, for all items, from bread to cotton cloth, were in desperately short supply. Throughout the country workers could not find meat, fish, milk or other sources of protein, either for themselves or for their children. Bread shops had long queues, and workers complained that the bread would run out before they had a chance to buy any. Workers were driven to private trade, where prices skyrocketed: By 1932 prices on private agricultural produce were eight times what they had been in 1928, and twelve times their level in 1926. The result was a fall in real wages between 1928 and

12 R. W. Davies, *Crisis and Progress in the Soviet Economy, 1931–1933* (Basingstoke: Macmillan, 1996), 538. The increase is from the census of 1926 to January 1934, after the famine had abated.

13 Solomon Schwarz, *Labor in the Soviet Union* (New York: Praeger, 1952), 136.

1932 of around 50 percent.[14] In fact, the fall was worse than this. Factories routinely paid wages with great delays – the arrears could be both lengthy and substantial, leaving workers without money to buy food. Money wages were further curtailed as workers were placed under constant pressure to make substantial contributions to state loans.[15] The situation reached crisis point during the 1932–33 famine. Although the vast majority of fatalities were among people living in the countryside, urban workers suffered greatly, and eye-witnesses reported seeing significant numbers of corpses on city streets. In an attempt to bring consumption into line with vastly reduced food supplies, the government cut urban rations in 1933. In Samara (later renamed Kuibyshev), which was in the process of becoming a large industrial center in the middle Volga region, workers in nonpriority enterprises had their bread ration cut to just 400 grams a day – enough to provide just 700 calories. Any remaining family members had to share 200 grams between them. Clerical workers were also reduced to just 200 grams of bread a day. Many urban residents, including workers, were purged from the ration lists altogether.[16]

Equally pressing was the acute shortage of housing. The Soviet Union's urban housing stock was already under pressure even before the Five-Year Plans, with factories claiming to be able to provide accommodation for barely 10–25 percent of their workers. It was common for workers to share a bunk in a dormitory, with one worker coming in to sleep as the former occupant was leaving for the next shift.[17] Once the industrialization drive was under way, the towns, and even more so the large construction projects, proved totally unable to cope with the influx of large numbers of new workers. Enterprises faced multiple problems. The first was the simple lack of space, as new housing construction lagged way behind the rise in demand for living space. From Leningrad to the Urals, factories reported that large contingents of workers were either sleeping in the factory or bedding down at the railway station. *Trud*, the trade union newspaper, warned in 1931 that some 4,500 workers at the Stalingrad tractor factory might have nowhere to live during the coming winter.[18] The second problem was the lack of amenities. Housing

14 Ibid., 137–39; Naum Jasny, *The Soviet 1956 Statistical Handbook: A Commentary* (East Lansing: Michigan State University Press, 1957), 41.

15 Donald Filtzer, *Soviet Workers and Stalinist Industrialization: The Formation of Modern Soviet Production Relations, 1928–1941* (London: Pluto, 1986), 70–71, 91. Davies, *Crisis and Progress*, 236–37.

16 Davies, *Crisis and Progress*, 368–70.

17 *Puti industrializatsii* 13–14 (1929), 40 (S. Kheinman).

18 Filtzer, *Soviet Workers and Stalinist Industrialization*, 95; Goldman, *Women at the Gates*, 236–40, here 238.

was not simply housing in the sense that we think of it today. Almost no Soviet cities had centralized sewerage systems. In larger towns people used courtyard outhouses, which were emptied of human excrement only irregularly. Barracks and dormitories might have outhouses, but it was common for people to relieve themselves on whatever spare ground they could find. Almost no residential buildings had indoor running water. People took water in buckets and pails from street pumps, only some of which drew water from uncontaminated sources. To wash – a major public health issue in a society where lice infestation and typhus were serious endemic hazards – most people had to rely on public bathhouses, which could nowhere nearly meet demand. The same was true of laundry facilities, which were almost nonexistent. Only the very luckiest workers would see their sheets and bedding laundered more frequently than once every two or three months. Finally, there was the problem of the quality of new housing construction, which was simply deplorable. Aside from the lack of essential facilities, barracks and dormitories were cold, poorly lit, with bare, unplastered walls. Nor were the more permanent residential buildings much better: At the Cheliabinsk tractor factory, apartment buildings put up in 1931 were already in need of major repairs one year later.[19]

This confluence of factors – the mass influx of peasant workers, the policy of sweated labor in the factories, the dire food shortages and the acute shortage of accommodation fit for human habitation – made for an explosive situation. One response was strikes and mass protests. These were always spontaneous demonstrations of anger over a range of related issues: delays in paying wages, cuts in wage rates, norm rises, and the dire shortages of food and essentials such as salt, matches and kerosene. The scope of strike activity extended from Moscow and Leningrad, to the Donbass coalfields, Kharkiv and Odessa in Ukraine, to Gor'kii (Nizhnii Novgorod) in Central Russia, and further east into the Urals' centers of heavy industry. Strike activity persisted from 1929 until at least 1934.[20] Usually the strikes were confined to a single factory or section of a factory, but this was not always the case. The most important outbreak of mass unrest occurred in the Ivanovo industrial region – the heart of the Soviet Union's textile industry – in April 1932. This was a pivotal period. Although still some months away from the catastrophic famine of winter 1932–33, the food situation was already desperate; protests over food shortages erupted in Leningrad, Nizhnii Novgorod (soon to be renamed Gor'kii), the Urals, Belorussia and the Donbass, where children led

19 *Trud*, 18 Aug. 1932. 20 Filtzer, *Soviet Workers and Stalinist Industrialization*, 81–87.

demonstrations demanding bread. The Ivanovo region was particularly hard hit because textiles, as a low-priority industry, received lower rations than heavy industry. A succession of wage cuts had already made it impossible for workers to buy supplemental food on the open market, and when, on 1 April 1932, 400,000 workers saw their bread rations reduced further to just 250–350 grams a day (that is, enough to provide between 450 and 650 calories, or barely a third to a half of what an adult needs to fend off starvation), workers struck.[21] In Teykovo and Vichuga workers virtually took over the towns for several days and held the authorities at bay. Eventually the authorities regained the upper hand, suppressed the strikes and arrested the strike leaders.[22]

As dramatic as strikes and mass protests may have been, the vast majority of workers were left to seek individual solutions to the hardships of industrialization. The most prominent of these was high labor turnover. The first Five-Year Plan had created strong push and pull factors for frequent job-changing. The push factors were the collapse of the standard of living, the housing crisis and the relentless intensification of labor. The pull factor was the labor shortage, which forced industrial managers to compete with one another to attract scarce workers through (usually false) promises of better housing, wages and rations. The competition for workers was so fierce that it became common practice for managers to poach workers from neighboring factories.

Although labor turnover had been high during the NEP, during the first Five-Year Plan it increased by 70 percent for industry as a whole, and more than doubled in key sectors such as coalmining, iron and steel, machine-building, textiles, petroleum and chemicals. This is shown in Table 15.2. The table gives two measures of turnover. The first is the percentage of an industry's average annual number of workers that quit their jobs during a calendar year. The second translates this into the number of months the average worker remained at her or his job before quitting.

For most of the industries listed here the worst year was 1930. In that year a coalminer stayed on the job a mere four months; a worker in iron and steel less than eight months; and workers in machine-building ten months. For managers this was a real crisis. It made workforce planning difficult, if not impossible, and accentuated the disruptions to production caused by acute

21 Davies, *Crisis and Progress*, 188.

22 Jeffrey J. Rossman, *Worker Resistance Under Stalin: Class and Revolution on the Shop Floor* (Cambridge, MA: Harvard University Press, 2005).

Table 15.2 *Turnover in Major Branches of Soviet Industry, 1924–1936*

For each industry the first column expresses turnover as the percentage of the average workforce leaving their jobs during the calendar year. The second column expresses turnover as the number of months the average worker stayed on the job before leaving.

	All industry		Coalmining		Petroleum		Chemicals		Iron and steel		Machine-building and metalworking		Cotton textiles	
Year	%	months	%	months	%	months	%	months	%	months	%	months	%	months
1924	98.5	12.2	139.3	8.6	–	–	74.6	16.1	89.7	13.4	63.3	19.0	47.5	25.3
1925	89.2	13.5	124.6	9.6	51.2	23.4	73.5	16.3	73.5	16.3	60.4	19.9	35.9	33.4
1926	101.2	11.9	161.4	7.4	47.4	25.3	103.2	11.6	75.9	15.8	61.5	19.5	30.6	39.2
1927	103.3	11.6	156.3	7.7	41.6	28.8	100.9	11.9	90.9	13.2	54.4	22.1	32.0	37.5
1928	92.4	13.0	132.0	9.1	42.0	28.6	107.3	11.2	69.6	17.2	62.4	19.2	31.2	38.5
1929	115.2	10.4	192.0	6.3	44.4	27.0	110.7	10.8	90.0	13.3	78.0	15.4	37.2	32.3
1930	152.4	7.9	295.2	4.1	90.0	13.3	159.0	7.5	145.2	8.3	120.0	10.0	62.4	19.2
1931	136.8	8.8	205.2	5.8	87.6	13.7	126.2	9.5	127.2	9.4	100.8	11.9	68.4	17.5
1932	135.3	8.9	187.9	6.4	112.4	10.7	131.8	9.1	117.1	10.2	103.2	11.6	72.2	16.6
1933	122.4	9.8	120.7	9.9	102.3	11.7	114.4	10.5	97.9	12.3	96.0	12.5	61.2	19.6
1934	96.7	12.4	95.4	12.6	92.1	13.0	84.2	14.3	69.9	17.2	74.4	16.1	43.1	27.8
1935	86.1	13.9	99.1	12.1	92.8	12.9	78.5	15.3	71.0	16.9	64.9	18.5	45.9	26.1
1936	87.5	13.7	112.7	10.6	95.5	12.6	75.1	16.0	70.6	17.0	67.9	17.7	–	–

Sources: 1924–35: *Trud v SSSR. Statischeskii sbornik* (Moscow, 1936), 95–96, 109–10, 116–17, 131, 145, 155, 187–88; 1936: Ya. Kats, "Tekuchest' rabochei sily v krupnoi promyshlennosti," *Plan* 9 (1937), 21–22.

shortages of fuel, raw materials, parts and equipment. It also led to a degradation of the workforce's skills with knock-on effects on discipline and quality. No sooner had a factory finished training a worker than the worker upped and left. For workers, however, the labor shortage gave them at least some limited ability to improve their situation by finding a locality or an enterprise where conditions were less oppressive.

That workers were able to exploit their own scarcity shows up not just in labor turnover, but in their frequent violations of internal discipline. The most often cited statistic in this regard is absenteeism. During the first Five-Year Plan the average number of days per year that workers were absent without leave rose from 4.09 in 1929 to 5.96 in 1931 and 1932; in coalmining during both 1930 and 1931, the average mineworker was truant the equivalent of two working weeks. To a significant extent absenteeism was part of a cat-and-mouse game between workers and managers: Labor laws stipulated that a worker could be fired from a job only for a third offense of truancy; if managers refused to give workers their release, they would go AWOL for three days to try to force managers to dismiss them.[23] On 15 November 1932 the regime imposed harsh penalties on absenteeism: A single case of truancy would lead to immediate dismissal and loss of ration cards and enterprise housing. At a time of impending famine these were harsh penalties indeed. Absenteeism rates plummeted, although the real fall was exaggerated by the fact that managers, desperate not to lose scarce workers and in many cases unwilling to cast people out to starve, often surreptitiously (and sometimes openly) refused to apply the new law.[24]

The importance of job-changing, absenteeism and general insubordination lay not just in the difficulties they created for the enterprise and for the economy as a whole, but in the fact that these were essentially individualized responses by individual workers who had no collective means to influence their situation. The Stalinist state, by making collective action impossible, forced workers to find other ways to counter the hardships they faced. High turnover and absenteeism were one manifestation of this, but a more important and longlasting one was the attitude that this fostered among workers within the workplace itself, namely in the way they used their work time.

23 Z. Mordukhovich, *Na bor'bu s tekuchest'iu rabochei sily* (Moscow and Leningrad: Gos. sots.-ėkon. izd-vo, 1931), 39.

24 For the details of the law, see Filtzer, *Soviet Workers and Stalinist Industrialization*, 111–12. On its circumvention, see ibid., 112–15, and Goldman, *Women at the Gates*, 255–60.

The Labor Process, Norm-Setting and Effort Bargaining

The turmoil of the initial period of industrialization eventually subsided. Unfinished factories finally came on line, living standards gradually improved after the 1932–33 famine, and for a brief period in the mid 1930s (1934–36) the leadership attempted to rebalance investment in favor of consumption, infrastructure and health care.[25] The decline in labor turnover reflected this stabilization. It is precisely here that we see a major shift in the concerns of the economic and labor literature, away from job-changing and overt manifestations of poor discipline toward problems within the work regime itself. Focus was on two closely related issues: the use of work time and norm-setting.

During the NEP skilled workers in both machine-building and textiles had enjoyed a large amount of control over the work process. They determined the organization and sequence of jobs and, together with work teams that they themselves hired (in textiles, mainly their families and relatives), carried out all operations in the production process, including the maintenance and modification of machinery. By relying on such customary practices these workers were largely able to defend themselves against attempts to intensify the labor process during the latter part of the NEP.[26] This system of work organization was clearly incompatible with the demands of the Stalinist industrialization drive, for three basic reasons. First, economists feared, with considerable justification, that the millions of inexperienced peasants taking up jobs in industry would find it difficult to master complex, integrated tasks. Second, the old system gave workers too much control over the conceptualization and organization of tasks, control which it was necessary to wrest away from operatives and place in the hands of a hierarchical managerial structure. Third, the experience of the NEP had shown that this system had made it too easy for workers to resist the wholesale application of piece rates and the radical individualization of wages and incentives. To this end industrialization saw work processes become highly specialized, with

25 R. W. Davies, with Oleg V. Khlevnyuk and Stephen G. Wheatcroft, *The Industrialisation of Soviet Russia*, vol. VI, *The Years of Progress: The Soviet Economy, 1934–1936* (Basingstoke: Palgrave Macmillan, 2014).

26 A. Rabinovich, *Problema proizvoditel'nosti truda* (Moscow: Ekonomicheskaia zhizn, 1925), 105–44; Walter Süss, *Der Betrieb in der UdSSR. Stellung, Organisation und Management 1917–1932* (Frankfurt am Main: Peter Lang, 1981), 189; B. Marsheva, A. Isaev, and E. Shteinbakh, *Zhenskii trud v mashinostroenii* (Moscow, 1933), 41–42; Chris Ward, *Russia's Cotton Workers and the New Economic Policy: Shop-Floor Culture and State Policy 1921–1929* (Cambridge: Cambridge University Press, 1990), ch. 4.

operations broken down into innumerable small jobs, with each worker carrying out just one specific operation. The wholesale application of piece work was central to this system, as it encouraged each worker to boost individual performance, although as already noted, this came at considerable cost. By individualizing incentives workers were pushed to overshoot their targets, with scant regard either for coordination between the different phases of an item's manufacture or for the quality of finished output. The same logic applied to the different sections and shops within the factory: Shop managers, driven to overfulfill their shop plans, concentrated on parts or products that were easiest to produce, ignoring more costly or complex items that were nevertheless essential to final assembly. The Russians even had a specific name for this phenomenon: *nekomplektnost'*, which can be translated variably as "incomplete batching" or "incomplete production." Of course one factory's partially assembled machine or defective component became a cause of stoppages in the factory that acquired them.

The irregular rhythms of Soviet production provided workers countless opportunities to break up the working day and seize large amounts of time for themselves. Workers frequently had to interrupt a job to hunt down missing parts or tools. They also lost inordinate amounts of time waiting for equipment to be repaired, for a foreman to come and give advice, or for a tool-setter to reset or adjust a lathe or a loom. Factory dining rooms almost everywhere had only a fraction of the seating capacity, tableware, or cutlery needed to cope with the actual number of workers. So workers had little choice but to sneak off early to beat the queues and almost invariably returned late. The same was true at the close of shifts. Workers might be housed far away from where they worked, and because public transport was not always coordinated with factory shift times workers would knock off early to catch the last bus or tram home. The fact that factories compensated for the general shortage of food and consumer goods in state stores by providing these things to their own workers also led to large losses of work time. Commenting on Moscow's Elektrozavod in 1937, the industrial newspaper noted:

> Throughout the day an unending flow of people spills along the factory corridors, through the shops, along the stairwells. This is the best index of both the level of discipline and the organization of production. In the corridor of Elektrozavod they trade books and sell ice cream. Sometimes it's a factory, sometimes it's a department store.[27]

27 *Za industrializatsiiu*, 2 Aug. 1937 (A. Khavin).

All of these would appear as "objective" factors that compelled workers to violate the normal shift regime, but they equally gave workers pretexts to steal time for themselves. Time and motion studies found that workers regularly spent long periods of time dawdling at the start of a shift, skiving off for a smoke, wandering around shops talking to workmates, or on night shifts abandoning their machines to catch a bit of extra sleep.[28]

Not all of these disruptions eased the pressure on workers. Long stoppages due to breakdowns or the nonarrival of supplies had to be made up through massive overtime at the end of the month or end of the quarter, what the Soviets called "storming." Stoppages could also eat into earnings, a point that was an almost permanent bone of contention between workers and line managers throughout the Soviet period. Yet there is no question that substantial amounts of production were lost because workers were able to exploit the situation to reduce the intensity of labor.

The use of work time therefore became an area of direct contestation between workers and management, and more importantly, between workers and the regime. The area where this conflict was most intense was norm-setting. For it was through the ongoing campaigns to push up norms that the state sought to regain control over the work regime.

The apex of this policy was the Stakhanov campaign of 1935–37. The campaign was named after the Donbass miner, Alexei Stakhanov, who, on the night shift of 30–31 August 1935, mined a "record" 102 tons of coal in a single shift. Stakhanov's achievement, which was not in fact unique or without precedent, had been carefully prepared, so that carters, roofers and other auxiliary workers were on hand to prepare the coalface and load and take away the coal that he hewed, thus freeing Stakhanov himself to concentrate solely on coal-cutting. The core idea was certainly logical: A well-organized division of labor within work teams would lead to higher output compared to the traditional system of one miner hewing coal and then collecting and loading it. However, once the regime adopted this initiative as the basis of a nationwide campaign to "rationalize" production, this logical core was soon subverted by two essential factors. First, the so-called Stakhanov movement was used as an extension of shock work. The records of the new Stakhanovites were set as the targets for ordinary workers, who now had to cope with very sharp norm rises, ranging anywhere from 20 to 55 percent, depending on the industry and the job in question. Second, the rationalization principle became impossible to apply in the context of Soviet industry.

28 *Voprosy profdvizheniia* 2–3 (1935), 69; 5–6 (1935), 35–36; *Trud*, 24 Feb. 1939.

Managers could organize the workplaces of individual workers so that they could become Stakhanovites, but this came at the expense of taking auxiliary workers, tools, raw materials, components and other supplies away from ordinary workers, who then found themselves unable to perform their own jobs properly. This cut into their earnings and destroyed internal coordination between the different links in the chain of production. In a similar vein, and just as shock work had done, it encouraged the overtaxing and abuse of equipment, and created bottlenecks impeding the smooth flow of production. Special "Stakhanovite campaigns" might register large numbers of participants, but they rarely led to an overall increase in production, and not infrequently to just the opposite. Finally, also like shock work, it provoked no small amount of resentment among ordinary workers against Stakhanovite rate busters. This is not to deny that at many factories Stakhanovism did encourage workers and engineers to devise genuine innovations that rationalized production, but on the whole the movement subverted its own ostensible goals. It reached its peak in late 1936, and although the title "Stakhanovite" continued to be used until Stalin's death, it carried little meaning.[29]

Although Stakhanov's record was not orchestrated by the national leadership, it came at an opportune time. Over the course of 1934 and 1935 the central leadership had been trying to slow down the pace of new investment in order to introduce financial discipline into the budget and planning processes. This meant that planned increases in output would have to come by increasing the productivity of equipment and the workers using it. The Stakhanov movement appeared as an ideal vehicle for forwarding this aim.[30] However, this necessarily meant a concerted assault on the work practices outlined above, primarily through the imposition of vastly higher norms.

Soviet industry worked with two sets of norms. Most were so-called statistical-empirical norms, and were calculated to take account of the frequency of stoppages, supply disruptions and the actual pace at which workers did their jobs. "Empirical" norms thus reflected the work day as it was actually used. Throughout the 1930s, in fact, during the entire Soviet period,

29 Lewis H. Siegelbaum, *Stakhanovism and the Politics of Productivity in the USSR, 1935–1941* (Cambridge: Cambridge University Press, 1988), chs. 2 and 6; Filtzer, *Soviet Workers and Stalinist Industrialization*, ch. 7; Victor Kravchenko, *I Chose Freedom: The Personal and Political Life of a Soviet Official* (London: Robert Hale, 1947), ch. 13.

30 R. W. Davies and Oleg Khlevnyuk, "Stakhanovism and the Soviet Economy," *Europe-Asia Studies* 54, 6 (Sep. 2002), 867–903.

the regime pressed managers to adopt what they called "scientifically based" norms, derived from the potential output of equipment (or in the case of wholly manual jobs, the potential output of the worker) if everything ran perfectly smoothly, with no delays or bottlenecks. Tighter norms and the adoption of "scientific" norms thereby became a weapon for intensifying the work regime and imposing stricter discipline.[31]

Over the course of the 1930s production processes obviously became more streamlined and modernized, but this had little to do with the almost annual upward revisions of output norms. On the contrary, managers were under intense pressure to meet their plans. As the internal factory environment was one of constant uncertainty due to irregular delivery of supplies and frequent but unpredictable equipment failures, managers needed the ongoing cooperation of their workers in order to deal with these problems. Given that the Soviet economy was equally marked by constant labor scarcity and high labor turnover, this gave workers significant opportunities to engage in what Western industrial sociologists term effort bargaining. Throughout industry line managers through a variety of devices endeavored to weaken, and sometimes totally ignore, prescribed norm increases. Where this proved too difficult they made informal adjustments to earnings through the award of fictitious bonuses, allowing workers to claim inflated output results. The aim in all cases was to allow workers – or at least those upon whom managers were more strategically dependent – to protect customary earnings and regulate the amount of effort they needed to expend in order to achieve these earnings. By the end of the 1930s this led to the seemingly paradoxical anomaly where norms were systematically set lower than plans. In other words, if workers fulfilled their norms by only 100 percent, the shop or factory plan would be underfulfilled, sometimes substantially. Conversely, where plans were met, norms were overfulfilled, often by very large amounts.[32]

Legal Controls over Workers' Behavior

By 1936 labor turnover, although still high and economically damaging in absolute terms, had fallen dramatically compared to the chaotic days of 1930–32 (Table 15.2). It fell still further during 1937 and 1938, but then again

31 Lewis H. Siegelbaum, "Soviet Norm Determination in Theory and Practice," *Soviet Studies* 36, 1 (Jan. 1984), 45–68.

32 Filtzer, *Soviet Workers and Stalinist Industrialization*, ch. 8; Siegelbaum, "Soviet Norm Determination," 61–63.

began to rise, so that by 1939 the average worker was changing jobs once every thirteen months. The increase was especially worrying in the strategically important industries of coalmining, construction, oil extraction, and iron and steel. Alarmingly, the workers who were leaving were not being replaced – more workers were quitting than were being hired. This was largely, although not exclusively, due to a shift of resources into defense production, which had a twofold impact. First, skilled workers were being transferred out of non-defense enterprises to defense factories. Second, the increase in military spending began to put severe pressure on living standards, which once again began to fall after the recovery of the mid 1930s. More workers were picking up stakes and looking for better conditions elsewhere. Factories, and the coalmines in particular, found it especially difficult to retain workers recruited – primarily from the collective farms – via organized recruitment, vast numbers of whom quit soon after arriving at their new place of employment.[33]

On 20 December 1938, the regime introduced the work book, which recorded the details of a worker's employment history and reasons for discharge. The worker had to present the book when taking up new employment, so that prospective employers could, at least in theory, vet any worker they deemed unreliable. On 28 December a much tougher decree placed new restrictions on job-changing and absenteeism. It reiterated the November 1932 sanction of immediate dismissal for truancy, a sanction that in the intervening years had fallen into disuse, but now broadened it to include arriving more than twenty minutes late for work. Insofar as there was a new element, it was to tie the receipt of pensions and sick pay (both administered by the trade unions) to a worker's length of service at the enterprise, a move taken in the hope that this would make workers think twice before changing jobs.[34] The decree had only limited success. Workers, managers, timekeepers and factory doctors all found ways to circumvent the sanctions against absenteeism and sick pay. Truants were able to stay at their jobs, and turnover continued to rise throughout 1939 and early 1940, as the military buildup accentuated the labor shortage and placed ever greater downward pressure on workers' consumption.

33 Filtzer, *Soviet Workers and Stalinist Industrialization*, 141–44.

34 Decree of the Council of People's Commissars of the USSR, Central Committee of the All-Union Communist Party (Bolsheviks) and the All-Union Central Council of Trade Unions, 28 Dec. 1938, "On Measures Concerning the Regulation of Labor Discipline, Improvement in the Practice of State Social Insurance, and Struggle Against Abuses in this Area," *Pravda*, 29 Dec. 1938.

The failure of the December 1938 laws left the regime with one final option: the outright criminalization of absenteeism and job-changing. An edict of the Presidium of the USSR Supreme Soviet of 26 June 1940 made absenteeism (now redefined to include any loss of work time within a shift of more than twenty minutes) punishable by up to six months' corrective labor at the worker's current enterprise with a cut in pay of up to 25 percent. This closed the loophole in the law that had allowed workers to commit truancy in order to force managers to dismiss them. Leaving one's job without managerial permission earned a much more severe penalty: two to four months in jail.[35] The new law produced two seemingly paradoxical results: a dizzying number of convictions alongside widespread circumvention. During the first six months of its application some 321,000 workers and clerical staff were prosecuted for illegally quitting their jobs, and 1.77 million were prosecuted for absenteeism.[36] Yet circumvention and subversion of the law by workers, managers, People's Court judges and local prosecutors were common. It was only when the regime threatened the enforcers, and People's Court judges in particular, with repression that the law began to be more strictly applied.[37]

The June 1940 edict in effect established a system of indentured labor. Workers were legally tied to their place of work. The move toward indenture was further strengthened in October 1940, when the regime introduced compulsory labor service for teenagers through a new system of State Labor Reserves.[38] This set up a network of vocational training schools: factory schools for training young teens in so-called mass trades, and trade schools that provided longer training in skilled trades. The schools were to be populated primarily through labor conscription of collective farm teenagers – the farms were to surrender each year two teenage boys for every 100 collective farm members, the equivalent of 4 percent of their working-age male population.

35 Edict of the Presidium of the USSR Supreme Soviet, "On the Transfer to the Eight-Hour Day and the Seven-Day Work Week, and on the Prohibition against Workers and Clerical Employees Willfully Leaving Enterprises and Institutions," 26 June 1940, *Izvestia*, 27 June 1940. As the title implies, the work day was increased from seven to eight hours, and the work week from six days to seven, while gross weekly or monthly pay was to stay the same. This meant massive norm increases for piece workers and a freeze on weekly and monthly pay for workers on time rates or salaried employees.

36 Gosudarstvennyi arkhiv Rossiiskoi federatsii (GARF), f. 9492, op. 6s, d. 14, l. 7, 11.

37 Peter H. Solomon, Jr., *Soviet Criminal Justice Under Stalin* (Cambridge: Cambridge University Press, 1997), ch. 9; Filtzer, *Soviet Workers and Stalinist Industrialization*, 236–52.

38 Edict of the Presidium of the USSR Supreme Soviet, 2 Oct. 1940, "On the State Labor Reserves of the USSR," *Pravda*, 3 Oct. 1940.

Epilogue

The system of indentured labor became greatly intensified during the war. For workers in defense-related sectors the penalties against illegal job-changing increased from a few months in jail to several years in a Gulag labor camp. The penalties for absenteeism remained unchanged, but with the added sanction that truants would suffer a drastic cut in their bread rations, literally a life-threatening punishment at a time of widespread food shortages and civilian malnutrition. Yet the harshness of the penalties provoked its own counterreaction. Although nearly 1 million defense-sector workers were officially convicted under the wartime laws, most "labor deserters" either were never brought to trial or were tried *in absentia* but never apprehended. Procuracy data suggest that less than 25 percent of offenders were ever made to serve time.[39] Labor conscription also reached its apex during the war, as all teenagers and adults not drafted into the army could be forcibly mobilized into industry and construction.

The wartime strictures remained in place until 1948; the June 1940 edict was relaxed in the early 1950s and repealed *in toto* by Khrushchev in 1956. The war and early postwar years also saw a change in the dynamics of informal shop-floor bargaining, as workers found themselves with far less leeway to attenuate the strains of the work regime. This proved to be only temporary, however. The strain that Stalinist methods of rule placed on the population proved unsustainable. Relaxation began virtually as soon as Stalin's corpse was cold. At this point the system of informal shop-floor bargaining that had emerged during the 1930s quickly reasserted itself. From then until the collapse of the Soviet Union, the authorities never found an effective means to impose tighter controls over norm fulfillment, wages and, most important of all, the speed and quality with which workers worked. These became a permanent source of instability in the Soviet economy and one of the primary causes of the system's long-term decline and eventual collapse.[40]

39 Martin Kragh, "Soviet Labour Law During the Second World War," *War in History* 18, 4 (Nov. 2011), 531–46, and "Stalinist Labour Coercion During World War II: An Economic Approach," *Europe-Asia Studies* 63, 7 (Sep. 2011), 1253–73; Donald Filtzer, "Reluctant Fighters on the Labour Front: Labour Mobilization and Labour Turnover in Soviet Industry During World War II," unpublished conference paper, Association for Slavic, East European and Eurasian Studies annual conference, Nov. 2013.

40 Filtzer, *Soviet Workers and De-Stalinization*; Donald Filtzer, *Soviet Workers and the Collapse of Perestroika: The Soviet Labour Process and Gorbachev's Reforms, 1985–1991* (Cambridge: Cambridge University Press, 1994).

Plate 1 Crowds on Nevskii Prospekt during the February Revolution in Petrograd. Slava Katamidze Collection / Getty

Plate 2 A political demonstration in Petrograd on 18 June 1917. "Peace All over the World, All Power to the People, All the Land to the People." Central Press Hulton Archive / Getty

Plate 3 Red Guards at the Triangle rubber works in Petrograd, October 1917. Stringer AFP / Getty

Plate 4 A column of soldiers demonstrating along Nikol'skii street under a banner proclaiming "Communism" in Moscow, November 1917. Sovfoto / Universal Images Group / Getty

В. И. Ленин за чтением „Правды". 1918 год.
14

Plate 5 Lenin reading *Pravda*, 1918. DEA PICTURE LIBRARY / Getty

Plate 6 The Council of the People's Commissars, Russia, 1918. Next to Lenin and Stalin, Alexandra Kollontai, the commissar of social welfare. Heritage Image Partnership Ltd. / Alamy

Plate 7 Lenin and Trotsky soon after the October Revolution. Keystone / Getty

Plate 8 Lenin and Stalin soon after the October Revolution. Keystone Pictures USA / Alamy

Plate 9 Clara Zetkin and Rosa Luxemburg, 1918. ITAR-TASS Photo Agency / Alamy

Plate 10 Street battles and barricades in Schutzen Strasse, Berlin, end of 1918. After Germany's defeat in World War I, social protest and revolutionary upheavals erupted there. In January 1919 the German communists (Spartacists) launched an insurrection in which their leaders Karl Liebknecht and Rosa Luxemburg were murdered. Culture Club / Getty

Plate 11 The founding congress of the Communist International (Comintern), Moscow, March 1919. Universal History Archive / Getty

Plate 12 The Hungarian communist Béla Kun surrounded by workers and students in 1919. He was the leader of the Soviet Republic in April–August 1919 and then a member of the Executive Committee of the Comintern in Moscow. DEA / A. DAGLI ORTI / Getty

Plate 13 "Long Live the Three-Million-Strong Red Army!" Poster, 1919. Heritage Images Hulton Archive / Getty

Plate 14 A group of Russian refugees at Tbilisi (Tiflis) railway station during the civil war, January 1920. I. Masini / Getty

Plate 15 Young civil war fighters, returning from Mongolia in 1921, vividly parade their sense of authority and empowerment. Vestnik Arkhiva Prezidenta Rossiiskoi Federatsii, *Krasnaia Armiia v 1920-e gody* (Moscow, 2007), 87.

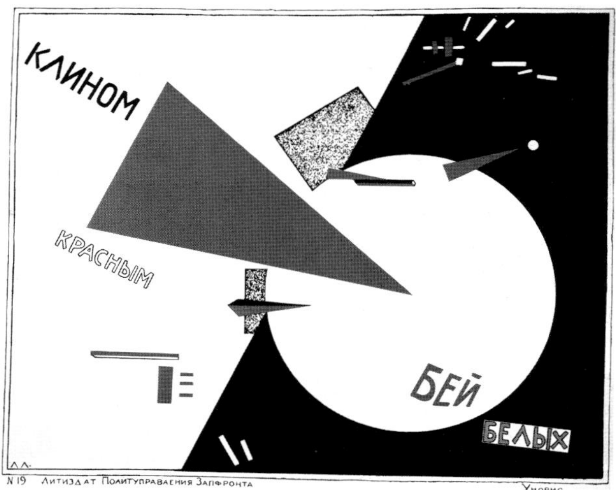

Plate 16 "Beat the Whites with the Red Wedge." Propaganda lithograph by Lazar' Lisitskii, a symbolic representation of the Red Army in the Russian Civil War, 1920. Photo 12 / Universal Images Group / Getty

Plate 17 "Be on Your Guard." Trotsky, symbol of the Red Army, fights off foreign interventionists, 1920, poster by Dmitrii Moor. De Agostini Picture Library / Getty

Plate 18 "To the Polish Front! Comrades, the commune is strengthening under a hail of bullets. With rifles we will treble our strength." Propaganda poster by Vladimir Maiakovskii and Ivan Maliutin, 1920. Photo 12 / Universal Images Group / Getty

Plate 19 Group portrait of the delegates of the Congress of Eastern Peoples posing around a meeting table, Baku, Azerbaijan, September 1920. American writer John Reed (in front, wearing a dark suit) sits second to the left of Soviet leader Grigorii Zinoviev (third from left). Hulton Archive / Getty

Plate 20 Lenin, Bukharin, Zinoviev and Paul Levi at the Comintern Third Congress, 1921. ullstein bild / Getty

Plate 21 "Long Live the Communist International!," poster, 1920s. Heritage Image Partnership Ltd. / Alamy

Plate 28 Red Front fighters march under the slogan, "Everywhere in the City and the Countryside: Red Unity for Anti-Fascist Action!," June 1932. Arbeiter-Illustrierte-Zeitung

Plate 29 Stalin, Bukharin and Grigorii Ordzhonikidze, 1929. Imagno / Getty

Plate 30 "The Communist Youth Organization Is the Shock Brigade of the Five-Year Plan." Poster by Vladimir Liushin, 1931. Photo 12 / Universal Images Group / Getty

Plate 31 Workers of Magnitogorsk, USSR, 1932. The city of Magnitogorsk in the Urals, with its large-scale mining and iron and steel industries, was at the forefront of Stalin's Five-Year Plan in the early 1930s. Hulton Archive Heritage Images / Getty

Plate 32 Bolshevik propagandists talk to Ukrainian peasants at the start of the collectivization of agriculture, 1929. SPUTNIK / Alamy

Plate 33 Forced labor in Ukhta on the Izhma River, circa 1930. SVF2 Universal Images Group / Getty

Plate 34 "Kolkhoznik, Guard Your Fields Against Class Enemies, Thieves and Idlers Wrecking the Socialist Harvest!" Poster by Viktor Ivanovich Govorkov, 1933. Heritage Image Partnership Ltd. / Alamy

Plate 35 George Bernard Shaw (R) during his visit to the Soviet Union, 1931. Here with Soviet People's Commissar Anatolii Lunacharskii (L) and theater director Konstantin Stanislavskii (C). Heritage Images Hulton Archive / Getty

Plate 36 "Dimitrov Lets in the Light." James Boswell ("Buchan"), *Daily Worker*, 21 October 1933. Communist Bulgarian leader Georgi Dimitrov became a symbol of anti-fascism in Europe as he famously refuted the Nazi accusation that he was responsible for the Reichstag fire six months earlier. Courtesy James Boswell Archive

Plate 37 Antonio Gramsci, secretary of the Communist Party of Italy (1924–26), was arrested and imprisoned by Mussolini's regime in November 1926. He spent ten years in prison and died in April 1937, leaving theoretical and philosophical writings which were published after World War II as his "Prison Notebooks." Postcard issued in 1934. World History Archive / Alamy

Plate 38 A group of survivors from the Long March after their arrival in Yan'an, northern Shaanxi, in 1935. An entire army of Chinese communists was forced to flee from the south to the northwest of the country by the Nationalists. Only a few thousand of the 100,000 people who set off survived, but the new territorial base was crucial to the destiny of Chinese communism. Keystone-France / Getty

Plate 39 The Executive Committee of the Comintern at its Seventh Congress, July–August 1935. Left to right standing: Otto Kuusinen, Klement Gottwald, Wilhelm Pieck, Dmitry Manuilsky. Left to right seated: Georgi Dimitrov, Palmiro Togliatti, Wilhelm Florin, Wang Ming. ITAR-TASS Photo Agency / Alamy

Plate 40 Demonstration in support of the Popular Front at Place de la Bastille, Paris, 14 July 1936. The left alliance of socialists, communists and radicals won the elections in France in May 1936. Photo 12 / Universal Images Group / Getty

Plate 41 Spanish Communist Party election poster urging voters to support the Popular Front, 1936. The alliance of left forces won the elections in Spain in February 1936. Universal History Archive / Getty

Plate 42 Dolores Ibárruri (*La Pasionaria*) speaking from a podium to members of the International Brigades during the Spanish Civil War, 1937. The war broke out in July 1936 after a rebellion of nationalist military against the Popular Front government and ended in defeat for the Republicans in March 1939. ullstein bild / Getty

Plate 43 British volunteers in the Spanish Civil War. Internationalist anti-fascist mobilization in support of the Republic and the Popular Front involved thousands of people from many countries. International Brigade Memorial Trust

Plate 44 Mao Zedong, the leader of the Chinese Communist Party, at the beginning of the Anti-Japanese War, Yan'an, late 1930s. Russian State Archives of Social and Political History, 495/225/71

Plate 45 "Soviet integrated education and paramilitary training." *Komsomol'skaia pravda*, 2 September 1935.

Plate 46 "Long Live Stalin's Generation of Stakhanovite Heroes!" Poster by Gustav Klutsis, 1936. Heritage Image Partnership Ltd. / Alamy

Plate 47 "We'll Dig Out the Spies and Diversionists, the Trotskyite–Bukharinite Agents of Fascism!" Poster, 1937. The wave of anti-Trotsky propaganda and persecution mounted in the Soviet Union after the assassination of Sergei Kirov (1 December 1934) and peaked in the show trials and mass terror of 1936–38. Heritage Images / Getty

Plate 48 The Ayach Yaginsk mine barracks in the Gulag work camp, 1930s. Photo from the State Central Archives of the October Revolution. SPUTNIK / Alamy

Plate 49 Signing of the Non-Aggression Pact between the Soviet Union and Nazi Germany. Molotov signs. Behind him, Ribbentrop (L) and Stalin (C), 23 August 1939, Moscow. Photo 12 / Universal Images Group / Getty

Plate 50 "Let Us Mercilessly Smash and Destroy the Enemy!" Poster by Kukryniksy workshop, 1941. Photo 12 / Universal Images Group / Getty

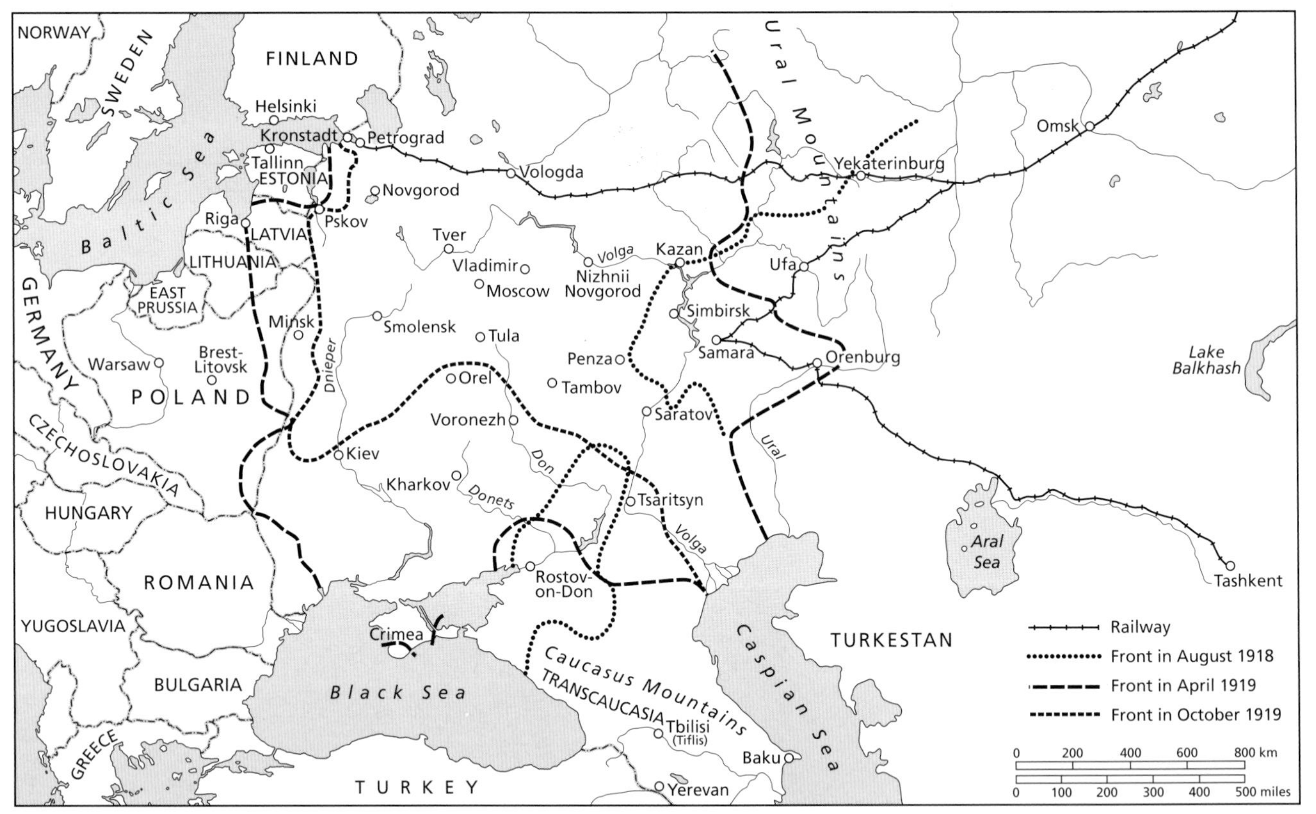

Plate 51 The Russian Civil War

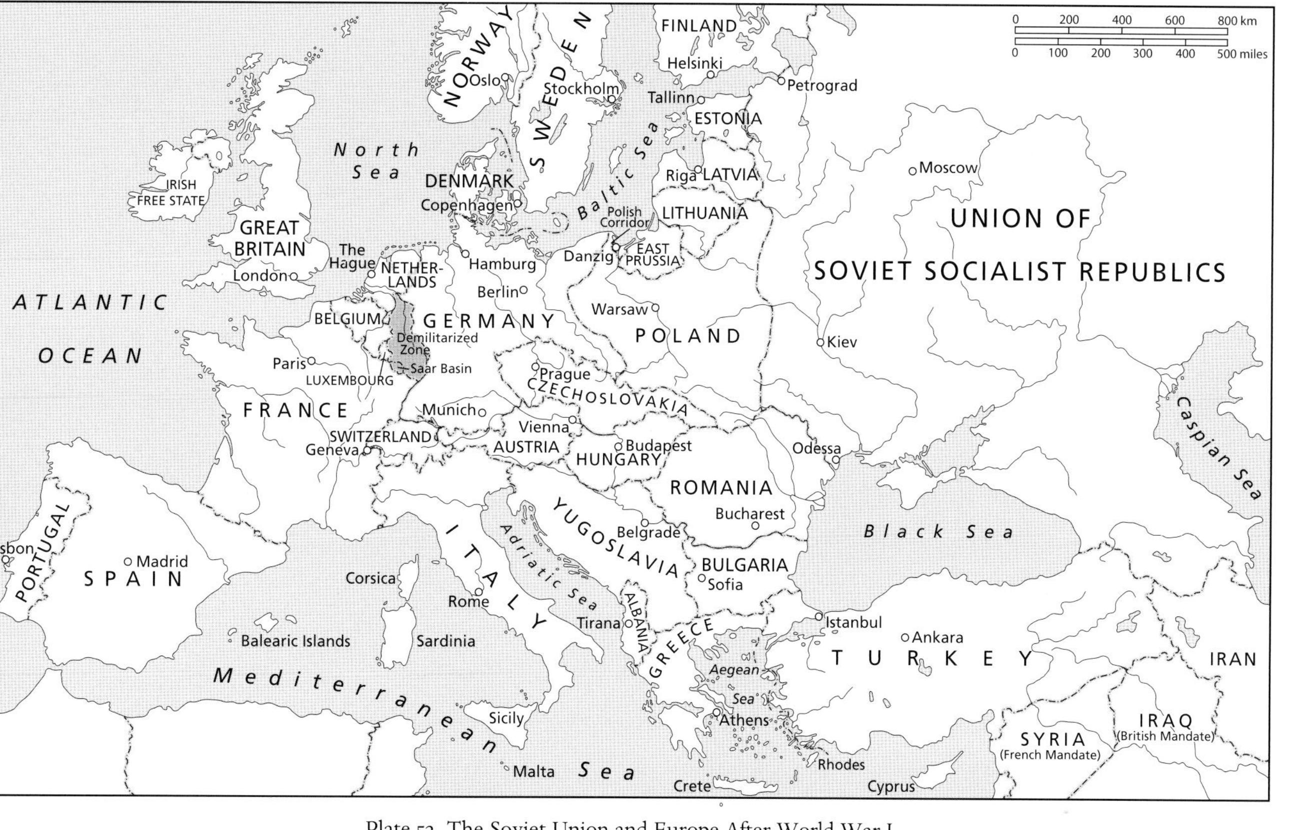

Plate 52 The Soviet Union and Europe After World War I

Plate 53 The Soviet Union in the Interwar Years

Bibliographical Essay

Anyone wanting a fuller grasp of the position of workers during the 1920s and 1930s should start with Solomon Schwarz's *Labor in the Soviet Union* (New York: Praeger, 1952). Schwarz was an ex-Menshevik and has a teleological interpretation of what he sees as a linear path from free to coerced labor, but the story he tells is empirically rich and offers an excellent introduction to the topic. Three outstanding memoirs of the 1930s are equally rewarding and full of accurate and insightful detail: Andrew Smith, *I Was a Soviet Worker* (London: Robert Hale, 1937); John Scott, *Behind the Urals: An American Worker in Russia's City of Steel*, enlarged edn. prepared by Stephen Kotkin (Bloomington: Indiana University Press, 1989); and Victor Kravchenko, *I Chose Freedom: The Personal and Political Life of a Soviet Official* (London: Robert Hale, 1947).

The 1980s and 1990s produced a number of well-researched monographs on Soviet workers during industrialization. Their interpretations differ, often considerably, but all are solid studies. Hiroaki Kuromiya, *Stalin's Industrial Revolution: Politics and Workers, 1928–1932* (Cambridge: Cambridge University Press, 1988), focuses mainly on the shock work movement. Lewis H. Siegelbaum, *Stakhanovism and the Politics of Productivity in the USSR, 1935–1942* (Cambridge: Cambridge University Press, 1988), examines Stakhanovism not just from the point of view of its impact on production, but also its social and cultural role in the context of the mid 1930s. A study of Stakhanovism from a radically different perspective is Robert Maier, *Die Stachanov-Bewegung 1935–1938: Der Stachanovismus als tragendes und verschärfendes Moment der Stalinisierung der Sowjetischen Gesellschaft* (Stuttgart: Franz Steiner Verlag, 1990). Donald Filtzer, *Soviet Workers and Stalinist Industrialization: The Formation of Modern Soviet Production Relations, 1928–1941* (London: Pluto, 1986), is a structural analysis of worker–state relations during the entire span of the first three Five-Year Plans from a Marxist perspective. Vladimir Andrle, *Workers in Stalin's Russia: Industrialization and Social Change in a Planned Economy* (New York: St. Martin's Press, 1988), advances arguments similar to those of Filtzer, but analyzes them within the framework of sociological theory.

All of the above books, with the partial exception of Maier, were written before historians had access to the former Soviet archives. Since then some important specialist studies have appeared. Wendy Z. Goldman, *Women at the Gates: Gender and Industry in Stalin's Russia* (New York: Cambridge University Press, 2002), is a comprehensive study of women workers and the politics of female labor during the first two Five-Year Plans (1928–37); it also offers a detailed account of the general situation within industry in these years. Stephen Kotkin, *Magnetic Mountain: Stalinism as a Civilization* (Berkeley: University of California Press, 1995), is a monumental study of the building and operation of Magnitogorsk and how workers constructed their lives there. Jeffrey J. Rossman, *Worker Resistance Under Stalin: Class and Revolution on the Shop Floor* (Cambridge, MA: Harvard University Press, 2005), is one of the few archive-based studies of worker protests during the first years of industrialization. Sarah Davies, *Popular Opinion in Stalin's Russia: Terror, Propaganda and Dissent, 1934–1941* (Cambridge: Cambridge University Press, 1997), is one of the only archive-based studies on workers' attitudes, although its representativeness is limited by its focus solely on Leningrad. These and other archive studies greatly enhance our grasp of the nuances and details of the period they cover. They also show that the memoirs and the earlier studies based only on published sources hold up rather well.

16
The Soviet State and Peasants

NICOLAS WERTH

The great Russian historian of agrarian affairs Viktor Petrovich Danilov called it "the tragedy of the Soviet countryside." This is the title he gave to the enormous collection of documents about the relation between the Soviet state and the peasantry (1927–39), which he edited with the help of an international team of historians, and published at the beginning of the twenty-first century.[1] He was right that the conflict-ridden relations between the Soviet party-state, taken over by Stalin at the end of the 1920s, and the peasantry constitute a tragedy: The compulsory collectivization initiated by the group around Stalin at the end of 1929 not only reactivated the deep split between the "two Russias" which Alexander Herzen had analyzed in the middle of the nineteenth century – a dominant urban and industrial Russia and a rural Russia which was politically oppressed, isolated and turned in upon itself – but it also completely and conclusively destroyed a culture and a mode of life, in fact an entire "peasant civilization." Yet in 1917, the peasants, or, more exactly, the peasant-soldiers, had significantly contributed to the victory of the Bolsheviks. Relations between the new regime and the peasantry seemed to have entered a new era with the end of the mass butchery of the Great War, the breakup of large rural estates and the much anticipated advent of a massive redistribution of land (*cernyi peredel*). How did the great hope of 1917 eventually end in the tragedy of the 1930s?

The Great Misunderstanding of October

During the course of 1917 a powerful peasant revolution unfolded which had its own dynamic, moved at its own speed, proceeded in ways no political

1 Viktor P. Danilov, Roberta Manning and Lynne Viola (eds.), *Tragediia sovetskoi derevni*, 5 vols. (Moscow: ROSSPEN, 1999–2006).

party had envisaged and was fueled by demands that were not in the program of any of the existing political groups. This revolution can be understood only against its particular historical background: The rural landowner was a longstanding object of hatred for Russian peasants, who until two generations before the Great War had been serfs, and the whole rural world was profoundly distrustful of the city, of the external world and of any form of intervention by the state.

The peasant revolution broke out in the autumn of 1917, when agrarian unrest, which up to then had been relatively limited, evolved into full-scale uprisings in a large number of regions. These were spontaneous and very violent affairs. The dwellings of a number of *pomeshchiki* (landlords) were destroyed, especially in the Volga area, where land-hunger was most intense. This rural revolt was in many of its aspects a continuation of that of 1905–07, but in 1917 physical violence against landowners became more frequent; in fact a certain number of them were lynched.

Peasant violence was directed in the first instance against the *pomeshchiki*, but it also extended to members of the class of peasant-owners (*otrubniki*) who had risen above the other members of the rural community thanks to the reforms of Pyotr Stolypin. These *otrubniki* were forced to give their lands back to the communal holding.

Starting in September 1917, that is two months *before* the seizure of power by the Bolsheviks in Petrograd, the provincial peasant assemblies approved proposals that would have led to the confiscation of the land, livestock and agricultural material of landowners. These measures represent the triumph of a decentralized and community-based conception of politics. The peasant delegates made no distinction between a government decree and a resolution adopted, either at a district or a provincial level, by a congress, an assembly or a peasant soviet. They were expressing their own ideals of social justice, while ignoring – or distorting – the new political vocabulary which was then current in the "democratic Russia" of the cities, and they recognized as legitimate only those institutions that ratified their demands.

In the autumn of 1917 the Bolshevik leaders, in the first instance Lenin himself, had the political intelligence to encourage this peasant revolution which they could not control; they put aside for the moment their own agrarian program, which envisaged the nationalization of land and its exploitation by large collectives. On the other hand, the leaders of the Socialist Revolutionary Party (SRs), who were hampered by their own participation in the Provisional Government, refused to endorse without question or discussion the peasant demands, even when these in fact were in line with their own political program. As a result, during the period that was decisive for their seizure of power, the Bolsheviks obtained the benevolent neutrality or even the active support of the peasantry. The peasants, who had scarcely any direct acquaintance with the Bolsheviks, because they were not generally very active in the countryside, were persuaded by what the peasant-soldiers said upon their return to the villages, namely that the Bolsheviks were the only ones who wanted "more" (*bol'she*) – more land, more liberty.[2]

Immediately after their seizure of power, the Bolsheviks had the Second All-Russian Congress of Soviets pass a "Land Decree." Its text took over to a large extent the model decree that had been elaborated by the SRs which was based on 242 motions passed by peasant soviets. This text, which did no more than legitimize what many rural committees and peasant soviets had already put into practice, required the dissolution, without indemnity, of the large rural estates. However, it also left a number of questions unanswered: To whom would this land, which was for the moment put at the "disposal of the agrarian committees," eventually revert? To "The Workers' and Peasants' State," as the Bolsheviks desired, or to the peasant communities, as the peasants demanded?

In the autumn of 1917 the bankruptcy of all forms of state authority and the collapse of the civil and military institutions allowed the peasants finally to realize their long-cherished aspirations, which were summed up in two words: Land and Freedom (*Zemlia i Volia*). For six months, until the beginning of the summer of 1918, the countryside experienced a unique period of "peasant power." The Bolsheviks had few partisans in rural areas and were consequently completely unable to control this peasant revolution by putting in place power structures of their own. So, for a brief moment, they allowed the peasants to organize themselves and to complete the destruction of their "old world." The many agrarian committees that had arisen during 1917 rebaptized themselves "soviets," and instituted a direct "peasant democracy" which demonstrated a remarkable political and organizational ability by immediately resolving a number of complex problems. The peasants organized militias, elected judges and regulated local commerce, but the greatest issue confronting peasant democracy was agrarian reform. The redistribution of land proceeded, however, starting in the winter of 1917–18, with a minimum of conflict and very few signs of a "class struggle" among the peasants.

2 Orlando Figes, "The Russian Revolution and Its Language in the Village," *Russian Review* 56, 3 (1997), 323–45.

The most frequent incidents arose not between "rich and poor" individuals, but between better and less well-off villages. This redistribution was based exclusively on the peasants' own idea of "justice": The land was distributed according to a complex set of criteria that took account both of the number of "mouths that needed to be fed" and the number of able-bodied adults capable of working the family plot. The peasant revolution was carried out in a spirit of egalitarianism and led to a leveling down of the standard of living of the peasantry, without, however, totally doing away with differences between those peasants who were poor and those who were "less poor." On average, a peasant family obtained one or two hectares of arable land, but much less than this in the rare cases in which the land was especially fertile. It was a paradoxical feature of this rural revolution that the most archaic aspects of the social organization of the peasantry were reinforced during the upheaval of 1917. Although it had been thought to be moribund, the peasant commune sprang back into life. By implementing a policy of egalitarian leveling down of the peasantry, this revolution undid all the effects, incomplete and fragile as they had been, of the reforms of Stolypin, and eventually had the effect of transforming rural society back into something more archaic than it had seemed to be in the process of becoming. To cite the very insightful formulation of Moshe Lewin, the new Bolshevik regime found itself "saddled with a peasantry which had just undone everything which capitalist development had brought it."[3]

The First Conflicts Between the Peasants and the Bolshevik State

"What we need," Lenin wrote in May 1918, "is to follow the example of German state capitalism and to assimilate its lessons with all our strength, and not to hesitate to use dictatorial methods to accelerate, even more than Peter I did, the assimilation by barbarous Russia of the West; we must not hesitate to employ barbarous methods to struggle against barbarism."[4] The "barbarism" he was speaking about was primarily peasant "barbarism," the "Asiatic form of life" of the rural masses, against which it was completely legitimate, in the eyes of the Bolshevik leaders, to use extreme violence.

How can one explain the apparent reversal? Why were the peasants who, by their revolt in the autumn of 1917, had contributed objectively to the

3 Moshe Lewin, *La formation du système soviétique* (Paris: Gallimard, 1985), 427.

4 V. I. Lenin, *Polnoe Sobranie Sochinenii*, vol. XXXVI (Moscow: Izdatel'stvo politicheskoi literatury, 1965), 301.

victory of the Bolsheviks, perceived six months later as a menace to the new regime? The main reason in the spring of 1918 was an economic one: The cities controlled by the Bolsheviks were on the point of starvation and the Bolshevik leaders were convinced – as had been their precursors in the Provisional Government who had succeeded one another during the whole long course of 1917 – that the peasants were "hoarding" grain and speculating on food shortages. The "battle for grain," which the Bolshevik leaders unleashed in May 1918 when they conferred full powers on the People's Commissariat for Provisioning, a state-within-the-state, was the political response to a specific situation: the crisis in economic exchange between the cities and rural areas which had begun well before the Bolshevik seizure of power, but which by spring 1918 had developed in such a way as to make the provisioning of the cities, the bastions of the new power, immensely difficult. However, this "battle for grain" was not exclusively an economic one. The Bolshevik leaders decided to reimpose the "principle of the state" on "small landowners who have a horror of organization and discipline" by means of a "dictatorship over the provision of foodstuffs." This "dictatorship" was to be enforced by hundreds of detachments of the Prodarmiia (Food Army) of the most varied kinds. "The time has come," Lenin wrote on 29 April 1918, "to conduct a pitiless struggle, one without mercy, against smallholders and small landowners."[5]

In addition to the detachments of the Prodarmiia who were essentially groups of unemployed workers and Bolshevik militants from the cities, the Bolsheviks, starting in June 1918, instituted Committees of Poor Peasants (Kombedy), who were charged with requisitioning agricultural surpluses from their more well-off neighbors. The organization of these Committees of Poor Peasants was difficult, reflecting the complete ignorance on the part of the Bolsheviks of the realities of peasant society. Following a rather simplistic Marxist view, they imagined that this society was profoundly divided by class antagonisms, between *bedniaki* (poor peasants), *seredniaki* (middle peasants) and *kulaki* (rich peasants), whereas in fact the peasants as a whole usually maintained a remarkable solidarity among themselves when confronted with the world outside their community.

As the operational reports of the Cheka, which have been published by Danilov and his team,[6] indicate, summary requisitions carried out by detachments of the *Prodarmia* and conscription into the Red Army in the zones

5 Ibid., 265.

6 Viktor P. Danilov and Aleksei Berelovich (eds.), *Sovetskaia derevnia glazami VChK, OGPU, NKVD*, vol. I, *1918–1922* (Moscow: ROSSPEN, 1998).

controlled by the Bolsheviks constituted the detonators for a series of confrontations between the new regime and large sections of the peasantry. It is important also to note that the peasants reacted in the very same way to all state or quasi-state forces who tried to requisition agricultural produce or livestock or to mobilize men in a war which the peasants considered to be "fratricidal" (*bratoubistvennaia voina*);[7] their resistance was directed not only at the Bolsheviks, but equally at the various "White" governments and the government of Komuch (Committee of the Members of the Constituent Assembly) which was composed in its majority of politicians close to the SRs. Men who evaded military service or deserters numbered as many as 200,000 a month in 1919, and they constituted the principal pool from which the "Greens" drew their strength. The importance of the "Greens" in this period – bands of lawless peasants who flourished in the unsettled countryside during the years of revolution and civil war – is an indication of how "archaic" conditions had become. All the elements favorable to generating an explosive form of "primitive revolt" of the kind analyzed by Eric Hobsbawm[8] came together: a traditional peasant society under attack by an emerging state which was trying to impose its authority and assert control over the inhabitants of a certain rural territory and their economy by force; at the local level, massive instability of established powers in the context of a civil war; and generalized impoverishment of the population resulting from the devastations of war, which stirred up millenarian expectations.

The first disturbances directed against the Bolshevik authorities were still rather limited; they broke out during the summer of 1918 in the central provinces of Russia (Tula, Riazan, Tambov, Kaluga, Tver). The Bolsheviks held power only in a small portion of the former Russian Empire: These were the areas that were most firmly under their control, and from which consequently grain and men had been most thoroughly extracted. A second and much more important wave of peasant unrest took place in the provinces of the Volga (Simbirsk, Samara, Kazan) and in part of Ukraine in the spring of 1919. In the provinces of Samara and Simbirsk, these protests developed into true insurrections; this was the so-called *Tchapannaia voina* or "kaftan war" which took its name from the *tchapan* or kaftan, the traditional dress of the peasants which distinguished them from the inhabitants of the cities.

7 This expression is frequently used in peasant petitions and resolutions. See Orlando Figes, *Peasant Russian, Civil War: The Volga Countryside in Revolution* (Oxford: Oxford University Press, 1989), 310–12.

8 Eric Hobsbawm, *Primitive Rebels: Studies in Archaic Forms of Social Movement in the 19th and 20th Centuries* (New York: Norton, 1965).

This rebellion permitted units of the White Army under Admiral Aleksandr Kolchak to advance toward the Volga, when the commanders of the Red Army were forced to withdraw men and materiel from the eastern front in order to deal with a well-organized peasant army led by soldiers who had fought in the Great War. The repression of the peasants after their defeat carried out by units of the Red Army supported by special detachments of the Cheka claimed thousands of victims.

The second large breeding-ground of peasant insurrections during the summer of 1919 was Ukraine, where, as Andrea Graziosi[9] has shown, one can find the "first national-socialist liberation movement based on the peasantry" which arose during the course of 1918 as part of the struggle against German occupation. After the defeat of Germany this movement redirected its energies against the Bolsheviks, the *Moskali* (Russians of Moscow), the Jews and the Whites. For the Bolsheviks the reconquest of Ukraine in the spring of 1919 was of vital importance, given its immense agricultural and industrial potential. It is significant that it was in Ukraine in 1919–20 that the Bolsheviks conducted the most extensive trials of the system of collective agriculture, and it was here that the opposition by the peasants against the *kommuny* (collectives) which were being imposed on them by the authorities was to be strongest. This opposition was to flare up one final time ten years later in the struggle against the compulsory collectivization of the countryside.

In 1920 two new factors contributed to an unprecedented increase in peasant militancy: a record high of requisitions and, in addition and more importantly, the defeat of the White armies which meant for the peasants that there was no longer any danger of a return to the old order. Against the background of endemic unrest, two specific episodes of large-scale insurrection stand out. In February–March 1920 the "Pitchfork Uprising" (also called "Uprising of the Black Eagle") broke out in large parts of the provinces of Kazan, Ufa and Samara, areas that had been subjected, after the defeat of Admiral Kolchak, to particularly heavy and brutal requisitions. One of the special features of this insurrection, which was carried out by a proper army of tens of thousands of peasants, was that it united Tatars, Bashkirs and Russians in common opposition to the policies of the regime. The intensity and extent of the fighting were such as to incite even Trotsky, the people's commissar of war, who visited the theater of operations in person, to propose the suspension of the requisitions and their replacement with a tax

9 Andrea Graziosi, *Bol'sheviki i krest'iane na Ukraine, 1918–1919* (Moscow: Airo-XX, 1997).

in kind, a measure that would eventually be adopted a year later, inaugurating the NEP (New Economic Policy).[10] Starting in the autumn of 1920 a second wave of peasant wars of unprecedented magnitude broke out in different localities over an extremely large area: The first major region affected extended from the province of Tambov to the middle Volga (the provinces of Saratov, Samara and Simbirsk); a second wave engulfed several provinces in the Urals and in western Siberia (Cheliabinsk, Yekaterinburg, Tiumen and Omsk). In the province of Tambov and in western Siberia armies of insurgent peasants held units of the Red Army and detachments of the Cheka at bay for months at a time. In Siberia the Bolsheviks even lost control of such important cities like Tobolsk, which was occupied for six months (from the end of February to the beginning of April 1921) by a "peasant government" of the "Federation of Tobolsk."

The opening of the archives containing material about the state of the peasantry in the former Russian Empire during the period of the civil wars has led to the publication of important collections of documents and of a number of important monographs.[11] These give a picture especially of the organization of these peasant armies, which were much more structured than was generally assumed to be the case. Often these armies were commanded by high officers of the Red Army who had mutinied; they had recourse to conscription of all men capable of bearing arms and they put into effect a complex system of supply and provisioning which was intended to avoid arousing the ire of the local population who generally supported their insurgency. It is also notable that the programs put forth by the insurgents of Tambov and those of Tobolsk, despite the immense distances that separated them, were coherent, were very much like each other, and did not really change. The peasants unanimously demanded an end to the requisitions and freedom of commerce, and they protested against the innumerable forms of forced labor which the authorities imposed on them, and which reminded them of the "time of serfdom"; they refused any idea of a collectivization of land. The peasants also rose up against the brutality, the exactions and the abusive behavior of the agents

10 On this little-known episode which one might call "proto-NEP," see Viktor P. Danilov and Teodor Shanin (eds.), *Antonovschina. Dokumenty i Materialy* (Tambov: Izd. TIO, 1994), 13–14.

11 In addition to the collections cited earlier in notes 6, 7 and 9, see Viktor P. Danilov and Teodor Shanin (eds.), *Filipp Mironov. Tikhii Don v 1917–1921* (Moscow: Iz. Demokratia, 1997); V. I. Shishkin, *Sibirskaia Vandeia*, 2 vols. (Moscow: Mezhdunarodnyi fond "Demokratiia," 2000–01); and V. P. Kondrashin, *Krestianstvo Rossii v grazhdanskoi voine: k voprosu ob istokakh stalinizma* (Moscow: ROSSPEN, 2009).

of the state who turned the countryside into a place where arbitrary, absolute power reigned supreme. One of the most frequent demands of the peasants was "soviets without communists." This slogan expressed both the fact that "soviet power," understood as a form of direct and decentralized democracy that was very like that practiced in the traditional peasant commune, was a popular idea, but also the idea, which was widespread in rural areas, that the Bolsheviks (who had encouraged the peasants to take control of the large estates in 1917) had been ejected from power by "communists" (who requisitioned everything, prohibited trade and wanted to force all the peasants into *kommuny*). This was the reason we find the peasants raising one of the great issues that had played a role in all the peasant revolts that had shaken the Russian Empire for centuries: the duplicity of those in power. In the Volga provinces a revolt broke out in the summer of 1920 led by a certain A. V. Sapozhkov, a commander who had mutinied and left the Red Army. He placed himself at the head of a peasant army, which called itself, significantly, "The First Army of Truth." Something similar happened in Siberia during the great insurrection of February–March 1921, when the peasants rose up in the name of "true socialism," "true liberty" and "true power for soviets without communists."

This great wave of peasant wars, which culminated in February–March 1921, was much more important than the revolt at the naval base of Kronstadt in forcing the Bolshevik leaders to adopt the NEP at the Tenth RKP(b) Congress. They then had to bring an end to the disturbances, which had not stopped, despite a promise to cease requisitioning and replace it with a tax in kind. To deal with these insurgencies, punitive detachments were used. These were often commanded by officers trained in the military academies of the tsar, who had rallied to the Bolshevik regime only when it seemed to them to provide the only bulwark against the power of the peasant hordes. The punitive detachments employed the most modern techniques of warfare which had been perfected on the battlefields of the Great War. These they now used in an attempt to annihilate the "inner enemy": bombardment of insurgent villages by artillery and aviation, use of gas to "clear" forests where peasant "bandits" had taken refuge, massive deportations of the civilian population and shooting of hostages. The great centers of peasant resistance were destroyed during the summer of 1921, except those in Central Asia and in Dagestan. In the Volga regions, famine, the result of years of combat, devastation of the countryside and requisition contributed greatly to quenching the fire of peasant resistance.

Soviet Power in the Face of the "Accursed Problem"

In his pioneering study *Russian Peasants and Soviet Power*,[12] Moshe Lewin has very aptly characterized the sentiment of the Bolshevik leaders in the face of the "peasant question": It was an "accursed problem" which remained at the very heart of all the political debates within the party during the 1920s. How, and at what speed, could one push this "backward" and refractory peasantry toward socialism? How was the differentiation and social stratification of the rural world going to evolve? How could one realize the "worker–peasant alliance" which was the fruit of the "compromise" embodied in the NEP? In the spirit of Lenin, the NEP was supposed to rest on a strong "worker–peasant alliance," the famous *smychka*, which was thought to be the only way to solve the problem of economic underdevelopment. Agriculture and industry were supposed to stand shoulder-to-shoulder and develop in tandem. The program of the alliance was: the development of industry, in the first instance of the sector devoted to the production of agricultural machinery and of the manufactured goods that were essential to rural life; and support of small rural industries. The rapid improvement of the material equipment available for farming was supposed to increase the general productivity of agriculture and also the quantity of agricultural products that could be sent to the market. This would mean that the provisioning of the cities with foodstuffs would be assured. Then Russia could export agricultural products and receive in exchange machines and industrial equipment. This would mean that one could hope for a harmonious growth of the two members of the "alliance" and a general development of the national economy.

In fact, the idealized program of the worker–peasant alliance was mostly based on an illusion and was unworkable because of the structural weaknesses of an agricultural sector that had just emerged from seven years of war and revolution, and also because of some grave errors in political economy on the part of the Bolshevik leaders during the whole of the NEP era and the distrust of the new regime that was deeply rooted among the peasants. The leveling down of the peasantry which followed the massive land redistribution of 1917–18 (the "black redistribution"), the reduction in the number and size of plots (16 million in 1914 as against 24 million in 1924, with

12 Moshe Lewin, *Russian Peasants and Soviet Power: A Study in Collectivization* (London: Allen & Unwin, 1968), ch. 5.

corresponding diminution in size), the disappearance of the large landowners, and the impoverishment of the whole class of well-off peasants put a break on any increase in productivity and drastically reduced the quantity of cereals, meat and dairy products available for sale outside the local village community. A direct result of this situation was that a country which in 1905–14 had exported on average tens of millions of tons of cereals each year, now exported none. As far as the provisioning of the cities was concerned, it remained dependent on the "economic goodwill" of a peasantry loath to sell, at a low price, their foodstuffs to the state. Manufactured products were expensive, of mediocre quality and scarce, whereas the prices paid by state agencies who purchased cereals were very low. In view of the extremely low quality of the manufactured goods on offer and the low prices for agricultural products, the peasants adopted the only economically coherent policy: They consumed what they grew themselves, and limited their production of cereals to what was required for necessary purchases. This attitude was also dictated by the traumatic experience of "war communism" and by their memory of the requisitions the Bolsheviks had practiced for so long.

The difficulties encountered by the NEP, and the increasingly evident failure of the worker–peasant alliance, gave rise to very heated debates with the party during the course of the 1920s. Two opposing views gradually emerged: the so-called leftist view, which was most consistently defended by Trotsky, Yevgenii Preobrazhenskii and G. L. Piatakov, and a "rightist" view whose principal theoretician was Bukharin. Oddly enough, Feliks Dzerzhinskii, head of the OGPU, defended the rightist view in the Supreme Council of National Economy (VSNKh), over which he presided until his death in 1926.

Ever since the Twelfth Party Congress (April 1923) Trotsky had put great emphasis on the need to give priority to industrial development, without which there could be no progress in agriculture. The Scissors Crisis (whose name derived from the way in which the price of manufactured goods got higher and higher, whereas the price of agricultural products remained low, so that the gap between them increased, as if the blades of a pair of scissors were gradually opening) showed, in his view, the weakness of industrial productivity, which was precisely what needed to be most strongly stimulated, even if this required the workers in the meantime to "extent credit to their state, if the state could not immediately pay them their full salary." In addition to the question of how to raise industrial productivity, there was also the fundamental issue of how to finance investments. It fell to Preobrazhenskii, in a work that appeared in 1926, *The New Economy*, to explain the problem which Trotsky had been pointing out since 1923: how one was to organize "primitive socialist accumulation." In a hostile international environment an economically underdeveloped country like Russia could acquire the capital necessary for industrialization only by siphoning off (*perekachka*) capital from the peasant private sector and injecting it into the socialist sector. The peasantry would need to pay for industrialization. This would be brought about by enforcing inequality of the terms of exchange (high prices for industrial goods; low prices for foodstuffs), but also by imposing a high level of taxation which would penalize the middle and more well-off peasants.

For Bukharin the only conceivable outcome of such a policy would be to "kill the goose that laid the golden egg." His view was that it was necessary to give priority to the satisfaction of the peasants' needs and encourage them to produce more; this amounted essentially to betting on the effectiveness of market forces. This was what he meant when, in his famous speech of 17 April 1925, he told the peasants to "enrich themselves without fearing any coercion." To overcome their technological backwardness, Bukharin appealed to the peasants to organize themselves, voluntarily, into cooperatives for production and distribution, which, he said, would be supported by the state. This form of cooperation would lead the peasants toward a socialist economy "at a snail's pace." Finally attaining this goal would, as Lenin predicted in his final writings, take several decades. Nevertheless, it was less dangerous than precipitous industrialization which would cause a brutal break in the relations of the Bolsheviks to the peasants; at this point forced collectivization was not even envisaged.

On this major issue the other main Bolshevik leaders, Stalin, Kamenev and Zinoviev, made a point of not taking a clear position. They did not commit themselves until they were forced to and then the position they took was based on tactical considerations of a political sort. So, until 1924, Zinoviev and Kamenev, allied with Stalin against Trotsky, took the "rightist position," but starting in 1925, when they had allied themselves with Trotsky against Stalin, they shifted to the "leftist" line.

As far as Stalin himself is concerned, he was able to maneuver very deftly so as to pose as a man of the "moderate middle,"[13] until he had firmly acquired power, when he implemented a solution that was more extreme than any envisaged or formulated by the "left": the forcible and accelerated collectivization of the peasantry.

13 Isaac Deutscher, *Stalin* (London: Penguin, 1966), 306.

The Peasantry and Soviet Power Under the NEP

While the Bolshevik leaders were trying to come to terms with the "accursed problem" without being able to arrive at a unitary position, the peasants tried to build up relations of exchange among themselves, to make the most of the fruits of their labor, and to live "far away from the state"; as Michael Confino put it, they tried to live "as if in a functioning peasant utopia."[14] The reports on the "state of rural areas," which were compiled by the political police and have now been published under the editorship of V. P. Danilov,[15] can serve in part as a corrective to the image of a rural life completely cut off from political reality and devoted to trying to implement a conservative and inward-looking "peasant utopia," based exclusively on the immutable round of everyday life in the villages. On the contrary, the picture that emerges is of a peasantry that was very much "playing the game," participating both in the market economy (within the limits of the NEP) and in local elections (within the limits of "soviet democracy"); the peasants were organizing themselves, formulating demands and resisting interventions they felt were unjustified. The peasant world did not have only one weapon in its oppositional struggle: the force of inertia; rather it showed an extraordinary capacity to absorb "external" elements which in reality meant "anything from outside the village." This was the origin of one of the nightmares of the central authorities, a nightmare that they had good reason to fear, namely that the local representatives of soviet power, who were already very thin on the ground (in 1928 there were 20,800 party cells containing only 84,000 active peasants in a country with 540,000 rural districts), would be completely dissolved and absorbed into the peasant milieu.[16] Deep distrust of the urban population and of workers, and also antagonism toward the cities, remained very strong among the peasantry. This antagonism, which had a long history well before 1917, got a new lease on life in the 1920s, when the peasants saw the striking inequality of the terms on which they were forced to exchange with the urban population and the high levels of taxation that were imposed on them. In terms of the price of rye, a scythe cost five times more, in 1925, than it had before the war, even though agricultural yields had declined. The peasants also had the sense of being second-class citizens in relation to the privileged

14 Michael Confino, "Le droit coutumier et l'étude des mentalités paysannes en Russie," in *Sociétés et mentalités collectives en Russie sous l'Ancien Régime* (Paris: Institut d'Études Slaves, 1991), 423–32.

15 Danilov and Berelowitch (eds.), *Sovetskaia derevnia glazami VChK, OGPU, NKVD.*

16 On the process of "degeneration" of Soviet functionaries who came into contact with the peasant world, see Lewin, *Russian Peasants and Soviet Power*, 125–26.

workers, who were perceived as enjoying the protection of "their" party, the "party of the proletariat."[17] They especially complained of being subjected to the arbitrary will of Soviet functionaries who "had come from elsewhere and multiplied like grasshoppers."[18] The peasants did not merely express their discontent; they also began to organize. Their active participation in the elections to rural soviets in 1925 and 1927 was a testimony to this; in these elections a large number of candidates "of no party," who were supported by the peasants, were elected. This success, which had no future and was of merely symbolic significance, brought to the fore again an old peasant demand, originally of social-revolutionary inspiration, which had seen its glory days in 1905–06. This was the demand for "peasant unions." These unions were conceived as something between a trade union and a political party, and were thought by the peasants to be an effective means for defending their interests.

The Breakdown of the Truce (1928–1929)

The peasants, then, were mobilizing and the inhabitants of rural areas reacted very negatively to the "war psychosis" that was orchestrated by the group around Stalin in the summer of 1927: Many peasants heartily wished the Bolsheviks would be defeated because they thought that this would free them from the "communist yoke."[19] Then, even more importantly there was the "grain crisis" which began in the autumn of 1927 when, despite a good harvest, the peasants sold to the state organs less than 5 million tons of cereals, very much less than in previous years. As a result of these events, Stalin and his supporters decided to break the truce with the peasantry. At the beginning of 1928, then, the second act of the confrontation with the peasantry began. "This was different from the first," as Andrea Graziosi very rightly puts it, "in that the initiative was totally with the state; the peasants as a social class could do nothing but

17 The reduction of the working day in factories to seven hours in 1927 generated a wave of discontent among the peasants who had already begun to make fun of workers who, since 1917, enjoyed a working day limited to eight hours.

18 This image appears frequently in the letters and petitions sent by peasants to the central authorities; see A. Livshin (ed.), *Pis'ma vo vlast' 1917–1927* (Moscow: ROSSPEN, 1998). One finds the same motif in comparable documents written in 1905–06 and 1917; see T. Shanin, *Revoliutsiia kak moment istiny* (Moscow: Ves' mir, 1997).

19 Numerous examples are to be found in the reports about attitudes in the countryside during 1927; see Viktor P. Danilov and Aleksei Berelovich (eds.), *Sovetskaia derevnia glazami VChK, OGPU, NKVD*, vol. II, *1923–1927* (Moscow: ROSSPEN, 2000).

react, in an increasingly feeble way, to the war being conducted against them."[20]

By January 1928 the group around Stalin once again had recourse to requisitions and to a whole series of repressive measures. "Plenipotentiaries" – the term itself recalled the era of "war communism" – and detachments of urban communist militants were dispatched to the countryside to search out the hidden "surpluses"; if necessary they used poor peasants as auxiliaries and promised these a share in the "booty." Taxes were increased by a factor of ten in two years on more well-off peasants. These measures had no effect except to exacerbate the crisis. As in 1920, the peasants reacted by reducing the amount of land they brought under cultivation. It took Stalin and his supporters a whole year to overcome resistance within the party to the policy of confrontation with the peasantry. The opposition to collectivization, which Stalin was now advocating more and more openly, was led by Bukharin and Rykov. They thought that even partial collectivization could lead only to a "military-feudal exploitation" of the peasantry, to peasant wars like those of 1919–20, to chaos and to famine. The opposition was finally defeated in 1929. While this struggle between opponents and supporters of the NEP was being played out within the leadership, the country fell further and further into crisis. In February 1929 ration cards, which had disappeared in 1921, were issued in the cities. The harvest of 1929 was the worst it had been during the second half of the 1920s, although the organs of the state succeeded in collecting, by force, 22 percent of it, that is, about twice as much as the peasants had voluntarily put on the market in the previous years. In parallel to this, the number of revolts and other disturbances among the peasantry increased twentyfold: In 1929 the OGPU counted 1,200 "mass demonstrations" in rural areas.

Nonetheless, despite this spectacular rise in peasant unrest, especially in Ukraine and the northern Caucasus, the richest agricultural areas, the authorities never lost control of the situation. By using a better system of obtaining and storing information, a rudimentary card-catalogue system of the "recalcitrants" in each village, the OGPU was able, starting in the autumn of 1929, to initiate a vast operation of preventative arrest: Almost 100,000 people were arrested in the countryside even before the policy of collectivization was officially launched.[21]

20 A. Graziosi, *The Great Soviet Peasant War: Bolsheviks and Peasants, 1917–1933* (Cambridge, MA: Harvard University Press/Ukrainian Research Institute, 1996).

21 On this campaign see the extensive report of the Department of Secret Operations of the OGPU, January 1930, in Danilov and Berelovich (eds.), *Sovetskaia derevnia glazami*, vol. II, 1016–21.

In the autumn of 1929, the groups around Stalin, who was now in complete control of the party, announced the start of a new phase in their program: "mass collectivization." The objectives of the first Five-Year Plan, which was ratified in April 1929 by the Sixteenth Party Conference, were revised significantly upward: Instead of trying to collectivize 20 percent of farms (5 million) by 1931, it was envisaged to collectivize 50 percent (13 million) by the end of 1930. On 31 October 1929 *Pravda* called for "total collectivization" without any limits. A week later, on the twelfth anniversary of the revolution, Stalin published his famous article "The Year of the Great Turning-Point" on page one of *Pravda*. This article was based on a completely erroneous assessment of the situation in that it asserted that "today the middle peasant has turned resolutely toward the kolkhozes."

Forcible Collectivization as an Anti-Peasant War

As Lynne Viola has shown,[22] forcible collectivization of the countryside was much more than just a way of expropriating the peasants and concentrating them in kolkhozes. In a country in which there was a serious rift between the dominant urban world and the dominated countryside, collectivization amounted to a declaration of war against the whole traditional peasant culture. Behind the slogans calling for the "construction of socialism," this was a counterrevolutionary offensive in the true sense of the word, because it attacked the principal revolutionary achievement of the peasantry in 1917 – the appropriation by the peasants of the land from its former owners. The realization of Stalin's plan to construct a modern industrialized state required the forcible extraction of what was actually "tribute" from the peasantry; this was done by means of destroying the market, forcing the peasants into collective farms, and then imposing on them an obligatory levy on harvests and livestock. But for the peasants, joining the hated *kommuny* represented a return to serfdom. In a few years this resulted in what the great Russian historian of the peasantry V. P. Danilov would later characterize as the "destruction of the peasant way of life" (*raskrestianivanie*) for the rural population. This was a genuine anthropological revolution which transformed the small peasant entrepreneur, the owner-occupier of his own farm (*khoziain*), into "the peasant of the kolkhoz," an indolent, lazy layabout, or even tramp, who had lost the taste for working the land and caring for the

22 Lynne Viola, *Peasant Rebels Under Stalin: Collectivization and the Culture of Peasant Resistance* (Oxford: Oxford University Press, 1996).

animals because they did not belong to him. This radical destruction of the peasant's way of life and ethos had consequences that were infinitely more profound than the policy of "de-kulakization" or the "liquidation of the kulaks as a class," which was also inaugurated by the group around Stalin at the same time as compulsory collectivization. "De-kulakization" had as its goal the neutralization of the elites in the villages – the most enterprising peasants, the well-off, the most influential, but also the orthodox priests and "village intellectuals" suspected of social-revolutionary sympathies (*eserovschina*). They were to be prevented from opposing collectivization. Between January and September of 1930 special units of the OGPU arrested 280,000 kulaks "of the first category," which was arbitrarily defined as "activists engaged in counterrevolutionary activities"; actually these were people who had already been in the files of the OGPU for years. After a quick appearance before a *troika* (a special court of the political police) most of these were condemned to forced labor, and so added to the increasing number of prisoners in work camps. In 1931–33 several hundred thousand more peasants were arrested and condemned to forced labor as "kulaks." However, the majority of those who were categorized by the Special Commission of the Politburo in charge of de-kulakization as "kulaks of the second category" ("rich peasants, but not engaged in counterrevolutionary activity") were simply administratively expropriated and deported with their families to inhospitable regions, such as the far north, the Urals, Kazakhstan or Siberia, which they were expected to "colonize."

In the beginning (winter 1930) the authorities were able to involve in the process of de-kulakization a certain number of the village poor, and also some criminal and downwardly mobile elements, who were attracted by the promise of gain and a share in the goods of those who were expropriated. However, village solidarity quickly reasserted itself in the face of pressure to force the peasants into kolkhozes.

The resistance to this offensive by the state power grew: For February 1930 alone the political police registered more than 1,000 disturbances and mass protests. This massive resistance of the peasantry caused Stalin to step back and proclaim a pause in the frenetic pace of collectivization. Officially 13 percent of farms had been collectivized in December 1929; the number reached 20 percent on 1 January 1930; 34.7 percent on 1 February; 58.7 percent on 1 March. These figures, to be sure, were inflated by local authority so they do not mean much; most the kolkhozes that figured in them existed only on paper.

Stalin published a long article on the front page of all Soviet newspapers on 2 March 1930 in which he placed the responsibility for any "excesses" committed during the previous months firmly on local communist authorities, and warned against the "dizziness of success." He also criticized the abuse of "de-kulakization," admitting that it had affected a large number of "middle peasants," and he condemned the "numerous infractions of the principle that entry by peasants into the kolkhozes should be voluntary." However, he did not criticize any of his own decisions and did not call into question the principle of collectivization itself. This tactical retreat did not immediately end the peasant disturbances, which reached their high point in the course of May 1930, for which the OGPU registered 6,500 riots and disturbances in which 1.5 million peasants participated. Although there were a large number of such expressions of discontent, the disturbances now had a different goal and a different character: By condemning the "excesses" of collectivization and authorizing, temporarily, the peasants to leave the kolkhozes (which they did massively, in their millions), the government succeeded in turning the wrath of the peasants against the authorities in their local districts and in limiting the most radical forms of political confrontation. In contrast to what had happened during the civil war, the peasant disturbances of 1930 never led to large-scale uprisings. In 1919–20 the insurgent peasants were almost all armed and organized by politically oriented leaders, SRs, anarchists, even sometimes former Bolsheviks who had broken with the party; in 1930, in contrast, the rioters had no arms, no wider organizational network and no leaders. There were relatively few real insurgencies, that is, armed protests with a clear revolutionary leadership who called for an overthrow of local soviet power by force and had some kind of intention to expand the territory they had liberated. There were only 176 of these among the 13,754 protests recorded during the course of 1930. What protests there were, were restricted in time, lasting for a few weeks at most, and in space, involving only a few districts. The most important revolts were in western Ukraine. There for a month (mid February to mid March) a strategically important region of 50,000 km^2 bordering Poland and Romania escaped from Soviet control. There were also large uprisings, though, in the Cossack regions of the Don and Kuban, and in certain districts of Kazakhstan, Dagestan, Chechnia, Uzbekistan and Azerbaijan which had never been entirely pacified in the 1920s. Essentially peasant resistance in this period was a matter of a few thousand demonstrations, protest marches, riots, improvised public meetings and short-term disturbances which mobilized only a few hundred people each. After the "fever period" of March,[23] peasant agitations remained at a high level in April (2,000 demonstrations) and May (1,400 demonstration), but then declined significantly during the summer months, when the peasants had to work the fields. In 1930 refusal to join a kolkhoz was the main reason for peasant unrest (7,400 incidents among 13,700). The solidarity of the villagers with persecuted kulaks was the second most prominent cause (more than 2,300 incidents). Finally almost 1,500 disturbances were provoked by the anti-religious vandalism of atheist activists who were sent into the villages or by the closure of churches. The most massive expression of the refusal to collectivize was simply flight: The peasants began an exodus to the cities. Between 1930 and 1933 at least 12 million peasants left their villages to seek a "better life" in the cities or in the huge work projects of the first Five-Year Plan.

During these years there was no diminution of the repression. In three years (1930–33) more than 2.2 million kulaks were deported. This required organization worthy of a military campaign; hundreds of rail convoys were needed and tens of thousands of OGPU agents had to be deployed. The first wave of deportation (February–May 1930, 550,000 deportees) suffered from the total absence of any coordination between the deportation itself, organized by the political police, and the accommodation at the destination of those deported. Accommodation was in the hands of overwhelmed local authorities who had in some cases not been informed except at the last minute that deportees were going to arrive. Often this meant that people were deported, and then simply abandoned at their destination. Hundreds of thousands of deportees were simply left to their fate in this way, installed in provisional barracks on railway sidings. Only a minimal proportion of them (that is, of the healthy males) were assigned to any productive work. A large number of those deported, mostly children and the elderly, died in the months that followed their deportation. In this chaotic situation a large number of those deported were able to escape and flee.

For the second wave of deportation, which was the most far-reaching (January–September 1931, 1,250,000 persons), the Politburo put in place a special commission (the "Andreev Commission") which was charged with organizing a "rational way of managing" the deportees (who were called "special displaced people"). This commission transferred to the OGPU the whole of the economic, administrative and organizational management of these "special displaced people."

23 Viola, *Peasant Rebels Under Stalin*, ch. 5.

These people were assigned residence in "special villages" and also sent to work in a certain number of economic combines which had the task of exploiting the natural resources and building the infrastructure in inhospitable regions. When on 1 January 1932 the OGPU carried out a first census of the "special displaced persons" they discovered that they could locate only 1,317,000 of the 1,803,000 persons deported in 1930–31. How many had escaped? How many had died? They estimated that losses were due in about equal measure to death and flight.

In 1932–33, 400,000 more people, mostly kulaks, were deported. The statistics collected by the OGPU register an overall figure of 240,000 deaths among deportees during those two years. In total, between 1930 and 1933 about half a million peasants, or a quarter of the 2.2 million deported, died.[24]

The deportation, or relegation to a labor camp, of the economic and cultural elite of the villages, on the grounds that they were kulaks, but also the various forms of pressure that were brought to bear on peasants who refused to join a kolkhoz (for instance, taxes high enough to cause the peasant to sell his livestock, refusal of the right to use common pasture and forests which were essential to the peasant economy, etc.) finally forced a majority of the peasants to join collectives. The percentage of collectivized farms, which had fallen to 21 percent in June 1930, rose again to the level it had reached on 1 March 1930: 57.5 percent. At the end of 1932, it reached 80 percent and exceeded 90 percent at the end of 1934. There was a record harvest in 1930 (77 million tons) due in large measure to the excellent climactic conditions, and also to the fact that in the spring the sowing had been carried out by peasants most of whom had left kolkhozes that had been "created" during the furious collectivization of the winter of 1929–30, but which existed only on paper. In contrast, the harvests of 1931 and 1932 (67–69 million tons each) were notably worse than the average for the period of the 1920s had been. The "mechanization" of agriculture in the collectives, that is, the use of tractors, which was so vaunted by the regime, could not compensate for the collapse in the number of livestock (down 40 percent in three years) and the brutal drop in the productivity of peasant labor. On the other hand, the percentage of the harvest collected directly by the state continued to rise significantly: 26 percent in 1930, 33 percent in 1931, 28 percent in 1932, 34 percent in 1933, 38 percent in 1934 and 45 percent in 1935. The figure for this last year is

24 The best synthesis of the figures on de-kulakization is that of V. N. Zemskov, *Spetsposelentsy v SSSR, 1930–1960* (Moscow: Nauka, 2003).

proportionally four times larger than the amount of the harvest the peasants put on the market during the years of the NEP. Export of grain was multiplied by a factor of twenty-five, and in 1931 exports amounted to almost 5 million tons. In five years, the state had succeeded in setting up and operating a formidable system of extortion of agricultural products from the peasants. These products were "bought" by the state at derisory prices, which scarcely covered 20 percent of the cost of production. Operating this system required the deployment of exceptionally coercive measures, which contributed greatly to the bureaucratic and repressive character of the regime. The state could announce victory; the peasants cried "famine."

The Heavy Responsibility of the Regime for "Man-Made Famines"

The result of the cycle of policies and events just described (predatory exactions–resistance–repression) were terrible famines that were completely hushed up by the regime. Between 1931 and 1933 tens of millions of people were affected; about 6 million died of starvation. Kazakhstan was the first area touched by famine. It had been the premier livestock raising region of the USSR, but the authorities initiated a brutal policy of collectivization of the livestock of the nomadic and semi-nomadic Kazakhs, imposing such excessive quotas of meat to supply Moscow, Leningrad and the other great industrial centers that the stock of animals dropped by 90 percent in three years. This was coupled with a huge plan of sedentarization. Between 1.2 and 1.4 million people disappeared in a total Kazakh population of less than 4 million. In 1932–33 severe famine struck the regions of the Volga and the central black earth provinces (at least 800,000 dead), Kuban (400,000 dead) and Ukraine (between 3.5 and 3.8 million dead); these were the richest agricultural areas in the country and those that had been most subject to state exactions. As numerous recent studies have shown,[25] in Kuban and Ukraine Stalin intentionally aggravated the famine, starting in the autumn of 1932, in order to break down the resistance of the Ukrainian peasantry, who were largely supported by the local cadres of the Ukrainian Communist Party, the people who were responsible for the kolkhozes, the local soviets, or for the administrative district. Moscow suspected these

25 See the many studies and collections of documents published by the Ukrainian historians S. Kulchitskii, I. Shapavol, V. Vassiliev and R. Pyrih and the work of A. Graziosi.

local communists of being supporters of "Ukrainian nationalism" which was thought to be the principal obstacle to the construction of a centralized, authoritarian Soviet state. For Stalin, the peasants – not just the kulaks but also the peasants in the kolkhozes – were engaged in a vicious "war of attrition" against the state, when they failed to provide their grain quota to the state agencies. The state had to respond to this with a "crushing blow" (*sokrushitelnyi udar*).[26] During three decisive months (end of October 1932 to the end of January 1933), a whole series of measures were taken by Stalin and his two "plenipotentiaries," Molotov and Kaganovitch, who had been sent respectively to Ukraine and to Kuban. The decisions they took aggravated the famine that was to break out during the following months. Some of the measures adopted were: requisition of the last reserves of grain (including seed-grain) from those kolkhozes that had not supplied their quota to the state agencies; punitive confiscations of all reserves of foodstuffs on the kolkhozes (including poultry, small domestic animals and food for immediate consumption); closure of all the shops selling foodstuffs; and blockading of villages (cordons of soldiers on the exit routes, suspension of the sale of rail tickets) in order to prevent the starving from leaving the villages. Famine had become a weapon of war intended to break the last vestiges of peasant resistance. But it also clearly was intended to have a pedagogical effect: It was to demonstrate to the peasants that it was futile to oppose the pitiless power of the state. This is admirably illustrated by the following passage in a letter which Stanislav Kossior, leader of the Ukrainian Communist Party, wrote to Stalin on 15 May 1933, while the famine was raging:

> The comrade who went into the villages in the Kiev region noted with satisfaction that the peasants no longer said "The bread has been confiscated": They recognize that they are to blame because they did not work hard enough . . . Nevertheless, the inadequate preparations for the spring sowing that is now under way show that hunger has not yet born its fruit and has not yet forced a majority of the peasants in the kolkhozes to choose the right path, that of honest labor.[27]

Having defeated the peasants by using the terrible weapon of hunger, the regime granted them two concessions. First, state levies on harvests and

26 This is the expression used by Stalin in his speech of 27 November 1932 before the Plenum of the Central Committee.

27 The complete text of this letter is to be found in Ruslan Pyrikh (ed.), *Golodomor 1932–1933 rokiv v Ukraini. Dokumenti i materiali* (Kiev: Kyievo-Mohylians'ka akademiia, 2007).

animal products were to be assimilated to a tax that could not be revised by local authorities; this measure was supposed to protect the members of the kolkhozes from the arbitrary imposition of new quotas to "fulfill the plan." Also peasants in the kolkhozes were authorized to keep a small farm-patch (less than half a hectare) and to raise animals on a very small scale (one cow and some poultry). This concession was too little to satisfy the kolkhoz peasants, but it was enough to permit them to cover their essential needs and to undermine the very foundations of the system of collectives. At the end of the 1930s, these family plots produced more than 70 percent of the meat and milk and almost 40 percent of the wool in the whole country. The typical kolkhoz family derived half its general income from its plot and virtually all of its monetary income (by selling some of its "surplus" on the free market). This is why the peasant in a kolkhoz neglected work for the collective, which brought him next to nothing (a few quartals of grain a year as payment in kind for days of work in the kolkhoz fields). The member of a kolkhoz felt himself to be doubly victimized: He had been an independent producer but had lost all economic independence, and he was a second-class citizen deprived of rights and subject to discriminatory measures. He was subject to forced labor for the benefit of the state – construction of roads, clearing of forests – and, after the promulgation of the law of 17 March 1933, which prohibited members of a kolkhoz from leaving it without a contract from a future employer which had been duly ratified by the administration, he did not even have freedom of movement. In law the peasant, who had no internal passport, was attached to the kolkhoz as the serf had been attached to the land of his master. Despite all these restrictions, millions of the most enterprising or the most threatened peasants left their kolkhoz without authorization. By doing this they put themselves in an illegal situation, which made them especially vulnerable on the labor market and exposed them to the danger of being arrested at any moment for vagrancy or some other small misdemeanor. Those who remained in the kolkhoz resigned themselves to their fate, made themselves as comfortable as possible on their small plots, which at least gave them a kind of minimal security, worked as little as possible in the collective fields, and retreated into the old relation of distrust which had for centuries characterized the attitude of the Russian peasant toward the external world and the hated state with its bureaucrats, judges and policemen. Thus the state found itself compelled to take direct responsibility for a whole spectrum of activities which peasants, everywhere else and from time immemorial, had been perfectly able to discharge on their own: labor in the field, sowing, harvesting and threshing of grain. Completely deprived of their autonomy and of any possibility of exercising initiative, the kolkhozes were condemned to stagnation. And Soviet agriculture entered a period of debility from which it would never recover.

Bibliographical Essay

Since the end of the 1990s, several important volumes of archival documents on the policy of the Soviet state toward peasants in the period of the civil war, the NEP and the 1930s have been published in Russia by eminent specialists of Soviet peasantry. The two most outstanding series are: V. P. Danilov, R. Manning and L. Viola (eds.), *Tragediia sovetskoi derevni, 1927–1939*, 6 vols. (Moscow: ROSSPEN, 1999–2006), and V. P. Danilov and A. Berelovich (eds.), *Sovetskaia derevnia glazami VChK, OGPU, NKVD, 1918–1939*, 6 vols. (Moscow: ROSSPEN, 1998–2012).

A short, but thought-provoking, essay on the relationship between the Soviet state and peasants during the first two decades of Soviet power is Andrea Graziosi, *The Great Soviet Peasant War* (Cambridge, MA: Harvard University Press/Ukrainian Research Institute, 1996).

On peasants and the Bolshevik state during war communism and the civil war, see V. P. Kondrashin, *Krestianstvo Rossii v grazhdanskoi voine: k voprosu ob istokakh stalinizma* (Moscow: ROSSPEN, 2009); Orlando Figes, *Peasant Russia, Civil War: The Volga Countryside in Revolution* (Oxford: Oxford University Press, 1989); V. P. Danilov and T. Shanin (eds.), *Antonovschina. Dokumenty i materialy* (Tambov: Izd. TIO, 1994); T. Osipova, *Rossiiskoe krest'ianstvo v revoliutsii i grazhdanskoi voine* (Moscow: Streletz, 2001); and, for the specific case of Ukraine, Andrea Graziosi, *Bolsheviki i krestiane na Ukraine, 1918–1919* (Moscow: Airo-XX, 1997).

On peasants and the Soviet state during the NEP, see Moshe Lewin, *La paysannerie et le pouvoir soviétique* (Paris: Mouton, 1966); Sigrid Grosskopf, *L'alliance ouvrière et paysanne en URSS (1921–1928): le problème du blé* (Paris: Éditions de l'EHESS, 1976); Viktor P. Danilov, *Rural Russia under the New Regime* (London: Hutchinson, 1988); and Nicolas Werth, *La vie quotidienne des paysans soviétiques de la Révolution à la collectivisation* (Paris: Hachette, 1984).

On peasants and the Soviet state during the 1930s, see Robert W. Davies, *The Socialist Offensive: The Collectivization of Soviet Agriculture, 1929–1930* (Basingstoke: Macmillan, 1980); Lynne Viola, *Peasant Rebels Under Stalin: Collectivization and the Culture of Peasant Resistance* (Oxford: Oxford University Press, 1996); and Sheila Fitzpatrick, *Stalin's Peasants: Resistance *and Survival in the Russian Village After Collectivization* (Oxford: Oxford University Press, 1994).

On the 1931–33 famine, see Robert Conquest, *Harvest of Sorrow: Soviet Collectivization and the Terror Famine* (Oxford: Oxford University Press, 1986); Robert W. Davies and Stephen G. Wheatcroft, *The Years of Hunger: Soviet Agriculture, 1931–1933* (New York: Palgrave Macmillan, 2004); V. Kondrashin, *Golod 1932–1933 godov: tragediia rossiiskoi derevni* (Moscow: ROSSPEN, 2008); R. Pyrih (ed), *Golodomor 1932–1933 rokiv v Ukraini. Dokumenti i materiali* (Kiev: Kyievo-Mohylians'ka akademiia, 2007); Andrea Graziosi, *Lettres de Kharkov* (Lausanne: Noir et Blanc, 2015); Terry Martin, "The National Interpretation of the 1933 Famine," in *The Affirmative Action Empire: Nations and Nationalism in the Soviet Union, 1923–1939* (Ithaca and London: Cornell University Press, 2001), ch. 7; and Andrea Graziosi, Lubomir A. Hajda and Halyna Hryn (eds.), *After the Holodomor: The Enduring Impact of the Great Famine on Ukraine* (Cambridge, MA: Harvard University Press, 2013). There is an interesting debate between Russian historians (V. Kondrashin, V. P. Danilov, N. Ivnitskii, I. Zelenin) who consider the famines of 1931–33 in Kazakhstan, the Volga region, the north Caucasus and Ukraine as a "tragedy of the Soviet countryside") and Ukrainian historians (S. Kul'chyts'kyi, V. Vasylyev, Y. Shapoval, R. Serbyn, H. Boriak et al.) who single out the famine in Ukraine ("Holodomor") as a genocide perpetrated by the Stalinist regime against the Ukrainian peasants in particular. On this debate, see Andrea Graziosi, "Les famines soviétiques de 1931–1933 et le *Holodomor* ukrainien," *Cahiers du monde russe* 46, 3 (2005), 453–73.

17

Bolshevik Feminism and Gender Agendas of Communism

ANNA KRYLOVA

In Fedor Gladkov's 1924 classic *Cement*, a Red Army soldier, Gleb, returns to his worker settlement near Novorossiysk and finds a dispiriting scene. The factory nearby, the birthplace of the new class of which Gleb is a proud member, stands idle, deserted and pillaged. Local workers are the mirror image of their surroundings: They are demoralized and lead an existence deprived of purpose. The physical and psychological ruin brought upon the Proletarian Republic by the Russian Civil War is difficult enough to stomach. And yet, it extends far beyond the walls of Gleb's beloved factory. It penetrates the intimate microcosm of his "family hearth" and dooms him, for the duration of the novel, to inexorable suffering. The fact that his own wife, Dasha, serves as the main agent of destruction of the familiar gender order makes the blow especially painful.

The young woman who meets Gleb at home is no longer the submissive wife that he once knew. During his absence, she has become a different kind of woman who no longer sees herself as a *baba* – a woman unaware of her individuality, unable to resist "the [sexual] power of her man," and happy to "feel herself deprived of her own will." This "new Dasha," foreign and unapproachable, is a complex case of a woman indeed. A Bolshevik, she works in the women's section of the local party cell and eats at the communal canteen of the Food Commissariat. She has handed their daughter, Niurka, over to a children's home, the institution she supervises. Gone most of the day, she spends her rare moments at home reading August Bebel's *Woman and Socialism*. Longing for Gleb, she is determined to curtail her sexual desire until Gleb recognizes her as a "person" and his "equal." A loving mother, she no longer sees motherhood as her primary calling. Her life is organized around a new set of priorities that enables her to be a woman whose life is of public consequence and no longer overdetermined by maternal instinct and household responsibilities. Even when Niurka dies at the children's home, Dasha, devastated by the loss, does not retreat back to the "hearth" – a plot Gladkov could have easily deployed but did not.[1]

In the first postrevolutionary decade, the language that Gladkov's heroine speaks was the lingua franca of the Soviet state itself while the devastation that she brings into Gleb's life was in full accord with the party-endorsed program of women's emancipation. A condensed image of the epoch, the Dasha character introduces us to basic premises and cardinal agendas of Bolshevik feminism in action. The history of the Soviet encounter with socialist feminism that this chapter writes is not a narrative that scholars versed in Soviet and communist gender history will find necessarily familiar. Drawing on the latest research and critical debate on feminist legacies of communism in and outside the Soviet Union, the story here does not unfold into either of the two habitual linear narratives. One – of the uninterrupted progress of women's liberation – comes to us from Soviet historiography. The other – a product of feminist scholarship outside the Soviet Union – traces the sharp de-radicalization of the Bolshevik agenda in the 1920s and its complete reversal in the midst of the Stalinist industrialization of the 1930s.[2]

This chapter is an experiment in nonlinear historical writing. It does not assign clear-cut shifts and complete reversals to the Soviet state's gender ideologies and policies. On the contrary, the chapter uncovers and traces different institutional lives of Bolshevik feminism and its uneven and contradictory impact on Soviet society and its generations throughout the interwar period. One of the greatest paradoxes explored here is the fact that the construction of state socialism in its 1930s Stalinist-totalitarian variety relied on varied and blatantly contradictory ways of viewing and instituting gender norms and, consequently, enabled varied and contradictory ways of imagining and enacting socialist ideals of womanhood and manhood.

Socialist Feminism

The cluster of feminist aspirations that Gladkov empowered his heroine Dasha with could have come from the first Soviet Code on Marriage, the Family and Guardianship that resolutely wrote the principle of gender equality and the notion of women's independent and self-reliant personhood into law. Passed in October 1918, the Code was the culmination of the first

1 Fedor Gladkov, *Tsement* (Moscow: Zemlia i fabrika, 1928), 11, 19–23, 37–41, 45.

2 Discussed in Anna Krylova, *Soviet Women in Combat: A History of Violence on the Eastern Front* (Cambridge: Cambridge University Press, 2010), 23.

revolutionary year of legislation that granted women an unprecedented package of rights in addition to the right to vote, already conferred by the Provisional Government several months before the Bolshevik seizure of power in October 1917. It eschewed the patriarchal tenets of the old regime by abolishing women's inferior legal status and establishing civil marriage based on individual rights. The previous restrictions on women's right to seek employment and pursue an education without the husband's consent were removed. As one historian put it, the wife's "unlimited obedience" was replaced with the woman's unlimited freedom to study and to work, and to create for herself economic conditions without which freedom either to enter and exit marriage or to become a political subject – a citizen – would be meaningless.[3]

The legislation relied on one of the most radical interpretations of the principle of gender equality. No-grounds divorce was now attainable at the request of either spouse. No special, protective provisions on behalf of women or women with children were introduced. The law presumed that both spouses would be economically self-sufficient and would retain control of their earnings during and after marriage. Either spouse was eligible to get child custody and receive alimony but the assistance was made available only if she or he was disabled or economically disadvantaged. The law strove not only to guarantee maximum freedom to end a marriage but also to reduce the amount of paperwork and time spent on divorce proceedings. It was no longer required that the party not filing for divorce be present. Speaking at the First All-Russia Congress of Working Women a month after the October Code was ratified, V. I. Lenin summed up that the accomplished "abolition of all restrictions on women's rights" had placed the Soviet republic ahead of "all civilized countries, even the most advanced."[4]

The Bolshevik agenda of women's emancipation, however, extended beyond the demands for legal and political equality that powered what historians today call "first-wave feminism" and what *fin de siècle* socialists disparagingly called "bourgeois feminism."[5] In the early years of the revolution, the Bolshevik theoreticians, politicians and public intellectuals, turned into high-powered lawmakers and administrators, strove to implement the

3 Wendy Z. Goldman, *Women, the State and Revolution: Soviet Family Policy and Social Life, 1917–1936* (Cambridge: Cambridge University Press, 1993), 49–57.

4 V. I. Lenin, speech at the First All-Russia Congress of Working Women, *Izvestiia*, 20 Nov. 1918.

5 Nancy F. Cott, *The Grounding of Modern Feminism* (New Haven: Yale University Press, 1987).

most radical version of women's emancipation that the transnational socialist tradition had to offer. They treated the establishment of women's legal equality in marital, educational, employment and political matters as the bare minimum. The larger goal of women's emancipation was to transform, "beyond contemporary imagination" – a favorite figure of speech of Marxist social theory – the social institutions of family and marriage themselves together with prevailing forms of gender relations. The very content of the notions of motherhood and parenthood, love and sex, and, consequently, womanhood and manhood was to undergo a revolutionary re-signification.[6] In the West, these beyond-formal-rights questions would have to wait until after World War II to become mainstream demands and would define "second- and third-wave feminisms."[7]

The Bolsheviks' radical agenda was already detectable in the 1918 Family Code. Its main preoccupations squarely lay not so much with upholding stability and durability of family life under socialism as with ensuring the right of citizens to make and unmake marital arrangements with virtually no questions asked. With its insistence that both women and men were eligible to get child custody, it also strove to revoke the very privileged association of parenthood with motherhood. In the eyes of prominent Bolshevik party and state leaders, social theorists-turned-functionaries, such as Nikolai Bukharin and Leon Trotsky (who need no special introduction); Alexandra Kollontai, commissar of social welfare and, later, head of the Women's Department of the Party Central Committee; Petr Stuchka, the commissar of justice; Nadezhda Krupskaia, Chair of the State Academic Council of the Commissariat of Education; economist Yevgenii Preobrazhenskii; legal theorist and jurist Aleksandr Goikhbarg and many others – this extraordinary legislation was still a regrettable compromise: a temporary solution, not to be around for a long time. Goikhbarg, author of the Code, for example, endorsed his legal creation on condition that it would gradually undermine itself and would pave the road toward a complete suspension, or "withering away" (in Russian, literally, "dying out") of the family and, consequently,

6 Gail Warshofsky Lapidus, *Women in Soviet Society: Equality, Development, and Social Change* (Berkeley: University of California Press, 1978), ch. 2; Richard Stites, *The Women's Liberation Movement in Russia: Feminism, Nihilism and Bolshevism (1860–1930)* (Princeton: Princeton University Press, 1988), ch. 10; Goldman, *Women, the State and Revolution*, 3–13; Elizabeth A. Wood, *The Baba and the Comrade: Gender and Politics in Revolutionary Russia* (Bloomington: Indiana University Press, 1997), ch. 1.

7 Dorothy Sue Cobble, Linda Gordon and Astrid Henry, *Feminism Unfinished: A Short, Surprising History of American Women's Movements* (New York: Liveright Publishing, 2014).

radical transformation of all social institutions and relations constitutive of the marital and parental realms.[8]

No one in a position of administrative or intellectual authority seemed to feel sorry for the family. For over half a century, the philosophical precepts of the international socialist movement had been firmly and – thanks to August Bebel's 1879 unmatched Marxist bestseller *Woman and Socialism* – legendarily predicated on the certainty that the family and all social relations and personality types necessitated by it were historically "contingent." Like any social institution, wrote Bebel, producing one of the most popular Marxist quotations of the nineteenth and twentieth centuries, the family was "subject to continuous transformation and reorganization and, eventually, termination."[9]

The second half of the nineteenth century played a special part in this otherwise abstract Marxist prophecy. The demolition of traditional forms of familial living took place in everyone's plain sight. Welcomed by radical socialists, the process, it was believed, pointed to a new stage of capitalist development. At its center, there stood the woman worker – a formidable social force. Pressed to leave her family by the Moloch of industrial capital which grew more and more dependent on her labor, the woman worker was at once a victim pained by the separation from her family and a new historical agent, gaining consciousness of her triple burden – wife, mother, worker – and joining the male proletariat in its class struggle. In accordance with this historical vision, the woman worker was never meant to go back to the "family hearth," that is, back to her degrading status as man's property, wasting her time in the endless drudgery of household and childrearing responsibilities. Nor was the man worker ever to find himself back in a traditional family setting either. Undermined by industrial capitalism itself, the institution of the family was to be replaced with new, more progressive forms of socialized housework and child care.[10]

The radiant optimism about the imminent demise of the family and the uninhibited flourishing of women's as well as men's individuality in the world of public dining and social upbringing that socialist feminist thinkers professed did not necessarily translate into concrete social policies before 1917. The Social Democratic Party of Germany (SPD), the home-base of such major socialist theorists and organizers as August Bebel himself and Clara

8 Cited in Goldman, *Women, the State and Revolution*, 1.

9 Avgust Bebel, *Zhenshchina i sotsializm* (Petrograd: Sovet rabochikh i krasnoarmeiskikh deputatov, 1919), 212.

10 Ibid., 211–21; Goldman, *Women, the State and Revolution*, 36–38.

Zetkin, the leading spokeswoman for Germany's and the international socialist women's movement, for decades popularized the radical socialist vision while advocating social reforms cleansed of direct challenges to traditional familial arrangements. In her 1896 programmatic speech on the woman question delivered to the SPD National Congress, Zetkin, for example, assured the gathering that "it must certainly not be the task of Socialist propaganda ... to alienate the proletarian woman from her duties as mother and wife," rather to have her "rights as wife and mother restored and permanently secured."[11]

This affirmative language of "restoration" and "permanency" of the woman's role as "wife and mother" was nowhere to be found in the early Bolshevik lingua franca. The language of the emergent Bolshevik party-state establishment was impatient of tradition. All grounding concepts in it – family, wife, mother, marriage, household, parenthood – were on the move either toward demolition and oblivion or a radical transformation. They were also invariably negatively charged. To compare the family with the institutions of "slavery" and "serfdom," to condemn motherhood as a "burden," a "cross" and a "source of [women's] endless disgrace, humiliation, dependence," to deny housework any value and abhor it as the "most unproductive, the most savage and the most arduous work a woman can do" did not sound scandalous but familiar and ordinary. Having factored the imminent "dying out" of the family into their first Family Code, the Bolsheviks communicated effectively their long-term agenda. In their propaganda and grassroots organizational work, they announced the family to be a social institution undergoing an immediate demolition. The lead role in this demolition scenario was assigned to the Soviet state as it entered the four years of the Russian Civil War and tried to counteract its social, economic and psychological rampage.[12]

Meeting during the four-year conflict in November 1918, the First All-Russian Congress of Women Workers and Peasants, where Lenin delivered his best-known speeches on the liberation of women, was thus a wartime

11 Clara Zetkin, "Only in Conjunction with the Proletarian Woman Will Socialism Be Victorious," in Philip S. Foner (ed.), *Clara Zetkin: Selected Writings* (New York: International Publishers, 1984), 81; Kathleen Canning, *Languages of Labor and Gender: Female Factory Work in Germany, 1850–1914* (Ann Arbor: University of Michigan Press, 2002), chs. 4–5.

12 Inessa Armand, "Zadachi rabotnits v sovetskoi Rossii," in *Kommunisticheskaia partiia i organizatsiia rabotnits* (Moscow, 1919), 17–19; V. I. Lenin, speech at the Fourth Moscow City Conference of Non-Party Working Women, *Pravda*, 25 Sep. 1919; A. Kollontai, "Sem'ia i kommunizm," *Kommunistka* 7 (1920), 16–19.

congress. Some of its over 1,000 women delegates came directly from the front. In the name of women's liberation and defense of the revolution the gathering called for the abolition of the family and presented the Bolshevik government with a list of urgent measures to aid the process: communal dining halls, public catering establishments, state-run laundry services, clothes-mending centers, nurseries, kindergartens, children's homes and colonies. Only when freed from the family, party theorists and rank-and-file activists insisted, was the woman worker free to cross traditional gender lines and to enter "all party committees" and trade union organizations, partake in "all councils" of municipal government, and, answering the urgent needs of the republic, become a Red nurse, "join bread-procurement squads, frontline and home-front corps."[13]

Elaborating on the revolutionary feminist rationale behind the list of concrete demands, Alexandra Kollontai, a leading Marxist theorist of the woman question, and the only woman in the first Soviet government – delivered the programmatic speech of the Congress. What would be left of the family, she inquired polemically, if and when its consumption, social insurance, feeding and childrearing functions were completely taken over by the state. She affirmed: "Not much," except for a "spiritual connection" between the spouses, not sufficient to save the family but sufficient to serve as a foundation for a new kind of a marital union. Taking the conversation one step further, Kollontai summarized the thirty years of socialist theory, including her own contribution, on the future of marriage and motherhood in the absence of traditional family life.[14]

In accordance with socialist expectations, marriage was to cease to be a lasting arrangement but to evolve into different forms with various content to fit the individual peculiarities of spouses. Motherhood too was to undergo a transformation of its own, akin to the family and marriage. Often sidestepped, the theory of motherhood formed the cardinal nexus of Bolshevik feminism and constitutes its most original and, to many, unsettling contribution to twentieth-century thought on reorganization of the social concept and practice of womanhood and, consequently, manhood.

Having published her monumental, 600-page *Society and Motherhood* in 1913, Kollontai was perhaps the best-known authority of the period on the "motherhood question." In *Society and Motherhood*, two prevalent ideologies of motherhood found in European welfare legislations were rejected: that of

13 The list of pressing demands was included in the Congress's resolutions, published in *Izvestiia* (20 Nov. 1918).

14 Kollontai, "Sem'ia i kommunizm," 217–20.

an "illness" overdetermining woman's personality and that of a woman's unique "service to society," warranted by her natural predispositions. In this first systematic attempt at formulating a socialist counter-theory, Kollontai posited motherhood as a "social responsibility" *shared* between a woman and society.[15]

In contemporary scholarship, this undoubtedly well-known socialist formula is deprived of much of its historical specificity and theoretical daringness. The *fin de siècle* concept, on the other hand, was a complex and counter-intuitive creature. Contrary to the established rules of feminist critique in gender history today, the concept allowed its authors and users to invoke and discuss the maternal instinct or female physiology without necessarily vindicating an essentialist notion of universal female nature. With its help, it was possible to treat motherhood as a woman's physiological function and, at the same time, as a variable condition, being different things to different women. How was this possible? In the Bolshevik case, the turn-of-the-century debates on sexual difference, human nature and maternal and child welfare that dominated European and Russian anthropological, political, legal and medical journals and the popular press played as much a defining role as classic Marxist tenets on the inevitable death of the family. Undergirding Kollontai's theorization, for example, soon to be tirelessly popularized, was a radical proposition. Not only was "womanhood" bigger than the woman's physiological and social role as a mother but, more specifically, a woman's nature – "nature-given" predispositions – was also not reducible to her maternal calling. Since Bebel, the discovery of what nature had in store for women once they entered en masse the realms of state governance, politics, sciences, arts and the professions had been posed in the language of contemporary social sciences, as an undetermined, experimental question.[16]

By the early 1920s, the corpus of Bolshevik thought on the woman question and the basis for Bolshevik welfare policy, as presented to students at the Sverdlov Communist University, included the following precepts. Motherhood played a significant but "supplementary" role in a life of a woman. Not optional, it was nevertheless shareable, and in need of

15 A. Kollontai, "Vvedenie," in *Obshchestvo i materinstvo,* in *Marksistskii Feminizm. Kollektsiia tekstov A. M. Kollontai* (Tver: Feminist Press-Rossia, 2003), 130–32.

16 Ibid., 136–39; A. Kollontai, "Liubov' i novaia moral'," in A. Kollontai, *Novaia moral' i rabochii klass* (Moscow: Izdatel'stvo Vserossiiskogo tsentral'nogo ispolnitel'nogo komiteta, 1918), 36–47. Bebel's *Woman and Socialism* (XXXV, 218–28, 233) contains an encyclopedia of socialist thinking on physiological, anthropological and medical research on human nature.

committed "statization" (*ogosudarstvovanie*). Motherhood in the life of a socialist woman was demarcated by prenatal and postnatal responsibilities that included giving birth to a healthy baby and taking care of it during the first year. After this period, the workers' state was to take the lead. In this radical vision, even the maternal instinct was not a fixed variable but responsive to societal change. Over time, the instinct was expected to diminish as women and men would reconsider the temporal boundaries and meaning of parenthood.[17]

Early Bolshevik feminist propaganda and educational literature predictably did not presuppose a perfect alignment between traditional maternal qualities and socialist "womanhood," treating the meaning of the "new proletarian woman" as an open-ended question. In the pages of *Kommunistka*, for example, a versatile theoretical and organizational journal edited by Nikolai Bukharin, Alexandra Kollontai and Nadezhda Krupskaia, "the woman-human being" (*zhenshchina-chelovek*) figured as a capacious identity concept. It arched over a multitude of social roles and types, personified by concrete women, previously seen as not belonging together: a "woman-supervisor" of state orphanages and canteens, a "woman Red nurse" and "caretaker of Red Army soldiers," a "woman-soldier" herself, a "woman-militia guard," a "woman-commissar" – all made possible by a reconfiguration of motherhood into a shared social responsibility, no longer claiming the totality of women's nature-given predispositions.[18] An intrinsic part of the larger universe of Bolshevik political culture and propaganda, the diversity of Bolshevik women-types disabled the security of traditional gender oppositions and hierarchies.[19] Given the range of encouraged ways of how to be a woman, Gladkov's Dasha was thus modeled not after the most radical womanhood available in revolutionary and civil war Russia.

The translation of Bolshevik theory into the language of state decrees and regulations took place expeditiously. The legislation on the protection of motherhood, socialized child care and social education preceded the 1918 October Code on Marriage, the Family and Guardianship. People's

17 A. Kollontai, "Revolutsiia byta," in *Marksistskii feminism*, 230–39; Inessa Armand, "Marks i Engels po voprosu sem'i i braka," ibid., 85.

18 "K tretei godovshchine Oktiabrkoi revolutsii," editorial, *Kommunistka* 5 (Oct. 1920); Barbara Evans Clements, *Bolshevik Women* (Cambridge: Cambridge University Press, 1997), ch. 4.

19 On studies foregrounding traditional representations and discourses on womanhood in interwar Russia, see Victoria Bonnell, *Iconography of Power: Soviet Political Posters Under Lenin and Stalin* (Berkeley: University of California Press, 1997); Eliot Borenstein, *Men Without Women: Masculinity and Revolution in Russian Fiction, 1917–1929* (Durham, NC: Duke University Press, 2000).

Commissariats of Social Welfare, Education, Health, Justice and Labor (which, at the time, also housed the Department of Social Security) used the vision of socially shareable motherhood as a guideline in their decrees and proposals on behalf of women and children.

Between December 1917 and February 1918, for example, the Commissariat of Social Welfare, led by Kollontai, ordered the creation of a special Department for the Protection of Mother and Child. True to the Bolshevik feminist vision, the department's work was divided between setting up an institutional network for taking care of women-mothers during their prenatal and postnatal months and organizing state-run children's crèches and homes in order "to lay the basis for social upbringing from the very first days of the child's life." Keeping up the momentum of revolutionary lawmaking, the Commissariat of Education put forward a proposal for a nationwide and free system of "people's kindergartens." A crucial component of this initiative was the organization of special courses for kindergarten teachers which were open, in defiance of traditional gender roles, to both women and men.[20] It was also during the first postrevolutionary years that the Commissariat of Labor passed its complementary decrees for the protection of women-workers who were pregnant and the Commissariat of Health lobbied for the construction of more mothers' homes, crèches and kindergartens.[21] However, the chronic lack of funds in the Workers' Republic whose two most urgent questions between 1917 and 1922 were those of bread and war, warranted compromise.

Compromises and Setbacks

The 1920 Decree of the Commissariats' of Health and Justice that legalized abortion was one of the first public admissions by the Soviet state that what was proclaimed on behalf of women's emancipation had to be amended. Having become the first government in Europe to grant women free medical assistance to terminate unwanted pregnancies, the Soviet government has been long criticized for this piece of legislation. The decree, critics point out correctly, protected women's health against poorly performed underground

20 Goldman, *Women, the State and Revolution*, ch. 2, esp. 61–65; Klara Zetkin, "Sotsial'noe obespechenie materi i rebenka v Rossii," *Kommunistka* 7 (Dec. 1920), 29–30; also Elizabeth Waters, "Modernization of Russian Motherhood, 1917–1936," *Soviet Studies* 44, 1 (1992), 123–35; Frances L. Bernstein, *The Dictatorship of Sex: Lifestyle Advice for the Soviet Masses* (DeKalb: Northern Illinois University Press, 2007).

21 Lapidus, *Women in Soviet Society*, ch. 4, esp. 123–35.

abortions and not the woman and her basic right to control her body. Or, in other words, the Bolsheviks have been reprimanded for disregarding the values that they did not profess to hold. The ideal of motherhood as a shared social responsibility made it exceedingly difficult to posit maternity as a choice and a private matter.[22] The same critique has been directed at every other government in post-World War I Europe, be it a liberal democracy or an emergent totalitarian regime, that neither deemed it thinkable to grant women the right to control their fertility nor legalized abortion. What made the Soviet case different was its radical reconceptualization of what it meant to be a mother and a woman once the two were no longer perfectly aligned. The 1920 legalization of abortion and the rationale behind it did not renege on this radical vision. By acknowledging publicly that the state lacked funds to fulfill its part in mothering Soviet children, the decree restated the ideal of socially shared motherhood for the socialist woman.

Compromises were endemic to the implementation of state policies on behalf of working women from the first days of the revolution. Cautionary advice as to what one could realistically expect from the Soviet state accompanied most postrevolutionary women's congresses and conferences. At the 1919 Moscow Conference of Non-Party Working Women, with over 3,000 women present, Lenin, having started his speech again with his staple points about the "definite legislative revolution" in the sphere of women's rights, moved on to his usual disclaimers about the Soviet republic's limited means to help women realize, in concrete, material terms, those rights. For the time being, the main work of organizing public institutions "that liberate women from their position as household slaves" was to "fall mainly to women" themselves: "We say that the emancipation of the workers must be effected by the workers themselves, and, in exactly the same way," stated Lenin, "the emancipation of working women is a matter for the working women themselves."[23]

Though not the only compromise proposed at the time, this formula ended up becoming a prominent direction in the work of the Women's Party Department – a controversial formation within the party's top-level administration. Established between 1918 and 1919, it was authorized to direct

22 Wendy Z. Goldman, "Women, Abortion, and the State," in Barbara Evans Clements, Barbara Alpern Engel and Christine Worobec (eds.), *Russia's Women: Accommodation, Resistance, Transformation* (Berkeley and Los Angeles: University of California Press, 1991), 243–66.

23 V. I. Lenin, "Zadachi zhenskogo rabochego dvizheniia v sovetskoi Rossii," *Pravda*, 25 Sep. 1919.

ideological, educational, social and mobilizing work among working women and to serve as administrative and de facto lobbying headquarters of the working women's movement. The controversial nature of such a subdivision was not unique to the Bolsheviks. The question of how to factor gender-specific issues into a class-based political agenda had been an Achilles' heel of transnational social democracy, despite its forceful demands for women's emancipation. Special women's structures within the socialist movement seemed to threaten its class unity. On the other hand, hopes to integrate proletarian women into regular party organizations without the help of those structures proved to be unworkable.[24]

The department's original strategy of rescuing women from their demoralizing triple enslavement – family, marriage and motherhood – proposed that special women's sections be organized in local party organizations and include both men and women. According to the department's first leader, Inessa Armand, such sections were to communicate that the "questions of motherhood, childhood, and housework" encompassed male and female worlds.[25] The shattering of tradition was to take place thanks to an innovative and methodically thought-out emancipation program, soon to be known as the women-delegates movement. A proud product of creative brainstorming by the department's coordinating committee, later shared with the Communist Women's International, it outlined concrete steps to accomplish the removal of working class and peasant women from behind the walls of the private sphere.

To accomplish this goal, the department's teams of field organizers helped set up women's sections in local party committees. Women's sections usually announced their presence by organizing meetings with nonparty women and had them elect their delegates. Each delegate represented 25–50 women and, according to the vision, embodied a live link between the party and the masses of working-class and peasant women and housewives. The elected were to agree to participate in three-month political-educational courses. A once-a-week commitment, the courses were combined with practical assignments and internships at local-level governmental bodies. Intended as an initiation into the world of administration, governance and politics, the delegate movement aspired to help women build up their self-confidence in the public sphere, discover their administrative-leadership potential and

24 Wood, *Baba and the Comrade*, ch. 3, esp. 73–80; Evans Clements, *Bolshevik Women*, 204–19.

25 Armand, "Zadachi rabotnits v sovetskoi Rossii," 68.

jumpstart their state and party careers, for which joining the party was a prerequisite. A crucial condition of practical assignments was that women-delegates were to be introduced to "all branches" and "all aspects" of state governance and administration.[26]

The implementation of the vision was, however, hindered not only by the Soviet state's limited resources. The help-yourself recommendation became a staple of the department's agitation which singled out the social services sector of dining, child care, schooling and medical care as women's number one priority. Grassroots resistance and hostility of male workers, local party committees, trade union organizations as well as women-delegates' understandable preference to seek assignments in governmental bodies "closer" to their traditional expertise also played a crucial role.[27]

By the early 1920s, the Women's Department was conflicted as to how to evaluate its work. The statistics of the women-delegates movement were "impressive." Over 70,000 women in twelve provinces had participated in the movement since 1919, which represented over 3 million women. At the same time, the leadership could not hide its disappointment that figured prominently in national and international communist newspapers and journals. The majority of women delegates underwent their internships in local governmental committees that assisted the work of "friendly" commissariats: those of Social Welfare, Education, Labor and Health. They worked as hospital, school and labor inspectors; organized and ran the emergent public sector of communal dining; established crèches, daycare centers and children's colonies; and took courses in nursing. Very few of them worked as factory inspectors or were in positions of authority either in local-level governments, or in trade unions or party cells. The trend was easy to see. The traditional gender division of labor seemed to be sneaking into local Soviet governments, people's commissariats and the so badly needed socialized sector.[28]

The unexpected comeback of what looked like traditional gender roles reconfigured and adjusted to new realities had a sobering effect on the leaders and activist-organizers. It revealed forces of societal inertia and resistance and

26 [A. Kollontai,] *Rabotnitsa i krestian'ka v sovetskoi Rossii* (Moscow: Gos. izd-vo, 1921), 5–6. On the Bolshevik-Soviet project of women's emancipation in Muslim Central Asia, see Douglas Northrop, *Veiled Empire: Gender and Power in Stalinist Central Asia* (Ithaca: Cornell University Press, 2004).

27 Diane P. Koenker, "Men against Women on the Shop Floor in Early Soviet Russia: Gender and Class in the Socialist Workplace," *American Historical Review* 100, 5 (Dec. 1995), 1438–64; Wood, *Baba and the Comrade*, 116–19.

28 *Rabotnitsa i krestian'ka v sovetskoi Rossii*, 7.

called for an adjustment of one's expectations. New strategies were proposed to offset the trend toward rebuilding the familiar division of labor on a national scale in Soviet Russia. Much hope was also placed on the anticipated end of the civil war and more generous allocation of state resources.[29]

In a stroke of historical irony, the department's plans to counterbalance the worrying gender dynamics in the spring of 1921 coincided with the party's preparations to shift toward a mode of economic reconstruction that relied on market mechanisms. The New Economic Policy (NEP) swept away the very foundation from underneath the department's and commissariats' efforts on behalf of working women. Pursuing the goals of reanimation of the agricultural market and industry, the policy brought back the commanding values of a market economy – productivity and profitability, and their side effects – unemployment and drastic curtailing of state funding for public services. The new direction hit working-class women particularly hard.

By the mid 1920s, the civil war social service sector that bore witness as to how much can be accomplished largely by women's labor, with limited state support and in a state of war was either drastically cut or discontinued. Its predominantly female personnel lost their jobs while working women lost the institutional basis of their emancipation. Between 1922 and 1925, for example, the sector lost nearly half of its factory and regional daycare centers. Having increased from 14 in 1917 to 914 by 1922, the number of daycare facilities dropped to 538 in 1925. Even more severe cuts were applied to children's homes where the number declined from 765 to 313 between 1922 and 1925. No longer were children whose parents or relatives were alive accepted into children's homes. The 237 houses for mother and infant – the brainchild of Kollontai's Commissariat of Social Welfare – did not weather the state's cuts well either and were reduced to 80.[30]

The parallel closing down of the vast network of communal dining was another blow to women workers who found themselves at once without a job and without their welfare institutions. The civil war dining halls of Petrograd and Moscow that annually serviced close to 1 million people became a thing of the past, together with various institutions of communal dining that fed more than one-third of the population in forty-nine provinces (4.5 million people).[31]

29 Inessa Armand, "Usloviia polnogo osvobozhdeniia rabotnits i krestianok," *Kommunistka* 3–4 (1920).

30 Goldman, *Women, the State and Revolution*, 126–29.

31 Ibid.

Having found themselves without a job, former welfare workers joined a growing army of unemployed men and women and learned that, in the Russia of the NEP, women were "first fired, and last hired." The Soviet statistics tell a demoralizing story of gender discrimination in the workplace. In the early 1920s, 62 percent of the registered unemployed were women while between 1921 and 1927, female unemployment increased sixfold. The ensuing situation was, strictly speaking, illegal: a result of a willful disregard of the Soviet labor legislation by Soviet managers pursuing the goals of cost accounting and rationalization at the expense of female workers. "Ironically," wrote historian Wendy Goldman, "the more progressive features of Soviet labor legislation, such as paid maternity leave, the ban on nightwork for women, and work restrictions for pregnant and nursing mothers, often prompted managers to fire women and replace them with men. Women were considered more costly to employ." Throughout the decade, no people's commissariat could effectively reverse this perfectly rational grassroots response to new economic imperatives.[32]

The emergent new social contract made the 1918 Family Code now look strikingly detached from economic and social realities of the 1920s. Built on the presumption of women's and men's personal freedom, economic independence and access to welfare networks, the Code was not only premature but harmful, as some of its former advocates began to argue as early as 1923. Having simplified marriage and divorce procedures, the Code made the Soviet Union an absolute champion in divorce granting and divorce itself – a social activity of phenomenal popularity. In the mid 1920s, the Soviet Union had the highest marriage and divorce rate in Europe: 3 times as high as Germany; 3.56 times as high as France; and 26 times that of England and Wales. The Soviet rates were especially high in cities and towns where there was one divorce for every three and a half marriages. But even in the countryside, the divorce rate exceeded that of any European country.[33] Behind the record-making divorce rates, as critics pointed out, there stood a single woman, a mother, unemployed and unlikely to find a job, in need of social assistance and deprived of it.

The plight of the female proletariat in the 1920s generated prolonged public controversy. The many critics proposed solutions that often canceled each other out. The second and last All-Russian Congress of Working Women in 1927, for example, firmly called upon the state to resume its emancipatory social contract and to bring the law and life into accord.

32 Ibid., 110–12, 115. 33 Ibid., 106–08, 228.

Many delegates, administrators, and ground-level activists reminded party leaders about the need to "make a basic revolution in our own families" which still ought to be based on the socialization of household chores and on untying women's hands tangled by motherhood. Another vocal camp of jurists and party and state officials, Trotsky being among the best known, fervently defended the 1918 legislation intuiting in the social chaos and the breakdown of the family a progressive transition toward new forms of marital relations, the women's plight notwithstanding. Yet, other voices in the debate held that a legal reform was necessary. As long as the state was not in the position to fulfill its social role and protect women, the traditional family, they argued, was not optional but a means of social survival.[34]

The 1920s advocates for a legal reform were right: In the absence of the promised state-run sector taking over familial and maternal responsibilities, the return of the family with its distribution, consumption, nurturing and safety functions was an urgent social necessity. In fact, since the early 1920s, the question of reintegrating the family institution into the socialist vision was thus not a question of "if" but of "when." And yet, for the rest of the decade, the basic principles of the 1918 Code continued to inform revisions, amendments and semi-amendments of family and marriage legislation. The Soviet government, even when it became Stalinist, took its time to acknowledge, in the language of law and public discourse, its default on the revolutionary program to free women and men from the family.

A "Complete Retreat"?

The definitive reform of the Soviet family code was finally carried out in the aftermath of another radical, socioeconomic reorganization of the country that made not only women's but also men's wellbeing dependent on the family institution. Launched by the Stalinist government in the late 1920s, the policy of rapid industrialization of the country pointed in the direction away from market mechanisms of the reconstruction period. The new goal was nothing less than the construction of a centralized planned economy and the establishment of a socialist society. To make such ambitious plans come true, the industrial push forward was carried out at an extraordinary pace and an

34 Goldman, *Women, the State and Revolution*, chs. 5–6, esp. 126–31, 250–53; L. Trotsky, "From the Old Family to the New Family," *Pravda*, 13 Jul. 1923; William G. Rosenberg (ed.), *Bolshevik Visions: First Phase of the Cultural Revolution in Soviet Russia* (Ann Arbor: University of Michigan Press, 1990).

extraordinary cost to millions of Soviet citizens, used up in collective farms, labor camps and the expanding industrial sector. Drastic reductions of real wages – by half – constituted a critical variable in the economic spreadsheets of Stalinist industrialization. Now, it took two paychecks – that is, a family – to attain the before-industrialization level of living of one male worker. Women workers and peasants who did enter the labor force in the late 1920s and early 1930s in record numbers could hardly count on achieving economic independence. They joined a mass of chronically underpaid workers for whom the traditional family was not a choice. Factored into the very implementation of Stalinist industrialization, the family was an institution that neither the citizen nor the state could do without.[35]

The legal vindication of the family followed. It took place *post factum* in one of the most notorious legislations of the 1930s – the 1936 decree "On the Protection of Motherhood and Childhood." For the first time in Soviet legal history, the law identified the family as a basic unit of socialist society, made divorce procedures more difficult, and created economic incentives for citizens to stay married (by raising state fees for each additional divorce). Its most ill-famed statute was a ban on abortion which brought into the national and local Soviet press, for the first time, the essentialist discourse on motherhood. Unlike the Bolshevik feminist approach to female biology as variable in women and motherhood as shareable with society, the essentialist rhetoric around the 1936 decree was old and familiar. Using it, journalists created images of women as being made of the same biological material and living lives ruled by the maternal instinct. Women's mothering responsibilities were extended indefinitely. The woman-mother by instinct was now advised to learn not how to let go of her children in the name of social upbringing but how to "combine" her work and family obligations.[36]

In scholarly and popular accounts of modern Russia, the 1936 legislation occupies a special place. For decades it has served historians as the cardinal event – the final nail in the coffin of Bolshevik feminism – around which a story of "complete reversal" of the Bolshevik emancipatory agenda and the return of traditional gender values is built. The remainder of this chapter, however, extends the story of Bolshevik feminism beyond the year 1936.

35 Goldman, *Women, the State and Revolution*, ch. 8, esp. 310–17; Wendy Z. Goldman, *Women at the Gates: Gender and Industry in Stalin's Russia* (Cambridge: Cambridge University Press, 2002).

36 Krylova, *Soviet Women*, 70–71; David L. Hoffmann, "Mothers in the Motherland: Stalinist Pronatalism in its Pan-European Context," *Journal of Social History* 34, 1 (Fall 2000), 35–54.

What happens to the account of the 1936 decree as a "complete reversal" if we expand the scope of our analysis beyond the institutional and social terrains that the early Bolshevik legislation and party initiatives treated as primary sites of state intervention? One such site is arguably at the heart of the socialist ideological project, encompassing those vast institutional terrains of the Soviet school system.

Established by the People's Commissariat of Education during the first month of the revolution, the United Labor Schools of the Soviet Republic constituted chronically underfunded backwaters until the early 1930s. Throughout the 1920s, the school system had been doggedly criticized for being neither "new" nor "labor" but "bourgeois." The situation changed dramatically in the early 1930s when the Soviet school became the largest state-sponsored project of the first half of the twentieth century built on the rejection of traditional gender roles. Better known for its termination of the experimental educational spirit of the earlier decade and promotion of standardized curriculum, classroom discipline and teachers' authority, the Stalinist school of the 1930s is rarely seen as a grand social laboratory where core socialist feminist ideals acquired their most radical institutionalized form.[37] And, yet, a laboratory it was thanks to key figures at the top of the People's Commissariat of Education, including Nadezhda Krupskaia, who had been directly involved with the Women's Department. A direct connection to the Women's Department, its publications and initiatives, was, of course, not a necessary condition for being well versed in the basics of Bolshevik feminism. Its main premises such as the historical contingency and open-endedness of female and male personalities had never left the center of the 1920s public and professional debates. In the institutional language of the 1930s, these premises became building blocks of a thoroughly integrated school system from the math class to the shooting range.

The goals of this integrated education were eloquently spelled out in professional pedagogical journals and teacher manuals as well as in the mainstream press. The integrated school was viewed as a powerful socializing and resocializing tool. Its spaces of shared interaction between boys and girls were believed to both prevent children from learning "bourgeois" and "backward" gender roles from their parents and help them create "new socialist gender relations." Educational theorists and educators asked Soviet

37 Larry E. Holmes, "School and Schooling Under Stalin, 1931–1953," in Ben Eklof, Larry E. Holmes and Vera Kaplan (eds.), *Education Reform in Post-Soviet Russia: Legacies and Prospects* (London: Frank Cass, 2005), 56–101.

teachers not only to cooperate with the project of dismantling the social components of conventional gender stereotypes in school but also to educate parents on how not to recreate "bourgeois" gender roles (via traditional division of domestic chores, for example) at home. In regard to girls, the stated intention was to allow the "hidden," suppressed aspects of female identity to reveal themselves. By definition, the Stalinist school had no home economics to offer for the girls.[38]

The institutionalization of new gender roles took on its most radical form in the sphere of integrated and obligatory paramilitary training which was collaboratively developed by the Ministry of Education, the Young Communist League (Komsomol) and the Ministry of Defense. Together with the rest of 1930s society, the "military-political school program" took the imminence of war with the capitalist West and East for granted. The youngsters made their first practical acquaintance with the military realm at the age of eight by "playing in elemental military games," by learning how to use a gas mask and by shooting arrows. Rifle training joined the curriculum when children turned thirteen. Practical classes in shooting inevitably provoked a competitive attitude as well as effectively designated this most basic military skill as no longer the conventional domain of the male gender alone.[39]

The spaces outside the walls of the Soviet school where young people spent much time preparing for war did not display as coherent a gender policy. Throughout the decade, the Komsomol, for example, insisted, with different degrees of commitment, on including young women in combat-related training on equal footing with young men and, thus, contributing to the re-gendering of the status of the modern citizen-soldier as shared between men and women.[40] The giant world of advanced, specialized paramilitary training administered by the Union of Societies of Assistance to Defense and Aviation-Chemical Construction of the USSR (OSOAVIAKHIM), generously funded by the Stalinist state, was an even more complex universe. With its vast infrastructure of firing ranges, parachute stands and flying schools, the OSOAVIAKHIM was a magnet for those young women and men who wanted to pursue such costly military skills and occupations as parachute jumping, gliding, piloting, and high precision and machine-gun shooting. And yet the organization seemed

38 See I. V. Chuvashev, "Vospitanie shkol'nika v sem'e," *Sovetskaia pedagogika* 25 (Feb. 1939), 40, 55; Krylova, *Soviet Women*, 49–51.

39 "Voenno-politicheskoe vospitanie v 1–10 klassakh," 1936, Russian State Archive of Social-Political History (RGASPI), f. 1M, op. 23, d. 1134, l. 22.

40 On Komsomol gender policies of the 1920s, see Anne E. Gorsuch, "'A Woman Is Not a Man': The Culture of Gender and Generation in Soviet Russia, 1921–1928," *Slavic Review* 55, 3 (Fall 1996), 636–60.

hopelessly inconsistent in its views on women and men and their role in the future war effort. Its gender policy varied from repeated rejections of young women who sought admission, on the one extreme, to focused recruitment and promotion of female youth, on the other. Foreshadowing wartime mobilization policies of young women by the Soviet state, the organization did not operate with one, uniform concept of the woman. [41]

The proliferation of such variable institutional stands on the question of male and female callings in peace and wartime saw young women hurrying to firing ranges, posing with rifles for newspaper cameras and giving interviews after a parachute jump, with parading in military and flying uniforms on the street a common sight in the prewar years. As such, they attested not only to the presence of state-funded opportunities and, in the case of the Soviet educational system, imperatives to try out nonconventional female and male personas but also to the perpetual open-endedness of the very question of what constituted appropriate, socialist womanhood and manhood. Lacking coherency, the educational and paramilitary terrains effected a profound change in the gender appearance of prewar Soviet society and the way it imagined itself in press, film and literature.

Soviet newspapers of the 1930s were busy producing a maze of contradictory representations of women in relation to the upcoming war and their maternal and family obligations. Images of wives waiting for their officer-husbands to come home from missions were joined by images of husbands staying home with children and waiting for the return of women officers and military sport activists. Representations of the future front in the prewar official culture offered other spectacular examples of gender ambiguities. Depictions of combat as a space shared between men and women and, at the same time, as a strictly male territory routinely collided with one another in literature and in film.[42]

In the midst of these contradictions, the Soviet film industry created probably the first cinematic images of the woman soldier for the mass Soviet audience. Anka the machine gunner, depicted in the act of

41 Krylova, *Soviet Women*, 52–60; Melanie Ilic, "Soviet Women and Civil Defense Training in the 1930s," *Minerva Journal of Women and War* 2 (Spring 2008), 100–13; Olga Nikonova, "Soviet Amazons: Women Patriots During Prewar Stalinism," *Minerva Journal of Women and War* 2 (Spring 2008), 84–99.

42 Krylova, *Soviet Women*, 60–70; on uneven representations of gender in Stalinist official culture, see Choi Chatterjee, *Soviet Heroines and Public Identities, 1930–1939* (Pittsburgh: University of Pittsburgh Press, 2000); Rebecca Balmas Neary, "Mothering Socialist Society: The Wife-Activists' Movement and the Soviet Culture of Daily Life, 1934–41," *Russian Review* 58, 3 (July 1999), 396–412.

mechanized destruction of the enemy in the Vasiliev brothers' film *Chapaev* (1936), devoted to the Russian Civil War, became an exceptionally popular icon of female otherness and soldierly calling. Another icon – Vasilisa from Sergei Eisenstein's 1938 *Alexander Nevsky*, a thirteenth-century "type" of a "woman warrior" – incarnates a prehistory of the multiplicity of ways to realize oneself as a woman and to gender military and familial endeavors. In the film, Vasilisa fights on the battlefield against the Teutonic Knights of the Holy Roman Empire both by herself and together with a courageous male warrior, Buslai. Having taken off her civilian dress and put on a chain-mail suit at the beginning of the film, Vasilisa, in the vision of the filmmakers, thus does not simply transition temporarily from a traditional female self to a traditional male self. She does not act like a warrior. Rather, she cannot help herself because she *is* one "by blood." As such, she embodies a reconfigured concept of the woman, a concept in accordance with which the soldierly and the womanly do not share a polarity. The film ends with the Russian people's victory and two weddings and celebrates more than one meaning of womanhood and married family life. One wedding creates a familiar family entity out of a young woman who never picks up a sword and a male warrior. The second wedding brings together Vasilisa and Buslai, the female and male defenders of the Russian land whose attraction develops after their encounter on the battlefield. Merging courage and military competence with heterosexual attractiveness and the potential consequence of married life – motherhood – the character of Vasilisa captures the expansion of the notion of the essential female character, for Vasilisa is a woman-warrior "by blood" – beyond the maternal calling in Soviet mass culture.[43]

The 1936 decree "On the Protection of Motherhood and Childhood," in other words, falls short of representing the full spectrum of the Soviet state's policies and Soviet society's gender ideals created by state-funded mass entertainment before the war. The paradoxes of Stalinist gender politics – the situation when one state policy utilized the platform of traditional gender roles that another state institution worked to overcome – underline the futility of fitting the prewar gender history of the Soviet Union into one coherent narrative. Nor does it appear to be appropriate to split it into two

43 P. Pavlenko and S. M. Eisenstein, "Alexander Nevsky," screenplay submitted to the Cinematographic Committee of the Council of Ministers (Izd. # 2654, 1938), 18, 30, 43, 51, 62–63. On gender dynamics under Soviet state socialism and rethinking the theoretical limits of the gender category in contemporary gender history, see Anna Krylova, "Gender Binary and the Limits of Poststructuralist Method," *Gender and History* 28, 2 (Aug. 2016), 307–23.

disconnected chapters devoted to the years before and after the presumed 1936 divide. In fact, it is precisely the contradictory nature of the gender agendas of the Stalinist regime that defines the prewar decade and explains the multiplicity (not usually expected from a totalitarian regime) of gendered ideals and lives that individual citizens managed to derive from it.

The variety of popular visions of what it meant to be a Soviet woman and mother and their embeddedness in the Bolshevik feminist challenge to traditional gender norms is perhaps best captured in the public discussion of the 1936 Decree draft itself. In flagship national newspapers, the discussion spoke more than one language of gender. It vividly demonstrated that even though the Bolshevik feminist ideal of the family-free society was no longer included among desirable and feasible socialist goals, the Bolshevik envisioning of socialist womanhood as larger than traditional accounts of female physiology and of motherhood as a shareable and prioritizable social duty was not foreclosed. For two months, *Pravda* and *Komsomolskaia Pravda*, for example, published letters that supported and opposed the Decree's most controversial proposal to ban abortion and that presented diametrically opposing views of the Soviet "woman-mother." Essentially framed ideals of women consumed by uncontrollable maternal urges, on the one hand, and views of motherhood as a plannable "state obligation," on the other, coexisted in the press, simultaneously disqualifying women from traditionally male pursuits and explicitly lobbying on behalf of women's aspirations to become engineers, scientists and soldiers.

Judging by the letter writers' backgrounds and aspirations, one could conclude that the Bolshevik feminist insistence that female nature was an open-ended variable, not fitting essentialist stereotypes, and that the role of mother in a woman's life ought to be fulfilled but also confined – was now nurtured by the Soviet school system and by conflict-ridden paramilitary sites. Thanks to these institutional sites, the first postrevolutionary generation did get its own, though abridged, dose of Bolshevik gender education. Even the very notion of the "natural" was an open question for those young women who agreed to be mothers by "civic duty" but claimed to be pilots and officers "by birth."[44]

* * *

What lessons are we to derive from this contradictory Bolshevik-Soviet project of women's emancipation that in all its different incarnations – either in its uncompromising rejection of the family after the revolution or its 1930s grand

44 Krylova, *Soviet Women*, 71–82.

institutionalization of integrated education informed by ideals of nonpolarized gender roles – assigned a preeminent role to the modern state? The inconsistent record of the Bolshevik-Soviet program with its at times breathtaking scale of implementation takes us into the middle of a critical contemporary debate among scholars of twentieth-century socialism. One query that fuels the discussion specifically interrogates the role that the modern state can and did play in the emancipation of women and transformation of gender stereotypes. Gender scholars of Chinese and East European encounters with communism in particular have begun to probe the limitations of the "uncritical Western feminist preference for autonomous women's organizing" by asking "whether advocacy for women's gender interests needs to be linked exclusively to any one organizational form." The a priori suspect role of the modern socialist state looms large in this critique launched on behalf of economically underdeveloped nations. Contrary to well-established Western accounts, these scholars recover what they call "inherently contradictory" histories, not unlike the Soviet case, in which the program of women's emancipation forms a "fundamental component of the overall communist program for rapid modernization" and does not stop at the threshold of rhetorical pronouncements.[45]

In this reconceptualization, the Soviet interwar period offers a unique platform to highlight the complexities and variability of twentieth-century gender agendas of socialist and communist governments. Embedded in the European socialist feminist tradition that was informed as much by Marxist tenets as by *fin de siècle* social sciences, the Bolshevik-Soviet trajectory foregrounds the need to deepen our understanding of its radical conceptual stance on the questions of womanhood, motherhood and human nature before we turn to its practical, state-funded realization. The discovered gender policies – contradictory and inconsistent as they were and defiant of a linear historical narration – can hardly be dismissed as largely inconsequential "lip service." The inherent contradictions notwithstanding, the impact of the Bolshevik feminist agenda on Soviet state institutions, mainstream political culture, mass entertainment and, ultimately, the society as a whole and its postrevolutionary generation was profound.

Throughout the 1930s, neither the Stalinist leadership nor educational and cultural workers attempted to either acknowledge or to resolve the

45 Kristen Ghodsee, "State-Socialist Women's Organizations in Cold War Perspective: Revisiting the Work of Maxine Molyneux," *Aspasia* 10 (2016), 115, 118; Francisca de Haan, "Continuing Cold War Paradigms in the Western Historiography of Transnational Women's Organizations: The Case of the Women's International Democratic Federation," *Women's History Review* 19, 4 (2010), 547–73; Wang Zheng, "'State Feminism'? Gender and Socialist State Formation in Maoist China," *Feminist Studies* 31, 3 (Fall 2005), 519–51.

inconsistencies of state gender policies and promoted gender ideals. No clear-cut, final statements on what the concept of a Soviet socialist woman or mother entailed or what an actual Soviet female teenager was to do in a case of war, for example, were made. No concrete advice on the reorganization of labor within the family, now when the family was back, was offered. How was the new Soviet woman to make sense of new opportunities, even imperatives, to step outside the tradition, on the one hand, and essentialist expectations, on the other? Encompassing traditional essentialism and its rejection, the official borders of the 1930s gender imagination and practice were less maximalist but more conflict-ridden than a decade earlier. The anxieties over the disappearance of familial and familiar gender orders of the early revolutionary years that Gladkov's *Cement* documented were replaced by a maze of contradictory but no longer imperative-for-all possibilities.

The en masse volunteering of young women, often together with young men of their generation, for combat in June 1941 – this crowning event of the prewar years – bears witness to how the first postrevolutionary generation interpreted the contradictory gender scripts of the 1930s as well as to how much power the modern state with its institutional and educational capabilities has to determine the gender order. In its Stalinist-totalitarian form, the Soviet state not only exerted a deep influence on popular understandings of gender differences, it also left a detailed record of how institutional spaces and cultural discourses, organized contrary to conventional gender logic, facilitate popular creative reworking of gender relations, even under the perpetually punitive conditions of civilian and military life in Stalin's Soviet Union. In this regard, the Soviet–German War of 1941–45 can no longer be perceived as a watershed facilitating a disruption in gender norms but as the venue in which the diversification of popular conceptions of appropriate gender roles, already accomplished, was unleashed and made plain.

Bibliographical Essay

For defining contributions to the fields of women's and gender history and the study of Bolshevik agendas of women's liberation, see Gail Warshofsky Lapidus, *Women in Soviet Society: Equality, Development, and Social Change* (Berkeley: University of California Press, 1978), and Wendy Z. Goldman, *Women, the State, and Revolution: Soviet Family Policy and Social Life, 1917–1936* (Cambridge: Cambridge University Press, 1993). For studies encompassing the *longue durée* of the women's movement and women's lives in imperial Russia and the Soviet Union, see Richard Stites, *The Women's Liberation Movement in Russia: Feminism,*

Nihilism and Bolshevism (1860–1930) (Princeton: Princeton University Press, 1988) and Barbara Alpern Engel, *Women in Russia, 1700–2000* (Cambridge: Cambridge University Press, 2004).

The works devoted to prominent figures of the Bolshevik working women's movement include Barbara Evans Clements, *Bolshevik Women* (Cambridge: Cambridge University Press, 1997); Beatrice Farnsworth, *Aleksandra Kollontai: Socialism, Feminism, and the Bolshevik Revolution* (Stanford: Stanford University Press, 1980); and R. C. Elwood, *Inessa Armand: Revolutionary and Feminist* (Cambridge: Cambridge University Press, 1992). Elizabeth A. Wood's *The Baba and the Comrade: Gender and Politics in Revolutionary Russia* (Bloomington: Indiana University Press, 1997) focuses on the conflict-ridden history of the Women's Department of the Secretariat of the Party Central Committee, its leaders and grassroots organizational work. On the Bolshevik-Soviet gender project of women's emancipation in Muslim Central Asia, see Douglas Northrop, *Veiled Empire: Gender and Power in Stalinist Central Asia* (Ithaca: Cornell University Press, 2004).

On ramifications of Bolshevik visions in their compromised, defaulted variations in public policy, popular culture, and the workplace of the 1920s and 1930s, see Anne E. Gorsuch, "'A Woman is Not a Man': The Culture of Gender and Generation in Soviet Russia, 1921–1928," *Slavic Review* 55, 3 (Fall 1996), 636–60; Eric Naiman, *Sex in Public: The Incarnation of Early Soviet Ideology* (Princeton: Princeton University Press, 1997); Victoria Bonnell, *Iconography of Power: Soviet Political Posters under Lenin and Stalin* (Berkeley: University of California Press, 1997); David L. Hoffmann, "Mothers in the Motherland: Stalinist Pronatalism in its Pan-European Context," *Journal of Social History* 34, 1 (Fall 2000), 35–54; Wendy Z. Goldman, *Women at the Gates: Gender and Industry in Stalin's Russia* (Cambridge: Cambridge University Press, 2002); Eliot Borenstein, *Men Without Women: Masculinity and Revolution in Russian Fiction, 1917–1929* (Durham, NC: Duke University Press, 2000); and Frances L. Bernstein, *The Dictatorship of Sex: Lifestyle Advice for the Soviet Masses* (DeKalb: Northern Illinois University Press, 2007).

On the recent scholarship questioning the prevalent historical account about marked de-radicalization of Soviet gender agendas by the mid 1930s, see Anna Krylova, *Soviet Women in Combat: A History of Violence on the Eastern Front* (Cambridge: Cambridge University Press, 2010); also her "Gender Binary and the Limits of Poststructuralist Method," *Gender and History* 28, 2 (2016), 307–23. On variegated representations of gender roles in Stalinist official culture, see Choi Chatterjee, *Soviet Heroines and Public Identities, 1930–1939* (Pittsburgh: University of Pittsburgh Press, 2000), and Rebecca Balmas Neary, "Mothering Socialist Society: The Wife-Activists' Movement and the Soviet Culture of Daily Life, 1934–41," *Russian Review* 58, 3 (1999), 396–412.

18

Communism, Nations and Nationalism

ANDREA GRAZIOSI

Introduction

Communism and nationalism have been seen as opposites. Even the former's supporters maintained that Marxism has not contributed much to the analysis of the latter, not least because it downplayed its importance. Communists and nationalists repeatedly clashed, and the nation, or the national, was repeatedly denied in the name of class, or of the social. Yet simply to counterpose the two is inaccurate, as there were many reciprocal borrowings and hybrids of various kinds, and communism was to play a key role in the twentieth century's national liberation movements.

If nationalism and its martyrs brought the sacred into politics, communists took the phenomenon to an extreme; in 1848 Marx and Engels adapted the liberation discourse created early in the century by German nationalist thinkers; and sixty years later Lenin's party of professional revolutionaries, charged with bringing socialist consciousness to the working class in order to transform it into a conscious proletariat, harked back to Mazzini's *Giovane Italia*, which aimed at bringing the nation into being by infusing its objective preconditions (common language, history, territory, etc.) with life-giving consciousness through revolutionary action.[1]

Above all, in the second half of the nineteenth century the social and the national spontaneously blended, especially in European multiethnic, multilingual and multireligious territories, where "nationalization" (e.g. of the land or of the means of production) coincided with the expulsion of dominant or privileged minorities.

Marxism's theoretical barrenness vis-à-vis nationalism has certainly been a feature of the currents stressing the role of classes in both social analysis and

1 O. Vossler, *Mazzinis politisches Denken und Wollen in den geistigen Strömungen seiner Zeit* (Berlin: Oldenburg, 1927).

political action. Yet the two most preeminent communist leaders, Lenin and Stalin, assigned national struggles a crucial role, and contributed to the understanding of the "national question" by combining the most innovative socialist thinking of the time, such as that of the Irish socialist leader James Connolly, with some of the basic tenets of the classical, continental nationalist tradition. The undervaluation of Marxism's analysis and use of the "national" factor thus derives from incomprehension of Lenin's and Stalin's thought and policies, rather than from reality.

The interpenetration between what must be seen as two aggregations of related phenomena, rather than as two discrete entities, is attested by a number of theories and movements, as well as by scores of socialist states evidently featuring a more or less "national" orientation, and by countless attempts at creating states on the basis of a mix of national and social aspirations. The first, crucial experience was of course the Soviet one: not just the pan-Soviet phenomenon, soon contaminated by Russian great-power chauvinism, but also the many "national socialisms" of the Soviet republics, where in the 1920s socialism was presented, and used, as a tool of national liberation. Their experience contributed much to the international discourse on national liberation outside Europe, which the Communist International (Comintern) started to actively build in that decade, and whose importance Stalin recognized by adding *"and the colonial"* to the title of his *Marxism and the National Question* (1913).

After 1945, with the rise of the socialist bloc, revolution in China and Cuba, decolonization and the emergence of many socialist states, the relationships between communism and nationalism became even closer, and the attempt to establish the primacy of the "international" by means of the socialist camp rapidly collapsed.[2] This is attested by the weight of the national factor in the make-up of the socialist leaderships of many of the new states, China included;[3] by the debates on the "national roads" to socialism; by the clashes between the national interests of the new socialist states; and by the many ways in which the communists of former colonies dealt with the national question before liberation, and nation-building – extending to war against neighboring states – after it.

The relationships between communism and nationalism also became crucial to foreign relations. And if the "Cold War" defined the terms of these relations, as well as the course taken by decolonization, it can be

2 Silvio Pons, *The Global Revolution: A History of International Communism 1917–1991* (Oxford: Oxford University Press, 2014).

3 Lucien Bianco, *La Récidive. Révolution russe, révolution chinoise* (Paris: Gallimard, 2014).

maintained that the latter – that is, the expulsion of former imperial powers, in which the combination of the national and the social played a prominent role – was indeed the defining feature of the postwar decades: so much so that the demise of communism coincided with the end of the great wave of decolonization from which the socialist bloc received much of its energy. Meanwhile, this bloc's rise and decline bred new combinations of nationalism and communism which surfaced during and after the collapse of its members.

Communism and nationalism thus had extremely varied, rapidly evolving and intimate relationships, embodied in countless historical experiences, which proved crucial to internal developments as well as to foreign relations. I will therefore privilege ideas and prototypes, in order to provide the reader with a guide to understanding the scope, plurality, relevance and evolution of the interpenetration of the two phenomena.

Background

The possibility of interpreting history as the product of social conflict, and explaining the latter as the consequence of ethnic/national enmity caused by conquest, was already present in Emmanuel Joseph Sieyès's booklets praising the *Tiers état* and inviting the supposedly Frankish, that is German, nobility to return to the Franconian forests. The theory was systematized thirty years later by Augustin Thierry in his *Lettres sur l'histoire de France* (1820), which presented French history as the product of a struggle between an alien Frankish nobility and a national Gaulish *roture* that culminated in the French Revolution. Social conflict thus rested upon an original ethnic, or national (in the continental European meaning of the term) clash, and could be resolved only by the removal/integration of the alien element.

This vision, popularized by novels like Walter Scott's *Ivanhoe*, incorporated an image of the European continent in which ethnic stratification antedated and explained the social one. A cognate thesis, formalized by Hegel, strengthened this image by surmising that peoples and nations (the borders between the two concepts remained blurred) could be divided into two groups: those which had been able to create a state, and thus had a proper history (since state history was the only relevant one), and those which did not have, or had very soon lost, their state, and were thus also deprived of history (such peoples were known as "small" peoples, independently of their size). This hierarchical vision admitted exceptions, like Poles and Magyars who had lost their states but still had their ruling classes, and middle-of-the-road cases, like Italians and Germans, that produced many statelets but did not have a state capable of defending them.

European intellectuals, therefore, already possessed before 1848 a model of historical explanation based on ethnic and social conflict, and a pyramid-like image of Europe's peoples, with but a few "historical" nations, some of which were felt to be unjustly oppressed and thereby possessing a right to rebuild their own state.

By showing that social conflicts could be independent of ethnic ones, and could make France tremble, 1848 Paris seemed to disprove Thierry, who had maintained that, having reunified the French people, 1789 had laid inner conflicts to rest. It also pushed Marx and Engels to proclaim that all history was a history of class struggle, and the proletariat had no national identity.

Contemporary Central and East European events, however, stressed instead the power of ethnic conflicts as well as their intersection with social ones, so much so that even Marx and Engels called in 1849 to annihilate counterrevolutionary *peoples*, not classes. These peoples were Hegel's peoples "without history" that were betraying the revolution by affirming their right to build their own state at the expense of "historical nations" like Germans, Magyars and Italians. Revolutionaries were thus entitled to take their revenge, and Czechs, Slovaks, Croats and other "barbaric Slavs" (Engels's words) – who refused to finish, as Czechs or Slovaks, in the dustbin of history – were to be destroyed, thus paving the way for their Germanization, Magyarization, etc.[4]

The only Slavic nation whose rights Marx and Engels upheld was Poland. Far from supporting national liberation movements in general, at first the two founders of communism thus opposed those of the "small peoples," whose destiny they saw in terms of assimilation. In 1865 this position was reaffirmed in the *Proclamation on the Polish Question*, endorsed by the First International, which stressed the need "to annihilate the growing influence of Russia . . . by assuring Poland the right of self-determination which belongs to every nation." As Walker Connor has noted, however, the universality of the call was limited by restricting the status of "nation" to Hegel's "historical" peoples.[5]

Things started to change with Marx's, and especially Engels's, involvement in the Irish question. Ireland, which could not be presented as an unjustly

4 Roman Rosdolsky, *Engels and the "Nonhistoric" Peoples: The National Question in the Revolution of 1848* [1934] (Glasgow: Critique, 1986).

5 Walker Connor, *The National Question in Marxist-Leninist Theory and Strategy* (Princeton: Princeton University Press, 1984).

oppressed historical nation, became the prototype of the oppressed peoples in which national and social liberation coincided. Besides, its liberation was seen as a precondition for revolution in Britain since, as Marx wrote, "any nation that oppresses another forges its own chains." In and through Ireland, therefore, communism laid the foundations for its support for national and social liberation movements the world over, a support that was, however, yet to come.

In those same years, a Polish intellectual of Jewish origins and German culture, Ludwig Gumplowicz, was rethinking the interpenetration of the social and the national under the influence of both Thierry and Marx, whose historical materialism he accepted, rejecting at the same time its teleological content. For Gumplowicz, social and national struggles were everlasting, and communism was but an illusion. In his scheme, those struggles started as conflicts among different human groups. Through conquest, however, such groups ceased to be ethnically homogeneous and, via the assimilation of the defeated, grew in size and inner articulation, thus opening the door to social conflicts. The theory, which won many followers and influenced – through Gaetano Mosca – the beginnings of political science, openly raised the question of "assimilation," implicit in Marx's and Engels's analysis of the "small" peoples' destiny. If different groups could be amalgamated, new entities could be born, and peoples and nations could be "built." The term "ethnographic material" then started to be used to refer to illiterate peasant masses which could be manipulated using new, powerful tools – like the draft or compulsory education – in order to either integrate them into existing high cultures, or to make them adhere to new national projects.[6]

Modernization, that is, the combination of industrialization and mass urbanization, was meanwhile proving that the "small" peoples, whom Marx had thought doomed to disappear, instead had a future. The Czechs' revival, accompanied by their conquest of Prague, was particularly momentous: On its basis Karl Kautsky, a native of the city and Marx's and Engels's heir, questioned his teachers' assumptions. Small, peasant peoples were proving their right to life, and social democracy could not ignore their plight, also because their struggles influenced the socialist parties, as proven by the Austrian one's split along national lines.

But if small peoples proved vital, and "historical" nations' minorities could not be assimilated into them, if both were (in Otto Bauer's terms) *active*

6 Ludwig Gumplowicz, *Der Rassenkampf. Soziologische Untersuchungen* (Innsbruck: Wagner'sche Univ. Buchhandlung, 1883).

nationalities, how could the conflicts among them be managed, so as to prevent these conflicts from distorting social ones, thereby endangering the socialist perspective?

The answer was provided by Karl Renner and Otto Bauer, who looked at Jewish self-government in the Habsburg Empire and at the Ottoman millet system. Their solution (nonterritorial national cultural autonomy) was to institute in multinational states national communities provided with rights in the fields of culture, education, etc., which citizens belonging to those nationalities could join independently of their residence. Kautsky, instead, proposed to reorganize the Austro-Hungarian Empire into a federal state composed of language-based units, with federally guaranteed minority rights.[7]

Both solutions required a definition of what a nation or a nationality was, and which were the features that qualified them as such. When discussing these problems, the Second International was confronted with the question of whether non-European "primitive peoples" were indeed such, and as such endowed with the right to become nations, a right few now denied to "barbaric Slavs." The answer was no: "Civilized" peoples alone were endowed with the right. Only the most enlightened socialists (and liberals) maintained that given time, and "development," "primitive peoples" too could gain that status, and therefore aspire to self-determination. Many more supported the idea that civilized nations had the right to build empires, also because imperial spaces alone could guarantee the survival of a socialist system in case the revolution did not triumph everywhere at the same moment, but only in a single, developed country. Georg von Vollmar's "socialism in one country" (which could thrive because of socialism's higher productivity vis-à-vis capitalism) thus became "socialism in one empire." In 1899 even Eduard Bernstein, often criticized because of his liberal leanings, admitted that "it may be desirable for [a socialist Germany] to procure at least part" of the products it needed from colonies that, also in the eyes of many socialists, were to guarantee the country that *Platz an der Sonne* that Britain and France were denying it.[8]

7 Otto Bauer, *The Question of Nationalities and Social Democracy* [1907], ed. E. J. Mimni (Minneapolis: University of Minnesota Press, 2000); T. B. Bottomore and Patrick Goode, *Austro-Marxism* (Oxford: Clarendon Press, 1978); René Gallissot, "Nazione e nazionalità nei dibattiti del movimento operaio," in *Storia del marxismo*, vol. II, *Il marxismo nell'età della Seconda Internazionale* (Turin: Einaudi, 1979), 787–864.

8 Erik van Ree, "'Socialism in One Country' Before Stalin: German Origins," *Journal of Political Ideologies* 15, 2 (2010): 143–59.

This rhetoric penetrated to Italy, where Enrico Corradini gave it a new formulation, which was to influence nationalist and socialist movements the world over. Corradini acknowledged that the new nationalism he proclaimed descended from collectivism, and recognized socialism's birthright and achievements. Socialism's mistake, he added, was the incapacity to see that the division into haves and have-nots which fueled class struggle within each state was duplicated without its borders by that between proletarian, like Italy with her emigrants, and capitalist nations, like France and the British Empire. Before fighting the class struggle within, each people had therefore to unite to fight the international class struggle, that is, war. Obviously, the real "proletarian nations," that is the majority of the oppressed, non-European peoples, escaped Corradini's attention, also because – in line with the Second International – he did not even consider them as such. The link to later, famous "Third World" theories – such as Frantz Fanon's – which read world history as a conflict between Western capitalistic nations and colonial, oppressed peoples, is, however, evident.[9]

In the Central and East European territories disputed by historical nations and "small" peoples, new and different hybrids, appealing to a combination of nationalism and socialism, emerged. They presented themselves as the organs of self-defense of the respective communities, and belonged to the left or the right of the political spectrum according to whether these communities were the oppressed or the oppressing ones. In Bohemia, for instance, the Czechs founded the progressive Czech National Socialist Party, and the Germans their anti-Slav, anti-Semitic Deutsche Arbeiterpartei, later to be renamed German National Socialist Workers' Party. Yet, in spite of fundamental differences, the conditions breeding these hybrids fueled in both cases the possibility of very unpleasant developments, which the Ukrainian socialist Mykhaylo Drahomanov perceptively analyzed, noting that in territories where national, social and religious cleavages coincided, conflicts could escalate and lead all sides to extermination policies.[10]

Connolly, whom Lenin admired, adopted instead a positive view: The countries in which national and social oppression dovetailed, such as Ireland, were those in which the socialist revolution could more easily triumph. In

9 Enrico Corradini, "Socialismo, classi proletarie; Nazionalismo, nazioni proletarie," in *Il nazionalismo italiano* (Florence: Quattrini, 1911); Frantz Fanon, *Les damnés de la terre* (Paris: Maspero, 1961).

10 Antonio Ferrara and Niccolò Pianciola, *L'età delle migrazioni forzate: esodi e deportazioni in Europa, 1853–1953* (Bologna: Il Mulino, 2012); Tomasz Kamusella, *The Politics of Language and Nationalism in Modern Central Europe* (Basingstoke: Palgrave Macmillan, 2009).

1896 he thus founded the Irish Republican Socialist Party, which aimed at fusing the national and the class struggle in order to reach the socialist revolution through the national one.[11]

Such was the climate in which the young Stalin grew up, studying in a seminary in which Russification was crudely enforced. His first political experiences were tied to the Georgian national movement, to whose periodical, *Iveria*, he contributed verses ("Blossom, lovely land, / Exult, country of Georgians. / And you, Georgian, / Gladden your motherland with learning") proving his participation in continental Europe's nineteenth-century nationalist culture, a culture he later abandoned for socialism, but did not forget. As Ronald Suny noted, in the Georgian literary works he read, national and social liberation blurred into each other, and Stalin came into contact with the model of the militant infusing from above consciousness into the people in a nationalist milieu.[12]

Lenin and Stalin as Innovators 1913–1929

In 1903 the Russian Social Democratic Workers' Party declared in favor of self-determination for the empire's nationalities. While Mensheviks later espoused Renner's and Bauer's policies, Bolsheviks stuck to that choice, carrying it to its logical conclusion. In *Marxism and the National Question* Stalin transcended the opposition between socialism and nationalism without compromising the former's supremacy. Defining the nation as "a historically constituted, stable community of people, formed on the basis of a common language, territory, economic life, and psychological make-up manifested in a common culture," a list that – through Bauer – harked back to Italian nationalist theories, Stalin acknowledged the role of noneconomic factors. He also fruitfully combined these ideas with Marxism's evolutionism, tying the forms taken by the national question to different historical stages: National claims were legitimate at a certain stage of development, and revolutionaries had therefore to support them, because, as Lenin wrote, "the struggle [of the masses] against all national oppression, for the sovereignty of the people, or the nation [is] progressive." The door was opened to the rights of all nonhistorical peoples.

In fact, a rare case among Russian revolutionaries, in 1914 Lenin supported Ukraine's national cause, applying to Russia Marx's dictum about the

11 James Connolly, *Collected Works*, 2 vols. (Dublin: New Books, 1987).

12 Ronald G. Suny, "Beyond Psychohistory: The Young Stalin in Georgia," *Slavic Review* 46, 1 (1991), 48–58.

impossibility for a nation oppressing other nations to liberate itself; and in 1916 he mourned Connolly's death in Dublin's Easter Rising, criticizing the Marxists who branded the Irish rebellion as bourgeois. Above all, following Herder's theory of the equality among peoples rather than Marx's hierarchy of nations, in his *Imperialism* (1916) Lenin stated that all the peoples of the worlds, not just European ones, enjoyed the same rights, including that to self-determination.

These positions greatly contributed to the Bolsheviks' victory. In October Lenin seized power by riding two slogans – land to the peasants and national self-determination up to separation (as in the Polish and Finnish cases) – that most Bolshevik leaders disliked because they went against the grain of collective ownership of the means of production and internationalism. He won, however, the favor of the countryside and of the non-Russian nationalities. Even when, in the course of the civil war, the new state's relationships with the latter soured because of Moscow's centralism, many non-Russians continued to prefer the Bolshevik solution over the Whites' "Russia one and indivisible." Besides, with the exception of Central Asia where peasants often were Slavic colonists coveting the land of local nomads, in the imperial peripheries support for the peasants' seizure of the land meant support for the dispossession of previously privileged alien minorities, like Polish-Lithuanian or German nobles. The Bolsheviks' social program thus coincided with national aspirations, winning the sympathies of local peasants and intellectuals.

In Moscow, instead, the new state consolidated its foundations by carrying to new extremes the German war economy model. The Soviet economic system thus developed out of a combination of practical emergencies and nationalist and socialist economic theories, in which the former – from Johann Gottlieb Fichte's *Closed Commercial State* and Friedrich List's *National System of Political Economy* down to German General Staff planners – played a seminal role alongside the works of Marxists like Rudolf Hilferding. It soon presented the traits of an autarchic, closed and almost fully "nationalized" economy, in which state interests trumped the traditional socialist demands for justice.[13]

The 1918 German defeat revived the hopes for an international revolution, which Béla Kun's victory in Hungary, favored by national resentment against the humiliation of the country, seemed to anticipate. The Central Powers'

13 Roman Szporluk, *Communism and Nationalism: Karl Marx Versus Friedrich List* (New York: Oxford University Press, 1988).

collapse opened the door also to the second Bolshevik government in Ukraine. Thinking that the world revolution was at hand, and that the national question had thereby lost its importance, Lenin supported that government's anti-Ukrainian and anti-peasant policies, backed by the Russian-speaking urban population. This fueled a wave of rural rebellions that in the summer of 1919 resulted in the most important Bolshevik defeat of the civil war. When communists reentered Ukraine, Lenin made sure the mistake was not repeated, adopting measures in support of the Ukrainian language and culture that imitated the nationalist ones. The seeds of the NEP indigenization policies were thus planted.

In 1919, the Third Communist International (Comintern) was founded. Its second 1920 Congress adopted the theses "on the national and colonial question" presented by Lenin and M. N. Roy, the former advocating support for national bourgeoisies in their fight for independence, the latter insisting on the revolutionaries' own initiative. A former Bengali nationalist, and the founder of both the Mexican and the Indian Communist Parties, Roy was then placed in charge of the Asian bureau, directing communist policies toward the Asian subjects of European empires. Once more the communists thus proved adept at maneuvering the national question, something that Western socialist parties were unable to do, as the incapacity of the Italian socialists to think *also* in national terms, thus opening the road to fascism, was indicating (a mistake that, also because of Stalin's advice, Togliatti was not to repeat in post-World War II Italy).[14]

In defeated Germany, instead, aggressive groups from both the extreme left and right combined "a commitment to class struggle and total nationalization of the means of production with extreme state chauvinism" under the banner of National Bolshevism. They soon found some Russian imitators, and influenced thinkers like Moeller van den Bruck, who imported Corradini's ideas about proletarian and bourgeois nations into Germany.[15]

The Bolsheviks' victory in the civil war coincided with defeat at Warsaw. Nationalism's capacity to bind social strata together proved superior to the communists' appeal to the Polish proletariat, as Moscow implicitly recognized by adopting for the first time, during the war against Poland, the trinkets of Great Russian nationalism. During the peace negotiations, Lenin and Stalin put the civil war's lessons on the national question to good use,

14 John P. Haithcox, *Communism and Nationalism in India: M. N. Roy and Comintern Policy, 1920–1939* (Princeton: Princeton University Press, 1971).

15 Louis Dupeux, *National bolchevisme. Stratégie communiste et dynamique conservatrice*, 2 vols. (Paris: H. Champion, 1979).

maintaining that "alien" cities (such as Polish and Jewish Wilno or Lwów, and by implication also German Danzig, Italian Trieste, etc.) "belonged" to the countryside surrounding them. It was therefore legitimate to envision a change, linguistic and cultural if not physical, in their make-up, a position that won Moscow the support of many "small" peoples, even though Moscow quickly clarified that the theory did not apply to Russian cities in Ukraine.

In spite of their strict collaboration, it was on the national question that Lenin and Stalin conflicted: In 1922 the latter continued to defend the traditional Bolshevik idea of a Russian Federation reuniting all the Soviet republics. Lenin proposed instead to create a new union without national or geographical connotation (the USSR) formed by language-based republics, including the federal Russian one, enjoying equal rights, and constitutionally preserving their rights to self-determination up to separation. Such a union, Lenin thought (and Stalin later conceded that he had been right), would guarantee a more stable solution to the national question in the former tsarist empire, and could serve as a model for all the oppressed peoples. At the same time, the party would remain a highly centralized institution, controlling the federal state and providing it with a strong unitary skeleton.

Lenin's USSR was thus organized as a set of Chinese boxes, the biggest one devoid of any national connotations, and the smaller ones (from federal republics down to autonomous regions, districts and even villages) defined instead on the basis of language-ethnicity, and guaranteeing special rights to their "titular nationalities." The latitude of these rights greatly varied over the course of Soviet history, but the principle was never questioned, even in the bleakest periods of Stalin's imperial despotism. In the 1920s the creation of these boxes and of their borders, which Stalin personally supervised, generated interesting debates among communist leaders, ethnographers, statisticians and others, during which many of the "national" problems that were to emerge during the Soviet period and after the Soviet collapse came to the fore.[16]

In 1926 these debates led to the identification – based on the 1913 criteria – of approximately 200 peoples (*narodnosti*), reduced to 172 in 1927, and halved in the following decade. At their height, in 1925, Stalin stated that "[it is] beyond doubt that, after all, the peasant question is the basis, the quintessence, of the national question. That explains the fact that the peasantry

16 Francine Hirsch, *Empire of Nations: Ethnographic Knowledge and the Making of the Soviet Union* (Ithaca: Cornell University Press, 2005); Niccolò Pianciola, "Gruppi senza etnicità: alla ricerca delle nazioni in Asia centrale (1917–1924)," *Storica* 15, 43–45 (2009), 257–311.

constitutes the main army of the national movement, that there is no powerful national movement without the peasant army, nor can there be." Without understanding this, he added, it was impossible to understand "the profoundly popular and profoundly revolutionary character of the national movement."[17]

The peasant and the national questions thus defined the NEP. The republics' national communists then launched impressive nation-building programs under the banner of indigenization: alphabets, languages, education systems and cultures went through rapid changes, so much so that national socialist leaders opposed to the Bolshevik regime like Józef Piłsudski and the Georgian Noe Zhordania noted that communists were making "the nations without history progress, and revive." Zhordania, in particular, stressed that Ukraine was "being created under our own eyes." Ukrainian communists also enlisted the support of émigré leaders like the historian Mykhailo Hrushevsky, who returned to Kyiv in 1924 to use the Soviet regime – which he had fought during the civil war – and Lenin's national policies to build Ukraine.[18]

The turn in favor of oppressed peoples also influenced the Soviet cultural debate. Mikhail Pokrovskii read tsarist history as a story of conquest and imperial oppression, while the Georgian linguist Nikolay Marr accused his European colleagues of abetting the oppression of Oriental peoples, and presented Indo-European philology as a pseudo-science conceived to perpetuate the West's dominance. He also applied the theory of class struggle to linguistics, claiming that different linguistic strata corresponded to different social classes, and that all the oppressed classes spoke language varieties that were closer among themselves than they were to the language of their respective ruling classes. Linguistic/ethnic and social stratification thus coincided, in what can be seen as an extreme version of Thierry's theories.[19]

Russian-speakers reacted: By 1925–26 Russian party leaders, intellectuals and urban strata in both non-Russian republics and Moscow were lamenting their belittlement and the disparagement of things Russian. Actually, the drawing of republican borders had favored the Russian republic, which acquired Ukrainian territories that were granted special rights in the field of

17 J. V. Stalin, "Concerning the National Question in Yugoslavia," in J. V. Stalin, *Works*, vol. VII, *1925* (Moscow: Foreign Languages Publishing House, 1954), 69–76.

18 James Mace, *Communism and the Dilemmas of National Liberation: National Communism in Soviet Ukraine, 1918–1933* (Cambridge, MA: Harvard University Press, 1983).

19 Mikhail N. Pokrovskii, *Russia in World History: Selected Essays*, ed. R. Szporluk (Ann Arbor: University of Michigan Press, 1970); Yuri Slezkine, "N. Ia. Marr and the National Origins of Soviet Ethnogenetics," *Slavic Review* 55, 4 (1996), 826–62.

language and education. Yet it is true that the Soviet solution, though allowing for the continuing of Moscow's predominance over the former Russian imperial space, did so by denying Russians what the other nationalities received. For instance, there was no Russian Communist Party, nor a Russian Academy of Science because to have them would have meant to undermine the importance of the central Soviet institutions, which would have become but shadows of their Russian counterparts. On the other hand, the formal Russification of the party or of the academy would have alarmed the non-Russian nationalities whose support Lenin's policies had won.[20]

At the international level, the communist approach to national struggles was marked by the coexistence of the lines that Lenin and Roy discussed in 1920, in their turn distorted by Soviet state interests. In Turkey as in China Moscow supported at first the pro-national bourgeoisie line, granting financial and military aid to Mustafa Kemal and the Kuomintang, and defending their modernization projects, including linguistic ones. However, in spite of the failure of the 1923 revolution in Germany, where Karl Radek in his "Schlageter speech" claimed that "the great majority of the nationalist-minded masses belong not to the camp of the capitalists but to the camp of the workers," an important section of the Comintern continued to stress the importance of a pure communist and worker policy, and considered the alliance with nationalists a betrayal potentially leading to massacres of communists like those of 1927 China.

The Soviet solution to the national question, and Lenin's extension of self-determination to all the peoples of the world, proved in the 1920s extremely appealing to colonial elites, also because of Willi Münzenberg's ability in presenting them, for instance, with his League against Imperialism. Like Zhordania, nationalist and socialist leaders such as Jawaharlal Nehru expressed their admiration for the Soviet model, which also attracted minority (Jewish, Armenian, Greek, etc.) intellectuals from the Middle East and Africa.[21]

The Comintern also proposed solutions for a number of national problems that were to play a significant role in subsequent years, for instance envisaging a "greater Ukraine" built at the expense of Poland, which Stalin was able to create with the Molotov–Ribbentrop Pact and to sanction with the 1945

20 Terry Martin, *An Affirmative Action Empire: Nations and Nationalism in the Soviet Union, 1923–1939* (Ithaca: Cornell University Press, 2001).

21 Sean McMeekin, *The Red Millionaire: A Political Biography of Willi Münzenberg* (New Haven: Yale University Press, 2003); T. Ter Minassian, *Colporteurs du Komintern. L'Union soviétique et les minorités au Moyen-Orient* (Paris: Presses de Sciences Po, 1997).

victory, and a Balkan Federation that constituted the kernel of Tito's plans in 1945–48. Questions such as that of black Americans were also considered: In 1928 the Comintern advanced the slogan of the "right of self-determination for negroes" in those "regions of the South in which compact negro masses are living," and later on called for their "national self-determination."[22]

Though a student of linguistics, Gramsci did not apply to his native Sardinia (whose people and language had been repeatedly oppressed by foreign conquerors) the categories of "dominant" and "subaltern" which he derived from the island's experience (Sardinians called Torino "*la dominante*"). Instead, he projected the category of hegemony, which Gumplowicz and Bauer used to explain the assimilation of "passive" peoples by active ones, to the analysis of Italian and European society and politics.

Stalinism and the National Question 1929–1953

Stalin's 1929 revolution from above caused a sharp turnabout also in national policies. Forced collectivization and industrialization required a stronger center, and this trend was reinforced by Stalin's perception of the unpopularity of his moves, which was especially strong in Ukraine, whose borders Stalin judged particularly dangerous, whose grain Moscow needed, whose peasants deeply resented collectivization and where national communism was deeply rooted. In 1930 repression struck the republics' intelligentsia. The Russian intelligentsia was not spared, but Ukrainian intellectuals were charged with nationalism, a clear signal that stricter limits were being imposed upon indigenization.

This turn disappointed Republican leaderships, especially in Ukraine, since at the beginning they had supported Stalin because they hoped that rapid industrialization and urbanization would allow them to conquer their "alien" cities. Their disappointment was compounded by Stalin's 1931 appropriation of Russian nationalist rhetoric to stem the crisis his policies had provoked, and by the fierceness of the confrontation in the countryside involving state peasants and nomads.

Tragedy struck first in Kazakhstan, where in 1931 Moscow's decision to use local herds to feed Slavic cities ruined an indigenous society already weakened by repeated assaults, precipitating a famine that was to wipe out one-third of the local population and to uproot the traditional Kazakh way of life.

22 Mark Solomon, *The Cry Was Unity: Communists and African Americans, 1917–1936* (Jackson: University Press of Mississippi, 1998).

In Ukraine, the confrontation between state and villages grew, and in the spring of 1932 local famines appeared. Ukrainian leaders questioned Moscow's policies and asked for help, but were reminded that state needs came first. In the fall, after Stalin convinced himself that there was a risk of "losing Ukraine," whose party he deemed penetrated by nationalism, a decision was taken to use hunger to force peasants to swallow collectivization, and to simultaneously reverse indigenization policies, arresting thousands of its cadres and intellectuals, and making the alphabet and the lexicon closer to the Russian one.[23]

As Naimark noted, events in Kazakhstan and Ukraine, to which the deportation of the peoples accused of abetting Germany, like Chechens and Tatars, in 1943–44 has to be added, raise the question of the presence of genocide within the communist experience. Whatever the answer, Stalin derived from the theory and practice of nation-building, which he promoted before 1929, the possibility of reversing that process, thus implementing nation-deformation, if not nation-destruction.[24]

The confrontation with national communism, and Stalin's growing perception of national origins as a security concern (in 1934–36 border areas were cleansed accordingly), is the background of the rehabilitation of Great Russian nationalism and of the tsarist past. In 1935 Russians were declared to be the elder brother in the Soviet fraternity of peoples, while the tsars' state-building activities started to be praised. Yet, especially in the north and in the east, nation-building policies were still enforced, even though it was made clear that local cultures had to be relegated to folklore, and that modernity, and the world, could be reached only through Russia and Moscow.

On the international level, the decision to concentrate on internal socialist state-building was accompanied by ultra-leftist policies, which favored Hitler's rise to power. The Comintern's role was marginalized, and its apparatus was even used as a tool of de facto imperial administration in Mongolia.[25] After 1933, the threat posed by Hitler, and by Japan, pushed

23 Niccolò Pianciola, *Stalinismo di frontiera. Colonizzazione agricola, sterminio dei nomadi e costruzione statale in Asia centrale, 1905–1936* (Rome: Viella, 2009); Andrea Graziosi, "The Uses of Hunger: Stalin's Solution of the Peasant and the National Questions in Soviet Ukraine, 1932 to 1933," in Declan Cullan, Lubomyr Luciuk and Andrew G. Newby (eds.), *Famines in European Economic History: The Last Great European Famines Reconsidered* (London: Routledge, 2015), 223–60.

24 Norman N. Naimark, *Stalin's Genocides* (Princeton: Princeton University Press, 2010).

25 Irina Y. Morozova, *The Comintern and Revolution in Mongolia* (Cambridge: White Horse, 2002).

Moscow to embrace a strategy of collaboration with the "progressive forces." The Popular Fronts Against Fascism and War, launched by Georgi Dimitrov in 1935, appealed to *peoples* in almost their entirety, and pushed communists, especially but not solely in France, to deal with the national problems and realities. At the same time, anti-fascism became the tool of a new internationalism, which found in the Spanish Civil War its first testing ground.

That war, which was seen as the prelude to a new European conflict, together with the notion of "fifth columns," heightened Stalin's perception of national/ethnic origins as a security risk. The "mass operations" that constituted the core of the 1937–38 Great Terror were therefore conducted also along national lines: Hundreds of thousands of people with the "wrong" ethnic backgrounds were shot or deported. Ethnic Koreans, for example, were forcibly moved to Central Asia in order to secure the border with Manchuria.[26]

Ethnic-based persecutions strengthened Soviet isolationism as well as the resort to Great Russian chauvinism as a legitimizing tool, also under the influence of the success of nationalist ideologies in Europe. Yet it was not simply a "great retreat" to traditional conceptions. In 1939 Stalin again proved his skill in the use of the national question by drawing the lines separating the Soviet and the German spheres of influence in the Molotov–Ribbentrop Pact. As Curzon had done in 1919, he followed a language/nationality criterion, and presented Soviet annexations as the liberation of Polish-oppressed Belorussian and Ukrainian territories (the new borders, solidified after 1944 by population exchanges, are still in existence today). In the same spirit, Stalin gave Vilnius to the Lithuanians, while at Katyn he reimplemented nation-unbuilding practices via the liquidation of the Polish elite.[27]

In May 1943 Stalin ordered the dissolution of the Comintern, granting more room to national considerations in the conduct of communist parties, as witnessed by the shift from popular to national fronts. Above all, the war pushed Stalin to reconsider the relative weight of the national and the social factors in history and politics. His belief in the stability of "national characters" was strengthened, and this contributed to determining the policies adopted toward this or that people: While Russians and their virtues were exalted, as in the famous 1945 toast, and Germans were appreciated, other

26 Terry Martin, "The Origins of Soviet Ethnic Cleansing," *Journal of Modern History* 70, 4 (1998), 813–61.

27 Jan T. Gross, *Revolution from Abroad: The Soviet Conquest of Poland's Western Ukraine and Western Belorussia* (Princeton: Princeton University Press, 1988).

peoples were considered to be treacherous, or unfit for socialism, and were thus punished, as Engels proposed to do in 1849.[28]

The resort to national considerations was also evident in the support Stalin gave to the extreme nationalist policies implemented by the new East European popular democracies. Poland and Czechoslovakia were authorized to forcibly deport German minorities, and Tito's anti-Italian ambitions were encouraged. Socialism thus fulfilled many of these countries' nationalistic aspirations for ethnolinguistic homogeneity, but for Romania, where Stalin supported the autonomy of Hungarians in Transylvania.[29]

In Soviet-annexed territories Ukrainians received an ethnically cleansed L'viv, yet communists and nationalist organizations ferociously fought each other, reviving the two ideologies' confrontational rhetoric. Events in European colonial empires, however, were fostering a new, powerful wave of hybridization, to which Moscow was not quick to react because World War II had fixed Stalin's eyes on Europe, a move sanctioned by the Cold War, the Marshall Plan, the founding of a new communist international organization, the Cominform, in fact limited to Europe, and the creation of the socialist bloc.

In 1948 the break with Tito, who tried to implement in his favor the Comintern's program for the Balkans, reinforced this trend, showing that the Cold War often contextualized conflicts that had their own causes, rather than provoking them, and that disputes within the socialist bloc could acquire state / national overtones.[30]

This was the case also without Europe, where the most important developments were taking place: Here the Cold War did provide the framework for decolonization, but it was the latter that shaped the world's future, by coupling socialism and nationalism in new, unexpected ways. India's independence and socialist choice in 1947, and the 1949 Revolution in China, led by a communist party inspired by national ambitions tinged with social radicalism, were but the two most glaring examples. Yet Stalin dismissed

28 Erik van Ree, "Heroes and Merchants: Stalin's Understanding of National Character," *Kritika* 8, 1 (2007), 41–65.

29 Norman M. Naimark and Leonid Gibianskii (eds.), *The Establishment of Communist Regimes in Eastern Europe, 1944–1949* (Boulder: Westview, 1997); Philipp Ther and Ana Siljak (eds.), *Redrawing Nations: Ethnic Cleansing in East-Central Europe, 1944–1948* (Lanham, MD: Rowman & Littlefield, 2001); Hugo Service, *Germans to Poles: Communism, Nationalism and Ethnic Cleansing after the Second World War* (Cambridge: Cambridge University Press, 2013).

30 G. M. Adibekov, *Kominform i poslevoennaia Evropa, 1947–1956* (Moscow: Rossiia molodaia, 1994); L. Ia. Gibianskii, *Sovetskii soiuz i novaia Yugoslaviia, 1941–1947 gg.* (Moscow: Nauka, 1987); Joze Pirjevec, *Tito in Tovariši* (Ljubljana: Skupina Mladinska knjiga, 2011).

Gandhi, Nehru, Nasser and other Third World leaders as American agents, helping Washington realize its plan to replace the UK as the world's leading imperial power.

In *Marxism and Problems of Linguistics* (1950) Stalin maintained that languages and nations were historical organisms lasting longer and thus more vital than social classes. He also inspired an anti-cosmopolitanism campaign, with strong anti-Jewish overtones, which extolled the Russian genius: Tsarist expansion was now presented as progressive, revolts against it as reactionary, and the reunification of peoples under Moscow as positive. Given the multinational nature of the USSR, however, Russian nationalism could not completely replace the Soviet official discourse on nationalities. Yet a new variant of the former coalesced, reuniting segments of the party, of the new Orthodox Church and of the new imperial bureaucracies: At its core stood Russian pride, Stalin's cult and the cult of force, hierarchy and the state that went with it. A new, aggressive hybrid between communism and nationalism, in the guise of Stalinism and Russian chauvinism, was thus born.[31]

The USSR and Communism Between the Cold War and Decolonization 1953–1968

After Stalin's death, Russian nationalism's hold upon the country relaxed. Lavrentii Beria accommodated other nationalities, and the trend was slowed down, but not arrested, by his liquidation: Republican leaderships' powers grew until 1957, while "punished peoples" profited from de-Stalinization to reacquire at least part of their rights. At first, therefore, Khrushchev's promotion of the concept of "Soviet people" as a nonethnic entity associated with progress and optimism did not violate the interests of the non-Russian nationalities.

This rhetoric reinforced the appeal of the Soviet model, already strengthened by victory and the country's capacity to emerge in the international arena, "solving" at the same time the national and the modernization questions. Third World elites in search for a solution to their new countries' problems thus turned to Moscow, ignoring the Soviet model's defects.

Moscow, however, was not ready. Late Stalinism's European focus combined with the crisis of Lenin's (and Stalin's) revolutionary theory – which tied revolution to a war that the hydrogen bomb had made impossible – in

31 David Brandenberger, *National Bolshevism: Stalinist Mass Culture and the Formation of Modern Russian National Identity, 1931–1956* (Cambridge, MA: Harvard University Press, 2002).

paralyzing Soviet initiative. Slowly, however, the pieces for the reconfiguration of a new theory, and thus of a new foreign policy, came together. Decolonization, and therefore the national question, played a crucial role in both. After condemning Georgy Malenkov's reinterpretation of "peaceful coexistence," Khrushchev appropriated the term, and tied it to decolonization, of whose importance he grew aware. The USSR was to coexist with the West, and at the same time protect – also militarily – national liberation struggles and the new states coming out of them. This way the world's equilibrium would switch in favor of socialism, to which an isolated West was to concede defeat.

This concept fully matured in the early 1960s, but its seeds were present in Khrushchev's speeches at the Twentieth Party Congress of 1956, in which the support for national liberation struggles went hand in hand with a reevaluation of the "national roads" to socialism. The benefits Moscow derived from the new international situation were already evident in the summer of that year, when the Third World's appreciation of Moscow's defense of Nasser limited the damages of the Hungarian crisis. Four years later, the UN Assembly – until then under Western control – started to swing in favor of the USSR, thanks to the votes of the new countries entering it.

Those years' great expectations, of which Sputnik was the symbol, fed leftist turns in both China – where they were embodied in the Great Leap Forward – and the USSR. Here Khrushchev sponsored anti-national policies in the fields of education, language and religion and at the Twenty-Second Party Congress of 1962 promised to build communism within twenty years, claiming that in the USSR a new "historical community" of peoples, the *sovetskii narod*, was born. The traits supposedly binding it echoed Stalin's 1913 list: a common homeland, the same economic foundation and social structure, Marxist-Leninist ideology, and the ideal and psychological affinity expressed in the shared aim of communism. The lack of a common language was to be remedied through a new push for Russification.

De-Stalinization and the Great Leap Forward's failure antagonized Sino-Soviet relationships, precipitating the 1960 split and showing once more to Moscow the dangers of the national roads to socialism.[32] The Chinese catastrophe was compounded in 1961 by the reluctant decision to build the Berlin Wall, thus implicitly admitting the failure of the socialist model, which only three years previously seemed triumphant. This while in Eastern

32 Lorenz Luthi, *The Sino-Soviet Split: Cold War in the Communist World* (Princeton: Princeton University Press, 2008).

Europe several varieties of national socialisms were developing, from the pro-Chinese Albanian and the nationalistic Polish and Romanian ones of Enver Hoxha, Władysław Gomułka (who had carried out the Polonization of former German territories after the war) and Nicolae Ceaușescu, to the later "human" Czechoslovak kind of Alexander Dubček. If Kim Il Sung's North Korea and other regimes are considered, it may be surmised that by the 1960s most socialist countries were in fact "national communisms," to use Zbigniew Brzezinski's 1962 definition: Everywhere communist leaders were forced to come to terms with state needs, including ideological ones, and found in nationalism a powerful tool in the furthering of their aims.

Peter Zwick proposed to group these national communisms into two categories: on the one hand those which developed in countries that tried to gain a certain independence from Moscow, and inspired Marxist national liberation movements; on the other, the communist chauvinisms that developed in the USSR or in China, but also in Vietnam or in the Yugoslavian republics. Some belonged to both categories, that is, they searched for autonomy but oppressed their own minorities; and in a way, the two varieties corresponded to the two national socialisms, that from below and that from above, that developed in nineteenth-century Europe (for instance in Ukraine and in Germany), the difference being that in the twentieth century they controlled a state.[33]

In 1962, Khrushchev's reaction to the Cuban Missile Crisis pushed Cuba, a prototype of "Third World" socialism with strong national undercurrents, to follow its own foreign policy, based upon support for guerrilla insurrections often predicated upon the union of social and national demands.[34] Many ended tragically, as did the 1965 pro-communist coup attempt in Indonesia. The catastrophe that followed seemed to put a stop to the energy communism derived from national liberation struggles. Yet the war in Vietnam soon proved that that season was not over.

Toward the End?

The post-1964 Soviet leadership dealt with the national question in a spirit of continuity and search for stability. Brezhnev too used the "Soviet people" rhetoric, yet he was careful to stress that this did not mean that national

33 Peter Zwick, *National Communism* (Boulder: Westview Press, 1983).

34 Timothy P. Wickham-Crowley, *Guerrillas and Revolution in Latin America: A Comparative Study of Insurgents and Regimes since 1956* (Princeton: Princeton University Press, 1992).

differences were to disappear: that a people was a creature composed of groups that not only preserved their features, but made them flourish, rather than the product of a fusion. The relaxing of ethnic tensions and the increase in interethnic marriages indicated these policies' effectiveness. They hid, however, a determined pressure for Russification that peaked in the Soviet western republics, and of which Brezhnev himself, a Ukrainian turned into a Russian, was the symbol. Leaders opposing it, like Petro Shelest in Ukraine, were dismissed, while the role of Russian in primary schools was strengthened, an implicit admission that the main players in the building of a national community were to be found in language and culture, rather than in class or ideology.

The provincialism of national, non-Russian cultures was also reinforced. At the same time, however, Brezhnev's decision to respect, as far as possible, local cadres, combined with the ethnic quota system operating in the republics in facilitating the consolidation of power networks that formed as many embryos of possible nation-building activities. In the prevailing conditions of systemic degradation, localist attitudes permeating an empty socialist container thus substituted for the expected replacement of national form by socialist content. Their carriers often were Russified, subservient leaderships, ready, however, to aggressively defend their grip on the republics, their different lifestyles and their shady behaviors.[35]

In the center, the alliance between parts of the Soviet leadership and Russian chauvinism, which had been for a while marginalized, gained new ground, in spite of the hostility of the remaining Marxist cadres. It had to confront different readings of Russian interests, like those of the pro-Western intellectual milieu, or of that faction of Russian nationalism that opposed any accommodation with the regime. Aleksandr Solzhenitsyn invited the Soviet leadership to replace Marxism-Leninism with nationalism, and resisted the "single stream" interpretation of history developed by the supporters of the alliance between the regime and Russian chauvinism. In this interpretation, which was to acquire an almost official status in Putin's Russia, all the state-building, imperial activities of Russia's rulers were accepted as positive, from Peter the Great to Stalin, whose Gulag Solzhenitsyn was instead denouncing. Events like the new wave of anti-Semitism, tied to Jewish emigration, and the growing influence of national feelings among Ukrainian, Baltic and Tatar

35 Victor Zaslavsky and Robert Brym, *Soviet-Jewish Emigration and Soviet Nationality Policy* (New York: St. Martin's Press, 1983); Yuri Slezkine, "The USSR as a Communal Apartment, or How a Socialist State Promoted Ethnic Particularism," *Slavic Review* 53, 2 (1994), 414–52.

dissidents, accelerated the trend toward the fusion of Soviet and Russian chauvinistic ideas, indicating that the most important, and most open national question was in fact the Russian one.[36]

In the Third World, after the crisis of the mid 1960s, a new generation of national liberation movements' Marxist leaderships expanded the boundaries of the socialist system in Indochina, Latin America and, above all, Africa, where the first European empire, the Portuguese one, was the last to collapse. The mid 1970s triumphs deluded Moscow into believing that the strategy of combining coexistence with capitalistic countries and aggressive support for national liberation struggles had allowed the socialist bloc to win the Cold War.[37]

That strategy was, however, leading to a new confrontation with the West, in conditions of weakness signaled by the social and economic misfortunes all socialist countries were going through. The reluctant invasion of Afghanistan, to save one of those Marxist leaderships, was its last product. But already two years previously, Khomeini's victory in Iran, and the massacre of local communists who had hoped to control the revolution, indicated the crisis of the communist capacity to influence revolutions in a Third World that was itself disappearing. Meanwhile, the completion of decolonization deprived communism of a precious support, leaving it to its own devices.

In the Soviet Union, the 1980s were marked by disaffection toward both the external sphere of influence and the internal empire. The Russian urban population, and part of the Soviet elite, convinced themselves that support for weak regimes that proved demanding and difficult to handle was not in Russia's interest; and the same belief started to develop also in relation to Central Asia and Transcaucasia. These feelings played a key role in the final convulsions of the Soviet state: Gorbachev could barely stand many of the socialist countries' leaders, and Yeltsin's Russia supported national movements within the USSR. In the final month of 1991 his government openly debated whether Russia should follow the British, or the French path, that is, relinquish its empire or fight for it, and adopted the former solution.

At the same time, however, from within the nationalist groups that had opted for the alliance with the Soviet system were developing new, and

36 Yitzhak Brudny, *Reinventing Russia: Russian Nationalism and the Soviet State, 1953–1991* (Cambridge, MA: Harvard University Press, 2000); Nikolai Mitrokhin, *Russkaia partiia. Dvizhenie russkikh natsionalistov v SSSR, 1953–1985* (Moscow: Novoe literaturnoe obozrenie, 2003).

37 Odd Arne Westad, *The Global Cold War: Third World Interventions and the Making of Our Times* (New York: Cambridge University Press, 2005).

aggressive national socialist hybrids, including national bolshevism. In Russia these movements were at first relegated to the fringes of the political system, but in Yugoslavia they influenced an important part of the Serbian and Croatian political and intellectual establishments already in the final years of the federation.[38]

In other countries too, the collapse of socialist regimes was accompanied by the switch of many communist cadres to a variety of nationalisms, with some of them growing into nation-builders. The interpenetration between communist leadership and nationalism thus developed into a new phenomenon, which in the USSR and in Yugoslavia derived from the need to survive the collapse of the federal state, but also and more generally from communism's ideological failure. Since at least the late 1960s, often crude nationalism has in fact proved the easiest substitute available on the ideological market for culturally deprived socialist elites, as in the case of Gomułka, Ceaușescu, Franjo Tuđman, Slobodan Milošević and that part of the Soviet leadership which was to found the Communist Party of the Russian Socialist Federative Soviet Republic (RSFSR) in 1990.[39]

The experience of the past 200 years thus shows that the interpenetration of socialism and nationalism has provided a key subset of the ideologies leading the extraordinary wave of state-building cum modernization and national liberation generated by the American and the French revolutions. It was also thanks to its capacity to ride – via Lenin and Stalin – this wave that communism became a crucial component of the twentieth-century experience. The end of the golden age of state-building thus powerfully contributed, by itself, to the demise of communist experiments.

Bibliographical Essay

Surveys of the relationships between communism and nationalism include those devoted to Marxism such as Charles C. Herod, *The Nation in the History of Marxian Thought: The Concept of Nations with History and Nations without History* (The Hague: Martinus Nijhoff, 1976), and Walker Connor, *The National Question in Marxist-Leninist Theory and Strategy* (Princeton: Princeton University Press, 1984), as well as to the history of communism,

38 Joze Pirjevec, *La guerre jugoslave, 1991–1999* (Turin: Einaudi, 2001).

39 Ronald G. Suny, *The Revenge of the Past: Nationalism, Revolution, and the Collapse of the Soviet Union* (Stanford: Stanford University Press, 1993); Marlène Laruelle, *Le rouge et le noir. Extrême droite et nationalisme en Russie* (Paris: CNRS, 2007).

like Silvio Pons, *The Global Revolution: A History of International Communism 1917–1991* (Oxford: Oxford University Press, 2014). These relationships have also been analyzed by intellectuals like Ludwig von Mises, *Nation, State, and Economy: Contributions to the Politics and History of our Time* [1919] (New York: New York University Press, 1983), Hans Kohn, *Living in a World Revolution: My Encounters with History* (New York: Trident Press, 1964), or Hugh Seton-Watson, *Nationalism and Communism: Essays, 1946–1963* (New York: Praeger, 1964). In 1934 Roman Rosdolsky, *Engels and the "Nonhistoric" Peoples: The National Question in the Revolution of 1848* (Glasgow: Critique, 1986), reconsidered Marx's and Engels's view of the national question, on which also see Ian Cummins, *Marx, Engels and the National Movements* (London: Croom Helm, 1980). René Gallissot, "Nazione e nazionalità nei dibattiti del movimento operaio," in *Storia del marxismo*, vol. II, *Il marxismo nell'età della Seconda Internazionale* (Turin: Einaudi, 1979), 787–864, remains the best study of the Second International's attitude toward the national question.

The Soviet pre-1939 experience has been the subject of important studies. Andreas Kappeler, *The Russian Empire: A Multiethnic History* (New York: Longman, 2001), is the key book on the Russian Empire, and Richard Pipes, *The Formation of the Soviet Union: Communism and Nationalism, 1917–1923* (Cambridge, MA: Harvard University Press, 1954) still is the fundamental work on the civil war. I reviewed the evolution of the national question in Soviet history in "La 'question nationale,'" in *Histoire de l'URSS* (Paris: PUF, 2010), while the best specific study on the topic remains Terry Martin, *An Affirmative Action Empire: Nations and Nationalism in the Soviet Union, 1923–1939* (Ithaca: Cornell University Press, 2001). Also noteworthy are Jeremy Smith, *The Bolsheviks and the National Question, 1917–1923* (New York: St. Martin's Press, 1999); Ronald G. Suny and Terry Martin (eds.), *A State of Nations: Empire and Nation-Making in the Age of Lenin and Stalin* (Oxford: Oxford University Press, 2001); Francine Hirsch, *Empire of Nations: Ethnographic Knowledge and the Making of the Soviet Union* (Ithaca: Cornell University Press, 2005); and Juliette Cadiot, *Le laboratoire imperial. Russie-URSS, 1860–1940* (Paris: CNRS, 2007).

Valuable studies of specific questions are Alexandre Bennigsen and Chantal Lemercier-Quelquejay, *Les mouvements nationaux chez les musulmans de Russie. Le "sultangalievisme" au Tatarstan* (Paris: Mouton, 1960); Zvi Gitelman, *Jewish Nationality and Soviet Politics: The Jewish Section of the CPSU, 1917–1930* (Princeton: Princeton University Press, 1972); James Mace, *Communism and the Dilemmas of National Liberation: National Communism in Soviet Ukraine, 1918–1933* (Cambridge, MA: Harvard University Press, 1983);

and Niccolò Pianciola, *Stalinismo di frontiera. Colonizzazione agricola, sterminio dei nomadi e costruzione statale in Asia centrale, 1905–1936* (Rome: Viella, 2009), while Jan T. Gross, *Revolution from Abroad: The Soviet Conquest of Poland's Western Ukraine and Western Belorussia* (Princeton: Princeton University Press, 1988), analyzes the use of the national question after the Molotov–Ribbentrop Pact. As for Stalin, the articles quoted in the text must be read together with Erik van Ree, *The Political Thought of Joseph Stalin: A Study in Twentieth-Century Revolutionary Patriotism* (London: Routledge, 2002).

Franz Borkenau, *The Communist International* [1938] (Ann Arbor: University of Michigan Press, 1962); Mikhail Narinsky and Jürgen Rojahn (eds.), *Centre and Periphery: The History of the Comintern in the Light of New Documents* (Amsterdam: International Institute of Social History, 1996); Pierre Broué, *Histoire de l'Internationale communiste, 1919–1943* (Paris: Fayard, 1997); and A. O. Chubarian (ed.), *Istoriia kommunisticheskogo Internatsionala, 1919–1943. Dokumental'nye ocherki* (Moscow: Nauka, 2002), introduce the history of the Third International, about which see also *The Diary of Georgi Dimitrov, 1933–1949* (New Haven: Yale University Press, 2003). On the Cominform, see G. M. Adibekov, *Kominform i poslevoennaia Evropa, 1947–1956* (Moscow: Rossiia molodaia, 1994), and G. Procacci et al. (eds.), *The Cominform: Minutes of the Three Conferences, 1947/1948/1949* (Milan: Feltrinelli, 1994).

Norman M. Naimark and Leonid Gibianskii (eds.), *The Establishment of Communist Regimes in Eastern Europe, 1944–1949* (Boulder: Westview, 1997), Philipp Ther and Ana Siljak (eds.), *Redrawing Nations: Ethnic Cleansing in East-Central Europe, 1944–1948* (Lanham, MD: Rowman & Littlefield, 2001), and Hugo Service, *Germans to Poles: Communism, Nationalism and Ethnic Cleansing After the Second World War* (Cambridge: Cambridge University Press, 2013), detail the emergence of the socialist bloc in Europe, while L. Ia. Gibianskii, *Sovetskii soiuz i novaia Yugoslaviia, 1941–1947 gg.* (Moscow: Nauka, 1987), and Joze Pirjevec, *Tito in Tovariši* (Ljubljana: Skupina Mladinska knjiga, 2011), are devoted to Tito's Yugoslavia, and François Fejtö, *A History of the People's Democracies: Eastern Europe since Stalin* (New York: Praeger, 1971), provides an overview of the evolution of socialist regimes, with Peter Zwick, *National Communism* (Boulder: Westview Press, 1983), looking especially at their relations with nationalism.

Lucien Bianco, *La Récidive. Révolution russe, révolution chinoise* (Paris: Gallimard, 2014) throws light on the Chinese leadership's relations with nationalism, while Lorenz Luthi, *The Sino-Soviet Split: Cold War in the Communist World* (Princeton: Princeton University Press, 2008), analyzes the Sino-Soviet split. David Engerman, *Staging Growth: Modernization,*

Development and the Global Cold War (Amherst: University of Massachusetts Press, 2003) looks at the value of the Soviet model for the leaders of the states emerging from decolonization. Walter Z. Laqueur, *Communism and Nationalism in the Middle East* (London: Routledge, 1961), pioneered the exploration of the topic in the Middle East, while Debnarayan Modak, *Dynamics of National Question in India: The Communist Approach (1942–64)* (Kolkata: Progressive Publishers, 2006), and Edmond J. Keller, *Revolutionary Ethiopia: From Empire to People's Republic* (Bloomington: Indiana University Press, 1988), study communist attitudes toward the national question in two large multinational settings. Odd Arne Westad, *The Global Cold War: Third World Interventions and the Making of Our Times* (New York: Cambridge University Press, 2005), analyzes Moscow's relationships with socialist regimes in the Third World in the 1970s.

Mikhail Agursky, *The Third Rome: National Bolshevism in the USSR* (Boulder: Westview, 1987), David Brandenberger, *National Bolshevism: Stalinist Mass Culture and the Formation of Modern Russian National Identity, 1931–1956* (Cambridge, MA: Harvard University Press, 2002), Yitzhak Brudny, *Reinventing Russia: Russian Nationalism and the Soviet State, 1953–1991* (Cambridge, MA: Harvard University Press, 2000), and Nikolai Mitrokhin, *Russkaia partiia. Dvizhenie russkikh natsionalistov v SSSR, 1953–1985* (Moscow: Novoe literaturnoe obozrenie, 2003), reconstruct the emergence of strong nationalist trends within the Soviet Russian elite, while Victor Zaslavsky and Robert Brym, *Soviet-Jewish Emigration and Soviet Nationality Policy* (New York: St. Martin's Press, 1983), and Yuri Slezkine, "The USSR as a Communal Apartment, or How a Socialist State Promoted Ethnic Particularism," *Slavic Review* 53, 2 (1994), 414–52, provide an account of the late Soviet approach to the national question. Mark R. Beissinger, *Nationalist Mobilization and the Collapse of the Soviet State* (Cambridge: Cambridge University Press, 2002), is still the best study of the national factor in the collapse of the USSR, on which see also Ronald G. Suny, *The Revenge of the Past: Nationalism, Revolution, and the Collapse of the Soviet Union* (Stanford: Stanford University Press, 1993). Roman Szporluk, *Russia, Ukraine, and the Breakup of the Soviet Union* (Stanford: Hoover Institution Press, 2000), and Serhii Plokhii, *The Last Empire: The Final Days of the Soviet Union* (New York: Basic Books, 2014), focus upon Russian–Ukrainian relationships, while Joze Pirjevec, *Le guerre jugoslave, 1991–1999* (Turin: Einaudi, 2001), is a solid study of the Yugoslavian catastrophe. Marlène Laruelle, *Le rouge et le noir. Extrême droite et nationalisme en Russie* (Paris: CNRS, 2007), follows the evolution of the interconnection between communism and nationalism in Russia after 1991.

19

Communism, Youth and Generation

MATTHIAS NEUMANN

The emergence of youth movements in the late nineteenth century was closely linked to the process of modernization and the socioeconomic upheaval caused by industrialization. Ever since the French Revolution, growing youth cohorts in Europe had led revolutionaries, nationalists and anti-imperialists alike, to identify youth as a crucial force in history. Youth was the future – seen as either a potentially major revolutionary force or as soldiers-to-be upholding a nationalist vision of the state. The communist movement associated itself from its beginnings with the image of "youth." Marxism taught that capitalism was moribund, dying and decaying while the communist movement represented the youthful forces who would build a new world. Indeed, Lenin understood its discursive political capital claiming: "We are the party of the future, and the future belongs to the youth."[1] Young people, uncorrupted by the old order and raised with communist ethics, were seen as the "guarantor of future social and political hegemony."[2]

The abstract imagery of youth as a pivotal revolutionary force was filled with youthful radicalism and anger directed at the older generation as a result of World War I. By the start of the war, socialist youth organizations had emerged in most European countries. The conflict, however, had shattered socialist internationalism and with it the Second International as well as the International Union of Socialist Youth Organizations (IUSYO). The genuine anti-militarism of the socialist youth movement was too weak to prevent many young socialists across the continent from taking up arms for their fatherlands. However, as the "short war" turned into one of prolonged senseless slaughter, resistance among working-class youth was on the rise.

1 V. I. Lenin, *Collected Works*, vol. XI (Moscow: Progress Publishers, 1965), 354.
2 Anne E. Gorsuch, *Youth in Revolutionary Russia: Enthusiasts, Bohemians, Delinquents* (Bloomington: Indiana University Press, 2000), 1.

Half a year into the war, some socialist youth leaders in Europe attempted to capitalize on the anti-militarism of a growing number of young workers by creating new organizational structures. In April 1915, the conference of the international socialist youth movement met in Bern and established an International Youth Bureau, effectively reconstituting the youth international (IUSYO). The conference fully committed itself to "revolutionary socialism," anti-militarism and socialist internationalism, but also crucially defined the youth international as an independent organization, rejecting subordination to the party or Second International. Its journal, *Jugend-Internationale* (Youth International), started publishing in September 1915 and promoted its work across Europe. The socialist youth was, in some respects, leading the way in a process that would culminate in the formation of the Third International, the Comintern. And it actively cultivated the idea of youth as a separate revolutionary force in the socialist camp.[3] The key tenets identified at the Bern meeting foreshadowed the crucial elements that would characterize the interwar communist youth movement and would prove controversial in respect of its identity and role within the communist movement. These key issues will serve as an analytical pathway for this chapter, which seeks to reconstruct the experience of being a young communist in interwar Europe. It will mainly concentrate on four countries: Germany, (Soviet) Russia, Britain and France. Because of their distinctive political, social and cultural developments in the period under consideration, and their importance in the theoretical evolution and practical pursuit of international revolution, this quartet provides a valuable basis for an analysis of the communist youth movement in the interwar period.

World War I and the Politics of Class and Generation

The implicit criticism of the old socialist leadership, who had betrayed internationalist principles, and the youthful vanguardism expressed in the recreation of the youth international in April 1915, brought the notion

3 Richard Cornell, *Revolutionary Vanguard: The Early Years of the Communist Youth International, 1914–1924* (Toronto: University of Toronto Press, 1982), 11–17; Thomas Ekman Jørgensen, "The Purest Flame of the Revolution: Working Class Youth and Left Wing Radicalism in Germany and Italy during the Great War," *Labor History* 50, 1 (2009), 26.

of generational divisions more to the forefront within the socialist movement. The interwar period would become, in many respects, an era of the politics of generation. Indeed, the idea of generational conflict as a force for social change was a recurring theme in contemporary conceptualizations of the legacy of the war. The irrational slaughter of the war, ruthlessly pursued by the elites, led many young people to lose their trust in, and respect for, the older generations. Young French communists vigorously expressed their generational anger toward older socialists in 1920 at the congress of the French Section of the Workers' International (SFIO), cementing their conscious self-identification as the revolutionary vanguard:

> Many of them are old, old as Clemenceau. They belong to the generation that sent us to the trenches. They're still alive and holding the reins. France is ruled by old men. That's what we are fighting today, here, at the Chamber, everywhere: the dictatorship of terrible old men [*la dictature des vieillards*].[4]

In the French communist youth movement in particular, but also elsewhere in Europe, the idea of a wider deep-rooted generational conflict in postwar society allowed young people to claim the role of the uncorrupted revolutionary vanguard. In many respects, they were often encouraged to do so by those older activists who pursued a more militant line within the socialist movement. For instance, Karl Liebknecht declared in November 1918: "The revolutionary proletarian youth, it was the hottest, the purest flame of the German revolution until now, and it will be the holiest, unquenchable flame of the revolution to come."[5] However, it is important to note that the discursive image of generational divisions was not replicated in the real pathways that brought youngsters into the communist youth movement. As numerous studies have revealed, young people who joined the movement in Europe did so as a result of "anticipatory socialization." They usually grew up in a working-class milieu, within families and communities that exposed them to working-class politics. Far from rebelling against their fathers, they followed in their footsteps. Indeed, the radicalism of the father is often mentioned in autobiographical records as a crucial stepping

4 Susan B. Whitney, *Mobilizing Youth: Communists and Catholics in Interwar France* (Durham, NC: Duke University Press, 2009), 21.

5 Jørgensen, "The Purest Flame," 19.

stone into the arena of militant communist politics.[6] A member of the Communist Youth League of Germany (KJVD) reflected in the late 1920s:

> My father is a worker. He is in the AEG Betriebsrat [work council] and at the same time a communist functionary . . . I am attached to the problems of communism as much as my father. In this respect, I am not patronized, I could have equally become a national socialist, if it could be reconciled with my class-consciousness.[7]

In the decade after World War I the communist youth movement in Europe was thus very much class-based, and found it hard to expand its social membership base beyond an urban working-class milieu. However, the great exception was the state-sponsored Soviet Communist Youth League (Komsomol), in which the proportion of students and white-collar workers steadily increased. Furthermore, a concerted "face to the countryside" campaign in 1924–25 brought significant numbers of rural youth into the movement. The influx of young peasants caused heated in-fighting in both its lower and upper echelons over the League's social identity, purpose and leadership.[8]

Vanguardism and Militancy: Youth, Party and the Communist Youth International

Communist youth organizations emerged in most European countries in the shadow of the war and the October Revolution. In 1918 communist youth organizations existed in Austria, Germany, Hungary, Russia, the Netherlands, Greece, Poland and Finland. Two years later they had also emerged in Denmark, Spain, France, Norway and Turkey. In Britain,

6 See autobiographical records of the *Erinnerungsbestand* in the Foundation Archives of Parties and Mass Organizations of the GDR in the Federal Archives (SAPMO-BArch), SgY 30. For example: SAPMO-BArch SgY 30/1976 (Artur Mannbar), SAPMO-BArch SgY 30/1103 (Karl Wloch); Jørgensen, "The Purest Flame," 33; Whitney, *Mobilizing Youth*, 29; Michael Waite, "Young People and Formal Political Activity. A Case Study: Young People and Communist Politics in Britain 1920–1991: Aspects of the Young Communist League" (MPhil dissertation, University of Lancaster, 1992), 206–07; Barbara Köster, "'Die Junge Garde des Proletariat': Untersuchungen zum Kommunistischen Jugendverband Deutschlands in der Weimarer Republik" (Ph.D. dissertation, University of Bielefeld, 2005), 182–84; Klaus Michael Mallmann, *Kommunisten in der Weimarer Republik. Sozialgeschichte einer revolutionären Bewegung* (Darmstadt: Wissenschaftliche Buchgesellschaft, 1996), 190–91.

7 Mallmann, *Kommunisten*, 190.

8 Matthias Neumann, "Class Ascription and Class Identity: *Komsomol'tsy* and the Policy of Class during NEP," *Revolutionary Russia* 19, 2 (2006), 175–96.

where several socialist youth groups still existed by 1921, the sense of being part of a growing global community of communists helped to unify scattered Marxist youth groups.[9] In those years, communism, with its internationalist outlook, was an attractive political alternative; a real cause for which people could mobilize. Ever since the April 1915 meeting in Bern, which led to the reconstitution of the youth international, the idea of a "Third International" became a central leitmotiv in the communist youth movement. Internationalism was the prime duty of every young communist, meaning they had to self-identify in international class terms. For example, in an article in *The Red Flag* from 1920, the official organ of the radical Young Communist League in Britain (YCLGB), the youthful James Stewart asserted:

> I cannot love England as it is to-day and I cannot love Englishmen as such; neither can I love Germans as such. I cannot love any men, women or child merely for their nationality; I can only love the working-class all the world over – that is my class, a slave class. I am a slave; all the world's workers are slaves. I am a slave in revolt. I am not a patriot, I am an internationalist.[10]

This was not just rhetoric. In Russia, during the summer of 1917, scattered youth groups in numerous urban areas were merged or founded under the banner of proletarian internationalism.[11] The idea was tangible on the streets. It resonated with young people and made them feel part of a global community of revolutionaries. Liusik Lisinova, a nineteen-year-old student, for example, wrote a letter to a friend recollecting the exhilarating experience of singing the *Internationale* at the May Day demonstration in 1917: "The very *Internationale*, which will soon lead the entire international proletariat to the great battle for the entire human race."[12] A few weeks later, Lisinova became the organizer of the Third International Union of Youth in Moscow's Zamoskvorech'e district.

The first program of the Komsomol, founded in October 1918, managed to merge genuine commitment to proletarian internationalism with a staunch

9 Waite, "Young People," 63.

10 Joel A. Lewis, *Youth Against Fascism: Young Communists in Britain and the United States, 1919–1939* (Saarbrücken: VDM Verlag Dr. Müller, 2007), 60–61.

11 *Slavnyi put' leninskogo komsomola, Tom 1.* (Moscow: Molodaia gvardiia, 1974), 84–91; Diane Koenker, "Urban Families, Working-Class Youth Groups, and the 1917 Revolution in Moscow," in David L. Ransel (ed.), *The Family in Imperial Russia* (Urbana: University of Illinois Press, 1978), 299.

12 Liusik Lisinova, "Togda ia zhvoi chelovek . . .," in M. L. Kataeva (ed.), *Dnevniki i pis'ma Komsomol'tsev* (Moscow: Molodaia gvardiia, 1983), 9–10.

faith in the possibility of constructing a new economic order in Russia. Identifying the construction of socialism in Russia with the cause of international revolution was not an exercise of squaring the circle. It was an expression of political faith. The same was also true for young and old communists in Western Europe. The October Revolution, and the creation of the Soviet Union, was of immense importance to them. The very existence of the Soviet Union had created a "Promised Land," a workers' paradise. It validated their teleological perspectives of a coming world revolution, legitimized their efforts at home, and provided an anchor point to deal with the inevitable setbacks.[13] The Soviet Union quickly became the central focus and mainstay of communist propaganda.

After the creation of the Communist International (Comintern) in March 1919, the enthusiastic leaders of socialist youth organizations from thirteen countries met in a shabby tavern in a working-class suburb of Berlin to establish the Communist Youth International (CYI) in November. This development was driven forward by young revolutionary socialists from Western Europe. Contrary to the process of the creation of the Comintern, Russian representatives were in no position to exert controlling influence over the congress proceedings that took place in Berlin, not Moscow. The young Western communists were in a buoyant mood, enthused by the events in Russia and instilled with millenarian optimism that world revolution was forthcoming. Their self-perception of being young revolutionary vanguards was expressed vividly in their strong commitment to revolutionary socialism, affirming a clear break with the reformist left, but also in vigorous criticism of the Komsomol representatives' view that all youth organizations should be directly subordinated to communist parties.

Until 1921, the Komsomol struggled to impose its leadership over the communist youth movement abroad. Its structure and relationship to the party was simply not regarded as a suitable role model for the movement in noncommunist countries by Western youth leaders. Indeed, national organizations repeatedly rejected the push for subordination as "acceptable for Russia, but not Western Europe."[14] The French Jeunesse Communiste, in particular, embraced the Berlin congress's position on organizational autonomy and political independence, asserting in its main publication, appropriately entitled *L'Avant-Garde*, that: "In the proletarian movement,

13 Mallmann, *Kommunisten*, 230
14 *Slavnyi put' leninskogo komsomola*, 207; Cornell, *Revolutionary Vanguard*, 63, 70, 104–06.

we will continue to be in the vanguard and to fulfill our historical mission of pushing the party toward action."[15] The young activist Margaret McCarthy remembered that similar attitudes were common in Britain: "We felt ourselves intellectually, emotionally, and in activity superior to the Party members. We felt ourselves not only leading the youth of the world, but we believed ourselves even leading the Party."[16] The Komsomol leadership, all of whom were party members, branded such assertiveness as dangerous "youthful vanguardism." However, a significant proportion of its members clearly shared the self-assertiveness of their European peers.

A Revolutionary Combat Unit

The Komsomol program of 1918 demonstrated this self-perception of Soviet young communists, their sense of power and revolutionary authority: "Youth, as the most active and revolutionary part of the working class, is the vanguard of the proletarian revolution."[17] This was a strong display of self-confidence and faith in one's own role. Many Komsomol members wholeheartedly adopted the revolutionary "vanguardism" proclaimed by the League's first program. Vladimir Dunaevskii, a leading youth labor activist in Moscow's Komsomol who enjoyed widespread popularity among working-class members, forcefully articulated this belief in a speech on the proletarian youth movement in autumn 1919: "Our movement is messianic. We are the avant-garde of the avant-garde."[18]

In the Soviet Union, the first generation of Komsomol members, those who had played an active role in the Russian Civil War, became a highly visible force among the communist youth. The young civil war veterans stood out from the masses and gave the Komsomol a face in the early 1920s. It was a face that was often received with open hostility from the older generations, particularly in the countryside.

Their shared formative experiences of the revolution and war helped to produce a strong sense of common belonging. It created a generational framework of experience that found expression in the subculture of young

15 Whitney, *Mobilizing Youth*, 34.
16 Margaret McCarthy, *Generation in Revolt* (London: Heinemann, 1953), 134–35.
17 "Program and Charter of the Communist Youth League, 1918," in Isabel Tirado, *Young Guard! The Communist Youth League, Petrograd 1917–1920* (New York: Greenwood Press, 1988), 231.
18 *Iunyi kommunist* 15 (Nov. 1919), 19.

militants, the so-called *bratushki* (little brothers), who passed on their admiration of the revolutionary struggle to the younger, mostly male, members of the Komsomol. The *bratushki* cultivated and expressed their sociocultural perspective shaped by the civil war, their sense of revolutionary vanguardism and class identity, through discourses of language, fashion and behavior in the time of the New Economic Policy (NEP) of the 1920s.[19] The ethos of the first generation of Komsomol members was masculine. This, very importantly, applied not only to the young Soviet communists, but more widely to the communist youth movement in Europe. Young women found themselves to be a small minority and faced a dominant culture of revolutionary and proletarian manliness expressed through mannerisms and behavior. Consequently, the communist youth movement in Europe struggled to attract female members in the 1920s.

While the youthful claim to a vanguard role in the communist movement was officially relinquished to the parties at the Third Congress of the Comintern in 1921, the attitudes of ordinary members proved more difficult to reconfigure. However, by then the clear subordination of the CYI under the Comintern quickly turned the former into a central tool in a system of multiple controls, which allowed the Bolshevik party to assert its influence on youth organizations abroad. In 1922, the Komsomol leader Lazar Shatskin, who became secretary of the CYI from 1922 to 1924 and had pushed to subject the CYI to Moscow's leadership ever since its creation, declared that communist youth organizations abroad were only obliged to obey the communist party of their own country when that native party was obeying the Comintern.[20] This position allowed the Comintern not only to use the CYI to eliminate oppositional views within youth organizations, but also to instrumentalize the militancy of many young communists in the process of Bolshevizing the communist parties. In France this tactic helped to Bolshevize the French Communist Party in 1925; in Britain it was applied to push through the "class against class" line in 1929.[21] The Italian communist leader Palmiro Togliatti was reported to have stated during Stalin's great turn of 1929: "If we don't give in, Moscow

19 Matthias Neumann, "'Youth, It's Your Turn!': Generations and the Fate of the Russian Revolution (1917–1932)," *Journal of Social History* 46, 2 (2012), 279–87; Anne Gorsuch, "'NEP Be Damned!' Young Militants in the 1920s and the Culture of Civil War," *Russian Review* 56, 4 (1997), 564–80.

20 Ralph T. Fisher, *Pattern for Soviet Youth: A Study of the Congresses of the Komsomol, 1918–1954* (New York: Columbia University Press, 1955), 103.

21 Whitney, *Mobilizing Youth*, 45–50; Waite, "Young People," 70–72.

won't hesitate to fix up a leadership with some kid out of the Lenin School."[22]

Significantly, the communist youth organizations across Europe never achieved a mass following in the first decade after World War I with the exception of the Komsomol. Their memberships were usually in the thousands and local cells were built around small networks of friends. Communist youth leagues across Europe found it hard to establish stable cells in factories and other workplaces. All of them, including the Komsomol, also grappled with the problem of a high turnover in membership. In Britain the membership stood at only 1,800 in 1926. By way of numerical comparison, the British Boy Scouts almost doubled their membership from 232,758 in 1920 to 422,662 in 1930.[23] Indeed, the continuing popularity of the Scout movement, even in Soviet Russia, meant communist children's organizations were set up under the tutelage of the youth organizations in most European countries to embrace 10- to 14-year-olds. In Germany, the country with the strongest socialist movement, the communist youth organization was significantly stronger than in Britain. However, it nevertheless had persistent problems in becoming a genuine mass organization, peaking in 1932 with a membership of 57,756.[24]

Even the Soviet Komsomol faced problems in becoming an undisputed mass organization for youth in the 1920s. As a state-sponsored organization it was deemed to play a central role in the creation of Soviet civil society, allowing young people to take part in the project of building communism of their own volition. Komsomol membership also offered great opportunities for social mobility. For young peasants it offered a potential path into further education, to escape from the countryside, and eventually join the ranks of the new Soviet intelligentsia. The Komsomol also became the prime organization that helped to ascribe class identity to young people. It was a key agent in the external identification of adolescents. Class identity was crucial in the first socialist state, since it determined not only a youngster's status within the social environment, but also whether an adolescent was part of the generation of builders of communism. This was quite different from Western Europe. Here membership in a communist youth organization would almost certainly result in some form of (self-) isolation, even from one's working-class peers. Organizations such as the YCLGB often led an

22 Waite, "Young People," 71.

23 Ibid., 67–68; Paul Wilkinson, "English Youth Movements, 1908–1930," *Journal of Contemporary History* 4, 2 (1969), 17.

24 Köster, "Die Junge Garde," 134, 185.

"internal looking, 'sect' like existence." As a letter by its National Bureau to all members in September 1930 explained, "we live in a world by ourselves, we talk a language different from that of the young workers."[25] The austere nature of political work in the YCLGB, effectively a self-styled mirror image of the adult party, was hardly attractive to young workers.

Yet despite the opportunities for upward social mobility in the Soviet Union, the youth as a whole did not necessarily subscribe to revolutionary ideas in the 1920s. Far from it, the 1.75 million Komsomol members in March 1926 represented only 5.5 percent of the youth in the relevant age group. Conversely, religious youth organizations remained popular in the 1920s.[26] The Komsomol was an organization of myriad contradictions in which the center struggled to control the periphery and lower echelons. On the ground, the organization maintained a life of its own in many places, often providing an autonomous space in which young people could live out their idiosyncratic ideas of revolution and communism, ranging from Komsomol communes establishing "Socialism in one apartment" to iconoclastic and violent anti-religious campaigns. The legacy of the civil war as a formative experience is all too evident in this context, but its seeds were watered and nurtured in the NEP era. The latter provided an environment for contested visions and expressions of Bolshevism which generated an unintended generational conflict that would act as a driving force behind Stalin's revolution.[27] The latter received strong support from within the Komsomol, sparking a rapid expansion that brought its membership to 10 million by 1940.[28]

Youthful Impatience: Looking for a Cause

The creation of children's and youth organizations "generationalized" the communist movement in discursive terms. In Germany, as in Britain and France, the relationship between the youth organization and the party was characterized by persistent tensions. Ernst Thälmann's vision of unity between the three generations – the children's organization, the youth organization and the party – turned out to be an illusion.[29] In day-to-day

25 Waite, "Young People," 74.

26 N. I. Bukharin, *K novomu pokoleniiu: doklady, vystupleniia i stat'i, posviashchennye problemam molodezhi* (Moscow: Progress Publishers, 1990), 485.

27 Neumann, "'Youth, It's Your Turn!'"; Matthias Neumann, *The Communist Youth League and the Transformation of the Soviet Union* (London: Routledge, 2011), chs. 4–6.

28 Neumann, *The Communist Youth League*, Appendix 1.

29 Ernst Thälmann, "Einige Bemerkungen zur Arbeit des Jugendverbandes," *Die Internationale* 2 (1932) SAPMO-BArch RY 1 I 4/1/56, 210.

politics, these organizations were often neglected and the demands of their leaders ignored. When the party intervened in the youth leagues' affairs this was often experienced as patronizing. This difficult and confused relationship caused some irritation but naturally created pockets of autonomy that allowed young communist activists to run their own affairs.[30] Yet age was not the dominant issue in the communist movement in the West. Like their Soviet counterparts, young communists were very much concerned with their class identity as a source for revolutionary commitment. In France, Germany and Britain this was becoming evident during the turn toward the ultra-leftist "class against class" tactics that found strong support among youth leaders – many of whom viewed most matters through the prism of Comintern high politics – and activists at the lower echelons alike.[31] By the late 1920s, young communists had not experienced the split of the worker movement, but they simply accepted it as fact. Indeed, the radicalism expressed in the "class against class" policy appealed to the vanguardist self-image of many activists who understood themselves to be a revolutionary combat unit.

The Comintern's "class against class" line, just as the German October of 1923 or the General Strike in Britain in 1926, provided a renewed cause around which young activists could mobilize. Magaret McCarthy, who was a prominent member of the YCLGB by 1929, commented that: "Young communists adopted ... the new [class against class] line ... without doubt or hesitation. It accorded completely with our mood of frustration and despair ... our desire for something sharp, short, and spectacular to end the hopeless stalemate of our existence."[32] Young people, and young men in particular, were predisposed to these feelings of anger and impatience with the revolutionary process as they were coming of age, going through the biographical period of "storm and stress," in a period of the interwar era which saw much entrenchment. It was not only the radicalism of the "class against class" policy that drew them to support it, but just as much the *activism* and *actions* promised by its acceptance.

The existence of a clear *cause* was crucial in terms of mobilization, because the day-to-day life in communist youth leagues was often tedious. Young

30 Köster, "Die Junge Garde," 80–81. For example: SAPMO-BArch RY 1 I 4/1/78, 216; SAPMO-BArch RY 1 I 4/51, 10.

31 Mallmann, *Kommunisten*, 187; Waite, "Young People," 70–72; Whitney, *Mobilizing Youth*, 45–50.

32 McCarthy, *Generation in Revolt*, 138.

activists across the continent, and indeed in the Soviet Union, threw themselves readily into campaigns and revolutionary actions when they were linked to a particular, and tangible, cause. The street was their domain – a training ground for the anticipated revolution. This enthusiasm for direct action was certainly noted by the parties. They used young communists as willing foot soldiers in the 1920s for much of the time-consuming propaganda work, such as selling papers, collections, painting banners, demonstrations and picketing. This naturally flattered young people at least initially and, in turn, further fostered their self-perception as a revolutionary vanguard. But it also alienated them from their working-class constituency because it made them look like a mere propaganda outlet.[33] Indeed, for the YCLGB "class against class" turned out to be a major debacle. While many leaders and activists initially embraced the new radical line, the wider membership collapsed completely as a result of it. The League was effectively closed down by the party in spring 1930 and reconstituted with a reported membership of only around 150 in June.[34] It had to be entirely reconstituted, but real progress was not made before the shift to the "popular front" policy.

For the German communist youth movement, the pivotal moment of the 1920s came earlier in the decade. In 1923, the German October unleashed the real prospect of creating a Soviet Germany and led to much youthful excitement and activism. Indeed, reflecting on the failure of the uprising, the youth leaders stressed that their organization had achieved a better mobilization and had acted with more discipline in the aftermath of the defeat.[35] Nevertheless, the defeat of the German October led to a significant drop in support by young workers from which the movement only recovered in the early 1930s. Until then engagement in militant labor politics, in streetfighting and revolutionary grandstanding, persistently undermined the communist youth movement's ambition to engage more young workers, particularly female youths. Indeed, young male communists, in particular workers aged between nineteen and twenty-two, were predominant among streetfighters in late Weimar Germany. Youth was an important social condition in the enactment of street violence. Streetfighting allowed youngsters to live out their feelings

33 Mallmann, *Kommunisten*, 189.

34 Thomas Linehan, *Communism in Britain 1920–39: From the Cradle to the Grave* (Manchester: Manchester University Press, 2007), 58–59.

35 Köster, "Die Junge Garde," 88.SAPMO-BArch RY 1 I 4/1/61, 116.

of "proletarian comradeship" grounded in neighborhood friendships in conjunction with the demands of national politics.[36]

While neighborhood networks remained the central pillar of day-to-day communist politics, the revolutionary setbacks in Western Europe meant that commitment to revolutionary internationalism, the faith in, and devotion to, the Soviet Union became one of the most important aspects of the identity of a young communist in the 1920s. The strong centralization pursued by the Comintern and CYI clearly ran contrary to the interests of young communists committed to autonomy and independence. However, the temptation to look to Moscow for leadership was increasing in the postrevolutionary world of the mid 1920s. This was not purely down to opportunism and careerism, but also, as Richard Cornell has suggested, stimulated by "the psychological need for unity and belonging," particularly important in times of repeated setbacks. The genuine commitment to revolutionary internationalism and solidarity of young communists made national and regional youth leaders accept some of the unwelcome effects of central Bolshevik leadership. Yet, looking toward Moscow also came at a clear cost. The freedom to express and act upon their idiosyncratic views within the youth movement was gradually, but steadily reduced. "Bolshevization" was either supported or accepted with no or very little protest.[37] Loyalty to the Soviet Union became a crucial anchor point in the identity of young communists abroad.

Heil Moscow: Defending the Socialist Motherland

As the hopes of revolution at home were shattered, the myth of the Soviet Union as the Promised Land – "socialism in one country" – became a vital aspect of the identity of every communist in the world. It shaped young people's emotional engagement with communist politics and ideology. Across the globe they began to dream of defending the Soviet land. The young German communist Fritz Grosse, for example, born in 1904, was introduced to communist politics in 1918 and started to contemplate going to Russia to fight for the revolution. In spring 1920, he and a friend illegally crossed the border to Poland and managed to join the Red Army "Internationalists" formation close to Minsk.[38] A few years later, in 1925, the enthusiasm for the Soviet state led another young German communist,

36 Eve Rosenhaft, *Beating the Fascists? The German Communists and Political Violence 1929–1933* (Cambridge: Cambridge University Press, 1983), 158–59, 164–66, 193–96.

37 Cornell, *Revolutionary Vanguard*, 297.

38 SAPMO-BArch SgY 30/0309, 6–9.

Wilhelm Fischer, to demand repeatedly to be allowed to emigrate to the Soviet Union to become "a soldier of the proletarian revolution."[39] These were extreme cases, but youthful vanguardism mixed with revolutionary idealism and romanticism meant that impatience with revolutionary progress often spurred youngsters into action. Indeed, throughout the 1920s it was ironically young Komsomol members who, frustrated with the inertia of the revolutionary project at home and enthused by romanticized visions of being heroic revolutionary fighters, volunteered to fight for world revolution in Germany, Poland and particularly China in letters sent to the authorities.[40]

Soviet youth activists were animated by developments abroad to express and enact their internationalist outlook. The German October of 1923 led to an upsurge of genuine enthusiasm and practices expressing international solidarity; its ultimate failure led to serious disappointment.[41] For instance, the Komsomol organization of the young sailors of Samara expressed their comradely support for the German communist youth in a letter in November 1923. They saw events in Germany as the "start of struggle, a fight of the world proletariat," declaring that they were ready to take up arms to defend the revolution.[42] Others took real action. The student Georgii Starchev explained in a letter to the Petrograd party leadership that he and forty-five of his peers had left university and joined the Red Army in anticipation of the outbreak of the German Revolution.[43] Komsomol members also took part in demonstrations, distributed literature and set up "corners of the German revolution" in youth clubs.[44] Furthermore, they organized fundraisers to support the German communist youth who, just a year earlier, had played a significant role in large campaigns by the Workers' International Relief Organization to relieve famine in the Soviet Union. The German communists saw youngsters as *Tatmenschen* (people of deeds) who were very much engaged in the solidarity campaigns. Indeed, communist children's newspapers had

39 SAPMO-BArch RY1 I 4/1/51, 46.

40 Russian State Archive of Socio-Political History (RGASPI), f. M1, op. 23, d. 507, ll. 55–57, 60, 61; d. 678, ll. 2, 6–8, 9, 10, 15, 16, 17–18, 19–20.

41 Gleb J. Albert, "'German October Is Approaching': Internationalism, Activists, and the Soviet State in 1923," *Revolutionary Russia* 24, 2 (2011), 111–42.

42 SAPMO-BArch RY1 I 4/1/66, 167–68.

43 Gleb J. Albert, *Das Charisma der Weltrevolution: Revolutionärer Internationalismus in der frühen Sowjetgesellschaft, 1917–1927* (Cologne; Böhlau Verlag, 2017), 532–33.

44 Albert, "'German October Is Approaching,'" 117; Albert, *Das Charisma der Weltrevolution*, 117–18.

printed appeals by Russian children to their German, Dutch and British counterparts calling them to join the campaign to provide aid for the Soviet Union.[45] Followed by real practices of transnational solidarity, this created an emotional bond with the first socialist state and between young communists from different countries. This sense of belonging was cemented through rituals and practices such as the frequent exchange of flags, fraternal messages, collective penpalships and public demonstrations to express solidarity with striking workers abroad.[46] They all become part of an "imagined community" of (young) revolutionaries, for whom the defense of the Soviet Union became increasingly the supreme internationalist duty.

The front page of the *Junge Garde*, the central organ of the KJVD, captured this image of transnational and cross-generational unity in November 1927 at the tenth anniversary of the revolution: "Defend the Soviet Union!" read the slogan, depicting an armed German worker, a Red Army soldier and a communist youth holding the Red Flag in front of the Lenin Mausoleum and the Kremlin. Being part of the imagined global community of communists – the "socialist fatherland of the proletarians of all countries" – gave members of the movement an important reference point in making sense of their own situation back home. The popular visions of the Soviet Union were very much shaped by the thousands of young and old communists from across Europe who traveled to the Soviet Union in the 1920s and 1930s.

Visiting the "Promised Land"

Many communist youth leaders traveled to the Soviet Union to attend congresses of the CYI or the International Lenin School. However, by the mid 1920s a growing number of workers' delegations allowed young communists from across Europe to visit the Soviet state. Indeed, in November 1925, the first German young workers' delegation embarked on a trip to see "socialism in one country." The enthusiastic accounts of these trips to the workers' paradise by young communists were disseminated

45 *Slavnyi put' leninskogo komsomola*, 282; Köster, "Die Junge Garde," 74; SAPMO-BArch RY9 I 6/7/1, 253; SAPMO-BArch RY9 I 6/7/1, 12, 125; SAPMO-BArch RY1 I 4/1/80, 5, 9. *Der Junge Genosse: Internationale Zeitung für Arbeiter* 16 (Aug. 1921), 1; 18 (Sep. 1921), 1; 20 (Oct. 1921), 1–2, 7.

46 For example: SAPMO-BArch RY1 I 4/1/3, 35–36; SAPMO-BArch RY1 I 4/1/78, 225–27. For a detailed examination of these practices see Albert, *Das Charisma der Weltrevolution*, 445–95.

widely in the youth press and through mass meetings and film screenings in Western Europe. In France, *L'Avant-Garde* celebrated the achievements of the Soviet state in improving the socioeconomic and cultural situation of young workers in an article entitled "What We Saw in Red Moscow."[47] Furthermore, *Junge Garde* in Germany printed numerous celebratory accounts from members of every youth delegation.[48] In Moscow, a member of the first youth worker delegation reported that they were welcomed by huge receptions at stations, an enthusiastic youth rally and a military orchestra playing the *Internationale*, which they joined in singing with their Russian comrades.[49] Indeed, the singing of the *Internationale*, the communist world anthem but also the national anthem of the Soviet Union, became an emotionally laden ritual. It was an important aspect of creating a community of communists, an expression of belief in the strength of the Soviet Union, but also a clear articulation of their faith in the superiority of the communist system which would eventually lead the revolution to be exported. Henri Barbé, a young French communist, recalled how moved he was by the thunderous rendition of the *Internationale* during a visit of a Komsomol club 1924, seeing the "will and invincible faith in the world revolution" in the faces of his Russian comrades.[50]

The trips to the Soviet Union resembled pilgrimages. Delegates, old and young, often faced really difficult journeys to the workers' paradise which "heightened the sense of excitement upon arrival."[51] Although the reality of transnational encounters did not necessarily live up to the expectations of either side, these problems did little to seriously challenge the preconceived interpretational frameworks through which young communists rationalized their experience.[52] Margaret McCarthy, for instance, recalled that she "enthusiastically . . . and truthfully . . . told the stories of shortages and queues, explaining this as a self-sacrificing gesture on the part of the Russian people at a party meeting back home in Lancashire." Her belief in the Soviet system had not been undermined by witnessing the severe socioeconomic problems, but at the meeting her honest and enthusiastic

47 Whitney, *Mobilizing Youth*, 58.

48 Köster, "Die Junge Garde," 279; examples: *Junge Garde* 9 (Jan. 1926), 1; 10 (Jan. 1926), 1; 5 (Nov. 1926), 1; 4 (Oct. 1927), 1; 5 (Nov. 1927), 2; 6 (Dec. 1927), 1.

49 Hans Riesert, "Meine Erlebnisse aud der Reise nach Sowjetrussland," *Junge Garde* 9 (Jan. 1926), 1.

50 Whitney, *Mobilizing Youth*, 59. 51 Ibid.

52 Köster, "Die Junge Garde," 281–82; Mallmann, *Kommunisten*, 233. A report of the 1930 delegation made proposals on how to improve the experience of the trips. SAPMO-BArch RY1 I 4/1/62, 257–59.

report was not welcome. To her amazement she was attacked for being a purveyor of anti-Soviet lies.[53]

With the launch of the first Five-Year Plan, the Soviet mystique reached new heights among young communists in the West. Youngsters visiting the workers' state during a time when the capitalist world had sunk into depression found their belief system validated. The experience of these visits and the wide dissemination of their successes within the movement strengthened the sense of being part of a genuine closely knit international community of young communists – a world movement whose capital was Moscow, and for which the Soviet youth served as a role model. However, in the 1930s the focus started to shift back more firmly to the continent with the rise of fascism. Fascist parties made "youth" a powerful symbol of the regeneration and rival of the nation; soldiers of an idea. This obviously presented a special challenge to communist youth who, ever since the reconstitution of the youth international in April 1915, had made anti-militarism one of its central programmatic tenets. Yet the problem was that none of the European communist youth organizations had assumed a real mass character. In order to become a crucial force in the fight against fascism, for which they were singled out by the Comintern, they had to broaden their appeal.

From Anti-Militarism to Popular Fronts

Anti-fascism became the central cause of communist internationalism in the 1930s. And it was the deep-rooted anti-militarist convictions of young communists that allowed it to connect with socialist and bourgeois youth organizations. With the World Committee against War and Fascism, founded in Amsterdam in 1932 and sponsored by the Comintern, an institutional framework was formed in which the communist youth movement in Europe created a broader and more gender-inclusive political constituency.[54]

It was the real tangible threat of war that brought back the politics of generation into the discourse. World War I returned as an important point of reference. It was *the* rallying point that could unite youngsters with conflicting political views. A youth committee poster from Reims, France, communicated this age-based attitude: "Youth will be the first victim of the impending carnage. We will not allow ourselves to be sacrificed in vain, as

53 McCarthy, *Generation in Revolt*, 238. 54 Whitney, *Mobilizing Youth*, 135.

was the case in the First World War."[55] Of course, in this context, young politically trained communists were also taking the opportunity to remind their socialist peers of the "original sin" their party had committed in 1914.[56] However, from 1932 onwards there was a gradual but steady shift in the movement to overcome sectarianism and form a wider alliance against fascism in Europe. In Germany, where young communists were operating illegally after March 1933, the Youth League eventually reached out to Christian youth organizations and groups.[57] In an appeal to the German youth in 1937, the KVJD made frequent references to the carnage of World War I and stated that modern wars would only lead to a "barbaric slaughter of youth."[58]

Many young German communist activists were quickly persecuted after Hitler came to power. Indeed, the movement showed admirable courage and strength in its ability to reestablish regional operations. For example, a Gestapo report from September 1933 noted that thirty-five young communist leaders of the regional organization of North Bavaria had been arrested, but nonetheless the League had managed to reconstitute its activities. It asserted that further arrests were needed to shut the organization down.[59] As the communist movement in Germany went underground, the lines between the youth organization and the party became very much blurred. While it had failed to fulfill the promise of generating a steady flow of new young party members, the KVJD clearly became a *Kaderschmiede*: a cadre school from which the future leaders of the communist party emerged.[60] For those young communists who put their lives on the line during the Nazi regime, the underground fight became a pivotal formative experience. It would become a chief leitmotiv in the articulation of self-identities by communist functionaries in postwar East Germany.

The Generational Front

A major step in forming a broader alliance against fascism and war was the World Youth Congress held in Paris in September 1933, which was attended by 1,092 delegates from thirty-three countries, including a delegation from the Soviet Union. At the congress delegates sung revolutionary songs and

55 Ibid., 151. 56 SAPMO-BArch RY1 I 4/1/56, 126.

57 For an example see the appeal from January 1935: SAPMO-BArch RY1 I 4/1/62, 325.

58 SAPMO-BArch RY1 I 4/1/43, 316–19. 59 SAPMO-BArch RY1 I 4/1/79, 21.

60 Köster, "Die Junge Garde," 90–108; Mallmann, *Kommunisten*, 191.

those from fascist countries told the congress about their heroic fight against reactionaries. Soviet youth were hailed as role models of a happy young generation living in a world of peace. The German delegation, which had traveled illegally, was reported to include young socialists, communists, Christians, policemen and even disillusioned Nazis. The British delegation too, included youngsters from different youth organizations and social backgrounds – trade unionists, socialists, communists, students and workers. The congress was hailed as a "united front in action," almost a year before the Comintern officially endorsed joint actions with socialist forces. Only 387 of the more than one thousand delegates identified as young communists.[61] Henri Barbusse, a leading French communist, assigned youth the pivotal role in the fight against the fascist threat:

> You are the shock-brigade of contemporary humanity, you are the masters of to-morrow, you are the victors of to-morrow. It is the love of your vast objective which must be the breath of this great congress of the united front of youth. This united front is the vanguard of the world's workers – it is only the image of the immense living reality. There is only one proletariat in the world, and humanity is one.[62]

The day after the congress had finished, 500 delegates traveled to the war memorial in Rethondes and swore a solemn oath to confront the war. The final lines were reported to have been: "We will no longer spill our blood to profit the rich! We announce the rallying of young people throughout the world! We will avenge the death! We summon the living!" As Whitney has rightly asserted, the congress and its final manifesto signaled an important shift in the communist youth movement. Age was stressed as an important aspect in the fight against fascism, not class background.[63] This was most vividly expressed by the manifesto of the congress "To the Youth of the World." Its opening lines read: "To you all young men, young girls, workers, students, peasants, employees, soldiers and sailors, unemployed"; it proclaimed that it is:

> our firm intention of widening considerably our movement of united action in order to bring together all the youth who are in revolt against War and Fascism, having different political connections, but without distinction of party or opinion, no matter to what section of the working population they may belong.[64]

61 Henri Barbusse, "You Are the Pioneers," *Report of the World Youth Congress Against Fascism*, Paris, 22–24 September 1933 (London: Utopia Press, 1933), 3–4, 9, 12–15.

62 Ibid., 7. 63 Whitney, *Mobilizing Youth*, 152–53.

64 Barbusse, "You Are the Pioneers," 13.

The mood for common action was tangible at the congress and it did not take long for this generational front to turn to real action. Indeed, already in 1932, young communists and socialists had spontaneously joined forces in street demonstrations in Paris on Armistice Day. Demonstrations and political violence on the streets became a basis for joint actions between young socialists and communists in 1934.[65] These actions highlighted persistent vanguardism and revolutionary radicalism among the young communists, but also their predisposition to take their struggle into the open – onto the streets. That said, the sectarianism of some members remained a problem in the youth movement's attempts to organize effective united and popular fronts. However, it was this youthful preference for real action, and the fact that they had not experienced for themselves the acrimonious divisions of the left during World War I, that ironically also provided the basis for the formation of a much broader Popular Front in the 1930s in Europe. Indeed, as demonstrated above, the Jeunesse Communiste anticipated the Popular Front well before it became Comintern policy.

In the process of building a broad opposition to the threat of fascism and war among the young, generational divisions became more pronounced, because the opposition to war and fascism was frequently framed in generational terms. For example, the "Declaration of Rights of the Young Generations" by the communist-supported Youth Committee against War and Fascism in October 1934, explicitly promoted the formation of a generational bloc, unequivocally reaching out to students and young women. This quite radical shift away from class struggle and revolution to the expression of special interests of a generational front was not welcomed by the CYI. The latter claimed that it highlighted "dangerous right opportunist tendencies."[66] This episode showed that national communist youth organizations still had the agency to pursue their own idiosyncratic policies, but ultimately Moscow was in a position to control and impose policy when needed. For example, the French young communists spearheaded the anti-militarist campaign vehemently opposing the law to extend military service in 1934; a law that would have affected young people in particular. But when the mutual assistance pact was signed in May 1935 between the Soviet Union and France, French communists had no option but to commit a complete U-turn. Its press organs stopped reporting on anti-militarist protests against the law, actions that, until Stalin's intervention, had been understood as revolutionary in

65 Whitney, *Mobilizing Youth*, 145, 155–56. 66 Ibid., 160–62.

character. A year later the youth press even praised the Republican Army and embraced the discourse on national defense.[67]

While the threat of war led to the growing militarization of Soviet youth in the second half of the 1930s, in Britain and France the anti-fascist campaigning had, in many respects, the opposite effect. With its core anti-militarist message the fight against the rise of fascism challenged the political culture of militant proletarian manliness in many communist organizations. In doing so, it successfully engaged greater numbers of young people from both genders in the popular front movement.[68] Young communists were still fighting on front lines where fascists were taken on in street brawls, but at the same time the movement as such reached out to a broader constituency. Embracing the notion of a popular front brought young communists into contact with more gender-balanced noncommunist organizations from which they recruited suitable youngsters. The membership of the Jeunesse Communiste reached 100,000 in the fall of 1936, while the recently established all-female communist Union des Jeune Filles de France had 20,000 members a year later.[69]

This success in France, as well as in other European countries, was also due to a shift in the approach to sport and leisure in the movement. In Britain too, physical education was redefined as an activity that could bring happiness to the young and was less seen as training for revolutionary combat. Sport and leisure became important pathways into the movement from the early 1930s onwards. They helped to challenge the rather ascetic and austere character the League had obtained in the 1920s, bringing youngsters gradually into the "orbit" of communist politics. The shift played a crucial role in the process of rebuilding the organization after the disastrous "class against class" line had led to its collapse. For example, in Manchester, young communists were successful in drawing in youngsters from the ramblers' movement. The club-like, nonpolitical setting of activities such as sport, dances and socials was attractive to all youth. Betty Bruce was encouraged by her communist mother to join the communist youth organization in Glasgow in the mid 1930s. She did not join it for the politics, but remembered that she "first became interested in social and hiking activities, then became involved in protest meetings and demos on the Spanish Civil War, and collecting for the foodships."[70] Indeed, the Spanish Civil War would become the most captivating international event of the 1930s for young people within the

67 Ibid., 166–67.

68 Waite, "Young People," 76–78, 211–12, 327–29; Whitney, *Mobilizing Youth*, 162, 196–208.

69 Whitney, *Mobilizing Youth*, 207.

70 Waite, "Young People," 211–12, 324–28.

communist movement. In Britain the new spirit of cooperation under the popular front policy and the shift toward leisure reenergized the movement and lifted the membership of the YCL to 4,600 in 1938.[71]

Communist Youth and the Spanish Civil War

In nonfascist countries across the continent but also in the Soviet Union mass campaigns to express solidarity with the Spanish republican forces were organized by the communist movement. They became an outlet for youthful idealism, adventurism and revolutionary romanticism. As Mike Waite asserted, "by making 'Spain' the nodal point of left activity, communists were able to symbolically define the great political choice of the day – democracy against fascism – in terms which presented themselves as the most consistent, committed and courageous defenders of what everybody on the left stood for."[72] Indeed, in spite of the shifting rhetoric in the 1930s and the growing ritualization of internationalist practices in the communist movement, the responses to the Spanish Civil War revealed how much communist internationalism and solidarity meant to young communists.

In the Soviet Union, internationalist practices had become very Russocentric but the genuine commitment of Soviet youth to international solidarity demonstrated the potency of communist internationalism in the epoch of "socialism in one country." The feeling of belonging to a transnational movement, which was repeatedly revitalized among youngsters during the solidarity campaigns of the interwar period, served as an important reference point in their understanding of communism. Age thus mattered in this context. Lev Kopelev, a young Soviet communist, recalled that, infected by "'childhood diseases' of Pioneer-Komsomol and Esperanto internationalism," the Spanish Civil War reignited his old ideals and dreams of international brotherhood. Kopelev and two of his fellow comrades eagerly studied Spanish and sent letters to Stalin, Voroshilov and Koltsov begging them to be allowed to fight in Spain.[73] The authorities found themselves inundated with letters from young and old people with similar requests.[74] For example, a letter by four Komsomol members, all in their

71 Linehan, *Communism in Britain*, 60. 72 Waite, "Young People," 101.

73 Lev Kopelev, *The Education of a True Believer* (London: Wildwood House, 1981), 122–23.

74 Gleb J. Albert, "'To Help the Republicans Not Just By Donations and Rallies, but with the Rifle': Militant Solidarity with the Spanish Republic in the Soviet Union, 1936–1937," *European Review of History – Revue européenne d'histoire* 21, 4 (2014), 502; Timur A. Mukhamatulin, "Formirovanie obraza Ispanii v sovetskom obshchestve v 1936–1939 gg." (Ph.D. dissertation, Moscow, 2012), 176.

twenties, asserted that they were prepared to lay down their lives "for the idea of international communism."[75]

While Soviet citizens, young or old, were not allowed to go to Spain, many British young communists were among the 2,000 volunteers serving in the British International Brigades. At least 126 members of the YCLGB died. French young communists played an even bigger role in the International Brigades which were dominated by communists from France. Those youngsters who remained home worked alongside a range of religious and bourgeois youth organizations to support the cause. In Britain, for example, young communists helped to set up Youth Foodship committees all over the country.[76]

The enthusiastic, emotional and passionate response of youngsters to the solidarity campaign with Spain highlighted the mobilization value of "internationalism" in the communist youth movement. Anti-militarism and anti-fascism allowed the communist youth movement to broaden its appeal in Europe, providing a cause which received a strong public response. It also meant that youngsters joined for different reasons. There were those who were motivated by a strong anti-fascist impulse that allowed them to work within the present order, and those for whom commitment to the Soviet Union superseded all other issues. It is also important to note, as Joel Lewis has pointed out, that in the quest to broaden an alliance against imperialist war and fascism, the inherently internationalist campaigns for solidarity with Spain were often linked to national interests to rally wider support. As John Gollan, born in 1911, succinctly put it to the YCLGB convention in 1938: "Defence of Spain means our defence."[77] In Britain as in France, the growing threat of war and shifts in Comintern policy meant that the communist youth movement eventually adopted the discourse on national defense. Not surprisingly, the Molotov–Ribbentrop Pact of August 1939 caused deep shock and confusion among young communists. The young activist Alan Sims recalled: "Soviet and Stalinist manoeuvrings were becoming increasingly difficult to keep up with. The 'acid test' of 'what is your attitude to the Soviet Union' became increasingly more difficult."[78] However, with Hitler's attack in June 1941, the cognitive dissonance that communists, young and old, had grappled with was removed. The harmony between being anti-fascist

75 RGASPI, f. 495 op. 73, d. 217a, 27–27 ob.

76 Waite, "Young People," 102; *Challenge: The Voice of Youth* 4, 23 (7 Jan. 1939), 8; Rémi Skoutelsky, *L'espoir guidait leurs pas* (Paris: Grasset, 1998), 154.

77 Lewis, *Youth Against Fascism*, 74.

78 Waite, "Young People," 107.

and being a communist internationalist loyal to the Soviet Union was reestablished. Young communists, irrespective of their class and gender, were now able to serve their country without giving up their internationalist outlook.

Conclusions

The interwar period became a defining era for a whole generation of communists. Their experience of being young and a communist in this tumultuous period differed widely depending on the specific sociopolitical environment in which they grew up and operated. As this chapter has shown, the development of communist youth movements was complex and multifaceted. In the Soviet Union, young communists were representative of the new order. Membership in the Komsomol offered great opportunities for upward social mobility, and for many it provided a ticket to escape the countryside and to access education. In contrast, in Western Europe, young communists were in many respects "outsiders." While they lived and operated within the working-class milieu – indeed in Germany young communists were joining an established counterculture – they were nevertheless defined by their opposition to the status quo. Far from providing social mobility, being a young communist could severely undermine one's chances in life. Being a young communist meant taking a stand. Furthermore, many young communists operated illegally under fascist regimes for a significant part of the interwar period. Those who did so showed admirable courage and resolution in their active resistance. Many paid with their lives.

While it is difficult to generalize, there are some common characteristics linked to the age-specific experience of being a young communist in this era. As this chapter has demonstrated, those youngsters who joined the communist cause during and immediately after World War I were idealists. They engaged with communism in a passionate, emotional and impulsive way. They perceived themselves as a revolutionary vanguard and their passion and idealism were tested by the entrenchment and stalemate in Western Europe as well as in the Soviet Union during the 1920s. It led many youngsters to escape into revolutionary romanticism, dreaming of a heroic fight for world revolution and of defending the socialist motherland of all proletarians – the Soviet Union. Indeed, as Eric Hobsbawm remembered, "the knowledge that we were essentially a global movement comforted us."[79] The successful industrialization of the Soviet Union at a time when the world sank into depression in the early 1930s validated their belief system. As a real manifestation of their hopes for the future, the Soviet Union provided a crucial point of reference in their self-identification. The communist youth's commitment to revolutionary internationalism, even in its Russocentric interpretation of the 1930s, fostered a sense of belonging across borders.

The relationship between the parties and the youth, between old and young, was often tenuous and, at times, chaotic and acrimonious. While generational conflict was not the key driver in communist politics, the widespread neglect of youth by local party activists in their day-to-day dealings meant that young communists were frequently able to operate autonomously and express their idiosyncratic views through a variety of practices and rituals. Communist youths were actors in their own right, with their own revolutionary identities. The militant vanguardism and restlessness of young communists, seeking revolutionary deeds, was periodically demonstrated in campaigns around a common cause. For example, this was the case in support of revolutionary events abroad, strike actions at home, or most clearly in volunteering for the Spanish Civil War. Facing dull and boring day-to-day work in their organizations, young communists clearly showed a predisposition for revolutionary deeds, not thoughts. The street was their domain.

The Bolshevization of the Comintern and CYI gradually reduced the freedom for free ideas and spontaneous actions within the communist movement. Nevertheless, the passionate embracing of the anti-fascist cause of the 1930s saw a conscious reorientation and depoliticization of activities, particularly in France and Britain. The anti-militarist cause and the reaching out to other organizations, including religious youth organizations, helped to create a more gender-inclusive environment as part of the drive to create a wider coalition against the rise of fascism. In contrast, in the Soviet Union, the threat of war led to the growing militarization of the activities of the Komsomol and its members. Furthermore, the power of the hegemonic Stalinist discourse made it increasingly difficult for young people to imagine alternatives to Soviet socialism. The language of the regime pervaded people's minds and led many young people to embrace Stalinist values, developing a deep sense of Soviet identity and citizenship.

79 Eric Hobsbawm, *Interesting Times: A Twentieth-Century Life* (London: Abacus, 2003), 72.

Millions of young Soviets, alongside thousands of young communists, would die in the fight against fascism during World War II on the battle-fields of Europe. The passionate struggle in the 1930s to prevent their generation from suffering the same fate as many young people in World War I turned out to be in vain. However, the ultimate defeat of fascism renewed the belief in the righteousness of the communist cause. Communism was, in many respects, reborn as a result of the war and the imagery of youth was once again at the center of this renewal. Paul Vaillant-Couturier captured this mood in his 1946 documentary *Les Lendemains qui chantent*, released to support the communist candidates in the French elections:

> Le communisme c'est la jeunesse du monde, il prépare des lendemains qui chantent.[80]

Bibliographical Essay

Recently the study of the history of youth has experienced a real boom. Historians have begun to approach youth as a social and cultural construct as well as an object and engine of change. For a general introduction to the historical study of youth as a social and cultural construct see Giovanni Levi and Jean-Claude Schmitt (eds.), *A History of Young People in the West* (Cambridge, MA: Harvard University Press, 1997), vol. 1, "Introduction," 1–11.

World War I and the revolutionary upheaval that followed it became an important formative experience for many young people in Europe. They brought the politics of generation to the forefront in the interwar period. The seminal intellectual history of the "generation of 1914," the European youth born around 1900, is Robert Wohl's *The Generation of 1914* (Cambridge, MA: Harvard University Press, 1979), in which the author demonstrates the commonality in their experience and thinking. More specifically focused on socialist youth is Thomas E. Jørgensen's article "The Purest Flame of the Revolution: Working Class Youth and Left Wing Radicalism in Germany and Italy during the Great War," *Labour History* 50, 1 (2009), 19–38, which deals with the radicalizing force of World War I. In my article "'Youth, It's Your Turn!': Generations and the Fate of the Russian Revolution (1917–1932)," *Journal of Social History* 46, 2 (2012), 279–87, I analyze the lasting legacy of

80 "Communism is the youth of the world, it prepares for tomorrows that will sing."

the Russian Civil War on communist youth. I demonstrate how the Komsomol became an outlet in which generational tensions were nurtured and expressed throughout the 1920s, producing a constituency for the Stalinist turn.

The standard study on the development of the early Communist Youth International is Richard Cornell, *Revolutionary Vanguard: The Early Years of the Communist Youth International, 1914–1924* (Toronto: University of Toronto Press, 1982). Following a similar approach, primarily based on an analysis of stenographic reports of Komsomol congresses is Ralph T. Fisher's *Pattern of Soviet Youth: A Study of the Congresses of the Komsomol, 1918–1954* (New York: Columbia University Press, 1959). More recently a number of studies on the interwar Komsomol have appeared that make extensive use of archival material. They examine the complicated interchange between ideology, policy and reality in the league's evolution and practices as well as explore the relationship between representation and the reality of Soviet youth: Anne E. Gorsuch, *Youth in Revolutionary Russia: Enthusiasts, Bohemians, Delinquents* (Bloomington: Indiana University Press, 2000); Matthias Neumann, *The Communist Youth League and the Transformation of the Soviet Union* (London: Routledge, 2011); Matthias Neumann, "Revolutionizing Mind and Soul? Soviet Youth and Cultural Campaigns during the New Economic Policy (1921–8)," *Social History* 33, 3 (2008), 243–67; Sean Guillory, "Profiles in Exhaustion and Pomposity: The Everyday Life of Komsomol Cadres in the 1920s,"*Carl Beck Papers* 2303 (2013). Gorsuch's monograph also includes an excellent chapter on gender and generation. On the issue of class identity, vanguardism and rural expansion see Matthias Neumann, "Class Ascription and Class Identity: *Komsomol'tsy* and the Policy of Class During NEP," *Revolutionary Russia* 19, 2 (2006), 175–96; and Isabel Tirado, "The Komsomol and the Young Peasants: The Dilemma of Rural Expansion 1921–1925," *Slavic Review* 52, 3 (1993), 460–76, and "The Komsomol's Village Vanguard: Youth and Politics in the NEP Countryside," *Russian Review* 72 (2013), 427–46. On the growing militarization of Soviet youth in the 1930s, see Seth Bernstein, *Raised Under Stalin: Young Communists and The Defense of Socialism* (Ithaca: Cornell University Press, 2017).

The literature on the communist youth movement in other European countries is less extensive. The two key works for Britain are Michael Waite's "Young People and Formal Political Activity. A Case Study: Young People and Communist Politics in Britain 1920–1991: Aspects of the Young Communist League" (M.Phil. dissertation, University of Lancaster, 1992), which uses archival material as well as oral history interviews, and Thomas Linehan's chapter on young communists in *Communism in Britain 1920–1930: From the Cradle to the Grave* (Manchester: Manchester University Press, 2007). Susan B. Withney's monograph *Mobilizing Youth: Communists and Catholics in Interwar France* (Durham, NC: Duke University Press, 2009) provides a fascinating analysis of the politics of generation in interwar France. The standard work on the communist youth movement in Weimar Germany is Barbara Köster's "'Die Junge Garde des Proletariat': Untersuchungen zum Kommunistischen Jugendverband Deutschlands in der Weimarer Republik" (Ph.D. dissertation, University of Bielefeld, 2005). A succinct overview can also be found in Klaus Michael Mallmann, *Kommunisten in der Weimarer Republik. Sozialgeschichte einer revolutionaeren Bewegung* (Darmstadt: Wissenschaftliche Buchgesellschaft, 1996), 182–93.

On the issue of revolutionary internationalism and practices of transnational solidarity the reader should consult the ground-breaking works by Gleb J. Albert, including *Das Charisma der Weltrevolution: Revolutionärer Internationalismus in der frühen Sowjetgesellschaft, 1917–1927* (Cologne: Böhlau Verlag, 2017), "'German October Is Approaching': Internationalism, Activists, and the Soviet State in 1923," *Revolutionary Russia* 24, 2 (2011), 111–42, and "'To Help the Republicans Not Just by Donations and Rallies, but with the Rifle': Militant Solidarity with the Spanish Republic in the Soviet Union, 1936–1937," *European Review of History – Revue européenne d'histoire* 21, 4 (2014), 501–18.

There are many fascinating autobiographies of former communists which cover their formative years in the communist youth movement. For the Soviet Union the most intriguing account has been provided by Lev Kopelev in his autobiography *The Education of a True Believer* (London: Wildwood House, 1981). Similarly, the British Marxist and historian Eric Hobsbawm vividly recollects his experience of youth in interwar Europe in *Interesting Times: A Twentieth-Century Life* (London: Abacus, 2003). Margarete Buber-Neumann recalls her path through the KJVD, to the Comintern and into the whirlwind of the Great Purges in the Soviet Union in *Von Potsdam nach Moskau: Stationen eines Irrweges* (Stuttgart: Deutsche Verlag-Anstalt, 1957). For an interesting autobiography of a young French communist, see Léo Figuères, *Jeunesse militante: chronique d'un jeune communiste des anneés 30–50* (Paris: Éditions Sociales, 1971).

20

Communism as Existential Choice

BRIGITTE STUDER

In the time of the Communist International, between 1919 and 1943, the decision to join a communist party was heavy with consequences, as is attested by many autobiographies: "Life-changing," in the words of Eric Hobsbawm.[1] To become a member was, in the first place, to act on – to make practical – a critique (in the dual sense of both objection and analysis) of the existing social world. Whether prompted by first-hand experience or second-hand witness, this critique of class oppression in capitalist society might find practical expression in a host of fields: in trade union work, in campaigns for the rights of women or young people, in peasant or anti-colonial struggles, in the provision of humanitarian aid to the oppressed or legal assistance to imprisoned activists, in the fight against war and fascism . . . While members' immediate motivations for joining were many and various and their subsequent experience within the party equally diverse, they all confronted certain core expectations and political practices inspired by the model of the Soviet party and diffused with more or less success through the channels of the Comintern. Norms and obligations varied in scope and intensity by country and rank in the party, and also changed with the prevailing political line. In all cases, however, in the name of political efficacy and of the ideological unity supposed to ensure it, communist parties strove constantly to counter the sociological, political and cultural diversity of the membership, which in the early years was indeed very marked as revolutionaries of many shades – syndicalists and feminists, anarchists and social democrats, intellectuals and avant-garde artists, even adventurers – found themselves attracted to the cause. To this end the communist parties relied on certain means of political socialization, among them party rules and techniques of cadre control. They imposed behavioral norms and deployed

1 Eric Hobsbawm, *Interesting Times: A Twentieth-Century Life* (London: Abacus, 2005), 129.

sanctions to bend individuals to a collective political rationality. Above all, they built on party members' own disposition to self-perfection in order to inculcate the required mind-set and attitudes.

Before looking at the key elements of the normative system governing the "communist world" and the party techniques that sustained it, it is worth considering that first moment of commitment.

Joining the Party: Reason and Emotion

To join the communist party (CP) was to seize the opportunity for education and self-expression it offered to workers as an oppressed and disadvantaged class, or to express solidarity with them in their struggle. It was to live political passion as a way of life. And finally, it was to sustain, by playing one's own part in it, the organization that was to realize the global revolutionary project – the Communist International, which ranged across every level of political space, from the international (in its ambition to cover every country of the globe) via the transnational (with its horizontal networks extending from one country to another) down to the national and the local, the basis for concrete political activity.

All the same, the factors that actually triggered the decision were diverse: the bankruptcy of the Second International in 1914, the barbarism of World War I, the new hope born of the Russian Revolution, the anti-colonial struggle, opposition to Nazism, solidarity with republican Spain, resistance in occupied France. Is it even possible to usefully categorize the cases of the millions of men and women who joined the party during the period of the Communist International's existence – almost all of whom would eventually leave it again?

One might ask, nonetheless, whether future communists were impelled to party membership by the general revolutionary or political tendencies of their time, or whether the decision was arrived at individually, or even against the prevailing current. Above all, were they joining a party in power, the representative of legitimate political authority, or a party in opposition or even clandestine? And finally, were they men or women? Women in fact remained a small minority, given the near absence (or rather the progressive rejection) of any serious reflection on women's political disqualification (too simply attributed to capitalist society). Indeed, despite its lip-service to the principle of equality, the communist movement was no exception to the exclusion of women from politics more widely, an instance of the more general dynamic characteristic of Western democracies described by Pierre Bourdieu: "The propensity to use political power (the power to vote, or 'talk politics' or 'get involved in politics') is commensurate with the reality of this power, or in other words ... indifference is only a manifestation of impotence."[2]

Georges Lavau distinguishes between "emotive enrollment" (often at a big event, even if mostly preceded by a longer or shorter period of incubation), "enrollment as regularization" (by those already arguing for communist positions in the organizations they were involved in), "enrollment as rectification" (by those who already belonged to a socialist organization but no longer felt happy there) and "enrollment through impregnation" (in the context of family, work, or neighborhood).[3] Annie Kriegel, doyenne of the historical ethnography of the French CP, distinguishes different kinds of subjective relationship to the institution. The first is *functional* in the case of properly political adherence, in which the CP simply represented the most radical party, a situation that presupposed a party already legitimate, enjoying a strong political and institutional presence, if not in power. The same kind of presence was presupposed by the *existential* – almost "natural" – adherence of those for whom the party was less a political party than a way of life, characteristic of the "Little Moscows,"[4] local communities whose very social fabric was structured by the party and its activities. *Ideological* adherence, finally, was generally reserved to students and intellectuals, who made a deliberate choice to align themselves with the interests of the working class.[5]

Useful as such ideal types are, in reality motivation was usually not so clear cut. In any case, joining the French party was not enough to become a communist. Even if the degree of involvement varied, the individual had to "politicize" his or her membership, that is, to appropriate specific norms of militancy in order to think, feel and act like a communist. We will first consider European communism in general and then the more restricted population of those who worked in the Comintern *apparat* or who were selected for cadre education in Moscow.

2 Pierre Bourdieu, *Distinction: A Social Critique of the Judgment of Taste*, trans. Richard Nice (Cambridge, MA: Harvard University Press, 1984), 406.

3 Georges Lavau, *A quoi sert le parti communiste français?* (Paris: Fayard, 1981), 103–05.

4 Stuart Macintyre, *Little Moscows: Communism and Working-Class Militancy in Interwar Britain* (London: Croom Helm, 1980). See also Richard Cross, Norry LaPorte, Kevin Morgan and Matthew Worley (eds.), *Twentieth Century Communism* 5 (2013), special issue on "Local Communisms."

5 Annie Kriegel, *Les communistes français dans leur premier demi-siècle 1920–1970. Nouvelle édition entièrement refondue et augmentée avec la collaboration de Guillaume Bourgeois* (Paris: Seuil, 1985), 169–80.

Belonging to the Party: A World of Meaning and Duty

Any political commitment involves a conscious, deliberate, personal choice that bears not only on the present but also on the future, with a direct impact on everyday life. In the case of the CP, the consequences were particularly weighty, and this for two reasons. It should be recalled, first, that communist parties are among the family of "total" institutions described by Erving Goffman, even if they represent the special case of an open total institution, both entry and exit being voluntary.[6] They nonetheless engaged their members in a coherent social framework that touched every aspect of life, both public and private, involving to varying degrees adjustment of habitus, the reconstruction of personal identity. Second, the communist nearly always faced a hostile or even dangerous environment: Most communist parties of the past had to act completely or at least partly clandestinely (only twenty-six of the seventy-six parties represented at the 7th World Congress of 1935 were able to send a legal delegation) or faced police repression, exclusion from trade unions and public opprobrium.

Membership of a communist party brought with it demands that went beyond those of any "ordinary" party. These were not limited to political tasks such as distributing leaflets, selling the paper, campaigning in elections, organizing strikes, or simply participating in the life of the party through regular attendance at meetings. The theses on the structure and methods of work of the communist parties adopted at the Third Congress of the International are explicit "On communists' obligation to be active": "In its effort to have a genuinely active membership, a Communist Party should ask of everyone in its ranks to commit their energy and time to the party, to the extent possible under given circumstances, and to always do their best in its service."[7] "Passivity" was reviled, mobilization more or less permanent as one campaign followed on the heels of another with the famine in Soviet

6 Erving Goffman, *Asylums: Essays on the Social Situation of Mental Patients and Other Inmates* (Garden City, NY: Anchor Books, 1961). For the qualification, see Claude Pennetier and Bernard Pudal, "Du parti bolchevik au parti stalinien," in Michel Dreyfus et al. (eds.), *Le siècle des communismes*, 2nd edn. (Paris: Seuil, 2004), 499–510, here 506.

7 "Theses on the Organisational Structure of Communist Parties and the Methods and Content of their Work," 12 July 1921, in John Riddell (ed.), *To the Masses: Proceedings of the Third Congress of the Communist International, 1921* (Leiden and Boston: Brill, 2015), 978–1006, here 980–81; see also the extracts in a rather more strongly formulated translation, in Jane Degras (ed.), *The Communist International 1919–1943: Documents*, vol. 1, *1919–1922* (London: Oxford University Press, 1956), 256–71, here 259.

Russia, the danger of war with Japan, the execution of Sacco and Vanzetti, the supposed imminent collapse of capitalism, the rise of fascism and the Spanish Civil War. There were always strikers or prisoners' families somewhere who needed support. And if there was no worldwide campaign, then there were the national and the local activities. As well as street demonstrations, protest marches, paper sales, stalls at public events and canvassing for elections (where they happened), the week was punctuated by numerous meetings: the local branch of the party, the workplace cell, the communist fraction in the union, Workers' International Relief, the party women's organization, the unemployed workers' assembly and more. Tasks accumulated as the member was accorded new responsibilities and rose through the hierarchy of the party and its organizations: cell bureau, fraction leadership in union or mass organization and so on. While it was an honor, becoming a fulltimer did not reduce the overload of work, even if it did solve the problem of combining conventional employment and such time-consuming militancy. In everything they did – not just in the everyday routine of political work, but in the smallest details of life – communists were to prove themselves serious and responsible, respectable even. Otherwise, how could the workers trust the party? Every meeting had to be prepared for by reading and above all "studying" the relevant party texts. Any intervention was to be structured, preferably delivered from notes. Party members were expected to be exemplary not only in their political engagement but also in their work and in their private lives. The party required that one be a conscientious worker and a good father . . . or indeed mother, in the case of the female members. A communist, finally, was to be moderate in the use of intoxicants or stimulants and morally irreproachable. Drunkenness was disapproved of and could be sanctioned. In 1932, the Swiss party expelled four unemployed young men for engaging in prostitution. This kind of thing could not be tolerated, not so much on account of the acts themselves, but on account of the risk they presented to the party's reputation.[8]

An Ethic for Life

To be a communist structured one's relationship to the world. To be a communist was to have priorities – in terms of the investment of time, and in terms of one's whole being. To be a communist was to have an ethic.

8 Brigitte Studer, *Un parti sous influence. Le Parti communiste suisse, une section du Komintern, 1931 à 1939* (Lausanne: L'Âge d'Homme, 1994), 373.

In sociological register, we can call the organization of life through a set of underlying principles a conduct of life, in the sense of Weber's *Lebensführung*. This involves making choices and exerting control over oneself so as to exhibit the attitudes and forms of behavior answering to the expectations of the community to which one belongs.

Beyond the great general principles of proletarian internationalism and solidarity with the oppressed, inherited from the European labor movement, international communism was marked by the values of the Russian experience. This meant first of all having a sense of the collective and a sense of discipline. As Nikolai Bukharin and Yevgenii Preobrazhenskii's *ABC of Communism* put it, as early as 1920, "The individual human being does not belong to himself, but to society, to the human race. The individual can only live and thrive owing to the existence of society."[9] A legacy of the Bolshevik party's clandestine existence under tsarism, discipline became a condition of membership of the CP during the civil war of 1918–21, when the Bolsheviks were caught between the need to defend their newly acquired power and the desire to lay the foundations for a communist society. While the prospect of revolution presented itself in Central Europe, Lenin wanted to move fast and strike hard. The Second Congress of the Communist International in 1920 thus adopted resolutions that forced communist parties to close ranks around the line of the International, weeding out "reformists and centrists." The famous "Twenty-One Conditions" called for "iron discipline," a notion that covered individual behavior. In fact, the "politically reliable" communist subordinated his or her own interests to those of "truly revolutionary propaganda and agitation." The sense of discipline instilled by these early documents was such that the power of administrative fiat always inherent in the communist conception of organization was all the more easily accepted by the membership taking it as a token of efficacy. In 1936, in an essay on the party's expectations of its members, Yemelian Yaroslavskii noted that any weakening of discipline would serve the enemy. But, he went on to insist, if this discipline recalled military discipline, it was a discipline freely assumed, a conscious, revolutionary discipline. Once the member had accepted it by joining, it was for him to show himself a model of party discipline.[10] This means that he accepted the party's decisions, executed its orders and defended its positions at all costs, though he might doubt or even disagree

9 www.marxists.org/archive/bukharin/works/1920/abc/.

10 E. Jaroslawski, *Was fordert die Partei vom Kommunisten* (Moscow: Verlagsgenossenschaft Ausländischer Arbeiter in der UdSSR, 1936), 48–49.

with them. And this even at the cost of disruption or even complete loss of family life.

"Party-Mindedness"

At the heart of it all was "the party" (as has often been noted, for the communists there was only ever one). Without what Bolshevik semantics called *partiinost'* – which can be translated as "party-mindedness," that is, a high level of political consciousness and devotion to the party[11] – none of the factors mentioned earlier would by itself have been enough to ensure the depth and sometimes long duration of the self-abnegation involved. In *What Is To Be Done?*, Lenin defined the party as a centralized "organization of struggle" composed of dedicated, professional revolutionaries. It represented the avant-garde of the working class, it alone being capable of developing a true class-consciousness. For this its unity was an absolute condition that had to be protected against the erosion that transactions with other worlds and ideologies could bring about.

After the Bolshevik party's conquest of power in Russia, this conception and the principles of "Leninist" party organization associated with it were imposed on all communist parties, being lifted from the context that had originally provided their *raison d'être* and turned into ends in themselves. They then served to discipline the communist parties and their members. The principle of democratic centralism adopted at the Second Congress of the Comintern in 1920 brought in a form of "authoritarian democracy" that allowed the formation of tendencies and the expression of minority positions during periods of formal debate only. Once a decision was taken by a leading body, it was to be implemented without further discussion, in disciplined fashion, the minority submitting to the majority. However, following the example of the Russian CP, which banned factions in 1921 – and with them any criticism of the line that went beyond silent individual dissent – all opposition came to be gradually banished, being met with sanctions that could go as far as expulsion, the 1930s seeing the Soviet language of crime, too, being taken up elsewhere. The party was always right; it had its reasons, and it had no need to justify them. When Manuilsky asked Jules Humbert-Droz what he thought of the decisions of the 7th World Congress, the latter replied that it was what he had advocated in 1928 and 1932. To which Manuilsky replied: "Comrade Humbert-Droz, we are never right

11 Richard Stites (ed.), *Culture and Entertainment in Wartime Russia* (Bloomington: Indiana University Press, 1995), 4.

against our own party. In 1928 and 1932, the policy was wrong. Today it is right."[12]

The Italian communist Angelo Tasca (party name Amilcare Rossi) spoke of a "mystique of the party" in characterizing the relationship between the member and the organization. "The party" was not simply an instrument of political struggle, but first of all the site of a dividing line between those who belonged and the others, the unorganized. It defined an inside and an outside. The sources testify to the very great strength of communists' relationship to the party: Its members belonged to an elite circle, a community knit together by adversity; and they were symbolically enclosed by it. The nature of the communist's relationship to the party needs to be historically situated though. With "Bolshevization" and even more so with Stalinization, it gradually came to be understood as a form of subordination – one whose logic was portrayed, in dramatically exaggerated form, by Bertolt Brecht 1929–30 in his learning-play *The Measures Taken*, which justifies, in the name of the party, the killing of the young communist whose imprudence and enthusiasm threaten the mission of the Comintern agents he is accompanying. Here "the party" is glorified as an indestructible collective body: "The individual has two eyes / The Party has a thousand eyes / . . . The individual can be wiped out / But the Party cannot be wiped out / For it rests on the teaching of the classic writers / Which is created from acquaintance with reality."[13] Conversely, in order to serve the party, which itself serves the revolution, all personal identity must be abandoned: "Then you are yourselves no longer. You are not Karl Schmitt from Berlin, you are not Anna Kjersk from Kazan, and you are not Peter Sawitch from Moscow. All of you are nameless and motherless, blank pages on which the Revolution writes its instructions."[14] Or, as it was more simply put by a young Austrian communist, a refugee in the Soviet Union: "As a communist, I am a soldier. Where the party sends me, I go. That's what a communist does."[15] Others, like the German communist Alfred Kurella, a writer himself and a cultural functionary of the Comintern,

12 Jules Humbert-Droz, *Dix ans de lutte antifasciste, 1931–1941* (Neuchâtel: La Baconnière, 1972), 139.

13 Bertolt Brecht, *The Measures Taken*, in Bertolt Brecht, *The Jewish Wife and other Short Plays*, trans. Eric Bentley (New York: Grove Press, 1967), 100.

14 Ibid., 81.

15 Minutes of the meeting of the Schutzbündlerkollektiv, 16 July 1936, in Rossiiskii gosudarstvennyi arkhiv sotsial'no-politicheskoi istorii (RGASPI), 495/187/587.

criticized Brecht's representation. Even if idealized and overstated, and more likely partial and temporary, as well as varying individually, the communist's dedication to the party remains extraordinary.

Gift of Self . . . or Fair Exchange?

This abdication or entrustment of the self to the party has always fascinated outside observers, though interpretations have differed. Was it the expression of a militarized political culture, as in the example above, or was it generated by a sense of revolutionary romanticism as Turkish communist poet Nazım Hikmet saw it?[16] Theories of totalitarianism see in it the effect of force. Understandings based on the idea of political religion focus on the irrationality of communists' life-choices and behaviors, conceptualizing the relationship between member and party as an attachment in the mode of faith. Setting aside these over-general claims, whose limits are evident (in the case of the first, its inadequacy for the situation in democratic countries, in that of the second, the nonidentity of the religious and the political), there remains another hypothesis worthy of attention. While emphasis was for a long time laid on the communist's selflessness, more recently the focus has shifted to the personal rewards of political engagement. As Pierre Bourdieu put it, expressing agreement with the ideas of Albert Hirschman, "political work . . . can be its own end and its own reward."[17]

The kinds of satisfaction provided by communists' political engagement were many, one being selflessness itself. Self-sacrifice for a cause can give coherence to an identity by aligning political belief and action, giving meaning to a life that otherwise might seem bleak and insignificant. In the abstract, the communist cause represented a struggle for global justice, the reinvention of the social world for the better; in the concrete, it was an everyday struggle to ensure better conditions of life for the exploited and oppressed. Involvement could bring personal advantages, either material or symbolic. A party activist acquired organizational and rhetorical skills. To be a communist was also to play a part in a historic process and to join a community symbolically united by shared references and common goals. It was to transcend social categories and to inscribe oneself into a new universalism. From this point of

16 As in his semi-autobiographical novel, *The Romantics* [1967] (Chicago: Banner Press, 1992).

17 Pierre Bourdieu, *Homo Academicus*, trans. Peter Collier (Cambridge: Polity Press, 1988), 317, n. 28; Albert O. Hirschman, *Shifting Involvements: Private Interest and Public Action* (Princeton: Princeton University Press, 1982); see also Daniel Gaxie, "Rétributions du militantisme et paradoxes de l'action collective," *Swiss Political Science Review* 11, 1 (2005), 157–88.

view, to accept the primacy of the collective, to give up individual interests in favor of the collective will was to become an integral part of a force that was to change the course of the world. And in exchange, the individual – however insignificant in him- or herself – gained the sense of importance and even of power that came from being one element in a greater whole in which every component counted.

This was all the more so as the world of communism was bound together in what Kris Manjapra terms an "economy of recognition."[18] Its transnational infrastructure, a global network of varying density whose detail cannot be gone into here, was largely funded by the Soviet state. The channels it provided created a space of exchange between different groups of actors struggling against colonialism. One should not of course overestimate the freedom enjoyed by these laboratories of anti-colonial struggle, especially as its limits were ever more tightly drawn as the 1920s progressed. Nor should one idealize the nature of the interpersonal relationships established, for they could be highly conflictual. It is nonetheless the case that the Comintern provided these activists with both logistical and ideological support, and facilitated North–South and East–West exchanges. The channels of communication and the funding it made available helped constitute an active solidarity between colonized and colonizing countries, as it did between the industrialized countries of the capitalist world. To individuals it provided opportunities for traveling. It was thanks to the International Liaison Department of the Comintern that the American writer and journalist Agnes Smedley, a birth-control activist and campaigner for Indian independence, was able to move to China.[19] Even for ordinary members of the party, international solidarity went beyond declarations and appeals, regularly expressing itself in concrete assistance to comrades abroad or to foreign comrades in the country. The limits on individual autonomy were counterbalanced by strong group support and practices of mutual aid. For the leaders, the existence of the International was the *sine qua non* of their political careers, and in many cases of their social advancement.

The world of the communists was thus fortified by transnational links both material and symbolic. The ritual of revolutionary celebration and demonstration, even of confrontation with the police, emblems such as the red flag, the raised fist, the slogan, the *Internationale*: All were signs of both distinction

18 See Kris Manjapra, "Communist Internationalism and Transcolonial Recognition," in Kris Manjapra and Sugata Bose (eds.), *Cosmopolitan Thought Zones: South Asia and the Global Circulation of Ideas* (Basingstoke: Palgrave Macmillan, 2010), 159–77.

19 Ruth Price, *The Lives of Agnes Smedley* (Oxford: Oxford University Press, 2005).

and belonging. Not only signs of unity and strength, but also practices creating fusional moments, as is illustrated by a story told by the Austrian communist Ruth von Mayenburg, the daughter of an aristocratic family who ended up working for Soviet army intelligence. Under cover of ski-touring, she was exploring frontier crossings between Nazi Germany and Schuschnigg's Austria. Without really thinking, moved by the beauty of the mountains, she began to sing the *Internationale*. Great was her surprise and joy to find herself answered, not by an echo, but by a man's voice joining her. There were still comrades in the Third Reich! Together, but without ever seeing each other, they then worked through all the well-known revolutionary songs.[20]

Nor were these the only rewards. Involvement in the party also answered to intellectual and cultural aspects of care of the self. The party schools offered access to knowledge to members of social classes deprived of cultural capital, but for all communists – men and women, workers and intellectuals – learning had a value, both intrinsically – the appropriation of symbolic cultural goods having a value in itself (even if in the late 1920s what was worthwhile became more tightly defined, as the "proletarian" in art and literature and the "Marxist-Leninist" in science and philosophy) – and instrumentally, in that the work on the self effected by study served the needs of the party. In both cases, learning was part of a process of self-improvement leading from mere spontaneity to consciousness. The Marxism propagated by the communist organizations in the form of dialectical materialism functioned as a key to understanding the world: "Marxism gave life a pattern. During the 1930s it had explained the abject behaviour of British Conservatives, as Hitler gobbled one country after another. It explained the bumbling slowness of the Labour Party in the face of these events. We, with our pattern, understood what was going on."[21] The explanatory power of the boiled-down Marxism put out by the communists in the 1930s equally appealed to intellectuals, who admired precisely its simplicity. Eric Hobsbawm confesses in his memoirs, without any false shame, to the aesthetic attraction of a coherent and all-embracing system of thought:

> When this section [on "Dialectical and Historical Materialism" in Stalin's notorious *History of the Communist Party of the Soviet Union (Bolsheviks): Short*

20 Ruth von Mayenburg, *Blaues Blut und rote Fahnen. Ein Leben unter vielen Namen*, 2nd edn. (Vienna, Munich and Zürich: Verlag Fritz Molden, 1969), 161–62.

21 Alison Macleod, *The Death of Uncle Joe* (Rendlesham: Merlin Press, 1997), 12.

> *Course* (1939)] appeared, I read it with enthusiasm, allowing for its pedagogic simplifications. It corresponded pretty much to what I, and perhaps most of the British intellectual reds of the 1930s, understood by Marxism. We liked to think of it as "scientific" in a rather nineteenth-century sense . . . "Dialectical materialism" provided, if not a "theory of everything", then at least a "framework of everything", linking inorganic and organic nature with human affairs, collective and individual, and providing a guide to the nature of all interactions in a world in constant flux.[22]

The young Austrian leader Ernst Fischer felt this too. What led intellectuals like him to admire Stalin, he says, what they succumbed to, was "the enormously helpful *simplification*." This dreadful simplicity of course put an end to all critical thinking, "but it gave us greater strength."[23]

Care for the self did not, though, extend to physical wellbeing. On the contrary, many were the communists who did not hesitate to risk their health or even life itself, through constant activity or in consequence of imprisonment. After the early days, communist parties were not generally welcoming to adventurers, but one cannot completely exclude the appeal of danger, especially among those engaged in clandestine activities or indeed espionage, even if they acted first and foremost from a sense of duty. Communists like Richard Sorge or Ruth Werner ("Sonja"), who spied for Soviet army intelligence, were taking enormous risks, but they escaped humdrum insignificance and in Werner's case the boredom of a non-employed wife accompanying her husband in China. But as she explains in her memoirs there was also a concern for social justice: "There were many positive factors to set against the dangers. We were helping the only country in the world where the working class had been victorious. We were fighting Japanese Fascism. Our hatred of capitalism, oppression and war was more than theory. We were witnessing their effects daily, with our own eyes, and we loved the Chinese people who had to suffer them – the coolies, the peasants, the children and the mothers."[24] It cannot be denied, in any event, that those who sought to build communist movements in the colonies and in semi-colonial countries showed courage. More generally, the Comintern and its global network offered many members the opportunity for a social and geographical mobility that would otherwise have remained inaccessible to most.

22 Hobsbawm, *Interesting Times*, 96–97.

23 Ernst Fischer, *Erinnerungen und Reflexionen* (Reinbek bei Hamburg: Rowohlt, 1969), 300–01 [emphasis in original].

24 Ruth Werner, *Sonya's Report* (London: Chatto & Windus, 1991), 144.

A Metaphysics of Progress

Political commitment undeniably rested on belief. Communists believed in the future and in their ability to change it. Central in this worldview was the existence of the Soviet Union. For communists living outside the Soviet Union, the "fatherland of socialism," which already covered one-sixth of the globe, served as a beacon in the struggle, a bastion against fascism and a screen for the projection of their hopes for another modernity.[25] Wherever they might be they shared with the Bolsheviks a "metaphysics of progress" (Raphael Samuel) that underlay the double project of creating a new society and a New Man.[26] Both would be perfectly rationalized, human self-discipline being part of this vision of modernity.

The instruments to this end were first science and technology, and second education and training. Though situated products of the 1920s general rational vision of modernity, they remained fundamental references over time and place. "We believed in the transforming power of knowledge, and the emancipatory potential of science," wrote Samuel.[27] The rationalization of work, the prevention of natural catastrophes through mechanization and engineering, "scientific" organization and social planning by means of cybernetics and statistics: These were among the first goals of the young Soviet state. In its utopian aspect, the belief that everything was possible, the Bolshevik imaginary foresaw a perfect future. It looked forward to a new age in which communism could shape and model an unresisting world, just as it could move rivers as it wished, nature being mastered by the ingenuity of man. What would the new society be like? Its features are less distinct than those of the New Man. Bukharin might wax lyrical in 1928, but it made the utopia no less abstract: "We are creating and will create a civilization in comparison with which the capitalist civilization will seem like a vulgar street dance in comparison with the heroic symphonies of Beethoven."[28] Indeed, in the vision of

25 On the concept of "alternative modernity" as a way of shifting attention from the Western model as the only conceivable modernity, see Michael David-Fox, "Multiple Modernities vs. Neo-Traditionalism: On Recent Debates in Russian and Soviet History," *Jahrbücher für Geschichte Osteuropas* 54, 4 (2006), 535–55.

26 On this dual enterprise see especially, among an extensive and diverse literature, Peter Holquist, *Making War, Forging Revolution: Russia's Continuum of Crisis, 1914–1921* (Cambridge, MA: Harvard University Press, 2002), and Richard Stites, *Revolutionary Dreams: Utopian Vision and Experimental Life in the Russian Revolution* (Oxford: Oxford University Press, 1989).

27 Raphael Samuel, *The Lost World of British Communism* (London: Verso, 2006), 50.

28 Cited in Svetlana Boym, *Common Places: Mythologies of Everyday Life in Russian* (Cambridge, MA, and London: Harvard University Press, 1994), 62.

a titanically empowered humanity shared by a whole range of authors from Gor'kii to Trotsky, men and women were completely transformed. It wasn't just a question of New Man: The Women's Department of the Bolshevik party promoted the image of the New Woman, active and independent. But for the most part the New Man was male, and he would be quicker, more vigorous and more productive, with nerves of steel and a will of iron. In his novel *How the Steel Was Tempered* (first published in serial form in 1932–34, and then as a book in 1936, rewritten in accordance with Socialist Realist prescriptions), Nikolai Ostrovskii represented these virtues in the person of the hero Pavel Korchagin. Translated into many languages, the book became compulsory reading for young communists the world over. In the scientistic version (mocked by Bulgakov in his short story "Heart of a Dog"), the change from the "Old Man" is ascribed to genetics; and in the more technicist (taken to its limits in Aleksei Gastev's machine-man) to rationalization.

A different though not incompatible approach put the accent on work on the self in producing the New Man. Reflecting the high proportion of intellectuals among the party leadership, but very much in the tradition of the workers' movement in Europe generally, the Russian party stressed the importance of education and training. Discussion circles, theoretical debate, and especially private reading were central to the everyday life of its leading figures, and – ideally – that of every member. In power, the Bolsheviks continued to uphold this ethos of study, seeking to promote popular education through the organization of literacy campaigns on the one hand and workers' universities (*rabfak*) on the other.

Under the first Five-Year Plan of 1928–32, training took on a new significance: As well as fulfilling an obligation to the party, it now meant social advance.[29] The Soviet effort at self-education, now even further reinforced, was viewed very positively by most foreign observers as it radicalized the old idea of workers' education. The French communist Paul Vaillant-Couturier, editor of *L'Humanité*, noted in *Les Bâtisseurs de la Russie nouvelle* (1932) that "school is everywhere, from the factory to the club, the theatre, the cinema and the culture park."[30] In 1933, the *Arbeiter-Illustrierte Zeitung*, whose many reports on the USSR found a large readership in German-speaking countries, reported the thinking of young Soviet citizens in the

29 Sheila Fitzpatrick, *Everyday Stalinism: Ordinary Life in Extraordinary Times: Soviet Russia in the 1930s* (Oxford: Oxford University Press, 1999), 18.

30 Paul Vaillant-Couturier, *Les Bâtisseurs de la Russie nouvelle* (Paris: Bureau d'éditions du PC, 1932).

words "There's nothing you can't learn."[31] And in 1935, this same newspaper of Willy Münzenberg's introduced Stalin with the title "The Great Educator."[32] The communist parties for their part shared a sense of the importance of political education and more generally of the necessity of producing more rounded, more cultivated men and women. But how was one to produce the communist militant of the Bolshevik type? The individuals and organizations that joined the Third International came from very diverse traditions and sometimes evidenced divergent political sensibilities.

Forming the Communist Cadre: Practices of Homogenization

To ensure ideological cohesion among its members, the Comintern adopted with "Bolshevization" a number of practices borrowed from the Bolshevik party, such cohesion being all the more important for an organization that functioned in accordance with the principle of unity in action and insisted on a form of "political consciousness" from which all social-democratic traces had been eliminated. Adopted for political reasons, these practices also had a social function, an ambiguity reflected in their effects, the boundaries between education, the creation of symbolic cohesion, the testing of loyalty, discipline and frank repression often being shifting and unclear.[33]

Selective Admission

A first step toward homogeneity was represented by selective admission to membership (a practice that was difficult to reconcile with the mass party conception). Candidates couldn't join just because they wanted to, but had to undergo a series of rites of passage. In the Soviet Union, they had to be sponsored by three existing members and also to prove themselves worthy. Before being admitted, one had to write an "autobiography," a more or less lengthy and detailed curriculum vitae that featured social origin (preferably worker or peasant), social engagement (in mass organizations) and reasons

31 *Arbeiter-Illustrierte Zeitung*, 27 July 1933.

32 "Der große Erzieher," *Arbeiter-Illustrierte Zeitung* (14 Mar. 1935), front page.

33 On the multiplicity of interactions between party organizations and Soviet state institutions and individuals see the multilingual volume Brigitte Studer and Heiko Haumann (eds.), *Stalinist Subjects: Individual and System in the Soviet Union and the Comintern, 1929–1953* (Zurich: Chronos, 2006).

for wanting to join the party. There followed an inquiry report and an interview with the leader of the cell or perhaps a committee. Then one had to take an examination in politics, which varied in difficulty with social class and with period (taking on in the 1930s the character of a police investigation).[34] Communist parties outside the Soviet Union were much less bureaucratically insistent on form, but they were nonetheless selective (except in those rare moments of mass mobilization), and admitted new members only on probation. They had no parallel, of course, to the distinctively Soviet practice of submitting the list of candidates to the state authorities for investigation. They did, however, eventually take up the Bolshevik practice of re-registration, that is, the withdrawal and reissue of membership cards, allowing the removal of those inactive members who were communists in name only. In addition to their selective function, these rites or acts of institution also had a performative effect, constituting the group in as much as the group constituted itself through them.[35] In emphasizing the significance of joining and submitting members to a first series of tests, the CP made clear the meaning of admission: They had been selected by the party organs to form part of the advance guard of the working class. These rituals thus had a second function, that of discouraging exit from the party, a danger that threatened all members over time, in the face of adversity, the personal costs of intensive political activity and the discipline the party insisted on.

Cadre Control

If, ideally, communists were to be entirely devoted to the cause, historical research has necessarily to distinguish between discourse and concrete reality. Even a party as hierarchically structured and disciplined as the CP had to deal with "individual activist potential," as it was termed by Victor Fay, the Polish-born head of political education of the French party from 1929 to 1936.[36] The leadership were well aware of this. Building a party of loyal and dedicated militants needed time, and above all good cadres. Turning norms of behavior into habitus was a long process, one that depended not just on structures but on collective interaction.

34 Nicolas Werth, *Être communiste en URSS sous Staline* (Paris: Gallimard, 1981), 15–41.

35 Pierre Bourdieu, "Rites of Institution," in John B. Thompson (ed.), *Language and Symbolic Power*, trans. G. Raymond and M. Adamson (Cambridge: Polity Press, 1991), 117–26.

36 Victor Fay, *La flamme et la cendre. Histoire d'une vie militante* (Saint-Denis: Presses universitaires de Vincennes, 1989), 102.

Cadre control began with cadre training. With the "Bolshevization" of the mid 1920s came the demand that communist parties establish central schools, into which the leadership directed politically promising young members. The best of these might then be selected to attend one of the clandestine international cadre schools in the USSR, the best known being the International Lenin School, established in 1926. But to get there, the student had to undergo an increasingly stringent selection process that was far from purely political. From the late 1920s onward, the list of positive and negative criteria grew longer. Among the negatives, lack of political experience was joined in 1931 by lack of transparency as regards one's past; other grounds for exclusion were present or past membership of an oppositional group, active participation in factional struggle, and poor health.[37] On arrival in the Soviet Union, candidates were subjected to further observation and control by organs of the Comintern and of the Soviet CP.

What students were then taught was not limited to politics and economics, as well as the practical knowledge useful to activists, in order to equip them for their future roles as leading party cadres. There were of course lectures on such subjects as political economy, building the party, work in the unions, organizational work, Leninism or Marxism-Leninism. However, in the training afforded by CP schools, it was as important to acquire a "correct" interpretation of social reality as to acquire knowledge itself. The students were to interiorize a self-restriction to only one meaning-context and to reject all alternative ideological frameworks. The corresponding shift in pedagogical objectives in the late 1920s, which becomes even more marked in the 1930s, is reflected in changes in course content. The work of the classical authors of the Marxist-Leninist tradition thus increasingly gave way to its exegesis by Soviet leaders, Stalin and his writings on "Leninism" foremost among them. The only "correct" interpretation was the "Marxist-Leninist" one, while "social democrat" or "bourgeois" interpretations were plainly wrong. Ideas and meanings were to circulate in the internal space of the party only. The play or labor of interpretation being forbidden and only one interpretation being correct, this last could only be that provided by the legitimate authorities. And if there were any doubt about where to turn, the *Short Course* made it plain that it was to the leaders of the Bolshevik party, namely Lenin and Stalin: "The CPSU(B) has always been guided by the revolutionary teachings of

37 For further detail see Brigitte Studer, "Penser le sujet stalinien," in Claude Pennetier and Bernard Pudal (eds.), *Le sujet communiste. Identités militantes et laboratoires du "moi"* (Rennes: Presses Universitaires de Rennes, 2014), 35–57.

Marxism-Leninism. In the new conditions of the era of imperialism, imperialist wars and proletarian revolutions, its leaders further developed the teachings of Marx and Engels and raised them to a new level."[38] For the teachers, there followed from this a simple rule. In the words of Ivan Titkin, the secretary of the Lenin School party committee, in 1936, in every subject one had to attend "to what Stalin had said in that connection."[39] Should students then show any inclination to venture upon their own interpretations, their reports would tax them with "self-centredness, arrogance or a sense of superiority."

A second rule attributed to Lenin, enjoining the unity of theory and practice, became, in Stalin's reading, the claim that there could be no theory without practice.[40] This meant providing the students with "practical" knowledge. Knowing the "correct" political line was not enough, one had to know how to apply it, to put it into practice in the "correct" way. Being "capable of drawing the right conclusions from experience on the ground" as the teachers kept insisting seems to be no more than common sense. Yet in the Stalinist context, the requirement was imposed on the grassroots member or future cadre in such a way as to devalue theory as a tool of critical reflection in favor of the automatic application of fixed schemes of thought.[41] The general line could not be criticized in terms of theoretical principles. There could be no debate on how it should be interpreted, as it flowed directly from practice. Given this, Isaac Deutscher's description of the Stalinist cognitive framework as "a mental labour-saving device" seems apt enough.[42]

At this point, it is worth entering a caution. As useful as Goffman's concept of the "total institution" may be, it has distinct limitations as applied to the international cadre schools. These were not, in fact, abstract mechanisms of social control but social spaces characterized by an asymmetry of power between the institution and those it governed in accordance with its internal hierarchies. All enjoyed a certain margin of maneuver, which they made use

38 Introduction to *History of the Communist Party of the Soviet Union (Bolsheviks): Short Course* (Moscow: International Publishers, 1939), 1.

39 Meeting of the cadre training sector of the Executive Committee of the Communist International, 13 Dec. 1936, RGASPI, 495/30/1118.

40 J. V. Stalin, "Foundations of Leninism," in J. V. Stalin, *Works*, vol. VI (Moscow: Foreign Languages Publishing House, 1953), 71–196; "Concerning Questions of Leninism," in J. V. Stalin, *Works*, vol. VIII (Moscow: Foreign Languages Publishing House, 1954), 13–96.

41 Bernard Pudal, *Prendre parti. Pour une sociologie historique du PCF* (Paris: Presses de la FNSP, 1989), 207.

42 Isaac Deutscher, *Stalin: A Political Biography* (Oxford: Oxford University Press, 1949), 137.

of as they could, given their social, cultural and intellectual skills. And as has been revealed by recent analyses of subjectivities under Stalinism,[43] actors had a personal investment – normally very strong even if varying in degree – in the normative field that governed them. They were ready to "kill the Old Man" or, in Stalinist language, to "struggle against the petty bourgeois within." In Foucauldian terms, technologies of power were negotiated through "technologies of the self," "instituted models of self-knowledge."[44] Quite unlike either Lenin's conception of the state as a "simple apparatus for administering things"[45] or the "totalitarian" notion of the police apparatus as steam-roller, the Soviet state and the communist parties were very interested in people as individuals. They therefore engaged them in a whole series of practices that brought them to speak of themselves. The cadre school candidate had thus first to write an autobiography (*avtobiografiya*), structured by a very comprehensive set of questions on all aspects of his or her social and political life, as did all future cadres in the communist parties elsewhere, where the practice was on the whole less prevalent than in the Soviet Union. At the international schools, students had to regularly present a self-report (*samootchët*) covering not only their progress in study but on the conformity of their behavior with the model of the "true Bolshevik." Finally, to conclude this brief typology of Soviet technologies of the self, there was also the self-criticism (*samokritika*) that foreign communists had to engage in alongside their Soviet comrades, another of the applied methods of education for "the Bolshevization of cadre."[46]

Learning these techniques was often difficult, as is evidenced by a wealth of documentation preserved in the Comintern archives, for every session devoted to these matters by party cells or student groups was taken down in shorthand and the autobiographies added to the personal file held on every foreign communist in the USSR.[47] Reporting to the collective on one's

43 See in this connection Choi Chatterjee and Karen Petrone, "Models of Selfhood and Subjectivity: The Soviet Case in Historical Perspective," *Slavic Review* 67, 4 (Winter 2008), 967–86, and Catherine Depretto, "La 'Soviet subjectivity': le journal personnel, laboratoire du moi dans l'URSS stalinienne," in Pennetier and Pudal (eds.), *Le sujet communiste*, 19–34.

44 Michel Foucault, "Subjectivity and Truth" and "Technologies of the Self," in Paul Rabinow (ed.), *The Essential Works of Michel Foucault*, vol. I, *Ethics* (New York: New Press, 1997), 87, 223–51.

45 As reported in Clara Zetkin, *Batailles pour les femmes*, ed. Gilbert Badia, trans. G. Badia et al. (Paris: Éditions sociales, 1980), 129.

46 Speech by André Marty to Sector I of the International Lenin School, 23 Nov. 1933, RGASPI, 531/2/67.

47 Brigitte Studer, *The Transnational World of the Cominternians*, trans. D. R. Roberts (Basingstoke: Palgrave Macmillan, 2015).

progress and one's errors and responding to the critical questioning of the comrades entailed measuring oneself up against the prevailing norms and codes of behavior, a form of work on the self to acquire the knowledge and the attitudes expected of a communist, or even the Soviet New Man. Novelist Panteleimon Romanov put it very neatly in his novel *Comrade Kisliakov* (1930): Every communist had to become "an inner laboratory." Some, of course, knew better how to present themselves in a good light than others. But whether one shared almost everything, a lot, or rather less about oneself, no party member was in a position to completely reject these techniques of co-production of knowledge of the person: first of all because they fell under a set of norms (trusting the party, hiding nothing from it, self-cultivation and self-education to become a better communist) and institutional rules (regarding conspiracy, vigilance, the "verification" of party cards); second because the party believed itself entitled to form its members, ensuring conformity to its rules and norms not only in observance but in conviction. To illustrate the full ambition of this pedagogical objective, as identified by recent research on the communist or more specifically the Stalinist subject, here again is Yaroslavskii: "The Party wants every one of its members to bring all the better inclinations, all their capacities to the highest development, in both their public and their private lives. If however they develop these inclinations and capacities in the wrong direction so as to bring *disgrace* upon the Party, then the Party has the right to rebuke them, to correct them, to call them to order."[48] Yet the party was always left in doubt. How could you be sure that someone hadn't escaped the party's control through deliberate dissimulation – playing a "double game," as Stalinist language had it?[49] Only by periodically confirming loyalty through new tests, known to history as "the purges," in which public confession, paradoxically, was a kind of final proof. In this context, anything could become a sign of detachment, or worse, of disloyalty, "treason," and "espionage."

Cadre control can also be looked at from another angle, as one aspect of the general tendency to the rationalization of organization and of practice more generally that reached its height at the turn of the century, in both East and West.[50] The Soviet Union was a civilization of the report, in which everything was recorded in writing, a practice that communist parties

48 Jaroslawski, *Was fordert die Partei*, 99.

49 Sheila Fitzpatrick, *Tear Off the Masks! Identity and Imposture in Twentieth-Century Russia* (Princeton: Princeton University Press, 2005).

50 On this see esp. Yves Cohen, *Le siècle des chefs. Une histoire transnationale du commandement et de l'autorité (1890–1940)* (Paris: Éditions Amsterdam, 2013).

elsewhere would adopt in the late 1920s, making shorthand records of every important meeting. The many reports and evaluations on students at the national and international cadre schools,[51] the minutes of meetings at every level of the party, from the cell to the highest leadership, as well as the shorthand records of meetings in Soviet enterprises met the needs of bureaucratic administration. The creation of a Cadre Department at the Comintern in 1932 saw the "professionalization" of the task of cadre control and selection, previously the responsibility of the Organization Department and now confided to a specialized staff. To give full effect to this symbolic power to categorize, legitimate and disqualify the cadre deployed at national and international levels, the communist parties were instructed to establish organs of the same kind. Under close observation by the Comintern and its emissaries at the time, the French CP complied. In other parties, however, the Swiss and the British among them, delays and shortcomings in implementation meant that cadre control remained disorganized and inconsistent. On the whole, cadres were more likely to be judged against Soviet norms rather than by standards more closely attuned to local realities the higher they rose in the hierarchy.

In the final analysis, despite its incontestable strength, the communist world of the 1920s and 1930s was already marked by the fissures that would shatter it after 1989. Concern for the unity of a fighting force and the imposition of fixed perspectives deriving from "Marxism-Leninism" led to the gradual establishment of a hierarchy of interpretations that would leave no room for internal debate or critique. The inevitable consequences of the diversity of political contexts and the differences in relations of forces on the ground were understood as the results of delay, "political error," or even "sabotage." Given the lack of any forum for the expression of political differences, any opposition had to go underground, thus fueling the notion of the hidden enemies who in the last analysis were the real obstacle to the construction of a new world. Furthermore, the changeability of the biographical criteria for the selection and legitimation of communist cadres could discourage even the well-inclined from doing the work on the self required to achieve conformity. The history of the

51 For party schools at the national level, for France see Danielle Tartakowsky, *Les premiers communistes français. Formation des cadres et bolchevisation* (Paris: Presses de la Fondation nationale des sciences politiques, 1980), and Claude Pennetier and Bernard Pudal, "La certification scolaire communiste dans les années trente," *Politix* 35 (1996), 69–88; and for Canada see Andrée Lévesque, *Red Travellers: Jeanne Corbin and her Comrades*, trans. Y. M. Klein (Montreal and Kingston: McGill-Queen's University Press, 2006), 16–26.

communist movement is thus marked by crises and more or less evident waves of disaffection, right through the 1920s and 1930s, not to speak of the early years of World War II.

On the other hand, so long as it existed, the Comintern provided communism and its sympathizers with an organizational framework for revolutionary struggle. With its dissolution in 1943, this hope would be entirely projected onto the USSR, thus completing a process of de-internationalization that had been set in train in the second half of the 1920s.

Bibliographical Essay

Before the opening of the Russian archives, scholars interested in the communist experience and the internal life of communist parties had to rely chiefly on oral history and the memoirs of former communists. Some further light was cast on the Soviet Communist Party by the party archives of the Smolensk Oblast, captured by the invading Germans and deposited after the war at Harvard University. These provided the material for Merle Fainsod's classic study, *Smolensk Under Soviet Rule* [1958] (Winchester, MA: Unwin Hyman, 1989), and Nicolas Werth's *Être communiste en URSS sous Staline* (Paris: Gallimard-Julliard, 1981). In France, Annie Kriegel, a former member, blazed a trail with her ethnological and sociological study of the French communists, who in her view formed a "party-society," a party that was a society in itself: *Les communistes français* (Paris: Seuil, 1968) – translated as *French Communists: Profile of a People* (Chicago: University of Chicago Press, 1972) – was several times reworked and expanded before achieving its final form in 1985. Bernard Pudal, in his *Prendre parti. Pour une sociologie historique du PCF* (Paris: Presses de la FNSP, 1989), made use of Bourdieu's praxeological sociology to analyze the role of Thorez as a model in activists' identification with the party.

The opening of the Russian party archive (RGASPI) in 1990–91 brought into view the intense interaction and circulation of cadres between national parties and the Comintern in Moscow, and with it the transfer of Soviet practices to parties elsewhere. On these particular themes, see for example Brigitte Studer, *Un parti sous influence. Le Parti communiste, une section du Komintern, 1931 à 1939* (Lausanne: L'Âge d'Homme, 1994) and Bert Hoppe, *In Stalins Gefolgschaft. Moskau und die KPD 1928–1933* (Munich: Oldenbourg, 2007). In exploiting the Russian and Western archives to explore the diversity of Communism, Michel Dreyfus et al. (eds.), *Le siècle des communismes* (Paris:

Seuil, 2004), proved to be a seminal work. It was followed by others that drew on the surprising wealth of personal files and autobiographical materials made available to reveal new aspects of communist life, from transnational exchanges to the biographical tabs kept on party members and the construction of communist subjectivities. Kevin Morgan, Gideon Cohen and Andrew Flinn's *Communists and British Society 1920–1991* (London: Rivers Oram Press, 2007) offers a collective biography of British communists; Brigitte Studer, *The Transnational World of the Cominternians* (Basingstoke: Palgrave Macmillan, 2015), looks at the experience of European communists in Stalin's Moscow and Lisa A. Kirschenbaum, *International Communism and the Spanish Civil War: Solidarity and Suspicion* (Cambridge: Cambridge University Press, 2015), at that of American communists, focusing on Spain; while Claude Pennetier and Bernard Pudal (eds.), *Le sujet communiste. Identités militantes et laboratoires du "moi"* (Rennes: Presses Universitaires de Rennes, 2014), offers a recent overview of the construction of communist identities and subjectivities.

21

Communism and Intellectuals

MICHAEL DAVID-FOX

Grappling with the relationship between intellectuals and communism after 1917 calls to mind two topics long treated as almost entirely distinct. The first concerns non-Soviet, generally noncommunist intellectuals around the world and, in particular, intense twentieth-century debates over the pro-Soviet "fellow travelers" in the decades after 1917. The second concerns the role and place of intellectuals living and working under communism itself as a new, postrevolutionary intelligentsia emerged. The two topics have been divorced from one another not only because they were studied by historians in separated fields, but because the differences between them seemed obvious. Foreign intellectuals, wooed as sympathizers or potential allies by the organs of Soviet cultural diplomacy, parts of the Comintern and the party-state, were outsiders not infrequently distant from the workings of the secretive Soviet system. Under Stalinism, the most pro-Soviet of them – known as fellow travelers abroad and "friends of the Soviet Union" at home – were celebrated rather than repressed. "Domestic" intellectuals, by contrast, were directly enmeshed in the political, cultural, scientific and ideological dimensions of Soviet power during a period when the intelligentsia and culture were drastically remade. In the most hackneyed, Cold War-era renditions of these two topics, foreign fellow travelers were naive dupes or "useful idiots" (an apocryphal phase attributed to Lenin), while the Soviet intellectuals were either dissident martyrs or "hacks."

It is the purpose of this chapter, by contrast, to hone in on a rich field of interactions, overlap and parallels in the ways the new Soviet regime approached intellectuals both domestic and foreign and, by the same token, to identify certain common ways in which intellectuals both subject to and distant from Soviet power approached communism. These rare, twin juxtapositions reveal the patterns of a consequential twentieth-century relationship rather than the easy answers of martyrology or demonization.

In the history of communism, intellectuals were anything but marginal, and the ways in which foreign and domestic intellectuals were linked were several. Most of the top Bolshevik leaders themselves emerged from the Russian revolutionary intelligentsia, and they attributed outsized importance to intellectuals even as they and other Marxists condemned most of them as servants of the bourgeoisie. Soviet Marxism entrenched a class framework for analyzing the intelligentsia as a wavering "stratum" that applied internationally as well as at home; the practices and institutions the new regime innovated to attract and police nonparty specialists at home had a major impact on the way intellectuals abroad were approached.[1] From the start, a nexus emerged between the internal and external dimensions of the Soviet system. This internal–external nexus ensured that both international and domestic factors, and in particular their interaction, shaped communist agendas and approaches to intellectuals. Both domestic and foreign intellectuals, in turn, shared a range of little-analyzed commonalities in their strategies toward and interactions with Soviet communism.

In other times and places, intellectuals have sometimes been seen as marginal or far from the core missions of the state. Under communism, and in the minds of party leaders, they became central. Both the determination of top Bolshevik theoreticians and politicians to create a "proletarian" intelligentsia in the 1920s and Antonio Gramsci's roughly contemporaneous theory of organic intellectuals contained in his prison notebooks reflected the importance the communist movement attributed to the role intellectuals would play in a new socialist order. As a practical matter, the international weakness and isolation of the early Soviet state heightened the importance of foreign intellectuals.

By the time a simple class analysis of the intelligentsia as a wavering stratum caught between the poles of the proletariat and bourgeoisie became entrenched in the early Soviet years, communist policymakers in practice confronted a complicated and diversified array of intellectual groups, professions and attitudes in their own and other countries. What was unusual was that the concept of "intelligentsia" inherited and reworked in the Soviet years was remarkably broad, ranging from

1 Michael David-Fox, *Showcasing the Great Experiment: Cultural Diplomacy and Western Visitors to the Soviet Union, 1921–1941* (New York: Oxford University Press, 2012).

composers and literary figures to engineers and scientists, and under Stalin extending even to bureaucrats and "white-collar workers."

This encompassing Soviet category thus united these varied groups conceptually and in terms of many policies, while in practice intellectuals played many roles, and hardly just those of visionaries and "thinkers." Heightening their importance for the Soviet party-state, they included experts and shapers of culture in an age of "cultural revolution," as well as publicists and public figures who could influence the "masses" in the wake of the international "propaganda revolution" of World War I. The era of total war made shaping popular opinion a top priority for states not just at home but also in other countries. The young Soviet state, in particular, held few international trump cards other than what we would today call its "soft power" among leftists and sympathetic opinion-makers.

At the same time, intellectuals represented a threat. Within the Russian Empire and well into the 1920s, the intelligentsia formed the backbone of civic and political groups and movements. Given the overpowering Bolshevik imperative to dismantle autonomous organizations and direct the construction of socialism, this too provided strong incentives either to coopt or to defeat old elites and launch the fateful project of creating a new intelligentsia.

As a result, there quickly emerged a striking dualism in Bolshevik and early Soviet approaches to intellectuals, an ambivalence that was very much present to varying degrees in the history of foreign communist parties and their personnel policies. Despite the crucial importance attributed to intellectuals by revolutionary leaders, the legacy of the workers' movement and the habits of Marxist political thought also created a propensity to dismiss intellectuals and cultural policy as matters less fundamental than the reconstruction of the economic base or issues related to mass mobilization. The result of a dualistic approach was dualistic results: The Bolshevik Revolution directed considerable political violence toward members of the intelligentsia from the start, yet equally quickly moved down the path of according them very significant privileges.

The duplexity of the communist approach was squarely rooted in longstanding splits within the revolutionary movement and social democracy. The two major constituencies within Russian social democracy were workers and intellectuals, and there were innumerable permutations within the sociocultural, political and ideological world of the revolutionary movement in response to this fraught cohabitation.[2] There was a continuum over the years ranging from workerist and anti-intelligentsia sentiment, on the one side, and *vozhdizm*, or a de facto cult of elite, often intelligentsia leaders and leadership, on the other. Marx had said that only the workers could emancipate themselves, but the theoretician of this autonomy was himself an intellectual.

Lenin's own position might be seen as a compromise, since his famous concept of professional revolutionary was accessible to workers and intellectuals alike. On the one hand, Lenin loathed the "bourgeois" intelligentsia; on the other, the revolutionary leader who once filled out a questionnaire about his own occupation by writing "litterateur" firmly believed in the need for political leadership of the masses by the interpreters of Marxism and the necessity for building socialism with white-collar, noncommunist hands. The first widespread use of "old" experts by the new regime may have been the "military specialists" in Trotsky's Red Army in 1918, but it was Lenin in the same year who forbade "mischief-making" around the old Academy of Sciences after it expressed willingness to cooperate with the red republic. Lenin also presided over the use of former factor managers, white-collar personnel, scientists and other "bourgeois specialists" even during the height of anti-intelligentsia sentiment and class-discriminatory social policies in the early Soviet years.

At the outset of the New Economic Policy (NEP), Bolshevik policymakers condemned *spetseedstvo* (specialist-baiting) and Lenin railed against "communist conceit" toward experts, while at the same time longstanding intelligentsia traditions of civic opposition were broken.[3] Between 1922 and 1924, a new *modus vivendi* with the old intelligentsia was put in place. For example, a 1924 VSNKh report commissioned on the initiative of Feliks Dzerzhinskii, the Cheka founder, who came to defend official yet embattled NEP-era practices of accommodation with the specialists at the end of his life, started with the premise that the majority of the technical personnel in the country came from the "old technical intelligentsia." Written by A. Z. Gol'tsman, it explicitly rejected the derogatory class connotations attached to "specialist" in favor of judging people by professional qualifications. At the same time, even this report followed the orthodoxy that new "red" specialists would take their place – but not,

2 Reginald E. Zelnik (ed.), *Workers and Intelligentsia in Late Imperial Russia: Realities, Representations, Reflections* (Berkeley: Institute for International Studies, 1999).

3 Stuart Finkel, *On the Ideological Front: The Russian Intelligentsia and the Making of the Soviet Public Sphere* (New Haven: Yale University Press, 2007).

however, overnight.[4] Thus did practices associated with awarding scientific and cultural elites material rewards and privileges become established even as the project of creating their potential gravediggers – a new, proletarian or socialist intelligentsia – was launched.

While Lenin railed against the rotten bourgeois intelligentsia yet found ways to launch a specialist policy aimed at winning their services for the new state, his lieutenant Stalin foreshadowed future features of Stalinism with his "Tsaritsyn approach," the civil war commissar's 1918 combination of harsh maneuvers against military specialists and fabricated counterrevolutionary plots on the southern front. Stalin's best biographers have emphasized his congenital suspiciousness of experts and intellectuals as manifested in this formative experience.[5] But Stalin too went on to tolerate the NEP-era *modus vivendi* with the specialists, even though he then presided over a great attack on specialists during the "Great Break"; by the same token, he rehabilitated the old specialists in 1932 and created vast new privileges for the intelligentsia during the two decades that followed, yet purged the intelligentsia ruthlessly and, as with all elites during the Great Terror, disproportionately.

A more convincing interpretation, therefore, is that Stalin, who as a seminary graduate definitively belonged to the intelligentsia wing of the party yet not its theoretical elite, reconfigured and expanded the fundamental Leninist dualism toward intellectuals. Like the other Bolshevik leaders, Stalin recognized and perhaps even overestimated their crucial importance yet saw most as unreliable if not enemies. As a result, he was ready at once to privilege and to repress them. Stalin did not only shape but was constrained and influenced by the successive policies of differing periods: war communism, NEP, the "Great Break." To be sure, after he consolidated his one-man dictatorship in the 1930s he then demonstrated more willingness to take extreme, unprecedented steps in both areas – privilege and repression. As Erik van Ree has written, Stalin, himself a revolutionary *intelligent* who had adopted the persona of a teacher vis-à-vis the workers, was "no Mao, no Pol Pot: He targeted these people not because they were an intelligentsia but because they were an intelligentsia of the wrong kind. To educate a politically

4 Discussed in N. N. Pavlova, "Repressirovannaia intelligentsia: Solovetskii izvod (1928–1934)," in D. B. Pavlov (ed.), *Repressirovannaia intelligentsiia 1917–1934 gg.* (Moscow: ROSSPEN, 2010), 407–13.

5 Stephen Kotkin, *Stalin, vol. 1, Paradoxes of Power, 1878–1928* (New York: Penguin Press, 2014), 300–07; Oleg V. Khlevniuk, *Stalin: New Biography of a Dictator*, trans. Nora S. Favorov (New Haven: Yale University Press, 2015), 55–59.

reliable new intelligentsia was even more important for him than to crush the old one."[6]

As of the early 1920s, the line between foreign and domestic intellectuals was blurred by the fact of a large emigration at the end of the civil war of a kaleidoscopic array of cultural and intellectual figures from the Russian Empire who appeared in Harbin, Berlin and other European capitals such as Belgrade. The Bolshevik leadership and the GPU in the early 1920s were more than a little obsessed with the Russian emigration, and their fears of Russian émigré influence on international opinion and Soviet initiatives abroad were heightened by the fact that the borders were not yet sealed. Some cultural and intellectual figures who traveled abroad did not come back, and others who had left returned. It was at this moment that the Changing Landmarks (*Smena vekh*) movement caused a sensation among Russian émigrés with their 1921 call for the Russian intelligentsia to "go to Canossa" and support the new Soviet state. The Bolsheviks were reuniting Russia, making it a great power on the world stage; in spite and not because of their ideology, Lenin and the Bolsheviks were in fact pursuing Russian national missions.[7] The article "Patriotica" by N. V. Ustrialov assumed a central place in *Smena vekh*. The author, a right-wing Kadet disillusioned with party politics, had been director of the press agency glorifying Aleksandr Kolchak's White dictatorship in Omsk. On the eve of his departure for Harbin, his movement defeated, Ustrialov underwent a conversion to his electrifying stance in favor of a strong Soviet state.[8]

Conflict and compromise between "reds" and experts became a hallmark of the era. The NEP-era "carrots" of a regularized place in the Soviet order and material incentives for the nonparty intelligentsia were accompanied by swings of the stick: International travel policy tightened up and a range of key figures were simply evicted. Several hundred major intellectuals and their families considered anti-Soviet, including numerous philosophers, religious thinkers, and civic activists, were famously expelled from the country in 1922 on the "philosopher's steamboat." Civil groups led by the old middle-left yet non-Bolshevik intelligentsia, whose activist ethos had been heightened by total war, were either banned or coopted, while the new university charter of 1922 put party appointees in charge.

6 Erik van Ree, "The Stalinist Self: The Case of Ioseb Jughashvili," *Kritika* 11, 2 (Spring 2010), 280.

7 S. S. Chakhotin, "V Kanossu!," in *Smena vekh* (Prague: Politika, 1921), 150–66.

8 N. V. Ustrialov, "Patriotica," in *Smena vekh*, 59, 63.

The first "bourgeois" foreigners to arrive for extended periods, such as the German scholar Otto Hoetzsch, were wooed, marking the emergence of a new system of cultural diplomacy focused on the reception of foreign visitors.

At this same time, the Bolsheviks met the *smenovekhovtsy* half-way and launched a policy of coopting members of the Russian intelligentsia, explicitly including those motivated to reconcile with the Soviets on national, patriotic and imperial grounds. In 1921, the party literary figure N. L. Meshcheriakov greeted the Changing Landmark intellectuals as "National-Bolsheviks" who would inevitably move closer to what he called true Bolshevik-Communists.[9] The ideas of the *smenovekhovtsy* were triumphantly propagated as well as harshly criticized in the Soviet 1920s, and the label *smenovekhovstvo* was deployed in Soviet parlance far beyond the original *Smena vekh* group to encompass many different types able to come to terms with the new regime. This included a range of prominent Ukrainian émigré intellectuals (the Ukrainian equivalent of the term was *zminovikhivtsy*) who either became Sovietophiles or found an accommodation with the Bolsheviks at a time when the "ideology of the far right came to dominate the political thought of the Ukrainian emigration." As a trail of Russian intelligentsia returnees received positions during the NEP, prominent members of the Ukrainian intellectual and political class returned to the Ukrainian SSR. These included the renowned historian and politician Mykhailo Hrushevsky; a section of his party, the Ukrainian Socialist Revolutionaries; a number of social democrats; and former members of the independent Ukrainian People's Republic (UNR).[10]

The ideological offensive of the "Great Break" after 1928 prompted an assault on both the Russian and Ukrainian returnees, and they were particularly vulnerable during the Great Terror. However, in the 1920s the precedent and success of early Soviet recruitment policies toward émigré intellectuals who were far from Bolshevism established a precedent for flexible maneuvering with ideologically distant foreign intellectuals willing to form partnerships with communism. These included nationalists and conservatives of various stripes in different countries, and, at key moments,

9 The foremost work of scholarship is Hilde Hardeman, *Coming to Terms with the Soviet Regime: The "Changing Signposts" Movement among Russian Émigrés in the Early 1920s* (DeKalb: Northern Illinois University Press, 1994); Meshcheriakov cited on 100.

10 Christopher Gilley, *The "Change of Signposts" in the Ukrainian Emigration: A Contribution to the History of Sovietophilism in the 1920s* (Stuttgart: ibidem-Verlag, 2009), quotation 22.

even far-right figures of Weimar Germany's "Eastern Orientation" who were close to fascism.[11]

In the common émigré miscalculation that the new regime would gradually moderate itself and serve either Russian, national, or great-power interests – not to mention their own agendas – these insiders with linguistic and political knowledge of Soviet communism in fact mirrored a response common among a number of foreign intellectuals, who faced many more linguistic and cultural barriers in accessing information and understanding the Bolsheviks. For example, a number of liberals in the US ARA (American Relief Administration) famine relief mission circa 1922 believed that economic aid for reconstruction would lead to a stronger Russia without Bolshevism. Later in the decade, some of them assumed pro-Soviet stances.[12] Conversely, a number of Mexican intellectuals, artists and writers, experiencing the maturing, compromise-ridden stages in the life cycle of their own very different revolution begun in 1910, flocked to the "first socialist society" with the underlying yearning to restart stalled revolutionary transformations at home.[13]

If there was overlap in the calculations leading émigré intellectuals from revolutionary Russia and foreign intellectual observers to engage the young Soviet state, analogies can also be found between Russian intellectuals and the non-Russian intelligentsias in the borderland regions. A tutelary mission to enlighten and mold the masses was a distinguishing feature of the Russian intelligentsia since the mid nineteenth century. In the Central Asian context, the liberal reformers known as Jadids, with their "aggressively modernist interpretation of Islam," developed a cult of knowledge and enlightenment hardly unfamiliar to the strong strain of *kul'turtregerstvo* in the Russian intelligentsia. But as Adeeb Khalid suggests, before 1917 the Jadids looked more to Istanbul than to St. Petersburg. After they were radicalized by the Bolshevik Revolution, they underwent a shift from liberal constitutionalism to the "politics of mobilization."

11 Michael David-Fox, "Leftists Versus Nationalists in Soviet–Weimar Cultural Diplomacy: Showcases, Fronts, and Boomerangs," in Susan Gross Solomon (ed.), *Doing Medicine Together: Germany and Russia between the Wars* (Toronto: University of Toronto Press, 2006), 103–58.

12 David Engerman, *Modernization from the Other Shore: American Intellectuals and the Romance of Russian Development* (Cambridge, MA: Harvard University Press, 2003), ch. 6 and *passim*.

13 William Richardson, "'To the World of the Future': Mexican Visitors to the USSR, 1920–1940," *Carl Beck Papers* 1002 (1993).

Jadid intellectuals thus became central players in a cultural revolution and Soviet war on backwardness that unfolded throughout the 1920s. Party leaders from the center knew little about the Muslim "East," and this opened a major space for the cooperation of indigenous intellectuals. But the Jadids' cultural revolutionary project revolved around nation rather than class and engaged a particular, "Turkestan-centered Turkism." In sum, their project became thoroughly intertwined with and ultimately subordinated to Bolshevik missions, but even so maintained its own logic and influence in the early Soviet decades, especially in Bukhara until 1924 and then in Uzbekistan.[14] The history of Jadidism and Bolshevism provides a case study of entangled modernities in the emergence of Soviet Central Asia.

Non-Russian intelligentsias more generally became prime agents in Soviet-sponsored "national construction." The involvement of non-Russian intelligentsias – whether Turkic, Slavic or Transcaucasian – in the broad Soviet project of cultural revolution throughout the 1920s also held international ramifications in that decade and beyond. Domestic non-Russian intelligentsias became involved in Soviet cultural and political outreach directed at related nations and nationalities across Soviet borders or in other regions of the developing world. There is an analogy here with the major input of nonparty intellectuals in the all-union center into the creation of Soviet culture and science, which also involved official and quasi-official external missions. In all these instances, intellectuals helped construct their own gilded cage and, once inside, suffered greatly, especially in two waves of anti-intelligentsia persecution during the Great Break and the Great Terror.

Once the Soviet order had stabilized in the 1920s, another type of internal–external dynamic emerged as well. Communism was scientistic and promised advanced results from rational planning and state-funded projects, and this feature of the new regime went well beyond the realm of ideas alone. The collapse of the tsarist state had paved the way for a wave of postrevolutionary institution-building that included not only new types of

14 Adeeb Khalid, *The Politics of Muslim Cultural Reform: Jadidism in Central Asia* (Berkeley: University of California Press, 1998); Adeeb Khalid, *Islam after Communism: Religion and Politics in Central Asia* (Berkeley: University of California Press, 2007), 56–59; and esp. Adeeb Khalid, *Making Uzbekistan: Nation, Empire, and Revolution in the Early USSR* (Ithaca: Cornell University Press, 2015), quotations 6, 15. On the East as a key communist category in the internal–external nexus, see Masha Kirasirova, "The 'East' in Bolshevik and Comintern Ideology: The Arab Section of the Communist University of the Toilers of the East," *Kritika* 18, 1 (Winter 2017), 7–34.

institutions – most notably, scientific research institutes – but also opened the door to previously stymied or novel methodologies and subfields. When disciplinary innovation occurred in fields that could be seen in harmony with Soviet Marxism, it benefited from declarations of support for Soviet goals. Often, new fields or approaches were simply pushed forward by visionaries and dreamers inspired by the revolution, and this occurred in a wide range of medical, social science and scientific fields. To cite only well-known examples, these ranged from social medicine and eugenics to more radical and utopian experiments, such as ex-Bolshevik Aleksandr Bogdanov's blood transfusion institute or the biologist Il'ia Ivanov's attempts to crossbreed humans and apes.[15] At the same time, impetus toward social engineering and the great project of creating a New Man inspired a range of social scientists in fields such as criminology, pedagogy and psychology to try to ride the tiger of the new Soviet state.[16] While a significant portion of the "old" intelligentsia went into emigration by 1920, another part of the professional and scientific intelligentsia came to participate in the Bolshevik Revolution, with its core projects of remolding society and creating a New Man, as either an inspiration, an opportunity, or a bit of both.

The mushrooming new institutes and novel disciplinary configurations created with state patronage by the Soviet scientific intelligentsia, in turn, attracted the interest and attention of a wide variety of foreign professionals, scientists, social scientists and cultural figures. While a number of them joined the interwar "pilgrimage to Russia" and visited the USSR, it was very common for those of them who viewed the USSR from afar to combine pro-Soviet political views with an overriding personal interest in a branch of Soviet science or culture connected to their own specific fields. Some of them, such as the French physicist Paul Langevin or the Czech musicologist Zdeněk Nejedlý, joined the ranks of the most ardent and activist fellow travelers of the interwar period. Here there is an analogy between the way the members of the Russian avant-garde, who were "outsiders" of the late tsarist period, became "insiders" after they

15 On social medicine, see Solomon (ed.), *Doing Medicine Together*; on Bogdanov, see Nikolai Krementsov, *A Martian Stranded on Earth: Alexander Bogdanov, Blood Transfusions, and Proletarian Science* (Chicago: University of Chicago Press, 2010); on crossbreeding, Kirill Rossianov, "Beyond Species: Il'ya Ivanov and his Experiments on Cross-Breeding Humans and Anthropoid Apes," *Science in Context* 15, 2 (2002), 277–316.

16 Daniel Beer, *Renovating Russia: The Human Sciences and the Fate of Liberal Modernity* (Ithaca: Cornell University Press, 2008).

supported the revolution (and took advantage of Narkompros and Soviet state patronage). The heyday of the young Soviet avant-garde then contributed to a wave of cultural-political interest in the Soviet experiment, starting with a sensational exhibition of Soviet avant-garde art in Berlin on Unter den Linden in 1921 and continuing through the Berlin–Moscow cultural axis of the first Five-Year Plan.[17]

On the right wing of the political spectrum, intelligentsia émigrés from the Russian Empire contributed to the most virulent new forms of anti-communism. Russian, Ukrainian and Baltic anti-Bolshevism, anti-Semitism and right-wing nationalism stimulated by the White struggle with the Red Army were transferred abroad via the Russian emigration, which included ideologues and intellectuals as well as political and military figures. In the Central European context this played a role in the rise of fascism. To be sure, the internationalism of extreme nationalisms was by definition limited, but circa 1920 key texts such as the notorious *Protocols of the Elders of Zion* were propagated through this dynamic.[18] Just as Soviet recruitment took advantage of émigré Russian nationalist intellectuals such as the Changing Landmark group, Soviet and Comintern operatives in certain times and circumstances courted those they conventionally considered bitter enemies – right-wing nationalists and fascist intellectuals, and in some cases before 1933, fascist intellectuals who were or later became Nazis.

The door was opened toward this little-known communist tactic because there was a strain of ideological fascination as well as enmity for Bolshevism and Stalinism on the extreme right of the political spectrum in interwar Europe. In Germany in particular, this was stimulated by the geopolitical "Eastern Orientation" and fascination with regimented mass mobilization for revolutionary goals. The aim on the Soviet side was not necessarily attempted conversion, but potential "neutralization" of the new nationalist, revolutionary intellectuals of the right.[19]

17 Katerina Clark, *Moscow, the Fourth Rome: Stalinism, Cosmopolitanism, and the Evolution of Soviet Culture, 1931–1941* (Cambridge, MA: Harvard University Press, 2011), ch. 1.

18 Michael Kellogg, *The Russian Roots of Nazism: White Émigrés and the Making of National Socialism, 1917–1945* (Cambridge: Cambridge University Press, 2008).

19 Michael David-Fox, "Annäherung der Extreme: Die UdSSR und rechtsradikalen Intellektuellen," *Osteuropa* 59, 7–8 (2009), 115–24; Michael David-Fox, "A 'Prussian Bolshevik' in Stalin's Russia: Ernst Niekisch at the Crossroads between Communism and National Socialism," in Michael David-Fox, *Crossing Borders: Modernity, Ideology, and Culture in Russia and the Soviet Union* (Pittsburgh: University of Pittsburgh Press, 2015), ch. 7.

Although such openings to right-wing intellectuals were not without controversy on the Soviet side, the flexibility to undertake them at all was enabled not only by Leninist politics, but also by Marxist-Leninist ideology – or, more exactly, an emergent doctrinal tenet that morphed into an early Soviet worldview. In the 1920s, as Marxism-Leninism became entrenched, Soviet writings on the intelligentsia widely disseminated a "class analysis" of the intelligentsia as a "wavering" stratum caught between the two great poles of the bourgeoisie and the proletariat.[20] This early Soviet doctrinal cliché served several purposes. It explained how some intellectuals could go over to the side of the working class while others remained enemies. It also fed a marked anti-intellectualism in communist political culture writ large that associated intellectuals with indecisiveness and weakness. The flip side of the communist on-again, off-again accommodation with specialists was that the "wavering" of intellectual Hamlets was counterposed to the steely proletarian or Bolshevik qualities of resolute action and necessary ruthlessness.

This quasi-official class definition of the intelligentsia, as it was dispersed, was internalized by important figures such as the writer and Old Bolshevik Aleksandr Arosev, a friend of Molotov from childhood who became head of VOKS (All-Union Society for Cultural Relations with Foreign Countries) during the years of the Popular Front. The stereotype of the wavering intellectual became a leitmotiv of Arosev's thinking on the intelligentsia in the 1920s and 1930s. His diary shows he even applied it to himself, seeing himself as a Hamlet-like figure caught between his cultural and political ambitions. Tellingly, however, in his public pronouncements in the mid 1930s Arosev only contrasted the wavering of foreign and European intellectuals to the virile, ideological unity of the Soviet intelligentsia.[21]

As Soviet notions of the "Western" or "foreign intelligentsia" came into use, they became conduits for projecting into international contexts a number of familiar tropes applied to intellectuals at home. Stalinism ratified

20 For an example of the early Soviet debate on the intelligentsia within an emerging Marxist-Leninist framework, see Boris Isaakovich Gorev, "Intelligentsiia, kak ekonomicheskaia kategoriia," in *Na ideologicheskom fronte: Sbornik statei* (Moscow: Gosizdat, 1923), ch. 1.

21 "Stenogramma doklada A. Ia. Aroseva, 'O vstrechakh i besedakh s vidneishimi predstaveiteliami zapadno-evropeiskoi intelligentsiia," 4 May 1935, in Rossiiskii gosudarstvennyi arkhiv literatury i iskusstva (RGALI), f. 631, o 14, ed. khr. 3, ll. 1–24, quotations 16, 22; Arosev, entries of 24 Sep. 1934 and 18 Jun. 1935, in Aleksandra Aroseva, *Bez grima* (Moscow: ZAO Izdatel'stvo Tsentrpoligraf, 1999), 65, 70.

a veritable cult of culture in the 1930s, in which achievements in the cultural realm became a key part of a broader Stalinist superiority complex. With this official celebration of culture and "culturedness" (*kul'turnost'*), mini-cults of foreign intellectual "friends of the Soviet Union" served to appropriate the trappings of world culture. The celebration of foreign intellectuals ranged from George Bernard Shaw (who visited the USSR with fanfare in 1930) to the French writer Romain Rolland (who acquired a mini-cult during his visit of 1935).

To be sure, the celebration of pro-Soviet foreign intellectuals was outdone by even grander forms of domestic hero-worship of a pantheon of domestic writers, scientists and professionals such as Maksim Gor'kii, Ivan Pavlov, the pedagogue Anton Makarenko and the rocket scientist Konstantin Tsiolkovskii.[22] In the case of nonparty or "bourgeois" intellectuals – both Soviet and foreign – narratives presented the famous intellectuals' biography as a teleological process of overcoming early social and political flaws. In a tendentious Russian translation of Rolland's autobiographical essay, for example, the French writer engaged in self-criticism of his "bourgeois individualist" youth, but set on the correct "path" toward embracing the Soviet Union after he overcame his pacifism and bourgeois intellectual "wavering."[23]

This general Marxist-Leninist framework for understanding the intelligentsia in practice became linked to specific modes of party-state information-gathering and analysis concerning intellectuals. A general party-state practice of political reportage, commonly applied in the international arena, for example, was to divide any given group into three – enemies, friends and those in between who could be swayed either way. This conventional triad fit neatly into the class analysis of the intelligentsia as a group caught in between.[24] In the cultural diplomatic and security organs tasked with dealing with foreign intellectuals, *apparatchiki* judged levels of friendship and enmity with statements and publications about the USSR centrally in mind.

22 On the cults of leading Soviet intellectuals in a wide range of fields, see Sheila Fitzpatrick, "Cultural Orthodoxies under Stalin," in Sheila Fitzpatrick (ed.), *The Cultural Front: Power and Culture in Revolutionary Russia* (Ithaca: Cornell University Press, 1992), ch. 10. On the cult of Tsiolkovskii, see Michael G. Smith, *Rockets and Revolution: A Cultural History of Early Spaceflight* (Lincoln: University of Nebraska Press, 2014), chs. 9–10.

23 Romen Rollan [Romain Rolland], "Moi put' k proletarskoi revoliutsii," *Internatsional'naia literatura* 3–4 (1934), 9–10.

24 For an example, see E. V. Mikhin, "Klassovaia bor'ba i nauchnye rabotniki," *Nauchnyi rabotnik* 5–6 (May–Jun. 1930), 15–18.

At home, they could rely on far more direct surveillance and loyalty tests. Thus, in practice, flexible and contingent classifications toward intellectuals could be inserted into a Manichean worldview. That said, foreign and nonparty intellectuals alike, even the most ardent of sympathizers could never be completely "ours." Famously, when André Gide published a book critical of the regime after his 1936 Soviet tour, one of the most celebrated friends of the decade became a maligned enemy faster than the blink of an eye.

By the late 1920s and 1930s, a range of party-state practices governing relations with the intelligentsia had solidified. These involved the carrot as well as the stick. Particularly in the case of utilitarian incentives, one can also discern a distinct overlap between the treatment of foreign and domestic intellectuals. Foreign intellectual sympathizers as well as members of the Soviet intelligentsia were offered economic incentives as well as non-monetary privileges. Policy toward the "bourgeois" specialists had ratified privileged pay differentials and a scientific "star" system already in the 1920s, and by the 1930s "intelligentsia privileges were often proudly announced."[25] For their part, foreign intellectuals were offered royalties from translations, invitations to tour the USSR at state expense, banquets and gifts. Other strategies involved flattery, such as exhibitions, wide distribution of the foreigners' works and press coverage.

The ritualistic, highly scripted aspects of Stalinist culture accentuated these early practices, but there is also evidence that Stalin's own proclivities fed the unprecedented scale of the privileges accorded the new intelligentsia elite. In his memoirs, the editor of *Izvestiia*, Ivan Gronskii, recalled how Stalin discussed preparations for Gor'kii's fortieth literary jubilee: "At one of the sessions, Stalin made a proposal: 'Give Nizhnii Novgorod and the oblast Gor'kii's name. Rename Tverskaia Street in Moscow after him.'" Gronskii reacted negatively, saying that this was laying it on too "thick," but Stalin replied: "'That doesn't matter. That doesn't matter.' Leaning over, very quietly, he said to me: 'He's an ambitious man. We have to bind him to the Party.'"[26]

In the 1930s, the visits of leading foreign intellectual "friends of the Soviet Union" became grandiose state visits filled with pomp, circumstance and

25 Sheila Fitzpatrick, *Everyday Stalinism: Ordinary Life in Extraordinary Times. Soviet Russia in the 1930s* (New York: Oxford University Press, 1999), 96, ch. 4 on privileges.

26 Quoted in Katerina Clark and Evgeny Dobrenko (eds.), *Soviet Culture and Power: A History in Documents, 1917–1953*, trans. Marian Schwartz (New Haven: Yale University Press, 2007), 87.

meetings with the *vozhd'*. These Kremlin receptions, along with the galaxy of mini-cults of cultural and scientific figures, supported the central Stalin cult in direct ways by displaying the symbiosis of culture and power. The Stalin cult itself glorified the man who had launched his career in the intelligentsia wing of the party as a great Marxist theoretician and, in a trend that reached its apogee with Stalin's 1950 tract, *Marxism and Problems of Linguistics*, a scientific genius in his own right.

Closely related to outright economic incentives for intellectuals were broader patterns of patronage. Patron–client relations in general became fundamental to Soviet intellectual life, because of both party-state direction of science and culture and the norms of the political system. But it was not just the domestic intelligentsia that had to have its own patrons in the guise of powerful politicians and key institutions; this phenomenon, too, was exported across state lines. A new form of transnational patronage emerged, in which institutions of the party-state charged with cultivating foreign intellectuals offered to favored or pro-Soviet figures such important tangible commodities such as travel and translations, or more intangible goods such as the political prestige or access to information that might accrue from high-level Soviet ties. Friendship societies abroad, the first of which was created in Berlin in 1923 under the concealed auspices of VOKS, and which in the course of the next decade spread to cities around the world, were one key conduit of this transnational patronage. Soviet embassies, especially at first in European capitals with significant Soviet colonies such as Berlin, Prague, Paris and London, became another vehicle. What is most clearly the case in the transactions of transnational patronage in turn holds true for domestic, Soviet phenomena: Patron–client relations were shaped by institutional and ideological rationales, and not only by personalistic favoritism, important as that may have been.

Another avenue along which domestic and foreign intellectuals became linked was in the innovative, indeed unique system in which the land of socialism was showcased abroad. On-site visits became the crown jewel of Soviet outreach to foreign intellectuals after noncommunist sympathizers began streaming in on their own accord after the end of civil war hostilities, at the very time the international practices of the new regime crystallized. It soon became clear that bringing outside observers in served key functions when it came to intellectuals. In what turned out to be a great advantage, members of the Soviet intelligentsia alike were mobilized to meet and greet their foreign counterparts. For example, when the American writer Theodore Dreiser visited in 1927, it was arranged for him to hobnob with the crème de la crème of cultural and intellectual life of the era, including the theater director Konstantin Stanislavskii, the poet Vladimir Maiakovskii and the filmmaker Sergei Eisenstein. Tours were tailored to the visiting intellectual's specific field: The American pragmatist philosopher and progressive educational reformer John Dewey met the leading educational officials and theorists of the day, from Lunacharskii and Krupskaia to S. T. Shatskii and V. N. Shul'gin. Overwhelmed by the extent to which his own theories were embraced and ostensibly put into practice, the future chair of the purge-era Commission of Inquiry into the Charges Made Against Leon Trotsky declared in 1927 that progressive pedagogy was more advanced in the USSR than in the USA.[27]

Perhaps most important, the presentation of Soviet socialism became centered on model sites that were presented as embodying the future or, in a key conflation, as typical of the Soviet present. The methodology of showing these models – which ranged from schools and institutes to prisons, collective farms and communes for reformed juvenile delinquents – was termed *kul'tpokaz*, or cultural show. *Kul'tpokaz* had overlapping origins with Socialist Realism, which in the 1930s became a pervasive ideological mode of seeing the future in the present as well as the official if capacious doctrine in literature and the arts.

Soviet intellectuals played a key role in the history of *kul'tpokaz*. For one thing, they and their agendas were instrumental in displaying many of the model sites, or founding institutions that later became presented as models inside and outside the country. For example, the pedagogue Anton Makarenko and the writer Maksim Gor'kii were both heavily involved in the OGPU/NKVD labor communes for rehabilitating homeless juvenile delinquents in the late 1920s, when they became a prime stop on the itineraries of visiting intellectual dignitaries. Furthermore, the guides and translators who were attached to the intellectual visitors through VOKS or other Soviet institutions were versed in foreign languages and some area of culture or science, so the methodology of cultural show was propagated by people who could be considered minor Soviet intellectuals in their own right.

More generally, the Soviet intelligentsia was mobilized to promote cultural ties abroad and the international image of Soviet socialism. This took on a more coercive cast when Stalin's Great Break of 1928–29 broke

27 David C. Engerman, "John Dewey and the Soviet Union: Pragmatism Meets Revolution," *Modern Intellectual History* 3, 1 (2006), 33–65, esp. 40–46.

the NEP-era *modus vivendi* with the "bourgeois specialists" and intergenerational, institutional and political in-fighting reached its apogee. As professions such as engineering were decimated by arrests, Soviet intellectuals were pressured, for example, to sign the latest declaration du jour and make themselves available for the reception of foreign luminaries. Of course, even then such international contacts could be seen as a privilege as well as an obligation on the Soviet side. Even in the periods of greatest repressiveness, members of the Soviet intelligentsia were far from mere cogs in the machine; they were highly skilled in pursuing their own priorities.

In the Stalin period in particular, Moscow assumed an extraordinary, unprecedented position of dominance that deeply affected cultural and intellectual life. While Leningrad and many non-Russian cities were cultural centers in the years between 1918 and the end of the 1920s, Moscow in the 1930s was represented as the showcase socialist city for foreigners and the epicenter of a superior culture with global pretensions. Economic and cultural hypercentralization drew provincial and non-Russian intellectuals like a magnet to the all-union center.[28]

Moscow was thus also the privileged meeting place for Soviet intellectual intermediaries and their foreign intellectual interlocutors. But for a charmed circle of leading Soviet intellectuals in the 1930s, the foreign intellectuals were cultivated abroad, *in situ*. As the first phase of the Stalin period after 1920 significantly tightened restrictions on international travel, the role of these elite Soviet mediators paradoxically increased. These were the privileged party and Soviet intellectuals, cultural officials, journalists and diplomats who were able to crisscross Europe or embark for more distant venues to shape what an entire country read on international developments.

The successful Soviet intellectual mediator had to be able to navigate simultaneously in two worlds: the cultural and intellectual life in the relevant international context, on the one hand, and the pressure-cooker of Soviet and Stalinist cultural politics and ideology, on the other. Mediators' close contacts with prominent Soviet sympathizers abroad put a certain class of these figures in a special position in both the institutions of Soviet cultural diplomacy and the extraordinarily

28 Clark, *Moscow, the Fourth Rome*; Mayhill Fowler, "Mikhail Bulgakov, Mykola Kulish, and Soviet Theater: How Internal Transnationalism Remade Center and Periphery," *Kritika* 16, 2 (Spring 2015), 263–90.

successful Comintern-based initiatives of Willi Münzenberg. Often several such figures were attached to every major pro-Soviet intellectual sympathizer.[29]

The most talented and impressive Soviet intellectuals, of course, had their own views about politics, culture and the figures from abroad with whom they interacted. In the era before most of them met their destruction in the Great Terror, a number of Stalinist Westernizers, as they might be called, discerned a chance to bring Soviet culture close to the leftist culture of Europe. Many Soviet intellectual mediators genuinely admired the writers and intellectuals they also influenced or manipulated.[30] As this suggests, Soviet cultural and intellectual elites had their own agendas that were distinct if overlapping with those of the political and foreign policy leadership. In pursuing them, they played a discernible role in making the interwar Soviet Union into a global preoccupation for intellectuals.

In non-Russian union republics, local intellectuals played a different kind of mediating role, part of what Mayhill Fowler has called internal transnationalism.[31] They found themselves in between Moscow-based ideologues and cultural *apparatchiki*, on the one hand, and their own national audiences, on the other. In the case of Ukraine and the construction of Soviet Ukrainian national identity, for example, Serhy Yekelchyk has talked about both Ukrainian ideologues and intellectuals in the Stalin era as occupying "the ambiguous position of mediator between the Kremlin and their non-Russian constituencies."[32] Ethnic intellectuals, as this makes clear, preserved their own cultural prominence while playing a key role in the Soviet order. The international role of non-Russian intellectuals remains to be further investigated. For example, Masha Kirasirova has explored how Central Asians "were

29 Sophie Coeuré, "'Comme ils disent SSSR': Louis Aragon et l'Union soviétique dans les années 1930," in Jacques Girault and Bernard Lecherbonnier (eds.), *Les engagements d'Aragon* (Paris: L'Harmattan, 1997), 59–67, esp. 62–65; Leonid Maksimenkov, "Ocherki nomenklaturnoi istorii sovetskoi literatury: Zapadnye pilgrimy u stalinskogo prestola (Feikhtvanger i drugie)," *Voprosy literatury* 2 (2004), 242–91; *Voprosy literatury* 3 (2004), 274–353; and Leonid Maksimenkov (ed.), *Bol'shaia tenzura: Pisateli i zhurnalisty v Strane sovetov 1917–1956* (Moscow: Materik, 2005), on Rolland 238, 300, 378–81, 389–90, 391, 411.

30 Michael David-Fox, "Stalinist Westernizer? Aleksandr Arosev's Literary and Political Depictions of Europe," *Slavic Review* 62, 4 (Winter 2003), 733–59.

31 Fowler, "Mikhail Bulgakov, Mykola Kulish, and Soviet Theater."

32 Serhy Yekelchyk, *Stalin's Empire of Memory: Russian–Ukrainian Relations in the Soviet Historical Imagination* (Toronto: University of Toronto Press, 2004), 6, 12.

recruited to produce Eastern images of Sovietness for export to the Middle East through media and film propaganda and, increasingly after World War II, through physical travel abroad and managing tourism at home."[33]

***

Looking at intellectuals and communism across borders raises valuable interpretive possibilities. But it also reveals major differences between foreign intellectuals not directly subject to the jurisdiction of Soviet power and Soviet intellectuals increasingly shaped by their perspectives as insiders within the Soviet political and economic system, their proximity to the extensive Soviet ideological and cultural establishment, and the direct application of coercion and political violence. Intelligentsia elites lived through three peaks of repression under Stalinism: the early 1930s, the Great Terror and the Zhdanov period. Even at the apex of anti-intellectual policies and ideological xenophobia at home, the project of wooing intellectuals abroad carried on.

While the domestic order was marked for the duration of the Soviet period by a shifting oscillation between crackdowns and thaws, intellectuals inside Soviet borders were ultimately affected even more by a long-term, linear intensification of institutional controls and self-censorship. The party-state built an elaborate and unprecedentedly intrusive arsenal of soft and hard levers that ran the gamut from political and ideological campaigns, economic privileges and incentives, centralized cultural unions, appointments and patronage, to the organization of institutions on the macro and micro level. Intellectuals developed elaborate strategies to deflect those instruments but at the same time engaged in self-mobilization, self-policing, lateral surveillance and ubiquitous appeals to authority. While the intelligentsia's self-image was one of a heroic force of resistance to preserve culture, it is important to reflect on how intellectuals themselves were caught up in their own repression. Finally, the history of Soviet scientific and cultural fields suggests that the internal configurations of disciplines, the actions of their leading figures and the proximity of their core methodologies to Marxist-Leninist ideology led to significant variations affecting the professional lives of Soviet intellectuals.

33 Masha Kirasirova, "The Eastern International: The 'Domestic East' and the 'Foreign East' in Soviet–Arab Relations, 1917–1968" (Ph.D. dissertation, New York University, 2014), xiii.

Another dynamic specific to the internal history of the Soviet intelligentsia revolves around generational conflict. Because of the major breaks in political life, science, education, culture and ideology that occurred both around the great turning-points of 1917–18 and 1929–30, a succession of distinct generational cohorts became central to the history of intellectuals in the Soviet space. Speaking in the broadest terms, those with prerevolutionary education and experience were separated from a younger, 1920s generation, which in turn was distinct from the rapidly promoted cadres (*vydvizhentsy*) of the Stalin period. This rough, tripartite generational division held for both the nonparty intelligentsia and the party intellectuals (Old Bolsheviks, 1920s party Marxists and, for lack of a more nuanced term, Stalinists) and, *mutatis mutandis*, was replicated among non-Russian intellectuals in the Union republics. For obvious reasons, the last of the three foundational generational cohorts in the early Soviet Union had the least amount of international experience and was least successful at brokering ties with foreign intellectuals. The first phase of Stalinism during the first Five-Year Plan and after was marked by intergenerational conflict among all three groups. The importance of distinct generational cohorts of Soviet intellectuals remained salient for decades to come.

The trajectory of non-Soviet intellectuals' relationship to Soviet communism was shaped by a very different set of dynamics. In the most general sense, what attracted foreign intellectuals and indeed all foreign observers in some way sympathetic to Soviet communism was the multifaceted appeal of an alternative modernity and noncapitalist path to the future. Without this element, for example, the new transnational patronage would have lost most of its effectiveness for foreign intellectuals. The NEP, with its domestic compromises, thus held far less appeal to many intellectuals abroad than the repressive "socialist offensive" of the first Five-Year Plan. Intellectuals in other countries were affected directly and in vastly different ways from domestic Soviet intellectuals by the twists and turns of Soviet foreign relations with their own countries and a succession of major conjunctural shocks, including the rise of fascism, the Great Depression, the terror, the Molotov–Ribbentrop Pact and the Grand Alliance. Speaking no less broadly, the Soviet Union's alternative modernity held its greatest appeal to intellectuals in Europe and the United States in the interwar period, while after World War II that appeal shifted to developing countries, whose elites perceived in the Soviet superpower a recipe for rapid, authoritarian and non-Western modernization.[34]

Despite the importance of these disjunctures between Soviet and non-Soviet intellectuals, this chapter has identified a number of overlooked commonalities in the relationship between Soviet communism and intellectuals inside and outside the USSR. In terms of Soviet policies and attitudes, or what might be termed intelligentsia policy, these commonalities emerged early on in part because the new regime crystallized at a time when the potential repatriation of émigré intellectuals blurred the line between domestic and international. They emerged also because the Marxist-Leninist analysis of the intelligentsia as a wavering stratum, which affected or justified some practices of recruitment of nonproletarian, nonparty intellectuals, was salient for intellectuals inside and outside the USSR. One can also posit that the pragmatic political and economic integration of nonparty "specialists" at home, however rocky that was, eased the way for the proletarian state to woo foreign "bourgeois" intellectuals with a good dose of ideological flexibility and scarce material incentives. From the point of view of the vast range of intellectuals who saw reason to cooperate with the first socialist society, attempts to link their own agendas in particular fields of culture and science to the new regime or to benefit from party-state patronage did not stop at the borders of the Soviet state.

All this suggests that the relationship between communism and intellectuals was not a question of ideas alone – the ideological or political attraction of Soviet communism as a system – as often portrayed in the discussion of fellow travelers and Western "dupes." Rather, ideas worked in tandem with a range of material interests, specific disciplinary or cultural considerations, the experiences of visits and the influence of networks of mediators. Of course, without ideological allure or political interest all other factors would have worked much less effectively.

As this chapter has also suggested, communist attitudes toward intellectuals were dualistic from the start: Large doses of suspicion and hostility toward the intelligentsia were present at every stage, but at the same time the crucial significance of the intelligentsia was an *idée fixe*. Given the deep

34 Steven Marks, *How Russia Shaped the Modern World: From Art to Anti-Semitism, Ballet to Bolshevism* (Princeton: Princeton University Press, 2003), ch. 7. But on conflicts in the Soviet relationship with intellectuals in the "global South" in the era of decolonialization, see Constantine Katsakioris, "The Soviet–South Encounter: Tensions in the Friendship with Afro-Asian Partners, 1945–1965," in Patryk Babiracki and Kenyon Zimmer (eds.), *Cold War Crossings: International Travel and Exchange across the Soviet Bloc, 1940s–1960s* (College Station: Texas A&M University Press, 2014), 134–65.

roots of this Janus-faced mentality, there was a logic to the resulting situation in which the Soviet intelligentsia became at once enormously privileged and harshly coerced.

At the end of the 1920s, the secret police's Solovetskii Camp of Special Designation in the far north White Sea archipelago became the prototype for the emergent Gulag and by far the most infamous holding ground for repressed members of the intelligentsia. Dmitrii Likhachev, the future academician who, decades later, supplied Aleksandr Solzhenitsyn with the Solovki-based title for his *Gulag Archipelago*, worked in a philological unit studying prisoner slang with a Russian scholar who held a doctorate from the Sorbonne.[35] In 1930, an OGPU special commission studying camp conditions produced a three-volume report recommending greater "use" of repressed specialists in the Gulag. Indeed, the Great Break marked one initial peak in the creation of the so-called *sharashki*, or special units of arrested scientists and engineers working on high-priority projects in relatively privileged conditions.[36]

The largest single category of prisoners at Solovki in 1930, which encompassed the incarcerated intellectuals, were "politicals" often classified in camp statistics as "counterrevolutionaries" (known as *kaery* after the acronym from the Russian letters k-r). Of 555 prisoners at Solovki on the books as informers in 1930 (the camp population reached 71,800 at the beginning of 1931), the OGPU commission concluded, too few derived from intelligentsia, specialist and "cultured" elements. The commission therefore issued a call for more recruitment among "counterrevolutionary authorities" (*k-r avtoritetov*). This formulation, on the face of it so bizarre, signified intellectuals imprisoned for political crimes who would have influence among the "counterrevolutionary masses."[37] Even in the Gulag, Soviet power looked to the intelligentsia as a crucial, influential stratum between the authorities and the people and its members were mobilized, privileged and used. Inside the camps, as without, willing partners were found.[38]

35 Dmitrii Likhachev, "Mesto pod narami: Solovki. 1928–1931 gody", interview in *Pervoe sentiabria* (6 Nov. 1999), 5; Dmitrii Likhachev, "Iz knigi Vospominaniia," in M. A. Babicheva (ed.), *"V Belom more krasnyi SLON": Vospominaniia uznikov Solovetskogo lageria osobogo naznacheniia i literatura o nem* (Moscow: Pashkov Dom, 2006), 264–96.

36 Asif Siddiqi, "Scientists and Specialists in the Gulag: Life and Death in Stalin's *Sharashka*," *Kritika* 16, 3 (Summer 2015), 557–88.

37 Cited in Pavlova, "Repressirovannaia intelligentsia," 420, 434–35.

38 Here see the neglected classic by Thomas Lahusen, *How Life Writes the Book: Real Socialism and Socialist Realism in Stalin's Russia* (Ithaca: Cornell University Press, 1997).

Bibliographical Essay

On the rise of the category of "intelligentsia" in Russia, see the original interpretation in Nathaniel Knight, "Was the Intelligentsia Part of the Nation? Visions of Society in Post-Emancipation Russia," *Kritika* 7, 4 (2006), 733–58. On the strain of anti-intelligentsia sentiment within Russian social democracy, see Marshall S. Shatz, *Jan Wacław Machajski: A Radical Critic of the Russian Intelligentsia and Socialism* (Pittsburgh: University of Pittsburgh Press, 1989).

On intellectuals and the Bolshevik Revolution, see Jane Burbank, *Intelligentsia and Revolution: Russian Views of Bolshevism, 1917–1922* (Oxford: Oxford University Press, 1986), and Stuart Finkel, *On the Ideological Front: The Russian Intelligentsia and the Making of the Public Sphere* (New Haven: Yale University Press, 2007).

The historiography on Soviet intellectuals across the range of cultural and scientific fields and professions is truly vast. Fundamental works in English include Sheila Fitzpatrick (ed.), *The Cultural Front: Power and Culture in Revolutionary Russia* (Ithaca: Cornell University Press, 1992); Kendall Bailes, *Technology and Society Under Lenin and Stalin: Origins of the Soviet Technical Intelligentsia, 1917–1941* (Princeton: Princeton University Press, 1978); Katerina Clark, *Petersburg, Crucible of Cultural Revolution* (Cambridge, MA: Harvard University Press, 1998); Nikolai Krementsov, *Stalinist Science* (Princeton: Princeton University Press, 1997); Evgeny Dobrenko, *The Making of the State Writer: Social and Aesthetic Origins of Soviet Literary Culture* (Stanford: Stanford University Press, 1997); and Vladislav Zubok, *Zhivago's Children: The Last Soviet Intelligentsia* (Cambridge, MA: Harvard University Press, 2011).

The literature on fellow travelers and foreign intellectual visitors to the USSR is large, although heavily focused on Europe and the United States at the expense of other regions. The best-known "pre-archival" work is Paul Hollander, *Political Pilgrims: Western Intellectuals in Search of the Good Society*, 4th edn. (New Brunswick, NJ: Transaction Publishers, 1998), which advanced a monocausal explanation centered on intellectuals' alienation from their home society at odds with the present essay. A classic work particularly strong on biographical factors is David Caute, *The Fellow-Travellers: Intellectual Friends of Communism*, rev. edn. (New Haven: Yale University Press, 1988). More recent studies include Sophie Coeuré, *La grande lueur à l'Est: les Français et l'Union soviétique, 1917–1939* (Paris: Seuil, 1999); David Engerman, *Modernization from the Other Shore: American Intellectuals and the Romance of Russian Economic Development* (Cambridge, MA: Harvard University Press, 2003); Liudmilla Stern, *Western Intellectuals and the Soviet Union, 1920–40: From*

Red Square to the Left Bank (Abingdon: Routledge, 2007); and Joy Carew, *Blacks, Reds, and Russians: Sojourners in Search of the Soviet Promise* (New Brunswick, NJ: Rutgers University Press, 2010). For an interesting take on a non-European case, see Sheila Fitzpatrick and Carolyn Rasmussen (eds.), *Political Tourists: Australian Visitors to the Soviet Union in the 1920s–1940s* (Melbourne: Melbourne University Press, 2008).

Katerina Clark's *Moscow, the Fourth Rome: Stalinism, Cosmopolitanism, and the Evolution of Soviet Culture, 1931–1941* (Cambridge, MA: Harvard University Press, 2011) reinterprets the international dimensions of Soviet culture and politics. Soviet cultural diplomacy, image-making and the reception of foreign intellectuals are treated in Michael David-Fox, *Showcasing the Great Experiment: Cultural Diplomacy and Western Visitors to the Soviet Union, 1921–1941* (New York: Oxford University Press, 2012); A. V. Golubev, *"... Vzgliad na zemliu obetovannuiu": Iz istorii sovetskoi kul'turnoi diplomatii 1920–1930-x godov* (Moscow: IRI RAN, 2004); and Jean-François Fayet, *VOKS: Le laboratoire helvétique. Histoire de la diplomatie culturelle soviétique dans l'entre-deux-guerres* (Chêne-Bourg: Georg Editeur, 2014).

Works on party-state policies toward the domestic intelligentsia include an important collection of documents edited by Andrei Artizov and Oleg Naumov, *Vlast' i khudozhestvennaia intelligentsiia: Dokumenty TsK RKP(b)-VKP(b), VChK-OGPU-NKVD o kul'turnoi politiki 1917–1953 gg.* (Moscow: Mezhdunarodnyi fond Demokratiia, 1999), translated in abridged form by Miriam Schwartz with commentaries by Katerina Clark and Evgeny Dobrenko (eds.), *Soviet Culture and Power: A History in Documents, 1917–1953* (New Haven: Yale University Press, 2007).

The literature on Russian émigré intellectuals after 1917 is large. The seminal synthetic work on the emigration is Marc Raeff, *Russia Abroad: A Cultural History of the Russian Emigration, 1919–1939* (New York: Oxford University Press, 1990). Literature on the fascination of fascist intellectuals and German "National Bolsheviks" with communism is scattered, but see the references in Michael David-Fox, *Crossing Borders: Modernity, Ideology, and Culture in Russia and the Soviet Union* (Pittsburgh: University of Pittsburgh Press, 2016), ch. 7, and Marlène Laruelle (ed.), *Unknown Pages of Russian History: Russia and the Fascist Temptation* (forthcoming).

Study of the non-Russian intelligentsias of the USSR and their international roles is also fragmented but developing in promising ways. The most suggestive works include (on the Ukrainian case) Serhy Yekelchyk, *Stalin's Empire of Memory: Russian–Ukrainian Relations in the Soviet Historical*

Imagination (Toronto: University of Toronto Press, 2004), and Tarik Cyril Amar, *The Paradox of Ukrainian Lviv: A Borderland City between Stalinists, Nazis, and Nationalists* (Ithaca: Cornell University Press, 2015); and (on Turkestan and Central Asia), Adeeb Khalid, *The Politics of Muslim Cultural Reform: Jadidism in Central Asia* (Berkeley: University of California Press, 1998), and Adeeb Khalid, *Making Uzbekistan: Nation, Empire, and Revolution in the Early USSR* (Ithaca: Cornell University Press, 2015).

22

Cults of the Individual

KEVIN MORGAN

The cult of the individual was a phrase that entered into general communist discourse in the years immediately following Stalin's death in 1953. Also translated as the cult of personality – and the terms are used here interchangeably – the *kul't lichnosti* was most famously the centerpiece of Nikita Khrushchev's so-called secret speech to the Twentieth CPSU Congress in February 1956. Acknowledging for the first time the enormity of Stalin's crimes, Khrushchev's aim was to signal a symbolic break with this legacy without bringing into question the basic legitimacy and historical necessity of Soviet rule itself. Both within and beyond the communist movement, the inadequacy of a form of explanation focusing on the flaws and excesses of an individual was immediately recognized. Nevertheless, the phrase has entered into general usage precisely because both the origins and effects of the cult phenomenon were not confined to the individual but were of a manifestly wider, systemic character. Historians of communism have therefore sought to engage with the phenomenon's complexities and ambiguities, not only as one of the defining features of Stalinist political culture, but as one periodically reappearing in its longer history and that of other radical movements.

Leaving to one side these longer-term developments, there were two, perhaps three, main phases of cult-building in the period of Stalin's ascendancy. The first, which for Khrushchev remained beyond criticism and was thus not mentioned, was the posthumous Lenin cult which Stalin succeeded in turning to his advantage. The second, already prefigured by the marking of Stalin's fiftieth birthday in 1929, is usually dated from 1933–34 and reached its prewar peak with the onset of the terror in 1936–37. Following a relative hiatus in activity during the war years, the cult then reached its apogee in a third phase coinciding with the Cold War and "high Stalinism," attaining its climax with the commemoration of Stalin's seventieth birthday in December 1949. Though Stalin was not the only dictator to relish such performances, what was of a different order was the truly global scale of the tributes that were now accorded him. As the British communist R. Palme Dutt proudly maintained, such recognition across all national, linguistic and racial barriers had hitherto had to await the verdict of posterity, and the Stalin cult should therefore be presented as the symbol of the communists' internationalism.[1]

The overview offered here will focus on this transnational aspect of the cult phenomenon. Already in the first of these three phases this was evident in the figure of a Lenin who was not just a state-builder but a world revolutionary, and whose living and posthumous cults were not merely a Soviet construction but involved multiple actors across national boundaries. Lenin's cult was at this point *sui generis*, and Stalin's in its embryonic form also had this singular character as Lenin's vaunted legatee. However, with the opening of the second phase of cult construction in 1933–34 there was a veritable turn to the individual throughout the Communist International, and increasingly at the head of each communist party there emerged a leader whose authority at this lower level seemed analogous to Stalin's own. It is on these earlier phases, particularly the second of them, that the narrative here will concentrate. Nevertheless, it was in its third, post-Comintern phase that the cult of the individual achieved a sort of culmination in the formalization of a pyramidal cult hierarchy which had Stalin at its apex, but also somehow at its center, and investing every part. *"Wherever a communist party or central committee is at work,"* wrote one French communist on the occasion of his seventieth birthday, *"Stalin is alive."*[2]

The transnational character of the cult phenomenon has hitherto attracted surprisingly little notice. Mao has lately excited interest as a global figure, and Napoleon as a European one.[3] It is odd, given the scale and scope of the Comintern's ambitions, that similar issues have impinged far less in respect of the Stalin and even Lenin cults. National-level cults have been considered at a primarily national level; but so too have cults which also functioned at an international level, while the

1 R. Palme Dutt, "Stalin and the Future," *Labour Monthly* 35, 4 (Apr. 1953), 146–47.

2 Georges Mounin, "Le marxisme et les grands hommes," *La Nouvelle Critique* 5 (Dec. 1949), 17.

3 Alexander C. Cook (ed.), *Mao's Little Red Book: A Global History* (Cambridge: Cambridge University Press, 2014); Émilie Robbe and François Lagrange (eds.), *Napoléon et l'Europe* (Paris: Somogy Éditions d'art, 2013).

interconnections which were intrinsic to communism's character as an international movement have not in this respect been much explored.

Of course, there exists the wider issue of what some have seen as an "intellectual iron curtain" in respect of Soviet studies, and the development of specialisms in Soviet and international communist history largely independently of each other.[4] That the need to reach across these barriers has been identified so clearly is also a sign of how much things are beginning to change. Nevertheless, the iron curtain is reinforced in this particular context by the prevailing conception of the personality cult as a sacralization of some established center of authority, and what the Soviet specialist J. Arch Getty refers to as a universal human tendency to anthropomorphize power.[5] Not only is it a center of sovereign power that is seen as being embodied in the figure of the leader. Its characterization as a cult is also made conditional on an underpinning of coercive as well as symbolic authority through its restriction to societies that are closed, as E. A. Rees has put it, "both domestically and in their relations to the outside world."[6]

The notion of the "modern personality cult" used in some of the major contributions in the field thus assumes a directed public sphere set apart from the world beyond and precluding any significant rivalry, dissension, or political competition.[7] Within the terms of this definition, a crucial transnational dimension is certainly recognized with the extension of Stalin's dominions to a second wave of communist states in the late

4 Katerina Clark, *Moscow, the Fourth Rome: Stalinism, Cosmopolitanism, and the Evolution of Soviet Culture, 1931–1941* (Cambridge, MA: Harvard University Press, 2011), 6; Brigitte Studer and Heiko Haumann, "Introduction," in Brigitte Studer and Heiko Haumann (eds.), *Stalinistische Subjekte. Individuum und System in der Sowjetunion und Der Komintern 1929–1953* (Zurich: Chronos, 2006), 40.

5 J. Arch Getty, *Practicing Stalinism: Bolsheviks, Boyars and the Persistence of Tradition* (New Haven: Yale University Press, 2013), 77. Like others working in this field, Getty cites as his authority the Chicago sociologist Edward Shils, in particular Shils's essay "Center and Periphery," originally published in 1961.

6 E. A. Rees, "Leader Cults: Varieties, Preconditions and Functions," in Balázs Apor, Jan C. Behrends, Polly Jones and E. A. Rees (eds.), *The Leader Cult in Communist Dictatorships: Stalin and the Eastern Bloc* (Basingstoke: Palgrave Macmillan, 2004), 8.

7 See for example Jan Plamper, *The Stalin Cult: A Study in the Alchemies of Power* (New Haven: Yale University Press, 2012), xvii–xviii; Daniel Leese, "The Cult of Personality and Symbolic Politics," in S. A. Smith (ed.), *The Oxford Handbook of the History of Communism* (Oxford: Oxford University Press, 2014), 339–54. One of the many strengths of Leese's *Mao Cult: Rhetoric and Ritual in China's Cultural Revolution* (Cambridge: Cambridge University Press, 2011) is that it is *not* confined to its closed-society aspect, but does recognize both its international aspect and its development in the period in which Mao did not yet exercise power.

1940s.[8] Moreover, it is within these territorial limits that Alexey Tikhomirov has introduced the highly serviceable notion of an international cult community with Stalin at its center.[9] With its recognition of the symbolic as well as material foundations of Stalin's authority, there seems no reason why such a notion should not also be extended to the nonruling parties of the Cold War years, or indeed to the imagined cult community already represented by the Comintern. One of the challenges of a wider communist history has been precisely to consider how far and in what circumstances an overarching communist identity was established and maintained in the absence of coercion. As Annie Kriegel once observed, the cult of the individual thus deserves our attention as an exercise in normative power which was available in some form or degree to any communist party, irrespective of its position vis-à-vis the state apparatus. As Kriegel also noted, it can also through its obvious variations furnish important comparative insights into the character and effectiveness of different communist parties.[10]

If the parameters of the discussion are extended in this way, concepts developed within a primarily Soviet context will inevitably require some adaptation. Whatever their ideological coloring or forms of legitimation, statist leader cults have tended to be described as integrating devices that served to bind some clearly defined population around a single central figure. Stalin himself would from time to time invoke this integrating role to justify the position he now occupied in Russia, as with the aphorism ascribed to him that "the people need a tsar."[11] As Kriegel suggested, functions of integration and control could equally be imagined at the level of the party as well as state, and thus too at the level of the world party or fraternity that went beyond the confines of the state. Nevertheless, these nonruling parties not only lacked significant means of coercion; they were also engaged in forms of political mobilization and

8 See notably Apor et al. (eds.), *Leader Cult*.

9 Alexey Tikhomirov, "The Stalin Cult Between Center and Periphery: The Structures of the Cult Community in the Empire of Socialism, 1949–1956 – the Case of GDR," in Benno Ennker and Heidi Hein-Kircher (eds.), *Der Führer im Europa des 20. Jahrhunderts* (Marburg, DE: Herder-Institut, 2010), 297–324.

10 Annie Kriegel, "Bureaucratie, culte de la personnalité et charisme. Le cas français: Maurice Thorez, secrétaire général du PCF (1900–1964)," in Annie Kriegel, *Communisme au miroir français.Temps, cultures et sociétés en France devant le communisme* (Paris: Gallimard, 1974), 132–58.

11 D. L. Brandenberger and A. M. Dubrovsky, "'The People Need a Tsar': The Emergence of National Bolshevism as Stalinist Ideology, 1931–1941," *Europe-Asia Studies* 50, 5 (1998), 873–92.

party-building that required a wider public to be drawn into communist campaigns, and ideally into the party itself. Even tsars like Alexander I have had their fleeting moments of popularity outside Russia. What movements of political transformation have needed, however, is not a tsar but a liberator, or a tribune, or a scourge; and as communist parties came forward in just this guise, this too could be anthropomorphized, either in a particular individual or in the wider heroization of the appeals of communism.

Surmounting the architectural epitome of Stalinist hubris, Boris Iofan's unbuilt Palace of the Soviets, an 80-meter-high figure of Lenin was to have been captured by sculptor Sergei Merkurov in the gesturing pose that was familiar to every communist. There was, however, an ambiguity: for the finger that from one perspective seemed to point to the sacral center of the Kremlin appeared from another – that of the worker still striving for emancipation – to be Lenin showing the path to a better future and away from "capitalist misery and oppression."[12] Clearly, one cannot reduce such cult figures as this to a simple classification. One can even so distinguish between the different roles and attributes that different conceptions of the cult community required. Borrowing a phrase from Eduard Bernstein, the notion of the integrating cult is therefore complemented here with the idea of an enkindling cult that did not so much bind a closed community as attempt to galvanize a larger one. The distinction is offered as a heuristic device, for in practice every cult figure considered here may be observed in diverse forms of interaction or transition between these different conceptions of their function, role and audience. At the risk of a degree of schematicism, the discussion that follows will nevertheless be structured around this broad distinction, beginning with the integration cult.

From a closed-society perspective, this may seem to muddy the distinction with openly contested forms of politics which play so crucial a role in accounts of communism's ruling-party cults. Often in these other cases there was not the access to the full range of modern communications assumed in notions of the modern personality cult. The language of deification, which one must in any case be careful not to employ too indiscriminately in this context, would certainly exclude those secular

12 Kevin Morgan, *International Communism and the Cult of the Individual: Leaders, Tribunes and Martyrs Under Lenin and Stalin* (Basingstoke: Palgrave Macmillan, 2016), ch. 2.

forms of hero-worship which in practice fell somewhat short of worship. The highly ritualized character of the ruling communist polity has its approximation elsewhere in looser conventions, or at least in ones requiring more sporadic observance; for the corollary of the closed society was a leader cult that was not only unchallenged but omnipresent and ubiquitous in a way that was unachievable where there was no monopoly of power.[13]

Nevertheless, the usage suggested here is not only familiar in a wider historiography; it is also, as we shall see, how the term was originally used. Though these older and wider usages have tended to lack precise definition, the cult of the individual can for present purposes be defined in slightly more expansive terms as representing the collective ascription to such figures of a distinctive emblematic quality deriving from their office, their personal history, or the postulation of extraordinary gifts and capabilities, whether these were innate or acquired. The relative breadth of this definition has the advantage that it helps to register communism's basic ambiguity as an international movement caught between a project that at its center was one of state-building, and the impulse to protest and "contentious politics" that over the years drew millions within its ambit. For the point about Lenin's statue was not that it was gesturing in different ways, but that it simply appeared to be, depending on where you were standing.

From Lenin to "the Lenin of Today"

Regimes promoting the organized veneration of a leader are usually held to have done so as an instrument of cohesion and control through provision of a stable symbolic center, often in circumstances of acute social flux or political uncertainty. The idea of an integrating cult is consequently one that may be encountered in a variety of historical contexts, from the fascist cults contemporaneous with Stalinism, to the "cult of royal personality" that has been posited as a function of the absolutist state.[14] Despite conflicting verdicts as to how far it answered a genuine impulse from

13 Rees, "Leader Cults," 4.

14 Ian Kershaw, *The "Hitler Myth": Image and Reality in the Third Reich* (Oxford: Oxford University Press, 1989); Emilio Gentile, *The Sacralization of Politics in Fascist Italy* (Cambridge, MA: Harvard University Press, 1996), ch. 6; Peter Burke, *The Fabrication of Louis XIV* (New Haven: Yale University Press, 1992), 198–203.

below, communism's founding cult of Lenin has also been described in just these terms.[15]

Its distinctiveness, of course, was that its full development occurred only after Lenin's death. Depending on the criteria one adopts, there was certainly evidence enough of Lenin's cult-like treatment during his lifetime. Nevertheless, it was Lenin's death in January 1924 that left a void in leadership and legitimation which could not be left unfilled without risk of peril to the regime he had founded. Partly this was therefore a succession crisis. However, the only one of Lenin's successors remotely of the stature to have filled this void was the Bolshevik latecomer Trotsky, whose rivals accused him of nurturing exactly such an ambition. In part to forestall such an outcome, but principally to secure their political cohesion and grip on power, the Bolsheviks therefore determined on replacing the living Lenin with a Lenin who could never die. Politically he lived on in the party he created. Ideologically he lived on in the canon of his writings, and in the edifice of theory combined with successful practice that was now called Leninism. Even physically, Lenin's body was embalmed and preserved for collective veneration in what certainly was the sacral center of his Red Square mausoleum. Unobtrusively abstracted, his brain was removed to a special laboratory, afterwards the Institute of the Brain, to analyze or simply genuflect before the cognitive apparatus of a genius.

Stalin's projection as a figure of comparable stature can be dated from the fiftieth birthday issue of an expanded *Pravda* that was given over to his accomplishments. Trotsky was now in exile, and Bukharin and his supporters removed from any significant leadership position. Crucially, the cult was not therefore the instrument by which Stalin prevailed over his rivals; rather it took their silencing, cooptation, or exclusion to allow the promotion of a Stalin myth that was otherwise plainly refutable. Already in 1920, Lenin's fiftieth birthday had occasioned a surfeit of eulogy and public ceremonial that took up most of that day's *Pravda*. The parallel intended was thus unmistakable. The ceremonialization of the leader's birthday, usually only on the decade markers, was not only to provide the three great landmarks of the Stalin cult. It was also the practice whose later adoption by the communists internationally would symbolize their acquiescence in rituals that in most countries were definitely

15 For contrasting readings see Nina Tumarkin, *Lenin Lives! The Lenin Cult in Soviet Russia* (Cambridge, MA: Harvard University Press, 1983); Benno Ennker, *Die Anfänge des Leninkults in der Sowjetunion* (Cologne: Bohlau Verlag, 1997).

esoteric.[16] No such observances were required of them in 1929; perhaps it was the hastiness of the preparations that did not allow it. Nevertheless, the Comintern did at this stage figure prominently in the rehearsal of Stalin's claimed achievements; and with the circulation of these materials internationally he was for the first time projected as leader, not only of the Soviet workers, but of every class-conscious worker.

For reasons that are still unclear, his cult then remained somewhat in abeyance until the latter part of 1933. One suggestion is that Stalin hesitated to be identified with the traumas of collectivization. It is certainly notable that he would later draw back once more from the spotlight during the darkest days of the war. In the intervening period, his cult had nevertheless become a matter of international notoriety. It was at the Seventeenth CPSU Congress of January 1934, the so-called Congress of Victors, that delegates were for the first time bound by rituals of encomium and ovation that were henceforth paralleled by the ubiquity of Stalin's image in the Soviet press and public spaces. Significantly, the opening of the Congress marked the tenth anniversary, not of Lenin's death, but of the memorial speech by Stalin which had come to symbolize his succession. Film representations also underlined the link with Lenin; for unlike Hitler and Mussolini – seemingly indeed unlike any comparable figure with the exception of Tito – Stalin approved his own impersonation in historical dramas by actors who played him better than he could himself. There is some suggestion of the cult having tailed off by the end of the decade. Nevertheless, Stalin's sixtieth birthday in 1939 was marked on a scale immeasurably exceeding that of a decade earlier. As Khrushchev observed, there were not only exhibitions, musical tributes and cult biographies, but Stalin surpassed even the tsars in establishing in his own lifetime prizes bearing his own name. Compared with a decade earlier, the Comintern figured far less in the construction of the persona, which by now was more than ever like the rippling out from Moscow of a state-centered leader cult. In the words of the New York *Daily Worker*, Stalin led the teeming millions of every continent, but he did so as "captain of the Socialist society" that was now their vanguard state.[17]

16 As witness the ambivalence of the Italian party leader Togliatti regarding the marking of his sixtieth birthday in 1953, see Togliatti to Luigi Longo, 11 Feb. 1953, in Palmiro Togliatti, *La guerra di posizione in Italia. Epistolario 1944–1964* (Turin: Einaudi, 2014), 182–85.

17 "Stalin's Birthday," *Daily Worker*, 22 Dec. 1939.

Within the USSR this did certainly appear as an integrating cult in which, as a disillusioned André Gide suggested, the elements of adoration, love and fear might all have been commingled.[18] When Stalin in 1937 sought to reassure such sensibilities in meeting with the German fellow traveler Lion Feuchtwanger, he protested that he was helpless to prevent the worship that was lavished upon him: "[T]hey see in me a unifying concept, and create foolish raptures around me."[19] The affectation of modesty was an integral part of the cult itself. Stalin in reality not only took a strenuous interest in the operations of his cult; in this first phase of cult-building, as subsequently in the postwar people's democracies, he also underpinned the construction of a unifying concept by the purging and vilification of those who, even without challenging him, might have cast a shadow over the symbiosis of party, state and people that he had now become. Nevertheless, this was also how the cult was rationalized by well-disposed observers like the Britons Sidney and Beatrice Webb and the French sociologist Georges Friedmann. Noting the explosion of the cult as he visited in 1936, Friedmann thus contended that a vast and heterogeneous population like the USSR's could not be brought together around an abstract notion or even a regime, but required a "concrete, living figure" whom one could relate to precisely as an individual.[20] In the years immediately following, culminating in Stalin's sixtieth birthday, the motif of leader of the peoples was not abandoned so much as redefined to signify the peoples of the USSR, and thus the redeployment of older formulae as a sort of internationalism in one country.[21]

This integrating logic might certainly have applied to the vast and potentially fractious population of the Comintern. Its remarkable cohesion across national boundaries was rooted in a common ideology, political identity, and sense of mission underpinned by an ethos of party discipline and the charisma of the revolution as embodied in the Soviet state.[22] Even so, a collective experience that was predominantly one of thwarted hopes and expectations would have offered this population sufficient cause for

18 André Gide, *Retour de l'URSS* (Paris: Gallimard, 1936), 70.

19 Cited in Sarah Davies, "Stalin and the Making of the Leader Cult in the 1930s," in Apor et al. (eds.), *Leader Cult*, 37.

20 Georges Friedmann, *De la Sainte Russie à l'URSS* (Paris: Gallimard, 1938), 213–18.

21 Jan Plamper, "Georgian Koba or Soviet 'Father of Peoples'? The Stalin Cult and Ethnicity," in Apor et al. (eds.), *Leader Cult*, 126–27.

22 For the last point, see Gleb J. Albert, "'Esteemed Comintern!': The Communist International and World-Revolutionary Charisma in Early Soviet Society," *Twentieth Century Communism* 8, 8 (Jan. 2015), 10–39.

dissension even without the Comintern's subjection to the brutal expediencies of the same Soviet state. Factionalism and deviationism were consequently treated as anathema, while the command ideology of Marxism-Leninism vested an *ex cathedra* authority in the word descending from above. Deferring to Stalin thus became part and parcel of the wider processes that are often referred to as Stalinization; and for the inner cadre of "Cominternians" who came directly into contact with Soviet practices through work or study in the Moscow apparatus, the experience in many cases was a profoundly affecting one.[23]

If the first great set-piece of the Soviet cult of Stalin was the Congress of Victors, its Comintern equivalent was the Seventh World Congress which assembled in August–September 1935. The Italian Palmiro Togliatti, generally held to be one of the most measured of Stalin's Western disciples, concluded his report by saluting his leadership on behalf of the Congress. "Military music with trumpets," the French delegate Marcel Cachin recorded in his journal:

> Impeccable and powerful processions. Warm and enthusiastic atmosphere. The homage to Stalin, unanimous, vibrant.[24]

Communists in France, and Cachin in particular, were already among those most prone to identify Soviet achievements with the guiding hand of the man whom Henri Barbusse famously described as standing at the helm.[25] What was equally striking about the Seventh World Congress was how other communist parties, as indeed the Comintern itself, were also now represented by some single figure clearly identifiable at their head. It was thus the Bulgarian Georgi Dimitrov, now secretary of the Comintern, who delivered the main Congress report, and who was followed by a succession of party leaders, beginning with the party of the moment – which in that first summer of the Popular Front meant Maurice Thorez and the French Communist Party (PCF). If already a sort of cultic hierarchy was implicit in the order in which these figures appeared, this is confirmed in the published proceedings

23 For Stalinization and the experience of the Cominternians, see respectively Norman LaPorte, Kevin Morgan and Matthew Worley (eds.), *Bolshevism, Stalinism and the Comintern: Perspectives on Stalinization* (Basingstoke: Palgrave Macmillan, 2008); Brigitte Studer, *The Transnational World of the Cominternians* (Basingstoke: Palgrave Macmillan, 2015).

24 Denis Peschanski (ed.), *Marcel Cachin. Carnets 1906–1947*, 4 vols. (Paris: CNRS Éditions, 1993–98), vol. IV, III, entry for 25 July 1935.

25 Henri Barbusse, *Staline: un monde nouveau vu à travers un homme* (Paris: Flammarion, 1936).

by the ratcheting up of the mere "applause" accorded some to the warm applause for the Briton Harry Pollitt (who followed Thorez) and the warm and prolonged applause for Thorez himself. "Tumultuous and prolonged applause, cheers and ovations" were reserved for Stalin, and for the imprisoned German communist leader Ernst Thälmann.[26] When three years later the undeceived former communist Franz Borkenau published his pioneering Comintern history, he picked out Thorez and Pollitt, along with the American Earl Browder and the Spaniard José Díaz, as leaders whom he claimed wielded the same "absolute power" within their own parties as Stalin did within his.[27]

Whether within the ruling or the nonruling communist party, the cult of the general secretary could thus provide a source of binding rituals and professions of loyalty that reinforced the disciplines of democratic centralism and could perhaps be said to have anthropomorphized them. Internationally, the cult of Stalin could function in much the same way: as in the recollections of one recalcitrant British communist that in opposing party policy one might according to the circumstances be warned that this was an "attack on comrade Pollitt" – or else on comrade Stalin.[28] Certain features can be identified that were conducive if not indispensable to this role. Most fundamental was the need for an unambiguous symbolic hierarchy, usually culminating in a single individual. Should comrades Pollitt and Stalin see things differently, for example, as famously at the start of World War II, comrade Pollitt would have to cede to Stalin's authority, or else the disciplines embodied in their two persons would cease to be effective. This, of course, was what subsequently happened in the case of a figure like Tito. In Stalin's case, even the legitimizing cult of the departed Lenin eventually needed cutting down to size: like the statues that now depicted him an inch or several shorter than his successor.

Because of their incarnating wider relations of power, cults of this type have also been described as a necessarily patricentric phenomenon.[29] In fact, the point is a broader one, for the individual performing such a role had typically to represent either some preeminent social or national identity or else an encompassing protean quality in which diverse qualities, associations and accomplishments were united in the figure of the leader.

26 Serge Wolikow, "Préface" to "Année 1935: Le VIIe congrès de l'Internationale communiste," in Peschanski (ed.), *Marcel Cachin*, vol. IV, 56–57.
27 Franz Borkenau, *The Communist International* (London: Faber, 1938), 395.
28 Kevin Morgan, *Harry Pollitt* (Manchester: Manchester University Press, 1993), 163, 180.
29 Plamper, *Stalin Cult*, xviii.

It was thus that Barbusse described Stalin as the "perfect blend" of intellectual and worker; and thus too that the Romanian communist Ana Pauker would, despite her political credentials, signal her triple unfitness for such a role as at once "a woman, a Jew, and an intellectual."[30] In the USA, the black communist James B. Ford could three times stand for the country's vice-presidency, but each time cede precedence to a white running mate. This also implied that the contingencies of individual biography could not simply be left uncorrected: as with the suppression of the Jewish identity of Pauker's Hungarian contemporary Mátyás Rákosi. Even Stalin, who could hardly forget that his one encomium from Lenin was as that "wonderful Georgian," used a multiple identity which in class and ethnic terms sought to neutralize the threat posed by wider divisions in Soviet society.[31] There thus had to be a symbiosis of leader and movement. This tended to mean the downplaying of any purely personal history, and a process of manufacturing or refashioning to meet these cultic desiderata, not only in respect of the central cult figure, but in the observances that their elevation to cultic status required. Communists were always wary of spontaneity; and the true integrating figure was not the one on which an impressible public happened to fasten, but the vehicle mandated for such a role with all the inexorable attention to protocol of a Congress panels commission.

Decade of Heroes

From the moment that Khrushchev delivered his secret speech, the idea of the cult of the individual became irrevocably associated with Stalin. This, for historians of communism, was the original personality cult; and if the concept has become linked with notions of sovereign power, coercion and the closed society, it is Stalin who is always lurking there as archetype or implied comparator. Nevertheless, when Khrushchev, seeking textual authority for his iconoclasm, recovered the expression from the Marxist canon, his source was Marx's disclaimer of the *Personenkultus* in a letter of 1877 referring to himself – not a sacralized despot but a revolutionary writer in exile. More familiar in Marx's day was the association of such a notion with Marx's rival as a founder of German socialism, Ferdinand Lassalle. In his book on Lassalle

30 Barbusse, *Staline*, 15–16; Robert Levy, *Ana Pauker: The Rise and Fall of a Jewish Communist* (Berkeley: University of California Press, 2001), 71–74.

31 Alfred J. Rieber, "Stalin, Man of the Borderlands," *American Historical Review* 106, 5 (Dec. 2001), 1651–91.

published in 1891, the revisionist Marxist Eduard Bernstein referred more specifically to a cult of personality – *Kultus der Persönlichkeit* – in evoking Lassalle's signal contribution in the earliest days of German social democracy. Lassalle's name, he wrote, became a standard which engendered ever more enthusiasm among the masses and enkindled hundreds of thousands to struggle for the rights of labor. "When all is said and done most persons like to see a cause, which, the more far-reaching its aims at any given moment, must seem the more abstract, embodied in one individual." How similar is this investiture in the individual to that described by Friedmann; and yet how different the object of this "craving to personify a cause" (*Perzonifizierungssucht*). Borrowing Eleanor Marx's translation, it is this that may be thought of as an enkindling cult.[32]

One may return to Merkurov's statue of a Lenin pointing at once to the state and to its overthrow. By the end of the 1930s, the Soviet cult of Lenin was in definite recession. Some would even date its supplantation a decade earlier – though the fact of Lenin's crowning the abortive Palace of the Soviets suggests that that should not be overstated. What is certain is that it was not at the mid 1920s peak of Soviet Leniniana but in the late 1920s–early 1930s that there appeared a publishers' boom of Lenin biographies in the West. Some, not all, were written by communists; what was true of most was that the Lenin they depicted was the one pointing the way out of capitalism, with the focus overwhelmingly on the years of agitation that culminated in the revolution. This was the Lenin whom Spanish socialists had in mind when they referred to their leader Francisco Largo Caballero as the Spanish Lenin; and this the Lenin who caused Tito to distinguish between Soviet workers looking to Stalin and those elsewhere still to achieve their revolution and continuing to see in Lenin their principal guide in achieving it.[33]

But of course, for his supporters in the West, Lenin, like Lassalle and Marx, had always pointed that way. Few were ever interested in what happened to his body. What Lenin represented was the incarnation of the revolution who in accomplishing that revolution had redeemed the faltering spirit of international socialism. In Britain, the first, effusively lyrical tribute to Lenin in the socialist press can be found as early

32 Eduard Bernstein, *Ferdinand Lassalle as a Social Reformer*, trans. Eleanor Marx (London: Swan Sonnenschein & Co, 1893), 188–89; also Eduard Bernstein, *Ferdinand Lassalle. Eine Würdigung des Lehres und Kämpfers* (Berlin: Bein Paul Cassirer, 1919), 299.

33 G. R. Swain, "Tito: The Formation of a Disloyal Bolshevik," *International Review of Social History* 34 (1989), 262.

as March 1918, hardly lagging behind even the earliest Soviet examples.[34] Gor'kii two years later used the pages of the *Communist International* to eulogize Lenin's intuitive genius, saintly asceticism and relentless will, and described him as mattering less within Russia itself than as a battering ram against world capitalism and its colonial empires.[35]

Looking back from the 1970s, the historian E. P. Thompson thought not of Lenin but of more recent examples of the enkindling cult. The years of anti-fascism, Thompson wrote, as one of thousands at that time recruited to the communist cause, were a "decade of heroes" with "Guevaras in every street and every wood."[36] It was certainly a decade of partisan heroes, like Mao, Tito and the Guevaras of the French *maquis*. But it was also a decade of courtroom tribunes, like Pauker, Rákosi and Dimitrov; of revolutionary martyrs, like Thälmann and the Italian Antonio Gramsci; and of popular tribune figures, of whom none surpassed the Spanish republic's legendary *Pasionaria*, Dolores Ibárruri. These figures were obviously central to the collective identity of communists like Thompson; but at the same time they also represented communism to a wider public, which, just as with Lassalle, might be drawn into one or other level of activity and the organizational ambit of the party itself.

Not all such figures were heroic; the American Browder appears to have cut anything but such a figure. Nevertheless, through his unassuming, midwestern demeanor and the even, placid quality of his coast-to-coast radio broadcasts, Browder did embody for this wider public the popular front buzzword that communism was "twentieth-century Americanism." Browder's biographer writes of a personality cult and a "miniature imitator of Stalin": ten-minute ovations, the singing of "Browder Is Our Leader," the recasting of Browder's family history as an American folk epic, the testimony to his command of theory that was the Browder Library – in forms commensurate with his cultural environment and his party's modest proportions, there was undeniably something attaching to Browder that located him somewhere between Stalin and Lassalle.[37] Thälmann in his prison cell meanwhile symbolized endurance in the face of oppression,

34 Ian Bullock, *Romancing the Revolution: The Myth of Soviet Democracy and the British Left* (Edmonton: Alberta University Press, 2011), 354.

35 There is a discussion in Tumarkin, *Lenin Lives!*, 105–06. Though Lenin protested at the article's uncommunist tone, it circulated on the widest scale internationally.

36 E. P. Thompson, "The Poverty of Theory: Or an Orrery of Errors," in *The Poverty of Theory and other Essays* (London: Merlin, 1978), 264.

37 James G. Ryan, *Earl Browder: The Failure of American Communism* (Tuscaloosa: University of Alabama Press, 1997); also Morgan, *International Communism*, ch. 3.

through a repertoire once more of biographies, leafletings and ovations necessarily in his absence. It was Thälmann, indeed, whose fiftieth birthday in April 1936 was the first such occasion in the capitalist world to be marked in a way that suggested the connection with Lenin and Stalin. There were, of course, tens of thousands of political prisoners in Nazi Germany. The turn to the individual was thus in this instance clearly evident in the focusing of a wider solidarity effort on the figure of the leader who was meant to symbolize their cause.[38]

Borkenau was one of the original anti-communists and a pioneer of the concept of totalitarianism. Nevertheless, even Borkenau singled out two figures as having restored for the Comintern some of the prestige it had lost in the period of Stalin's ascendancy.[39] The first of them was Dimitrov, who had earned his reputation as the hitherto little-known Comintern functionary who had defied the Nazis at the Leipzig trial in the latter months of 1933. The use of such occasions as a public platform had a long radical pedigree, and as communists in these years staked their claim to it, Dimitrov was at the heart of this claim.[40] Acquitted in triumph, he was given asylum in the USSR early in 1934 and immediately installed by Stalin in a leading position in the Comintern. As Dimitrov himself observed, his achievement at Leipzig was invaluable political capital for the Comintern, and with the assistance of the agit-prop veteran Alfred Kurella he made every effort to exploit it. Productions included a biography, a prospective autobiography, a volume of prison letters and a dramatized feature film, *Kämpfer* (Fighters), made by German émigrés in Moscow with the initial assistance of Dutch documentarist Joris Ivens. Through his report to the Seventh World Congress, it was Dimitrov, not Stalin, who was clearly the Congress's dominant personality for all who had not personally witnessed the proceedings. "Three years ago Dimitrov fought alone," wrote the young British communist John Cornford before his death in Spain:

> And we stood taller when he won.
> But now the Leipzig dragon's teeth
> Sprout strong and handsome against death
> And here an army fights where there was one.

38 On the Thälmann cult, see Russel Lemmons, *Hitler's Rival: Ernst Thälmann in Myth and Memory* (Lexington: University of Kentucky Press, 2013).

39 Borkenau, *Communist International*, 405.

40 See for example Marcel Willard, *La défense accuse ... De Babeuf à Dimitrov* (Paris: Éditions Sociales Internationales, 1938); the discussion of Dimitrov here draws on Morgan, *International Communism*, ch. 5.

If it were only the enkindling of verse, it was Dimitrov who achieved its unforced expression far more than Stalin. By this time, he had even begun to be saluted as the leader and "tested pilot" of the workers in the capitalist countries, as if he were the counterpart to Stalin at the head of the Soviet state.

The integrating cult, in a communist context, was inextricably a cult at once of office and of office-holder; indeed, where the symbiosis of party and leader was disturbed, as subsequently in China's Cultural Revolution, cultic practices could have a disintegrative and even anarchic effect.[41] Dimitrov as secretary of the Comintern also came to represent such a symbiosis, and the authority of the one clearly underpinned the other. Nevertheless, if Dimitrov in this sense was the beneficiary of Stalin's preferment, he achieved it through a political capital which was inalienably his own. Moreover, Stalin's own rationale for thus favoring Dimitrov was quite explicitly to reach out to the social democratic workers whom he believed would abandon their present leaders only to the extent that better ones were available. It is impossible to understand the international resonance of Dimitrov's stand except in the context of the collapse in Germany of Europe's strongest communist party, and the subjugation of its strongest labor movement seemingly without a fight. The Comintern, however, could not simply manufacture such a figure; in Europe's liberal press, and the publishers who sought the rights to Dimitrov's autobiography, and the dramatist Elmer Rice who turned to the Leipzig trial for a successful Broadway play, a fascination with a figure truly bearing the kudos of the hero broke out like an upsurge from below that the Comintern had failed to anticipate. Moreover, although Dimitrov stood in the dock as every inch the communist, he also made much of his own authentic personal history, and in campaigning internationally this was corroborated and reinforced by the prominence of his sister and his mother. Dimitrov was now a yardstick and exemplar; Rákosi, for example, was proudly designated the "Hungarian Dimitrov." But the point about the Leipzig trial, unlike the cult of a leader's birthday, was that it was not simply reproducible at the party's will.

The other figure mentioned by Borkenau was Ibárurri. Indeed, there is no better witness to Ibárurri's enkindling qualities than Borkenau himself. In August 1936, he attended a Popular Front demonstration in Valencia which Ibárurri addressed coming straight from the front. Though she was

41 Daniel Leese, *Mao Cult: Rhetoric and Ritual in China's Cultural Revolution* (Cambridge: Cambridge University Press, 2011), pt. 3.

one of Spain's foremost communist leaders, and Borkenau one of communism's most seasoned observers, he described her as one who was not even politically minded, but moved only by the "simple, self-sacrificing faith which emanates from every word she speaks." The one communist leader who was known and loved by the masses, they worshipped her, he said, "not for her intellect, but as a sort of saint who is to lead them in the days of trial and temptation." Borkenau was not the only one to react to *La Pasionaria* in this way. Like Dimitrov before the Leipzig trial, she was not her party's general secretary or acknowledged leader, and when later she became so, the intrigues it took to achieve this would never have been sufficient without the legend of *La Pasionaria*. Moreover, where Dimitrov the Bulgarian had come to overshadow Germany's own communist leaders as the paradoxical symbol of the "other" anti-fascist Germany, the role of tribune figure was accessible to Ibárurri even as a woman. Indeed, as Borkenau like many others saw, this was integral to the charisma that she exercised, as in every word and gesture she combined a "profound motherliness" with the defiance of a communist and the religious personality of a medieval ascetic.[42]

Instruments of Stalinization

What influenced Stalin to revive his cult in 1933–34 remains a matter of conjecture. One suggestion is that with the establishment of the Nazi dictatorship in Germany he both influenced and was influenced by the Hitler cult.[43] It is nevertheless unclear why this should have registered so much more quickly than the example of Italian fascism. This, after all, not only predated the Nazi regime by a decade. Its symbiosis of leader and vaunted revolution also offered more obvious analogies with Bolshevism, as latterly with Mussolini's *Decennale* celebrations of 1932 which so clearly echoed those which the Bolsheviks had organized on the tenth anniversary of their own revolution. What Hitler did represent, far more than Mussolini, was not so much exemplar as threat. Too late the Comintern awoke to the reality of that threat. Even then, there was at first no relenting in the claim that communist leadership alone could meet that threat. It was in these circumstances that

42 Franz Borkenau, *The Spanish Cockpit: An Eye-Witness Account of the Political and Social Conflicts of the Spanish Civil War* (London: Faber, 1937), 120–21.
43 Yves Cohen, *Le Siècle des chefs: Une histoire transnationale du commandement et de l'autorité* (Paris: Éditions Amsterdam, 2013), 727.

Stalin appeared to emerge from the international shadows in the guise of a counter-cult.

He was certainly conscious of the need to reach out to an international public. Already in December 1931 he had entertained the bestselling German biographer and journalist, Emil Ludwig. This seems to indicate a direct rivalry with Mussolini, whose *Autobiography* of the 1920s had appeared in English but not Italian, and whose concerns with the same international public would result in 1932 in Ludwig's *Talks with Mussolini*. Both leaders were evidently moved in part to counteract hostile portrayals circulating internationally – in Stalin's case those notably of the defector Boris Bazhanov and the former Georgian Social Revolutionary who wrote as Essad Bey.[44] It is perhaps suggestive of the wider audience that he principally had in mind that within the USSR Stalin's interview with Ludwig initially appeared only in the Central Committee journal *Bol'shevik* with its relatively modest circulation.[45]

Doubtless to the gratification of Stalin's *amour-propre*, he would later consent to further public audiences with such intellectual heavyweights as H. G. Wells, in 1934, and Romain Rolland in 1935. Immediately following the meeting with Ludwig, he had also had Gor'kii sounded out as a prospective biographer of similar repute. Though Gor'kii was not to be drawn, in the summer of 1933 Stalin turned to France and Barbusse for provision of the hitherto elusive cult biography. No Western communist had a wider reading public than the well-known author of *Le Feu*; as Barbusse himself observed, his object was a life of Stalin "capable of getting everywhere and being understood by all and influencing what is called 'public opinion' or 'the general public.'"[46]

The moment, however, was not to last. Barbusse's papers record his considerable frustration in attempting to produce such a living portrait under the oversight of the CPSU's head of Kultprop, Aleksei Stetskii, and with the niggardly documentation that was alone available to him. Barbusse's *Staline* did at least appear shortly before his death in the summer of 1935, and the several translations that followed included a Russian one with a preface by Stetskii. Nevertheless, the volume was rapidly withdrawn because of its

44 Miklós Kun, *Stalin: An Unknown Portrait* (Budapest: Central European University Press, 2003), 70–71.

45 Wolfgang Schieder, "Von Stalin zu Mussolini. Emil Ludwig bei Diktatoren des 20. Jahrhunderts," in Dan Diner, Gideon Reuveni and Yfaat Weiss (eds.), *Deutsche Zeiten: Geschichte und Lebenswelt* (Göttingen: Vandenhoeck & Ruprecht, 2012), 111–31.

46 Barbusse to Alfred Kurella, 6 Feb. 1934, Barbusse papers, PCF archives, Paris.

compromising allusions to sundry victims of the terror, the sometime Bukharinite Stetskii among them. Stalin's interview with Rolland, meanwhile, was not approved for publication, presumably because of the critical lines of questioning that it included. The interview with Feuchtwanger, whose well-disposed *Moskau 1937* referred openly if indulgently to the excessiveness of Stalin's cult, was to prove the last in this series of transnational encounters.[47]

Mussolini at this stage preferred depiction before this external public in more conventional pose and attire than was often the case within Italy itself.[48] Stalin in more subtle ways was also aware that there were different sensitivities in addressing a closed domestic audience and an international one.[49] Nevertheless, it is difficult to see that these sensitivities registered in any significant way by the end of the 1930s. His revisions to the famous *Short Course* history of the Soviet party in 1938 have latterly been identified as a watershed moment in this decline of internationalism.[50] During the subsequent Molotov–Ribbentrop Pact (1939–41) this was epitomized by Stalin's exchange of birthday greetings with Hitler, in a sort of ghastly parody of the caste recognition of an earlier age of kings. A failure as an enkindling figure, Stalin's was now the integrating cult at once of leader and of leading state, and only through this state of the wider cult community beyond.

What such a cult also required was the explicit subordination of any personality who in rivaling it might detract from it. In this respect, it is notable that specifically Dimitrov and Ibárruri were the only leading Comintern figures who contributed to the sixtieth-birthday accolades paid to Stalin in *Pravda*. "Better than any writer or biographer," Ibárruri wrote, "the people themselves express the significance of Stalin, when in the words of their rank-and-file representatives, they say: 'For us Stalin is more than our own father.'"[51] It was like the making over to Stalin of her own symbolic capital; for if power and protest alike could be symbolized

47 Lion Feuchtwanger, *Moskau 1937. Ein Reisebericht für meine Freunde* (Amsterdam: Querido Verlag, 1937), 76, 83.

48 Maurizio Serra, "Présentation," in Emil Ludwig, *Entretiens avec Mussolini* (Paris: Perrin, 2016), 33–34.

49 Davies, "Stalin and the Making of the Leader Cult," 39–40.

50 David Brandenberger, "The Fate of Interwar Soviet Internationalism: A Case Study of the Editing of Stalin's 1938 *Short Course on the History of the ACP(b)*," *Revolutionary Russia* 29, 1 (2016), 1–23.

51 Translated as "Pasionaria Tells of First Meeting People's Leader," *Daily Worker*, 21 Dec. 1939.

by the individual, so could acquiescence and the recognition of a still higher authority.

So early into Thompson's decade of heroes, the imperatives were already clearly evident that would bring it to an end. The passing of the communist hero did not, however, mean the end of the cult of the individual, but only of a particular version of it that had always existed in a state of tension with the bureaucratic cult of office. In a sense this is therefore a narrative of Stalinization, but one that could never be fully accomplished while the contradictions of the Popular Front remained, and whose usual connotations of a finished process are restricted to the more truncated phase of high Stalinism.

It was consequently the two-camps mentality of the Cold War which at both national and international level provided the heyday of the integrating cult. These were the years that saw Ibárruri at the head of her party, and Dimitrov following Lenin into his own mausoleum, and a posthumous Thälmann cult that coincided with Germany's division into two, and the excoriation of the backsliders Tito and Browder. Communism in effect had become its own cult community, and almost every one of the figures mentioned here can be used to illustrate the fact. Nevertheless, the longer history of the cult phenomenon, as outlined here, is one that cannot simply be reduced to such a teleology. As sometime martyrs and party tribunes were installed in power, the singularity and complexity of international communism was not just the interlocking of such figures within a movement of unprecedented cohesion, but the encompassing over time of multiple transitions from one such figure to another. The challenge of a transnational communist history is to try to develop a conceptual apparatus that is at once rigorous and flexible enough to accommodate them.

Bibliographical Essay

There are a number of important studies of the founding Lenin cult focusing on its Soviet aspect and the immediate aftermath of Lenin's death. Nina Tumarkin, *Lenin Lives! The Lenin Cult in Soviet Russia* (Cambridge, MA: Harvard University Press, 1983), stresses the Russian roots of the phenomenon at the expense of its communist character. Benno Ennker, *Die Anfänge des Leninkults in der Sowjetunion* (Cologne: Bohlau Verlag, 1997), uses Soviet archives to demonstrate the cult's conscious instrumentalization by Lenin's successors. Olga Velikanova,

Making of an Idol: On Uses of Lenin (Göttingen: Muster-Schmidt Verlag, 1996), incorporates a longer perspective and has a valuable documentation but suffers from a poor-quality translation.

Writings on the Stalin cult also focus on its Soviet aspect, and surprisingly there seems to be no major study of Stalin as an international figure. Jan Plamper, *The Stalin Cult: A Study in the Alchemies of Power* (New Haven: Yale University Press, 2012), is authoritative on Soviet visual culture. The essays in Sarah Davies and James Harris (eds.), *Stalin: A New History* (Cambridge: Cambridge University Press, 2005) offer a broad perspective including David Brandenberger's discussion of the all-important cult biography. Stalin is also discussed at length in Yves Cohen's monumental *Le Siècle des chefs. Une histoire transnationale du commandement et de l'autorité (1890–1940)* (Paris: Éditions Amsterdam, 2013), a comparative and transnational study of the broader fixation on the figure of the leader in different societies and fields of activity. Cohen does also register the importance of the international aspect of Stalin's cult, but this falls beyond the already monumental scope of his own treatment.

A number of recent studies of non-Soviet cults touch at least in passing on the Comintern period. Balázs Apor, *The "Invisible Shining": The Cult of Mátyás Rákosi in Stalinist Hungary, 1945–1956* (Budapest: Central European University Press, 2017), is excellent on the later state cult though it deals only briefly with the earlier period. While focusing on the period of the Cultural Revolution, Daniel Leese's *Mao Cult: Rhetoric and Ritual in China's Cultural Revolution* (Cambridge: Cambridge University Press, 2011) offers important insight into the earlier development of Mao's cult in an international as well as a national context. Adopting a political religions perspective, Russel Lemmons's *Hitler's Rival: Ernst Thälmann in Myth and Memory* (Lexington: University of Kentucky Press, 2013) deals with both the Weimar phase as party leader and the Nazi-era phase as political prisoner, as well as the importance of the posthumous Thälmann cult in communist East Germany.

The best collections and overviews tend to reflect the closed-society perspective of the state personality cult. Balázs Apor, Jan C. Behrends, Polly Jones and E. A. Rees (eds.), *The Leader Cult in Communist Dictatorships: Stalin and the Eastern Bloc* (Basingstoke: Palgrave Macmillan, 2004), covers a variety of East European cases and includes outstanding contributions on the Stalin cult. Klaus Heller and Jan Plamper (eds.), *Personality Cults in Stalinism – Personenkulte im Stalinismus* (Göttingen: V&R Unipress, 2004), also extends to fascist comparators and has a helpful introduction outlining the notion of the "modern personality cult." Benno Ennker and Heidi Hein-Kircher (eds.), *Der Führer im Europa des 20. Jahrhunderts* (Marburg: Herder-Institut, 2010), also includes comparators of the authoritarian right. The same volume contains a useful exposition of the notion of the international cult community by Alexey Tikhomirov on Stalin and the GDR: "The Stalin Cult Between Center and Periphery: The Structures of the Cult Community in the Empire of Socialism, 1949–1956 – the Case of GDR" (297–324). Kevin Morgan and Matthew Worley (eds.), *Twentieth Century Communism* 1 (2009), is a special issue on "Communism and the Leader Cult" bringing together work on nonruling parties including those in Belgium, Finland, Vietnam, France and Brazil. Kevin Morgan, *International Communism and the Cult of the Individual: Leaders, Tribunes and Martyrs Under Lenin and Stalin* (Basingstoke: Palgrave Macmillan, 2016), builds upon this in attempting a transnational and comparative study of the type presented more summarily here. The same account also provides full references for some of the arguments that are here only briefly alluded to.

23

German Communism

ERIC D. WEITZ

In the 1920s and early 1930s, Germans built the first mass-based communist party outside the Soviet Union. At its height, the Communist Party of Germany (KPD) attracted 17 percent of the electorate. In some working-class neighborhoods around the country, its support reached upwards of one-third of the voters. Russian revolutionaries, other foreign communists and KPD members themselves expected the party to lead the next phase of the worldwide proletarian revolution. But in the 1930s, the party would be crushed by both Nazi repression and the Soviet Great Terror.

Like all communist parties, the KPD increasingly came under the sway of the Communist Party of the Soviet Union (CPSU) and the Communist International (Comintern). However, the character of the KPD was also deeply rooted in German social, political and economic conditions extending back into the nineteenth century and, closer at hand, in the fateful events of World War I, the German Revolution of 1918–19 and the founding of the Weimar Republic. The KPD can never be understood in isolation from the history of the Bolshevik Revolution and the Soviet Union, nor can it be understood as merely a dependant of the CPSU and the Comintern.

Germany not only had a mass communist party. In the late nineteenth century, it also had produced the largest and most significant socialist party in the world. The Social Democratic Party of Germany (SPD) had been founded in 1875, and soon became a model for socialists worldwide. The party, firmly committed to Marxism, advocated a democratic, socialist and egalitarian future that would resolve all social and political problems. German socialists (or social democrats) created a movement that reached deep into working-class lives through educational programs; sport, hobby and art associations; and trade union affiliations. For workers with talent and ambition, the party could be a place of social mobility. They might leave the mine pit or the workbench and become party administrators, elected officials, or union advisors regarding Germany's myriad social welfare programs. The KPD would recreate this kind of movement, though with a far more radical bent.

The background to this great surge of socialism in Germany lay in the particular characteristics of imperial Germany. Founded in 1871 under the powerful direction of the Prussian minister-president Otto von Bismarck, imperial Germany combined strongly democratic with pronounced authoritarian features. At the same time, Germany's industrial economy grew at a powerful rate. By the turn of the century Germany's industrial might had surpassed Britain's and lagged only behind the United States. Its coalmines provided unending resources for the steel industry; its innovative chemical and electro-technical industries, which surged after 1890, also led the world.

This hotbed of industry had an almost insatiable demand for labor. From the German countryside, from Poland and from other European countries, people surged into Saxony, the Ruhr, the Saar and Silesia, all the regional sites of rapid industrialization, and into the major cities of Berlin, Munich, Mainz and many others. By 1900, the German population had become predominantly urban rather than rural.

Industrialization provided the SPD and later the KPD with their working-class base. By the 1890s the SPD had become Germany's largest political party in terms of popular votes. The key question for the party became how to transform Germany into a democratic socialist country. Many party leaders, notably Eduard Bernstein, the leader of the so-called revisionist wing, believed in a gradualist approach, working within the system to the extent possible, waging electoral campaigns and conducting educational work that would ultimately win the party the support of a majority of the German population. Bernstein pointed out that modern society had become more complex, with an ever-growing middle class of technically trained, white-collar workers and skilled workers whose living conditions were improving. The unrevised Marxist worldview, argued Bernstein, no longer fit social reality and strongly limited the SPD's appeal.

A middle stream in the party, led by Karl Kautsky, tried to have it both ways. It remained committed to Marxism and the inevitability of revolution. Yet it believed the path toward revolution had to be slowly and carefully prepared. Only when the time was right – whenever that was and however the "right time" was to be determined – could the SPD support revolution.

The left wing of the party vociferously contested Bernstein, and it is here that the origins of German communism are most directly to be found. Led by Rosa Luxemburg, Karl Liebknecht, Franz Mehring and Clara Zetkin, the left adhered to Marxism and the belief in revolution as the only path forward for Germany. Luxemburg's intellectual and rhetorical prowess was especially inspiring to those on the left. Her rejection of any hint of nationalist and imperialist politics and her celebration of working-class activism, notably mass strikes, provided a powerful counter to an SPD that was becoming increasingly integrated into German society and politics, even though it remained barred from political power. Among a small group of skilled workers and intellectuals, Luxemburg and her colleagues found significant support. Many of her supporters would go on to play key roles in German communism, some into the 1960s in the German Democratic Republic.

Then came World War I. No German family remained unaffected by this great catastrophe. Millions of young men were drafted into the army; some 2 million died, over 4 million came back physically and psychologically wounded. Hundreds of thousands of women streamed into the war-production factories, often working fourteen-hour days, seven days a week. By the winter of 1916–17, famine conditions were rampant. Women waited for hours on bread lines. By the next winter, strikes had become a common phenomenon as workers demanded better food rations and better working conditions. Quickly their demands escalated to the political level, with calls for an end to the war and the removal of the Kaiser. Radical workers, some influenced by Luxemburg and her friends, organized a Revolutionary Shop Stewards group. News of the Russian revolutions inspired workers, worn down by a seemingly unending war that had only created misery for working people.

The SPD leadership had lent its support to the Reich government at the outbreak of war. To the bitter end, it held on to that position, while at the same time, in alliance with the liberal Progressive Party and the Catholic Center Party, it tried to move the government to negotiate peace terms. That policy failed miserably. Germany became dominated by an officer corps increasingly reckless and increasingly removed from the reality of Germany's weak military position. With the country ruled under martial law, the government and the military did not shy away from active repression. Luxemburg and Liebknecht were only the most prominent socialists who spent a good part of the war years in prison. Striking workers were often sent directly to the front. As fearful as that measure was, it failed to stem the tide of protest in the factories and the mines, as well as in marketplaces and the streets, where women played the decisive role in the burgeoning protest movement.

The SPD's support for the war cost it dearly. A significant segment of the working class became alienated from the party, and its international reputation as the bastion of socialism and the hope for the future lay in tatters. In January 1916, a small group of radicals around Luxemburg and Liebknecht began distributing clandestine anti-war, socialist tracts. Known as the *Spartacist Letters*, the writers, printers and distributors gradually became known as the Spartacist group, and they would form the core of the KPD. In 1917, other dissident socialists, dismayed by their party's continued support of the war, organized the Independent Social Democratic Party (USPD), and the Spartacists joined it though retained their status as an autonomous group.

Four years into the war, in late summer and early autumn 1918, the Supreme High Command, the military leadership and effectively the dictatorial authority in the country, finally recognized that the war was lost. The military turned power over to a civilian government, setting the stage for the infamous stab-in-the-back legend, namely, that the German military had been victorious but was betrayed at home by Jews and socialists.

Kaiser Wilhelm II named a new chancellor, Prince Max von Baden, who took office on 3 October 1918. Prince Max formed a coalition government that, for the first time in German history, included social democrats. It began the process of democratization, which included the release from prison of many radical socialists. They streamed back home and to Berlin, the capital city.

At the same time, the government initiated contacts with the United States. President Woodrow Wilson proved more intractable than the Germans had imagined. The USA demanded an immediate ceasefire and withdrawal of all German forces to Germany's 1914 borders. German troops had been stuck at more or less the same line on the western front since autumn 1914. In the East, however, they were far into Russian territory, an occupation legitimized, in their eyes, by the Treaty of Brest-Litovsk that Germany had forced upon the young Bolshevik regime.

On 29 October 1918, sailors at the naval port of Kiel mutinied. They had been ordered to stoke the ships' boilers. Everyone knew that the war was coming to a close. The sailors did not know whether their officers were going to attempt one last battle or whether they were going to scuttle the ships, forcing collective suicide upon the sailors in some last-minute heroics. The sailors would have none of it. They refused, quickly seized control of the ships, and formed a council (*sovet* in Russian), the institution that would be at the heart of the German Revolution of 1918–19. SPD leaders rushed to Kiel to try to calm the situation; sailors rushed home, and on the way spread the word of revolution. In towns and cities throughout Germany, workers and soldiers formed councils, creating a grassroots, rough-and-tumble form of democracy. The mass meeting was the typical expression of council democracy. It usually led to a set of demands involving an end to the war, socialization of industry and a council democracy (whatever that meant specifically). It also entailed rough action against particularly hated foremen or officers, who might find themselves thrown onto a garbage heap, down a mine shaft, or into a river, or worse.

Under the press of revolution, Prince Max, after only one month in office, resigned. Tens of thousands had gathered in demonstrations in Berlin; tens of thousands more were marching on the capital city. The Revolutionary Shop Stewards and other groups were planning a revolution. On 9 November 1918, Prince Max turned power over to the social democrats under Friedrich Ebert. The Kaiser abdicated and went into exile. From the balcony of the Reichstag building, SPD leader Philipp Scheidemann proclaimed the German republic. A few hundred meters away, Liebknecht proclaimed a socialist republic, the two divergent proclamations capturing the conflicts that would ensue over the next two years.

Ebert constituted a new government composed of SPD and USPD leaders. It quickly concluded an armistice on 11 November 1918, which at least brought the fighting of World War I to an end. But it was a fateful move. The representatives of the civilian government, not those of the Kaiser and military, signed the armistice. For its entire existence, the Weimar Republic, as it came to be known, would be subject to the slur that it had betrayed Germany.

Ebert issued the slogan, "No experiments!" The government placed primacy on internal order, economic revival, democratization and the conclusion of a final peace treaty, not radical social change. Ebert negotiated with the military, the civilian bureaucracy and industrialists, all of whom were deeply shaken by the specter of revolution. Fearing something worse, namely Bolshevism, the same fear that rippled through the SPD, these forces of conservatism agreed to support the SPD government while the SPD sought to contain the tide of radicalism. The conservatives were biding their time, while the SPD thought it could build on conservative support and move Germany on the road to democracy with broad-based support. It was a fool's bargain on the part of social democrats, because the conservative elites were only making tactical concessions at a moment when their power was threatened.

Luxemburg was released from prison on the day of the German Revolution, 9 November 1919. She quickly made for Berlin and gathered together her small group of comrades. On 11 November, the day of the armistice, they formally constituted themselves as the Spartacist League. Their strategy was, in many ways, quite simple: Push the revolution forward. In contrast to "No experiments!" they called for a radical transformation of German society and support for the Bolshevik Revolution. They demanded a government constituted by the workers' and soldiers' councils and the immediate socialization of industry. Their hostility toward social democracy, articulated with great flourish by Luxemburg, became even more pronounced.

All around the country, councils were formed, even by artists and actors. Workers demanded first the eight-hour, then the seven-hour (six hours in the mines) workday. A national General Congress of Workers' and Soldiers' Councils met in Berlin in mid December. Its demands were moderate, but the meeting raised the specter of a social revolution that went far beyond SPD leaders sitting in the seat of power in the Reich Chancellery.

On 30 December 1918, the Spartacist League, along with members of the Revolutionary Shop Stewards and various other radical groups, gathered in Berlin and formed the Communist Party of Germany. Luxemburg gave the rousing keynote speech, in which she castigated the cowardice of the SPD and placed the KPD in line with Marx and the laws of history, which prescribed a future defined, worldwide, by socialism and communism. Luxemburg said:

> Now, comrades, today . . . we are again at Marx's side, under his banner. When we declare today in our program: The immediate task of the proletariat is nothing less than . . . to make socialism fact and reality, to eliminate capitalism root and branch, then we place ourselves on the same ground on which Marx and Engels stood in 1848 and from which they . . . never diverged.[1]

A sharper contrast to the timid steps of the SPD would be hard to find.

On the eve of the turn into 1919, with Germany as well as other European countries upended by mass strikes and demonstrations, with Bolsheviks in

1 Hermann Weber (ed.), *Der Gründungsparteitag der KPD: Protokoll und Materialien* (Frankfurt am Main: Europäische Verlagsanstalt, 1969), 179.

power in Russia, the confidence of the very small group of radicals who formed the KPD is easily understandable. Yet that confidence brewed a penchant for action and further revolution that was out of line with the sentiments of the vast majority of German workers, let alone the population at large. At best, workers constituted one-third of the German populace. Moreover, civilian bureaucrats remained at their posts, officers in command of the army and industrialists in possession of their properties. Meanwhile, the SPD government was pushing for quick elections – the very mark of democracy, in their eyes – to a constitutional convention. The forces were aligned against German communists, but they could not see the reality.

In the first weeks of January 1919, the situation in Berlin became even more heated. Radical shop stewards and others were planning a second revolution. The SPD was gathering paramilitary and police units to contain radicalism. Liebknecht, never one to shy away from action, threw the weight of the young party behind the revolutionary forces. So began the first of the three failed attempts by the KPD to seize power through revolution. The story told in the KPD for decades afterwards was that when Liebknecht returned to headquarters and told Luxemburg that he had pledged the party's support for immediate revolution – the KPD just two weeks old – she responded, "Karlyusha [the Russian diminutive], Karlyusha, how could you?"

Yet Luxemburg, too, was never one to shy away from a battle. She believed that once radical workers had set the course, the KPD had to support them. The government forces quickly defeated the Spartacist Uprising (a misleading name for a revolution begun by radicals outside the KPD). Liebknecht and Luxemburg went into hiding, but were soon found out and brutally murdered. A fair amount of *Schadenfreude* (malicious pleasure) rippled through the SPD leadership, which had always found the brilliant pair of Luxemburg and Liebknecht an immense bother. They were now gone, and, so it seemed, the work of order, reconstruction and democratization could proceed apace.

In her last article for *Rote Fahne* (Red Flag), the party newspaper, Luxemburg had written:

> "Order rules in Berlin!" You obtuse gendarmes! Your "order" is built on sand. Tomorrow the Revolution will "again climb the heights" and, to your horror, announce with trumpet blasts: *I was, I am, I shall be!*[2]

But it was all wishful thinking.

2 Rosa Luxemburg, "Die Ordnung herrscht in Berlin," *Rote Fahne*, 14 Jan. 1919.

The assassination of its two leaders – and two months later, of Luxemburg's sometime companion Leo Jogiches, a brilliant organizer – had profound consequences for the history of German communism. As much as they fought the SPD, all three were deeply rooted in prewar social democracy (and for Luxemburg and Jogiches, the Polish and Russian parties as well as the German one). They had a much broader field of experience than those who would join the KPD later in the decade and in the 1930s. Along with their experience – writing, orating, organizing, teaching – they had independent intellects and stature. They would have fought the rise of Stalinism and advocated a more independent path toward a German communist future. No doubt they would have lost, the victims either of Stalinism or Nazism or both. But they would have made a different KPD.

Just days after the Spartacist Uprising, Germans went to the polls to elect a Constitutional Assembly. The KPD, over Luxemburg's opposition, had decided not to contest the election. The USPD attracted only 8 percent of the electorate; the SPD won the largest bloc of voters with 38 percent. It formed the Weimar Coalition with the German Democratic Party and the Catholic Center Party. Together they forged the new constitution that would be proclaimed in July 1919. It gave Germans the most liberal, democratic order they had ever experienced. A raucous public sphere had emerged in Germany, and it would not be suppressed despite various executive and emergency powers that both the national and the state (*Länder*) governments retained. The KPD, despite periodic bans and police actions, would be able to publish its newspapers, hold rallies and demonstrations, and run cultural and social organizations. The strong, democratic cast of Weimar gave the KPD the opportunity to move in the public realm, a huge advantage in comparison to communist parties that had to operate under dictatorships, as the KPD would be forced to do in the 1930s.

In spring 1919, alongside successful elections, economic revival and the labor of constitution-writing, virtual civil war raged in the country. Workers were still going out on strike; left-wing paramilitary units began to operate. The right became ever-more active. The SPD government had authorized the formation of the Freikorps, paramilitary formations composed largely of army veterans. In numerous working-class regions and neighborhoods, they, along with the Reichswehr, the regular army, conducted a virtual White Terror, and would do so again in 1920, 1921 and 1923.

That experience also decisively shaped the KPD. From the murders of Luxemburg and Liebknecht onward, communists endured state repression and terror – at the same time that they experienced the openness of a democratic system. The repressive forces they faced were often led by social democrats, and the entire Weimar system was identified with the SPD. Prussia was Germany's largest state. For virtually the entire Weimar period, the Prussian Ministry of the Interior, which ran the major police forces, was led by social democrats. Prussia's Office for the Supervision of Public Order, also directed mainly by SPD members, spied on communist activities and often shut down the KPD press and workers' rallies. Nowhere else in Europe did communists face a police force and a state identified with social democrats. That experience gave German communists a life-long, deep-seated hostility toward the SPD, despite occasional examples of cooperation at the local level.

The other dramatic event in spring 1919 was the negotiation of the Versailles Peace Treaty, which brought World War I to its final conclusion. When Germany's delegates arrived at Versailles in late April 1919, still believing that they would be able to negotiate, they were shocked by the terms of defeat simply delivered to them. And the terms were onerous. Germany lost territory in its east and west and all of its overseas colonies. It had to assume full responsibility for the outbreak of the war – the famous "war guilt clause" – and agree to pay reparations to the Allies, though the amount was not fixed. The uproar in the country was immense. Some called for a revival of hostilities. Ultimately, cooler heads prevailed. Germany's delegates grimaced and signed the Peace Treaty on 28 June 1919.

Once again, it was the representatives of the new, democratic, SPD-led government who signed the terms of defeat, not those who had led Germany into a devastating war. The Weimar Republic would never shake off the stigma that it had sold out Germany. Communists too joined in the attack, hostility to the Versailles Treaty probably the only issue on which all Germans, from extreme left to extreme right, could agree. The discontent and disaffection generated by the Treaty benefited the KPD (and the right even more so).

In 1919, the KPD was a minor party on the edge of the political spectrum. In autumn 1919 it had 106,656 members; in autumn 1920, its numbers had fallen to 66,323.[3] It competed not only with the USPD and SPD, but also with more

3 Hermann Weber, *Die Wandlung des deutschen Kommunismus: Die Stalinisierung der KPD in der Weimarer Republik*, 2 vols. (Frankfurt am Main: Europäische Verlagsanstalt, 1969), vol. I, 362.

radical parties and groups, many of them anarchist or syndicalist oriented. For ten months after the Spartacist Uprising, the government banned the KPD. Paul Levi, Luxemburg's close associate, had assumed the mantle of leadership after her and Liebknecht's killings. Levi sought to build a broad-based left coalition, including social democrats, and to create a German communism that would be supportive of but also independent from the Soviet Union. His efforts were not graced with success.

Meanwhile, Germany's civil war continued through 1919 and 1920. The USPD, long absent from the government, attracted increasing support, largely from workers disenchanted with the moderate policies of the SPD. All around them, workers saw businessmen and managers still in control of factories and mines, old-style officers still ordering around rank-and-file soldiers and holdovers from the Kaiser's time still running state bureaucracies.

In March 1920, army officers and various right-wing forces attempted to overthrow the Weimar government. The event, known as the Kapp Putsch for its leader, Wolfgang Kapp, set off a wave of unrest in Germany. The government fled to Stuttgart, while industrial and public sector workers around the country went on strike. In parts of the country, notably the heavy industrial region of the Ruhr, radical workers organized a Red Army. The KPD leadership, unsure what to do, had to play catch-up, but the party had neither the depth of penetration nor the leadership capacity to assume control of the movement. Meanwhile, regular army and Freikorp units, unable to seize control of the government, went on the attack against the German Red Army and other manifestations of radical revolution. The government, in a state of panic, promised concessions to the unions and to workers generally while it authorized the attacks on radicals. Ultimately, workers faced down the attempted right-wing overthrow of the republic, but the right emerged stronger despite its failure to reach its ultimate goal.

Revolutionary Russia was engaged in its own brutal civil war, one in which the Bolsheviks would eventually triumph, but at enormous cost to the economic and social fabric of the country. As loyal workers fought in the Red Army and others fled cities that could barely feed their populations, the Bolsheviks' base of support deteriorated. The Bolsheviks' openly dictatorial and terrorist politics also caused the party to lose a good deal of the backing it had won in the revolutionary moment of autumn 1917.

The Russian revolutionaries still banked on world revolution to save them from their isolation, and that meant from Germany in particular. In an effort to propel forward the world revolution, the Bolsheviks had organized the Communist International and, in 1920, demanded that all member parties adhere to Bolshevik strictures of organization and ideology. What Lenin had accomplished in the Russian Social Democratic and Labour Party before World War I, he now sought to accomplish on the global scale: Create parties of disciplined revolutionaries, hierarchically organized and ideologically pure, all under the aegis of the Bolsheviks, who dominated the Comintern.

All this was enunciated in Lenin's Twenty-One Conditions, issued in July 1920 by the Comintern's Second Congress. The Conditions landed like a bombshell on the German left. Huge debates broke out in the USPD and the KPD, while the SPD watched with a good deal of glee, believing and hoping that in the conflict, the radical left would destroy itself. In some ways, the controversy over the Twenty-One Conditions represented democracy in action, as rank-and-file workers as well as party leaders wrote, rallied and debated the issue. Should a German communist party remain independent of Moscow, follow its own traditions, less disciplined, less hierarchical, more democratic? Or did the future really lie to the east, in Bolshevik Russia? If so, that meant getting on board with Bolshevik ideas and tactics, and the Bolshevik way of organizing the party.

The stakes were high when the USPD convened for its party congress in October 1920. High-level Bolsheviks, Mensheviks in exile and socialists from around Europe argued for and against the Bolshevik model. Ultimately, a majority of the USPD voted for adhesion to the Comintern along the lines of the Twenty-One Conditions. In December, the USPD and KPD merged. The KPD became a mass party through an acquisition, the smaller of the two fish, the KPD, absorbing the larger fish, the USPD. The United KPD (as it was called for a year) could now claim over 350,000 members, strong positions in the unions, and representation in the Reichstag as well as in numerous state parliaments.

For some on the German left, the unification marked a moment of joy. Finally, the KPD had become a party of consequence, one anointed to lead the next step of world revolution. For others, who sought, and ultimately failed, to maintain the USPD as an independent party, the conference was an utter disaster, a very public act of subservience to the Russians, the advocates of terror and discipline.

The question for the KPD was, as always: how to make that revolution in Germany? Essentially two tendencies emerged, neither of them particularly fixed and stable. Those who had been closely allied with Luxemburg and

Liebknecht, predominantly intellectuals and skilled workers, believed that party first had to build mass support before it could stage a revolution. The key figures here were Heinrich Brandler and August Thalheimer. More radical elements were constantly pushing for a revolution sooner rather than later, if not today then tomorrow. Notable figures here were Ruth Fischer, Arkadii Maslow, Karl Radek and, for a time, Ernst Thälmann, though his ideological and strategic predilections would change over time. The internal arguments were vociferous. Far from the disciplined party imagined in the Twenty-One Conditions, the KPD was wracked by internal conflict.

The working-class uprising in reaction against the Kapp Putsch had been beyond the direction and influence of the KPD. But since the merger with the USPD, the KPD was now a stronger party, and it made two more attempts to seize power through violence. In March 1921, yet another wave of worker unrest broke out, largely in the industrial region of Prussian Saxony, with Halle-Merseburg at its core. The argument between the two tendencies within the party reached fever pitch. The left radicals argued that the uprising was the sign of revolution for which they had all been waiting. The party, in good Leninist fashion, now had to give direction to an inchoate rebellion and move toward the seizure of power in Germany.

Yet this stance was shot through with illusions about the balance of forces in the country. The organized working class constituted a minority of the population, radical workers a small sliver of that. Germany had, of course, a far more developed and complex society than Russia had had in 1917. The forces of order, including the SPD, were far more powerful than anything the KPD could muster – as the more moderate wing in the party reiterated time and again. The inevitable disaster ensued, with a White Terror against workers in Prussian Saxony and elsewhere.

The defeat made the conflicts in the party even more virulent. Those convinced that the times were revolutionary argued that it was only the failure of the party leadership to be more decisive that had led to the defeat. Brandler, Thalheimer and others argued that the time had not been right, the party still too weak and isolated to stage a revolution.

In 1921, the disputes no longer remained an internal affair. The heavy hand of the Russian comrades came down on the KPD leadership. Various German communists were dragged to Moscow to explain their actions and defend themselves. The Bolshevik Party, soon to be named Russian Communist Party and then CPSU, was also mired in factional conflicts, which became worse as Lenin suffered a series of strokes and became largely incapacitated. The Russians would not yet intervene dramatically in the German party, but their presence and power could be felt.

All these issues were revived in 1923, the year of the German hyperinflation. French and Belgian forces had moved into the Ruhr because Germany, their governments claimed, had reneged on its reparations obligations. The German government declared a policy of passive resistance. Step by step, the industrial economy shut down while the government printed money in a vain effort to keep things afloat. Another round of misery ensued for the German population, especially the middle class and skilled workers, who saw whatever savings they had evaporate. Inflation on this scale, with prices for basic commodities like bread and shoes changing on an hourly basis, made everyone feel insecure and deprived them of the ability to plan their lives.

Now even the more moderate wing of the KPD began to believe that the time had come for a revolution in Germany. Brandler as party leader shuttled back and forth to Moscow. The Russian comrades, Trotsky in particular, advised the Germans to follow their recipe, even to the extent of choosing an October date that mimicked the Bolshevik Revolution. Through the summer and early autumn, as conditions in the country continued to deteriorate, the KPD leadership, with their Russian advisors, plotted revolution.

Inevitably, the effort failed. Individuals who were supposed to take over key institutions of power – army barracks, postal stations, banks – faltered. Hamburg communists jumped the gun, allowing the forces of order to pick them off. The entire effort to create a German October proved a fiasco.

Now the Russians moved decisively. They forced the removal of the Brandler–Thalheimer leadership and placed, in their stead, the radical left of Fischer and Maslow.[4]

The two intellectuals gave a shrill tone to German communism, which only further isolated the party. Their belief that radical agitation would inspire ever greater numbers to take up the cry of revolution, and that only the pusillanimous actions of Brandler and Thalheimer were to blame for the failure of the German October, was increasingly removed from reality, especially as a general exhaustion with social upheaval and defeat set in among workers.

4 See Mario Kessler, *Ruth Fischer: Ein Leben mit und gegen Kommunisten (1895–1961)* (Vienna, Cologne and Weimar: Böhlau, 2013).

In fact, in 1924, the forces of order triumphed. The government managed to get the inflation under control and negotiated a withdrawal of the French and Belgian troops in return for a regular schedule of reparations payments. American banks agreed to provide loans to Germany. So began the five years of relative stability and economic revival, the so-called Golden Years of the Weimar Republic.

Even the Russians had to admit that the revolutionary wave that had begun in 1917 had receded. Their original hope, that Germany, then other countries, would follow Russia's lead, creating global communism, had proved a chimera. Stalin was consolidating his power within the CPSU and the Soviet state, and had proclaimed that Russia would build "socialism in one country." The times had changed.

As a consequence, the radical leadership of the KPD lasted for little more than a year. The Comintern issued an open letter, condemning Fischer and Maslow for "left-wing communism," drawing on Lenin's pamphlet of the same name with the subtitle, *An Infantile Disorder*. Whiffs of anti-Semitism were evident in the attacks on Fischer, along with more straightforward condemnations of intellectuals (like Fischer, Maslow and others) who had no roots in the working class.

The Soviets turned to Thälmann, a Hamburg worker who had been part of the radical left, and anointed him the leader of the KPD. Thälmann was popular with the party rank and file and loyal to the Soviets. He would twist and turn with changes in Soviet and Comintern strategy over the next years, until his capture and imprisonment by the Nazis in March 1933.

Amid all this turmoil, in German and international communism as well as in German politics and society, the KPD managed to build a significant party and movement. The Zentrale (essentially what was known in other parties and subsequently in German communism as the Politburo) made critical decisions in consultation with the Soviets, sent out agents to the local organizations to check up on things, and chose party members who would stand for elections. But the essence of party life happened among communist groups in industrial communities and workplaces (very rarely in agrarian villages) around Germany.

With around 300,000 members in the mid 1920s, communists recreated the social-democratic party culture of the prewar years, though in more radical fashion. For committed communists, life revolved around the party. There were constant rounds of meetings and demonstrations to attend, and the party newspaper to hawk on the streets. Local and national elections marked the fever points of activism, as party members agitated in support of KPD candidates, going door-to-door and standing on street corners distributing leaflets and other propaganda material. In the workplace they fought to elect their own people to the works councils and to replace the unions associated with the social democratic, center, or liberal party with their own. For leisure activity, communists formed glee clubs and theater groups, sports teams, hiking and nudist associations, radio and film clubs. The SPD had the exact same kinds of associations, but almost never did communist and socialist hiking associations, for example, go out together into the forests and mountains of Germany. The political divisions on the left ran deeply, down to daily interactions.

The largest communist association was the Red Front Fighters League, formed in 1926. Its members trained in military fashion and sported army-like uniforms, complete with leather jackboots. The Red Front Fighters were given more to street brawls, especially once the Depression hit in 1929, than actual military combat. They gave a decidedly masculine and militaristic temperament to the KPD. The KPD articulated an ideology of women's emancipation, but the top leadership remained overwhelmingly male, and the personal lives of most communists were highly conventional in gender terms. Despite leading articles in the press about "comradely marriages," rare to nonexistent was the male communist who helped out with household labor.

The KPD, like other labor parties, in Germany and elsewhere, opened up a sphere of self-articulation and self-development for ambitious workers, women and men. In the party they learned to express themselves, orally and in print, and how to organize, a vital skill that developed only after a great deal of experience agitating among workers. They lived lives of commitment, firmly engaged in forging a new world that, they believed, would be equitable and democratic, and far less worrisome and grievous than their present existence. Their world broadened far beyond the neighborhood, factory and mine. Delegations traveled to the Soviet Union to experience communism first hand. *Rote Fahne*, the party newspaper, contained a great deal of propaganda castigating everyone but communists, but it also linked Germans workers' struggles around the globe. The *Arbeiter-Illustrierte-Zeitung* (Workers' Illustrated Magazine), developed by the KPD's propaganda genius, Willi Münzenberg, proved highly successful. Even more than *Rote Fahne*, it provided a window onto a larger world. Its lively, interesting and highly professional photos and photomontages were especially popular.

The KPD attracted numerous intellectuals as well, whether as formal members or as fellow travelers. Bertolt Brecht, Karl Korsch, Ernst Bloch, Walter Benjamin and many others moved in and around the party. They lent an air of intellectual and cultural sophistication to the KPD. But especially after 1925, when Thälmann was placed at its head, the KPD had a decidedly proletarian character, a source of attraction to some workers but also a feature that profoundly limited the party's appeal.

Through the latter half of the 1920s, when the situation in Germany had stabilized, the KPD could do little to break out beyond a core number of members and voters. The actual membership was notably unstable. People came and went; the overall number stayed around the same.

The mid and late 1920s was also the era of rationalization, when German firms began applying in earnest technical and managerial innovations designed to increase productivity. Economically the results were decidedly uneven; socially, rationalization led to a very high level of structural unemployment even before the onset of the Great Depression in 1929. Communists were disproportionately affected, in part because managers used the lower demand for workers to rid the workplace of KPD members, in part because overall, communists were less skilled than SPD members. Of course, there remained numerous skilled workers in the KPD ranks. In some firms and industrial regions, communists still made up a significant proportion of the workforce, as in Halle-Merseburg. However, overall and even before 1929, the KPD was becoming a party of the unemployed.

This trend had profound effects on the politics of German communism. In general terms – again, with numerous local exceptions – employment created a more deliberate, less adventuresome politics among party activists. Communists who held on to their jobs were continually involved in their unions and works councils. They sought to improve the daily working conditions and wages of the workforce. They were less inclined to see a revolution brewing every day, less willing to engage in rebellions and street battles that were doomed to failure.

The unemployed had no such options, especially when they lacked jobs for months and years on end. Their venue of activism became the streets, not the workplace. In the streets they marched, demonstrated and engaged in hit-and-run brawls with the police and various political antagonists, including social democrats but also, especially after 1928, the Nazis. The primacy was on action, sometimes with brass knuckles, knives, clubs and revolvers. These involvements intensified the radicalism and the masculine character of the KPD. However far-fetched it seems in hindsight, for communists around 1930, it was possible to see these street battles as preparation for revolution. As one communist pamphlet ran, "every street demonstration should accustom workers to struggles against ... state power."[5] This kind of activism garnered support from a slice of the working class, now essentially an unemployed underclass, and further alienated social-democratic workers from the KPD. The great divide between the two parties of the left turned into an unbridgeable chasm, especially since the police with whom communists came into conflict were so often commanded by social democrats.

The intensifying radicalism of the KPD, rooted in the social, economic and political history of the Weimar Republic, happened to move in tandem with developments in the Soviet Union and the Comintern. At the end of 1928, with his power now nearly secure, Stalin launched the forced collectivization and rapid industrialization policies that would mark the Soviet Union until the outbreak of World War II. Stalin's war against the peasantry necessitated the full mobilization of the CPSU and the Red Army. One cannot really compare KPD street battles with the systematic transformation of an entire society under Stalin. But the tenor and temperament of both parties was similar. Radical action, not deliberation, negotiations and compromise, was the order of the day for the KPD as it was for the CPSU.

At the same moment, the Comintern also underwent a radical shift. Its progenitor was none other than the "rightist" Nikolai Bukharin, who identified a "third period," the onset of capitalism's final crisis.[6] The outbreak of the Great Depression seemed to vindicate his analysis. If capitalism was in its death-throes, then the task for communists was to accelerate the process. The times called for decisive action by the communist bearers of the future order. No compromises, no collaboration with social democrats. The party had pierced the truth of history, and all that remained was for it to demonstrate that truth to other workers who would see the light and, in the German case, join the KPD and push capitalism to its final demise.

In this context, the Thälmann leadership, prompted by the CPSU and the Comintern, carried out a purge of the moderates, the so-called rightists and

5 Quotation in Eric D. Weitz, *Creating German Communism, 1890–1990: From Popular Protests to Socialist State* (Princeton: Princeton University Press, 1997), 160.

6 See Nicholas N. Kozlov and Eric D. Weitz, "Reflections on the Origins of the 'Third Period': Bukharin, the Comintern, and the Political Economy of Weimar Germany," *Journal of Contemporary History* 24, 3 (1989), 387–410.

"conciliators" in the party. Brandler and Thalheimer, in the shadows since the defeat of the party uprising in 1923, were now formally expelled from the KPD. The action also virtually destroyed the last communist presence in the workplace, since union and works council leaders tended to be allied with the more moderate wing of the party. The living links to the Luxemburg–Liebknecht heritage were largely severed by the internal purge.

Under Thälmann, the KPD became ever more authoritarian, ever more Stalinist in tone, ever more subject to Soviet directives. But never was the KPD a mere mirror of the CPSU. It was always shaped as much by German developments as by the Soviet model.

In Germany, however, it was the Nazis, not the communists, who reaped the fruits of the great crisis spawned by the Depression. From a marginal party in 1928, the National Socialist German Workers' Party (NSDAP) quickly rose to become a powerful movement. Increasingly, communists and Nazis fought in streets and taverns all over Germany, creating a sense of unease and instability – a deliberate strategy executed by both parties, each of which believed that the future lay exclusively in its hands.

The Nazi wave reached its peak in July 1932, when the NSDAP garnered 37 percent of the vote in a national election. In the succeeding electoral campaign in November 1932, its tally declined to 33 percent. It was saved from the political wilderness by a group of bankers, businessmen, estate owners, army officers and high-level state officials, who prevailed upon President Paul von Hindenburg to name Adolf Hitler chancellor of Germany.

On 30 January 1933, torchlight-bearing Nazis paraded around the country, celebrating Hitler's assumption of power. For communists, the consequences were quick and severe. Until the very end of the Third Reich, they were a hunted, persecuted political minority. Quickly, communists were rounded up and herded into jails and the first concentration camps. Many were tortured. Others went underground or fled into exile. Thälmann himself was caught and imprisoned for eleven years, only to be executed by the Nazis in 1944. By 1945, fully half of the roughly 300,000 party members had endured Nazi jails and concentration camps. Some 20,000 German communists were killed by the Nazis, many under the most brutal circumstances.[7]

Communists in the underground managed for a few years to write, print and distribute anti-Nazi leaflets and other printed materials, some smuggled

7 Horst Duhnke, *Die KPD von 1933 bis 1945* (Cologne: Kiepenheuer & Witsch, 1972), 104, 525.

in from the nearby places of exile like the Netherlands and Czechoslovakia. A few engaged in acts of sabotage, especially during the war years. All to no avail. By 1936, the Nazis' powerful repressive apparatus had essentially destroyed the KPD in Germany. A few communist resistance cells continued to function or were born anew during the war years. The famous Red Orchestra, the work of a handful of individuals, dispatched military intelligence to the Soviet Union. Virtually every one of these groups was uncovered by the Gestapo and its members tortured and executed.

Still, communists harbored illusions. As late as 1937 and 1938, some communists still believed that Nazi rule was highly tenuous, that one way or another, the NSDAP would fall from power, and the KPD would be the next in line in the halls of German state power.

It was not to be. Nazi racism and the revival of the economy exercised a powerful attraction on workers. The worldview of German communists, however, remained largely unchanged, chiefly a function of their experiences in the Weimar Republic. The French and Italian communist parties developed into mass parties under the Popular and National Front policies of the 1930s and 1940s, which meant coalitions with socialist, liberals, and even, during the war years, conservative nationalists.[8] Not so the KPD. It had become a mass party in the Weimar Republic and in direct, sometimes brutal conflict with the SPD. Despite the Comintern shift to the popular front strategy, German exile communists in Paris, the future leader Walter Ulbricht chief among them, torpedoed any effort to create such an anti-Nazi alliance among Germans of various political leanings. Only a few communists who had gone further into exile in the West, like Paul Merker in Mexico, began a fundamental reevaluation of KPD politics and sought to construct a broad, anti-Nazi alliance that would, they hoped, lay the groundwork for a postwar socialist and progressive Germany.[9]

Meanwhile, the roughly 2,000 German communists who had gone into exile in the Soviet Union also faced a tragic destiny. About 60 percent were caught up in the Stalinist terror and killed in the Soviet Union.[10] Others

8 See Eric D. Weitz, *Popular Communism: Political Strategies and Social Histories in the Formation of the German, French, and Italian Communist Parties, 1919–1948* (Ithaca: Cornell University Institute for European Studies, 1992).

9 See Jeffrey Herf, *Divided Memory: The Nazi Past in the Two Germanys* (Cambridge, MA: Harvard University Press, 1997).

10 Hermann Weber, "Aufstieg und Niedergang des deutschen Kommunismus," *Aus Politik und Zeitgeschichte* 40 (27 Sep. 1991), 29, and Duhnke, *Die KPD von 1933 bis 1945*, 348, n. 175.

survived torture and the Gulag, some still as convinced communists. All told, almost 40 percent of the functionary corps of 1932 were dead by 1945, the vast majority victims of the Nazi or Soviet dictatorships.[11]

Others were trained for the return to Germany in the company of the Red Army, to serve as the administrators of the Soviet occupation and the future leaders of what would become, in 1949, the German Democratic Republic (GDR). With few exceptions, all of them were Weimar veterans. Throughout the history of the GDR, that experience, along with their experience in the Soviet Union, had taught them that social democrats were as much the enemy as the Nazis; that democracy and Nazism were simply two forms of capitalism, both of which had to be fought; and that the future lay with a disciplined party devoted to the Soviet Union and a communist future as communism had become defined through the Bolshevik and Stalinist Revolutions. The Weimar experience of German communism resonated until the very demise of the GDR in 1989–90.

Bibliographical Essay

The first history of the KPD was written by Ossip K. Flechtheim, a former member who went on to a distinguished academic career in postwar West Germany. *Die KPD in der Weimarer Republik* [1949] (Frankfurt am Main: Europäische Verlagsanstalt, 1969) is still worth reading. In the same year as Flechtheim's book was reprinted, Hermann Weber published *Die Wandlung des deutschen Kommunismus: Die Stalinisierung der KPD in der Weimarer Republik*, 2 vols. (Frankfurt am Main: Europäische Verlagsanstalt, 1969), an indispensable work and one of his many books and articles on the KPD, its successor, the Socialist Unity Party, and the GDR. However, Weber's emphasis on the Soviet Union as the ultimate source for every development in the history of the KPD is limiting.

In the 1990s a new generation of scholars began emphasizing the social and cultural history of German communism without neglecting its political history. They rooted the development of the KPD in its German as well as its Soviet context. Critical here are Klaus-Michael Mallmann, *Kommunisten in der Weimarer Republik: Sozialgeschichte einer revolutionären Bewegung* (Darmstadt: Wissenschaftliche Buchgesellschaft, 1996), and Eric D. Weitz,

11 Hermann Weber, "Die deutschen Kommunisten 1945 in der SBZ," *Aus Politik und Zeitgeschichte* 31 (5 Aug. 1978), 30.

Creating German Communism, 1890–1990: From Popular Protests to Socialist State (Princeton: Princeton University Press, 1997). Pathbreaking in this regard is Eve Rosenhaft, *Beating the Fascists? The German Communists and Political Violence, 1929–1933* (Cambridge: Cambridge University Press, 1983). Atina Grossmann is illuminating on the KPD's involvement in the Depression-era struggle for abortion reform in *Reforming Sex: The German Movement for Birth Control and Abortion Reform, 1920–1950* (New York: Oxford University Press, 1995). Pamela Swett, *Neighbors and Enemies: The Culture of Radicalism in Berlin, 1929–1933* (Cambridge: Cambridge University Press, 2004), is also noteworthy, as is, from a different perspective, Conan J. Fischer, *German Communists and the Rise of Nazism* (New York: St. Martin's Press, 1991).

Much of the literature since the late 1990s has focused on the history of the German Democratic Republic, often with little attention to the party's roots in the Weimar period. Mario Kessler, in contrast, has authored a host of works that cover the long span of the twentieth century. Most concern dissident and exiled communists. Particularly relevant for the Weimar period, but also for the history of the Cold War and the beginnings of the West German New Left, is *Ruth Fischer: Ein Leben mit und gegen Kommunisten (1895–1961)* (Vienna: Böhlau, 2013). J. P. Nettl's biography *Rosa Luxemburg*, 2 vols. (Oxford: Oxford University Press, 1966) is a classic, even if he exaggerates her democratic proclivities. (A one-volume abridged version is available.) Marcel Bois provides a history of the KPD left in *Kommunisten gegen Hitler und Stalin: Die Linke Opposition der KPD in der Weimarer Republik. Eine Gesamtdarstellung* (Essen: Klartext-Verlag, 2014).

The German Left and the Weimar Republic: A Selection of Documents (Leiden: Brill, 2014), translated and edited by Ben Fowkes, is an excellent collection of primary sources, as is, more extensively, Hermann Weber, *Der deutsche Kommunismus: Dokumente 1915–1945* (Cologne and Berlin: Kiepenheuer & Witsch, 1963).

24
The Chinese Communist Movement 1919–1949

ALEXANDER V. PANTSOV

The earliest news on Marxism appeared in the Middle Kingdom toward the very end of the nineteenth century, but until 1919 the overwhelming majority of Chinese intellectuals had been skeptical about the new teaching. Chinese radicals did not believe that Marx's thoughts about the "world historical mission of the working class" were applicable to China. At the time China was extremely backward, and capitalism had not yet made a serious impact on society. There were slightly more than 12 million workers out of a total population of about 400 million. At the same time paupers and the rural underclass, including vagabonds, homeless beggars and other riff-raff, comprised roughly 40–45 million. Peasants constituted the overwhelming majority of the population: over 320 million.

The attitude began changing in 1919 following a popular anti-Japanese movement started on 4 May because of the leading European powers' support of Japan's annexation of the Chinese city Qingdao. Illusions about Western liberalism that thousands of Chinese patriots had shared now evaporated. Just then, about 100,000 workers had taken part in the May 4th movement. Their awakening appeared to those Chinese radicals who were already acquainted with Marxism as a clear affirmation of the truth of Marxist theory.

The more critical factors determining the interest of Chinese public opinion in Marxism were the triumphant character of the October Revolution in Russia, the radically anti-imperialist and anti-capitalist policy of the Soviet government, and the successes of the Soviet Red Army in its struggle against imperialist interventionists and domestic counterrevolutionaries. "With the Russian Revolution, Marxism demonstrated that it was a force that could rock the world," the first Chinese Bolshevik Li Dazhao emphasized in 1919.[1] He was essentially correct.

1 Li Dazhao, *Izbrannye proizvedeniia* (Moscow: Nauka, 1989), 204.

Patriotic Chinese intellectuals began to study the Bolshevik experiment, searching for a theory they could use as a lever to move China. Marxism, in essence, began to be disseminated and accepted in China through the prism of the Bolshevik experiment. Many years later the future communist leader Mao Zedong wrote, "It was through the Russians that the Chinese found Marxism . . . Follow the path of the Russians – that was their conclusion."[2]

The Founding of the Chinese Communist Party

The Russian communists were also deeply interested in developing the Chinese communist movement. They promoted worldwide revolution and for this purpose in March 1919 set up in Moscow an organization to unite and coordinate the efforts of all radical revolutionary parties that adopted Bolshevik principles. It was the Communist International (Comintern). In April 1920, a group of Bolsheviks headed by Grigorii Voitinskii arrived in China. Voitinskii met Li Dazhao and then another radical, Chen Duxiu, the editor of the popular journal *Xin qingnian* (New Youth). It was decided to make use of *Xin qingnian* as a tributary for the dissemination of communist ideas with the objective of uniting all radical revolutionary forces around the journal. In May 1920 Chen and Voitinskii established the Revolutionary Bureau, which began working to create party circles. On 19 July 1920, a meeting of the most active comrades took place in Shanghai at which it was decided to organize a communist cell. Chen Duxiu became its secretary. In September 1920, Chen and Voitinskii organized a so-called School of Foreign Languages for socialist-minded youth who wanted to study in Moscow. Voitinskii supplied graduates with funding to pay for their travel to Russia.

In October a Beijing communist group headed by Li Dazhao was formed, and by the summer of 1921, there were already six communist cells in China. In addition to Shanghai and Beijing, there were also party groups in Changsha, Canton, Wuhan and Jinan. A tiny cell was also organized in Japan. Chen Duxiu circulated a letter to all these organizations to set "an agenda for a [united] conference as well as a time and place."[3] Shanghai was chosen as the venue.

2 Mao Tse-tung, *Selected Works of Mao Tse-tung*, vol. IV (Beijing: Foreign Languages Press, 1969), 413.

3 M. L. Titarenko et al. (eds.), *VKP(b), Komintern i Kitai: Dokumenty*, vol. I (Moscow: AO "Buklet," 1994), 27.

In June 1921, two new Comintern representatives, Hendricus Maring and Vladimir Neiman, arrived in China. Their assignment included helping the Chinese Bolsheviks with running this conference. By 23 July, the twelve delegates assembled. Maring and Neiman were present along with a special representative from Chen Duxiu who was not in Shanghai at this time. Among the delegates was Mao Zedong.

The congress opened on 23 July and discussed the Program of the Chinese Communist Party (CCP), the Decision About the Objectives of the CCP, and the Manifesto that called for an immediate socialist revolution and the dictatorship of the proletariat in China.[4]

The delegates endorsed the isolationist position toward other Chinese political parties, including such a national revolutionary organization as the Guomindang, headed by the first provisional president of the Republic of China, Sun Yat-sen. This demonstrates how great was their desire to declare their ideological and organizational autonomy.

Even Maring and Neiman were giddy with revolutionary fervor. The former tried to explain that there are many different kinds of national democrats, and to bolster his point of view he cited the basic resolutions on the national and colonial questions adopted at the Second Comintern Congress (July–August 1920).

At that Congress Lenin set forth his special theory of the anti-colonial revolutions in Asian and African countries given that the majority of intellectuals in the East adhered to ideas of nationalism, rather than the abstract idea of internationalism as their countries were in colonial or semi-colonial dependence on the West. Consequently, revolutions in the East, including in China, in Lenin's view, would be nationalist, not socialist, in nature. In the course of these revolutions, the local communists were obligated to support the bourgeois liberation movements of their colonial and dependent nations. Elucidating this concept from the tribunal of the Second Comintern Congress, Lenin emphasized the temporary character of the new course and underlined its purely tactical character.[5]

Maring tried to convey all of this to the delegates in Shanghai, but his speech had no effect whatsoever upon them. The first adherents of communism in China found it extraordinarily difficult to understand the need simultaneously to grasp the theory of class conflict of the proletariat against the bourgeoisie and the concept of anti-imperialist cooperation.

4 See C. Martin Wilbur (ed.), *The Communist Movement in China: An Essay Written in 1924 by Ch'en Kung-po* (New York: Columbia University Press, 1960), 106.

5 See V. I. Lenin, *Selected Works*, vol. X (New York: International Publishers, 1943), 231–44.

On 31 July, the participants in the forum held the last meeting in the small town Jiaxing near Shanghai to adopt the Program, the Decision About the Objectives of the CCP, and a Manifesto, all in ultra-revolutionary versions. Then they unanimously selected Chen Duxiu as secretary of the Central Bureau of the party. (In 1922 the position of secretary was changed to chairman of the Central Executive Committee [CEC], and in 1925 was renamed general secretary of the CEC.) At the time the CCP numbered fifty-three members.

The CCP and the United National Front

In late 1921, Maring, ignoring the resolutions of the CCP Congress, set off for South China to gauge the prospects for organizing an anti-imperialist united front between the CCP and Sun Yat-sen. At the end of December 1921 he met with Dr. Sun in Guilin in Guangxi province.

Maring was impressed with Sun who achieved great results in protecting the workers' movement. The Comintern envoy concluded that the CCP should enter the Guomindang. He figured that that would make it easier for the CCP to forge ties with the workers and soldiers of South China where power was in the hands of Sun's supporters. It went without saying, Maring emphasized, that the CCP did not have to "give up its independence, on the contrary, the comrades must together decide which tactics they should follow within the KMT [Guomindang] ... The prospects for propaganda by the small groups [of communists], as long as they are not linked to the KMT, are dim," he resolved.[6]

Maring's initiative was approved by Sun Yat-sen who assured the Comintern representative that he would not obstruct communist propaganda inside his own party. At the end of April 1922, Maring left for Moscow to inform the Executive Committee of the Comintern (ECCI). Shortly thereafter, in July 1922, in Shanghai the Chinese communists held their Second Congress that passed over in silence Maring's earlier suggestion about the entry into the Guomindang. By that time the party had grown to 175 members.

In the middle of the next month Maring returned to China. He brought with him an instruction written by the secretary of the ECCI Karl Radek, which wholly supported his initiative. It emphasized that the CCP should

6 Tony Saich, *The Origins of the First United Front in China: The Role of Sneevliet (alias Maring)*, vol. I (Leiden: Brill, 1991), 323.

preserve its complete independence within the Guomindang and remain there only until such time as it developed into a mass political organization. The second paper was a directive from Voitinskii who was now the head of the Far Eastern Department of the ECCI. It stated flatly, "The Central Committee of the Communist party of China according to the decision of the Presidium of Comintern of July 18 must . . . do all its work in close contact with Comr. PHILIPP."[7] (This was one of Maring's many pseudonyms.)

At Maring's request, the members of the CEC of the party all got together for a meeting on 29 August. It was convened in Hangzhou. The participants rented a boat and for the next two days, with time off for eating and sleeping, they sailed on the picturesque West Lake situated at the edge of the city. The meeting was stormy and dramatic. All of the members of the CEC present at the meeting opposed the proposal of the Comintern agent who peremptorily demanded the implementation of the ECCI resolutions. Finally, Maring threatened to expel the dissidents from the Communist International demanding that those assembled submit to Comintern discipline.[8]

The CCP was wholly dependent upon Moscow, which demanded one thing only – absolute obedience. The expenditures of the communists were constantly growing, and if, at the beginning of 1921, they amounted to only 200 Chinese dollars, by the end of the year they had reached almost 18,000 dollars![9] In 1922 the Chinese communists were unable to scrape together any money at all while they had to receive 15,000 dollars from Moscow by the end of the year.[10] The Kremlin funded not only Chen Duxiu, whose monthly payment was 30 yuan, but also the regional party organizations. So the party was not in a position to demur. Reconsidering their position, the participants in the meeting came to the only reasonable conclusion: They unanimously voted to enter the Guomindang.

Sun Yat-sen approved of this decision and in early September 1922 received the first four communists including Chen Duxiu and Li Dazhao into the ranks of his party. On 1 January 1923, he published a declaration concerning the reorganization of the Guomindang. The next day a meeting was convened in Shanghai on Guomindang affairs and the party program and statutes were

7 Ibid., 327.

8 See Wang Jianmin, *Zhongguo gongchandang shigao*, vol. I (Taipei: The Author, 1965), 94.

9 See Saich, *The Origins of the First United Front in China*, vol. I, 53.

10 See Yang Kuisong, "Obshchaia kharakteristika otnoshenii mezhdu VKP(b) (KPSS), Kominternom i KPK do 1949 goda," *Problemy Dal'nego Vostoka* 6 (2004), 103.

published. In these documents Sun laid special stress on anti-imperialism, on defense of the rights of workers, and on the democratic transformation of China.

Shortly thereafter, in June 1923, the Chinese communists held their Third Congress in Canton, the location of Sun's headquarters. The Congress backed the policy of entrism. The forty delegates represented 420 members of the CCP. Since the Second Congress the party had more than doubled in size.

In early October 1923, the main political advisor to Sun Yat-sen, Mikhail Borodin, arrived in Canton. Simultaneously he served as the Comintern's new envoy to the CEC of the CCP. Following Borodin other Soviet political and military advisors arrived to serve in Sun's government of South China.

In January 1924, Sun held a Unification Congress of the Guomindang in Canton. There were 165 delegates present at the sessions. Of these, twenty-three were CCP members or almost 14 percent. Chen Duxiu, Li Dazhao and Mao Zedong were among the most active participants. The overwhelming majority of the participants in the Congress voted for the entry of communists into the Guomindang. Ten communists were chosen for the CEC of the Guomindang, which consisted of forty-one individuals.

Li Dazhao and two other communists became full members of the CEC. One communist, Tan Pingshan, even became a member of the highest organ of the party – the Standing Committee (Politburo). Mao Zedong and six other communists were chosen as candidate members of the CEC.

The cooperation between two parties progressed steadily. The Fourth CCP Congress, which took place in Shanghai in January 1925, confirmed the policy of entrism. Very few of the twenty delegates, who represented 994 members of the party, dared to utter any protest. In the meantime, Sun with the help of the Soviet advisors was making preparations for the Northern Expedition from Canton to unite China that had been in a state of constant feud between various militarists since 1916. However, in the midst of the preparations Sun died on 12 March 1925. He did not die in Canton, but in Beijing where he had gone to take part in a peace conference to unify the country. At the time peaceful unification seemed feasible.

After Sun's death a struggle for power erupted within the Guomindang among the supporters of various factions, but by the middle of the summer 1925 the leftists triumphed. The leader of the Guomindang leftists, Wang Jingwei, who was one of Sun's closest collaborators, became the leader of the

Guomindang and head of the Canton government, which on 1 July 1925 was named the National Government.

These events made Stalin change the CCP united front policy. From now on the CCP should use its sojourn within the Guomindang not only to transform itself into a mass political organization but also to radically transform the Guomindang by having Wang Jingwei's leftists and communists totally oust "representatives of the bourgeoisie" from leading posts and then purge them from the Guomindang. Stalin now wanted to transform the Guomindang itself into as "leftist" a party as possible, into a "people's (worker–peasant) party."

In essence, such a conception of a united front was purely bureaucratic, based almost entirely on armchair calculations about the balance of forces in the Guomindang. As someone extremely skilled in intra-party intrigues, Stalin must have been convinced of the inevitable success of his policy as he was occupied at this time with getting rid of his chief antagonists – Trotsky, Zinoviev and Kamenev – from the leadership of the Bolshevik party. However, this policy could not be effective in China, which was consumed by the flames of nationalist revolution. Unlike the degraded Russian Communist Party, the Guomindang was a revolutionary party and the anti-communist military faction within it was popular not only in the officer corps, but also among significant segments of Chinese society. It was simply impossible to squeeze the members of the group out of their own political organization.

The Chinese communists objectively were the hostages of Stalin's line. They were unable not to accept it for, as we have seen, they were totally dependent upon Soviet financial assistance. However, it was likewise impossible to implement the orders to communize the Guomindang without risking a rupture of the united front. Judging by the reminiscences of one CCP leader Zhang Guotao, a majority of the CCP leaders eventually understood this, and therefore were compelled to maneuver, bluff and twist about.[11] But this did not always help, and the only possible outcome was defeat.

A serious warning to the CCP was the outburst of anti-communist emotion on the part of the commander of the First Corps of the Guomindang National Revolutionary Army (NRA), Chiang Kai-shek, that took place in Canton on 20 March 1926. He arrested a number of communists and sent

11 See Chang Kuo-t'ao, *The Rise of the Chinese Communist Party, 1921–1927: Volume One of the Autobiography of Chang Kuo-t'ao* (Lawrence: University Press of Kansas, 1971), 484–85.

troops to surround the residences of the Soviet military advisors. The incident ended peacefully. Three Soviet military advisors had to leave Canton, and Chiang freed the arrested. On his part, it was just a demonstration of power. In consequence the position not only of the communists but also of the Guomindang leftists grouped around Wang Jingwei, was significantly weakened. Chiang became the commander-in-chief of the NRA and in July 1926 started the Northern Expedition.

The united front, however, survived. The communists retreated for a few months, but in late 1926–early 1927 they resumed their attempts to seize power within the Guomindang. In the areas occupied by the NRA they also stirred up the paupers, the rural lumpenproletariat and the poor clans against the wealthier peasantry. As a result, "class organizations" in the countryside grew like mushrooms after rain. If in July 1926 there were 400,000 members of various peasant organizations in Hunan, by December the number had grown to more than 1.3 million.[12] In the spring of 1927, in the words of Zhang Guotao, this radical movement reached a "stage of madness."[13] The riff-raff that flocked to these organizations even attacked the relatives of influential Guomindang members and communists.

In early March 1927, Stalin, sensing the coming victory of the CCP sent a directive to Chen Duxiu to "oust the rightist Guomindang members with all vigor."[14] In late March Borodin suggested the Guomindang leftists who grouped in the city of Wuhan should arrest Chiang Kai-shek who was at the front near Shanghai. But it was too late.

At the end of March, Chiang's troops took Shanghai and Nanjing and shortly thereafter, in the early morning of 12 April, Chiang Kai-shek staged an anti-communist *coup d'état*. "[C]ountless people ... died during the purge. It was the bloodthirsty war to eliminate the enemy within," Chiang's secretary recalled.[15]

The communist leadership that had stayed in Shanghai moved to "left" Wuhan. Here they held the Fifth CCP Congress in April–May 1927. This was the largest congress the CCP had held so far with eighty delegates and more

12 See Mao Tse-tung, *Selected Works*, vol. I, 24; Angus W. McDonald, *The Urban Origins of Rural Revolution: Elites and the Masses in Hunan Province, China, 1911–1927* (Berkeley: University of California Press, 1978), 271.

13 Chang, *The Rise of the Chinese Communist Party*, 606.

14 M. L. Titarenko et al. (eds.), *VKP(b), Komintern i Kitai: Dokumenty*, vol. II (Moscow: AO "Buklet," 1996), 632.

15 Ch'en Li-fu, *The Storm Clouds Clear over China: The Memoir of Ch'en Li-fu 1900–1993* (Stanford: Hoover Institution Press, 1994), 62.

than twenty guests. The assembled delegates represented 57,967 members of the party.

Before and after the Congress Stalin continued to bombard Chen Duxiu with his adventurist directives aimed at the seizure of power in the Guomindang. However, on 15 July Wang Jingwei also launched an anti-communist purge in Wuhan. So did other Guomindang leaders and NRA commanders in other parts on China under Guomindang control. The defeat of the CCP and with it the Stalinist line on China became a reality.

The CCP and the Soviet Movement in China

Stalin laid most of the blame for the defeat on the leadership of the CCP. He summoned Chen Duxiu to Moscow but Chen refused to go. In early July he had already given up his post to Qu Qiubai, who had close connections with the Soviet leaders.

Qu, backed by other members of the CCP new leadership, decided to carry out a series of armed ventures in the countryside of Hunan, Hubei, Guangdong and Jiangxi as well as within the Guomindang army. The Comintern also demanded the speedy organization of the armed uprisings.

The first revolt took place on the night of 31 July/1 August among the troops of the NRA quartered in Nanchang, Jiangxi. Party leadership of the uprising was exercised by Zhou Enlai, a leading member of Central Committee (CC). The mutineers, numbering over 20,000 officers and men, took the city, but did not stay there. After two days they left Nanchang for Guangdong to proclaim a new revolutionary government there. In late September–early October 1927, the insurgents, however, suffered a crushing defeat in the region of the port of Swatow (eastern Guangdong) where they had gone to receive arms from the USSR. After this their troops fell to pieces. One of their military leaders, Zhu De, at the head of a detachment of 1,000 men undertook a difficult march to the Guangdong–Jiangxi border.

Shortly thereafter, on 9 September 1927, in northeastern Hunan Mao Zedong raised the so-called Autumn Harvest Uprising of local paupers, poor peasants, soldiers and miners. That also ended in a crushing defeat. Gathering the remnants of his forces, Mao announced his intention of striking through to the south along the Hunan–Jiangxi border in the direction of the high mountainous region of Jinggang (literally "wells and ridges").

In this poor area, far from the provincial administrations of Hunan and Jiangxi, people lived according to their own traditional laws. The economy of the region, in Mao's words, was "still in the age of the mortar and pestle."[16] Most people who lived in the area belonged to dependent, indigent *hakka* (or *kejia*, guest people) clans whose ancestors had settled in this region from other areas at a time when the fertile valleys had already been taken over by local clans (*bendi*, core inhabitants). In China as a whole there were more than 30 million *hakka*, but their clans were scattered throughout a vast territory of southern China from Sichuan in the west to Fujian in the east. The local clans did not give the migrants access to fertile lands, so the *hakka* were forced to live in the hill country that was poorly suited to agriculture. Consequently, from generation to generation they were forced to rent land from the old residents who did not pass up the opportunity to enrich themselves at the expense of the migrants. In general a quarter of the new arrivals had no work. These people either turned to banditry or begged for their living.

Mao began developing the communist movement in this social milieu and had to establish friendly relations with the local bandits. He set up the first Chinese soviet, a communist legislative body in the form of an assembly of poor peasants, paupers and soldiers' deputies. At the end of April 1928, Zhu De's troops reached the Jinggang area and merged with Mao's guerrillas.

In the meantime, in December 1927, the CCP organized an armed uprising in Canton. This action, known to history as the Canton Commune, likewise ended in defeat. Only through a lucky accident was Ye Ting, the military leader of the uprising, able to flee.

The White Terror and the adventurist policy of uprisings in general exacted a heavy price from the communist party. By the end of 1927 it had lost about four-fifths of its membership. The numbers dropped from almost 58,000 to 10,000. Because of the White Terror in China, the Comintern convened the Sixth CCP Congress in the USSR, in Pervomaiskoe, a village in Moscow province. It took place in June–July 1928. Of the 118 delegates who came to the Congress eighty-four were full delegates and thirty-four were alternates.

Mao and Zhu De were not among them. At the time they were promoting radical socioeconomic reforms in the Jinggang area. By the late autumn of

16 Stuart R. Schram (ed.), *Mao's Road to Power: Revolutionary Writings 1912–1949*, vol. III (Armonk, NY: M. E. Sharpe, 1995), 109.

1928, all land in the region had been confiscated and redistributed. This kind of rough-and-ready redistribution, of course, evoked resistance on the part of many people. It was not only the landlords who had no taste for egalitarianism, but also the great mass of the peasantry, first of all the peasant proprietors who belonged to the wealthier native clans. Most of them fled. The result was that practically all markets shut down. It became necessary to introduce requisitioning of daily necessities including salt, cloth, medicines and many other commodities. However, despite the terror, the problem of acquiring provisions remained acute.

This fundamentally anti-peasant policy finally led to a profound crisis. By December 1928, the economic resources of Jinggang were almost completely exhausted. Mao could not stay there any longer.

On 14 January 1929, his troops, numbering barely more than 3,600 men, headed south from Jinggang. Until October 1930, they wandered Jiangxi looting local towns and robbing the rich and *bendi* clans. Finally, they settled down in the mountainous area on the Jiangxi–Fujian–Guangdong border, unofficially called the "Hakka Country." The CC CCP named this territory the Central Soviet Area (CSA).

From late 1927 to 1931 in addition to Mao's Soviet Area, the CCP also organized a number of other soviets. Among them were the western Hubei–Hunan Soviet under He Long, the Hunan–Hubei–Jiangxi Soviet under Peng Dehuai, the Hubei–Henan–Anhui Soviet under Zhang Guotao, the northwestern Guangxi Soviet under Deng Xiaoping and the western Fujian Soviet under Fang Zhimin. Various corps of the Chinese Red Army operated there numbering about 54,000 men.[17]

The party's central leadership, however, worked clandestinely in Shanghai. After the Sixth Congress its general secretary was Xiang Zhongfa, a leader of the workers' movement. To assist Xiang, the ECCI included such major intellectuals as Zhou Enlai and Li Lisan. The funds from Moscow grew steadily. By the 1930s it amounted to millions of rubles and dollars. Under these circumstances the CCP leaders had to listen carefully to the Moscow bosses.

When the Tenth ECCI Plenum (July 1929) clearly pointed to "the symptoms of a new revolutionary upsurge" in the world, identifying "the rightist danger" as the main one in the international communist movement, the CCP leaders wanted to be absolutely certain that this time their Russian

17 See A. M. Grigoriev, *Kommunisticheskaia partiia Kitaia v nachal'noi period sovetskogo dvizheniia (iul' 1927g.–sentiabr' 1931g.)* (Moscow: IDV AN SSSR Press, 1976), 338.

bosses would not find fault with them. The New York stock market crash (October 1929) exacerbated the situation. It seemed that the inevitable downfall of world capitalism was fast approaching.

On 11 June 1930, the CCP leadership adopted a resolution entitled "The New Revolutionary High Tide and an Initial Victory in One or More Provinces," drafted by Li Lisan. The resolution directed the Chinese Red Army to attack big cities to seize power in China. However, the CCP leaders completely miscalculated with respect to both political and military matters. The Chinese Red Army was defeated.

Infuriated, Stalin again reorganized the CCP leadership. Li Lisan was called to Moscow to "study," and in January 1931 a new Comintern representative, Pavel Mif, the former rector of the Comintern's Communist University of the Toilers of China formed a new CCP leadership. He promoted his former student Chen Shaoyu, who later became known under the pseudonym Wang Ming. After the execution of Xiang Zhongfa by the Guomindang police (24 June 1931) Chen played the leading role in CCP policymaking, but at the end of September 1931 he left for Moscow fearing arrest. His former classmate Bo Gu replaced him as the de facto leader of the CCP.

Meanwhile, from late 1930 to September 1931, Mao's forces repelled Chiang Kai-shek's three punitive expeditions against the CSA. To defeat the enemy Mao used a "people's war" tactic following a formula: "The enemy advances, we retreat; the enemy camps, we harass; the enemy tires, we attack; the enemy retreats, we pursue."[18]

In November 1931, Mao assembled the First All-China Congress of Soviets to pronounce the Chinese Soviet Republic (CSR), uniting all of the "red" districts in the country. He became chairman of the Central Executive Committee of the CSR and also headed the Council of People's Commissars.

Meanwhile, the situation in Shanghai was constantly worsening, and at the end of January 1933, Bo Gu and some other members of the party leadership were forced to relocate to the CSA. Bo Gu was jealous of Mao's successes. On his orders his associates in the CSA had already dismissed Mao from the positions of general political commissar of the First Front Army in September 1930, and secretary of the General Front Committee. Now he totally isolated Mao from policymaking. However, in February–March 1933 Zhu De managed to repel Chiang Kai-shek's fourth

18 Schram (ed.), *Mao's Road to Power*, vol. III, 154–56.

punitive expedition against the CSA by applying Mao's formula of the "people's war."

In the autumn of 1933 a Comintern military advisor to the CC CCP Otto Braun arrived in the CSA. He immediately opposed Mao's military tactics as "passive" and won Bo Gu over to his side. Braun imposed on the Red Army the senseless tactic of positional warfare under the slogan of "Do not yield an inch of ground!" As a result the communist troops began to lose one battle after another when Chiang Kai-shek launched the fifth punitive expedition in September 1933. Finally, in October 1934, the Red Army had to depart from the CSA.

The Long March

At the very beginning of November 1934, units of the Red Army, having broken through the second line of blockhouses, emerged into southeastern Hunan. At this time they numbered more than 86,000 troops. Many of the officers and men, who were deeply affected by the retreat, grumbled. This created a unique opportunity for Mao to return to power. By taking advantage of this mood and channeling it in the right direction, he would be able to take revenge on Bo Gu.

Mao managed this task brilliantly. He succeeded in winning over a majority of the members of the party leadership. Almost all the army commanders were on his side. He even was able to conclude secret alliances with Wang Jiaxiang and Luo Fu, the former close comrades-in-arms of Bo Gu who were also upset with the retreat.

On 15 January 1935 in the city of Zunyi, north Guizhou, Bo Gu was forced to convene a conference of the party and army leadership to discuss the results of the struggle against the Guomindang's fifth punitive campaign. He and Zhou Enlai, who served as general political commissar, tried to justify their actions. But Luo Fu, Mao, Wang Jiaxiang, Zhu De, Peng Dehuai and others attacked them. In the end Zhou Enlai switched sides and became engaged in self-criticism. Bo Gu was defeated.

Right after the conference the members of the party leadership held the second session, at which Mao was coopted into the Standing Committee of the Politburo, the highest ruling body of the CCP. He was also appointed assistant to General Political Commissar Zhou who no longer posed a danger to him.

At the beginning of February at a meeting of the Standing Committee, Luo Fu unexpectedly demanded that Bo Gu yield the position of general secretary to him. Mao immediately supported him. Bo Gu capitulated. A month later, on 4 March, the new party leader established a special Front Command and designated Mao as front political commissar.[19] Now most of the power was again in the hands of Mao. From that time on, his word in the CCP became decisive.

Meanwhile, the Long March proceeded. Gradually, its goal came into focus, namely, to unite with Zhang Guotao's forces, which were in northwestern Sichuan. Zhang, facing attacks from Chiang Kai-shek, had been forced to evacuate there from his former soviet area on the Hubei–Henan–Anhui border in October 1932.

On 25 June 1935, Mao's and Zhang's troops finally met but soon new problems emerged. Zhang had under arms seven or eight times as many troops as those in Mao's army. Out of Mao's 86,000 troops only 10,000 managed to get to northwestern Sichuan. Zhang demanded the post of general political commissar of the united Red Army, and Zhou Enlai yielded it to him. But shortly thereafter, Mao and Luo Fu decided to strike back at Zhang. At a meeting of the Politburo Luo Fu and Mao accused Zhang of committing serious errors in surrendering the old base area. Infuriated, Zhang suggested dividing the army into two columns and advancing into southern Gansu. One column would proceed along the left flank of the swamp that lay before them and the other along the right. In Gansu they would meet up.

The right column, including Mao and most of the Politburo members, crossed the swamp, but Zhang's left column got stuck. Zhang decided to head back south and send an order to Mao to return. However, Mao let Zhang know that he did not intend to bow to his orders. Then Zhang sent a secret telegram to his former fellow officers in the right column, requesting that they "initiate a struggle" against the Politburo. The split in the Red Army, and with it in the CCP leadership, had become a fact. (Later, in 1938, Zhang Guotao would leave the CCP.)

Soon, Mao and his comrades learned from recent Guomindang newspapers that a rather substantial soviet area existed in northern Shaanxi, close to the northeast border of Gansu. They decided to head there. In mid October, Mao's troops crossed the border of the north Shaanxi soviet area and on 22 October Mao declared the Long March over. He announced that the Red Army had traversed 25,000 *li*, that is, more than 6,000 miles. Actually it was 12,000 *li*, itself an impressive accomplishment, but

19 *Zunyi huiyi wenxian* (Beijing: Renmin chubanshe, 1985), 134.

25,000 sounded more heroic.[20] Out of 86,000 officers and men no more than 5,000 made it all the way to northern Shaanxi.

The CCP and China's War Against Japan

While Mao and other communists had been building their soviets, on 18 September 1931, Japan's Kwantung Army in northeast China had started its conquest of this Chinese region. By late autumn all of Manchuria, with a population of 30 million, was under Japanese control. Chiang Kai-shek, immersed in military action against the soviet areas, was unable to offer any resistance to the incursion, but the Soviet Government of China in late January 1932 officially declared war upon Japan. Of course, this action was purely formal in nature.

From January to March 1933 the Japanese army had seized Rehe and two years later moved into eastern Hebei. At that time Mao realized that only by giving voice to strong patriotic sentiments could the communists secure wide support among the people. This policy was completely in line with that of the Comintern. In the summer of 1935, Stalin himself had performed a similar shift. Fearing German and Japanese aggression against the USSR, he sharply altered the policy of the Comintern. From now on the communists were directed not to seek the overthrow of the ruling classes, but rather to organize a new united front with them – in the West an anti-fascist united front and in the East an anti-Japanese united front.

At the end of November 1935, Mao for the first time addressed a proposal for a truce and joint action against the Japanese to an officer of one of the Guomindang armies deployed in Shaanxi. In essence, this was a goodwill gesture toward Zhang Xueliang, commander of this army and the former Manchurian warlord whose 200,000 troops were now based in the southern and central parts of Shaanxi.

Zhang Xueliang started negotiating with the communists despite Chiang Kai-shek's preparations for a new, sixth, campaign against the CCP. On 4 December 1936, Chiang went to Xi'an to talk with Zhang Xueliang. Zhang insisted on the need to unite with the communists in the struggle against the Japanese. Chiang objected, indicating that the destruction of the CCP was precisely the key to successful resistance against foreign aggression. Attempting to exert pressure on Chiang, on

20 See Ed Jocelyn and Andrew McEwen, *The Long March: The True Story Behind the Legendary Journey that Made Mao's China* (London: Constable, 2006), 326–27.

12 December Zhang arrested Chiang Kai-shek. Mao was ecstatic. But Stalin, who was interested in the unification of China in a war against Japan, intervened. He ordered Mao to stand "decisively for a peaceful resolution of the conflict."[21]

The peaceful resolution of the Xi'an incident helped to establish an anti-Japanese united front between the Guomindang and the CCP. After the outbreak of full-scale Sino-Japanese war on 7 July 1937, a united front was finally inaugurated. On 22 August Chiang issued an order to include the Red Army in the table of organization of the NRA as the Eighth Route Army. Zhu De was appointed commander of the army and Peng Dehuai his deputy. A month later, on 22–23 September, the CCP and the Guomindang exchanged declarations regarding the establishment of an anti-Japanese united front.

However, there continued to be problems with regard to genuine unification. The sticking point was that neither Chiang Kai-shek nor Mao Zedong trusted each other. Mao took advantage of the war to establish communist power in a number of districts located deep in the Japanese rear. There were too few men in the Japanese army to enable it to maintain a firm grasp of all the Chinese territory it had seized. It only occupied the cities and other important strategic objectives as well as the lines of communication. The countryside mostly went its own way. The Japanese only rarely went there for provisions, and Guomindang officials had completely lost control. It was into these rural areas that Mao began to send armed detachments, in essence to fill the power vacuum. His strategy was successful. By 1940, more than ten CCP base areas had been established behind Japanese lines – for propaganda purposes, the communists called these "liberated areas" – and new ones were quickly added.[22]

At the same time Mao began changing his political and ideological stance. In 1938, he formulated a thesis about the need to "sinify Marxism," asserting that Marxism should take a Chinese national form. "From Confucius to Sun Yat-sen, we . . . must constitute ourselves the heirs to this precious legacy," he stated.

Mao's policy corresponded to Stalin's tactical line. It helped the CCP expand its influence among the masses. Moreover, it expressed Mao's desire to present himself to the members of his party as a great theoretician, something Stalin understood.

21 M. L. Titarenko (ed.), *Kommunisticheskii internatsional i kitaiskaia revoliutsiia: Dokumenty i materialy* (Moscow: Nauka, 1986), 270.

22 Stuart R. Schram (ed.), *Mao's Road to Power: Revolutionary Writings 1912–1949*, 7 vols. (Armonk, NY: M. E. Sharpe, 2005), vol. VI, 538.

While continuing to work on "the unification of Marxism with Chinese reality," in late 1939 / early 1940, he succeeded in formulating the idea of the "New Democratic revolution" as a special stage in the development of the liberation movement in China. Mao started with the proposition that because China was a "colonial, semi-colonial, and semi-feudal" country, what China needed to achieve was not a socialist but rather what he called a "Neo-Democratic" revolution. Appealing more to the nationalist sensibilities than to the social strivings of his fellow countrymen, he talked about the need for social reforms, promising to guarantee the right of private property after the revolution, to stimulate national entrepreneurship and to pursue a strict policy of protectionism. He called for tax reduction, the development of a multiparty system, the organization of a coalition government and the implementation of democratic freedoms. The theory of "New Democracy" differed from old-style Western democracy, according to Mao, because it would be implemented under the leadership of the communist party. However, the party was no longer presenting itself as the political organ of the working class, but rather as the organization of the united revolutionary front striving to unite "all the revolutionary people." Postrevolutionary China, Mao asserted, would not be a dictatorship of the proletariat but "a joint dictatorship of all revolutionary classes"; in the economy of the new country, state, cooperative and private capitalist property would coexist.[23]

Mao's concept was in accordance with Stalin's directives sent to him in November 1937: "The odds of speaking about a *noncapitalist* [socialist] path of development for China are worse now than they were before. (After all, capitalism is developing in China!)."[24]

Stalin's and Mao's tactics were based upon deception. The Chinese communists' new policy would enable the communist party to expand its mass base significantly by attracting the many Chinese who opposed any sort of dictatorship, whether communist or Guomindang. This theory was not strategic, but purely tactical. Mao's paradigm of social progress was fictional. Neither Mao, nor the majority of his subordinates intended to implement it. They just wanted to weaken the Guomindang by calling Chiang Kai-shek a dictator and portraying themselves as true democrats.

23 Schram (ed.), *Mao's Road to Power,* vol. VII, 330–69.

24 Ivo Banac (ed.), *The Diary of Georgi Dimitrov 1933–1949*, trans. Jane T. Hedges, Timothy D. Sergay and Irina Faion (New Haven: Yale University Press, 2003), 67–69.

In 1942–45, Mao launched a broad-scale "purge" of the party (*zhengfeng*) to unite it around himself ideologically on the foundation of "Sinicized Marxism." He did not initiate arrests and executions, but rather ideological study. All his former opponents had to write confessions. In July 1943, Mao's "Sinicized Marxism" was named *Mao Zedong sixiang* (Mao Zedong Thought). Its core was the theory of New Democracy. The choice of the term reflected the attempt by Mao to create a purely Chinese ideology that would reflect equally the interests of all strata in Chinese society. The Chinese term *sixiang* (thought) was much more comprehensible and closer to the broad masses of the Chinese people who had experienced the heavy burden of the past even in recent times than the foreign term *zhuyi* (ism).

In April–June 1945, in Yan'an city in northern Shaanxi Mao convened the Seventh CCP Congress. At this Congress the 755 delegates representing 1.2 million party members seemed to view Mao as the unquestionable leader of the party. The Congress asserted that the CCP "guides its entire work by the teaching" of Mao Zedong Thought.[25]

On the eve of the Congress Mao and his subordinates adopted a "Resolution on Certain Historical Questions." In this canonical history of the party the chief role, of course, was given to Mao, and the entire course of the CCP prior to the Zunyi Conference was depicted as a chain of continuous deviations from Mao's correct line, either to the right, or to the left.[26]

The CCP and the Neo-Democratic Revolution

When World War II ended in mid August 1945, China was still divided. The Guomindang's Central Government, backed by the United States, controlled only two-thirds of the country. The CCP held the Shaanxi–Gansu–Ningxia Special Region as well as eighteen "liberated areas" in the north, east and south of China.[27] Manchuria was occupied by the Soviet army.

Neither Mao nor Chiang could come to an agreement. Armed clashes between CCP and Guomindang troops even occurred behind Japanese lines

25 Liu Shao-chi, *On the Party* (Beijing: Foreign Languages Press, 1950), 157.

26 See "Resolution of the CCP CC on Certain Historical Questions," in Tony Saich (ed.), *The Rise to Power of the Chinese Communist Party: Documents and Analysis* (Armonk, NY: M. E. Sharpe, 1996), 1164–79.

27 See Mao Tse-tung, *Selected Works of Mao Tse-tung*, vol. III (Beijing: Foreign Languages Press, 1967), 219.

during the war against Japan notwithstanding the formal existence of a united front. New "frictions" began in August 1945 over which side would accept the Japanese. The full-scale war commenced in the spring of 1946.

The 4.3 million Guomindang troops greatly outnumbered the communist army of barely 1.2 million that at the end of March 1947 was renamed the Chinese People's Liberation Army (PLA). Initially, Chiang conducted a broad offensive from Shaanxi province in the west to the Pacific shore on the east. He also fought in Manchuria. The Americans, however, considered his action "over-ambitious," threatening economic chaos and the very survival of his government.[28] Chiang's army was also inferior to Mao's forces in respect of morale. Unlike the CCP troops, the Guomindang forces had little will to fight. Despite Chiang's numerical superiority, his generals often avoided engagements so as not to risk their units, which were the sources of their political influence and their own enrichment. Corruption and local particularism flourished and the vestiges of militarism were also strong. Closely observing the situation in China, Truman felt compelled to declare to the members of his cabinet, "Chiang Kai-shek will not fight it out. [The] Communists will fight it out – they are fanatical. It would be pouring sand in a rat hole [to give aid] under present conditions."[29] Nonetheless, given the Cold War, the USA continued to support Chiang. Up to the end of 1949, they provided him credits and loans worth around US$ 2 billion (more than to any country in Western Europe after World War II), and sold him US$ 1.2 billion of weapons.[30] At the same time Stalin turned Manchuria into a base for the CCP. He also transferred some Japanese arms seized by Soviet soldiers to CCP troops worth hundreds of millions of dollars.

Meanwhile, the war continued. In mid March 1947, Mao was forced to abandon Yan'an and for the reminder of the year he led the exhausted units of the Yan'an garrison and his personal guard detachment along the mountainous roads of northern Shaanxi. Communist troops in Shandong also began to suffer defeats. Then Mao executed a brilliant plan: to use troops under a talented commander Liu Bocheng for a deep penetration to the south, via the Yellow River, to Chiang Kai-shek's rear, to force Chiang to redeploy military units from the northwestern and northeastern fronts

28 Dean Acheson, "Letter of Transmittal," in *United States Relations with China: With Special Relations to the Period 1944–1949* (New York: Greenwood Press, 1968), xv.

29 Quoted from Douglas J. Macdonald, *Adventures in Chaos: American Intervention for Reform in the Third World* (Cambridge, MA: Harvard University Press, 1992), 107–08, 110.

30 See Acheson, "Letter of Transmittal," xv.

to defend Wuhan, Nanchang, Shanghai and the capital Nanjing itself. This ruined Chiang's strategic plans. On 7 August 1947, Liu's army set out on a march. It remained in the south until February 1948 constituting a threat to Chiang's rear.

In 1948 the situation of the Guomindang became critical not only because of the actions of Liu's forces. The Chinese government turned out to be unable to manage the economy. Inflation took off in 1946. From September 1945 to February 1947, the value of the yuan collapsed. In 1947, monthly inflation was 26 percent. The Guomindang army had begun a hasty retreat and Chiang was powerless to reverse the situation. The strike movement rose sharply; in Shanghai alone in 1946, there were 1,716 strikes. In the spring of 1948 the government introduced ration cards for basic provisions in all major cities as well as compulsory purchases of grain at artificially low prices to increase the grain reserves. This latter measure alienated the Guomindang's natural ally, namely wealthy peasants.

At the same time, in early 1948, Mao launched a Neo-Democratic agrarian reform that received popular support. Chinese and Western liberals also backed the "liberal Mao" against the dictator Chiang Kai-shek. The Guomindang found itself isolated and finally lost.

From September 1948 through January 1949, the communist forces conducted three major successful operations. In early 1949, PLA troops streamed south in a mighty torrent. The Guomindang government moved consecutively to Canton, Chongqing, and Chengdu. On 10 December, Chiang Kai-shek finally escaped to Taiwan. He lost the battle for Mainland China.

The revolution triumphed in most of the country. Three months before the end of the war, on 30 September 1949, the CCP organized a multiparty coalition government; Mao Zedong became the chairman. On 1 October, in Beijing, Mao proclaimed the establishment of the People's Republic of China.

Thus, it took the CCP only twenty-eight years to conquer China. During the entire period it relied on Soviet financial help and political guidance. At the same time, Mao skillfully and in a timely manner changed tactics to win over to his side various social and political forces and isolate Chiang Kai-shek. The CCP came to power not under the banner of socialism, communism, or Stalinism, but under the slogan of New Democracy, which was of decisive importance.

Bibliographical Essay

The revolutionary history of the Chinese Communist Party has been the object of numerous studies. The opening of the secret Comintern archives caused by the collapse of the communist system in the USSR facilitated the documentary study of CCP history. Many new documents became available. The Russian scholars compiled the most comprehensive collection that simultaneously came out in Russia, Germany, China and Taiwan: M. L. Titarenko et al. (eds.), *VKP(b), Komintern i Kitai: Dokumenty*, 5 vols. (Moscow: AO "Buklet", 1994–2007). Tony Saich (ed.), *The Rise to Power of the Chinese Communist Party: Documents and Analysis* (Armonk, NY: M. E. Sharpe, 1996), is also valuable as an English-language translation of printed Chinese documents. Donald Klein and Anne Clark, *Biographic Dictionary of Chinese Communism. 1921–1969*, 2 vols. (Cambridge, MA: Harvard University Press, 1971) is still the best Western encyclopedia of CCP activists.

For the detailed documentary analysis of the foundation of CCP history, see the Maring's archives published in Tony Saich, *The Origins of the First United Front in China: The Role of Sneevliet (Alias Maring)*, 2 vols. (Leiden: Brill, 1991). Recent research that received worldwide recognition is Ishikawa Yoshihiro, *The Formation of the Chinese Communist Party*, trans. Joshua A. Fogel (New York: Columbia University Press, 2013). Chang Kuo-t'ao, *The Rise of the Chinese Communist Party. Volumes One & Two of the Autobiography of Chang Kuo-t'ao* (Lawrence: University Press of Kansas, 1971), is the most detailed first-hand account of CCP history in the 1920s and the 1930s. The Bolshevik impact on the CCP is meticulously examined in Alexander Pantsov, *The Bolsheviks and the Chinese Revolution 1919–1927* (Honolulu: University of Hawai'i Press, 2000). This book is almost entirely based on archives. An outstanding study of the training of CCP cadres in Moscow, based on archive sources, is Daria A. Spichak, *Kitaiskii avangard Kremlia: Revoliutsionery Kitaia v moskovskikh shkolakh Kominterna (1921–1939)* (Moscow: "Veche," 2012).

For a detailed account of the 1920s communist movement in the countryside, see Angus W. McDonald, Jr., *The Urban Origins of Rural Revolution: Elites and the Masses in Hunan Province, China, 1911–1927* (Berkeley: University of California Press, 1978), and for a comprehensive analysis on CCP activity in cities, see Stephen A. Smith, *A Road Is Made: Communism in Shanghai, 1920–1927* (Honolulu: University of Hawai'i Press, 2000).

A history of the Soviet movement in China is examined in a monumental study: Hsiao Tso-liang, *Power Relations Within the Chinese Communist*

Movement, 1930–1934, 2 vols. (Seattle: University of Washington Press, 1967), and the role of the *hakka* in the Chinese communist revolution is discussed in full detail in the magisterial article by Mary S. Erbaugh, "The Secret History of the Hakkas: The Chinese Revolution as a Hakka Enterprise," *China Quarterly* 132 (1992), 937–68. The fullest documentary account on the CC CCP clandestine work in Shanghai in the 1930s is Frederick S. Litten, "The Noulens Affair," *China Quarterly* 138 (1994), 492–512. For the Comintern's role in the Chinese communist movement in the 1930s and 1940s, see Ivo Banac (ed.), *The Diary of Georgi Dimitrov 1933–1949*, trans. Jane T. Hedges, Timothy D. Sergay and Irina Faion (New Haven: Yale University Press, 2003).

The role of the CCP in the Sino-Japanese War is thoroughly examined in the most recent study: Dagfinn Gatu, *Village China at War: The Impact of Resistance to Japan, 1937–1945* (Vancouver: UBS Press, 2007). The classic work Tetsuya Kataoka, *Resistance and Revolution in China: The Communists and the Second United Front* (Berkeley: University of California Press, 1974) is still quite useful. For Mao's concept of "Sinicized Marxism," see P. P. Vladimirov, *Osobyi raion Kitaia, 1942–1945* (Moscow: APN, 1975) and Raymond F. Wylie, *The Emergence of Maoism: Mao Tse-tung, Ch'en Po-ta, and the Search for Chinese Theory 1935–1945* (Stanford: Stanford University Press, 1980).

Steven I. Levine, *Anvil of Victory: The Communist Revolution in Manchuria, 1945–1948* (New York: Columbia University Press, 1987), is the pathbreaking work on the CCP's last civil war against the Guomindang. The most recent studies based on the new archival documents are Odd Arne Westad, *Decisive Encounters: The Chinese Civil War, 1946–1950* (Stanford: Stanford University Press, 2003) and Dieter Heinzig, *The Soviet Union and Communist China 1945–1950: The Arduous Road to the Alliance* (Armonk, NY: M. E. Sharpe, 2004).

For Mao Zedong's rise to power in the CCP see his most recent biography by Alexander V. Pantsov with Steven I. Levine, *Mao: The Real Story* (New York: Simon & Schuster, 2012) based on previously unknown archives. Mao's writings are also of great importance for the understanding of the history of the CCP. The most valuable collections are Mao Tse-tung, *Selected Works of Mao Tse-tung*, 4 vols. (Beijing: Foreign Languages Press, 1967) and Stuart Schram (ed.), *Mao's Road to Power: Revolutionary Writings 1912–1949*, 7 vols. (Armonk, NY: M. E. Sharpe, 1992–2005).

25

Communism on the Frontier: The Sovietization of Central Asia and Mongolia

ADEEB KHALID

One of the odder developments of the years following the Russian Revolution was the establishment of communism in a large swathe of territory from the Caspian Sea to the Mongol steppe. These borderlands of the former Russian Empire were overwhelmingly rural and in large part nomadic, and they boasted almost no industry and no proletariat. What did communism mean in such a context and how was it established? This chapter seeks to explore these questions.

To a certain extent, the establishment of communism in these imperial borderlands was a matter of "Sovietization," the imposition of new forms of rule by the Soviet state through military means, often accompanied with a great deal of violence. Seen thus, Sovietization was the re-annexation of Central Asia to the Russian state under new conditions and the wresting of Mongolia away from the Chinese orbit for the first time. But Sovietization is only part of the explanation. It fails to provide insight into what communism meant to local actors. Some of them articulated various forms of heretical Marxian theoretical stances that combined anti-colonialism and the nation with the desire for modernity and progress. Such actors worked with the Soviets and fought against "reaction" in their own societies. Communism meant many different things on the imperial frontier and it was deeply intertwined with anti-colonialism. The Soviets both recruited among local actors and were disquieted by them and their lack of ideological steadfastness. The resulting distrust was a fundamental dynamic in the process of Sovietization in these regions.

A Colonial Revolution

The events described in this chapter took place in three different zones of political ecology. In the west, Turkestan was the last major territorial acquisition of the Russian Empire. It had been formed into a province of the empire in 1867, but its conquest had continued until 1889. Turkestan included Transoxiana, with its ancient cities and an agrarian population, as well as the nomadic populations of the Turkmens in the south and the Kazakhs in the north. The khanates of Bukhara and Khiva had not been annexed to the empire and remained protectorates with their rulers enjoying wide autonomy in internal affairs. To the northeast lay the steppe region, comprising most of the Kazakh steppe and having a predominantly nomadic population. The steppe *krai* (region) had been under Russian control longer and since the 1890s had turned into a target of Slavic peasant settlement. Mongolia in the east was not part of the Russian Empire but a buffer separating it from the Qing Empire. The era of the Russian Revolution saw its final separation from Chinese rule and the installation of a people's republic, which made it a Soviet satellite. Unlike Russian Central Asia, whose population was solidly Muslim, Mongolia belonged to the Buddhist world and was part of a different geopolitical arena. It will be discussed separately at the end of the chapter.

In Turkestan, a nascent modernist intelligentsia called the Jadids had staked a claim to leadership in a public space made possible by the press and theater. Fascinated by notions of progress and civilization, the intelligentsia cast its message in the language of Islamic reform. Only a reformed Islam, synthesized with modernity, could lead the colonized society to progress. Modern education and the cultivation of knowledge were the panaceas. This claim to leadership was haughtily dismissed by established elites in society, led by Islamic scholars, the *ulama*.[1] This *Kulturkampf* was to have a profound effect on Muslim politics in and after 1917. At the same time, Turkestan's Muslim society coexisted alongside a settler society of Russians and other Europeans who had arrived in the aftermath of the Russian conquest and the difference between "Russians" and "natives" structured society far more significantly than did class. While there were complex patterns of economic interaction, the two groups seldom interacted socially. The political imagination of the two groups also differed. While socialist underground circles existed among the settler population in Central Asia, there was not the slightest trace of socialism in indigenous political discourse, where socialism was seen as a divisive doctrine injurious to Muslim unity.

1 Adeeb Khalid, *The Politics of Muslim Cultural Reform: Jadidism in Central Asia* (Berkeley: University of California Press, 1998).

The situation was somewhat different in the steppe *krai* where since the 1890s, tsarist authorities had been settling Slavic peasants on land occupied by Kazakh nomads. For the authorities, planned resettlement of Slavic peasants would achieve two goals. It would solve the problem of what they saw as overpopulation in European Russia and it would integrate the Kazakh steppe into the empire by implanting in it a more loyal population. Resettlement was accompanied by the expropriation of land deemed to be in excess of the needs of the nomads. Kazakhs resented not just the expropriation of land, which threatened the viability of the nomadic economy, but also a long-term demographic shift. Leadership in Kazakh society was less contested. Members of the Kazakh aristocracy had been sending their sons to Russian schools for many decades, and it was from among this group that a Kazakh national movement emerged. Far less engaged with Islamic reform (the *ulama* were a much weaker force in Kazakh society) and more conversant with Russian political life than their Turkestani counterparts, the Kazakh elites developed a political movement centered on the land question.

All these political arrangements were upended by the collapse of the Russian monarchy in February 1917. In Turkestan, the first weeks after the abdication of the tsar saw a massive political mobilization among the indigenous urban population whose demands coalesced around national autonomy. A Congress of Muslims of Turkestan resolved to make Turkestan an autonomous part of a federal democratic Russia, but that unity quickly collapsed and the modernists and their conservative foes quickly came to be at daggers drawn and spent much of 1917 in bitter disputes. The opposition from their conservative opponents radicalized the Jadids and gave them a fascination with revolution as a modality for change. Yet their struggle with the conservatives was not fought out in a vacuum. The settler population organized in parallel to the Muslims and was often inimical to them. Although there were divisions among the settlers too – between the privileged and the poor, between urban dwellers and peasants – they all started with the assumption that they would not have to share power with the natives. Even the liberals balked at the prospect of equal representation, which would have put power in native hands. As conditions deteriorated throughout Russia over the course of 1917, the enthusiasm of the early weeks of the revolution was replaced by unrestrained ethnic conflict between settlers and the indigenous population. The soviets that arose in 1917 to represent "democracy" were all dominated by Russians. To make matters worse, a famine loomed in

Turkestan and made control of food supply a matter of life and death. The struggle against "hoarding" and "speculation" by native merchants provided a useful "revolutionary" argument for local Russians (many of whom were soldiers bearing arms) to secure the food supply for themselves. When the Russian-dominated Tashkent Soviet seized power in October, the move had as much to do with food supply as anything else.[2] Tashkent remained a bastion of Soviet power from October 1917 on, the only place outside the Russian heartland where this was the case.

The seizure of power by Europeans drove the Muslim leadership to declare autonomy within the parameters promised by the Provisional Government. In November 1917, a Muslim congress established a Provisional Government of Turkestan in the city of Kokand.[3] The Kokand Autonomy, as this government came to be known, lasted less than three months. It had no money and no arms, and it was overrun by Soviet forces from Tashkent in February 1918. Large parts of Kokand were destroyed and the dreams of autonomy vanquished. Soon afterwards, the center intervened through plenipotentiary emissaries and forced the Tashkent Soviet to accept Muslim representatives. The Fifth Congress of Soviets of Turkestan declared Turkestan an autonomous Soviet republic within a socialist Russia in May 1918. This Soviet-style autonomy opened up a space for Muslims in the new order. As we shall see, the Muslims who entered the party brought their own understanding of its mission with them. Meanwhile, ethnic conflict continued, especially in the countryside where settlers continued the confiscation of land and food from the indigenous population. In Marco Buttino's apt phrase, this was the revolution turned upside down, in which settlers had come out on top in the colonial periphery of the empire.[4]

Moscow was able to reestablish control over Turkestan only in 1920. After the Red Army broke through to Turkestan late in 1919, a Turkestan Commission of the Central Committee (Turkkomissiia) arrived in Turkestan

2 On the complicated politics of Turkestan in 1917, see Khalid, *Politics of Muslim Cultural Reform*, ch. 8, and *Turkestan v nachale XX veka: k istorii istokov natsional'noi nezavisimosti* (Tashkent: Sharq, 2006), 18–112; on the ethnic dimension of the conflict, see Marco Buttino, "Turkestan 1917. La révolution des Russes," *Cahiers du monde russe et soviétique* 32, 1 (Jan.–Mar. 1991), 61–77, and Jeff Sahadeo, *Russian Colonial Society in Tashkent, 1865–1923* (Bloomington: Indiana University Press, 2007), 187–207.

3 Saidakbar Agzamkhodzhaev, *Istoriia Turkestanskoi avtonomii: Turkiston muxtoryiati* (Tashkent: Toshkent Islom universteti, 2006).

4 Marco Buttino, *La rivoluzione capovolta. L'Asia centrale tra il crollo dell'impero zarista e la formazione dell'URSS* (Naples: L'Ancora del Mediterraneo, 2003).

to assume control of soviet and party organizations in the region. One of its targets was the settlers, many of whom were removed from their positions and deported to Russia. Over the summer of 1920, all party committees were reelected and a new leadership installed in Turkestan. Among the new leadership were a number of Muslims, including some at the very highest levels. The Turkestan Bureau of the Central Committee, the plenipotentiary organ of central oversight created in 1920, acquired its first Muslim members in 1921.[5]

The situation in the Kazakh lands was murkier. An all-Kazakh conference in Orenburg in July 1917 called for national territorial autonomy for Kazakhs within a democratic Russia. After the seizure of power by the Bolsheviks, a second congress proclaimed the formation of an autonomous Kazakh republic on the territory of the steppe *krai*, with ultimate hopes of uniting the Kazakhs living in Turkestan with the republic. The executive body for this government was called Alash Orda and was to have guaranteed representation for non-Kazakh inhabitants of the republic. There were numerous similarities between Alash Orda and the Kokand Autonomy: Both sought territorial autonomy within the parameters of the February Revolution; both were led by modernist intellectuals; and both faced insurmountable obstacles in turning their proclamations into tangible political reality. Alash Orda lasted longer than its Turkestani counterpart because, unlike in Tashkent, Soviet power was always contested by various White forces on the Kazakh steppe. This circumstance allowed Alash Orda to maneuver in a way that was not possible for the Kokand Autonomy. During 1918 and 1919, Alash Orda raised a militia and fought alongside the Whites, but was forced to negotiate with the Bolsheviks as they emerged victorious on the steppe over the course of 1919. By January 1920, the Bolsheviks had formed a tactical alliance with Alash Orda, whereby Alash organizations were incorporated into Soviet and party units, and prominent Alash leaders acquired positions within the Soviet framework.[6] In October 1920, the Soviets proclaimed a Kazakh autonomous republic on Soviet lines. Much as in Turkestan, the center had trumped "bourgeois" autonomy with its Soviet counterpart. Communism was thus established on the ruins of national movements in Central Asia.

5 Adeeb Khalid, *Making Uzbekistan: Nation, Empire, and Revolution in the Early USSR* (Ithaca: Cornell University Press, 2015), 113–16.

6 D. Amanzholova, *Na izlome: Alash v etnopoliticheskoi istorii Kazakhstana* (Almaty: Taymas, 2009).

"Revolutionizing the East"

The Bolsheviks had from the beginning courted non-Russians in the empire. Lenin in particular was driven by an urge to distance the new regime from its tsarist predecessor, to show non-Russians that Soviet power was not synonymous with Russians. In November 1917, the Soviet government issued a proclamation "To All Toiling Muslims of Russia and the East" that exhorted Muslims to support the new government: "All you, whose mosques and shrines have been destroyed, whose faith and customs have been violated by the tsars and oppressors of Russia! Henceforward your beliefs and customs, your national and cultural institutions, are declared free and inviolable! Build your national life freely and without hindrance."[7] Lenin and Stalin, the signatories of this declaration, intertwined the national question in Russia with the colonial question abroad. This connection pushed itself to the fore in 1918 when the European proletariat failed to rise up in revolution and the Bolsheviks began to see revolution in the colonies as the principal means of defeating the bourgeoisie in Europe. If "the road [to revolution in] Paris and London [lay] via the towns of Afghanistan, the Punjab and Bengal,"[8] as Trotsky put it in 1919, then Central Asia was the "front door to the East," and a possible catalyst for revolution not just in Afghanistan and India, but also in Iran and China. As Lenin put it in an exhortation to "the [European] Communists of Turkestan" in November 1919, "It is no exaggeration to say that the establishment of proper relations with the peoples of Turkestan is now of immense, epochal importance for the Russian Socialist Federative Soviet Republic. The attitude of the Soviet Workers' and Peasants' Republic to the weak and hitherto oppressed nations is of very practical significance for the whole of Asia and for all the colonies of the world, for thousands and millions of people."[9] There followed a number of concrete steps to revolutionize the East, although they were often marked more by enthusiasm than by precision and did not add up to a cohesive whole. The "national and colonial questions" were a major topic at the Second Congress of the Comintern in July 1920. The recent experience of Turkestan informed these debates, even if Central Asia did not figure large in them. The Congress summoned a Congress of the Peoples of the

7 *Dekrety sovetskoi vlasti*, vol. I (Moscow: Izd. Politicheskoi literatury, 1957), 113–15.

8 Trotsky to Central Committee of the Russian Communist Party, 5 Aug. 1919, in Jan M. Meijer (ed.), *The Trotsky Papers, 1917–1922*, vol. I (The Hague: Mouton, 1964), 625.

9 V. I. Lenin, *Collected Works*, 4th edn., vol. XXX (Moscow: Progress Publishers, 1965), 138.

East in Baku and established a Turkestan Bureau of the Comintern in Tashkent. A Council for International Propaganda (Sovinterprop) and a Council for Activity Among Peoples of the East (Sovet deistviia narodov Vostoka) were formed, and a military school established in Tashkent to train "Indian revolutionaries." Social revolution would liberate the colonies and thus Europe. Central Asia was to be the showcase for the Soviet promise.

National Communism

It was the idea of revolution that brought the first Central Asians to communism. They too made the connection between revolution and colonial liberation that Lenin and Stalin had made, but they invested it with rather different meaning. The revolution held a great deal of *promise*: of inclusion, of equality, and of rapid modernization. In Turkestan, the bitter conflict of 1917 with traditionalist elites had further strengthened the Jadids' fascination with the idea of revolution, in which the institutions of a modernizing state could be used to bring about the sort of change that the Jadids had long exhorted their compatriots to undertake. Yet, this revolution had rather little to do with class. Most of the first Muslim communists to emerge in Turkestan came to the party via national organization or pedagogical work. They also tended to form their own cells when the Communist Party of Turkestan (KPT) was finally organized in June 1918. These cells came together in early 1919 to form the Bureau of Muslim Communist Organizations of Turkestan (Musburo). Until early 1920, the Musburo was, to all intents and purposes, a separate party, communicating directly with the Central Committee in Moscow and asserting itself against the European-dominated Central Committee of the KPT. Its members galvanized around the cause of the native population in the political chaos that had broken out in Turkestan. The struggle against this assertion of settler power – *kolonizatorstvo* – provided the main platform for Musburo.[10] For Tŭrar Rïsqŭlov (Russ. Ryskulov), the head of the Musburo, it was the central issue in the revolution and he went on to derive a theory of anti-colonial revolution from this basic fact. Speaking at the Fourth Congress of the KPT in September 1919, he argued that imperial powers sent "their best exploiters and functionaries" to the colonies, people who liked to think that "even a worker is a representative of a higher culture than the natives, a so-called Kulturträger." To counter this legacy of colonialism, Soviet power in

10 Khalid, *Making Uzbekistan*, 107–08.

Central Asia had to be based on "the broad, active participation in state activity" of the native population.[11] In May 1920, in a memorandum to Lenin, he wrote: "In Turkestan, as in the entire colonial East, two dominant groups have existed and [continue to] exist in the social struggle: the oppressed, exploited colonial natives, and European capital, struggling among themselves. Therefore, the October revolution in Turkestan should have been accomplished not only under the slogans of the overthrow of the existing bourgeois power, *but also of the final destruction of all traces of the legacy of all possible colonialist efforts on the part of tsarist officialdom and kulaks*."[12] Rïsqŭlov was in effect arguing that liberating the colonial world had to start in Turkestan by the application of anti-colonial policies there. Only then could Turkestan become the vanguard of revolution in the colonial world. That revolution would also make use of national unity. Rïsqŭlov argued that a major goal of the party should be to "propagandize the idea of the unity of Turkic nationalities beyond the RSFSR around their hearth Turkestan in a single, mighty Turkic Soviet Republic of the Russian Soviet Federation."[13] Indeed, at the Fifth Congress of the KPT in January 1920, the Musburo managed to rename the KPT "the Communist Party of Turkic Peoples," and Turkestan "the Turkic Republic."

This was "national communism," a common phenomenon in the early years of the Russian Revolution, when many non-Russians saw social revolution as intertwined with national liberation. It is best known to us through the figure of Mirsayät Soltangaliyev (Russ., Sultan-Galiev), the Tatar communist who rose to be a leading member of the Commissariat for Nationalities Affairs, and who formulated the idea of a "colonial international."[14] In Azerbaijan, Näriman Närimanov articulated remarkably similar views on nation and revolution.[15] Rïsqŭlov's national communism was similarly an independent invention. The Russian Revolution was a postcolonial moment and national liberation and anti-colonialism inhered in the revolution itself.

11 Gosudarstvennyi arkhiv Rossiiskoi federatsii (GARF), f. 1318, op. 1, d. 441, l. 79.

12 "Doklad polnomochnoi delegatsii Turkestanskoi Respubliki V. I. Leninu," in T. R. Ryskulov, *Sobranie sochinenii v trekh tomakh* (Almaty: Qazaqstan, 1997), vol. III, 175–76 [emphasis in the original].

13 GARF, f. 130, op. 4, d. 786, l. 3.

14 Alexandre Bennigsen and S. Enders Wimbush, *Muslim National Communism in the Soviet Union: A Revolutionary Strategy for the Colonial World* (Chicago: University of Chicago Press, 1979).

15 Jörg Baberowski, *Der Feind ist überall: Stalinismus im Kaukasus* (Munich: DVA, 2003), 225–313.

National communists were not the only ones to be fascinated by the idea of revolution. The Jadids, frustrated with opposition from within their own society, also saw in the universalist promises of the revolution a path to rapid modernization and cultural change. Indeed, the years 1918–20 saw heightened cultural activity in fields that were central to the Jadid program. Many new schools were founded in Tashkent and Samarqand and teacher-training courses established to train new teachers. Theater flourished even in the darkest days of the civil war and famine. Writers threw themselves into creating a modern literature that celebrated progress and the new life, but which was also unabashedly national. The 1920s was the golden age of Uzbek literature, when luminaries such as Fitrat, Cholpan and Abdulla Qodiriy, along with a host of other writers, created works of prose, poetry and drama that are still unrivaled. Creating a national literature required the reform of language itself. The 1920s saw committed efforts to simplify the grammar and the orthography of the Uzbek language. Kazakh was established as a literary language in the 1920s, while Kyrgyz and Turkmen emerged as written languages for the first time in this decade. Writers experimented with new forms and introduced new themes. The decade was one of cultural revolution, a result of enthusiasms unleashed by the revolution. A great deal of this creativity took place outside official Soviet institutions (which remained poorly funded and often in the hands of Russian functionaries who had little interest in native culture) and was a result of the revolution, not of communism. And all of it was aimed at the nation.

The Bolsheviks were always wary of such unauthorized understandings of the revolution. The debates leading up to the formal proclamation of the USSR as a federal entity in 1922 featured demands for greater autonomy for the national republics than the center was willing to concede. Stalin summoned cadres from national republics to a special gathering in the aftermath of the Twelfth Party Congress in April 1923 and attempted to rein in recalcitrant figures.[16] As the line hardened, many national cadres found themselves in trouble. Soltangaliyev was accused in 1923 of masterminding a nationalist "anti-party" faction and arrested. Närimanov was kicked upstairs to become head of the Soviet of Nationalities in Moscow. Rïsqŭlov was ousted in 1920 by the Turkkomissiia and demoted to a desk job in Moscow. He returned to Turkestan in 1922 but was exiled again in 1924, this time as Comintern

16 The confidential proceedings of this gathering were published as *Tainy natsional'noi politiki TsK RKP: stenograficheskii otchet sekretnogo IV soveshchaniia TsK RKP, 1923 g.*, ed. B. F. Sultanbekov (Moscow: Insan, 1992).

representative to Mongolia.[17] That was not enough to solve the problem, for the men who replaced Rïsqŭlov in Turkestan or the Alash Orda activists in the Kazakhstan after 1920 had very similar backgrounds and the same propensity to see the revolution through the prism of the nation. Even when they saw themselves as loyal members of the party, these national communists still saw colonial difference as a fundamental problem to be overcome in Central Asia. The nation could not simply vanish from their political imagination.

Historians have tended to speak of Bolshevik "collaboration" with various local actors in Central Asia in the tumultuous decade after 1917. This view is in need of revision. The Bolsheviks were never keen on collaboration or compromise, although until the late 1920s, they were willing to make tactical concessions and "use" technically competent people if they were loyal. Similarly, the policy of "indigenization" (*korenizatsiia*) of the government apparatus in non-Russian areas, officially implemented in 1923, was meant to produce politically reliable functionaries from indigenous nationalities, not to dilute the ideological purity of the party. The Bolsheviks therefore remained deeply suspicious of the ideological leanings of national communists. Yet, the new universalist order that the Bolsheviks promised was attractive to many in Central Asia, who hoped it was a path to modernity, development and equality. This was a fundamentally different understanding of communism than that of the party and it proved to be a source of distrust toward "national cadres" that culminated in a number of purges that proved fatal to the first generation of national communists. By 1938, most of the actors who had been active in the establishment of Soviet rule in Central Asia had been eliminated.

"Socialist Construction" in Soviet Central Asia

The establishment of Soviet power in Central Asia also raised theoretical questions. Could socialism be built in a region without industry? How did Central Asian agrarian relations map on to the categories used in Russia? Were Central Asian merchants a true bourgeoisie? Most importantly, where did nomads and nomadism fit in the Marxian scheme of history?

17 Xavier Hallez, "Communisme national et mouvement révolutionnaire en Orient. Parcours croisés de trois leaders soviétiques orientaux" (Ph.D. dissertation, Paris: École des hautes études en sciences sociales, 2012), 64–76, 253–64.

There were a few academic debates on the subject, but theory always gave way to politics, and the party's steadfast desire to extend power over all territories of the former tsarist empire was not curtailed by theoretical niceties. Categories developed in the Russian context were usually made to do service in Central Asia too. Uzbek merchants (*bai*), rendered into the abstract by the collective noun *baistvo*, served as counterparts to both the bourgeoisie and the landed aristocracy. Nomadic societies were even trickier. They were made to fit the Marxist evolutionary scheme by being classified as "patriarchal feudalism," in which nomadism itself had been the barrier to further evolution, for it disguised class exploitation in kinship terms ("clan in form, class in content" became a popular slogan in the early 1920s). Sedentarization was thus essential to the liberation of the Kazakhs from the dead end of nomadism. Still, clan elders, called *bais* in Kazakhstan and *manaps* in Kyrgyzstan, stood in for both the bourgeoisie and the kulaks in official analysis of the situation in the nomadic parts of Central Asia. Campaigns for the "liquidation of kulaks as a class" had their equivalents in "demanapization" in Kyrgyzstan and a vicious attack on *bais* in Kazakhstan.

Some of this lay in the future, for large parts of Central Asia remained beyond Soviet control for several years after 1920. White Russian forces were not defeated in the Kazakh steppe until 1921, while the Basmachi insurgency flourished in the Fergana Valley and its surrounding mountains until late 1923. The Basmachi were armed bands who first emerged as a defense against the seizure of land and food supplies by Russian settlers in 1917–18. State collapse had brought about a resurgence of local solidarities and forms of authority often deeply inimical to anything the fifty years of Russian rule had brought about. The Basmachi represented a very different form of leadership than urban Muslims, Jadids and communists alike. The defeat of the Basmachi was possible only through prolonged military action that amounted to a second conquest of Central Asia. It was only by the autumn of 1923 that the Soviets felt confident in their hold over the region; the Turkestan front of the civil war was deactivated only in 1925.

Socialist construction involved building up the communist party and its women's and youth divisions, as well as the establishment of a Soviet apparatus of administrative institutions, from the village level up to that of the republic. These new institutions were meant to reshape society, which required challenging the authority of established elites and destroying the basis of their support. The Soviets mobilized support on the margins of society, among landless peasants, among women who had fled abusive marriages or the oppression of their families, and among urban youth impatient for change and chafing against the authority of their elders. Quite a few recruits were orphans who had grown up outside the strictures of traditional family life. The dislocations of war, civil war and famine had loosened many social bonds and opened up many faultlines. Soviet institutions provided the new arena in which contests over authority in local society were to be played out. And yet, those who entered new institutions often saw their goals through the prisms of their own interests. Party authorities and even more so the political police constantly worried about the infiltration and clogging (*zasorenie*) of Soviet and party institutions by "alien elements," and sought to cleanse (or purge) them. The party's perpetual mistrust of native cadres was a fundamental part of the political reality of the period.

Integrally connected to the process of implanting Soviet institutions in Central Asia was the creation of ethnonational republics in the region. Nationalism, the Soviets had learnt, was a necessary evil that had to be dealt with. If it wouldn't go away, it had to be harnessed to revolutionary goals. Each nationality had to be recognized officially and granted some degree of territorial autonomy. Giving each nation its own homeland would curb ethnic conflict and focus everyone's attention on the right kind of conflict – that between social classes of the same nation. It would also make administration easier and more efficient.[18] Implementing this policy in Central Asia, it was hoped, would also solve the problem of interethnic conflict and spur the economic development of the region. "The separate, uncoordinated masses of toilers of one and the same nation scattered all over Central Asia are now being gathered by us into their own single, soviet, national states," enthused Juozas Vareikis at a party gathering in 1924. "By revolutionary means, we are correcting all the distortions of national history of Central Asia committed by the policies of the khans, beks, emirs, or Russian imperialism."[19] In 1924, the Soviets carried out the so-called national-territorial delimitation of Soviet Central Asia, which replaced the older administrative units by ethnonational republics. The process was initiated by the center but carried out

18 Yuri Slezkine, "The USSR as a Communal Apartment, or How a Socialist State Promoted Ethnic Particularism," *Slavic Review* 53, 2 (Summer 1994), 414–52.

19 In I. Vareikis and I. Zelenskii, *Natsional'noe-gosudarstvennoe razmezhevanie Srednei Azii* (Tashkent: Sredne-Aziatskoe Gos. Izd., 1924), 42.

by indigenous cadres.[20] The creation of nationally homogeneous republics was often touted at the time as Central Asia's "second revolution," one that would consolidate the tasks of social revolution the October Revolution was supposed to have begun. The process gave the party a greater sense of control over the region and the confidence to plunge deeper into policies of transformation.

The years after the national-territorial delimitation saw a number of initiatives to strengthen Soviet institutions. In Uzbekistan, the party launched a project of land reform in 1925 that sought to redistribute land among the peasantry. The redistribution of land was supposed to increase economic productivity, but the main goals of the reform were political, to isolate and dispossess the upper strata in the countryside, deemed to be inimical to the regime, and instead to strengthen the position of landless and land-poor peasants. This was accompanied by the opening of an "ideological front," a campaign to ensure the ideological purity of the party and of Soviet institutions. In practice, this meant attacks on prerevolutionary figures both in the party and in the cultural field. A wave of arrests in 1926 swept away activists connected to the Kokand Autonomy, while a campaign in the press mounted attacks on intellectuals whose commitment to socialism was found to be suspect. A new cohort of self-identified Soviet Uzbek "cultural workers" (*madaniyatchilar*) attacked their elders as the "old intelligentsia" (*eski ziyolilar*), who were accused of nationalism and local patriotism.[21] Nationalism, in fact, became the cardinal sin ascribed to all suspect figures. A virulent campaign of denunciation culminated in a purge of the Uzbek Commissariat of Education in 1929–30. Parallel purges also struck at party organizations across Uzbekistan and wracked the Soviet apparatus, from the village to the republic level.

The ideological front was accompanied by a number of campaigns in the realm of culture that reshaped southern Central Asia. The most important among them targeted all manifestations of Islam. Beginning in 1927, hundreds of mosques, madrasas and Sufi lodges were closed and in many cases destroyed; pious foundations (*waqf*) confiscated; and religious scholars (the *ulama*) were mercilessly persecuted. This campaign dealt a body blow to older means of the reproduction of Islam. The culmination of this assault on the traditional way of life was the *hujum*, the campaign for unveiling women inaugurated in Uzbekistan in 1927. The main focus of

20 Arne Haugen, *The Establishment of National Republics in Soviet Central Asia* (Basingstoke: Palgrave Macmillan, 2003).
21 Khalid, *Making Uzbekistan*, 317–38.

the *hujum* was the veil – thousands of women unveiled in public acts of defiance of tradition – but the campaign was a basic metaphor for the state's relationship to local customs and traditions, which it sought to abolish and replace with more "rational" and modern practices.[22]

In Kazakhstan, the situation was even more drastic. The turning-point came in 1925, when Filipp Goloshchekin arrived to take up the position of the first secretary of the Central Committee of the Communist Party of the Kazakh ASSR. Immediately upon his arrival, he declared that Soviet power did not exist in Kazakhstan. Rather, things had to begin from zero, and Kazakhstan needed a "little October" (*malyi oktiabr'*) to initiate a social revolution. This meant fomenting civil war in the countryside to break the authority of the established social elites (the *bais*) as well as a bitter campaign against "national deviation" in the ranks of the party. As in Uzbekistan, numerous figures from the prerevolutionary and early revolutionary cohorts were arrested and exiled from the republic. While Islamic institutions were much less numerous among the nomadic Kazakhs, the campaign against mosques and shrines also extended into Kazakhstan.[23]

By the late 1920s, Central Asia had been knit back into the Soviet economy, which was increasingly centralized and autarkic, and based on the principle of regional specialization. Uzbekistan and the other republics of southern Central Asia were assigned the role of ensuring the Soviet Union's "cotton independence," that is, of producing as much cotton as was possible. This "cottonization" of the region's economy meant both that grain would be supplied from elsewhere and that industrialization would be put on the back burner. Collectivization further strengthened the center's stranglehold on Central Asia. The campaign started in 1929 along with the rest of the Soviet Union but took markedly different forms in the agricultural and nomadic parts of Central Asia. In agrarian Uzbekistan, collectivization was carried out first in the cotton-growing regions (thus cementing the center's position as the monopoly buyer of the cash crop). Like all other campaigns, the foot soldiers of collectivization were Uzbeks – radical youths from the Komsomol, poorer peasants in the countryside, communist party members – and they reshaped much more

22 Khalid, *Making Uzbekistan*, 343–62; on the *hujum*, see also Marianne Kamp, *The New Woman in Uzbekistan: Islam, Modernity, and Unveiling under Communism* (Seattle: University of Washington Press, 2006), 150–85.

23 Niccolò Pianciola, *Stalinismo di frontiera. Colonizzazione agricola, stermino dei nomadi e costruzione statale in Asia centrale (1905–1936)* (Rome: Viella, 2009), 271–79, 286–88.

in the countryside than its economy. Collectivization was tied also to the closure of mosques and shrines in the countryside and to the unveiling of rural women. In predominantly nomadic Kazakhstan, collectivization led to a massive decline in livestock and caused a catastrophic famine that lasted for three years. Over these years, about 1.5 million Kazakhs (about 40 percent of the total Kazakh population) died, while as many as 1.1 million people left the republic for Russia, Uzbekistan, or Chinese Turkestan. (The famine struck non-Kazakhs too in the republic, but the losses were not symmetrical across national lines, and Kazakhs suffered disproportionately more than settlers.)[24] These losses had devastating consequences for Kazakh society, for nomadism was no longer an option without the livestock and with the reduced population. More than any official campaign, the loss of livestock drove the sedentarization of the nomads. The demographic disaster also shifted the population balance in the republic, turning the Kazakhs into a minority in their own republic.

By the time the Kazakh famine was over in 1933, Central Asia had been Sovietized. The great transformations of the years between 1928 and 1933 had subjugated the region to the demands of the center, displaced its prerevolutionary elites from public life, largely sealed its borders and transformed its cultural life. In the 1920s, indigenous communists had striven to keep greater control on the economy of the region – greater rights of raising and retaining revenues locally and securing better prices for cotton. By the end of the decade, as those hopes were dashed, many indigenous members of the party grumbled that Central Asia had become a "Red colony," fated only to supply raw materials to the metropole at a pittance. For such cadres, Central Asia had gone from being the agent of the liberation of the entire colonial world to its most benighted part. The real end to this chapter of Central Asia's history came in 1937–38, when the leaderships of the republics were eviscerated with arrests and executions. The summer of 1937 saw the arrests of Fayzulla Xo'jayev and Akmal Ikromov, the long-serving first head of the Uzbek government and the first secretary of the Uzbek Communist Party respectively. Their arrests were followed by another round of arrests of the intelligentsia. Xo'jayev

24 The numbers are, of course, impossible to define with precision. The most thoughtful estimates for casualties are in Zh. B. Abylkhozhin, M. K. Kozybaev and M. B. Tatimov, "Kazakhstanskaia tragediia," *Voprosy istorii* 7 (1989), 53–71; and S. Maksudov, "Migratsii v SSSR v 1926–1939 godakh," *Cahiers du monde russe* 40, 4 (1999), 763–92; and Pianciola, *Stalinismo di frontiera*, 463–67.

and Ikromov were among the defendants of the Moscow show trial in March 1938 (alongside Bukharin and Rykov) and were duly executed. Other Uzbek figures languished in jail until October of that year, when they too were executed. In Kazakhstan and Turkmenistan, too, 1937–38 saw the arrest and execution of numerous figures, including those who had held leadership positions since the national-territorial delimitation. By the time the purges were over at the end of 1938, the political landscape had been drastically reshaped. Anyone with a political presence dating back to before 1924 had been banished from this world. Their place was taken by a new cohort of functionaries who had come of age entirely within the Soviet context, who were familiar with the new rules of the game, and who knew better than to rock the boat with unorthodox understandings of communism.

The Sovietization of Mongolia

The installation of communism in Mongolia was tied to the course of the Russian Civil War as it spilled over Russia's imperial boundaries. Until 1911, Mongolia had been an outlying part of the Qing Empire. In the instability unleashed by end of the Qing, a group of prominent nobles and Buddhist clerics declared Mongolia independent under the kingship of Jebtsundamba Khutuktu, the Tibetan-born head of the Buddhist hierarchy in Mongolia, who took the title of Bogd Khagan. In seeking to distance itself from China, the new theocratic monarchy sought Russian protection. Not willing to alienate China, the Russians negotiated far-reaching autonomy for Mongolia within the Chinese orbit, but with substantial Russian influence. Much like Manchuria and northern Iran, Mongolia became part of Russia's "external" empire. The collapse of the tsarist regime in 1917, however, allowed the Chinese to reclaim their influence in Mongolia. As Chinese garrisons moved in, a national movement began to take shape among urban youth, some of whom had received a Russian education. They came together to form the Mongol People's Party (MPP) in 1920, with a program that revolved around national independence and suspicion of China. A delegation traveled to Verkhneudinsk (now Ulan Ude) to seek Soviet help (some members of the delegation traveled on to Moscow). The MPP had looked to the Soviets out of purely geopolitical motives; there was no prior tradition of socialist thought in Mongolia. The Soviet connection made the MPP articulate its demands in a language closer to that of socialism, however, and protestations of the plight of the poor in the face of exploitation entered the program of the party.

At this moment, the Russian Civil War spilled over into Mongolia. Siberia had been a battlefield between Red and White forces. In February 1921, as the Reds made impressive gains, the White warlord Baron Roman Ungern-Sternberg invaded Mongolia, where he proceeded to scatter the Chinese garrisons and to proclaim the Bogd as the ruler of an independent Mongolia. Sternberg's actions, carried out with his characteristic brutality, were ultimately tied to his broader struggle with the Reds, against whom he launched a campaign in the spring of 1921.[25] The campaign was unsuccessful – Ungern himself was taken prisoner and executed – but it provided the opportunity for the Red Army to enter Mongolia to rid it of the Whites. The Red Army invasion paved the way for the final departure of the Chinese and the creation of a Provisional Government with the Bogd Khagan as a constitutional monarch and the MPP in charge. The Bogd's death in 1924 allowed the MPP to sever the link between the state and the Buddhist establishment and to proclaim a People's Republic. The MPP was driven by a desire for sovereignty and modernization and clearly saw the revolution through the prism of the nation. In fact, its second congress in 1923 even declared the unification of all people of the Mongol race and the "rejuvenation of Mongol culture" to be its main goals. It also sought to maximize its room for maneuver, establishing relations with France and Germany, and dispatching a trade mission to the latter country. Yet, its ability to control events, internally let alone externally, remained in question. The party was small in numbers and largely confined to Urga (now Ulaanbaatar). The task of building a party organization and structures of statehood, of transport infrastructure and modern education all lay ahead. In these circumstances, Soviet influence was unavoidable. It was exercised partly through Soviet advisors but much of it was channeled through the Comintern. A number of Buriats (who as Russian subjects of long standing had a small intelligentsia with a Russian education) also played a key role, both in the MPP and in government.

The MPP had its radical tendencies, most notably in its wariness toward the Buddhist establishment. Nevertheless, there can be no doubt that it was the Soviet connection that pushed Mongolia in the direction that it took in the 1920s. The MPP had arrived at socialism not just via the nation, but also

25 Ungern's Mongolian adventures are recounted in the context of his career by Willard Sunderland, *The Baron's Cloak: A History of the Russian Empire in War and Revolution* (Ithaca: Cornell University Press, 2014).

through its inescapable geopolitical embrace by the Soviet Union. Increasingly, its policies were dictated by Comintern emissaries, leading to significant disgruntlement among Mongol cadres, who complained that their state was being shaped "by the hands of aliens" and who also grumbled about "Red imperialism."[26] Yet, the MPP remained divided and its factions faced the same imperatives of proving their ideological purity against their opponents that communists did in the Soviet Union itself. In 1928, the left wing triumphed and, having purged "rightists," embarked on a policy of "building socialism through noncapitalist development." This meant a turn to full-blown collectivization of livestock, the creation of a planned economy and the liquidation of the "feudal nobility." The results were disastrous, and the policy was curtailed in 1933 by a New Turn Policy, which nevertheless continued to pursue the destruction of church property. By the end of the decade, all lamaseries had been dismantled and Mongolian society radically reshaped.

World War II

Mongolia occupied a unique place on the eve of World War II. Unlike Soviet Central Asia, it was not part of the USSR, and the fiction of its sovereignty was maintained. Nevertheless, an "Agreement on the Main Principles of Mutual Relations Between the USSR and Mongolia," signed in 1929, had turned Mongolia into a Soviet satellite, a buffer in Central Eurasia against the threat of Japanese expansion. Such geopolitical considerations meant that, when World War II began, the only socialist state in the world other than the USSR existed in one of the more remote and underdeveloped parts of the world. The war was to transform much about the Soviet Union and its communist frontier. Had the Soviet state collapsed under the Nazi onslaught, the future of Central Asia and Mongolia would have been very different. But it did not, and the war, for all of its devastation and privations, knit Central Asia into the Soviet state as never before.

For Central Asians, the most fundamental feature of the war was the conscription of all men of military age for the war effort. Recruits who might not know what or where Germany was went off to fight it as Soviet citizens. By all accounts, service in the war transformed individual

26 Quoted in Irina Y. Morozova, *The Comintern and Revolution in Mongolia* (Cambridge: White Horse Press, 2002), 61, 64.

subjectivities, as Uzbek peasants returned from the war as Soviet citizens. Nor was it simply a matter of subjectivity. The evacuation of citizens and industry to Central Asia from the western parts of the Soviet Union had lasting effects on the region. It brought heavy industry to the region and diversified its economy.[27] Mongolia did not formally enter the war until August 1945, when it declared war on Japan and its armies saw battle for a week in Manchuria. The years of the war were nevertheless of great hardship, as capital inflows from the Soviet Union dried up and were replaced by "gifts" and collections for the Soviet war effort. Nevertheless, the settlement at Yalta provided for eventual Chinese recognition of the independence of Mongolia, a recognition that the Chinese communists honored after their victory in 1949. World War II was thus instrumental in the full international recognition of Mongolian sovereignty.

Conclusions

It was the Russian Revolution – the collapse of the tsarist autocracy – that created communism in Central Asia and Mongolia. The establishment of the new order on the imperial frontier was largely the work of the Soviet state acting on both ideological and geopolitical imperatives. It was, however, also an anti-colonial moment in which indigenous elites saw in the new ideology a path to progress and modernity. The hopes and aspirations of local actors interacted in complex ways with Soviet imperatives, and together they reshaped local societies. Ultimately, however, the record of the interwar period is one of destruction – of older institutions and social groups, of alternatives, and of indigenous intelligentsias and alternative understandings of the revolution. By 1941, the major achievement of the Soviet regime was to have ensured its monopoly over the definition of communism in the region. Even the connection with anti-colonialism had been modulated. The passion for inciting colonial revolution calmed down after the signature of a trade pact with Britain in 1921, in which the British made the cessation of revolutionary propaganda a condition. It was only under Khrushchev and Brezhnev that Central Asia was touted again to the decolonizing world as a case of Soviet modernization that had bypassed capitalism and undone the injustices of colonialism.

27 Paul Stronski, *Tashkent: Forging a Soviet City, 1930–1966* (Pittsburgh: University of Pittsburgh Press, 2010), 84–96.

We have to look instead to the postwar years for the emergence of Soviet institutions in the region. In Mongolia, a planned socialist economy took root only after the war. In Soviet Central Asia, too, key Soviet institutions solidified only after the war. In the era of Khrushchev and Brezhnev, national political elites had the space and the self-confidence to assert their presence and to oversee cultural formations that were both Soviet and national at the same time. In the late Soviet period, Central Asia was completely intertwined with Soviet forms of culture and politics, and Central Asians proved to be the most resilient Soviets, voting overwhelmingly in 1991 to remain in the Soviet Union.

Bibliographical Essay

The literature on Central Asia and Mongolia was transformed by the collapse of the Soviet Union, which allowed historians to ask new questions and to answer them on the basis of unprecedented access to the archives. Nevertheless, the historiography remains thin and spotty, with large areas still awaiting monographic treatment. For developments in Central Asia in the late tsarist period, see Adeeb Khalid, *The Politics of Muslim Cultural Reform: Jadidism in Central Asia* (Berkeley: University of California Press, 1998), and Daniel Brower, *Turkestan and the Fate of the Russian Empire* (London: RoutledgeCurzon, 2003). Also useful is Steven Sabol, *Russian Colonization and the Genesis of Kazak National Consciousness* (Basingstoke: Palgrave Macmillan, 2003). Jeff Sahadeo, *Russian Colonial Society in Tashkent, 1865–1923* (Bloomington: Indiana University Press, 2007), provides an excellent account of settler society and covers the era of the revolution. The complex politics of the revolution in Turkestan are explored by Marco Buttino, *La rivoluzione capovolta. L'Asia centrale tra il crollo dell'impero zarista e la formazione dell'URSS* (Naples: L'Ancora del Mediterraneo, 2003), and Saidakbar Agzamkhodzhaev, *Istoriia Turkestanskoi avtonomii: Turkiston muxtoryiati* (Tashkent: Toshkent Islom universteti, 2006).

For the early Soviet period, Adeeb Khalid, *Making Uzbekistan: Nation, Empire, and Revolution in the Early USSR* (Ithaca: Cornell University Press, 2015), provides the most comprehensive account of events in Turkestan and Bukhara in 1917 and the decade and a half that followed it. Marianne Kamp, *The New Woman in Uzbekistan: Islam, Modernity, and Unveiling under Communism* (Seattle: University of Washington Press, 2006), and Douglas Northrop, *Veiled Empire: Gender and Power in Stalinist Central Asia* (Ithaca: Cornell University Press, 2004), offer contrasting takes on the *hujum*. On Kazakhstan, Niccolò Pianciola, *Stalinismo di frontiera.*

Colonizzazione agricola, stermino dei nomadi e costruzione statale in Asia centrale (1905–1936) (Rome: Viella, 2009) provides a sweeping account that spans the revolution. The political history of the revolutionary era is recounted by D. Amanzholova, *Na izlome: Alash v etnopoliticheskoi istorii Kazakhstana* (Almaty: Taymas, 2009). There is still very little on the 1920s in Kazakhstan, but two excellent monographs offer detailed accounts of collectivization and sedentarization: Isabelle Ohayon, *Le sédentarisation des Kazakhs dans l'URSS de Staline. Collectivisation et changement social (1928–1945)* (Paris: Maisonneuve & Larose, 2006), and Sarah Cameron, *The Hungry Steppe: Famine, Violence and the Making of Soviet Kazakhstan* (forthcoming). Excellent studies exist on the other republics in the early Soviet period. See Adrienne Edgar, *Tribal Nation: The Making of Soviet Turkmenistan* (Princeton: Princeton University Press, 2004); Ali İğmen, *Speaking Soviet with an Accent: Culture and Power in Kyrgyzstan* (Pittsburgh: University of Pittsburgh Press, 2012); and Benjamin Loring, "Building Socialism in Kyrgyzstan: Nation-Making, Rural Development, and Social Change, 1921–1932" (unpublished thesis, Brandeis University, 2008).

The foundational texts for the study of Soviet nationalities policies are Yuri Slezkine, "The USSR as a Communal Apartment, or How a Socialist State Promoted Ethnic Particularism," *Slavic Review* 53, 2 (1994), 414–52; Terry Martin, *The Affirmative Action Empire: Nations and Nationalism in the Soviet Union, 1923–1939* (Ithaca: Cornell University Press, 2001); and Francine Hirsch, *Empire of Nations: Ethnographic Knowledge and the Making of the Soviet Union* (Ithaca: Cornell University Press, 2005). For the national-territorial delimitation of Central Asia, Arne Haugen's *The Establishment of National Republics in Soviet Central Asia* (Basingstoke: Palgrave Macmillan, 2003) is indispensable. There is no adequate treatment of Soviet attempts at "revolutionizing the East," but the relevant sections of M. N. Roy's *Memoirs* (Bombay: Allied Publishers, 1964) offer fascinating insights.

Mongolia has not shared in the post-Soviet archival bonanza and the output on the years of the establishment of communism is quite thin. See Christopher Kaplonski, *The Lama Question: Violence, Sovereignty, and Exception in Early Socialist Mongolia* (Honolulu: University of Hawai'i Press, 2014). Also useful is Irina Y. Morozova, *The Comintern and Revolution in Mongolia* (Cambridge: White Horse Press, 2002). The best source on the Baron Ungern episode is Willard Sunderland's *The Baron's Cloak: A History of the Russian Empire in War and Revolution* (Ithaca: Cornell University Press, 2014).

Index